THE TWO BABYLONS

THE TWO BABYLONS

OR

THE PAPAL WORSHIP

PROVED TO BE

THE WORSHIP OF NIMROD AND HIS WIFE

With Sixty-one Woodcut Illustrations from

NINEVEH, BABYLON, EGYPT, POMPEII, &c.

BY THE LATE

REV. ALEXANDER HISLOP

OF EAST FREE CHURCH ARBROATH

KALPAZ

ISBN: 978-93-5128-592-2

First Published in 1903
Indian Reprint in 2017

Published by

Kalpaz Publications
C-30, Satyawati Nagar,
Delhi – 110052
E-mail: kalpaz@hotmail.com
Website: kalpazpublications.com
Ph.: +91-9212142040

Cataloging in Publication Data—DK
Courtesy: D.K. Agencies (P) Ltd. <docinfo@dkagencies.com>

Hislop, Alexander, 1807-1865, **author.**
The two Babylons, or, The papal worship proved to be the worship of Nimrod and his wife : with sixty-one woocut illustrations from Nineveh, Babylon, Egypt, Pompeii, &c. / by the Late Rev. Alexander Hislop.
pages cm
"First published in 1903"—Title page verso.
Includes index.
ISBN 9789351285922

1. Catholic Church—Controversial literature. 2. Papacy. I. Title.

BX1765.2.H45 2017 DDC 282 23

CONTENTS.

CHAPTER V.

Rites and Ceremonies.

CHAPTER VI.

Religious Orders.

CHAPTER VII.

The Two Developments Historically and Prophetically Considered.

NOTE BY THE EDITOR.

Had the lamented Author been spared to superintend the issue of the Fourth Edition of his work, it is probable he would have felt himself called upon to say something in reference to the political and ecclesiastical events that have occurred since the publication of the last Edition. By the authoritative promulgation of the dogma of the Pope's Infallibility, his argument as to the time of the slaying of the Witnesses, and his identification of the Roman pontiff as the legitimate successor of Belshazzar have been abundantly confirmed.

It is gratifying to the Author's friends to know that the work has been so favourably received hitherto, and that no one, so far as we are aware, has ventured to challenge the accuracy of the historical proofs adduced in support of the startling announcement on the title page. But it is deplorable to think that, notwithstanding all the revelations made from time to time of the true character and origin of Popery, Ritualism still makes progress in the Churches, and that men of the highest influence in the State are so infatuated as to seek to strengthen their political position by giving countenance to a system of idolatry. If Britons would preserve their FREEDOM and their pre-eminence among the nations, they should never forget the Divine declaration, "Them that honour Me I will honour, and they that despise Me shall be lightly esteemed."

It only remains for the Editor to say that the work has been carefully revised throughout, and a few trifling errors in the references have, in consequence, been corrected. One or two notes also, enclosed in brackets, have been added, and the Index has been somewhat extended.

R. H.

Blair Bank, Polmont Station, N.B.,
January, 1871.

PREFACE TO THE SECOND EDITION.

SINCE the appearing of the First Edition of this work, the Author has extensively prosecuted his researches into the same subject; and the result has been a very large addition of new evidence. Somewhat of the additional evidence has already been given to the public, first through the columns of the *British Messenger*, and then in the publication entitled "The Moral Identity of Babylon and Rome," issued by Mr. Drummond of Stirling. In the present edition of "The Two Babylons," the substance of that work is also included. But the whole has now been re-written, and the mass of new matter that has been added is so much greater than all that had previously appeared, that this may fairly be regarded as an entirely new work. The argument appears now with a completeness which, considering the obscurity in which the subject had long been wrapped, the Author himself, only a short while ago, could not have ventured to anticipate as a thing capable of attainment.

*   *   *   *   *

On the principle of giving honour to whom honour is due, the author gladly acknowledges, as he has done before, his obligations to the late H. J. Jones, Esq.—to whose researches Protestantism is not a little indebted—who was the first that directed his attention to this field of inquiry. That able, and excellent, and distinguished writer, however, was called to his rest before his views were matured. His facts, in important instances, were incorrect; and the conclusions at which he ultimately arrived were, in very vital respects, directly the reverse of those that are unfolded in these pages. Those who have read, in the *Quarterly Journal of Prophecy*, his speculations in regard to the Beast from the Sea, will, it is believed, readily perceive that, in regard to it, as well as other subjects, his argument is fairly set aside by the evidence here adduced.

In regard to the subject of the work, there are just two remarks the author would make. The first has reference to the Babylonian legends. These were all intended primarily to commemorate facts that took place in the early history of the *post*-diluvian world. But along with them were mixed up the momentous events in the history of our first parents. These events, as can be distinctly proved, were commemorated in the secret system of Babylon with a minuteness and particularity of detail of which the ordinary student of antiquity can have little conception. The post-diluvian divinities were connected with the ante-diluvian patriarchs, and the first progenitors of the human race, by means of the metempsychosis; and the names given to them were skilfully selected, so as to be capable of divers meanings, each of these meanings having reference to some remarkable feature in the history of the different patriarchs referred to. The knowledge of this fact is indispensable to the unravelling of the labyrinthine subject of Pagan mythology, which, with all its absurdities and abominations, when narrowly scrutinised, will be found exactly to answer to the idea contained in the well-known line of Pope in regard to a very different subject:—

> "A mighty maze, but not without a plan."

In the following work, however, this aspect of the subject has, as much as possible, been kept in abeyance, it being reserved for another work, in which, if Providence permit, it will be distinctly handled.

The other point on which the author finds it necessary to say a word, has reference to the use of the term "Chaldee," as employed in this work. According to ordinary usage, that term is appropriated to the language spoken in Babylon in the time of Daniel and thereafter. In these pages the term Chaldee, except where otherwise stated, is applied indiscriminately to whatever language can be proved to have been used in Babylonia from the time that the Babylonian system of idolatry commenced. Now, it is evident from the case of Abraham, who was brought up in Ur of the Chaldees, and who doubtless brought his native language along with him into Canaan, that, at that period, Chaldee and Hebrew were substantially the same. When, therefore, a pure Hebrew word is found mixed up with a system that confessedly had its origin in Babylonia, the land of the Chaldees, it cannot be doubted that that term, in that very form, must have originally belonged to the Chaldee dialect, as well as to that which is now commonly known as Hebrew. On this ground, the author has found himself warranted to give a wider application to the term "Chaldee" than that which is currently in use.

And now, in sending forth this new Edition, the author hopes he can say that, however feebly, he has yet had sincerely an eye, in the whole of his work, to the glory of "that name that is above every name," which is dear to every Christian heart, and through which all tribes, and peoples, and kindreds, and tongues, of this sinful and groaning earth, are yet destined to be blest. In the prosecuting of his researches, he has found his own faith sensibly quickened. His prayer is, that the good Spirit of all grace may bless the work for the same end to all who may read it.

PREFACE TO THE THIRD EDITION.

In giving the Third Edition of this work to the public, I have little else to do than to express my acknowledgments to those to whom I am under obligations, for enabling me thus far to bring it to a successful issue.

To Mr. Murray, of Albemarle Street, London; Mr. Vaux, of the British Museum; and Messrs. Black and Messrs. Chambers, Edinburgh, I am specially indebted for permission to copy woodcuts belonging to them. Individual woodcuts, from other sources, are acknowledged in the body of the work. To Mr. John Adam, the artist, who has executed the whole of the woodcuts, with a few exceptions, I have to express my obligations for the spirit and artistic skill displayed in their execution; and I do so with the more pleasure, that Mr. Adam is a native of Arbroath, and the son of a worthy elder of my own.

I have also acknowledgments of another kind to make. Considering the character of this work—a work that, from its very nature, required wide, and, at the same time, minute research, and the consultation of works of a very recondite character; and, taking also into view not only the very limited extent of my own library, but the distance of my abode from any of the great libraries of the land, where rare and expensive works may be consulted, the due preparation of such a work was attended with many difficulties. The kindness of friends, however, has tended wonderfully to remove these difficulties. From all quarters I have met with the most disinterested aid, of which I retain a grateful and pleasing remembrance. To enumerate the different sources whence help has come to me, in the prosecution of my task, would be impossible. There are three individuals, however, who stand out from the rest whom I cannot pass over without notice. Each of them has co-operated (and all spontaneously), though in different ways, in enabling me thus far to accomplish my task, and their aid has been of the most essential importance.

To Mrs. Barkworth, of Tranby Hall, Yorkshire (whose highly cultivated mind, enlightened zeal for Protestant truth, and unwearied beneficence need no testimony of mine), I am signally indebted, and it gives me pleasure to acknowledge it.

I have also to acknowledge my deep and peculiar obligations to one who chooses to be unknown,* who, entirely on public grounds, has taken a very lively interest in this work. He has spared neither expense nor pains, that, every incidental error being removed, the argument might be presented to the public in the most perfect possible form. For this purpose he has devoted a large portion of his time, during the last three years, to the examination of every quotation contained in the last edition, going in every case where it was at all possible, to the fountain-head of authority. His co-operation with me in the revisal of the work has been of the greatest advantage. His acute and logical mind, quick in detecting a flaw, his determination to be satisfied with nothing that had not sufficient evidence to rest upon, and yet his willing surrender to the force of truth whenever that evidence was presented, have made him a most valuable coadjutor. "As iron sharpeneth iron," says Solomon, "so doth a man sharpen the countenance of his friend." I have sensibly found it so. His correspondence, by this stimulus, has led to the accumulation of an immense mass of new evidence, here presented to the reader, which, but for his suggestions, and objections too, might never have been discovered. In the prosecution of his investigation he has examined

[* Edward Joshua Cooper, Esq., of Markree Castle, Ireland, the gentleman here alluded to, died 23rd April, 1863. He was "one of our most distinguished amateur astronomers. After leaving Oxford, he travelled extensively, with a sextant, chronometer, and telescope, as his inseparable companions. . . . . In the year 1831, he purchased from Cauchoix, of Paris, an object glass of 13·3 inches aperture, and 25 feet focus, the largest then existing, which, in 1834, was mounted, with perfect success, at his magnificent mansion of Markree." The labours of himself and his assistant were rewarded by "the discovery of the planet Metis; but his greatest work is his 'Catalogue of Ecliptic Stars.' This (which was published by aid from the Government grant placed at the disposal of the Royal Society, and which the Royal Irish Academy honoured with their Cunningham Medal) contains upwards of 60,000 stars down to the twelfth magnitude, of which very few had been previously discovered."

Mr. Cooper was a Fellow of the Royal Society and of the Royal Astronomical Society, as well as a Member of the Royal Irish Academy. "He represented the County of Sligo in Parliament for many years, and was a kind and good landlord, making great exertions to educate and improve his numerous tenantry. His personal qualities were of a high order. Blameless and fascinating in private life, he was a sincere Christian, no mean poet, an accomplished linguist, an exquisite musician, and possessed a wide and varied range of general information."—*See Obituary Notice in the Proceedings of the Royal Society*, 1864.]

no fewer than 240* out of the 270 works contained in the accompanying list of "Editions," many of them of large extent, all of which are in his own possession, and not a few of which he has procured for the purpose of verification. His object and mine has been, that the argument might be fairly stated, and that error might, as far as possible, be avoided. How far this object has been attained, the references and list of "Editions" will enable each reader competent to the task, to judge for himself. For myself, however, I cannot but express my high sense of the incalculable value of the service which the extraordinary labours of my kind and disinterested friend have rendered to the cause of universal Protestantism.

But while making mention of my obligations to the living, I may not forget what I owe to the dead. To him whose name stands on the front of this work, I am, in some respects, pre-eminently indebted, and I cannot send forth this edition without a tribute of affection to his memory. It is not for me to speak of his wit, and the brilliancy of his conversational powers, that captivated all who knew him; of the generous unselfishness of his nature, that made him a favourite with every one that came in contact with him; or of the deep interest that he took in the efforts at present being made for improving the dwellings of the working-classes, and especially of those of his own estate, as well as in their moral and religious improvement. But I should be liable to the charge of ingratitude if I contented myself, in the circumstances, with the mere formal dedication, which, though appropriate enough while he was alive, is now no more so when he is gone.

The time and the circumstances in which his active friendship was extended to me, made it especially welcome. His keen eye saw at a glance, as soon as the subject of this work came under his attention, the importance of it; and from that time forward, though the work was then in its most rudimentary form, he took the deepest interest in it. He did not wait till the leading organs of popular opinion, or the great dispensers of fame, should award their applause; but, prompted by his own kindly feeling, he spontaneously opened up a correspondence with me, to encourage and aid me in the path of discovery on which I had entered.

His own studies qualified him to appreciate the subject and pronounce upon it. For many years he had deeply studied the

* The whole number of works actually examined by the eminent individual above referred to, in connection with this subject, is upwards of 260; but space does not permit me to avail myself of anything like the full amount of the new evidence that has been gathered. The above number, therefore, refers only to the works actually quoted in this edition.

Druidical system, which, with the haze and mystery around it, and with its many points of contact with the patriarchal religion, had a strange and peculiar fascination for him. For the elucidation of this subject, he had acquired most valuable works; and what he possessed he was most ready to communicate. In the prosecution of my inquiries, I had met with what to me seemed insuperable difficulties. He had only to know of this to set himself to remove them; and the aid derived from him was at once precious and opportune; for through his acquaintance with Druidism, and the works received from him, difficulties disappeared, and a flood of light irradiated the whole subject. If, therefore, the reader shall find the early history of superstition, not only in our native land, but in the world at large, set in a new and instructive light in these pages, he must know that he is essentially indebted for that to Lord John Scott. In one, who was an entire stranger, being thus prompted to render efficient assistance to me at such a time, I could not but thankfully recognise the hand of a gracious Providence; and when I reflect on the generous, and humble, and disinterested kindness with which the four years' correspondence between us was conducted on his part,—a correspondence in which he always treated me with as much confidence as if I had been his friend and brother,—I cannot but feel warm and tender emotions, mingling with the thoughts that spring up in my bosom. Friendship such as his was no ordinary friendship. His memory, therefore, must be ever dear to me; the remembrance of his kindness ever fragrant.

Unexpected was the stroke—now, alas! near three years ago—by which our correspondence was brought to an end; but painful though that stroke was, and solemnising, there was no gloom attending it. The "hope full of immortality" cheered his dying bed. For years back he had found the emptiness of the world, and had begun to seek the better part. His religion was no sentimental religion; his fear of God was not taught by the commandment of men. His faith was drawn directly from the inspired fountain of Divine truth. From the time that the claims of God to the homage of his heart had laid hold on him, the Word of God became his grand study, and few men have I ever known who held with a more firm and tenacious grasp the great truth that the Word of God, and that Word *alone*, is the light and rule for the guidance of Christians; and that every departure from that Word, alike on the part of Churches and individuals, implies, as he himself expressed it, "going off the rails," and consequently danger of the highest kind. As his religion was Scriptural, so it was spiritual. In one of his earliest letters to me, he avowed that the bond of "spiritual religion" was that by which he felt himself specially bound to those whose character and spirit showed them to be the true sheep of Christ's pasture; and in accepting the dedication of my work, he particularly stated, that the interest that he took in it was not as a mere matter of literary curiosity, but as being "fitted to teach great truths, which the world is not very willing to learn." This, in the connection in which he wrote it, evidently had special reference to the great doctrine of "regeneration." His mind was deeply penetrated with a sense of the majesty of God, and the "awfulness" of our relations to Him, in consequence of the sin that has entered the world, and has infected the whole human race, and therefore he vividly realised the indispensable necessity of Mediation and Atonement, to give hope to sinful man in prospect of the grand account.

The origin of that earnestness and attachment to spiritual religion which he manifested in his last years, was, as I was assured by a relative now also gone to his reward, the perusal of the tract entitled "Sin no Trifle." Deep was the impression that tract had made. He read it, and re-read it, and continually carried it about with him, till it was entirely worn away. Under the impressions springing from such views of sin, he said to an intimate friend, when in the enjoyment of health and vigour, "It is easy to die the death of a gentleman, *but that will not do.*" His death was not the death of a mere gentleman. It was evidently the death of a Christian.

The circumstances in which he was removed were fitted to be peculiarly affecting to *me*. In reply to a letter—the last which I received from him—in which he expressed deep interest in the spread of vital religion, I was led, in pursuance of the theme to which he himself had specially referred, to dwell more than ever before on the necessity not merely of having hope towards God, but of having the question of personal acceptance decisively settled, and the consequent habitual possession of the "joy of salvation," and as one special reason for this, referred to the fact, that all would be needed in a dying hour. "And who can tell," I added, "how suddenly those who are surrounded with all the comforts of life may be removed from the midst of them?" In illustration of this, I referred to the affecting case of one whom I had known well, just a short while before, lost along with his family in the *Royal Charter*. Having made a large fortune in Australia, he was returning home, and when on the point of setting foot on his native shores, with the prospect of spending his days in ease and affluence, suddenly father and mother, son and daughter, were all engulfed in a watery grave. My letter concluded with these words: "In view of such a solemnising event, well may we say, What is man? But oh, man is great, if he walks with God, and the divine words are fulfilled in his experience, 'God, who commanded the light to shine out of darkness, hath shined in our hearts, to give the light of the knowledge of the glory of God in the face of Jesus Christ.' That this may be more and more the experience of your Lordship, is my earnest desire." When I wrote this I had not the least suspicion that I was writing to a dying man. But so it proved to be. Only a few days after he received this, he was smitten with his death-sickness. From his dying bed he sent me a kindly memorial of his affectionate remembrance, and in his painful illness he manifested the supporting power of faith, when faith has respect to the truth as it is in Jesus, and appropriates Him as a personal and Almighty Saviour.

EDITIONS OF WORKS

QUOTED OR REFERRED TO IN THIS WORK.

Adam's Roman Antiquities,	*London,*	1835
Æliani Historiæ,	*Rome,*	1545
Ælianus de Nat. Animal,	*Tubingen,*	1768
Æschylus,	*Paris,*	1557
Æschylus,		1552
Agathias (Corp. Script. Byzant.),	*Bonn,*	1828
Alford's Greek Test.,	*London,*	1856
Ambrosii Opera,	*Paris,*	1836
Ammianus Marcellinus,	*Paris,*	1681
Anacreon,	*Cambridge,*	1705
Apocalypse, Original Interpretation,	*London,*	1857
Apocriphi (Diodati, Bibbia),	*London,*	1819
Apollodorus,	*Gottingen,*	1803
Apuleius,	*Leipsic,*	1842
Arati Phœnomena,	*Leipsic,*	1793
Aristophanes,	*Amsterdam,*	1710
Arnobius,	*Paris,*	1836
Athenæus,	*Leyden,*	1612
Athenagoras,	*Wurtzburg,*	1777
Asiatic Journal,	*London,*	1816
——— Researches,	*London,*	1806
Augustini Opera Omnia,	*Bassano,*	1807
Augustine's City of God, with Lud. Vives's Comment.,	*London,*	1620
Aulus Gellius,	*Leyden,*	1666
Aurelius Victor,	*Utrecht,*	1696
Ausonii Opera,	*Amsterdam,*	1669
Barker and Ainsworth's Lares and Penates of Cilicia,	*London,*	1853
Barker's Hebrew Lexicon,	*London,*	1811
Baronii Annales,	*Cologne,*	1609
Bede's Works,	*Cambridge,*	1722
Begg's Handbook of Popery,	*Edinburgh,*	1856
Bell's (Robert) Wayside Pictures,	*London,*	1849
—— (John) Italy,	*Edinburgh,*	1825
Berosus,	*Leipsic,*	1825
Betham's Etruria Celtica,	*Dublin,*	1842
——— Gael and Cymbri,	*Dublin,*	1834

Bilney (British Reformers),	*London,*	S. D.
Bion (Poet. Græc. Min.),	*Cambridge,*	1661
Blakeney's Popery in its Social Aspect,	*Edinburgh,*	S. D.
Borrow's Gipsies,	*London,*	1843
Bower's Lives of the Popes,	*London,*	1750
Bryant's Mythology,	*London,*	1807
Bulwark, The,	*Edin.,*	1852-53
Bunsen's Egypt,	*London,*	1848
Cæsar,	*London,*	1770
Callimachus,	*Utrecht,*	1697
Catechismus Romanus,	*Lyons,*	1659
Catlin's American Indians,	*London,*	1841
Catullus,	*Utrecht,*	1659
Cedreni Compendium,	*Bonn,*	1838
Charlotte Elizabeth's Personal Recollections,	*London,*	1847
———— Sketches of Irish History,	*Dublin,*	1844
Chesney's Euphrates Expedition,	*London,*	1850
Chronicon Paschale,	*Bonn,*	1832
Chrysostomi Opera Omnia,	*Paris,*	1738
Ciceronis Opera Omnia,	*Paris,*	1740
Clemens Alexandrinus, Opera,	*Wurtzburg,*	1778
Clemens Protrepticos,	*Lutetiæ,*	1629
Clericus (Johannes) de Chaldæis et de Sabæis,	*Amsterdam,*	1700
Clinton, Fasti Hellenici,	*Oxford,*	1834
Codex Theodosianus,	*Bonn,*	1842
Coleman's Hindoo Mythology,	*London,*	1832
Cory's Fragments,	*London,*	1732
Courayer's Council of Trent,	*London,*	1736
Covenanter, Irish,	*Belfast,*	1862
Crabb's Mythology,	*London,*	1854
Crichton's Scandinavia,	*Edinburgh,*	1838
Cummianus (Patr. Patrum),	*Paris,*	1851
Daubuz's Symbolical Dictionary,	*London,*	1842
D'Aubigné's Reformation,	*Brussels,*	1839
David's Antiquités Etrusques, &c.,	*Paris,*	1787
Davies's Druids,	*London,*	1809
Davis's (Sir J. F.) China,	*London,*	1857
Didron's Christian Iconography,	*London,*	1851
Diodori Bibliotheca,	*Paris,*	1559
Diogenes Laertius,	*London,*	1664
Dionysius Afer,	*London,*	1658
Dionysius Halicarn,	*Oxford,*	1704
Dryden's Virgil,	*London,*	1709
Dupuis, Origine de tous les Cultes,	*Paris,*	1822
Dymock's Classical Dictionary,	*London,*	1833
Elliott's Horæ Apocalypticæ,	*London,*	1851
Ennodii Opera,	*Paris,*	1611
Epiphanii Opera Omnia,	*Cologne,*	1682
Eunapius,	*Geneva,*	1616
Euripides,	*Cambridge,*	1694
Eusebii Præpar. Evangel.,	*Leipsic,*	1842

Eusebii Chronicon,	*Venice,*	1818
——— Chron.,	*Basle,*	1529
——— Vita Constantin.,	*Paris,*	1677
Eustace's Classical Tour,	*London,*	1813
Eutropius (Rom. Hist. Script. Græc. Min.),	*Frankfort,*	1590
Evangelical Christendom,	*London,*	1853
Do. do.,	*London,*	1855
Firmicus, Julius,	*Oxford,*	1678
Flores Seraphici,	*Coloniæ Agrippinæ,*	1640
Furniss's What Every Christian must Know,	*London,*	S. D.
Fuss's Roman Antiquities,	*Oxford,*	1840
Garden of the Soul,	*Dublin,* / *London,*	1850 / S. D.
Gaussen's Daniel,	*Paris,*	1848-49
Gebelin, Monde Primitif,	*Paris,*	1773-82
Gesenii Lexicon,	*London,*	1855
Gibbon's Decline and Fall,	*Dublin,*	1781
Gibson's Preservative,	*London,*	1848
Gieseler's Eccles. History,	*Edinburgh,*	1846
Gill's Commentary,	*London,*	1852-54
Gillespie's Sinim,	*Edinburgh,*	1854
Golden Manual,	*London,*	1850
Gregorii Nazianzeni Opera,	*Antwerp,*	1612
Greswell's Dissertations,	*Oxford,*	1837
Guizot's European Civilisation,	*London,*	1846
Hanmer's Chronographia; appended to translation of Eusebius, &c.,	*London,*	1636
Hardy, Spence, Buddhism,	*London,*	1853
Harvet, Dr. Gent., Review of Epistle of,	*London,*	1598
Hay's Sincere Christian,	*Dublin,*	1783
Heathen Mythology,	*London,*	S. D.
Herodoti Historia,	*Paris,*	1592
Hesiodus,	*Oxford,*	1737
Hesychii Lexicon,	*Leyden,*	1688
Hieronymi Opera,	*Paris,*	1643
Hislop's Light of Prophecy,	*Edinburgh,*	1846
Homer,	*Cambridge,*	1711
——— (Pope's),	*London,*	1715
Horapollo's Hieroglyphics,	*Amsterdam,*	1835
Horatius,	*Paris,*	1691
Huc's Voyage dans la Tartarie et Thibet,	*Paris,*	1857
Humboldt's Mexican Researches,	*London,*	1814
Hurd's Rites and Ceremonies,	*London,*	S. D.
Hyde's Religio Persarum,	*Oxford,*	1700
Hygini Fabulæ,	*Leipsic,*	1856
Irenæi Opera,	*Leipsic,*	1853
Jamblichus on the Mysteries,	*Chiswick,*	1821
Jamieson's Scottish Dictionary,	*Edinburgh,*	1808
Jewell (British Reformers),	*London,*	S. D.
Jones's (Sir W.) Works,	*London,*	1807

Josephus (Græcé),	*Basle,*	1544
Justini Hist. (Hist. Rom. Script.),	*Aurelii,* *Allobrog.*	1609
Justinus Martyr,	*Wurtzburg,*	1777
Justus Lipsius,	*London,*	1698
Juvenal,	*London,*	1728
Kennedy's Ancient and Hindoo Mythology,	*London,*	1831
Kennett's Roman Antiquities,	*London,*	1696
Kitto's Cyclopædia,	*Edinburgh,*	1856
Kitto's Illustrated Commentary,	*London,*	1840
Knox's History of Reformation,	*Edin.,*	1846-48
Knox (British Reformers),	*London,*	S. D.
Lactantius,	*Cambridge,*	1685
Lafitau, Mœurs des Sauvages Americains,	*Paris,*	1724
Landseer's Sabean Researches,	*London,*	1823
Layard's Babylon and Nineveh,	*London,*	1853
——— Nineveh,	*London,*	1849
Livius,	*Amsterdam,*	1710
Lorimer's Manual of Presbytery,	*Edinburgh,*	1842
Lucan. de Bell. Civ.,	*Leyden,*	1658
Lucianus,	*Amsterdam,*	1743
Lucretius,	*Oxford,*	1695
Lycophron (Poet. Græc. Min.),	*Geneva,*	1814
Macrobius,	*Sanct. Colon.*	1521
M'Gavin's Protestant,	*Glasgow,*	1850
Maimonides More Nevochim,	*Basle,*	1629
Maitland on the Catacombs,	*London,*	1846
Mallet's Northern Antiquities,	*London,*	1770
Mallet,	*London,*	1847
Manilius,	*Berlin,*	1846
Martialis Epigrammata,	*Leyden,*	1656
Massy, Memoir of Rev. G.,	*London,*	1859
Maurice's Indian Antiquities,	*London* (*See Note*).	
Mede's Works,	*London,*	1672
Middleton's Letter from Rome,	*London,*	1741
Milner's Church History,	*London,*	1712
Milton's Paradise Lost,	*London,*	1695
Minutius Felix,	*Leyden,*	1672
Missale Romanum,	*Paris,*	1677
Do. do.,	*Vienna,*	1506
Missionary Record of Free Church,	*Edinburgh,*	1855
Moor's Hindoo Pantheon,	*London,*	1810
Morgan's (Lady) Italy,	*London,*	1824
Moses of Chorené,	*London,*	1736
Müller's Dorians,	*Oxford,*	1830
Mulleri Fragmenta,	*Paris,*	1846-51
Newman's Development,	*London,*	1846
Niebuhr's Roman History,	*London,*	1855
Nonnus de Phil. Oriental. et Dionysiaca,	*Leipsic,*	1857
Orphic Hymns (Poet. Græc.),	*Paris,*	1556
Ouvaroff's Eleusinian Mysteries,	*London,*	1817

Ovidii Opera,	*Leyden,*	1661
Pancarpium Mariæ,	*Antwerp,*	1618
Paradisus Sponsi et Sponsæ,	*Antwerp,*	1618
Parkhurst's Heb. Lexicon,	*London.*	1799
Parson's Japhet,	*London,*	1767
Pausanias,	*Leipsic,*	1696
Paxton's Illustrations, Geography,	*Edinburgh,*	1842
Persius,	*Leyden,*	1696
Petri Suavis Polani, Concilium Tridentinum,	*Gorinchemi,*	1658
Pfeiffer's (Ida) Iceland,	*London,*	1853
Photii Bibliotheca,	*Berlin,*	1824
——— Lexeōn Synagogé,	*London,*	1822
Pindarus,	*Oxford,*	1697
Pinkerton's Voyages,	*London,*	1808-14
Platonis Opera,	*Paris,*	1578
Plinii Opera,	*Frankfort,*	1599
Plutarchi Opera,	*Frankfort,*	1599
Pococke's India in Greece,	*London,*	1852
Pompeii,	*London,*	1831
Pontificale Romanum,	*Venice,*	1543
Do. do.,	*Venice,*	1572
Poor Man's Manual,	*Dublin,*	S. D.
Porphyrius de Antro Nympharum,	*Utrecht,*	1765
Potter's Greek Antiquities,	*Oxford,*	1697
Prescott's Conquest of Peru,	*London,*	1855
——— Mexico,	*London,*	1843
Prisciani Opera,	*Leipsic,*	1819
Proclus in Timæo,	*Vratislaviæ,*	1847
——— on Plat. Theology,	*London,*	1816
Propertius,	*Utrecht,*	1659
Quarterly Journal of Prophecy,	*London,*	1852
Quintus Curtius,	*Amsterdam,*	1684
Redhouse's Turkish Dictionary,	*London,*	1856
Rome in the Nineteenth Century,	*London,*	1823
Russell's Egypt,	*Edinburgh,*	1831
Ryle's (Rev. J.) Commentary,	*Ipswich,*	1858
Salverté, Eusebe, Sciences Occultes,	*Paris,*	1856
——— Essai sur les Noms,	*Paris,*	1824
Sanchuniathon,	*Bremen,*	1837
Scottish Protestant,	*Glasgow,*	1852
Septuagint,	*Paris,*	1628
Servius,	*Gottingen,*	1826
Savary's Letters on Egypt,	*London,*	1786
Seymour's Evenings with Romanists,	*London,*	1854
Sinclair's (Sir George) Letters to Protestants,	*Edinburgh.*	1852
Smith's Classical Dictionary,	*London,*	1859
Socrates Ecclesiasticus,	*Paris.*	1686
Sophocles,	*London,*	1747
Stanley's History of Philosophy,	*London,*	1687
Statius,	*Leyden,*	1671
Stephen's Central America,	*London,*	1841

Stockii Clavis,	*Lipsiæ,*	1753
Strabo,	*Basle,*	1549
Suidas,	*Geneva,*	1619
Symmachi Epistolæ,	*Douai,*	1587
Tacitus,	*Dublin,*	1730
Taylor's Mystic Hymns of Orpheus,	*Chiswick,*	1824
——— Pausanias	*London,*	1794
Tertulliani Opera,	*Paris,*	1844
Theocritus (Poet. Græc. Min.),	*Cambridge,*	1661
Theopompus (Müller),	*Paris,*	1853
Thevenot, Voyages,	*Paris,*	1689
Thuani Historia,	*London,*	1733
Todd's Western India,	*London,*	1839
Toland's Druids,	*Edinburgh,*	1815
Tooke's Pantheon,	*London,*	1806
Trimen's Architecture,	*London,*	1849
Trogus Pompeius (Hist. Rom. Script.),	*Aurel. Allobrog.*	1609
Turner's Anglo-Saxons,	*London,*	1823
Usher's Syllogé,	*Dublin,*	1632
Valerius Maximus,	*Venice,*	1505
Vaux's Nineveh,	*London,*	1851
——— Antiquities of the British Museum,	*London,*	1851
Virgilius,	*Paris,*	1675
Vitruvius de Architectura,	*Leipsic,*	1807
Vossius de Idololatria,	*Amsterdam,*	1668
Walpole's Ansayri,	*London,*	1849
Wilkinson's Egyptians,	*London,*	1837-41
Williams's Missionary Enterprises,	*London,*	1847
Wilson's India 3000 Years Ago,	*Bombay,*	1858
——— Parsee Religion,	*Bombay,*	1843
Wylie's Great Exodus,	*London,*	1862
Xenophontis Opera,	*Paris,*	1625
Zonaras,	*Bonn,*	1841
Zosimus (Rom. Hist. Script. Græci. Min.),	*Frankfort,*	1590

Note.—Of Maurice's "Indian Antiquities" in the copy quoted, except where otherwise stated, the 1st, 2nd, and 7th vols. are 1806; the 3rd, 1794; the 4th and 5th, 1800, and the 6th, 1812.

LIST OF ILLUSTRATIONS.

THE TWO BABYLONS.

"And upon her forehead was a name written, MYSTERY, BABYLON THE GREAT, THE MOTHER OF HARLOTS AND ABOMINATIONS OF THE EARTH."—REV. xvii. 5.

INTRODUCTION.

THERE is this great difference between the works of men and the works of God, that the same minute and searching investigation, which displays the defects and imperfections of the one, brings out also the beauties of the other. If the most finely polished needle on which the art of man has been expended be subjected to a microscope, many inequalities, much roughness and clumsiness, will be seen. But if the microscope be brought to bear on the flowers of the field, no such result appears. Instead of their beauty diminishing, new beauties and still more delicate, that have escaped the naked eye, are forthwith discovered; beauties that make us appreciate, in a way which otherwise we could have had little conception of, the full force of the Lord's saying, "Consider the lilies of the field, how they grow; they toil not, neither do they spin: and yet I say unto you, That even Solomon, in all his glory, was not arrayed like one of these." The same law appears also in comparing the *Word* of God and the most finished productions of men. There are spots and blemishes in the most admired productions of human genius. But the more the Scriptures are searched, the more minutely they are studied, the more their perfection appears; new beauties are brought into light every day; and the discoveries of science, the researches of the learned, and the labours of infidels, all alike conspire to illustrate the wonderful harmony of all the parts, and the Divine beauty that clothes the whole.

If this be the case with Scripture in general, it is especially the case with prophetic Scripture. As every spoke in the wheel of Providence revolves, the prophetic symbols start into still more bold and beautiful relief. This is very strikingly the case with the prophetic language that forms the groundwork and corner-stone of the present work. There never has been any difficulty in the mind of any enlightened Protestant in identifying the woman "sitting on seven mountains," and having on her forehead the name written, "Mystery, Babylon the Great," with the

Roman apostacy. "No other city in the world has ever been celebrated, as the city of Rome has, for its situation on seven hills. Pagan poets and orators, who had no thought of elucidating prophecy, have alike characterised it as 'the seven hilled city.'" Thus Virgil refers to it: "Rome has both become the most beautiful (city) in the world, and alone has surrounded for herself seven heights with a wall."* Propertius, in the same strain, speaks of it (only adding another trait, which completes the Apocalyptic picture) as "The lofty city on seven hills, which governs the whole world."† Its "governing the whole world" is just the counterpart of the Divine statement—"which reigneth over the kings of the earth" (Rev. xvii. 18). To call Rome the city "of the seven hills" was by its citizens held to be as descriptive as to call it by its own proper name. Hence Horace speaks of it by reference to its seven hills alone, when he addresses, "The gods who have set their affections on the seven hills."‡ Martial, in like manner, speaks of "The seven dominating mountains."§ In times long subsequent, the same kind of language was in current use; for when Symmachus, the prefect of the city, and the last acting Pagan Pontifex Maximus, as the Imperial substitute, introduces by letter one friend of his to another, he calls him "De septem montibus virum"—"a man from the seven mountains," meaning thereby, as the commentators interpret it, "Civem Romanum," "A Roman Citizen."|| Now, while this characteristic of Rome has ever been well marked and defined, it has always been easy to show, that the Church which has its seat and headquarters on the seven hills of Rome might most appropriately be called "Babylon," inasmuch as it is the chief seat of idolatry under the New Testament, as the ancient Babylon was the chief seat of idolatry under the Old. But recent discoveries in Assyria, taken in connection with the previously well-known but ill-understood history and mythology of the ancient world, demonstrate that there is a vast deal more significance in the name Babylon the Great than this. It has been known all along that Popery was baptised Paganism; but God is now making it manifest, that the Paganism which Rome has baptised is, in all its essential elements, *the very Paganism* which prevailed in the ancient literal Babylon, when Jehovah opened before Cyrus the two-leaved gates of brass, and cut in sunder the bars of iron.

That new and unexpected light, in some way or other, should be cast, about this very period, on the Church of the grand Apostacy, the very language and symbols of the Apocalypse might have prepared us to anticipate. In the Apocalyptic visions, it is *just before the judgment upon her* that, for the first time, John sees the

* Scilicet et rerum facta est pulcherrima Roma
Septemqueuna sibi muro circumdedit arces.
—*Georg.*, lib. ii. v. 534, 535.

† Septem urbs alta jugis toto quæ præsidet orbi.—Lib. iii. Eleg. 9, p. 721.

‡ Diis, quibus septem placuere colles.—*Carmen Seculare*, v. 7, p. 497.

§ Septem dominos montes.—Lib. iv. Ep. 64, p. 254.

|| SYMMACHUS, lib. ii. Epis. 9, *Note*, p. 63.

Apostate Church with the name Babylon the Great "written upon her forehead" (Rev. xvii. 5). What means the writing of that name "*on the forehead*"? Does it not naturally indicate that, just before judgment overtakes her, her real character was to be so thoroughly developed, that everyone who has eyes to see, who has the least spiritual discernment, would be compelled, as it were, on ocular demonstration, to recognise the wonderful fitness of the title which the Spirit of God had affixed to her. Her judgment is now evidently hastening on; and just as it approaches, the Providence of God, conspiring with the Word of God, by light pouring in from all quarters, makes it more and more evident that Rome is in very deed the Babylon of the Apocalypse; that the essential character of her system, the grand objects of her worship, her festivals, her doctrine and discipline, her rites and ceremonies, her priesthood and their orders, have all been derived from ancient Babylon; and, finally, that the Pope himself is truly and properly the lineal representative of Belshazzar. In the warfare that has been waged against the domineering pretensions of Rome, it has too often been counted enough merely to meet and set aside her presumptuous boast, that she is the mother and mistress of all churches—the one Catholic Church, out of whose pale there is no salvation. If ever there was excuse for such a mode of dealing with her, that excuse will hold no longer. If the position I have laid down can be maintained, she must be stripped of the name of a Christian Church altogether; for if it was a Church of Christ that was convened on that night, when the pontiff-king of Babylon, in the midst of his thousand lords, "praised the gods of gold, and of silver, and of wood, and of stone" (Dan. v. 4), then the Church of Rome is entitled to the name of a Christian Church; but not otherwise. This to some, no doubt, will appear a very startling position; but it is one which it is the object of this work to establish; and let the reader judge for himself, whether I do not bring ample evidence to substantiate my position.

CHAPTER I.

DISTINCTIVE CHARACTER OF THE TWO SYSTEMS.

In leading proof of the Babylonian character of the Papal Church, the first point to which I solicit the reader's attention, is the character of Mystery which attaches alike to the modern Roman and the ancient Babylonian systems. The gigantic system of moral corruption and idolatry, described in this passage under the emblem of a woman with a "golden cup in her hand" (Rev. xvii. 4), "making all nations drunk with the wine of her fornication" (Rev. xvii. 2; xviii. 3), is divinely called "Mystery, Babylon the Great" (Rev. xvii. 5). That Paul's "Mystery of iniquity," as described in 2 Thess. ii. 7, has its counterpart in the Church of Rome, no man of candid mind, who has carefully examined the subject, can easily doubt. Such was the impression made by that account on the mind of the great Sir Matthew Hale, no mean judge of evidence, that he used to say, that if the apostolic description were inserted in the public "Hue and Cry," any constable in the realm would be warranted in seizing, wherever he found him, the Bishop of Rome as the head of that "Mystery of iniquity." Now, as the system here described is equally characterised by the name of "Mystery," it may be presumed that both passages refer to the same system. But the language applied to the New Testament Babylon, as the reader cannot fail to see, naturally leads us back to the Babylon of the ancient world. As the Apocalyptic woman has in her hand a cup, wherewith she intoxicates the nations, so was it with the Babylon of old. Of that Babylon, while in all its glory, the Lord thus spake, in denouncing its doom by the prophet Jeremiah: "Babylon hath been a golden cup in the Lord's hand, that made all the earth drunken: the nations have drunken of her wine; therefore the nations are mad" (Jer. li. 7). Why this exact similarity of language in regard to the two systems? The natural inference surely is, that the one stands to the other in the relation of type and antitype. Now, as the Babylon of the Apocalypse is characterised by the name of "Mystery," so the grand distinguishing feature of the ancient Babylonian system was the Chaldean "Mysteries," that formed so essential a part of that system. And to these mysteries, the very language of the Hebrew prophet, symbolical though of course it is, distinctly alludes, when he speaks of Babylon as a "golden cup." To drink of "mysterious beverages," says Salverté, was indispensable on the part of all who sought initiation in these Mysteries.* These "mysterious beverages" were composed of "*wine*, honey, water, and flour."† From the ingredients avowedly used, and from the nature of others not avowed, but certainly used,‡ there can be no doubt that they were of an intoxicating nature; and till the aspirants had come under their power, till their understandings had been dimmed, and their passions excited by the medicated draught, they were not duly prepared for what they were either to hear or to see. If it be inquired what was the object and design of these ancient "Mysteries," it will be found that there was a wonderful analogy between them and that "Mystery of iniquity" which is embodied in the Church of Rome. Their primary object was to introduce privately, by little and little, under the seal of secrecy and the sanction of an oath, what it would not have been safe all at once and openly to propound. The *time* at which they were instituted proves that this must have been the case. The Chaldean Mysteries can be traced up to the days of Semiramis, who lived only a few centuries after the flood, and who is known to have impressed upon them the image of her own depraved and polluted mind.§ That beautiful but abandoned queen of Babylon was not only herself a paragon of unbridled lust and licentiousness, but in the Mysteries which she had a chief hand in forming, she was worshipped as Rhea,‖ the great "MOTHER" of the gods,¶ with such atrocious rites as identified her with Venus, the MOTHER of all impurity, and raised the very city where she had reigned to a bad eminence among the nations, as the grand seat at once of idolatry and consecrated prostitution.†† Thus

Fig. 1.

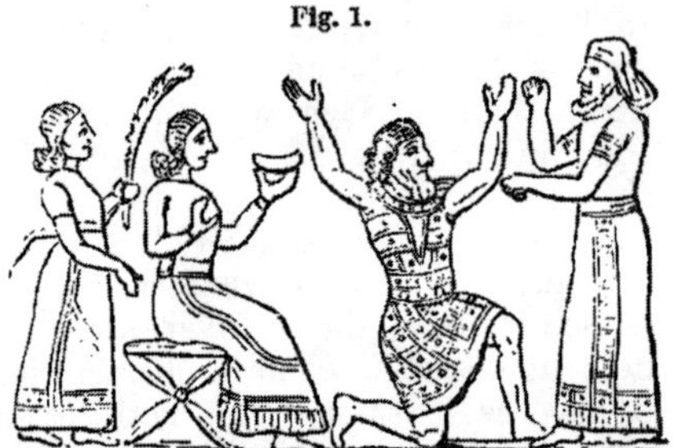

Woman with cup ** from Babylon.—(KITTO'S *Biblical Cyclopædia.*)

* EUSÈBE SALVERTÉ, *Des Sciences Occultes*, p. 259.

† GEBELIN, *Monde Primitif*, vol. iv. p. 319.

‡ See SALVERTÉ, pp. 258, 259.

§ AMMIANUS MARCELLINUS, lib. xiv. cap. 6, p. ad. 26, and lib. xxiii. cap. 6, pp. 371, 374, compared with JUSTINUS, *Historia*, lib. i. cap. 1, p. 615, and EUSEBIUS'S *Chronicle*, vol. i. pp. 40, 70, &c. Eusebius says that Ninus and Semiramis reigned in the time of Abraham. See vol. i. p. 41, and vol. ii. p. 65. In regard to the age of Semiramis, see further in note on next page.

‖ *Chronicon Paschale*, vol. i. p. 65. ¶ HESIOD, *Theogonia*, v. 453, p. 36.

** The shape of the cup in the woman's hand is the same as that of the cup held in the hand of the Assyrian kings; and it is held also in the very same manner.—See VAUX, pp. 243, 284.

[A correspondent has pointed out a reference by Pliny to the cup of Semiramis, which fell into the hands of the victorious Cyrus. Its gigantic proportions must have made it famous among the Babylonians and the nations with whom they had intercourse. It weighed fifteen talents, or 1200 pounds.—PLINII, Hist. Nat., lib. xxxiii. cap. 15.]

†† HERODOTUS, *Historia*, lib. i. cap. 199, p. 92; QUINTUS CURTIS, v. 1.

was this Chaldean queen a fit and remarkable prototype of the "*Woman*" in the Apocalypse, with the golden cup in her hand, and the name on her forehead, "Mystery, Babylon the Great, the MOTHER of harlots and abominations of the earth." (Fig. 1.) The Apocalyptic emblem of the Harlot woman with the cup in her hand was even embodied in the symbols of idolatry derived from ancient Babylon, as they were exhibited in Greece; for thus was the Greek Venus originally represented,* and it is singular that in our own day, and so far as appears for the first time, the Roman Church has actually taken this very symbol as her own chosen emblem. In 1825, on the occasion of the jubilee, Pope Leo XII. struck a medal, bearing on the one side his own image, and on the other, that of the Church of Rome symbolised as a "Woman," holding in her left hand a cross, and in her right a CUP, with the legend around her, "*Sedet super universum,*" "The whole world is her seat."† (Fig. 2.) Now the period when Semiramis lived,—a period when the patriarchal faith was still fresh in the minds of men, when Shem was still alive,‡ to rouse the minds of the faithful to rally around the banner for the truth and cause of God, made it hazardous all at once and publicly

Fig. 2.

Woman with cup from Rome, on reverse of medal.—(ELLIOTT's *Horæ*.)

to set up such a system as was inaugurated by the Babylonian queen. We know, from the statements in Job, that among

* For evidence on this subject, see Appendix, Note A.

† ELLIOTT's *Horæ*, vol. iv. p. 30.

‡ For the age of Shem see Genesis xi. 10, 11. According to this, Shem lived 502 years after the flood, that is, according to the Hebrew chronology, till B.C. 1846. The age of Ninus, the husband of Semiramis, as stated in a former note, according to Eusebius, synchronised with that of Abraham, who was born B.C. 1996. It was only about nine years, however, before the end of the reign of Ninus, that the birth of Abraham is said to have taken place.—(SYNCELLUS, p. 170. Paris, 1652.) Consequently, on this view, the reign of Ninus must have terminated, according to the usual chronology, about B.C. 1987. Clinton, who is of high authority in chronology, places the reign of Ninus somewhat earlier. In his *Fasti Hellenici* (vol. i. p. 263) he makes his age to have been B.C. 2182. Layard (in his *Nineveh and its Remains*, vol. ii. p. 217) subscribes to this opinion. Semiramis is said to have survived her husband forty-two years.—(SYNCELL., p. 96.) Whatever view, therefore, be adopted in regard to the age of Ninus, whether that of Eusebius, or that at which Clinton and Layard have arrived, it is evident that Shem long survived both Ninus and his wife. Of course, this argument proceeds on the supposition of the correctness of the Hebrew chronology. For conclusive evidence on that subject, see Appendix, Note B.

patriarchal tribes that had nothing whatever to do with Mosaic institutions, but which adhered to the pure faith of the patriarchs, idolatry in any shape was held to be a crime, to be visited with signal and summary punishment on the heads of those who practised it. "If I beheld the sun," said Job, "when it shined, or the moon walking in brightness; and my heart hath been secretly enticed, and* my mouth hath kissed my hand; *this also were an iniquity to be punished by the judge;* for I should have denied the God that is above" (Job xxxi. 26–28). Now if this was the case in Job's day, much more must it have been the case at the earlier period when the Mysteries were instituted. It was a matter, therefore, of necessity, if idolatry were to be brought in, and especially such foul idolatry as the Babylonian system contained in its bosom, that it should be done stealthily and in secret.† Even though introduced by the hand of power, it might have produced a revulsion, and violent attempts might have been made by the uncorrupted portion of mankind to put it down; and at all events, if it had appeared at once in all its hideousness, it would have alarmed the consciences of men, and defeated the very object in view. That object was to bind all mankind in blind and absolute submission to a hierarchy entirely dependent on the sovereigns of Babylon. In the carrying out of this scheme, all knowledge, sacred and profane, came to be monopolised by the priesthood,‡ who dealt it out to those who were initiated in the "Mysteries" exactly as they saw fit, according as the interests of the grand system of spiritual despotism they had to administer might seem to require. Thus the people, wherever the Babylonian system spread, were bound neck and heel to the priests. The priests were the only depositaries of religious knowledge; they only had the true tradition, by which the writs and symbols of the public religion could be interpreted; and without blind and implicit submission to them, what was necessary for salvation could not be known. Now compare this with the early history of the Papacy, and with its spirit and *modus operandi* throughout, and how exact was the coincidence! Was it in a period of patriarchal light that the corrupt system of the Babylonian "Mysteries" began? It was in a period of still greater light that that unholy and unscriptural system commenced, that has found such rank development in the Church of Rome. It began in the very age of the apostles, when the primitive Church was in its flower, when the glorious fruits of Pentecost were everywhere to be seen, when martyrs were sealing their testimony for the truth with their blood. Even then, when the Gospel shone so brightly, the Spirit of God bore this clear and distinct testimony by Paul: "THE MYSTERY OF INIQUITY DOTH ALREADY WORK"

* That which I have rendered "*and*" is in the authorised version "or," but there is no reason for such a rendering, for the word in the original is the very same as that which connects the previous clause, "*and* my heart," &c.

† It will be seen by-and-by what cogent reason there was, in *point of fact*, for the profoundest secrecy in the matter.—See Chapter II.

‡ EUSÈBE SALVERTÉ, *Des Sciences Occultes, passim.*

(2 Thess. ii. 7). That system of iniquity which then began it was divinely foretold was to issue in a portentous apostacy, that in due time would be awfully "revealed," and would continue until it should be destroyed "by the breath of the Lord's mouth, and consumed by the brightness of His coming" (*Ibid.* v. 8). But at its first introduction into the Church, it came in secretly and by stealth, with "all DECEIVABLENESS of unrighteousness." It wrought "mysteriously" under fair but false pretences, leading men away from the simplicity of the truth as it is in Jesus. And it did so secretly, for the very same reason that idolatry was secretly introduced in the ancient Mysteries of Babylon; it was not safe, it was not prudent to do otherwise. The zeal of the true Church, though destitute of civil power, would have aroused itself, to put the false system and all its abettors beyond the pale of Christianity, if it had appeared openly and all at once in all its grossness; and this would have arrested its progress. Therefore it was brought in secretly, and by little and little, one corruption being introduced after another, as apostacy proceeded, and the backsliding Church became prepared to tolerate it, till it has reached the gigantic height we now see, when in almost every particular the system of the Papacy is the very antipodes of the system of the primitive Church. Of the *gradual* introduction of all that is now most characteristic of Rome, through the working of the "*Mystery of iniquity*," we have very striking evidence, preserved even by Rome itself, in the inscriptions copied from the Roman catacombs. These catacombs are extensive excavations underground in the neighbourhood of Rome, in which the Christians, in times of persecution during the first three centuries, celebrated their worship, and also buried their dead. On some of the tombstones there are inscriptions still to be found, which are directly in the teeth of the now well-known principles and practices of Rome. Take only one example: What, for instance, at this day is a more distinguishing mark of the Papacy than the enforced celibacy of the clergy? Yet from these inscriptions we have most decisive evidence, that even in Rome, there was a time when no such system of clerical celibacy was known. Witness the following, found on different tombs:—

1. "To Basilius, the *presbyter*, and Felicitas, *his wife*. They made this for themselves."

2. "Petronia, a *priest's wife*, the type of modesty. In this place I lay my bones. Spare your tears, dear husband and daughter, and believe that it is forbidden to weep for one who lives in God."* A prayer here and there for the dead: "May God refresh thy spirit," proves that even then the Mystery of iniquity had *begun* to work; but inscriptions such as the above equally show that it had been slowly and cautiously working,—that up to the period to which they refer, the Roman Church had not proceeded the length it has done now, of absolutely "forbidding its priests to 'marry.'" Craftily and gradually did Rome lay the foundation of its system of priest-

* DR. MAITLAND'S *Church in the Catacombs*, pp. 191, 192.

craft, on which it was afterwards to rear so vast a superstructure. At its commencement, "*Mystery*" was stamped upon its system.

But this feature of "Mystery" has adhered to it throughout its whole course. When it had once succeeded in dimming the light of the Gospel, obscuring the fulness and freeness of the grace of God, and drawing away the souls of men from direct and immediate dealings with the One Grand Prophet and High Priest of our profession, a mysterious power was attributed to the clergy, which gave them "dominion over the faith" of the people—a dominion directly disclaimed by apostolic men (2 Cor. i. 24), but which, in connection with the confessional, has become at least as absolute and complete as was ever possessed by Babylonian priest over those initiated in the ancient Mysteries. The clerical power of the Roman priesthood culminated in the erection of the confessional. That confessional was itself borrowed from Babylon. The confession required of the votaries of Rome is entirely different from the confession prescribed in the Word of God. The dictate of Scripture in regard to confession is, "Confess your faults *one to another*" (James v. 16), which implies that the priest should confess to the people, as well as the people to the priest, if either should sin against the other. This could never have served any purpose of spiritual despotism; and therefore, Rome, leaving the Word of God, has had recourse to the Babylonian system. In that system, secret confession to the priest, according to a prescribed form, was required of all who were admitted to the "Mysteries;" and till such confession had been made, no complete initiation could take place. Thus does Salverté refer to this confession as observed in Greece, in rites that can be clearly traced to a Babylonian origin: *—"All the Greeks, from Delphi to Thermopylæ, were initiated in the Mysteries of the temple of Delphi. Their silence in regard to everything they were commanded to keep secret was secured both by the fear of the penalties threatened to a perjured revelation, and by the general CONFESSION exacted of the aspirants after initiation—a confession which caused *them* greater dread of the indiscretion of the priest, than gave *him* reason to dread *their* indiscretion."† This confession is also referred to by Potter, in his "Greek Antiquities," though it has been generally overlooked. In his account of the Eleusinian mysteries, after describing the preliminary ceremonies and instructions before the admission of the candidates for initiation into the immediate presence of the divinities, he thus proceeds:—"Then the priest that initiated them called Ἱεροφαντης [the Hierophant], proposed certain QUESTIONS, as, whether they were fasting, &c., to which they returned answers in a set form."‡ The etcetera here might not strike a casual reader; but it is a pregnant etcetera, and contains a great deal. It means, Are you free from every violation of chastity? and that not merely

* For *Babylonian* origin of these Mysteries, see next chapter, first two sections.

† EUSÈBE SALVERTÉ, *Des Sciences Occultes*, chap. xxvi. p. 428.

‡ POTTER, vol. i. *Eleusinia*, p. 356.

in the sense of moral impurity, but in that factitious sense of chastity which Paganism always cherishes.* Are you free from the guilt of murder?—for no one guilty of slaughter, even accidentally, could be admitted till he was purged from blood, and there were certain priests, called Köes, who "heard confessions" in such cases, and purged the guilt away.† The strictness of the inquiries in the Pagan confessional is evidently implied in certain licentious poems of Propertius, Tibullus, and Juvenal.‡ Wilkinson, in his chapter on "Private Fasts and Penance," which, he says, "were strictly enforced," in connection with "certain regulations at fixed periods,"§ has several classical quotations, which clearly prove *whence* Popery derived the kind of questions which have stamped that character of obscenity on its confessional, as exhibited in the notorious pages of Peter Dens. The pretence under which this auricular confession was required, was, that the solemnities to which the initiated were to be admitted were so high, so heavenly, so holy, that no man with guilt lying on his conscience, and sin unpurged, could lawfully be admitted to them. For the safety, therefore, of those who were to be initiated, it was held to be indispensable that the officiating priest should thoroughly probe their consciences, lest coming without due purgation from previous guilt contracted, the wrath of the gods should be provoked against the profane intruders. This was the pretence; but when we know the essentially unholy nature, both of the gods and their worship, who can fail to see that this was nothing more than a pretence; that the grand object in requiring the candidates for initiation to make confession to the priest of all their secret faults and shortcomings and sins, was just to put them entirely in the power of those to whom the inmost feelings of their souls and their most important secrets were confided? Now, exactly in the same way, and for the very same purposes, has Rome erected the confessional. Instead of requiring priests and people alike, as the Scripture does, to "confess their faults one to another," when either have offended the other, it commands all, on pain of perdition, to confess to the priest,‖ whether they have transgressed against him or no, while the priest is under no obligation to confess to the people at all. Without such confession, in the Church of Rome, there can be no admission to the Sacraments, any more than in the days of Paganism there could be admission without confession to the benefit of the Mysteries. Now, this confession is made

* For the arbitrary prohibitions, in consequence of which guilt might be contracted, see POTTER, vol. i. p. 356, a few sentences before the last quotation.

† DUPUIS, *De tous les Cultes*, vol. iv. Part I. p. 312. Paris. L'an III. de la Republique.

‡ See particularly JUVENAL, *Satires*, vi. 535, p. 129.

§ WILKINSON'S *Egyptians*, vol. v. pp. 335, 336.

‖ Bishop HAY'S *Sincere Christian*, vol. ii. p. 68. In this work, the following question and answer occur:—"*Q.* Is this confession of our sins necessary for obtaining absolution? *A.* It is ordained by Jesus Christ as *absolutely necessary* for this purpose." See also *Poor Man's Manual*, a work in use in Ireland, pp. 109, 110.

by every individual, in SECRECY AND IN SOLITUDE, to the priest sitting in the name and clothed with the authority of God,* invested with the power to examine the conscience, to judge the life, to absolve or condemn according to his mere arbitrary will and pleasure. This is the grand pivot on which the whole "Mystery of iniquity," as embodied in the Papacy, is made to turn; and wherever it is submitted to, admirably does it serve the design of binding men in abject subjection to the priesthood.

In conformity with the principle out of which the confessional grew, the Church, that is, the clergy, claimed to be the sole depositaries of the true faith of Christianity. As the Chaldean priests were believed alone to possess the key to the understanding of the Mythology of Babylon, a key handed down to them from primeval antiquity, so the priests of Rome set up to be the sole interpreters of Scripture; they only had the true tradition, transmitted from age to age, without which it was impossible to arrive at its true meaning. They, therefore, require implicit faith in their dogmas; all men were bound to believe as the Church believed, while the Church in this way could shape its faith as it pleased. As possessing supreme authority, also, over the faith, they could let out little or much, as they judged most expedient; and "RESERVE" in teaching the great truths of religion was as essential a principle in the system of Babylon, as it is in Romanism or Tractarianism at this day.† It was this priestly claim to dominion over the faith of men, that "imprisoned the truth in unrighteousness" ‡ in the ancient world, so that "darkness covered the earth, and gross darkness the people." It was the very same claim, in the hands of the Roman priests, that ushered in the dark ages, when, through many a dreary century, the Gospel was unknown, and the Bible a sealed book to millions who bore the name of Christ. In every respect, then, we see how justly Rome bears on its forehead the name, "*Mystery*, Babylon the Great."

* *Light of Prophecy*, Appendix, Note C.

† Even among the initiated there was a difference. Some were admitted only to the "Lesser Mysteries;" the "Greater" were for a favoured *few*.—WILKINSON'S *Ancient Egyptians*, vol. i. pp. 266, 267.

‡ Romans i. 18. The best interpreters render the passage as given above. It will be observed Paul is expressly speaking of the heathen.

CHAPTER II.

OBJECTS OF WORSHIP.

SECTION I.—TRINITY IN UNITY.

If there be this general coincidence between the systems of Babylon and Rome, the question arises, Does the coincidence stop here? To this the answer is, Far otherwise. We have only to bring the ancient Babylonian Mysteries to bear on the whole system of Rome, and then it will be seen how immensely the one has borrowed from the other. These Mysteries were long shrouded in darkness, but now the thick darkness begins to pass away. All who have paid the least attention to the literature of Greece, Egypt, Phenicia, or Rome are aware of the place which the "Mysteries" occupied in these countries, and that, whatever circumstantial diversities there might be, in all *essential* respects these "Mysteries" in the different countries were the same. Now, as the language of Jeremiah, already quoted, would indicate that Babylon was the primal source from which all these systems of idolatry flowed, so the deductions of the most learned historians, on mere historical grounds, have led to the same conclusion.* From Zonaras† we find that the concurrent testimony of the ancient authors he had consulted was to this effect; for, speaking of arithmetic and astronomy, he says: "It is said that these came from the Chaldees to the Egyptians, and thence to the Greeks." If the Egyptians and Greeks derived their arithmetic and astronomy from Chaldea, seeing these in Chaldea were sacred sciences, and monopolised by the priests, that is sufficient evidence that they must have derived their religion from the same quarter. Both Bunsen and Layard in their researches have come to substantially the same result. The statement of Bunsen is to the effect that the religious system of Egypt was derived from Asia, and "the primitive empire in Babel."‡ Layard, again, though taking a somewhat more favourable view of the system of the Chaldean Magi, than, I am persuaded, the facts of history warrant, nevertheless thus speaks of that system:—"Of the great antiquity of this primitive worship there is abundant evidence, and that it originated among the inhabitants of the Assyrian plains, we have the united testimony of sacred and profane history. It obtained the epithet of *perfect*, and was

* See Herodotus, lib. ii. cap. 109, and Diogenes Laertius, *Proëm.* p. 2.
† Lib. i. 6, p. 34.
‡ Bunsen's *Egypt*, vol. i. p. 444.

believed to be the most ancient of religious systems, having preceded that of the Egyptians (Egyptiis vero antiquiores esse MAGOS Aristoteles auctor est in primo de Philosophia libro.—*Theopompi Frag.*)."* "The identity," he adds, "of many of the Assyrian doctrines with those of Egypt is alluded to by Porphyry and Clemens;" and, in connection with the same subject, he quotes the following from Birch on Babylonian cylinders and monuments:—"The zodiacal signs . . . . show unequivocally that the Greeks derived their notions and arrangements of the zodiac [and consequently their Mythology, that was intertwined with it] from the Chaldees. The identity of Nimrod with the constellation Orion is not to be rejected."† Ouvaroff, also, in his learned work on the Eleusinian mysteries, has come to the same conclusion. After referring to the fact that the Egyptian priests claimed the honour of having transmitted to the Greeks the first elements of Polytheism, he thus concludes:—"These positive facts would sufficiently prove, even without the conformity of ideas, that the Mysteries transplanted into Greece, and there united with a certain number of local notions, never lost the character of their origin derived from the cradle of the moral and religious ideas of the universe. All these separate facts—all these scattered testimonies, recur to that fruitful principle which places in the East the centre of science and civilisation."‡ If thus we have evidence that Egypt and Greece derived their religion from Babylon, we have equal evidence that the religious system of the Phenicians came from the same source. Macrobius shows that the distinguishing feature of the Phenician idolatry must have been imported from Assyria, which, in classic writers, included Babylonia. "The worship of the Architic Venus," says he, "formerly flourished as much among the Assyrians as it does now among the Phenicians." §

Now to establish the identity between the systems of ancient Babylon and Papal Rome, we have just to inquire in how far does the system of the Papacy agree with the system established in these Babylonian Mysteries. In prosecuting such an inquiry there are considerable difficulties to be overcome; for, as in geology, it is impossible at all points to reach the deep, underlying strata of the earth's surface, so it is not to be expected that in any one country we should find a complete and connected account of the system established in that country. But yet, even as the geologist, by examining the contents of a fissure here, an upheaval there, and what "crops out" of itself on the surface elsewhere, is enabled to determine, with wonderful certainty, the order and general contents of the different strata over all the earth, so is it with the subject of the Chaldean Mysteries. What is wanted in one country is supplemented in another; and what actually "crops out" in different

* LAYARD'S *Nineveh and its Remains*, vol. ii. p. 440.

† *Ibid.* pp. 439, 440.

‡ OUVAROFF'S *Eleusinian Mysteries*, sect. ii. p. 20.

§ *Saturnalia*, lib. i. cap. 21, p. 79.

directions, to a large extent necessarily determines the character of much that does not directly appear on the surface. Taking, then, the admitted unity and Babylonian character of the ancient Mysteries of Egypt, Greece, Phenicia, and Rome, as the clue to guide us in our researches, let us go on from step to step in our comparison of the doctrine and practice of the two Babylons—the Babylon of the Old Testament and the Babylon of the New.

And here I have to notice, first, the identity of the *objects of worship* in Babylon and Rome. The ancient Babylonians, just as the modern Romans, recognised in *words* the unity of the Godhead; and, while worshipping innumerable minor deities, as possessed of certain influence on human affairs, they distinctly acknowledged that there was ONE infinite and Almighty Creator, supreme over all.* Most other nations did the same. "In the early ages of mankind," says Wilkinson in his "Ancient Egyptians," "the existence of a sole and omnipotent Deity, who created all things, seems to have been the *universal belief;* and tradition taught men the same notions on this subject, which, in later times, have been adopted by all civilised nations."† "The Gothic religion," says Mallet, "taught the being of a supreme God, Master of the Universe, to whom all things were submissive and obedient."—(*Tacit. de Morib. Germ.*) The ancient Icelandic mythology calls him "the Author of every thing that existeth, the eternal, the living, and awful Being; the searcher into concealed things, the Being that never changeth." It attributeth to this deity "an infinite power, a boundless knowledge, and incorruptible justice."‡ We have evidence of the same having been the faith of ancient Hindostan. Though modern Hinduism recognises millions of gods, yet the Indian sacred books show that originally it had been far otherwise. Major Moor, speaking of Brahm, the supreme God of the Hindoos, says: "Of Him whose Glory is so great, there is no image" (Veda). He "illumines all, delights all, whence all proceeded; that by which they live when born, and that to which all must return" (Veda).§ In the "Institutes of Menu," he is characterised as "He whom the mind alone can perceive; whose essence eludes the external organs, who has no visible parts, who exists from eternity . . . . the soul of all beings, whom no being can comprehend."‖ In these passages, there is a trace of the existence of Pantheism; but the very language employed bears testimony to the existence among the Hindoos at one period of a far purer faith.

Nay, not merely had the ancient Hindoos exalted ideas of the *natural* perfections of God, but there is evidence that they were well aware of the *gracious* character of God, as revealed in His dealings with a lost and guilty world. This is manifest from the very name

* JAMBLICHUS, sect. viii. chap. ii. MACROBIUS, *Saturnalia*, p. 65.
† WILKINSON, vol. iv. p. 176.
‡ MALLET'S *Northern Antiquities*, vol. i. pp. 78, 79.
§ MOOR'S *Pantheon*, p. 4.
‖ Col. VANS KENNEDY'S *Hindoo Mythology*, p. 270.

Brahm, appropriated by them to the one infinite and eternal God. There has been a great deal of unsatisfactory speculation in regard to the meaning of this name, but when the different statements in regard to Brahm are carefully considered, it becomes evident that the name Brahm is just the Hebrew Rahm, with the digamma prefixed, which is very frequent in Sanscrit words derived from Hebrew or Chaldee. Rahm in Hebrew signifies "The merciful or compassionate one."* But Rahm also signifies the WOMB† or the *bowels;*‡ as the seat of compassion. Now we find such language applied to Brahm, the one supreme God, as cannot be accounted for, except on the supposition that Brahm had the very same meaning as the Hebrew Rahm. Thus, we find the God Crishna, in one of the Hindoo sacred books, when asserting his high dignity as a divinity and his identity with the Supreme, using the following words: "The great Brahm is my WOMB, and in it I place my fœtus, and from it is the procreation of all nature. The great Brahm is the WOMB of all the various forms which are conceived in every natural womb."§ How could such language ever have been applied to "The supreme Brahm, the most holy, the most high God, the Divine being, before all other gods; without birth, the mighty Lord, God of gods, the universal Lord,"|| but from the connection between Rahm "the womb" and Rahm "the merciful one"? Here, then, we find that Brahm is just the same as "Er-Rahman," "The all-merciful one,"—a title applied by the Turks to the Most High, and that the Hindoos, notwithstanding their deep religious degradation *now*, had *once* known that "the most holy, most high God," is also "The God of Mercy," in other words, that he is "a just God and a Saviour."¶ And proceeding on this interpretation of the name Brahm, we see how exactly their religious knowledge as to the creation had coincided with the account of the origin of all things, as given in Genesis. It is well known that the Brahmins, to exalt themselves as a priestly, half-divine caste, to whom all others ought to bow down, have for many ages taught that, while the other castes came from the arms, and body and feet of Brahmà—the visible representative and manifestation of the invisible Brahm, and identified with him—*they alone* came from the mouth of the creative God. Now we find statements in their sacred books which prove that *once* a very different doctrine must have been taught. Thus, in one of the Vedas, speaking of Brahmà, it is expressly stated that "ALL beings" "are created from his MOUTH."** In the passage in question an attempt is made to mystify the matter; but, taken in connection with the meaning of the name Brahm, as already given, who can doubt what was the

* See PARKHURST'S *Hebrew Lexicon, sub voce*, No. V.

† *Ibid.* No. II.

‡ *Ibid.* No. IV.

§ MOOR'S *Pantheon*, "Crishna," p. 211.

|| GITA, p. 86, *apud* MOOR.

¶ For further evidence as to Hindu knowledge on this subject, see near the end of next section.

** *Asiatic Researches*, vol. vii. p. 294. London, 1807.

real meaning of the statement, opposed though it be to the lofty and exclusive pretensions of the Brahmins? It evidently meant that He who, ever since the fall, has been revealed to man as the "Merciful* and Gracious One" (Exod. xxxiv. 6), was known at the same time as the Almighty One, who in the beginning "*spake* and it was done," "*commanded* and all things stood fast," who made all things by the "*Word* of His power." After what has now been said, any one who consults the "Asiatic Researches," vol. vii. p. 293, may see that it is in a great measure from a wicked perversion of this Divine title of the One Living and True God, a title that ought to have been so dear to sinful men, that all those moral abominations have come that make the symbols of the pagan temples of India so offensive to the eye of purity.†

So utterly idolatrous was the Babylonian recognition of the Divine unity, that Jehovah, the Living God, severely condemned His own people for giving any countenance to it: "They that sanctify themselves, and purify themselves in the gardens, after the rites of the ONLY ONE,‡ eating swine's flesh, and the abomination, and the mouse, shall be consumed together" (Isaiah lxvi. 17). In the unity of that one Only God of the Babylonians, there were three persons, and to symbolise that doctrine of the Trinity, they employed, as the discoveries of Layard prove, the equilateral triangle, just as it is well known the Romish Church does at this day.§ In both cases

* The word in the original of Exodus is the very same as *rahm*, only in a participial form.

† While such is the meaning of Brahm, the meaning of Deva, the generic name for "God" in India, is near akin to it. That name is commonly derived from the Sanscrit, *Div*, "to shine,"—only a different form of *Shiv*, which has the same meaning, which again comes from the Chaldee, *Ziv*, "brightness or splendour" (Dan. ii. 31); and, no doubt, when sun-worship was engrafted on the Patriarchal faith, the visible splendour of the deified luminary might be suggested by the name. But there is reason to believe that "Deva" has a much more honourable origin, and that it really came originally from the Chaldee, *Thav*, "good," which is also legitimately pronounced *Thev*, and in the emphatic form is *Theva* or *Thevo*, "The Good." The first letter, represented by *Th*, as shown by Donaldson in his *New Cratylus*, is frequently pronounced *Dh*. Hence, from *Dheva* or *Theva*, "The Good," naturally comes the Sanscrit, *Deva*, or, without the digamma, as it frequently is, *Deo*, "God," the Latin, *Deus*, and the Greek, *Theos*, the digamma in the original *Thevo-s* being also dropped, as *novus* in Latin is *neos* in Greek. This view of the matter gives an emphasis to the saying of our Lord (Matt. xix. 17): "There is none *good* but One, that is (*Theos*) God"—"The Good."

‡ The words in our translation are, "behind one tree," but there is no word in the original for "tree"; and it is admitted by Lowth, and the best orientalists, that the rendering should be, "after the rites of *Achad*," *i.e.*, "*The Only One.* I am aware that some object to making "Achad" signify, "The Only One," on the ground that it wants the article. But how little weight is in this, may be seen from the fact that it is this very term "Achad," and that without the article, that is used in Deuteronomy, when the Unity of the Godhead is asserted in the most emphatic manner, "Hear, O Israel, Jehovah our God is one Jehovah," *i.e.*, "*only* Jehovah." When it is intended to assert the Unity of the Godhead in the strongest possible manner, the Babylonians used the term "Adad."—*Macrobii Saturnalia*, lib. i. cap. 23, p. 73.

§ LAYARD'S *Babylon and Nineveh*, p. 605. The Egyptians also used the triangle as a symbol of their "triform divinity." See MAURICE'S *Indian Antiquities*, vol. iv. p. 445. London, 1794.

such a comparison is most degrading to the King Eternal, and is fitted utterly to pervert the minds of those who contemplate it, as if there was or could be any similitude between such a figure and Him who hath said, "To whom will ye liken God, and what likeness will ye compare unto Him?"

The Papacy has in some of its churches, as, for instance, in the monastery of the so-called Trinitarians of Madrid, an image of the Triune God, with three heads on one body.* The Babylonians had something of the same. Mr. Layard, in his last work, has given a specimen of such a triune divinity, worshipped in ancient Assyria † (Fig. 3). The accompanying cut (Fig. 4) of such another divinity, worshipped among the Pagans of Siberia, is taken from a medal in the Imperial Cabinet of St. Petersburg, and given in Parson's "Japhet."‡ The three heads are differently arranged in Layard's specimen, but both alike are evidently intended to symbolise the same great truth, although all such representations of the Trinity

Fig. 3.

Fig. 4.

necessarily and utterly debase the conceptions of those, among whom such images prevail, in regard to that sublime mystery of our faith. In India, the supreme divinity, in like manner, in one of the most

* PARKHURST'S *Hebrew Lexicon, sub voce,* "Cherubim." From the following extract from the *Dublin Catholic Layman*, a very able Protestant paper, describing a Popish picture of the Trinity, recently published in that city, it will be seen that something akin to this mode of representing the Godhead is appearing nearer home :—" At the top of the picture is a representation of the Holy Trinity. We beg to speak of it with due reverence. God the Father and God the Son are represented as a MAN with *two heads*, one body, and two arms. One of the heads is like the ordinary pictures of our Saviour. The other is the head of an old man, surmounted by a triangle. Out of the middle of this figure is proceeding the Holy Ghost in the form of a dove. We think it must be painful to any Christian mind, and repugnant to Christian feeling, to look at this figure."—*Catholic Layman*, 17th July, 1856.

† *Babylon and Nineveh*, p. 160. Some have said that the *plural* form of the name of God, in the Hebrew of Genesis, affords no argument for the doctrine of plurality of persons in the Godhead, because the same word in the plural is applied to heathen divinities. But if the supreme divinity in almost all ancient heathen nations was triune, the futility of this objection must be manifest.

‡ *Japhet*, p. 184.

ancient cave-temples, is represented with three heads on one body, under the name of "Eko Deva Trimurtti," "One God, three forms."* In Japan, the Buddhists worship their great divinity, Buddha, with three heads, in the very same form, under the name of "San Pao Fuh."† All these have existed from ancient times. While overlaid with idolatry, the recognition of a Trinity was universal in all the ancient nations of the world, proving how deep-rooted in the human race was the primeval doctrine on this subject, which comes out so distinctly in Genesis.‡ When we look at the symbols in the triune figure of Layard, already referred to, and minutely examine them, they are very instructive. Layard regards the circle in that figure as signifying "Time without bounds." But the hieroglyphic meaning of the circle is evidently different. A circle in Chaldea was zero;§ and zero also signified "the seed." Therefore, according to the genius of the mystic system of Chaldea, which was to a large extent founded on double meanings, that which, to the eyes of men in general, was only zero, "a circle," was understood by the initiated to signify zero, "the seed." Now, viewed in this light, the triune emblem of the supreme Assyrian divinity shows clearly what had been the original patriarchal faith. First, there is the head of the old man; next, there is the zero, or circle, for "the seed;" and lastly, the wings and tail of the bird or dove;|| showing, though blasphemously, the unity of Father, Seed, or Son, and

* Col. KENNEDY'S *Hindoo Mythology*, p. 211. Col. Kennedy objects to the application of the name "Eko Deva" to the triform image in the cave-temple at Elephanta, on the ground that that name belongs only to the supreme Brahm. But in so doing he is entirely inconsistent, for he admits that Brahmà, the first person in that triform image, is *identified* with the supreme Brahm; and further, that a curse is pronounced upon all who distinguish between Brahmà, Vishnu, and Seva, the three divinities represented by that image.

† GILLESPIE'S *Sinim*, p. 60.

‡ The threefold invocation of the sacred name in the blessing of Jacob bestowed on the sons of Joseph is very striking: "And he blessed Joseph, and said, God, before whom my fathers Abraham and Isaac did walk, the God which fed me all my life long unto this day, the Angel which redeemed me from all evil, bless the lads" (Gen. xlviii. 15, 16). If the angel here referred to had not been God, Jacob could never have invoked him as on an equality with God. In Hosea xii. 3-5, "The Angel who redeemed" Jacob is expressly called God: "He (Jacob) had power with God: yea, he had power over the Angel, and prevailed; he wept and made supplication unto him: he found him in Bethel, and there he spake with us; even the Lord God of Hosts; The Lord is his memorial."

§ In our own language we have evidence that Zero had signified a circle among the Chaldeans; for what is Zero, the name of the cypher, but just a circle? And whence can we have derived this term but from the Arabians, as they, without doubt, had themselves derived it from the Chaldees, the grand original cultivators at once of arithmetic, geometry, and idolatry? Zero, in this sense, had evidently come from the Chaldee, *zer*, "to encompass," from which, also, no doubt, was derived the Babylonian name for a great cycle of time, called a "*saros*."—(BUNSEN, vol. i. pp. 711, 712.) As he, who by the Chaldeans was regarded as the great "Seed," was looked upon as the *sun* incarnate (see chap. iii. sect. i.), and as the emblem of the sun was a *circle* (BUNSEN, vol. i. p. 335, and p. 537, No. 4), the hieroglyphical relation between zero, "the circle," and zero, "the seed," was easily established.

|| From the statement in Gen. i. 2, that "the Spirit of God *fluttered* on the face of the deep" (for that is the expression in the original), it is evident that the *dove* had very early been a Divine emblem for the Holy Spirit.

Holy Ghost. While this had been the original way in which Pagan idolatry had represented the Triune God, and though this kind of representation had survived to Sennacherib's time, yet there is evidence that, at a very early period, an important change had taken place in the Babylonian notions in regard to the divinity; and that the three persons had come to be, the Eternal Father, the Spirit of God incarnate in a human mother, and a Divine Son, the fruit of that incarnation.

SECTION II.—THE MOTHER AND CHILD, AND THE ORIGINAL OF THE CHILD.

While this was the theory, the first person in the Godhead was practically overlooked. As the Great Invisible, taking no immediate

Fig. 5.

From Babylon.*

Fig. 6.

From India.†

concern in human affairs, he was "to be worshipped through silence alone,"‡ that is, in point of fact, he was not worshipped by the multitude at all. The same thing is strikingly illustrated in India at this day. Though Brahmà, according to the sacred books, is

* From KITTO'S *Illustrated Commentary*, vol. iv. p. 31.

† Indrani, the wife of the Indian god Indra, from *Asiatic Researches*, vol. vi. p. 393.

‡ JAMBLICHUS, *On the Mysteries*, sect. viii. chap. iii.

the first person of the Hindoo Triad, and the religion of Hindostan is called by his name, yet he is never worshipped, and there is scarcely a single Temple in all India now in existence of those that were formerly erected to his honour.* So also is it in those countries of Europe where the Papal system is most completely developed. In Papal Italy, as travellers universally admit (except where the Gospel has recently entered), all appearance of worshipping the King Eternal and Invisible is almost extinct, while the Mother and the Child are the grand objects of worship. Exactly so, in this latter respect, also was it in ancient Babylon. The Babylonians, in their *popular religion*, supremely worshipped a Goddess Mother and a Son, who was represented in pictures and in images as an infant or child in his mother's arms (Figs. 5 and 6). From Babylon, this worship of the Mother and the Child spread to the ends of the earth. In Egypt, the Mother and the Child were worshipped under the names of Isis and Osiris.† In India, even to this day, as Isi and Iswara; ‡ in Asia, as Cybele and Deōius; § in Pagan Rome, as Fortuna and Jupiter-puer, or Jupiter, the boy; ‖ in Greece, as Ceres, the Great Mother, with the babe at her breast,¶ or as Irene, the goddess of Peace, with the boy Plutus in her arms; ** and even in Thibet, in China, and Japan, the Jesuit missionaries were astonished to find the counterpart of Madonna†† and her child as devoutly

* WARD'S *View of the Hindus, apud* KENNEDY'S *Researches into Ancient and Modern Mythology*, p. 196.

† Osiris, as the child called most frequently Horus. Bunsen, vol. i. p. 438, compared with pp. 433, 434.

‡ KENNEDY'S *Hindoo Mythology*, p. 49. Though Iswara is the husband of Isi, he is also represented as an infant at her breast. *Ibid.* p. 338, Note.

§ DYMOCK'S *Classical Dictionary*, "Cybele" and "Deōius."

‖ CICERO'S Works, *De Divinatione*, lib. ii. cap. 41, vol. iii. p. 77.

¶ SOPHOCLES, *Antigone*, v. 1133.

** PAUSANIAS, lib. i. ATTICA, cap. 8.

†† The very name by which the Italians commonly designate the Virgin, is just the translation of one of the titles of the Babylonian goddess. As Baal or Belus was the name of the great male divinity of Babylon, so the female divinity was called Beltis.—(HESYCHIUS, *Lexicon*, p. 188.) This name has been found in Nineveh applied to the "Mother of the gods"—(VAUX'S *Nineveh and Persepolis*, p. 459); and in a speech attributed to Nebuchadnezzar, preserved in EUSEBII *Præparatio Evangelii*, lib. ix. cap. 41, both titles "Belus and Beltis" are conjoined as the titles of the great Babylonian god and goddess. The Greek Belus, as representing the highest title of the Babylonian god, was undoubtedly Baal, "The Lord." Beltis, therefore, as the title of the female divinity, was equivalent to "Baalti," which, in English, is "My Lady," in Latin, "Mea Domina," and, in Italian, is corrupted into the well-known "Madonna." In connection with this, it may be observed, that the name of Juno, the classical "Queen of Heaven," which, in Greek, was Hēra, also signified "The Lady;" and that the peculiar title of Cybele or Rhea at Rome, was Domina or "The Lady."—(OVID, *Fasti*, lib. iv. v. 340.) Further, there is strong reason to believe, that Athena, the well-known name of Minerva at Athens, had the very same meaning. The Hebrew Adon, "The Lord," is, with the points, pronounced Athon. We have evidence that this name was known to the Asiatic Greeks, from whom idolatry, in a large measure, came into European Greece, as a name of God under the form of "Athan." Eustathius, in a note on the Periergesis of Dionysius (v. 915, *apud* BRYANT, vol. iii. p. 140), speaking of local names in the district of Laodicea, says that "Athan is god." The feminine of Athan, "The

worshipped as in Papal Rome itself; Shing Moo, the Holy Mother in China, being represented with a child in her arms, and a *glory* around her, exactly as if a Roman Catholic artist had been employed to set her up.*

SUB-SECTION I.—THE CHILD IN ASSYRIA.

The original of that mother, so widely worshipped, there is reason to believe, was Semiramis,† already referred to, who, it is well known, was worshipped by the Babylonians,‡ and other eastern nations,§ and that under the name of Rhea,|| the great Goddess "Mother."

It was from the son, however, that she derived all her glory and her claims to deification. That son, though represented as a child in his mother's arms, was a person of great stature and immense bodily powers, as well as most fascinating manners. In Scripture he is referred to (Ezek. viii. 14) under the name of Tammuz, but he is commonly known among classical writers under the name of Bacchus, that is, "The Lamented one."¶ To the ordinary reader

Lord," is Athāna, "The Lady," which in the Attic dialect, is Athēna. No doubt, Minerva is commonly represented as a virgin; but, for all that, we learn from Strabo (Lib. x. cap. 3, p. 405. Paris, 1853), that at Hierapytna in Crete (the coins of which city, says Müller, *Dorians*, vol. i. p. 413, have the Athenian symbols of Minerva upon them), she was said to be the mother of the Corybantes by Helius, or "The Sun." It is certain that the *Egyptian* Minerva, who was the prototype of the Athenian goddess, was a mother, and was styled "Goddess Mother," or "Mother of the Gods."—See WILKINSON, vol. iv. p. 285.

* CRABB's *Mythology*, p. 150. Gutzlaff thought that Shing Moo must have been borrowed from a Popish source; and there can be no doubt, that in the individual case to which he refers, the Pagan and the Christian stories had been amalgamated. But Sir J. F. Davis shows that the Chinese of Canton find such an analogy between their own Pagan goddess Kuanyin and the Popish Madonna, that, in conversing with Europeans, they frequently call either of them indifferently by the same title.—DAVIS's *China*, vol. ii. p. 56. The first Jesuit missionaries to China also wrote home to Europe, that they found mention in the Chinese sacred books—books unequivocally Pagan—of a mother and child, very similar to their own Madonna and child at home.—See LE PERE LAFITAN, *Les Mœurs des Sauvages Ameriquains*, vol. i. p. 235, Note.

One of the names of the Chinese Holy Mother is Ma Tsoopo; in regard to which, see Appendix, Note C.

† Sir H. Rawlinson having found evidence at Nineveh, of the existence of a Semiramis about six or seven centuries before the Christian era, seems inclined to regard her as the *only* Semiramis that ever existed. But this is subversive of all history. The fact that there was a Semiramis in the primeval ages of the world, is beyond all doubt (see JUSTIN, *Historia*, p. 615, and the historian CASTOR in *Cory's Fragments*, p. 65), although some of the exploits of the latter queen have evidently been attributed to her predecessor. Mr. Layard dissents from Sir H. Rawlinson's opinion.

‡ See DIODORUS SICULUS, lib. ii. p. 76.

§ ATHENAGORAS, *Legatio*, pp. 178, 179.

|| PASCHAL, *Chronicle*, vol. i. p. 65.

¶ From Bakhah "to weep" or "lament." Among the Phenicians, says Hesychius, "Bacchos means weeping," p. 179. As the women wept for Tammuz, so did they for Bacchus.

the name of Bacchus suggests nothing more than revelry and drunkenness, but it is now well known, that amid all the abominations that attended his orgies, their grand design was professedly "the purification of souls,"* and that from the guilt and defilement of sin. This lamented one, exhibited and adored as a little child in his mother's arms, seems, in point of fact, to have been the *husband* of Semiramis, whose name, Ninus, by which he is commonly known in classical history, literally signified "The Son."† As Semiramis, the wife, was worshipped as Rhea, whose grand distinguishing character was that of the great goddess "Mother,"‡ the conjunction with her of her husband, under the name of Ninus, or "The Son," was sufficient to originate the peculiar worship of the "Mother and Son," so extensively diffused among the nations of antiquity; and this, no doubt, is the explanation of the fact which has so much puzzled the inquirers into ancient history, that Ninus is sometimes called the *husband*, and sometimes the *son* of Semiramis.§ This also accounts for the origin of the very same confusion of relationship between Isis and Osiris, the mother and child of the Egyptians; for as Bunsen shows, Osiris was represented in Egypt as at once the son and husband of his mother; and actually bore, as one of his titles of dignity and honour, the name "Husband of the Mother."‖ This

* SERVIUS, in *Georg.*, lib. i. vol. ii. p. 197, and in *Æneid*, lib. vi. vol. i. p. 400.

† From *Nin*, in Hebrew, "A Son."

‡ As such Rhea was called by the Greeks, Ammas; see HESYCHIUS, *sub voce* "Ammas." Ammas is evidently the Greek form of the Chaldee *Ama*, "Mother."

§ LAYARD's *Nineveh and its Remains*, vol. ii. p. 480.

‖ BUNSEN, vol. i. pp. 438, 439. It may be observed that this very name "Husband of the Mother," given to Osiris, seems even at this day to be in common use among ourselves, although there is not the least suspicion of the meaning of the term, or whence it has come. Herodotus mentions that when in Egypt, he was astonished to hear the very same mournful but ravishing "Song of Linus," sung by the Egyptians (although under another name), which he had been accustomed to hear in his own native land of Greece (HEROD., lib. ii. cap. 79). Linus was the same god as the Bacchus of Greece, or Osiris of Egypt; for Homer introduces a boy singing the song of Linus, while the vintage is going on (*Ilias*, lib. xviii. v. 569-571, pp. 725, 726), and the Scholiast says that this song was sung in memory of Linus, who was torn in pieces by dogs. The epithet "*dogs*," applied to those who tore Linus in pieces, is evidently used in a mystical sense, and it will afterwards be seen how thoroughly the other name by which he is known—Narcissus—identifies him with the Greek Bacchus and Egyptian Osiris. In some places in Egypt, for the song of Linus or Osiris, a peculiar melody seems to have been used. Savary says that, in the temple of Abydos, "the priest repeated the seven vowels in the form of hymns, and that musicians were forbid to enter it."—*Letters*, p. 566. Strabo, whom Savary refers to, calls the god of that temple Memnon, but we learn from Wilkinson, vol. iv. pp. 344, 345, that Osiris was the great god of Abydos, whence it is evident that Memnon and Osiris were only different names of the same divinity. Now the name of Linus or Osiris, as the "husband of his mother," in Egypt, was Kamut (BUNSEN, vol. i. pp. 373, 374). When Gregory the Great introduced into the Church of Rome what are now called the Gregorian Chants, he got them from the Chaldean mysteries, which had long been established in Rome; for the Roman Catholic priest, Eustace, admits that these chants were largely composed of "Lydian and Phrygian tunes" (*Classical Tour*, vol. i. p. 379), Lydia and Phrygia being among the chief seats in later times of those mysteries, of which the Egyptian mysteries were only a branch. These tunes were sacred—the music of the great god, and still further casts light on the fact already noticed, that the Indian God Iswara is represented as a babe at the breast of his own wife Isi, or Parvati.

Now, this Ninus, or "Son," borne in the arms of the Babylonian Madonna, is so described as very clearly to identify him with Nimrod. "Ninus, king of the Assyrians,"* says Trogus Pompeius, epitomised by Justin, "first of all changed the contented moderation of the ancient manners, incited by a new passion, the desire of conquest. He was the *first who carried on war against his neighbours*, and he conquered all nations from Assyria to Lybia, as they were yet unacquainted with the arts of war." † This account points directly to Nimrod, and can apply to no other. The account of Diodorus Siculus entirely agrees with it, and adds another trait that goes still further to determine the identity. That account is as follows:—"Ninus, the most ancient of the Assyrian kings mentioned in history, performed great actions. Being naturally of a warlike disposition, and ambitious of glory that results from valour, he armed a considerable number of young men that were brave and vigorous like himself, trained them up a long time in laborious exercises and hardships, and by that means accustomed them to bear the fatigues of war, and to face dangers with intrepidity." ‡ As Diodorus makes Ninus "the most ancient of the Assyrian kings," and represents him as beginning those wars which raised his power to an extraordinary height by bringing the *people* of Babylonia under subjection to him, while as yet the *city* of Babylon was not in existence, this shows that he occupied the very position of Nimrod, of whom the Scriptural account is, that he *first* "began to be mighty on the earth," and that the "*beginning* of his kingdom was Babylon." As the Babel builders, when their speech was confounded, were scattered abroad on the face of the earth, and therefore deserted both the city and the tower which they had commenced to build, Babylon as a *city*, could not properly be said to exist till Nimrod, by establishing his power there, made it the foundation and starting-point of his greatness. In this respect, then, the story of Ninus and of Nimrod exactly harmonise. The way, too, in which Ninus gained his power is the very way in which Nimrod erected his. There can be no doubt that it was by inuring his followers to the toils and dangers of the chase, that he gradually formed them to the use of arms, and so prepared them for aiding him in establishing his dominion; just as Ninus, by training his companions

in introducing them Gregory introduced the music of Kamut. And thus, to all appearance, has it come to pass, that the name of Osiris or Kamut, "the husband of the mother," is in every-day use among ourselves as the name of the musical scale; for what is the melody of Osiris, consisting of the "seven vowels" formed into a hymn, but—the Gamut?

* The name "Assyrians," as has already been noticed, has a wide latitude of meaning among the classic authors, taking in the Babylonians as well as the Assyrians proper.

† JUSTIN'S *Trogus Pompeius*, *Hist. Rom. Script.*, vol. ii. p. 615.

‡ DIODORUS, *Bibliotheca*, lib. ii. p. 63.

for a long time "in laborious exercises and hardships," qualified them for making him the first of the Assyrian kings.

The conclusions deduced from these testimonies of ancient history are greatly strengthened by many additional considerations. In Gen. x. 11, we find a passage, which, when its meaning is properly understood, casts a very steady light on the subject. That passage, as given in the authorised version, runs thus:—"Out of that land went forth Asshur, and builded Nineveh." This speaks of it as something remarkable, that Asshur went out of the land of Shinar, while yet the human race in general went forth from the same land. It goes upon the supposition that Asshur had some sort of divine right to that land, and that he had been, in a manner, expelled from it by Nimrod, while no divine right is elsewhere hinted at in the context, or seems capable of proof. Moreover, it represents Asshur as setting up in the IMMEDIATE NEIGHBOURHOOD of Nimrod as mighty a kingdom as Nimrod himself, Asshur building *four* cities, one of which is emphatically said to have been "great" (ver. 12); while Nimrod, on this interpretation, built just the same number of cities, of which none is specially characterised as "great." Now, it is in the last degree improbable that Nimrod would have quietly borne so mighty a rival so near him. To obviate such difficulties as these, it has been proposed to render the words, "out of that land he (Nimrod) went forth into Asshur, or Assyria." But then, according to ordinary usage of grammar, the word in the original should have been "Ashurah," with the sign of motion to a place affixed to it, whereas it is simply Asshur, without any such sign of motion affixed. I am persuaded that the whole perplexity that commentators have hitherto felt in considering this passage, has arisen from supposing that there is a proper name in the passage, where in reality no proper name exists. Asshur is the passive participle of a verb, which, in its Chaldee sense, signifies "to make *strong*,"* and, consequently, signifies "being strengthened," or "made strong." Read thus, the whole passage is natural and easy (ver. 10), "And the beginning of his (Nimrod's) kingdom was Babel, and Erech, and Accad, and Calneh." A *beginning* naturally implies something to succeed, and here we find it (ver. 11); "Out of that land he went forth, being made strong, or when he had been made strong (Ashur), and builded Nineveh," &c. Now, this exactly agrees with the statement in the ancient history of Justin: "Ninus *strengthened* the greatness of his acquired dominion by continued possession. Having subdued, therefore, his neighbours, when, by an accession of forces, being still further *strengthened*, he *went* forth against

* See *Chaldee Lexicon* in *Clavis Stockii*, where the verb "asher" is rendered "*firmavit roboravit.*" Ashur, the passive participle, is consequently "firmatus, roboratus." Even in Hebrew this sense seems to be inherent in the verb, as may be concluded from the noun *te-ashur*, the name of the box-tree (Isaiah lx. 13), the wood of that tree being remarkable for its *firmness* and *compactness.* Even in the ordinary Hebrew sense, the meaning is substantially the same; for as Asher means "to prosper," or "make prosperous," Ashur, in the participle passive, must signify "prospered," or "made prosperous."

other tribes, and every new victory paved the way for another, he subdued all the peoples of the East."* Thus, then, Nimrod, or Ninus, was the builder of Nineveh; and the origin of the name of that city, as "the habitation of Ninus," is accounted for,† and light is thereby, at the same time, cast on the fact, that the name of the chief part of the ruins of Nineveh is Nimroud at this day.‡

Now, assuming that Ninus is Nimrod, the way in which that assumption explains what is otherwise inexplicable in the statements of ancient history greatly confirms the truth of that assumption itself. Ninus is said to have been the son of Belus or Bel, and Bel is said to have been the founder of Babylon. If Ninus was in reality the first king of Babylon, how could Belus or Bel, his father, be said to be the founder of it? Both might very well be, as will appear if we consider who was Bel, and what we can trace of his doings. If Ninus was Nimrod, who was the historical Bel? He must have been Cush; for "Cush begat Nimrod" (Gen. x. 8); and Cush is generally represented as having been a ringleader in the great apostacy.§ But again, Cush, as the son of Ham, was Her-mes or Mercury; for Hermes is just an Egyptian synonym for the "son of Ham."|| Now, Hermes was the great original prophet of idolatry; for he was

* JUSTIN, *Hist. Rom. Script.*, vol. ii. p. 615. The words of the original are the following:—"Ninus magnitudinem quæsitæ dominationis continua possessione *firmavit.* Cum *accessione virum fortior*, ad alios transiret, et proxima quæque victoria instrumentum sequentis esset totius Orientis populos subegit."

† Nin-neveh, "The habitation of Ninus."

‡ LAYARD'S *Nineveh and its Remains*, vol. i. p. 7, *et passim.*

§ See GREGORIUS TURONENSIS, *De rerum Franc.*, lib. i., *apud*, BRYANT, vol. ii. pp. 403, 404. Gregory attributes to Cush what was said more generally to have befallen his son; but his statement shows the belief in his day, which is amply confirmed from other sources, that Cush had a pre-eminent share in leading mankind away from the true worship of God.

|| The composition of Her-mes is, first, from "Her," which, in Chaldee, is synonymous with Ham, or Khem, "The burnt one." As "Her" also, like Ham, signified "The hot or burning one," this name formed a foundation for covertly identifying Ham with the "Sun," and so deifying the great patriarch, after whose name the land of Egypt was called, in connection with the sun. Khem, or Ham, in his own name was openly worshipped in later ages in the land of Ham (BUNSEN, vol. i. p. 373); but this would have been too daring at first. By means of "Her," the synonym, however, the way was paved for this. "Her" is the name of Horus, who is identified with the sun (BUNSEN, vol. i. p. 507), which shows the real etymology of the name to be from the verb to which I have traced it. Then, secondly, "Mes" is from Mesheh (or, without the last radical, which is omissible, see PARKHURST, *sub voce*, p. 416), Mesh, "*to draw forth.*" In Egyptian, we have *Ms* in the sense of "to bring forth" (BUNSEN, vol. i., *Hieroglyphical Signs*, Append., b. 43, p. 540), which is evidently a different form of the same word. In the passive sense, also, we find *Ms* used (BUNSEN, *Vocabulary*, Appendix i. p. 470, at bottom, &c., "*Ms . . . . born*"). The radical meaning of Mesheh in *Stockii Lexicon*, is given in Latin "*Extraxit*," and our English word "*extraction*," as applied to birth or descent, shows that there is a connection between the generic meaning of this word and *birth.* This derivation will be found to explain the meaning of the names of the Egyptian kings, Ramesses and Thothmes, the former evidently being "The son of Ra," or the Sun; for Ramesses is *Ἡλιου παις* (AMMIANUS MARCELLINUS, lib. 17, cap. 4, p. 162); the latter, in like manner, being "The son of Thoth." For the very same reason Her-mes is the "Son of Her, or Ham," the burnt one—that is, Cush.

recognised by the pagans as the author of their religious rites, and the interpreter of the gods. The distinguished Gesenius identifies him with the Babylonian Nebo, as the prophetic god; and a statement of Hyginus shows that he was known as the grand agent in that movement which produced the division of tongues. His words are these: "For many ages men lived under the government of Jove [evidently not the Roman Jupiter, but the Jehovah of the Hebrews], without cities and without laws, and all speaking one language. But after that Mercury interpreted the speeches of men (whence an interpreter is called Hermeneutes), the same individual distributed the nations. Then discord began."* Here there is a manifest enigma. How could Mercury or Hermes have any need to interpret the speeches of mankind when they "all spake one language"? To find out the meaning of this, we must go to the language of the Mysteries. Peresh, in Chaldee, signifies "to interpret;" but was pronounced by old Egyptians and by Greeks, and often by the Chaldees themselves, in the same way as "Peres," to "divide." Mercury, then, or Hermes, or Cush, "the son of Ham," was the "DIVIDER of the speeches of men." He, it would seem, had been the ringleader in the scheme for building the great city and tower of Babel; and, as the well-known title of Hermes,—"the *interpreter* of the gods," would indicate, had encouraged them, in the name of God, to proceed in their presumptuous enterprise, and so had caused the language of men to be divided, and themselves to be scattered abroad on the face of the earth. Now look at the name of Belus or Bel, given to the father of Ninus, or Nimrod, in connection with this. While the Greek name Belus represented both the Baal and Bel of the Chaldees, these were nevertheless two entirely distinct titles. These titles were both alike often given to the same god, but they had totally different meanings. Baal, as we have already seen, signified "The Lord;" but Bel signified "The Confounder." When, then, we read that Belus, the father of Ninus, was he that built or founded Babylon, can there be a doubt, in what sense it was that the title of Belus was given to him? It must have been in the sense of Bel the "Confounder." And to this meaning of the name of the Babylonian Bel, there is a very distinct allusion in Jeremiah i. 2, where it is said "Bel is confounded," that is, "The Confounder is brought to confusion." That Cush was known to Pagan antiquity under the very character of Bel, "The Confounder," a statement of Ovid very clearly proves. The statement to which I refer is that in which Janus "the god of gods,"† from whom all the other gods had their origin,‡ is made to say of himself: "The ancients . . . . called me Chaos."§ Now, first this decisively shows that Chaos was known

* HYGINUS, *Fab.* 143, p. 114. Phoroneus is represented as king at this time.

† Janus was so called in the most ancient hymns of the Salii.—MACROB., *Saturn*, lib. i. cap. 9, p. 54, col. 2, H.

‡ By Terentianus Maurus he is called "Principium Deorum."—BRYANT, vol. iii. p. 82.

§ *Me Chaos antiqui nam res sum prisca vocabant.*—*Fasti*, lib. i. v. 104, vol. iii. p. 19.

not merely as a *state* of confusion, but as the "*god* of Confusion." But, secondly, who that is at all acquainted with the laws of Chaldaic pronunciation, does not know that Chaos is just one of the established forms of the name of Chūs or Cush?* Then, look at the symbol of Janus (see Fig. 7 †), whom "the ancients called Chaos," and it will be seen how exactly it tallies with the doings of Cush, when he is identified with Bel, "The Confounder." That symbol is a club; and the name of "a club" in Chaldee comes from the very word which signifies "to break in pieces, or *scatter abroad*."‡ He who caused the confusion of tongues was he who "broke" the previously united earth (Gen. xi. 1) "in pieces," and "scattered" the fragments abroad. How significant, then, as a symbol, is the club, as commemorating the work of Cush, as Bel, the "Confounder"? And that significance will be all the more apparent when the reader turns to the Hebrew of Gen. xi. 9, and finds that the very word from which a club derives its name is that which is employed when it is said, that in consequence of the confusion of tongues, the children of men were "scattered abroad on the face of all the earth."§ The word there used for scattering abroad is Hephaitz, which, in the Greek form

Fig. 7.

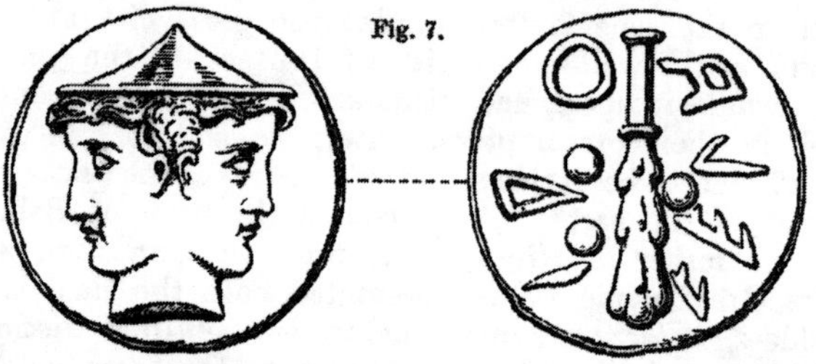

becomes Hephaizt,|| and hence the origin of the well-known but little understood name of Hephaistos, as applied to Vulcan, "The father of the gods."¶ Hephaistos is the name of the ringleader in the first

* The name of Cush is also Khūs, for *sh* frequently passes in Chaldee into *s*; and Khus, in pronunciation, legitimately becomes Khawos, or, without the digamma, Khaos.

† From Sir Wm. Betham's *Etruscan Literature and Antiquities Investigated*, Plate II., vol. ii. p. 120. 1842. The Etruscan name on the reverse of the above medal—Bel-athri, "Lord of spies," is probably given to Janus, in allusion to his well-known title "Janus Tuens," which may be rendered "Janus the Seer," or "All-seeing Janus."

‡ In Prov. xxv. 18, a maul or club is "Mephaitz." In Jer. li. 20, the same word, without the Jod, is evidently used for a *club* (though, in our version, it is rendered *battle-axe*); for the use of it is not to cut asunder, but to "break in pieces." See the whole passage.

§ Genesis xi. 9.

|| There are many instances of a similar change. Thus Botzra becomes in Greek, Bostra; and Mitzraim, Mestraim. For last, see Bunsen, vol. i. pp. 606-609.

¶ Vulcan, in the classical Pantheon, had not commonly so high a place, but in Egypt Hephaistos, or Vulcan, was called "Father of the gods."—Ammianus Marcellinus, lib. xvii.

rebellion, as "The Scatterer abroad," as Bel is the name of the same individual as the "Confounder of tongues." Here, then, the reader may see the real origin of Vulcan's Hammer, which is just another name for the club of Janus or Chaos, "The god of Confusion;" and to this, as breaking the earth in pieces, there is a covert allusion in Jer. i. 23, where Babylon, as identified with its primeval god, is thus apostrophised: "How is the hammer of the whole earth cut asunder and broken!" Now, as the tower-building was the first act of open rebellion after the flood, and Cush, as Bel, was the ringleader in it, he was, of course, the first to whom the name Merodach, "The great Rebel,"* must have been given, and, therefore, according to the usual parallelism of the prophetic language, we find both names of the Babylonian god referred to together, when the judgment on Babylon is predicted: "Bel is confounded: Merodach is broken in pieces" (Jer. i. 2). The judgment comes upon the Babylonian god according to what he had done. As Bel, he had "confounded" the whole earth, therefore *he* is "confounded." As Merodach, by the rebellion he had stirred up, he had "broken" the united world in pieces; therefore he *himself* is "broken in pieces."

So much for the historical character of Bel, as identified with Janus or Chaos, the *god* of confusion, with his symbolical club.† Proceeding, then, on these deductions, it is not difficult to see how it might be said that Bel or Belus, the father of Ninus, founded Babylon, while, nevertheless, Ninus or Nimrod was properly the builder of it. Now, though Bel or Cush, as being specially concerned in laying the first foundations of Babylon, might be looked upon as the first king, as in some of the copies of "Eusebius's Chronicle" he is represented, yet it is evident, from both sacred history and profane, that he could never have reigned as king of the Babylonian monarchy, properly so called; and accordingly, in the Armenian version of the "Chronicle of Eusebius," which bears the undisputed palm for correctness and authority, his name is entirely omitted in the list of Assyrian kings, and that of Ninus stands first, in such terms as exactly correspond with the Scriptural account of Nimrod. Thus, then, looking at the fact that Ninus is currently made by antiquity the son of Belus, or

* Merodach comes from *Mered*, to rebel; and *Dakh*, the demonstrative pronoun affixed, which makes it emphatic, signifying "That" or "The great."

† While the names Bel and Hephaistos had the origin above referred to, they were not inappropriate names also, though in a different sense, for the war-gods descending from Cush, from whom Babylon derived its glory among the nations. The warlike deified kings of the line of Cush gloried in their power to carry *confusion* among their enemies, to *scatter* their armies, and to "break *the earth in pieces*" by their resistless power. To this, no doubt, as well as to the acts of the primeval Bel, there is allusion in the inspired denunciations of Jeremiah on Babylon. The physical sense also of these names was embodied in the club given to the Grecian Hercules—the very club of Janus—when, in a character quite different from that of the original Hercules, he was set up as the great reformer of the world, by mere physical force. When two-headed Janus with the club is represented, the two-fold representation was probably intended to represent old Cush, and young Cush or Nimrod, as combined. But the two-fold representation with other attributes, had reference also to another "Father of the gods," afterwards to be noticed, who had specially to do with water.

Bel, when we have seen that the historical Bel is Cush, the identity of Ninus and Nimrod is still further confirmed.

But when we look at what is said of Semiramis, the wife of Ninus, the evidence receives an additional development. That evidence goes

Fig. 8.

Diana of Ephesus.*

conclusively to show that the wife of Ninus could be none other than the wife of Nimrod, and, further, to bring out one of the grand characters in which Nimrod, when deified, was adored. In Daniel

* From KITTO's *Illustrated Commentary*, vol. v. p. 205.

xi. 38, we read of a god called *Ala Mahozine**—*i.e.*, the "god of fortifications." Who this god of fortifications could be, commentators have found themselves at a loss to determine. In the records of antiquity the existence of any *god* of fortifications has been commonly overlooked; and it must be confessed that no such god stands forth there with any prominence to the ordinary reader. But of the existence of a *goddess* of fortifications, every one knows that there is the amplest evidence. That goddess is Cybele, who is universally represented with a mural or turreted crown, or with a fortification, on her head. Why was Rhea or Cybele thus represented? Ovid asks the question and answers it himself; and the answer is this: The reason he says, why the statue of Cybele wore a crown of towers was, "because she first erected them in cities."† The first city in the world after the flood (from whence the commencement of the world itself was often dated) that had towers and encompassing walls, was Babylon; and Ovid himself tells us that it was Semiramis, the first queen of that city, who was believed to have "surrounded Babylon with a wall of brick."‡ Semiramis, then, the first deified queen of that city and tower whose top was intended to reach to heaven, must have been the prototype of the goddess who "*first* made towers in cities." When we look at the Ephesian Diana, we find evidence to the very same effect. In general, Diana was depicted as a virgin, and the patroness of virginity; but the Ephesian Diana was quite different. She was represented with all the attributes of the Mother of the gods (see Fig. 8), and, *as* the Mother of the gods, she wore a turreted crown, such as no one can contemplate without being forcibly reminded of the tower of Babel. Now this tower-bearing Diana is by an ancient scholiast expressly identified with Semiramis.§ When, therefore we remember that Rhea, or Cybele, the tower-bearing goddess, was, in point of fact, a Babylonian goddess,‖ and that Semiramis, when deified, was worshipped under the name of Rhea,¶ there

* In our version, Ala Mahozim is rendered alternatively "god of forces," or "gods protectors." To the latter interpretation, there is this insuperable objection, that Ala is in the singular. Neither can the former be admitted; for Mahozim, or Mauzzim, does not signify "forces," or "armies," but "munitions," as it is also given in the margin—that is "fortifications." Stockius, in his *Lexicon*, gives as the definition of *Mahoz* in the singular, *robur*, *arx*, *locus munitus*, and in proof of the definition, the following examples:—Judges vi. 26, "And build an altar to the Lord thy God upon the top of this rock" (Mahoz, in the margin "strong place"); and Dan. xi. 19, "Then shall he turn his face to the fort (Mahoz) of his own land." See also GESENIUS, *Lexicon*, p. 533.

† OVID, *Opera*, vol. iii.; *Fasti*, iv. 219-221.

‡ *Ibid.* vol. ii., *Metam.*, lib. iv., *Fab. Pyramus and Thisbe.*

§ A scholiast on the *Periergesis* of Dionysius, says Layard (*Nineveh and its Remains*, vol. ii. p. 480, Note), makes Semiramis the same as the goddess Artemis or Despoina. Now, Artemis was Diana, and the title of Despoina given to her, shows that it was in the character of the Ephesian Diana she was identified with Semiramis; for Despoina is the Greek for Domina, "The Lady," the peculiar title of Rhea or Cybele, the tower-bearing goddess, in ancient Rome.—OVID, *Fasti*, lib. iv. 340.

‖ See LAYARD'S *Nineveh*, &c., vol. ii. pp. 451, 457.

¶ See *ante*, p. 21.

will remain, I think, no doubt as to the personal identity of the "*goddess* of fortifications."

Now there is no reason to believe that Semiramis alone (though some have represented the matter so) built the battlements of Babylon. We have the express testimony of the ancient historian, Megasthenes, as preserved by Abydenus, that it was "Belus" who "surrounded Babylon with a wall."* As "Bel," the Confounder, who began the city and tower of Babel, had to leave both unfinished, this could not refer to *him*. It could refer only to his son Ninus, who inherited his father's title, and who was the first actual king of the Babylonian empire, and, consequently Nimrod. The real reason that Semiramis, the wife of Ninus, gained the glory of finishing the fortifications of Babylon, was, that she came in the esteem of the ancient idolaters to hold a preponderating position, and to have attributed to her all the different characters that belonged, or were supposed to belong, to her husband. Having ascertained, then, one of the characters in which the deified *wife* was worshipped, we may from that conclude what was the corresponding character of the deified *husband*. Layard distinctly indicates his belief that Rhea or Cybele, the "tower-crown" goddess, was just the female counterpart of the "deity presiding over bulwarks or fortresses;" † and that this deity was Ninus, or Nimrod, we have still further evidence from what the scattered notices of antiquity say of the first deified king of Babylon, under a name that identifies him as the husband of Rhea, the "tower-bearing" goddess. That name is Kronos or Saturn. ‡ It is well known that Kronos, or Saturn, was Rhea's husband; but it is not so well known who was Kronos himself. Traced back to his

* CORY's *Fragments*, pp. 45, 46.

† LAYARD's *Nineveh and its Remains*, vol. ii. pp. 456, 457.

‡ In the Greek mythology, Kronos and Rhea are commonly brother and sister. Ninus and Semiramis, according to history, are not represented as standing in any such relation to one another; but this is no objection to the real identity of Ninus and Kronos; for, 1st, the relationships of the divinities, in most countries, are peculiarly conflicting—Osiris, in Egypt, is represented at different times, not only as the son and husband of Isis, but also as her father and brother (BUNSEN, vol. i. p. 438); then, secondly, whatever the deified mortals might be before deification, on being deified they came into new relationships. On the *apotheosis* of husband and wife, it was necessary for the dignity of both that both alike should be represented as of the same celestial origin—as both supernaturally the children of God. Before the flood, the great sin that brought ruin on the human race was, that the "Sons of God" married others than the *daughters of God*,—in other words, those who were not spiritually their "*sisters*."—(Gen. vi. 2, 3.) In the new world, while the influence of Noah prevailed, the opposite practice must have been strongly inculcated; for a "son of God" to marry any one but a daughter of God, or his own "*sister*" in the faith, must have been a *mesalliance* and a disgrace. Hence, from a perversion of a spiritual idea, came, doubtless, the notion of the dignity and purity of the royal line being preserved the more intact through the marriage of royal brothers and sisters. This was the case in Peru (PRESCOTT, vol. i. p. 18), in India (HARDY, p. 133), and in Egypt (WILKINSON, vol. iv. p. 385). Hence the relation of Jupiter to Juno, who gloried that she was "*soror et conjux*"—"sister and wife"—of her husband. Hence the same relation between Isis and her husband Osiris, the former of whom is represented as "lamenting her *brother* Osiris."—(BUNSEN, vol. i. p. 419.) For the same reason, no doubt, was Rhea, made the *sister* of her husband Kronos, to show her divine dignity and equality.

original, that divinity is proved to have been the first king of Babylon. Theophilus of Antioch shows that Kronos in the east was worshipped under the names of Bel and Bal;* and from Eusebius we learn that the first of the Assyrian kings, whose name was Belus, was also by the Assyrians called Kronos.† As the genuine copies of Eusebius do not admit of any Belus, as an actual king of Assyria, prior to Ninus, king of the Babylonians, and distinct from him, that shows that Ninus, the first king of Babylon, was Kronos. But, further, we find that Kronos was king of the Cyclops, who were his brethren, and who derived that name from him,‡ and that the Cyclops were known as "the inventors of tower-building."§ The king of the Cyclops, "the inventors of tower-building," occupied a position exactly correspondent to that of Rhea, who "first erected (towers) in cities." If, therefore, Rhea, the *wife* of Kronos, was the *goddess* of fortifications, Kronos or Saturn, the *husband* of Rhea, that is, Ninus or Nimrod, the first king of Babylon, must have been Ala mahozin, "the god of fortifications."||

The name Kronos itself goes not a little to confirm the argument. Kronos signifies "The Horned one."¶ As a horn is a well-known Oriental emblem for power or might, Kronos, "The Horned one," was, according to the mystic system, just a synonym for the Scriptural epithet applied to Nimrod—viz., *Gheber*, "The mighty one." (Gen. x. 8), "He began to be mighty on the earth." The name Kronos, as the classical reader is well aware, is applied to Saturn as the "Father of the gods." We have already had another "father of the gods" brought under our notice, even Cush in his character of Bel the Confounder, or Hephaistos, "The Scatterer abroad;"** and it is easy to understand how, when the deification of mortals began, and the "mighty" Son of Cush was deified, the father, especially considering the part which he seems to have had in concocting the whole idolatrous system, would have to be deified too, and of course, in his character as the Father of the "Mighty one," and of all the "immortals" that succeeded him. But, in point of fact, we shall find, in the course of our inquiry, that Nimrod was the *actual* Father of the gods, as being the *first* of deified mortals; and that, therefore, it is

* Clericus, *De Philosophia Orientali*, lib. i. sect. ii. cap. 37.

† Eusebii, *Chronicon*, p. 6.

‡ The scholiast upon Euripides, *Orest.*, v. 963, p. 85, says that "the Cyclops were so called from Cyclops their king." By this scholiast the Cyclops are regarded as a Thracian nation, for the Thracians had localised the tradition, and applied it to themselves; but the following statement of the scholiast on the *Prometheus* of Æschylus, p. 56, shows that they stood in such a relation to Kronos, as proves that he was their king: "The Cyclops . . . . were the brethren of Kronos, the father of Jupiter."

§ "*Turres ut Aristoteles, Cyclopes* (invenerunt)."—Pliny, lib. vii., cap. 56, p. 171.

|| For further evidence in regard to the "God of fortifications," see Appendix, Note D.

¶ From *Krn*, a horn. The epithet Carneus applied to Apollo (Pausanias, lib. iii., *Laconica*, cap. 13), is just a different form of the same word. In the *Orphic Hymns*, Apollo is addressed as the "Two-horned god" (*Hymn to Apollo*).

** See *ante*, p. 28.

in exact accordance with historical fact that Kronos, the Horned, or Mighty one, is, in the classic Pantheon, known by that title.

The meaning of this name Kronos, "The Horned one," as applied to Nimrod, fully explains the origin of the remarkable symbol, so frequently occurring among the Nineveh sculptures, the gigantic HORNED man-bull, as representing the great divinities in Assyria. The same word that signified a *bull*, signified also a *ruler* or *prince*.* Hence the "Horned bull" signified "The Mighty Prince," thereby pointing back to the first of those "Mighty ones," who, under the name of Guebres, Gabrs, or Cabiri, occupied so conspicuous a place in the ancient world, and to whom the deified Assyrian monarchs covertly traced back the origin of their greatness and might. This explains the reason why the Bacchus of the Greeks was represented as wearing horns, and why he was frequently addressed by the epithet "Bull-horned," as one of the high titles of his dignity.† Even in comparatively recent times, Togrul Begh, the leader of the Seljukian Turks, who came from the neighbourhood of the Euphrates, was in a similar manner represented with three horns growing out of his head, as the emblem of his sovereignty (Fig. 9).‡ This, also, in a remarkable way accounts for the origin of one of the divinities worshipped by our Pagan Anglo-Saxon ancestors under the name of Zernebogus. This Zernebogus was "the black, malevo-

Fig. 9.

Fig. 10.

* The name for a bull or ruler, is in Hebrew without points, Shur, which in Chaldee becomes Tur. From Tur, in the sense of a bull, comes the Latin Taurus; and from the same word, in the sense of a ruler, Turannus, which originally had no evil meaning. Thus, in these well-known classical words, we have evidence of the operation of the very principle which caused the deified Assyrian kings to be represented under the form of the man-bull.

† *Orphic Hymns:* Hymn li., *To Trietericus, Greek*, p. 117.

‡ From HYDE's *Religio Veterum Persarum*, cap. 4, p. 116.

lent, ill-omend divinity,"* in other words, the exact counterpart of the popular idea of the Devil, as supposed to be black, and equipped with horns and hoofs. This name, analysed and compared with the accompanying woodcut (Fig. 10), from Layard,† casts a very singular light on the source from whence has come the popular superstition in regard to the grand Adversary. The name Zer-Nebo-Gus is almost pure Chaldee, and seems to unfold itself as denoting "The seed of the prophet Cush." We have seen reason already to conclude that, under the name Bel, as distinguished from Baal, Cush was the great soothsayer or false prophet worshipped at Babylon. But independent inquirers have been led to the conclusion that Bel and Nebo were just two different titles for the same god, and that a prophetic god. Thus does Kitto comment on the words of Isaiah xlvi. 1: "Bel boweth down, Nebo stoopeth," with reference to the latter name: "The word seems to come from Nibba, to deliver an oracle, or to prophesy; and hence would mean an 'oracle,' and may thus, as Calmet suggests ('Commentaire Literal,' *in loc.*), be no more than another name for Bel himself, or a characterising epithet applied to him; it being not unusual to repeat the same thing, in the same verse, in equivalent terms."‡ "Zer-Nebo-Gus," the great "seed of the prophet Cush," was, of course, Nimrod; for Cush was Nimrod's father. Turn now to Layard, and see how this land of ours and Assyria are thus brought into intimate connection. In the woodcut referred to, first we find "the Assyrian Hercules,"§ that is "Nimrod the giant," as he is called in the Septuagint version of Genesis, without club, spear, or weapons of any kind, attacking a bull. Having overcome it, he sets the bull's horns on his head, as a trophy of victory and a symbol of power; and thenceforth the hero is represented, not only with the horns and hoofs above, but from the middle downwards, with the legs and cloven feet of the bull. Thus equipped he is represented as turning next to encounter a lion. This, in all likelihood, is intended to commemorate some event in the life of him who first began to be mighty in the chase and in war, and who, according to all ancient traditions, was remarkable also for bodily power, as being the leader of the Giants that rebelled against heaven. Now Nimrod, as the son of Cush, was black, in other words, was a negro. "Can the Æthiopian change his skin?" is in the original, "Can the Cushite" do so? Keeping this, then, in mind, it will be seen that in that figure disentombed from Nineveh, we have both the prototype of the Anglo-Saxon Zer-Nebo-Gus, "the seed of the prophet Cush," and the real original of the black Adversary of mankind, with horns and hoofs. It was in a different character from that of the Adversary that Nimrod was originally worshipped; but among a people of a fair complexion, as the Anglo-Saxons, it was inevitable

* SHARON TURNER'S *Anglo-Saxons*, vol. i. p. 217.
† LAYARD'S *Nineveh and Babylon*, p. 605.
‡ KITTO'S *Illustrated Commentary*, vol. iv. p. 53.
§ In *Lares and Penates of Cilicia*, p. 151, Barker identifies the Assyrian Hercules with "Dayyad the Hunter," that is evidently Nimrod.

that, if worshipped at all, it must generally be simply as an object of fear; and so Kronos, "The Horned one," who wore the "horns," as the emblem both of his physical might and sovereign power, has come to be, in popular superstition, the recognised representative of the Devil.

Fig. 11.

Horn Head Dresses.

In many and far-severed countries, horns became the symbols of sovereign power. The *corona* or *crown*, that still encircles the brows of European monarchs, seems remotely to be derived from the emblem of *might* adopted by *Kronos*, or Saturn, who, according to Pherecydes, was "the first before all others that ever wore a crown."*

* "Saturnum Pherecydes ante omnes refert coronatum."—TERTULLIAN, *De Corona Militis*, cap. 7, vol. ii. p. 85.

The first regal crown appears to have been only a band, in which the horns were set. From the idea of power contained in the "horn," even subordinate rulers seem to have worn a circlet adorned with a single horn, in token of their derived authority. Bruce, the Abyssinian traveller, gives examples of Abyssinian chiefs thus decorated (Fig. 11), in regard to whom he states that the horn attracted his particular attention, when he perceived that the *governors of provinces* were distinguished by this head-dress.* In the case of sovereign powers, the royal head-band was adorned sometimes with a double, sometimes with a triple horn. The double horn had evidently been the original symbol of power or might on the part of sovereigns; for, on the Egyptian monuments, the heads of the deified royal personages have generally no more than the two horns to shadow forth their power. As sovereignty in Nimrod's case was founded on physical force, so the two horns of the bull were the symbols of that physical force. And, in accordance with this, we read in "Sanchuniathon," that "Astarte put on her own head a bull's head as the ensign of royalty." † By-and-by, however, another and a higher idea came in, and the expression of that idea was seen in the symbol of the *three* horns. A cap seems in course of time to have come to be associated with the regal horns. In Assyria the three-horned cap was one of the "*sacred emblems*," ‡ in token that the power connected with it was of celestial origin,—the three horns evidently pointing at the power of the trinity. Still, we have indications that the horned band, without any cap, was anciently the *corona* or royal crown. The crown borne by the Hindoo god Vishnu, in his *avatar* of the Fish, is just an open circle or band, with three horns standing erect from it, with a knob on the top of each horn (Fig. 12). § All the *avatars*

Fig. 12.

* See KITTO's *Illustrated Commentary*, vol. iv. pp. 280-282. In Fig. 11, the two male figures are Abyssinian Chiefs. The two females, whom Kitto has grouped along with them, are ladies of Mount Lebanon, whose horned head-dresses Walpole regards as relics of the ancient worship of Astarte. (See above, and WALPOLE's *Ansayri*, vol. iii. p. 16.)

† EUSEBIUS, *Præparatio Evangelii*, lib. i. cap. 10, vol. i. p. 45.

‡ LAYARD's *Nineveh*, vol. ii. p. 446.

§ MAURICE, vol. iii. p. 353. London, 1793.

are represented as crowned with a crown that seems to have been modelled from this, consisting of a coronet with three points, standing erect from it, in which Sir William Jones recognises the Æthiopian or Parthian coronet.* The open tiara of Agni, the Hindoo god of fire, shows in its lower round the double horn, † made in the very same way as in Assyria,‡ proving at once the ancient custom, and whence that custom had come. Instead of the three horns, three horn-shaped leaves came to be substituted (Fig. 13);§ and thus the horned band gradually passed into the modern coronet or crown with the three leaves of the fleur-de-lis, or other familiar three-leaved adornings.

Among the Red Indians of America there had evidently been something entirely analogous to the Babylonian custom of wearing the horns; for, in the "buffalo dance" there, each of the dancers had his head arrayed with buffalo's horns;‖ and it is worthy of especial remark, that the "Satyric dance,"¶ or dance of the Satyrs in Greece, seems to have been the counterpart of this Red Indian solemnity; for the satyrs were horned divinities, and consequently those who imitated their dance must have had their heads set off in imitation of theirs. When thus we find a custom that is clearly founded on a form of speech that characteristically distinguished the region where Nimrod's power was wielded, used in so many different countries far removed from one another, where no such form of speech was used in *ordinary life*, we may be sure that such a custom was not the result of mere accident, but that it indicates the wide-spread diffusion of an influence that went forth in all directions from Babylon, from the time that Nimrod first "began to be mighty on the earth."

Fig. 13.

There was another way in which Nimrod's power was symbolised besides by the "horn." A synonym for Gheber, "The mighty one," was "Abir," while "Aber" also signified a "wing." Nimrod, as Head and Captain of those men of war, by whom he surrounded himself, and who were the instruments of establishing his power, was "Baal-aberin," "Lord of the mighty ones." But "Baal-abirin"

* *Asiatic Researches*, vol. i. p. 260.

† *Ibid.* "Agni," Plate 80.

‡ Layard's *Nineveh*, &c., vol. ii. p. 451.

§ From Kitto's *Illust. Com.*, vol. ii. p. 301. The groove in the middle of the central prominence seems to prove that it is not really a horn, but a leaf.

‖ Catlin's *North American Indians*, vol. ii. p. 128.

¶ Bryant, vol. iv. p. 250. The Satyrs were the companions of Bacchus, and "*danced* along with him" (*Ælian Hist.*, p. 22). When it is considered who Bacchus was, and that his distinguishing epithet was "Bull-horned," the horns of the "Satyrs" will appear in their true light. For a particular mystic reason the Satyr's horn was commonly a goat's horn, but originally it must have been the same as Bacchus's.

(pronounced nearly in the same way) signified "The winged one,"* and therefore in symbol he was represented, not only as a horned bull, but as at once a horned and winged bull—as showing not merely that he was mighty himself, but that he had mighty ones under his command, who were ever ready to carry his will into effect, and to put down all opposition to his power; and to shadow forth the vast extent of his might, he was represented with great and wide-expanding wings. To this mode of representing the mighty kings of Babylon and Assyria, who imitated Nimrod and his successors, there is manifest allusion in Isaiah viii. 6-8: "Forasmuch as this people refuseth the waters of Shiloah that go softly, and rejoice in Rezin and Remaliah's son; now therefore, behold, the Lord bringeth up upon them the waters of the river, strong and mighty, even the king of Assyria, and all his glory; and he shall come up over all his banks. And he shall pass through Judah; he shall overflow and go over; he shall reach even unto the neck; and the STRETCHING OUT OF HIS WINGS shall FILL the breadth of thy land, O Immanuel." When we look at such figures as those which are here

Fig. 14.

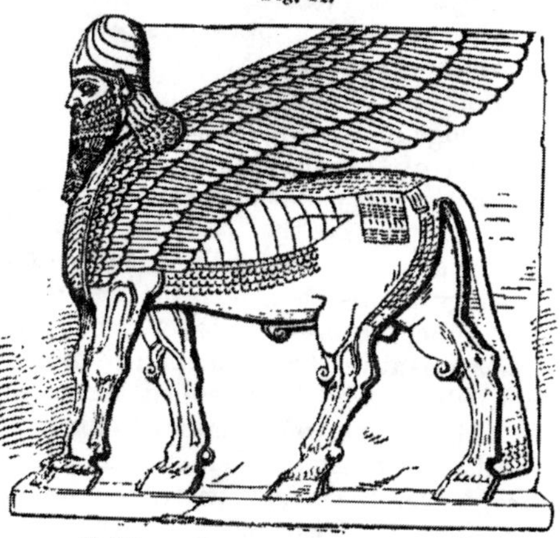

Bull from Nimrúd. From VAUX, p. 236.

Fig. 15.

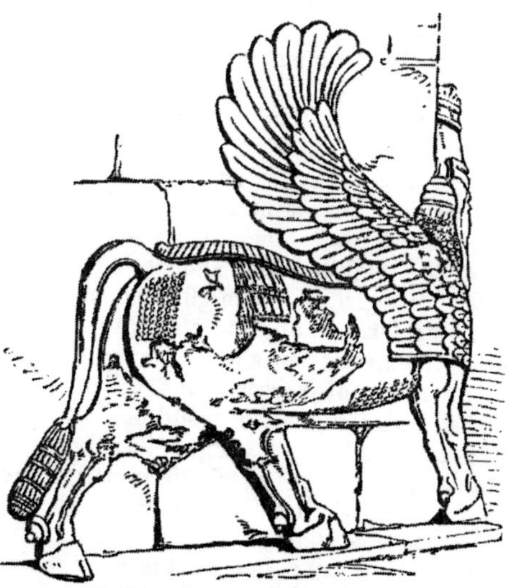

Bull from Persepolis. *Ibid.* p. 320.

* This is according to a peculiar Oriental idiom, of which there are many examples. Thus, *Baal-aph*, "Lord of wrath," signifies "an angry man;" *Baal-lashon*, "lord of tongue," "an eloquent man;" *Baal-hatzim*, "lord of arrows," "an archer;" and in like manner, *Baal-aberin*, "lord of wings," signifies "a winged one."

presented to the reader (Figs. 14 and 15), with their great extent of expanded wing, as symbolising an Assyrian king, what a vividness and force does it give to the inspired language of the prophet! And how clear is it, also, that the stretching forth of the Assyrian monarch's WINGS, that was to "*fill* the breadth of Immanuel's land," has that very symbolic meaning to which I have referred—viz., the overspreading of the land by his "mighty ones," or hosts of armed men, that the king of Babylon was to bring with him in his overflowing invasion! The knowledge of the way in which the Assyrian monarchs were represented, and of the meaning of that representation, gives additional force to the story of the dream of Cyrus the Great, as told by Herodotus. Cyrus, says the historian, dreamt that he saw the son of one of his princes, who was at the time in a distant province, with two great "wings on his shoulders, the one of which overshadowed Asia, and the other Europe,"* from which he immediately concluded that he was organising *rebellion* against him. The symbols of the Babylonians, whose capital Cyrus had taken, and to whose power he had succeeded, were entirely familiar to him; and if the "wings" were the symbols of sovereign power, and the possession of them implied the *lordship* over the *might*, or the armies of the empire, it is easy to see how very naturally any suspicions of disloyalty affecting the individual in question might take shape in the manner related, in the dreams of him who might harbour these suspicions.

Now, the understanding of this equivocal sense of "Baal-aberin" can alone explain the remarkable statement of Aristophanes, that at the beginning of the world "the birds" were *first* created, and *then*, *after* their creation, came the "race of the blessed immortal gods."† This has been regarded as either an atheistical or nonsensical utterance on the part of the poet, but, with the true key applied to the language, it is found to contain an important historical fact. Let it only be borne in mind that "the birds"—that is, "the winged ones" —symbolised "the Lords of the mighty ones," and then the meaning is clear—viz., that men *first* "began to be mighty on the earth;" and *then*, that the "Lords" or Leaders of "these mighty ones" were *deified*. The knowledge of the mystic sense of this symbol accounts also for the origin of the story of Perseus, the son of Jupiter, miraculously born of Danaë, who did such wondrous things, and who passed from country to country on wings divinely bestowed on him. This equally casts light on the symbolic myths in regard to Bellerophon, and the feats which he performed on his winged horse, and their ultimate disastrous issue; how high he mounted in the air, and how terrible was his fall; and of Icarus, the son of Dædalus, who, flying on wax-cemented wings over the Icarian Sea, had his wings melted off through his too near approach to the sun, and so gave his name to the sea where he was supposed to have fallen. The fables all referred to those who trode, or were supposed

* HERODOTUS, lib. i. cap. 209, p. 96.

† ARISTOPHANES *Aves*, v. 695-705, p. 404.

to have trodden, in the steps of Nimrod, the first "Lord of the mighty ones," and who in that character was symbolised as equipped with wings.

Now, it is remarkable that, in the passage of Aristophanes already referred to, that speaks of the birds, or "the winged ones," being produced *before* the gods, we are informed that he from whom both "mighty ones" and gods derived their origin, was none other than the winged *boy* Cupid.* Cupid, the son of Venus, occupied, as will afterwards be proved, in the mystic mythology the very same position as Nin, or Ninus, "the son," did to Rhea, the mother of the gods.† As Nimrod was unquestionably the *first* of "the mighty ones" after the Flood, this statement of Aristophanes, that the *boy-god* Cupid, himself a *winged* one, produced all the birds or "winged ones," while occupying the very position of Nin or Ninus, "the son," shows that in this respect also Ninus and Nimrod are identified. While this is the evident meaning of the poet, this also, in a strictly historical point of view, is the conclusion of the historian Apollodorus; for he states that "Ninus is Nimrod."‡ And then, in conformity with this identity of Ninus and Nimrod, we find, in one of the most celebrated sculptures of ancient Babylon, Ninus and his wife Semiramis represented as actively engaged in the pursuits of the chase,§—"the quiver-bearing Semiramis" being a fit companion for "the mighty Hunter before the Lord."

SUB-SECTION II.—THE CHILD IN EGYPT.

When we turn to Egypt we find remarkable evidence of the same thing there also. Justin, as we have already seen, says that "Ninus subdued all nations, as far as Lybia," and consequently Egypt. The statement of Diodorus Siculus is to the same effect, Egypt being one of the countries that, according to him, Ninus brought into subjection to himself.‖ In exact accordance with these historical statements, we find that the name of the third person in the primeval triad of Egypt was Khons. But Khons, in Egyptian, comes from a word that signifies "to chase."¶ Therefore, the name of Khons, the son of Maut, the goddess-mother, who was adorned in such a way as to

* Aristophanes says that Eros or Cupid produced the "birds" and "gods" by "*mingling* all things." This evidently points to the meaning of the name Bel, which signifies at once "the *mingler*" and "the confounder." This name properly belonged to the father of Nimrod, but, as the son was represented as identified with the father, we have evidence that the name descended to the son and others by inheritance.

† See Chap. V. Sect. IV.

‡ APOLLODORI, *Fragm.* 68, in MÜLLER, vol. i. p. 440.

§ DIODORUS, lib. ii. p. 69.

‖ See BRYANT, vol. ii. p. 377.

¶ BUNSEN, vol. i. p. 392, and *Vocabulary*, p. 488. The Coptic for "to hunt" is Κωνc, c being pronounced as *s*.

identify her with Rhea, the great goddess-mother of Chaldea,* properly signifies "The Huntsman," or god of the chase. As Khons stands in the very same relation to the Egyptian Maut as Ninus does to Rhea, how does this title of "The Huntsman" identify the Egyptian god with Nimrod? Now this very name Khons, brought into contact with the Roman mythology, not only explains the meaning of a name in the Pantheon there, that hitherto has stood greatly in need of explanation, but causes that name, when explained, to reflect light back again on this Egyptian divinity, and to strengthen the conclusion already arrived at. The name to which I refer is the name of the Latin god Consus, who was in one aspect identified with Neptune,† but who was also regarded as "the god of hidden counsels," or "the concealer of secrets," who was looked up to as the patron of horsemanship, and was said to have produced the horse.‡ Who could be the "god of hidden counsels," or the "concealer of secrets," but Saturn, the god of the "mysteries," and whose name as used at Rome, signified "The hidden one"?§ The father of Khons, or Khonso (as he was also called), that is, Amoun, was, as we are told by Plutarch, known as "The hidden God;"|| and as father and son in the same triad have ordinarily a correspondence of character, this shows that Khons also must have been known in the very same character of Saturn, "The hidden one." If the Latin Consus, then, thus exactly agreed with the Egyptian Khons, as the god of "mysteries," or "hidden counsels," can there be a doubt that Khons, the Huntsman, also agreed with the same Roman divinity as the supposed producer of the horse? Who so likely to get the credit of producing the horse as the great huntsman of Babel, who no doubt enlisted it in the toils of the chase, and by this means must have been signally aided in his conflicts with the wild beasts of the forest? In this connection, let the reader call to mind that fabulous creature, the Centaur, half-man, half-horse, that figures so much in the mythology of Greece. That imaginary creation, as is generally admitted, was intended to commemorate the man who first taught the art of horsemanship.¶ But that creation was not the offspring of Greek

* The distinguishing decoration of Maut was the vulture head-dress. Now the name of Rhea, in one of its meanings, signifies a vulture. For the *mystic* meaning of this name, see Appendix, Note C.

† How Nimrod came to be regarded as the god of the sea will afterwards appear. See Chap. IV. Sect. I.

‡ Fuss's *Roman Antiquities*, chap. iv. p. 347.

§ The meaning which the Romans attached to the name Saturn is evident from the account they give of the origin of the name of Latium. It was given, they said, because "Saturn had safely *lain hid* in its coasts." Virgil, *Æneid*, lib. viii. See also Ovid, *Fasti*, lib. i.

|| Plutarch, *De Iside et Osiride*, vol. ii. p. 354.

¶ In illustration of the principle that led to the making of the image of the Centaur, the following passage may be given from Prescott's *Mexico*, vol. i. p. 259, as showing the feelings of the Mexicans on first seeing a man on horseback: "He [Cortés] ordered his men [who were cavalry] to direct their lances at the faces of their opponents, who, terrified at the monstrous apparition—for they supposed the rider and the horse, which they had never before seen, *to be one and the same*—were seized with a panic."

fancy. Here, as in many other things, the Greeks have only borrowed from an earlier source. The Centaur is found on coins struck in Babylonia (Fig. 16),* showing that the idea must have originally come from that quarter. The Centaur is found in the Zodiac (Fig. 17),† the antiquity of which goes up to a high period, and which had its origin in Babylon. The Centaur was represented, as we are expressly assured by Berosus, the Babylonian historian, in the temple of Babylon,‡ and his language would seem to show that so also it had been in primeval times. The Greeks did themselves admit this antiquity and derivation of the Centaur; for though Ixion was commonly represented as the father of the Centaurs, yet they also acknowledged that the primitive Centaurus was the same as Kronos, or Saturn, the father of the gods.§ But we have seen that Kronos was the first King of Babylon, or Nimrod; consequently, the first Centaur was the same. Now, the way in which the Centaur was represented on the Babylonian coins, and in the Zodiac, viewed in this light, is very striking. The Centaur was the same as the sign Sagittarius, or "The Archer."‖ If the founder of Babylon's glory was "The mighty Hunter," whose name, even in the days of Moses, was a proverb—(Gen. x. 9, "Wherefore, *it is said*, Even as Nimrod, the mighty hunter before the Lord")—when we find the "Archer," with his bow and arrow, in the symbol of the supreme Babylonian divinity,¶ and the "Archer," among the signs of the Zodiac that originated in Babylon, I think we may safely conclude that this Man-horse or Horse-man Archer primarily referred to *him*, and was intended to perpetuate the memory at once of his fame as a huntsman and his skill as a horse-breaker.

Fig. 16.

Now, when we thus compare the Egyptian Khons, the "Huntsman," with the Latin Consus, the god of horse-races, who "produced the horse," and the Centaur of Babylon, to whom was attributed the

* See *Nineveh and Babylon*, p. 250, and BRYANT, vol. iii. Plate, p. 245.

† *Nineveh and its Remains*, vol. ii. p. 440, Note. The name there given is Sagittarius. See Note below.

‡ BEROSUS *apud* BUNSEN, p. 708.

§ Scholiast in *Lycophron*, v. 1200, *apud* BRYANT, vol. iii. p. 315. The Scholiast says that Chiron was the son of "Centaurus, that is, Kronos." If any one objects that, as Chiron is said to have lived in the time of the Trojan war, this shows that his father Kronos could not be the father of gods and men, Xenophon answers by saying "that Kronos was the brother of Jupiter."—*De Venatione*, p. 973.

‖ See coins already referred to, also the figure in the Zodiac. See also *Manilius*, i. 270, where he describes *Sagittarius as "mixtus equo."* Hence, says Smith, in his *Classical Dictionary*, Sagittarius is "frequently termed Centaurus."

¶ LAYARD's *Nineveh and its Remains*, vol. ii. p. 448. For the meaning of the name Centaurus, see Appendix, Note E.

honour of being the author of horsemanship, while we see how all the lines converge in Babylon, it will be very clear, I think, whence the primitive Egyptian god Khons has been derived.

Khons, the son of the great goddess-mother, seems to have been generally represented as a full-grown god.* The Babylonian divinity was also represented very frequently in Egypt in the very same way as in the land of his nativity—*i.e.*, as a child in his mother's arms.† This was the way in which Osiris, "the son, the husband of his mother," was often exhibited, and what we learn of this god, equally as in the case of Khonso, shows that in his original he was none other than Nimrod. It is admitted that the secret system of Free Masonry was originally founded on the Mysteries of the Egyptian Isis, the goddess-mother, or wife of Osiris. But what could have led to the union of a Masonic body with these Mysteries, had they not had particular reference to architecture, and had the god who was worshipped in them not been celebrated for his success in perfecting the arts of fortification and building? Now, if such were the case, considering the relation in which, as we have already seen, Egypt stood to Babylon, who would naturally be looked up to there as the great patron of the Masonic art? The strong presumption is, that Nimrod must have been the man. He was the first that gained fame in this way. As the child of the Babylonian goddess-mother, he was worshipped, as we have seen, in the character of Ala mahozim, "The god of fortifications." Osiris, in like manner, the child of the Egyptian Madonna, was equally celebrated as "the strong chief of the buildings."§ This strong chief of the buildings was originally worshipped in Egypt with every physical characteristic of Nimrod. I have already noticed the fact that Nimrod, as the son of Cush, was a negro. Now, there was a tradition in Egypt, recorded by Plutarch, that "Osiris was *black*,"|| which, in a land where the general complexion was dusky, must have implied something more than ordinary in its darkness. Plutarch also states that Horus, the son of Osiris, "was of a fair complexion,"¶ and it was in this way, for the most part, that Osiris was represented. But we have unequivocal evidence that Osiris, the son and husband of the great goddess-queen of Egypt, was also represented as a veritable negro. In Wilkinson may be found a representation of him (Fig. 18)** with the unmistakable features of the genuine Cushite or negro. Bunsen would have it that

Fig. 17.‡

* See Wilkinson, vol. vi. Plate 20.

† One of the symbols with which Khonso was represented, shows that even he was identified with the *child-god*; "for," says Wilkinson, "at the side of his head fell the plaited lock of Harpocrates, or *childhood*." Vol. v. p. 19.

‡ The above is the Hindoo Sagittarius, as found in the Indian Zodiac, which is proved by Sir William Jones to be substantially the same as the Zodiac of the Greeks. See *Asiatic Researches*, vol. ii. p. 303.

§ Bunsen, vol. i. p. 425.

|| Plutarch, *De Isid. et Os.*, vol. ii. p. 359.

¶ *Ibid.*

** Wilkinson, vol. vi. Plate 33.

this is a mere random importation from some of the barbaric tribes; but the dress in which this negro god is arrayed tells a different tale. That dress directly connects him with Nimrod. This negro-featured Osiris is clothed from head to foot in a *spotted* dress, the upper part being a leopard's skin, the under part also being spotted to correspond with it. Now the name Nimrod* signifies "the subduer of the leopard." This name seems to imply, that as Nimrod had gained fame by subduing the horse, and so making use of it in the chase, so his fame as a huntsman rested mainly on this, that he found out the art of making the leopard aid him in hunting the other wild beasts.

Fig. 13.

A particular kind of tame leopard is used in India at this day for hunting; and of Bagajet I., the Mogul Emperor of India, it is recorded that in his hunting establishment he had not only hounds of various breeds, but leopards also, whose "collars were set with jewels."† Upon the words of the prophet Habakkuk, chap. i. 8, "swifter than leopards," Kitto has the following remarks:—"The swiftness of the leopard is proverbial in all countries where it is found. This, conjoined with its other qualities, suggested the idea in the East of partially training it, that it might be employed in hunting. . . . . Leopards are now rarely kept for hunting in Western Asia, unless by kings and governors; but they are more common in the eastern parts of Asia. Orosius relates that one was sent by the king of Portugal to the Pope, which excited great astonishment by the way in which it overtook, and the facility with which it killed, deer and wild boars. Le Bruyn mentions a leopard kept by the Pasha who governed Gaza, and the other territories of the ancient Philistines, and

* "Nimr-rod"; from *Nimr*, a "leopard," and *rada* or *rad* "to subdue." According to invariable custom in Hebrew, when two consonants come together as the two *rs* in Nimr-rod, one of them is sunk. Thus Nin-neveh, "The habitation of Ninus," becomes Nineveh. The name Nimrod is commonly derived from Mered, "to rebel;" but a difficulty has always been found in regard to this derivation, as that would make the name Nimrod properly passive not "the rebel," but "he who was rebelled against." There is no doubt that Nimrod *was* a rebel, and that his rebellion was celebrated in ancient myths; but his name in that character was not Nimrod, but Merodach, or, as among the Romans, Mars, "the rebel;" or among the Oscans of Italy, Mamers (SMITH, *sub voce*), "The causer of rebellion." That the Roman Mars was really, in his original, the Babylonian god, is evident from the name given to the goddess, who was recognised sometimes as his "sister," and sometimes as his "wife"—*i.e.*, Bellona (see *Ibid.*, *sub voce*), which, in Chaldee, signifies, "The Lamenter of Bel" (from *Bel* and *onah*, to lament). The Egyptian Isis, the sister and wife of Osiris, is in like manner represented, as we have seen, as "*lamenting* her brother Osiris."—BUNSEN, vol. i. p. 419, Note.

† WILKINSON, vol. iii. p. 17.

which he frequently employed in hunting jackals. But it is in India that the *cheetah*, or hunting leopard, is most frequently employed, and is seen in the perfection of his power."* This custom of taming the leopard, and pressing it into the service of man in this way, is traced up to the earliest times of primitive antiquity. In the works of Sir William Jones, we find it stated from the Persian legends, that Hoshang, the father of Tahmurs, who built Babylon, was the "first who bred dogs and leopards for hunting."† As Tahmurs, who built Babylon, could be none other than Nimrod, this legend only attributes to his father what, as his name imports, he got the fame of doing himself. Now, as the classic god bearing the lion's skin is recognised by that sign as Hercules, the slayer of the Nemean lion, so in like manner, the god clothed in the leopard's skin, would naturally be marked out as Nimrod, the "Leopard-subduer." That this leopard skin, as appertaining to the Egyptian god, was no occasional thing, we have clearest evidence. Wilkinson tells us, that on all high occasions when the Egyptian high priest was called to officiate, it was indispensable that he should do so wearing, as his robe of office, the leopard's skin (Fig. 19). ‡ As it is a universal principle in all idolatries that the high priest wears the insignia of the god he serves, this indicates the importance which the spotted skin must have had attached to it as a symbol of the god himself. The ordinary way in which the favourite Egyptian divinity Osiris was *mystically* represented was under the form of a young bull or calf—the calf Apis—from which the golden calf of the Israelites was borrowed. There was a reason why that calf should not commonly appear in the appropriate symbols of the god he represented, for that calf represented the divinity in the character of Saturn, "The HIDDEN one," "Apis" being only another name for Saturn.§ The cow of Athor, however, the female divinity corresponding to Apis, is well known as a "spotted cow,"‖ and it is singular that the Druids of Britain also worshipped "a spotted cow."¶ Rare though it be, however, to find an instance of the deified calf or young bull represented with the spots, there is evidence still in existence, that

Fig. 19.

* KITTO'S *Illustrated Commentary*, vol. iv. pp. 271, 272.

† *Works*, vol. xii. p. 400.

‡ WILKINSON, vol. iv. pp. 341, 353.

§ The name of Apis in Egyptian is Hepi or Hapi, which is evidently from the Chaldee "*Hap*," "to cover." In Egyptian, *Hap* signifies "to conceal."—BUNSEN, vol. i. *Vocab.* p. 462.

‖ WILKINSON, vol. iv. p. 387, and vol. vi. Plate 36.

¶ DAVIES'S *Druids*, p. 121.

even it was sometimes so represented. The accompanying figure (Fig. 20) represents that divinity, as copied by Col. Hamilton Smith "from the original collection made by the artists of the French Institute of Cairo."* When we find that Osiris, the grand god of Egypt, under different forms, was thus arrayed in a leopard's skin or spotted dress, and that the leopard-skin dress was so indispensable a part of the sacred robes of his high priest, we may be sure that there was a deep meaning in such a costume. And what could that meaning be, but just to identify Osiris with the Babylonian god, who was celebrated as the "Leopard-tamer," and who was worshipped even as he was, as Ninus, the CHILD in his mother's arms?

SUB-SECTION III.—THE CHILD IN GREECE.

Fig. 20.

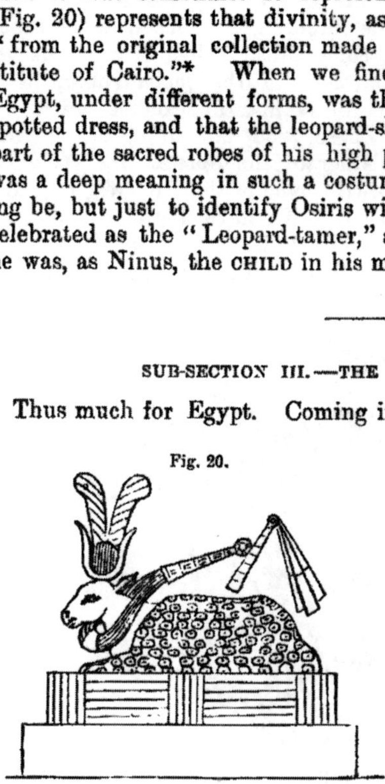

Egyptian Calf Idol.

Thus much for Egypt. Coming into Greece, not only do we find evidence there to the same effect, but increase of that evidence. The god worshipped as a child in the arms of the great Mother in Greece, under the names of Dionysus, or Bacchus, or Iacchus, is, by ancient inquirers, expressly identified with the Egyptian Osiris. This is the case with Herodotus, who had prosecuted his inquiries in Egypt itself, who ever speaks of Osiris as Bacchus.† To the same purpose is the testimony of Diodorus Siculus. "Orpheus," says he, "introduced from Egypt the greatest part of the mystical ceremonies, the orgies that celebrate the wanderings of Ceres, and the whole fable of the shades below. The rites of Osiris and Bacchus are the same; those of Isis and Ceres (Δημητρα) exactly resemble each other, except in name."‡ Now, as if to identify Bacchus with Nimrod, "the Leopard-tamer," leopards were employed to draw his car; he himself was represented as clothed with a leopard's skin; his priests were attired in the same manner, or when a leopard's skin was dispensed with, the *spotted* skin of a fawn was used as a priestly robe in its stead. This very custom of wearing the spotted fawn-skin seems to have been imported into Greece originally from Assyria, where a spotted fawn was a sacred emblem, as we learn from the Nineveh

* *Biblical Cyclopædia*, vol. i. p. 368. The flagellum or lash—the emblem of the great Egyptian god—suspended to the yoke about the neck of the calf, shows that this calf represented that god in one of his different forms.

† HERODOTUS, lib. ii. cap. 42.

‡ *Bibliotheca*, lib. i. p. 9.

sculptures; for there we find a divinity bearing a spotted fawn, or spotted fallow-deer (Fig. 21), in his arm, as a symbol of some mysterious import.* The origin of the importance attached to the spotted fawn and its skin had evidently come thus: When Nimrod, as "the Leopard-tamer," began to be clothed in the leopard-skin, as the trophy of his skill, his spotted dress and appearance must have impressed the imaginations of those who saw him; and he came to be called not only the "Subduer of the *Spotted one*" (for such is the precise meaning of Nimr—the name of the leopard), but to be called "The spotted one" himself. We have distinct evidence to this effect borne by Damascius, who tells us that the Babylonians called "the only son" of the great goddess-mother "Mōmis, or

Fig. 21.

Moumis."† Now, Mōmis, or Moumis, in Chaldee, like Nimr, signified "The spotted one." Thus, then, it became easy to represent Nimrod by the symbol of the "spotted fawn," and especially in Greece, and wherever a pronunciation akin to that of Greece prevailed. The name of Nimrod, as known to the Greeks, was Nebrod.‡ The name of the fawn, as "the spotted one," in Greece was Nebros;§ and thus nothing could be more natural than that Nebros, the

* VAUX's *Nineveh and Persepolis*, chap. viii. p. 233.

† DAMASCIUS, in CORY's *Fragments*, p. 318.

‡ In the Greek Septuagint, translated in Egypt, the name of Nimrod is "Nebrod."—(P. 17.)

§ Nebros, the name of the fawn, *signifies* "the spotted one." *Nmr*, in Egypt, would also become *Nbr*; for Bunsen shows that *m* and *b* in that land were often convertible. See vol. i. p. 449.

"spotted fawn," should become a synonym for Nebrod himself. When, therefore, the Bacchus of Greece was symbolised by the Nebros, or "spotted fawn," as we shall find he was symbolised, what could be the design but just covertly to identify him with Nimrod?

We have evidence that this god, whose emblem was the Nebros, was known as having the very lineage of Nimrod. From Anacreon, we find that a title of Bacchus was Aithiopais*—*i.e.*, "the son of Æthiops." But who was Æthiops? As the Æthiopians were Cushites, so Æthiops was Cush. "Chūs," says Eusebius, "was he from whom came the Æthiopians."† The testimony of Josephus is to the same effect. As the father of the Æthiopians, Cush was Æthiops, by way of eminence. Therefore Epiphanius, referring to the extraction of Nimrod, thus speaks: "Nimrod, the son of Cush, the Æthiop."‡ Now, as Bacchus was the son of Æthiops, or Cush, so to the *eye* he was represented in that character. As Nin "the Son," he was portrayed as a youth or child; and that youth or child was generally depicted with a *cup* in his hand. That cup, to the multitude, exhibited him as the god of drunken revelry; and of such revelry in his orgies, no doubt there was abundance; but yet, after all, the cup was mainly a hieroglyphic, and that of the *name* of the god. The name of a cup, in the sacred language, was khūs, and thus the *cup* in the hand of the youthful Bacchus, the son of Æthiops, showed that he was the *young* Chūs, or the *son* of Chūs.

Fig. 22.

In the accompanying woodcut (Fig. 22),§ the cup in the right hand of Bacchus is held up in so significant a way, as naturally to suggest that it must be a symbol; and as to the branch in the other hand, we have express testimony that it is a symbol. But it is worthy of notice that the branch has no leaves to determine what precise kind of a branch it is. It must, therefore, be a generic emblem for a branch, or a symbol of a branch in general; and, consequently, it needs the cup as its complement, to determine specifically what sort of a branch it is. The two symbols, then, must be read together;

* Anacreon, p. 296. The words of Anacreon are Διονυσον 'Αιθιοπαιδα.

† Eusebius, *Chronicon*, vol. i. p. 109.

‡ Epiphanius, lib. i. vol. i. p. 7.

§ From Smith's *Classical Dictionary*, p. 208.

and read thus, they are just equivalent to—the "Branch of Chūs" —*i.e.*, "the scion or son of Cush." *

There is another hieroglyphic connected with Bacchus that goes not a little to confirm this—that is, the Ivy branch. No emblem was more distinctive of the worship of Bacchus than this. Wherever the rites of Bacchus were performed, wherever his orgies were celebrated, the Ivy branch was sure to appear. Ivy, in some form or other, was essential to these celebrations. The votaries carried it in their hands,† bound it around their heads,‡ or had the Ivy leaf even indelibly stamped upon their persons.§ What could be the use, what could be the meaning of this? A few words will suffice to show it. In the first place, then, we have evidence that Kissos, the Greek name for Ivy, was one of the *names* of Bacchus; ‖ and further, that though the name of Cush, in its proper form, was known to the priests in the Mysteries, yet that the established way in which the name of his descendants, the Cushites, was ordinarily pronounced in Greece, was not after the Oriental fashion, but as "Kissaioi," or "Kissioi." Thus, Strabo, speaking of the inhabitants of Susa, who were the people of Chusistan, or the ancient land of Cush, says: "The Susians are called Kissioi," ¶—that is beyond all question, Cushites. Now, if Kissioi be Cushites, then Kissos is Cush. Then, further, the branch of Ivy that occupied so conspicuous a place in all Bacchanalian celebrations was an express symbol of Bacchus himself; for Hesychius assures us that Bacchus, as represented by his priest, was known in the Mysteries *as* "The branch." ** From this, then, it appears how Kissos, the Greek name of Ivy, became the name of Bacchus. As the son of Cush, and as identified with him, he was sometimes called by his father's name—Kissos.†† His actual relation,

* Everyone knows that Homer's *odzos Arēos*, or "Branch of Mars," is the same as a "Son of Mars." The hieroglyphic above was evidently formed on the same principle. That the *cup* alone in the hand of the *youthful* Bacchus was intended to designate him "as the young Chūs," or "the boy Chus," we may fairly conclude from a statement of Pausanias, in which he represents "the *boy* Kuathos" as acting the part of a *cup*-bearer, and presenting a *cup* to Hercules.—(PAUSANIAS, lib. ii.; *Corinthiaca*, cap. 13, p. 142.) Kuathos is the Greek for a "cup," and is evidently derived from the Hebrew Khus, "a cup," which, in one of its Chaldee forms, becomes Khuth or Khuath. Now, it is well known that the name of Cush is often found in the form of Cuth, and that name, in certain dialects, would be Cuath. The "boy Kuathos," then, is just the Greek form of the "boy Cush," or "the young Cush." The reader will not fail to notice the *spots* on the robe of the figure on opposite page.

[The berries or unopened flower-buds at the end of the twigs (Fig. 22), may indicate the Ivy plant. This, however, would not invalidate, but rather strengthen the general argument.]

† SMITH'S *Classical Dictionary*, "Dionysus," p. 227.

‡ EURIPID., in STRABO, lib. x. p. 452.

§ KITTO'S *Illust. Com.*, vol. iv. p. 144.—POTTER, vol. i. p. 75. Edin. 1808.

‖ PAUSANIAS, *Attica*, cap. 31, p. 78.

¶ STRABO, lib. xv. p. 691. In Hesychius, the name is Kissaioi, p. 531. The epithet applied to the land of Cush in Æschylus is Kissinos—ÆSCHYL., *Pers.* v. 16. The above accounts for one of the unexplained titles of Apollo. "Kisseus Apollon" is plainly "The Cushite Apollo."

** HESYCHIUS, p. 179.

†† See *ante*, for what is said of Janus, Note, p. 28.

however, to his father was specifically brought out by the Ivy branch, for "the branch of Kissos," which to the profane vulgar was only "the branch of Ivy," was to the initiated "The branch of Cush."*

Now, this god, who was recognised as "the scion of Cush," was worshipped under a name, which, while appropriate to him in his vulgar character as the god of the vintage, did also describe him as the great Fortifier. That name was Bassareus, which, in its two-fold meaning, signified at once "The houser of grapes, or the vintage gatherer," and "The Encompasser with a wall,"† in this latter sense identifying the Grecian god with the Egyptian Osiris, "the strong chief of the buildings," and with the Assyrian "Belus, who encompassed Babylon with a wall."

Thus from Assyria, Egypt, and Greece, we have cumulative and overwhelming evidence, all conspiring to demonstrate that the child worshipped in the arms of the goddess-mother in all these countries in the very character of Ninus or Nin, "The Son," was Nimrod, the son of Cush. A feature here, or an incident there, may have been borrowed from some succeeding hero; but it seems impossible to doubt, that of that child Nimrod was the prototype, the grand original.

The amazing extent of the worship of this man indicates something very extraordinary in his character; and there is ample reason to believe, that in his own day he was an object of high popularity. Though by setting up as king, Nimrod invaded the patriarchal system, and abridged the liberties of mankind, yet he was held by many to have conferred benefits upon them, that amply indemnified them for the loss of their liberties, and covered him with glory and renown. By the time that he appeared, the wild beasts of the forest multiplying more rapidly than the human race, must have committed

* The chaplet, or *head-band* of Ivy, had evidently a similar hieroglyphical meaning to the above, for the Greek "Zeira Kissou" is either a "band or circlet of Ivy," or "The seed of Cush." The formation of the Greek "Zeira," a zone or enclosing band, from the Chaldee *Zer*, to encompass, shows that Zero "the seed," which was also pronounced *Zeraa*, would, in like manner, in some Greek dialects, become Zeira. Kissos, "Ivy," in Greek, retains the radical idea of the Chaldee Khesha or Khesa, "to cover or hide," from which there is reason to believe the name of Cush is derived, for Ivy is characteristically "The coverer or hider." In connection with this, it may be stated that the second person of the Phenician trinity was Chusorus (Wilkinson, vol. iv. p. 191), which evidently is Chus-zoro, "The seed of Cush." We have already seen (p. 13) that the Phenicians derived their mythology from Assyria.

† Bassareus is evidently from the Chaldee Batzar, to which both Gesenius, pp. 150, 151, and Parkhurst, p. 77, give the two-fold meaning of "gathering in grapes," and "fortifying." Batzar is softened into Bazzar in the very same way as Nebuchadnetzar is pronounced Nebuchadnezzar. In the sense of "rendering a defence inaccessible," Gesenius adduces Jeremiah li. 53, "Though Babylon should *mount up to heaven*, and though she should *fortify* (tabatzar) the height of her strength, yet from me shall spoilers come unto her, saith the Lord." Here is evident reference to the two great elements in Babylon's strength, first her tower; secondly, her massive fortifications, or encompassing walls. In making the meaning of Batzar to be, "to render *inaccessible*," Gesenius seems to have missed the proper generic meaning of the term. Batzar is a compound verb, from *Ba*, "in," and *Tzar*, "to compass," exactly equivalent to our English word "en-compass."

great depredations on the scattered and straggling populations of the earth, and must have inspired great terror into the minds of men. The danger arising to the lives of men from such a source as this, when population is scanty, is implied in the reason given by God Himself for not driving out the doomed Canaanites before Israel at once, though the measure of their iniquity was full (Exod. xxiii. 29, 30): "I will not drive them out from before thee in one year, lest the land become desolate, and the beast of the field multiply against thee. By little and little I will drive them out from before thee, until thou be increased." The exploits of Nimrod, therefore, in hunting down the wild beasts of the field, and ridding the world of monsters, must have gained for him the character of a pre-eminent benefactor of his race. By this means, not less than by the bands he trained, was his power acquired, when he *first* began to be mighty upon the earth; and in the same way, no doubt, was that power consolidated. Then, over and above, as the first great city-builder after the flood, by gathering men together in masses, and surrounding them with walls, he did still more to enable them to pass their days in security, free from the alarms to which they had been exposed in their scattered life, when no one could tell but that at any moment he might be called to engage in deadly conflict with prowling wild beasts, in defence of his own life and of those who were dear to him. Within the battlements of a fortified city no such danger from savage animals was to be dreaded; and for the security afforded in this way, men no doubt looked upon themselves as greatly indebted to Nimrod. No wonder, therefore, that the name of the "mighty hunter," who was at the same time the prototype of "the god of fortifications," should have become a name of renown. Had Nimrod gained renown only thus, it had been well. But not content with delivering men from the fear of wild beasts, he set to work also to emancipate them from that fear of the Lord which is the beginning of wisdom, and in which alone true happiness can be found. For this very thing, he seems to have gained, as one of the titles by which men delighted to honour him, the title of the "Emancipator," or "Deliverer." The reader may remember a name that has already come under his notice. That name is the name of Phoroneus. The era of Phoroneus is exactly the era of Nimrod. He lived about the time when men had used one speech, when the confusion of tongues began, and when mankind was scattered abroad.* He is said to have been the first that gathered mankind into communities,† the first of mortals that reigned,‡ and the first that offered idolatrous sacrifices.§ This character can agree with none but that of Nimrod. Now the name given to him in connection with his "gathering men

* See *ante*, p. 25, and Note.

† PAUSANIAS, lib. ii.; *Corinthiaca*, cap. 15, p. 145.

‡ HYGINUS, *Fab.* 143, p. 114.

§ LUTATIUS PLACIDUS, in *Stat. Theb.*, lib. iv. v. 589, *apud* BRYANT, vol. iii. p. 65, Note. The words are "Primus *Junoni* sacrificasse dicitur." The meaning of this probably is, that he first set up the dove (Iunè) as a material and visible symbol of the Holy Spirit. See next Section.

together," and offering idolatrous sacrifice, is very significant. Phoroneus, in one of its meanings, and that one of the most natural, signifies the "Apostate."* That name had very likely been given him by the uninfected portion of the sons of Noah. But that name had also another meaning, that is, "to set free;" and therefore his own adherents adopted it, and glorified the great "Apostate" from the primeval faith, though he was the first that abridged the liberties of mankind, as the grand "Emancipator!"† And hence, in one form or other, this title was handed down to his deified successors as a title of honour.‡ All tradition from the earliest times bears testimony to the apostacy of Nimrod, and to his success in leading men away from the patriarchal faith, and delivering their minds from that awe of God and fear of the judgments of heaven that must have rested on them while yet the memory of the flood was recent. And according to all the principles of depraved human nature, this too, no doubt, was one grand element in his fame; for men will readily rally around any one who can give the least appearance of plausibility to any doctrine which will teach that they can be assured of happiness and heaven at last, though their hearts and natures are unchanged, and though they live without God in the world.

How great was the boon conferred by Nimrod on the human race, in the estimation of ungodly men, by emancipating them from the impressions of true religion, and putting the authority of heaven to a distance from them, we find most vividly described in a Polynesian tradition, that carries its own evidence with it. John Williams, the well-known missionary, tells us that, according to one of the ancient traditions of the islanders of the South Seas, "the heavens

* From Pharo, also pronounced Pharang, or Pharong, "to cast off, to make naked, to apostatise, to set free." These meanings are not commonly given in this *order*, but as the sense of "casting off" explains all the other meanings, that warrants the conclusion that "to cast off" is the generic sense of the word. Now "*apostacy*" is very near akin to this sense, and therefore is one of the most natural.

† The Sabine goddess Feronia had evidently a relation to Phoroneus, as the "Emancipator." She was believed to be the "goddess of liberty," because at Terracina (or Anxur) slaves were emancipated in her temple (Servius, in *Æneid*, viii. v. 564, vol. i. p. 490), and because the freedmen of Rome are recorded on one occasion to have collected a sum of money for the purpose of offering it in her temple.—SMITH's *Classical Dictionary* (the larger one), *sub voce* "Feronia."

The Chaldee meaning of the name "Feronia," strikingly confirms this conclusion. Her contemplar divinity, who was worshipped along with her in a grove, was, like Ninus, a youthful divinity. He was regarded as a "youthful Jupiter." —SMITH's *Classical Dictionary*, *sub voce* "Anxurus," p. 60.

‡ Thus we read of "Zeus Aphesio" (PAUSANIAS, lib. i. *Attica*, cap. 44), that is "Jupiter Liberator" (see also ARRIAN, who speaks of "Jovi *Aphesio* Liberatori scilicet," *apud* BRYANT, vol. v. p. 25), and of "Dionysus Eleuthereus" (PAUSANIAS, *Attica*, cap. 20, p. 46), or "Bacchus the Deliverer." The name of Theseus seems to have had the same origin, from *nthes* "to loosen," and so to set free (the *n* being omissible). "The temple of Theseus" [at Athens] says POTTER (vol. i. p. 36) . . . . "was allowed the privilege of being a Sanctuary for slaves, and all those of mean condition that fled from the persecution of men in power, in memory that Theseus, while he lived, *was an assister and protector of the distressed*."

were originally so close to the earth that men could not walk, but were compelled to crawl" under them. "This was found a very serious evil; but at length an individual conceived the sublime idea of elevating the heavens to a more convenient height. For this purpose he put forth his utmost energy, and by the first effort raised them to the top of a tender plant called *teve*, about four feet high. There he deposited them until he was refreshed, when, by a second effort, he lifted them to the height of a tree called Kauariki, which is as large as the sycamore. By the third attempt he carried them to the summits of the mountains; and after a long interval of repose, and by a most prodigious effort, he elevated them to their present situation." For this, as a mighty benefactor of mankind, "this individual was deified; and up to the moment that Christianity was embraced, the deluded inhabitants worshipped him as the 'Elevator of the heavens.'"* Now, what could more graphically describe the position of mankind soon after the flood, and the proceedings of Nimrod as Phoroneus, "The Emancipator,"† than this Polynesian fable? While the awful catastrophe by which God had showed His avenging justice on the sinners of the old world was yet fresh in the minds of men, and so long as Noah, and the upright among his descendants, sought with all earnestness to impress upon all under their control the lessons which that solemn event was so well fitted to teach, "heaven," that is, God, must have seemed very near to earth. To maintain the union between heaven and earth, and to keep it as close as possible, must have been the grand aim of all who loved God and the best interests of the human race. But this implied the restraining and discountenancing of all vice and all those "pleasures of sin," after which the natural mind, unrenewed and unsanctified, continually pants. This must have been secretly felt by every unholy mind as a state of insufferable bondage. "The carnal mind is enmity against God," is "not subject to His law," neither indeed is "able to be" so. It says to the Almighty, "Depart from us, for we desire not the knowledge of Thy ways." So long as the influence of the great father of the new world was in the ascendant, while his maxims were regarded, and a holy atmosphere surrounded the world, no wonder that those who were alienated from God and godliness, felt heaven and its influence and authority to be intolerably near, and that in such circumstances they "could not walk," but only "crawl,"—that is, that they had no freedom to "walk after the sight of their own eyes and the imaginations of their own hearts." From this bondage Nimrod emancipated them. By the apostacy he introduced, by the free life he developed among those who rallied around him, and by separating them from the holy influences that had previously less or more controlled them, he helped them to put God and the strict spirituality of His law at a distance,

* WILLIAM'S *Narrative of Missionary Enterprises*, chap. xxxi. p. 142.

† The bearing of this name, Phoroneus, "The Emancipator," will be seen in Chap. III. Sect. I., "Christmas," where it is shown that slaves had a temporary *emancipation* at his birthday.

and thus he became the "Elevator of the heavens," making men feel and act as if heaven were afar off from earth, and as if either the God of heaven "could not see through the dark cloud," or did not regard with displeasure the breakers of His laws. Then all such would feel that they could breathe freely, and that now they could walk at liberty. For this, such men could not but regard Nimrod as a high benefactor.

Now, who could have imagined that a tradition from Tahiti would have illuminated the story of Atlas? But yet, when Atlas, bearing the *heavens* on his shoulders, is brought into juxtaposition with the deified hero of the South Seas, who blessed the world by heaving up the superincumbent heavens that pressed so heavily upon it, who does not see that the one story bears a relation to the other?* Thus,

* In the Polynesian story the heavens and earth are said to have been "bound together with cords," and the "*severing*" of these cords is said to have been effected by myriads of "dragon-flies," which, with their "wings," bore an important share in the great work.—(WILLIAMS, p. 142.) Is there not here a reference to Nimrod's "mighties" or "winged ones"? The deified "mighty ones" were often represented as winged serpents. See WILKINSON, vol. iv. p. 232, where the god Agathodæmon is represented as a "winged asp." Among a rude people the memory of such a representation might very naturally be kept up in connection with the "dragon-fly"; and as *all* the mighty or winged ones of Nimrod's age, the *real* golden age of paganism, when "dead, became dæmons" (HESIOD, *Works and Days*, v. 120, 121), they would of course all alike be symbolised in the same way. If any be stumbled at the thought of such a connection between the mythology of Tahiti and of Babel, let it not be overlooked that the name of the Tahitian god of war was Oro (WILLIAMS, *Ibid.*), while "Horus (or Orus)," as Wilkinson calls the son of Osiris, in Egypt, which unquestionably borrowed its system from Babylon, appeared in that very character.—(WILKINSON, vol. iv. p. 402.) Then what could the severing of the "cords" that bound heaven and earth together be, but just the breaking of the bands of the covenant by which God bound the earth to Himself, when on smelling a sweet savour in Noah's sacrifice, He renewed His covenant with him as head of the human race. This covenant did not merely respect the promise to the earth securing it against another universal deluge, but contained in its bosom a promise of all spiritual blessings to those who adhere to it. The smelling of the sweet savour in Noah's sacrifice had respect to his *faith in Christ*. When, therefore, in consequence of smelling that sweet savour, "God blessed Noah and his sons" (Gen. ix. 1), that had reference not merely to temporal but to spiritual and eternal blessings. Every one, therefore, of the sons of Noah, who had Noah's faith, and who walked as Noah walked, was divinely assured of an interest in "the everlasting covenant, ordered in all things and sure." Blessed were those bands by which God bound the believing children of men to Himself—by which heaven and earth were so closely joined together. Those, on the other hand, who joined in the apostacy of Nimrod broke the covenant, and in casting off the authority of God, did in effect say, "Let us break His bands asunder, and cast His cords from us." To this very act of *severing* the covenant connection between earth and heaven there is very distinct allusion, though veiled, in the Babylonian history of Berosus. There Belus, that is Nimrod, after having dispelled the primeval darkness, is said to have *separated* heaven and earth from one another, and to have orderly arranged the world.—(BEROSUS, in BUNSEN, vol. i. p. 709.) These words were intended to represent Belus as the "*Former* of the world." But then it is a *new* world that he forms; for there are creatures in existence before his Demiurgic power is exerted. The new world that Belus or Nimrod formed, was just the *new order of things* which he introduced when, setting at nought all Divine appointments, he rebelled against *Heaven*. The rebellion of the Giants is represented as peculiarly a rebellion against *Heaven*. To this ancient quarrel between the Babylonian potentates and *Heaven*, there is

then, it appears that Atlas, with the heavens resting on his broad shoulders, refers to no mere distinction in astronomical knowledge, however great, as some have supposed, but to a quite different thing, even to that great apostacy in which the Giants rebelled against *Heaven*,* and in which apostacy Nimrod, "the mighty one,"† as the acknowledged ringleader, occupied a pre-eminent place.‡

According to the system which Nimrod was the grand instrument in introducing, men were led to believe that a real spiritual change of heart was unnecessary, and that so far as change was needful, they could be regenerated by mere external means. Looking at the subject in the light of the Bacchanalian orgies, which, as the reader has seen, commemorated the history of Nimrod, it is evident that he led mankind to seek their chief good in sensual enjoyment, and showed them how they might enjoy the pleasures of sin, without any fear of the wrath of a holy God. In his various expeditions he was always accompanied by troops of women; and by music and song, and games and revelries, and everything that could please the natural heart, he commended himself to the good graces of mankind.

SUB-SECTION IV.—THE DEATH OF THE CHILD.

How Nimrod died, Scripture is entirely silent. There was an ancient tradition that he came to a violent end. The circumstances of that end, however, as antiquity represents them, are clouded with fable. It is said that tempests of wind sent by God against the Tower of Babel overthrew it, and that Nimrod perished in its ruins.§ This could not be true, for we have sufficient evidence that the Tower of Babel stood long after Nimrod's day. Then, in regard to the death of Ninus, profane history speaks darkly and mysteriously, although one account tells of his having met with a violent death similar to that of Pentheus,‖ Lycurgus,¶ and Orpheus,** who were

plainly an allusion in the words of Daniel to Nebuchadnezzar, when announcing that sovereign's humiliation and subsequent restoration, he says (Daniel iv. 26), "Thy kingdom shall be sure unto thee, when thou hast known that the HEAVENS do rule."

* SMITH'S Lesser *Dictionary*, "Gigantes," pp. 282, 283.

† In the Greek Septuagint, translated in Egypt, the term "mighty" as applied in Gen. x. 8, to Nimrod, is rendered γιγας, the ordinary name for a "Giant."

‡ IVAN and KALLERY, in their account of Japan, show that a similar story to that of Atlas was known there, for they say that once a-day the Emperor "sits on his throne upholding the world and the empire." Now something like this came to be added to the story of Atlas, for PAUSANIAS shows (lib. v. cap. 18, p. 423) that Atlas also was represented as upholding both *earth* and heaven.

§ BRYANT, vol. iv. pp. 61, 62.

‖ HYGINUS, *Fab.* 184, p. 138.

¶ *Ibid.* *Fab.* 132, p. 109. Lycurgus, who is commonly made the enemy of Bacchus, was, by the Thracians and Phrygians, identified with Bacchus, who it is well known, was torn in pieces. See STRABO, lib. x. p. 453.

** APOLLODORUS, *Bibliotheca*, lib. i. cap. 3 and 7, p. 17.

said to have been torn in pieces.* The identity of Nimrod, however, and the Egyptian Osiris, having been established, we have thereby light as to Nimrod's death. Osiris met with a violent death, and that violent death of Osiris was the central theme of the whole idolatry of Egypt. If Osiris was Nimrod, as we have seen, that violent death which the Egyptians so pathetically deplored in their annual festivals was just the death of Nimrod. The accounts in regard to the death of the god worshipped in the several mysteries of the different countries are all to the same effect. A statement of Plato seems to show, that in his day the Egyptian Osiris was regarded as identical with Tammuz; † and Tammuz is well known to have been the same as Adonis,‡ the famous HUNTSMAN, for whose death Venus is fabled to have made such bitter lamentations. As the women of Egypt wept for Osiris, as the Phenician and Assyrian women wept for Tammuz, so in Greece and Rome the women wept for Bacchus, whose name, as we have seen, means "The bewailed," or "Lamented one." And now, in connection with the Bacchanal lamentations, the importance of the relation established between Nebros, "The spotted fawn," and Nebrod, "The mighty hunter," will appear. The Nebros, or "spotted fawn," was the symbol of Bacchus, as representing Nebrod or Nimrod himself. Now, on certain occasions, in the mystical celebrations, the Nebros, or "spotted fawn," was torn in pieces, expressly, as we learn from Photius, as a commemoration of what happened to Bacchus,§ whom that fawn represented. The tearing in pieces of Nebros, "the spotted one," goes to confirm the conclusion, that the death of Bacchus, even as the death of Osiris, represented the death of Nebrod, whom, under the very name of "The Spotted one," the Babylonians worshipped. Though we do not find any account of Mysteries observed in Greece in memory of Orion, the giant and mighty hunter celebrated by Homer, under that name, yet he was represented symbolically as having died in a similar way to that in which Osiris died, and as having then

* LUDOVICUS VIVES, *Commentary on Augustine*, lib. vi. chap. ix. Note, p. 239. Ninus as referred to by Vives is called "King of India." The word "India" in classical writers, though not always, yet commonly means Æthiopia, or the land of Cush. Thus the Choaspes in the land of the eastern Cushites is called an "Indian river" (DIONYSIUS AFER. *Periergesis*, v. 1073-4, p. 32); and the Nile is said by Virgil to come from the "coloured Indians" (*Georg.*, lib. iv. v., 293, p. 230)—*i.e.*, from the Cushites, or Æthiopians of Africa. Osiris also is by Diodorus Siculus (*Bibliotheca*, lib. i. p. 16), called "an Indian by extraction." There can be no doubt, then, that "Ninus, king of India," is the Cushite or Æthiopian Ninus.

† See WILKINSON'S *Egyptians*, vol. v. p. 3. The statement of Plato amounts to this, that the famous Thoth was a counsellor of Thamus, king of Egypt. Now Thoth is universally known as the "counsellor" of Osiris. (WILKINSON, vol. v. c. xiii. p. 10.) Hence it may be concluded that Thamus and Osiris are the same.

‡ KITTO'S *Illustrated Commentary*, vol. iv. p. 141.

§ Photius, under the head "Nebridz ōn" quotes Demosthenes as saying that "spotted fawns (or nebroi) were torn in pieces for a certain mystic or mysterious reason;" and he himself tells us that "the tearing in pieces of the nebroi (or spotted fawns) was in imitation of the suffering in the case of Dionysus" or Bacchus.—PHOTIUS, *Lexicon*, Pars. i. p. 291.

been translated to heaven.* From Persian records we are expressly assured that it was Nimrod who was deified after his death by the name of Orion, and placed among the stars.† Here, then, we have large and consenting evidence, all leading to one conclusion, that the death of Nimrod, the child worshipped in the arms of the goddess-mother of Babylon, was a death of violence.

Now, when this mighty hero, in the midst of his career of glory, was suddenly cut off by a violent death, great seems to have been the shock that the catastrophe occasioned. When the news spread abroad, the devotees of pleasure felt as if the best benefactor of mankind were gone, and the gaiety of nations eclipsed. Loud was the wail that everywhere ascended to heaven among the apostates from the primeval faith for so dire a catastrophe. Then began those weepings for Tammuz, in the guilt of which the daughters of Israel allowed themselves to be implicated, and the existence of which can be traced not merely in the annals of classical antiquity, but in the literature of the world from Ultima Thule to Japan.

Of the prevalence of such weepings in China, thus speaks the Rev. W. Gillespie: "The dragon-boat festival happens in midsummer, and is a season of great excitement. About 2000 years ago there lived a young Chinese Mandarin, Wat-yune, highly respected and beloved by the people. To the grief of all, he was suddenly drowned in the river. Many boats immediately rushed out in search of him, but his body was never found. Ever since that time, on the same day of the month, the dragon-boats go out in search of him." "It is something," adds the author, "like the bewailing of Adonis, or the weeping for Tammuz mentioned in Scripture."‡ As the great god Buddh is generally represented in China as a *Negro,* that may serve to identify the beloved Mandarin whose loss is thus annually bewailed. The religious system of Japan largely coincides with that of China. In Iceland, and throughout Scandinavia, there were similar lamentations for the loss of the god Balder. Balder, through the treachery of the god Loki, the spirit of evil, according as had been written in the book of destiny, "was slain, although the empire of heaven depended on his life." His father Odin had "learned the terrible secret from the book of destiny, having conjured one of the

* See OVID'S *Fasti*, lib. v. lines 540-544. Ovid represents Orion as so puffed up with pride on account of his great strength, as vain-gloriously to boast that no creature on earth could cope with him, whereupon a scorpion appeared, "and," says the poet, "he was added to the stars." The name of a scorpion in Chaldee is Akrab; but Ak-rab, thus divided, signifies "THE GREAT OPPRESSOR," and this is the hidden meaning of the Scorpion as represented in the Zodiac. That sign typifies him who cut off the Babylonian god, and *suppressed* the system he set up. It was while the sun was in Scorpio that Osiris in Egypt "*disappeared*" (WILKINSON, vol. iv. p. 331), and great lamentations were made for his *disappearance.* Another subject was mixed up with the death of the Egyptian god; but it is specially to be noticed that, as it was in consequence of a conflict with a *scorpion* that Orion was "added to the stars," so it was when the *scorpion* was in the ascendant that Osiris "*disappeared.*"

† See *Paschal Chronicle*, tom. i. p. 64.

‡ GILLESPIE'S *Sinim*, p. 71.

Volar from her infernal abode. All the gods trembled at the knowledge of this event. Then Frigga [the wife of Odin] called on every object, animate and inanimate, to take an oath not to destroy or furnish arms against Balder. Fire, water, rocks, and vegetables were bound by this solemn obligation. One plant only, the misletoe, was overlooked. Loki discovered the omission, and made that contemptible shrub the fatal weapon. Among the warlike pastimes of Valhalla [the assembly of the gods] one was to throw darts at the invulnerable deity, who felt a pleasure in presenting his charmed breast to their weapons. At a tournament of this kind, the evil genius putting a sprig of the misletoe into the hands of the blind Hoder, and directing his aim, the dreaded prediction was accomplished by an unintentional fratricide.* The spectators were struck with speechless wonder; and their misfortune was the greater, that no one, out of respect to the sacredness of the place, dared to avenge it. With tears of lamentation they carried the lifeless body to the shore, and laid it upon a ship, as a funeral pile, with that of Nanna his lovely bride, who had died of a broken heart. His horse and arms were burnt at the same time, as was customary at the obsequies of the ancient heroes of the north." Then Frigga, his mother, was overwhelmed with distress. "Inconsolable for the loss of her beautiful son," says Dr. Crichton, "she despatched Hermod (the swift) to the abode of Hela [the goddess of Hell, or the infernal regions], to offer a ransom for his release. The gloomy goddess promised that he should be restored, provided everything on earth were found to weep for him. Then were messengers sent over the whole world, to see that the order was obeyed, and the effect of the general sorrow was 'as when there is a universal thaw.'"† There are considerable variations from the original story in these two legends; but at bottom the essence of the stories is the same, indicating that they must have flowed from one fountain.

SUB-SECTION V.—THE DEIFICATION OF THE CHILD.

If there was one who was more deeply concerned in the tragic death of Nimrod than another, it was his wife Semiramis, who, from an originally humble position, had been raised to share with him the throne of Babylon. What, in this emergency shall she do? Shall she quietly forego the pomp and pride to which she has been raised? No. Though the death of her husband has given a rude shock to her power, yet her resolution and unbounded ambition were in nowise checked. On the contrary, her ambition took a still higher flight. In life her husband had been honoured as a hero; in death she will have him worshipped as a god, yea, as the woman's promised

* In THEOCRITUS, also, the boar that killed Adonis is represented as having done so accidentally. See next section.

† *Scandinavia*, vol. i. pp. 93, 94.

seed, "Zero-ashta,"* who was destined to bruise the serpent's head, and who, in doing so, was to have his own heel bruised. The patriarchs, and the ancient world in general, were perfectly acquainted with the grand primeval promise of Eden, and they knew right well that the bruising of the heel of the promised seed implied his death, and that the curse could be removed from the world only by the death of the grand Deliverer. If the promise about the bruising of the serpent's

* Zero—in Chaldee, "the seed"—though we have seen reason to conclude that in Greek it sometimes appeared as Zeira, quite naturally passed also into Zoro, as may be seen from the change of Zerubbabel in the Greek Septuagint to Zoro-babel; and hence Zuro-ashta, "the seed of the woman" became Zoroaster, the well-known name of the head of the fire-worshippers. Zoroaster's name is also found as Zeroastes (JOHANNES CLERICUS, tom. ii., *De Chaldæis,* sect. i. cap. 2, p. 194). The reader who consults the able and very learned work of Dr. Wilson of Bombay, on the Parsi Religion, will find that there was a Zoroaster long before that Zoroaster who lived in the reign of Darius Hystaspes.—(See note to WILSON's *Parsi Religion*, p. 398.) In general history, the Zoroaster of Bactria is most frequently referred to; but the voice of antiquity is clear and distinct to the effect that the first and great Zoroaster was an Assyrian or Chaldean (SUIDAS, tom. i. p. 1138), and that he was the founder of the idolatrous system of Babylon, and therefore Nimrod. It is equally clear also in stating that he perished by a violent death, even as was the case with Nimrod, Tammuz, or Bacchus. The identity of Bacchus and Zoroaster is still further proved by the epithet Pyrisporus, bestowed on Bacchus in the *Orphic Hymns* (Hymn xliv. 1). When the primeval promise of Eden began to be forgotten, the meaning of the name Zero-ashta was lost to all who knew only the *exoteric* doctrine of Paganism; and as "ashta" signified "fire" in Chaldee, as well as "the woman," and the rites of Bacchus had much to do with fire-worship, "Zero-ashta" came to be rendered "the seed of fire;" and hence the epithet Pyrisporus, or Ignigena, "fire-born," as applied to Bacchus. From this misunderstanding of the meaning of the name Zero-ashta, or rather from its wilful perversion by the priests, who wished to establish one doctrine for the initiated, and another for the profane vulgar, came the whole story about the unborn infant Bacchus having been rescued from the flames that consumed his mother Semele, when Jupiter came in his glory to visit her.—(Note to OVID's *Metam.*, lib. iii. v. 254, tom. ii. p. 139.)

There was another name by which Zoroaster was known, and which is not a little instructive, and that is Zar-adas, "The only seed."—(JOHANNES CLERICUS, tom. ii. *De Chaldæis,* sect. i. cap. 2, p. 191.) In WILSON's *Parsi Religion* the name is given either Zoroadus, or Zarades (p. 400). The ancient Pagans, while they recognised supremely one only God, knew also that there was one only *seed*, on whom the hopes of the world were founded. In almost all nations, not only was a great god known under the name of Zero or Zer, "the seed," and a great goddess under the name of Ashta or Isha, "the woman;" but the great god Zero is frequently characterised by some epithet which implies that he is "The only One." Now what can account for such names or epithets? Genesis iii. 15 can account for them; nothing else can. The name Zar-ades, or Zoro-adus, also strikingly illustrates the saying of Paul: "He saith not, And to seeds, as of many; but as of one, and to thy seed, which is Christ."

It is worthy of notice, that the modern system of Parseeism, which dates from the reform of the old fire-worship in the time of Darius Hystaspes, having rejected the worship of the goddess-mother, cast out also from the name of their Zoroaster the name of the "woman"; and therefore in the Zend, the sacred language of the Parsees, the name of their great reformer is Zarathustra (see WILSON, p. 201, and *passim*)—*i.e.*, "The Delivering Seed," the last member of the name coming from Thusht (the root being—Chaldee—nthsh, which drops the initial *n*), "to loosen or set loose," and so to free. Thusht is the infinitive, and *ra* appended to it is, in Sanscrit, with which the Zend has much affinity, the well-known sign of the doer of an action, just as *er* is in English. The Zend Zarathushtra, then, seems just the equivalent of Phoroneus, "The Emancipator."

head, recorded in Genesis, as made to our first parents, was actually made, and if all mankind were descended from them, then it might be expected that some trace of this promise would be found in all nations. And such is the fact. There is hardly a people or kindred on earth in whose mythology it is not shadowed forth. The Greeks represented their great god Apollo as slaying the serpent Pytho, and Hercules as strangling serpents while yet in his cradle. In Egypt, in India, in Scandinavia, in Mexico, we find clear allusions to the same great truth. "The evil genius," says Wilkinson, "of the adversaries of the Egyptian god Horus is frequently figured under the form of a snake, whose head he is seen piercing with a spear. The same fable occurs in the religion of India, where the malignant serpent Calyia is slain by Vishnu, in his avatar of Crishna (Fig. 23); and the Scandinavian deity Thor was said to have bruised the head of the great serpent with his mace." "The origin of this," he adds, "may be readily traced to the Bible."* In reference to a similar

Fig. 23.

An Egyptian goddess piercing the serpent's head, and the Indian Crishna crushing the serpent's head.†

belief among the Mexicans, we find Humboldt saying, that "The serpent crushed by the great spirit Teotl, when he takes the form of one of the subaltern deities, is the genius of evil—a real Kakodæmon."‡ Now, in almost all cases, when the subject is examined to the bottom, it turns out that the serpent destroying god is represented as enduring hardships and sufferings that end in his death. Thus the god Thor, while succeeding at last in destroying the great serpent, is represented as, in the very moment of victory, perishing from the venomous effluvia of his breath.§ The same would seem to be the way in which the Babylonians represented their great serpent-destroyer among the figures of their ancient sphere. His mysterious suffering is thus described by the Greek poet Aratus, whose

* WILKINSON, vol. iv. p. 395.

† The Egyptian goddess is from WILKINSON, vol. vi. Plate 42; Crishna from COLEMAN'S *Indian Mythology*, p. 34.

‡ HUMBOLDT'S *Mexican Researches*, vol. i. p. 228.

§ MALLET'S *Northern Antiquities*, Fab. li. p. 453.

language shows that when he wrote, the meaning of the representation had been generally lost, although, when viewed in the light of Scripture, it is surely deeply significant :—

> "A human figure, 'whelmed with toil, appears ;
> Yet still with name uncertain he remains ;
> Nor known the labour that he thus sustains ;
> But since upon his knees he seems to fall,
> Him ignorant mortals Engonasis call ;
> And while sublime his awful hands are spread,
> Beneath him rolls the dragon's horrid head,
> And his right *foot* unmoved appears to rest,
> Fixed on the writhing monster's burnished crest."*

The constellation thus represented is commonly known by the name of "The Kneeler," from this very description of the Greek poet; but it is plain that, as "Engonăsis" came from the Babylonians, it must be interpreted, not in a Greek, but in a Chaldee sense, and so interpreted, as the action of the figure itself implies, the title of the mysterious sufferer is just "The Serpent-crusher."† Sometimes, however, the actual crushing of the serpent was represented as a much more easy process; yet, even then, death was the ultimate result; and that death of the serpent-destroyer is so described as to leave no doubt whence the fable was borrowed. This is particularly the case with the Indian God Crishna, to whom Wilkinson alludes in the extract already given. In the legend that concerns him, the whole of the primeval promise in Eden is very strikingly embodied. First, he is represented in pictures and images with his foot on the great serpent's head,‡ and then, after destroying it, he is fabled to have died in consequence of being shot by an arrow in *the foot;* and, as in the case of Tammuz, great lamentations are annually made for his death.§ Even in Greece, also, in the classic story of Paris and Achilles, we have a very plain allusion to that part of the primeval promise, which referred to the bruising of the conqueror's "heel." Achilles, the only son of a goddess, was invulnerable in all points *except the heel*, but there a wound was deadly. At that his adversary took aim, and death was the result.

Now, if there be such evidence still, that even Pagans knew that it was by dying that the promised Messiah was to destroy death and him that has the power of death, that is the Devil, how much more vivid must have been the impression of mankind in general in regard to this vital truth in the early days of Semiramis, when they were so much nearer the fountain-head of all Divine tradition. When, therefore, the name Zoroastes, "the seed of the woman," was given to him who had perished in the midst of a prosperous career of false

* LANDSEER'S *Sabean Researches*, pp. 132-134.

† From *E*, "the," *nko*, "to crush," and *nahash*, "a serpent,"—"E-nko-nahash." The Arabic name of the constellation, "the Kneeler," is "Al-Gethi," which, in like manner, signifies "The Crusher."

‡ COLEMAN'S *Indian Mythology*, Plate xii. p. 34. See *ante*, p. 60.

§ POCOCKE'S *India in Greece*, p. 300.

worship and apostacy, there can be no doubt of the meaning which that name was intended to convey. And the fact of the violent death of the hero, who, in the esteem of his partisans, had done so much to bless mankind, to make life happy, and to deliver them from the fear of the wrath to come, instead of being fatal to the bestowal of such a title upon him, favoured rather than otherwise the daring design. All that was needed to countenance the scheme on the part of those who wished an excuse for continued apostacy from the true God, was just to give out that, though the great patron of the apostacy had fallen a prey to the malice of men, he had freely offered himself for the good of mankind. Now, this was what was actually done. The Chaldean version of the story of the great Zoroaster is that he prayed to the supreme God of heaven to take away his life; that his prayer was heard, and that he expired, assuring his followers that, if they cherished due regard for his memory, the empire would never depart from the Babylonians.* What Berosus, the Babylonian historian, says of the cutting off of the head of the great god Belus, is plainly to the same effect. Belus, says Berosus, commanded one of the gods to cut off his head, that from the blood thus shed by his own command and with his own consent, when mingled with the earth, new creatures might be formed, the first creation being represented as a sort of a failure.† Thus the death of Belus, who was Nimrod, like that attributed to Zoroaster, was represented as entirely voluntary, and as submitted to for the *benefit of the world.*

It seems to have been now only when the dead hero was to be deified, that the secret Mysteries were set up. The previous form of apostacy during the life of Nimrod appears to have been open and public. Now, it was evidently felt that publicity was out of the question. The death of the great ringleader of the apostacy was not the death of a warrior slain in battle, but an act of judicial rigour, solemnly inflicted. This is well established by the accounts of the deaths of both Tammuz and Osiris. The following is the account of Tammuz, given by the celebrated Maimonides, deeply read in all the learning of the Chaldeans: "When the false prophet named Thammuz preached to a certain king that he should worship the seven stars and the twelve signs of the Zodiac, that king ordered him to be put to a terrible death. On the night of his death all the images assembled from the ends of the earth into the temple of Babylon, to the great golden image of the Sun, which was suspended between heaven and earth. That image prostrated itself in the midst of the temple, and so did all the images around it, while it related to them all that had happened to Thammuz. The images wept and lamented all the night long, and then in the morning they flew away, each to his own temple again, to the ends of the earth. And hence arose the custom every year, on the first day of the month Thammuz, to mourn and to weep for Thammuz."‡ There is here, of course, all

* SUIDAS, tom. i. pp. 1133, 1134. † BEROSUS, *apud* BUNSEN, vol. i. p. 709.
‡ MORE NEVOCHIM, p. 426.

the extravagance of idolatry, as found in the Chaldean sacred books that Maimonides had consulted; but there is no reason to doubt the fact stated either as to the manner or the cause of the death of Tammuz. In this Chaldean legend, it is stated that it was by the command of a "certain king" that this ringleader in apostacy was put to death. Who could this king be, who was so determinedly opposed to the worship of the host of heaven? From what is related of the Egyptian Hercules, we get very valuable light on this subject. It is admitted by Wilkinson that the most ancient Hercules, and truly primitive one, was he who was known in Egypt as having, "by the power of the gods"* (*i.e.*, by the SPIRIT) fought against and overcome the Giants. Now, no doubt, the title and character of Hercules were afterwards given by the Pagans to him whom they worshipped as the grand deliverer or Messiah, just as the adversaries of the Pagan divinities came to be stigmatised as the "Giants" who rebelled against Heaven. But let the reader only reflect who *were* the real Giants that rebelled against Heaven. They were Nimrod and his party; for the "Giants" were just the "Mighty ones," of whom Nimrod was the leader. Who, then, was most likely to head the opposition to the apostacy from the primitive worship? If Shem was at that time alive, as beyond question he was, who so likely as he? In exact accordance with this deduction, we find that one of the names of the primitive Hercules in Egypt was "Sem."†

If "Sem," then, was the primitive Hercules, who overcame the Giants, and that not by mere physical force, but by "the power of God," or the influence of the Holy Spirit, that entirely agrees with his character; and more than that, it remarkably agrees with the Egyptian account of the death of Osiris. The Egyptians say, that the grand enemy of their god overcame him, not by open violence, but that, having entered into a *conspiracy* with seventy-two of the leading men of Egypt, he got him into his power, put him to death, and then cut his dead body into pieces, and sent the different parts to so many different cities throughout the country.‡ The real meaning of this statement will appear, if we glance at the judicial institutions of Egypt. Seventy-two was just the number of the judges, both civil and sacred, who, according to Egyptian law, were required to determine what was to be the punishment of one guilty of so high an offence as that of Osiris, supposing this to have become a matter of judicial inquiry. In determining such a case, there were necessarily two tribunals concerned. First, there were the ordinary judges, who had power of life and death, and who amounted to thirty,§ then there was, over and above, a tribunal consisting of forty-two judges, who, if Osiris was condemned to die, had to determine whether his body should be buried or no, for, before burial,

* The name of the true God (Elohim) is plural. Therefore, "the power of the gods," and "of God," is expressed by the same term.

† WILKINSON, vol. v. p. 17.

‡ *Ibid.* vol. iv. pp. 330-332.

§ DIODORUS, lib. i. p. 48.

every one after death had to pass the ordeal of this tribunal.* As burial was refused him, both tribunals would necessarily be concerned; and thus there would be exactly seventy-two persons, under Typho the president, to condemn Osiris to die and to be cut in pieces. What, then, does the statement amount to, in regard to the conspiracy, but just to this, that the great opponent of the idolatrous system which Osiris introduced, had so convinced these judges of the enormity of the offence which he had committed, that they gave up the offender to an awful death, and to ignominy after it, as a terror to any who might afterwards tread in his steps. The cutting of the dead body in pieces, and sending the dismembered parts among the different cities, is paralleled, and its object explained, by what we read in the Bible of the cutting of the dead body of the Levite's concubine in pieces (Judges xix. 29), and sending one of the parts to each of the twelve tribes of Israel; and the similar step taken by Saul, when he hewed the two yoke of oxen asunder, and sent them throughout all the coasts of his kingdom (1 Sam. xi. 7). It is admitted by commentators that both the Levite and Saul acted on a patriarchal custom, according to which summary vengeance would be dealt to those who failed to come to the gathering that in this solemn way was summoned. This was declared in so many words by Saul, when the parts of the slaughtered oxen were sent among the tribes: "Whosoever cometh not forth after Saul and after Samuel, so shall it be done to his oxen." In like manner, when the dismembered parts of Osiris were sent among the cities by the seventy-two "conspirators"—in other words, by the supreme judges of Egypt, it was equivalent to a solemn declaration in their name, that "whosoever should do as Osiris had done, so should it be done to him; so should he also be cut in pieces."

When irreligion and apostacy again rose into the ascendant, this act, into which the constituted authorities who had to do with the

* Diodorus, lib. i. p. 58. The words of Diodorus, as printed in the ordinary editions, make the number of the judges simply "more than forty," without specifying how many more. In the *Codex Coislianus*, the number is stated to be "*two* more than forty." The earthly judges, who tried the question of burial, are admitted both by Wilkinson (vol. v. p. 75) and Bunsen (vol. i. p. 27), to have corresponded in number to the judges of the infernal regions. Now, these judges, over and above their president, are proved from the monuments to have been just forty-two. The earthly judges at funerals, therefore, must equally have been forty-two. In reference to this number as applying equally to the judges of this world and the world of spirits, Bunsen, speaking of the judgment on a deceased person in the world unseen, uses these words in the passage above referred to: "Forty-two gods (*the number composing the earthly tribunal of the dead*) occupy the judgment-seat." Diodorus himself, whether he actually wrote "two more than forty," or simply "more than forty," gives reason to believe that forty-two was the number he had present to his mind; for he says, that "the whole of the fable of the shades below," as brought by Orpheus from Egypt, was "copied from the ceremonies of the Egyptian funerals," which he had witnessed at the judgment before the burial of the dead.—(Diodorus, lib. i. p. 58.) If, therefore, there were just forty-two judges in "the shades below," that even, on the showing of Diodorus, whatever reading of his words be preferred, proves that the number of the judges in the *earthly* judgment must have been the same.

ringleader of the apostates were led, for the putting down of the combined system of irreligion and despotism set up by Osiris or Nimrod, was naturally the object of intense abhorrence to all his sympathisers; and for his share in it the chief actor was stigmatised as Typho, or "The Evil One."* The influence that this abhorred Typho wielded over the minds of the so-called "conspirators," considering the physical force with which Nimrod was upheld, must have been wonderful, and goes to show, that though his deed in regard to Osiris is veiled, and himself branded by a hateful name, he was indeed none other than that primitive Hercules who overcame the Giants by "the power of God," by the persuasive might of his Holy Spirit.

In connection with this character of Shem, the myth that makes Adonis, who is identified with Osiris, perish by the tusks of a wild boar, is easily unravelled.† The tusk of a wild boar was a symbol. In Scripture, a tusk is called "a horn;"‡ among many of the Classic Greeks it was regarded in the very same light.§ When once it is known that a tusk is regarded as a "horn" according to the symbolism of idolatry, the meaning of the boar's tusks, by which Adonis perished, is not far to seek. The bull's horns that Nimrod wore were the symbol of physical power. The boar's tusks were the symbol of *spiritual* power. As a "horn" means *power*, so a tusk, that is, a horn in the mouth, means "power in the mouth;" in other words, the power of persuasion; the very power with which "Sem," the primitive Hercules, was so signally endowed. Even from the ancient traditions of the Gael, we get an item of evidence that at once illustrates this idea of power in the mouth, and connects it with that great son of Noah, on whom the blessing of the Highest, as recorded in Scripture, did specially rest. The Celtic Hercules was called

* Wilkinson admits that different individuals at different times bore this hated name in Egypt. One of the most noted names by which Typho, or the Evil One, was called, was Seth (EPIPHANIUS, *Adv. Hæres.*, lib. iii.). Now Seth and Shem are synonymous, both alike signifying "The appointed one." As Shem was a younger son of Noah, being "the brother of Japhet the *elder*" (Gen. x. 21), and as the pre-eminence was divinely destined to him, the name Shem, "the appointed one," had doubtless been given him by Divine direction, either at his birth or afterwards, to mark him out as Seth had been previously marked out as the "child of promise." Shem, however, seems to have been known in Egypt as Typho, not only under the name of Seth, but under his own name; for Wilkinson tells us that Typho was characterised by a name that signified "to destroy and render desert."—(*Egyptians*, vol. iv. p. 434.) Now the name of Shem also in one of its meanings signifies "to desolate" or lay waste. So Shem, the appointed one, was by his enemies made Shem, the Desolator or Destroyer—*i.e.*, the Devil.

† In India, a demon with a "boar's face" is said to have gained such power through his *devotion*, that he oppressed the "*devotees*" or worshippers of the gods, who had to hide themselves.—(MOOR'S *Pantheon*, p. 19.) Even in Japan there seems to be a similar myth. For Japanese boar, see *Illustrated News*, 15th Dec., 1860.

‡ Ezek. xxvii. 15: "They brought thee for a present *horns* of ivory."

§ Pausanias admits that some in his day regarded tusks as teeth; but he argues strongly, and, I think, conclusively, for their being considered as "*horns*."—See PAUSANIAS, lib. v., *Eliaca*, cap. 12, p. 404; also, VARRO, *De Lingua Latina*, lib. vi. *apud* PARKHURST, *sub voce* "Krn."

Hercules Ogmius, which, in Chaldee, is "Hercules the Lamenter."* No name could be more appropriate, none more descriptive of the history of Shem, than this. Except our first parent, Adam, there was, perhaps, never a mere man that saw so much grief as he. Not only did he see a vast apostacy, which, with his righteous feelings, and witness as he had been of the awful catastrophe of the flood, must have deeply grieved him; but he lived to bury SEVEN GENERATIONS of his descendants. He lived 502 years after the flood, and as the lives of men were rapidly shortened after that event, no less than SEVEN generations of his lineal descendants died before him (Gen. xi. 10-32). How appropriate a name Ogmius, "The Lamenter or Mourner," for one who had such a history! Now, how is this "Mourning" Hercules represented as putting down enormities and redressing wrongs? Not by his club, like the Hercules of the Greeks, but by the force of persuasion. Multitudes were represented as following him, drawn by fine chains of gold and amber inserted into their ears, and which chains proceeded from his mouth.† There is a great difference between the two symbols—the tusks of a boar and the golden chains issuing from the mouth, that draw willing crowds by the ears; but both very beautifully illustrate the same idea—the might of that persuasive power that enabled Shem for a time to withstand the tide of evil that came rapidly rushing in upon the world.

Now when Shem had so powerfully wrought upon the minds of men as to induce them to make a terrible example of the great Apostate, and when that Apostate's dismembered limbs were sent to the chief cities, where no doubt his system had been established, it will be readily perceived that, in these circumstances, if idolatry was to continue—if, above all, it was to take a step in advance, it was indispensable that it should operate in secret. The terror of an execution, inflicted on one so mighty as Nimrod, made it needful that, for some time to come at least, the extreme of caution should be used. In these circumstances, then, began, there can hardly be a doubt, that system of "Mystery," which, having Babylon for its

* The Celtic scholars derive the name Ogmius from the Celtic word Ogum, which is said to denote "the secret of writing;" but Ogum is much more likely to be derived from the name of the god, than the name of the god to be derived from it.

† Sir W. BETHAM'S *Gael and Cymbri*, pp. 90-93. In connection with this Ogmius, one of the names of "Sem," the great Egyptian Hercules who overcame the Giants, is worthy of notice. That name is Chon. In the *Etymologicum Magnum, apud* BRYANT, vol. ii. p. 33, we thus read: "They say that in the Egyptian dialect Hercules is called Chon." Compare this with WILKINSON, vol. v. p. 17, where Chon is called "Sem." Now Khon signifies "to lament" in Chaldee, and as Shem was Khon—*i.e.*, "Priest" of the Most High God, his character and peculiar circumstances as Khon "the lamenter" would form an additional reason why he should be distinguished by that name by which the Egyptian Hercules was known. And it is not to be overlooked, that on the part of those who seek to turn sinners from the error of their ways, there is an eloquence in tears that is very impressive. The tears of Whitefield formed one great part of his power; and, in like manner, the tears of Khon, "the lamenting" Hercules, would aid him mightily in overcoming the Giants.

centre, has spread over the world. In these Mysteries, under the seal of secrecy and the sanction of an oath, and by means of all the fertile resources of magic, men were gradually led back to all the idolatry that had been publicly suppressed, while new features were added to that idolatry that made it still more blasphemous than before. That magic and idolatry were twin sisters, and came into the world together, we have abundant evidence. "He" (Zoroaster), says Justin the historian, "was said to be the first that invented magic arts, and that most diligently studied the motions of the heavenly bodies."* The Zoroaster spoken of by Justin is the Bactrian Zoroaster; but this is generally admitted to be a mistake. Stanley, in his *History of Oriental Philosophy*, concludes that this mistake had arisen from similarity of name, and that from this cause *that* had been attributed to the Bactrian Zoroaster which properly belonged to the Chaldean, "since it cannot be imagined that the Bactrian was the inventor of those arts in which the Chaldean, who lived contemporary with him, was so much skilled."† Epiphanius had evidently come to the same substantial conclusion before him. He maintains, from the evidence open to him in his day, that it was "*Nimrod*, that established the sciences of magic and astronomy, the invention of which was subsequently attributed to (the Bactrian) Zoroaster."‡ As we have seen that Nimrod and the Chaldean Zoroaster are the same, the conclusions of the ancient and the modern inquirers into Chaldean antiquity entirely harmonise. Now the secret system of the Mysteries gave vast facilities for imposing on the senses of the initiated by means of the various tricks and artifices of magic. Notwithstanding all the care and precautions of those who conducted these initiations, enough has transpired to give us a very clear insight into their real character. Everything was so contrived as to wind up the minds of the novices to the highest pitch of excitement, that, after having surrendered themselves implicitly to the priests, they might be prepared to receive anything. After the candidates for initiation had passed through the confessional, and sworn the required oaths, "strange and amazing objects," says Wilkinson, "presented themselves. Sometimes the place they were in seemed to shake around them; sometimes it appeared bright and resplendent with light and radiant fire, and then again covered with black darkness, sometimes thunder and lightning, sometimes frightful noises and bellowings, sometimes terrible apparitions astonished the trembling spectators."§ Then, at last, the great god, the central object of their worship, Osiris, Tammuz, Nimrod or Adonis, was revealed to them in the way most fitted to soothe their feelings and engage their blind affections. An account of such a manifestation is thus given by an ancient Pagan, cautiously indeed, but yet in such a way as shows the nature of the magic secret by which such an

* JUSTINUS, *Historia*, lib. i. cap. 1, vol. ii. p. 615.

† STANLEY, p. 1031, col. 1.

‡ EPIPHANIUS, *Adv. Hæres.*, lib. i. tom. i., vol. i. p. 7 c.

§ WILKINSON'S *Manners and Customs of Egyptians*, vol. v. p. 326.

apparent miracle was accomplished: "In a manifestation which one must not reveal . . . . there is seen on a wall of the temple a mass of light, which appears at first at a very great distance. It is transformed, while unfolding itself, into a visage evidently divine and supernatural, of an aspect severe, but with a touch of sweetness. Following the teachings of a mysterious religion, the Alexandrians honour it as Osiris or Adonis."* From this statement, there can hardly be a doubt that the magical art here employed was none other than that now made use of in the modern phantasmagoria. Such or similar means were used in the very earliest periods for presenting to the view of the living, in the secret Mysteries, those who were dead. We have statements in ancient history referring to the very time of Semiramis, which imply that magic rites were practised for this very purpose;† and as the magic lantern, or something akin to it, was manifestly used in later times for such an end, it is reasonable to conclude that the same means, or similar, were employed in the most ancient times, when the same *effects* were produced. Now, in the hands of crafty, designing men, this was a powerful means of imposing upon those who were willing to be imposed upon, who were averse to the holy spiritual religion of the living God, and who still hankered after the system that was put down. It was easy for those who controlled the Mysteries, having discovered secrets that were then unknown to the mass of mankind, and which they carefully preserved in their own exclusive keeping, to give them what might seem ocular demonstration, that Tammuz, who had been slain, and for whom such lamentations had been made, was still alive, and encompassed with divine and heavenly glory. From the lips of one so gloriously revealed, or what was practically

* DAMASCIUS, *apud* PHOTIUM, *Bibliotheca*, cod. 242, p. 343.

† One of the statements to which I refer is contained in the following words of Moses of Chorene in his *Armenian History*, referring to the answer made by Semiramis to the friends of Aræus, who had been slain in battle by her: "Diis inquit [Semiramis] meis mendata dedi, ut Aræi vulnera lamberent, et ab inferis excitarent. . . . . Dii, inquit, Aræum lamberunt, et ad vitam revocarunt;" "I have given commands, says Semiramis, to my gods to lick the wounds of Aræus, and to raise him from the dead. The gods, says she, *have* licked Aræus, and recalled him to life."—(MOSES CHORONEN, lib. i. cap. 14, p. 42.) If Semiramis had really done what she said she had done, it would have been a miracle. The effects of magic were *sham* miracles; and Justin and Epiphanius show that sham miracles came in at the very birth of idolatry. Now, unless the sham miracle of raising the dead by magical arts had already been known to be practised in the days of Semiramis, it is not likely that she would have given such an answer to those whom she wished to propitiate; for, on the one hand, how could she ever have thought of such an answer, and on the other, how could she expect that it would have the intended effect, if there was no current belief in the practices of necromancy! We find that in Egypt, about the same age, such magic arts must have been practised, if Manetho is to be believed. "Manetho says," according to Josephus, "that he [the elder Horus, evidently spoken of as a human and mortal king] was admitted to *the sight of the gods*, and that Amenophis desired the same privilege." *Θεων γενεσθαι θεατην ʼωσπερ Ωρ*; so it stood in the old copies.—(JOSEPHUS, *contra* APION, lib. i. p. 932.) This pretended admission to *the sight of the gods* evidently implies the use of the magic art referred to in the text.

the same, from the lips of some unseen priest, speaking in his name from behind the scenes, what could be too wonderful or incredible to be believed? Thus the whole system of the secret Mysteries of Babylon was intended to glorify a dead man; and when once the worship of one dead man was established, the worship of many more was sure to follow. This casts light upon the language of the 106th Psalm, where the Lord, upbraiding Israel for their apostacy, says: "They joined themselves to Baalpeor, and ate the sacrifices of the *dead*." Thus, too, the way was paved for bringing in all the abominations and crimes of which the Mysteries became the scenes; for, to those who liked not to retain God in their knowledge, who preferred some visible object of worship, suited to the sensuous feelings of their carnal minds, nothing could seem a more cogent reason for faith or practice than to hear with their own ears a command given forth amid so glorious a manifestation apparently by the very divinity they adored.

The scheme, thus skilfully formed, took effect. Semiramis gained glory from her dead and deified husband; and in course of time both of them, under the names of Rhea and Nin, or "Goddess-Mother and Son," were worshipped with an enthusiasm that was incredible, and their images were everywhere set up and adored.* Wherever the negro aspect of Nimrod was found an obstacle to his worship, this was very easily obviated. According to the Chaldean doctrine of the transmigration of souls, all that was needful was just to teach that Ninus had reappeared in the person of a posthumous son, of a fair complexion, supernaturally borne by his widowed wife after the father had gone to glory. As the licentious and dissolute life of Semiramis gave her many children, for whom no ostensible father on earth would be alleged, a plea like this would at once sanctify sin, and enable her to meet the feelings of those who were disaffected to the true worship of Jehovah, and yet might have no fancy to bow down before a negro divinity. From the light reflected on Babylon by Egypt, as well as from the form of the extant images of the Babylonian child in the arms of the goddess-mother, we have every reason to believe that this was actually done. In Egypt the *fair* Horus, the son of the *black* Osiris, who was the favourite object of worship, in the arms of the goddess Isis, was said to have been miraculously born in consequence of a connection, on the part of that goddess, with Osiris after his death,† and, in point of fact, to have been a new incarnation of that god, to avenge his death on his murderers. It is wonderful to find in what widely-severed countries, and amongst what millions of the human race at this day, who never saw a negro, a negro god is worshipped. But yet, as we shall afterwards see, among the civilised nations of antiquity, Nimrod almost everywhere fell into disrepute, and was deposed from his original

* It would seem that no *public* idolatry was ventured upon till the reign of the grandson of Semiramis, Arioch or Arius.—*Cedreni Compendium*, vol. i. pp. 29, 30.

† *Plutarchi Opera*, vol. ii. p. 366.

pre-eminence, expressly *ob deformitatem,** "on account of his ugliness." Even in Babylon itself, the posthumous child, as identified with his father, and inheriting all his father's glory, yet possessing more of his mother's complexion, came to be the favourite type of the Madonna's divine son.

This son, thus worshipped in his mother's arms, was looked upon as invested with all the attributes, and called by almost all the names of the promised Messiah. As Christ, in the Hebrew of the Old Testament, was called Adonai, The Lord, so Tammuz was called Adon or Adonis. Under the name of Mithras, he was worshipped as the "Mediator."† As Mediator and head of the covenant of grace, he was styled Baal-berith, Lord of the Covenant (Fig. 24)—(Judges viii. 33). In this character he is represented in Persian monuments as seated on the rainbow, the well-known symbol of the covenant.‡ In India, under the name of Vishnu, the Preserver or Saviour of men, though a god, he was worshipped as the great "Victim-Man," who before the worlds were, because there was nothing else to offer, offered *himself* as a sacrifice.§ The Hindu

Fig. 24.

sacred writings teach that this mysterious offering before all creation is the foundation of all the sacrifices that have ever been offered since.‖ Do any marvel at such a statement being found in the sacred books of a Pagan mythology? Why should they? Since sin entered the world there has been only one way of salvation, and that through the blood of the everlasting covenant—a way that all mankind once knew, from the days of righteous Abel downwards. When Abel, "by faith," offered unto God his more excellent sacrifice than that of Cain, it was his faith "in the blood of the Lamb slain," in the purpose of God "from the foundation of the world," and in

* These are the words of the *Gradus ad Parnassum*, referring to the cause of the downfall of Vulcan, whose identity with Nimrod is shown in Chapter VII. Section I.

† PLUTARCH, *De Iside*, vol. ii. p. 369.

‡ THEVENOT, *Voyages*, Partie ii., chap. vii. p. 514.

§ Col. KENNEDY'S *Hindoo Mythology*, pp. 221 and 247, with Note.

‖ *Ibid.* pp. 200, 204, 205. In the exercise of his office as the *Remedial* god, Vishnu is said to "extract the thorns of the three worlds."—MOOR'S *Pantheon*, p. 12. "Thorns" were a symbol of the curse—(Gen. iii. 18).

due time to be actually offered up on Calvary, that gave all the "excellence" to his offering. If Abel knew of "the blood of the Lamb," why should Hindoos not have known of it? One little word shows that even in Greece the virtue of "the blood of God" had once been known, though that virtue, as exhibited in its poets, was utterly obscured and degraded. That word is Ichor. Every reader of the bards of classic Greece knows that Ichor is the term peculiarly appropriated to the blood of a divinity. Thus Homer refers to it:—

> "From the clear vein the immortal Ichor flowed,
> Such stream as issues from a wounded god,
> Pure emanation, uncorrupted flood,
> Unlike our gross, diseased terrestrial blood."*

Now, what is the proper meaning of the term Ichor? In Greek it has no etymological meaning whatever; but, in Chaldee, Ichor signifies "The precious thing." Such a name, applied to the blood of a divinity, could have only one origin. It bears its evidence on the very face of it, as coming from that grand patriarchal tradition, that led Abel to look forward to the "precious blood" of Christ, the most "precious" gift that love Divine could give to a guilty world, and which, while the blood of the only genuine "Victim-Man," is at the same time, in deed and in truth, "The blood of God" (Acts xx. 28). Even in Greece itself, though the doctrine was utterly perverted, it was not entirely lost. It was mingled with falsehood and fable, it was hid from the multitude; but yet, in the secret mystic system it necessarily occupied an important place. As Servius tells us that the grand purpose of the Bacchic orgies "was the purification of souls,"† and as in these orgies there was regularly the tearing asunder and the shedding of the blood of an animal, in memory of the shedding of the life's blood of the great divinity commemorated in them, could this symbolical shedding of the blood of that divinity have no bearing on the "purification" from sin, these mystic rites were intended to effect? We have seen that the sufferings of the Babylonian Zoroaster and Belus were expressly represented as voluntary, and as submitted to for the benefit of the world, and that in connection with crushing the great serpent's head, which implied the removal of sin and the curse. If the Grecian Bacchus was just another form of the Babylonian divinity, then his sufferings and blood-shedding must have been represented as having been undergone for the same purpose—viz., for the "purification of souls." From this point of view, let the well-known name of Bacchus in Greece be looked at. The name was Dionysus or Dionusos. What is the meaning of that name? Hitherto it has defied all interpretation. But deal with it as belonging to the language of that land from which the god himself originally came,

* POPE'S *Homer*, corrected by PARKHURST. See the original in *Iliad*, lib. v. ll. 339, 340, pp. 198, 199.

† See *ante*, p. 22.

and the meaning is very plain. *D'ion-nuso-s* signifies "THE SIN-BEARER,"* a name entirely appropriate to the character of him whose sufferings were represented as so mysterious, and who was looked up to as the great "purifier of souls."

Now, this Babylonian God, known in Greece as "The sin-bearer," and in India as the "Victim-Man," among the Buddhists of the East, the original elements of whose system are clearly Babylonian, was commonly addressed as the "Saviour of the world."† It has been all along well enough known that the Greeks occasionally worshipped the supreme god under the title of "Zeus the Saviour;" but this title was thought to have reference only to deliverance in battle, or some such-like temporal deliverance. But when it is known that "Zeus the Saviour" was only a title of Dionysus,‡ the "sin-bearing Bacchus," his character, as "The Saviour," appears in quite a different light. In Egypt, the Chaldean god was held up as the great object of love and adoration, as the god through whom "goodness and truth were revealed to mankind."§ He was regarded as the predestined heir of all things; and, on the day of his birth, it was believed that a voice was heard to proclaim, "The Lord of all the earth is born."‖ In this character he was styled "King of kings, and Lord of lords," it being as a professed representative of this hero-god that the celebrated Sesostris caused this very title to be added to his name on the monuments which he erected to perpetuate the fame of his victories.¶ Not only was he honoured as the great "World King," he was regarded as Lord of the invisible world, and "Judge of the dead;" and it was taught that, in the world of spirits, all must appear before his dread tribunal, to have their destiny assigned them.** As the

* The expression used in Exodus xxviii. 38, for "bearing iniquity" or sin in a vicarious manner is "*nsha eon*" (the first letter *eon* being *ayn*). A synonym for *eon*, "iniquity," is *aon* (the first letter being aleph).—(See PARKHURST *sub voce* '*An*,' No. IV.) In Chaldee the first letter *a* becomes *i*, and therefore *aon*, "iniquity," is *ion*. Then nsha "to bear," in the participle active is "nūsha." As the Greeks had no *sh*, that became *nūsa*. *De*, or *Da*, is the demonstrative pronoun signifying "That" or "The great." And thus "*D'ion-nusa*" is exactly "The great sin-bearer." That the classic Pagans had the very idea of the imputation of sin, and of vicarious suffering, is proved by what Ovid says in regard to Olenos. Olenos is said to have taken upon him and willingly to have borne the blame of guilt of which he was innocent:—

> "Quique in se crimen traxit, voluitque videri,
> Olenos esse nocens."

(OVID, *Metam.*, vol. ii. p. 486.) Under the load of this imputed guilt, voluntarily taken upon himself, Olenos is represented as having suffered such horror as to have perished, being petrified or turned into stone. As the stone into which Olenos was changed was erected on the *holy* mountain of Ida, that shows that Olenos must have been regarded as a *sacred* person. The real character of Olenos, as the "sin-bearer," can be very fully established. See Appendix, Note F.

† MAHAWANSO, xxxi. *apud* POCOCKE's *India in Greece*, p. 185.

‡ ATHENÆUS, lib. xv. p. 675.

§ WILKINSON's *Egyptians*, vol. iv. p. 189.

‖ *Ibid.* p. 310.

¶ RUSSELL's *Egypt*, p. 79.

** WILKINSON, vol. iv. pp. 310, 314.

true Messiah was prophesied of under the title of the "Man whose name was the branch," he was celebrated not only as the "Branch of Cush," but as the "Branch of God," graciously given to the earth for healing all the ills that flesh is heir to.* He was worshipped in Babylon under the name of El-Bar, or "God the Son." Under this very name he is introduced by Berosus, the Chaldean historian, as the second in the list of Babylonian sovereigns.† Under this name he has been found in the sculptures of Nineveh by Layard, the name Bar "the Son," having the sign denoting El or "God" prefixed to it.‡ Under the same name he has been found by Sir H. Rawlinson, the names "Beltis" and the "Shining Bar" being in immediate juxtaposition.§ Under the name of Bar he was worshipped in Egypt in the earliest times, though in later times the god Bar was degraded in the popular Pantheon, to make way for another more popular divinity.|| In Pagan Rome itself, as Ovid testifies, he was worshipped under the name of the "Eternal Boy."¶ Thus daringly

* This is the esoteric meaning of Virgil's "Golden Branch," and of the Misletoe Branch of the Druids. The proof of this must be reserved to the *Apocalypse of the Past.* I may remark, however, in passing, on the wide extent of the worship of a sacred branch. Not only do the Negroes in Africa in the worship of the Fetiche, on certain occasions, make use of a sacred branch (HURD's *Rites and Ceremonies*, p. 375), but even in India there are traces of the same practice. My brother, S. Hislop, Free Church Missionary at Nagpore, informs me that the late Rajah of Nagpore used every year, on a certain day, to go in state to worship the branch of a particular species of tree, called Apta, which had been planted for the occasion, and which, after receiving divine honours, was plucked up, and its leaves distributed by the native Prince among his nobles. In the streets of the city numerous boughs of the same kind of tree were sold, and the leaves presented to friends under the name of *sona*, or "gold."

† BEROSUS, in BUNSEN's *Egypt*, vol. i. p. 710, Note 5. The name "El-Bar" is given above in the Hebrew form, as being more familiar to the common reader of the English Bible. The Chaldee form of the name is Ala-Bar, which in the Greek of Berosus, is Ala-Par, with the ordinary Greek termination *os* affixed to it. The change of Bar into Par in Greek is just on the same principle as *Ab*, "father," in Greek becomes *Appa*, and *Bard*, the "spotted one," becomes Pardos, &c. This name, Ala-Bar, was probably given by Berosus to Ninyas as the legitimate son and successor of Nimrod. That Ala-Par-os was really intended to designate the sovereign referred to, as "God the Son," or "the Son of God," is confirmed by another reading of the same name as given in Greek (in p. 712 of BUNSEN, Note). There the name is Alasparos. Now Pyrisporus, as applied to Bacchus, means Ignigena, or the "Seed of Fire;" and Ala-sporos, the "Seed of God," is just a similar expression formed in the same way, the name being Grecised. It is well known that the Greek σπειρω comes from the Hebrew Zero, both signifying as verbs *to sow.* The formation of σπειρω comes thus: The active participle of Zero is Zūro, which, used as a verb, becomes Zwero, Zvero, and Zpero. "Alasparos," then, naturally signifies, "The Seed of God"—a mere variation of Ala-Par-os, "God the Son," or "the Son of God."

‡ *Nineveh and Babylon*, p. 629.

§ VAUX's *Nineveh*, p. 457.

|| BUNSEN, vol. i. p. 426. Though Bunsen does not *mention* the degradation of the god Bar, yet by making him Typhon he *implies* his degradation. See EPIPHANIUS, *Adv. Hæreses*, lib. iii. tom. ii., vol. i. p. 1093.

¶ To understand the true meaning of the above expression, reference must be had to a remarkable form of oath among the Romans. In Rome the most sacred form of an oath was (as we learn from AULUS GELLIUS, i. 21, p. 192), "Per Jovem LAPIDEM," "By Jupiter the STONE." This, as it stands, is nonsense. But trans-

and directly was a mere mortal set up in Babylon in opposition to the "Son of the Blessed."

SECTION III.—THE MOTHER OF THE CHILD.

Now while the mother derived her glory in the first instance from the divine character attributed to the child in her arms, the mother in the long-run practically *eclipsed* the son. At first, in all likelihood, there would be no thought whatever of ascribing divinity to the mother. There was an express promise that necessarily led mankind to expect that, at some time or other, the Son of God, in amazing condescension, should appear in this world as the Son of man. But there was no promise whatever, or the least shadow of a promise, to lead any one to anticipate that a *woman* should ever be invested with attributes that should *raise* her to a level with Divinity. It is in the last degree improbable, therefore, that when the mother was first exhibited with the child in her arms, it should be intended to give divine honours to her. She was doubtless used chiefly as a pedestal for the upholding of the divine Son, and holding him forth to the adoration of mankind; and glory enough it would be counted for her, alone of all the daughters of Eve, to have given birth to the promised seed, the world's only hope. But while this, no doubt, was the design, it is a plain principle in all idolatries that that which most appeals to the senses must make the most powerful impression. Now the Son, even in his new incarnation, when Nimrod was believed to have reappeared in a fairer form, was exhibited merely as a child, without any very particular attraction; while the mother in whose arms he was, was set off with all the art of painting and sculpture, as invested with much of that extraordinary beauty which in reality belonged to her. The beauty of Semiramis is said on one occasion to have quelled a rising rebellion among her subjects on her sudden appearance among them; and it is recorded that the memory of the admiration excited in their minds by her appearance on that occasion was perpetuated by a statue erected in Babylon, representing her in the guise in which she had fascinated them so much.* This Babylonian queen was not merely in character

late *lapidem* back into the sacred tongue, or Chaldee, and the oath stands, "By Jove, the Son," or "By the son of Jove." *Ben*, which in Hebrew is Son, in Chaldee becomes *Eben*, which also signifies a *stone*, as may be seen in "Ebenezer," "The *stone* of help." Now as the most learned inquirers into antiquity (Sir G. Wilkinson evidently being included among them, see *Egyptians*, vol. iv. p. 186), have admitted that the Roman Jovis, which was anciently the nominative, is just a form of the Hebrew Jehovah, it is evident that the oath had originally been, "by the son of Jehovah." This explains how the most solemn and binding oath had been taken in the form above referred to; and, it shows, also, what was really meant when Bacchus, "the son of Jovis," was called "The Eternal Boy." —OVID, *Metam.*, iv. 17, 18.

* VALERIUS MAXIMUS, lib. ix., cap. 3, leaf 193, p. 2. Valerius Maximus does not mention anything about the representation of Semiramis with the child in her arms; but as Semiramis was deified as Rhea, whose distinguishing character was

coincident with the Aphroditè of Greece and the Venus of Rome, but was, in point of fact, the historical original of that goddess that by the ancient world was regarded as the very embodiment of everything attractive in female form, and the perfection of female beauty; for Sanchuniathon assures us that Aphrodite or Venus was identical with Astartè,* and Astarte being interpreted, is none other than "The woman that made towers or encompassing walls"—*i.e.*, Semiramis. The Roman Venus, as is well known, was the Cyprian Venus, and the Venus of Cyprus is historically proved to have been derived from Babylon. (See Chap. IV. Sect. III.) Now, what in these circumstances might have been expected actually took place. If the child was to be adored, much more the mother. The mother, in point of fact, became the favourite object of worship.‡ To justify this worship, the mother was raised to divinity as well as her son, and she was looked upon as destined to complete that bruising of the serpent's head, which it was easy, if such a thing was needed, to find abundant and plausible reasons for alleging that Ninus or Nimrod, the great Son, in his mortal life had only begun.

The Roman Church maintains that it was not so much the *seed* of the woman, as the woman *herself*, that was to bruise the head of the serpent. In defiance of all grammar, she renders the Divine denunciation against the serpent thus: "*She* shall bruise thy head, and thou shalt bruise *her* heel." The same was held by the ancient Babylonians, and symbolically represented in their temples. In the uppermost storey of the tower of Babel, or temple of Belus, Diodorus Siculus tells us there stood three images of the great divinities of

that of goddess *Mother*, and as we have evidence that the name, "Seed of the *Woman*," or Zoroastes, goes back to the earliest times—viz., her own day (CLERICUS, *De Chaldæis*, lib. i. sect. i., cap. 3, tom. ii. p. 199), this implies that if there was any image-worship in these times, that "Seed of the *Woman*" must have occupied a prominent place in it. As over all the world the Mother and the child appear in some shape or other, and are found on the early Egyptian monuments, that shows that this worship must have had its roots in the primeval ages of the world. If, therefore, the mother was represented in so fascinating a form when singly represented, we may be sure that the same beauty for which she was celebrated would be given to her when exhibited with the child in her arms.

* SANCHUNIATHON, p. 25.

† From Asht-trt. See Appendix, "On the meaning of the name Astarte."

‡ How extraordinary, yea, frantic, was the devotion in the minds of the Babylonians to this goddess queen, is sufficiently proved by the statement of Herodotus, lib. i. cap. 199, as to the way in which she required to be propitiated. That a whole people should ever have consented to such a custom as is there described, shows the amazing hold her worship must have gained over them. Nonnus, speaking of the same goddess, calls her "The hope of the whole world,"—'Ελπις 'ολου κοσμοιο.—(DIONUSIACA, lib. xli., in BRYANT, vol. iii. p. 226.) It was the same goddess, as we have seen (pp. 29, 30), who was worshipped at Ephesus, whom Demetrius the silversmith characterised as the goddess "whom all Asia and the world worshipped" (Acts xix. 27). So great was the devotion to this goddess queen, not of the Babylonians only, but of the ancient world in general, that the fame of the exploits of Semiramis has, in history, cast the exploits of her husband Ninus or Nimrod, entirely into the shade.

In regard to the identification of Rhea or Cybele and Venus, see Appendix, Note G.

Babylon; and one of these was of *a woman grasping a serpent's head.** Among the Greeks the same thing was symbolised; for Diana, whose real character was originally the same as that of the great Babylonian goddess,† was represented as bearing in one of her hands a serpent *deprived of its head.*‡ As time wore away, and the facts of Semiramis's history became obscured, her son's birth was boldly declared to be miraculous: and therefore she was called "*Alma* Mater,"§ "the *Virgin* Mother." That the birth of the Great Deliverer was to be miraculous, was widely known long before the Christian era. For

* DIODORUS, *Bibliotheca*, lib. ii. p. 70. See Fig. 23, p. 60, *ante*, where an Egyptian goddess, in imitation of Horus, pierces a serpent's head.

† See *ante*, pp. 29, 30.

‡ See SMITH's *Classical Dictionary*, p. 320.

§ The term *Alma* is the precise term used by Isaiah in the Hebrew of the Old Testament, when announcing, 700 years before the event, that Christ should be born of a Virgin. If the question should be asked, how this Hebrew term *Alma* (not in a Roman, but a Hebrew sense) could find its way to Rome, the answer is, Through Etruria, which had an intimate connection with Assyria (see LAYARD, *Nineveh and Babylon*, p. 190). The word "mater" itself, from which comes our own "mother," is originally Hebrew. It comes from Heb. *Msh*, "to draw forth," in Egyptian *Ms*, "to bring forth" (BUNSEN, vol. i. p. 540), which in the Chaldee form becomes *Mt*, whence the Egyptian *Maut*, "mother." *Erh* or *Er*, as in English (and a similar form is found in Sanscrit), is, "The doer." So that Mater or Mother signifies "The bringer forth."

It may be thought an objection to the above account of the epithet Alma, that this term is often applied to Venus, who certainly was no virgin. But this objection is more apparent than real. On the testimony of Augustine, himself an eye-witness, we know that the rites of Vesta, emphatically "the *virgin* goddess of Rome," under the name of Terra, were exactly the same as those of Venus, the goddess of impurity and licentiousness (Aug., *De Civitate Dei*, lib. ii. cap. 26). Augustine elsewhere says that Vesta, the virgin goddess, "was by some called Venus" (*Ibid.* lib. iv. cap. 10).

Even in the mythology of our own Scandinavian ancestors, we have a remarkable evidence that *Alma* Mater, or the Virgin Mother, had been originally known to them. One of their gods called Heimdal, who is described in the most exalted terms, as having such quick perceptions as that he could hear the grass growing on the ground, or the wool on the sheep's back, and whose trumpet, when it blew, could be heard through all the worlds, is called by the paradoxical name, "the son of nine virgins."—(MALLET, p. 95.) Now this obviously contains an enigma. Let the language in which the religion of Odin was originally delivered—viz., the Chaldee, be brought to bear upon it, and the enigma is solved at once. In Chaldee "the son of nine virgins" is Ben-Almut-Teshaah. But in pronunciation this is identical with "Ben-Almet-Ishaa," "the son of the virgin of salvation." That son was everywhere known as the "saviour seed." "Zera-hosha" (in Zend, "cra-osha"), and his virgin mother consequently claimed to be "the virgin of salvation." Even in the very heavens the God of Providence has constrained His enemies to inscribe a testimony to the great Scriptural truth proclaimed by the Hebrew prophet, that a "virgin should bring forth a son, whose name should be called Immanuel." The constellation Virgo, as admitted by the most learned astronomers, was dedicated to Ceres (Dr. JOHN HILL, in his *Urania*, and Mr. A. JAMIESON, in his *Celestial Atlas*, see LANDSEER's *Sabean Researches*, p. 201), who is the same as the great goddess of Babylon, for Ceres was worshipped with the babe at her breast (SOPHOCLES, *Antigone*, v. 1133), even as the Babylonian goddess was. Virgo was originally the Assyrian Venus, the *mother* of Bacchus or Tammuz. Virgo then, was the Virgin *Mother*. Isaiah's prophecy was carried by the Jewish captives to Babylon, and hence the *new* title bestowed upon the Babylonian goddess.

centuries, some say for thousands of years before that event, the Buddhist priests had a tradition that a *Virgin* was to bring forth a child to bless the world.* That this tradition came from no Popish or Christian source, is evident from the surprise felt and expressed by the Jesuit missionaries, when they first entered Thibet and China, and not only found a mother and a child worshipped as at home, but that mother worshipped under a character exactly corresponding with that of their own Madonna, "Virgo Deipara," "the *Virgin* mother of God,"† and that, too, in regions where they could not find the least trace of either the name or history of our Lord Jesus Christ having ever been known.‡ The primeval promise that the "seed of the *woman* should bruise the serpent's head," naturally suggested the idea of a miraculous birth. Priestcraft and human presumption set themselves wickedly to anticipate the fulfilment of that promise; and the Babylonian queen seems to have been the first to whom that honour was given. The highest titles were accordingly bestowed upon her. She was called the "queen of heaven." (Jeremiah xliv. 17, 18, 19, 25.)§ In Egypt she was styled Athor—*i.e.*, "the Habitation of God,"‖ to signify that in her dwelt all the "fulness of the Godhead." To point out the great goddess-mother, in a Pantheistic sense, as at once the Infinite and Almighty one, and the *Virgin* mother, this inscription was engraven upon one of her temples in Egypt: "I am all that has been, or that is, or that shall be. No mortal has removed my veil. The fruit which I have brought forth is the Sun."¶ In Greece she had the name of Hestia, and amongst the Romans, Vesta, which is just a modification of the same name—a name which, though it has been commonly understood in a different sense, really meant "*The Dwelling-place.*"** As the Dwelling-place of Deity, thus is Hestia or Vesta addressed in the *Orphic Hymns* :—

* *Asiatic Researches*, vol. x. p. 27.

† See Sir J. F. Davis's *China*, vol. ii. p. 56, and Lafitan, who says that the accounts sent home by the Popish missionaries bore that the sacred books of the Chinese spoke not merely of a Holy Mother, but of a *Virgin* Mother (vol. i. p. 235, Note). See also Salverté, *De Sciences Occultes*, Appendix, Note A, Sect. 12, p. 490. The reader may find additional testimonies to the very same effect in Prescott's *Conquest of Mexico*, vol. i. pp. 53, 54, Note. For further evidence on this subject, see Appendix, Note H.

‡ Parson's *Japhet*, pp. 205, 206.

§ When Ashta, or "the woman," came to be called the "queen of heaven," the name "woman" became the highest title of honour applied to a female. This accounts for what we find so common among the ancient nations of the East, that queens and the most exalted personages were addressed by the name of "woman." "Woman" is not a complimentary title in our language; but formerly it had been applied by our ancestors in the very same way as among the Orientals; for our word "Queen" is derived from Cwino, which in the ancient Gothic just signified a woman.

‖ Bunsen, vol. i. p. 401.

¶ *Ibid.* vol. i. pp. 386, 387.

** Hestia, in Greek, signifies "a house" or "dwelling."—(See Schrevelius and Photius, *sub voce.*) This is usually thought to be a secondary meaning of the word, its proper meaning being believed to be "fire." But the statments made in regard to Hestia, show that the name is derived from Hes or Hesè, "to cover, to shelter," which is the very idea of a house, which "covers" or "shelters" from

"Daughter of Saturn, venerable dame,
Who dwell'st amid great fire's eternal flame,
In thee the *gods* have fix'd their DWELLING-PLACE,
Strong stable basis of the mortal race." *

Even when Vesta is *identified* with fire, this same character of Vesta as "The Dwelling-Place" still distinctly appears. Thus Philolaus, speaking of a fire in the middle of the centre of the world, calls it "The Vesta of the universe, The HOUSE of Jupiter, The mother of the gods."† In Babylon, the title of the goddess-mother as the Dwelling-place of God was Sacca,‡ or in the emphatic form, Sacta, that is, "The Tabernacle." Hence, at this day, the great goddesses in India, as wielding all the power of the god whom they represent, are called "Sacti," or the "Tabernacle."§ Now in her, as the Tabernacle or Temple of God, not only all power, but all grace and goodness were believed to dwell. Every quality of gentleness and mercy was regarded as centred in her; and when death had closed her career, while she was fabled to have been deified and changed into a pigeon,‖ to express the celestial benignity of her nature, she was called by the name of "D'Iuné,"¶ or "The Dove," or without the

the inclemency of the weather. The verb "Hes" also signifies "to protect," to "show mercy," and from this evidently comes the character of Hestia as "the protectress of suppliants."—(See SMITH.) Taking Hestia as derived from Hes, "to cover," or "shelter," the following statement of Smith is easily accounted for:—"Hestia was the goddess of domestic life, and the giver of all domestic happiness; as such she was believed to dwell in the inner part of every house, and *to have invented the art of building houses.*" If "fire" be supposed to be the original idea of Hestia, how could "fire" ever have been supposed to be "the builder of houses"? But taking Hestia in the sense of the Habitation or Dwelling-place, though derived from Hes, "to shelter," or "cover," it is easy to see how Hestia would come to be identified with "fire." The goddess who was regarded as the "Habitation of God" was known by the name of Ashta, "The Woman;" while "Ashta" also signified "The fire;" and thus Hestia or Vesta, as the Babylonian system was developed, would easily come to be regarded as "Fire," or "the goddess of fire." For the reason that suggested the idea of the Goddess-mother being a Habitation, see Appendix, Note I.

* TAYLOR'S *Orphic Hymns: Hymn to Vesta*, p. 175. Though Vesta is here called the *daughter* of Saturn, she is also identified in all the Pantheons with Cybele or Rhea, the wife of Saturn.

† Note to TAYLOR'S *Orphic Hymns*, p. 156.

‡ For the worship of Sacca, in the character of Anaitis—*i.e.*, Venus, see CHESNEY'S *Euphrates Expedition*, vol. i. p. 381.

§ KENNEDY and MOOR, *passim.* A synonym for Sacca, "a tabernacle," is "Ahel," which, with the points, is pronounced "Ohel." From the first form of the word, the name of the wife of the god Buddha seems to be derived, which, in KENNEDY, is Ahalya (pp. 246, 256), and in MOOR'S *Pantheon*, Ahilya (p. 264). From the second form, in like manner, seems to be derived the name of the wife of the Patriarch of the Peruvians, "Mama Oëllo." (PRESCOTT'S *Peru*, vol. i. pp. 7, 8.) Mama was by the Peruvians used in the Oriental sense; Oëllo, in all likelihood, was used in the same sense.

‖ DIODORUS SIC., lib. ii. p. 76. In connection with this the classical reader will remember the title of one of the fables in OVID'S *Metamorphoses*. "Semiramis in columbam" (*Metam.* iv.) "Semiramis into a pigeon."

¶ Dioné, the name of the mother of Venus, and frequently applied to Venus herself, is evidently the same name as the above. Dione, as meaning Venus, is clearly applied by Ovid to the Babylonian goddess. *Fasti*, lib. ii. 461-464, vol. iii. p. 113.

article, "Juno,"—the name of the Roman "queen of heaven," which has the very same meaning; and under the *form* of a dove as well as her own, she was worshipped by the Babylonians. The dove, the chosen symbol of this deified queen, is commonly represented with an olive branch in her mouth (Fig. 25), as she herself in her human form also is seen bearing the olive branch in her hand; * and from this form of representing her, it is highly probable that she has derived the name by which she is commonly known, for "Z'emir-amit" means "The branch-bearer."† When the goddess was thus represented as the Dove with the olive branch, there can be no doubt that the symbol had partly reference to the story of the flood; but there was much more in the symbol than a mere memorial of that great event. "A branch," as has been already proved, was the symbol of the deified son, and when the deified mother was represented as a Dove, what could the meaning of this representation be but just to identify *her* with the Spirit of all grace, that brooded, dove-like, over the deep at the creation; for in the sculptures at Nineveh, as we have seen, the wings and tail of the dove represented the *third* member of the idolatrous Assyrian trinity. In confirmation of this

Fig. 25. ‡

view, it must be stated that the Assyrian "Juno," or "The Virgin Venus," as she was called, was identified with the *air*. Thus Julius Firmicus says:—"The Assyrians and part of the Africans wish the *air* to have the supremacy of the elements, for they have consecrated this same [element] under the name of Juno, or the Virgin Venus."§ Why was *air* thus identified with Juno, whose symbol was that of the third person of the Assyrian trinity? Why, but because in Chaldee the same word which signifies the *air* signifies also the "*Holy Ghost.*" The knowledge of this entirely accounts for the

* LAYARD'S *Nineveh and Babylon*, p. 250.

† From *Ze*, "the" or "that," *emir*, "branch," and *amit*, "bearer," in the *feminine.*—HESYCHIUS, *sub voce*, says that Semiramis is a name for a "wild pigeon." The above explanation of the original meaning of the name Semiramis, as referring to Noah's wild pigeon (for it was evidently a wild one, as the tame one would not have suited the experiment), may account for its application by the Greeks to *any* wild pigeon.

‡ BRYANT, vol. iii. p. 84. The branch in the hand of Cybele in the above cut is only a conventional branch; but in the figure given by Layard it is distinctly an olive branch.

§ FIRMICUS, *De Errore*, cap. 4, p. 9.

statement of Proclus, that "Juno imports the generation of soul." * Whence could the soul—the spirit of man—be supposed to have its origin, but from the Spirit of God. In accordance with this character of Juno as the incarnation of the Divine Spirit, the source of life, and also as the goddess of the *air*, thus is she invoked in the "Orphic Hymns":—

"O royal Juno, of majestic mien,
Aërial formed, divine, Jove's blessed queen,
Throned in the bosom of cærulean *air*,
The race of mortals is thy constant care;
The *cooling gales*, thy power alone inspires,
Which nourish *life*, which every *life* desires;
Mother of showers and *winds*, from thee alone
Producing all things, mortal *life* is known;
All natures show thy temperament divine,
And universal sway alone is thine,
With sounding blasts of wind, the swelling sea
And rolling rivers roar when shook by thee." †

Thus, then, the deified queen, when in all respects regarded as a veritable woman, was at the same time adored as the incarnation of the Holy Ghost, the Spirit of peace and love. In the temple of Hierapolis in Syria, there was a famous statue of the goddess Juno, to which crowds from all quarters flocked to worship. The image of the goddess was richly habited, on her head was a golden dove, and she was called by a name peculiar to the country, "Semëion." ‡ What is the meaning of Semëion? It is evidently "The Habitation;" § and the "golden dove" on her head shows plainly who it was that was supposed to dwell in her—even the Spirit of God. When such transcendent dignity was bestowed on her, when such winning characters were attributed to her, and when, over and above all, her images presented her to the eyes of men as Venus Urania, "the heavenly Venus," the queen of beauty, who assured her worshippers of salvation, while giving loose reins to every unholy passion, and every depraved and sensual appetite—no wonder that everywhere she was enthusiastically adored. Under the name of the "Mother of the gods," the goddess queen of Babylon became an object of almost universal worship. "The Mother of the gods," says Clericus, "was worshipped by the Persians, the Syrians, and all the kings of Europe and Asia, with the most profound religious

* PROCLUS, lib. vi. cap. 22, vol. ii. p. 76.

† TAYLOR'S *Orphic Hymns*, p. 50. Every classical reader must be aware of the identification of Juno with the *air*. The following, however, as still further illustrative of the subject from Proclus, may not be out of place:—"The series of our sovereign mistress Juno, beginning from on high, pervades the last of things, and her allotment in the sublunary region is the air; for air is a symbol of soul, according to which also soul is called a *spirit*, *πνευμα*."—PROCLUS, *Ibid.* p. 197.

‡ BRYANT, vol. iii. p. 145.

§ From Ze, "that," or "the great," and "Maaon," or Maïon, "a habitation," which, in the Ionic dialect, in which Lucian, the describer of the goddess, wrote, would naturally become Meïon.

veneration."* Tacitus gives evidence that the Babylonian goddess was worshipped in the heart of Germany,† and Cæsar, when he invaded Britain, found that the priests of this same goddess, known by the name of Druids, had been there before him.‡ Herodotus, from personal knowledge, testifies, that in Egypt this "queen of heaven" was "the greatest and most worshipped of all the divinities."§ Wherever her worship was introduced, it is amazing what fascinating power it exerted. Truly, the nations might be said to be "made drunk" with the wine of her fornications. So deeply, in particular, did the Jews in the days of Jeremiah drink of her wine, cup, so bewitched were they with her idolatrous worship, that even after Jerusalem had been burnt, and the land desolated for this very thing, they could not be prevailed on to give it up. While dwelling in Egypt as forlorn exiles, instead of being witnesses for God against the heathenism around them, they were as much devoted to this form of idolatry as the Egyptians themselves. Jeremiah was sent of God to denounce wrath against them, if they continued to worship the queen of heaven; but his warnings were in vain. "Then," saith the prophet, "all the men which knew that their wives had burnt incense unto other gods, and all the women that stood by, a great multitude, even all the people that dwelt in the land of Egypt, in Pathros, answered Jeremiah, saying, As for the word that thou hast spoken unto us in the name of the Lord, we will not hearken unto thee; but we will certainly do whatsoever thing goeth forth out of our own mouth, to burn incense unto the queen of heaven, and to pour out drink-offerings unto her, as we have done, we, and our fathers, our kings, and our princes, in the cities of Judah, and in the streets of Jerusalem: for then had we plenty of victuals, and were well, and saw no evil" (Jer. xliv. 15-17). Thus did the Jews, God's

* JOANNES CLERICUS, *Philos. Orient.*, lib. ii., *De Persis*, cap. 9, vol. ii. p. 340.

† TACITUS, *Germania*, ix. tom. ii. p. 386.

‡ CÆSAR, *De Bello Gallico*, lib. vi. cap. 13, p. 121. The name Druid has been thought to be derived from the Greek *Drus*, an oak tree, or the Celtic *Deru*, which has the same meaning; but this is obviously a mistake. In Ireland, the name for a Druid is Droi, and in Wales Dryw; and it will be found that the connection of the Druids with the oak was more from the mere similarity of their name to that of the oak, than because they derived their name from it. The Druidic system in all its parts was evidently the Babylonian system. Dionysius informs us, that the rites of Bacchus were duly celebrated in the British Islands—(PERIERGESIS, v. 565, p. 29)—and Strabo cites Artemidorus to show that, in an island close to Britain, Ceres and Proserpine were venerated with rites similar to the orgies of Samothrace.—(Lib. iv. p. 190.) It will be seen from the account of the Druidic Ceridwen and her child, afterwards to be noticed—(see Chap. IV. Sect. III.)—that there was a great analogy between her character and that of the great goddess-mother of Babylon. Such was the system; and the name Dryw, or Droi, applied to the priests, is in exact accordance with that system. The name Zero, given in Hebrew or the early Chaldee, to the son of the great goddess queen, in later Chaldee became "Dero." The priest of Dero, "the seed," was called, as is the case in almost all religions, by the name of his god; and hence the familiar name "Druid" is thus proved to signify the priest of "Dero"—the woman's promised "*seed.*" The classical Hamadryads were evidently in like manner priestesses of "Hamed-dero,"—"the *desired* seed"—*i.e.*, "*the desire of all nations.*"

§ HERODOTUS, *Historia*, lib. ii. cap. 66, p. 117, D.

own peculiar people, emulate the Egyptians in their devotion to the queen of heaven.

The worship of the goddess-mother with the child in her arms continued to be observed in Egypt till Christianity entered. If the Gospel had come in power among the mass of the people, the worship of this goddess-queen would have been overthrown. With the generality it came only in name. Instead, therefore, of the Babylonian goddess being cast out, in too many cases her name only was changed. She was called the Virgin Mary, and, with her child, was worshipped with the same idolatrous feeling by professing Christians, as formerly by open and avowed Pagans. The consequence was, that when, in A.D. 325, the Nicene Council was summoned to condemn the heresy of Arius, who denied the true divinity of Christ, that heresy indeed was condemned, but not without the help of men who gave distinct indications of a desire to put the creature on a level with the Creator, to set the Virgin-mother side by side with her Son. At the Council of Nice, says the author of "Nimrod," "The Melchite section"—that is, the representatives of the so-called Christianity of Egypt—"held that there were three persons in the Trinity—the Father, the Virgin Mary, and Messiah their Son."* In reference to this astounding fact, elicited by the Nicene Council, Father Newman speaks exultingly of these discussions as tending to the glorification of Mary. "Thus," says he, "the controversy opened a question which it did not settle. It discovered a new sphere, if we may so speak, in the realms of light, *to which the Church had not yet assigned its inhabitant.* Thus, there was a wonder in Heaven; a throne was seen far above all created powers, mediatorial, intercessory, a title archetypal, a crown bright as the morning star, a glory issuing from the eternal throne, robes pure as the heavens, and a sceptre over all. And who was the predestined heir of that majesty? Who was that wisdom, and what was her name, *the mother of fair love*, and fear, and holy hope, exalted like a palm-tree in Engaddi, and a rose-plant in Jericho, created from the beginning before the world, in God's counsels, and in Jerusalem was her power? The vision is found in the Apocalypse 'a Woman clothed with the sun, and the moon under her feet, and upon her head a crown of twelve stars.'"† "The votaries of Mary," adds he, "do not exceed the true faith, unless the blasphemers of her Son came up to it. The Church of Rome is not idolatrous, unless Arianism is orthodoxy."‡ This is the very poetry of blasphemy.

* *Nimrod*, iii. p. 329, quoted in *Quarterly Journal of Prophecy*, July, 1852, p. 244.

† NEWMAN'S *Development*, pp. 405, 406. The intelligent reader will see at a glance the absurdity of applying this vision of the "woman" of the Apocalypse to the Virgin Mary. John expressly declares that what he saw was a "sign" or "symbol" (*semeion*). If the woman here is a literal woman, the woman that sits on the seven hills must be the same. "The woman" in both cases is a "symbol." "The woman" on the seven hills is the symbol of the false church; the woman clothed with the sun, of the true church—the Bride, the Lamb's wife.

‡ *Ibid.*

It contains an argument too; but what does that argument amount to? It just amounts to this, that if Christ be admitted to be truly and properly God, and worthy of Divine honours, His mother, from whom He derived merely His humanity, must be admitted to be the same, must be raised far above the level of all creatures, and be worshipped as a partaker of the Godhead. The divinity of Christ is made to stand or fall with the divinity of His mother. Such is Popery in the nineteenth century; yea, such is Popery in England. It was known already that Popery abroad was bold and unblushing in its blasphemies; that in Lisbon a church was to be seen with these words engraven on its front, "To the virgin goddess of Loretto, the Italian race, devoted to her DIVINITY, have dedicated this temple."* But when till now was such language ever heard in Britain before? This, however, is just the exact reproduction of the doctrine of ancient Babylon in regard to the great goddess-mother. The Madonna of Rome, then, is just the Madonna of Babylon. The "Queen of Heaven" in the one system is the same as the "Queen of Heaven" in the other. The goddess worshipped in Babylon and Egypt as the *Tabernacle* or Habitation of God, is identical with her who, under the name of Mary, is called by Rome "the HOUSE consecrated to God," "the awful Dwelling-place,"† "the Mansion of God,"‡ the "Tabernacle of the Holy Ghost,"§ the "Temple of the Trinity."|| Some may possibly be inclined to defend such language, by saying that the Scripture makes every believer to be a temple of the Holy Ghost, and, therefore, what harm can there be in speaking of the Virgin Mary, who was unquestionably a saint of God, under that name, or names of a similar import? Now, no doubt it is true that Paul says (1 Cor. iii. 16), "Know ye not that ye are the temple of God, and that the Spirit of God dwelleth in you?" It is not only true, but it is a great truth, and a blessed one—a truth that enhances every comfort when enjoyed, and takes the sting out of every trouble when it comes, that every genuine Christian has less or more experience of what is contained in these words of the same apostle (2 Cor. vi. 16), "Ye are the temple of the living God; as God hath said, I will dwell in them and walk in them, and I will be their God, and they shall be my people." It must also be admitted, and gladly admitted, that this implies the indwelling of all the Persons of the glorious Godhead; for the Lord Jesus hath said (John xiv. 23), "If a man love me, he will keep my words; and my Father will love him, and WE will come unto him, and make our abode with him." But while admitting all this, on examination it will be found that the Popish and the Scriptural ideas conveyed

* Journal of Professor GIBSON, in *Scottish Protestant*, vol. i. p. 464.

† The *Golden Manual*, in *Scottish Protestant*, vol. ii. p. 271. The word here used for "Dwelling-place" in the Latin of this work is a pure Chaldee word—"Zabulo," and is from the same verb as Zebulun (Gen. xxx. 20), the name which was given by Leah to her son, when she said "Now will my husband *dwell* with me."

‡ *Pancarpium Mariæ*, p. 141.

§ *Garden of the Soul*, p. 488.

|| *Golden Manual*, in *Scottish Protestant*, vol. ii. p. 272.

by these expressions, however apparently similar, are essentially different. When it is said that a believer is "a temple of God," or a temple of the Holy Ghost, the meaning is (Eph. iii. 17) that "Christ dwells in the heart by faith." But when Rome says that Mary is "The Temple" or "Tabernacle of God," the meaning is the exact Pagan meaning of the term—viz., that the union between her and the Godhead is a union akin to the hypostatical union between the divine and human nature of Christ. The human nature of Christ *is* the "Tabernacle of God," inasmuch as the Divine nature has veiled its glory in such a way, by assuming our nature, that we can come near without overwhelming dread to the Holy God. To this glorious truth John refers when he says (John i. 14), "The Word was made flesh, and dwelt (literally *tabernacled*) among us, and we beheld His glory, the glory as of the only begotten of the Father, full of grace and truth." In this sense, Christ, the God-man, is the only "Tabernacle of God." Now, it is precisely in this sense that Rome calls Mary the "Tabernacle of God," or of the "Holy Ghost." Thus speaks the author of a Popish work devoted to the exaltation of the Virgin, in which all the peculiar titles and prerogatives of Christ are given to Mary: "Behold the tabernacle of God, the mansion of God, the habitation, the city of God is with men, and in men and for men, for their salvation, and exaltation, and eternal glorification. . . . . Is it most clear that this is true of the holy church? and in like manner also equally true of the most holy sacrament of the Lord's body? Is it (true) of every one of us in as far as we are truly Christians? Undoubtedly; but we have to contemplate this mystery (as existing) in a *peculiar manner* in the most holy Mother of our Lord."* Then the author, after endeavouring to show that "Mary is rightly considered as the Tabernacle of God with men," and that in a peculiar sense, a sense different from that in which all Christians are the "temple of God," thus proceeds with express reference to *her* in this character of the Tabernacle: "Great truly is the benefit, singular is the privilege, that the Tabernacle of God should be with men, IN WHICH men may safely come near to God become man."† Here the whole mediatorial glory of Christ, as the God-man in whom dwelleth all the fulness of the Godhead bodily, is given to Mary, or at least is shared with her. The above extracts are taken from a work published upwards of two hundred years ago. Has the Papacy improved since then? Has it repented of its blasphemies? No, the very reverse. The quotation already given from Father Newman proves this; but there is still stronger proof. In a recently published work, the same blasphemous idea is even more clearly unfolded. While Mary is called "The HOUSE consecrated to God," and the "TEMPLE of the Trinity," the following versicle and response will show in what sense she is regarded as the temple of the Holy Ghost: "*V.* Ipse [deus] creavit illam in Spiritu Sancto. *R.* Et EFFUDIT ILLAM inter omnia opera sua. *V.* Domina, exaudi," &c., which is

* *Pancarpium Mariæ*, or *Marianum*, pp. 141, 142.
† *Ibid.* p. 142.

thus translated: "*V.* The Lord himself created HER in the Holy Ghost, and POURED HER out among all his works. *V.* O Lady, hear," &c.* This astounding language manifestly implies that Mary is *identified* with the Holy Ghost, when it speaks of *her* "being poured out" on "all the works of God;" and that, as we have seen, was just the very way in which the Woman, regarded as the "Tabernacle" or House of God by the Pagans, was looked upon. Where is such language used in regard to the Virgin? Not in Spain; not in Austria; not in the dark places of Continental Europe; but in London, the seat and centre of the world's enlightenment.

The names of blasphemy bestowed by the Papacy on Mary have not one shadow of foundation in the Bible, but are all to be found in the Babylonian idolatry. Yea, the very features and complexions of the Roman and Babylonian Madonnas are the same. Till recent times, when Raphael somewhat departed from the beaten track, there was nothing either Jewish or even Italian in the Romish Madonnas. Had these pictures or images of the Virgin Mother been intended to represent the mother of our Lord, naturally they would have been cast either in the one mould or the other. But it was not so. In a land of dark-eyed beauties, with raven locks, the Madonna was always represented with blue eyes and golden hair, a complexion entirely different from the Jewish complexion, which naturally would have been supposed to belong to the mother of our Lord, but which precisely agrees with that which all antiquity attributes to the goddess queen of Babylon. In almost all lands the great goddess has been described with golden or yellow hair, showing that there must have been one grand prototype, to which they were all made to correspond. "*Flava ceres*," the "yellow-haired Ceres," might not have been accounted of any weight in this argument if she had stood alone, for it might have been supposed in that case that the epithet "yellow-haired" was borrowed from the corn that was supposed to be under her guardian care. But many other goddesses have the very same epithet applied to them. Europa, whom Jupiter carried away in the form of a bull, is called "The yellow-haired Europa."† Minerva is called by Homer "the blue-eyed Minerva,"‡ and by Ovid "the yellow-haired;"§ the huntress Diana, who is commonly identified with the moon, is addressed by Anacreon as "the yellow-haired daughter of Jupiter,"|| a title which the pale face of the silver moon could surely never have suggested. Dioné, the mother of Venus, is described by Theocritus as "yellow-haired."¶ Venus herself is frequently called "Aurea Venus," the "golden Venus."** The Indian goddess Lakshmi, the "Mother of the Universe," is described

* *Golden Manual*, p. 649. This work has the *imprimatur* of "Nicholas, Bishop of Melipotamus," now Cardinal Wiseman.

† OVID, *Fasti*, lib. v. l. 609, tom. iii. p. 330.

‡ *Iliad*, lib. v. v. 420, tom. i. p. 205.

§ OVID, *Tristium*, lib. i.; *Elegia*, p. 44; and *Fasti*, lib. vi. v. 652, tom. iii. p. 387.

|| ANACREON, *Od.* lx. p. 204.

¶ *Idyll* vii. v. 116, p. 157.

** HOMER's *Iliad*, lib. v. v. 427.

as of "a golden complexion."* Ariadne, the wife of Bacchus, was called "the yellow-haired Ariadne."† Thus does Dryden refer to her golden or yellow hair:—

> "Where the rude waves in Dian's harbour play,
> The fair forsaken Ariadne lay;
> There, sick with grief and frantic with despair,
> Her dress she rent, and tore her golden hair."‡

The Gorgon Medusa before her transformation, while celebrated for her beauty, was equally celebrated for her golden hair:—

> "Medusa once had charms: to gain her love
> A rival crowd of anxious lovers strove.
> They who have seen her, own they ne'er did trace
> More moving features in a sweeter face;
> But above all, her length of hair they own
> In golden ringlets waved, and graceful shone."§

The mermaid that figured so much in the romantic tales of the north, which was evidently borrowed from the story of Atergatis, the fish goddess of Syria, who was called the mother of Semiramis, and was sometimes identified with Semiramis herself,‖ was described with hair of the same kind. "The Ellewoman," such is the Scandinavian name for the mermaid, "is fair," says the introduction to the "Danish Tales" of Hans Andersen, "and gold-haired, and plays most sweetly on a stringed instrument."¶ "She is frequently seen sitting on the surface of the waters, and combing her long golden hair with a golden comb."** Even when Athor, the Venus of Egypt, was represented as a cow, doubtless to indicate the complexion of the goddess that cow represented, the cow's *head* and *neck* were *gilded.*†† When, therefore, it is known that the most famed pictures of the Virgin Mother in Italy represented her as of a fair complexion and with golden hair, and when over all Ireland the Virgin is almost invariably represented at this day in the very same manner, who can resist the conclusion that she must have been thus represented, only because she had been copied from the same prototype as the Pagan divinities.

Nor is this agreement in complexion only, but also in features. Jewish features are everywhere marked, and have a character peculiarly their own. But the original Madonnas have nothing at all of Jewish form or feature; but are declared by those who have personally compared both,‡‡ entirely to agree in this respect, as well as in complexion, with the Babylonian Madonnas found by Sir Robert Ker Porter among the ruins of Babylon.

* *Asiatic Researches*, vol. xi. p. 184. † Hesiod, *Theogonia*, v. 947, p. 74.
‡ *Heathen Mythology Illustrated*, p. 58. § *Ibid.* p. 90.
‖ *Lucian de Dea Syria*, vol. iii. pp. 460, 461. The name mentioned by Lucian is Derketo, but it is well known that Derketo and Atergatis are the same.
¶ *Danish Tales*, p. 36. ** *Ibid.* p. 37.
†† Herodotus, lib. ii. p. 158, and Wilkinson, vol. i., Note to p. 128.
‡‡ H. J. Jones, in *Quarterly Journal of Prophecy*, October, 1852, p. 331.

There is yet another remarkable characteristic of these pictures worthy of notice, and that is the nimbus or peculiar *circle* of light that frequently encompasses the head of the Roman Madonna. With this *circle* the heads of the so-called figures of Christ are also frequently surrounded. Whence could such a device have originated? In the case of our Lord, if His head had been merely surrounded with rays, there might have been some *pretence* for saying that that was borrowed from the Evangelic narrative, where it is stated, that on the holy mount His face became resplendent with light. But where, in the whole compass of Scripture, do we ever read that His head was surrounded with a *disk*, or a *circle* of light? But what will be searched for in vain in the Word of God, is found in the artistic representations of the great gods and goddesses of Babylon. The disk, and particularly the *circle*, were the well-known symbols of the Sun-divinity, and figured largely in the symbolism of the East. With the circle or the disk the head of the Sun-divinity was encompassed. The same was the case in Pagan Rome. Apollo, as the child of the Sun, was often thus represented. The goddesses that claimed kindred with the Sun were equally entitled to be adorned with the nimbus or luminous circle. We give from *Pompeii* a representation of Circe, "the daughter of the Sun" (see Fig. 26), with her head surrounded with a circle, in the very same way as the head of the Roman Madonna is at this day surrounded. Let any one compare the nimbus around the head of Circe, with that around the head of the Popish Virgin, and he will see how exactly they correspond.*

Now, could any one possibly believe that all this coincidence could be accidental. Of course, if the Madonna had ever so exactly

* The explanation of the next woodcut is thus given in *Pompeii*, vol. ii. pp. 91, 92: "One of them [the paintings] is taken from the *Odyssey*, and represents Ulysses and Circe, at the moment when the hero, having drunk the charmed cup with impunity, by virtue of the antidote given him by Mercury [it is well known that Circe had a 'golden cup,' even as the Venus of Babylon had], draws his sword, and advances to avenge his companions," who, having drunk of her cup, had been changed into swine. The goddess, terrified, makes her submission at once, as described by Homer; Ulysses himself being the narrator:—

"'Hence, seek the sty, there wallow with thy friends,'
She spake, I drawing from beside my thigh
My falchion keen, with death-denouncing looks,
Rushed on her; she, with a shrill scream of fear,
Ran under my raised arm, seized fast my knees,
And in winged accents plaintive, thus began:
'Say, who art thou,'" &c.—COWPER'S *Odyssey*, x. 320.

"This picture," adds the author of *Pompeii*, "is remarkable, as teaching us the origin of that ugly and unmeaning glory by which the heads of saints are often surrounded. . . . This glory was called nimbus, or aureola, and is defined by Servius to be 'the luminous fluid which encircles the heads of the gods.' (On ÆNEID, lib. ii. v. 616, vol. i. p. 165.) It belongs with peculiar propriety to Circe, as the daughter of the Sun. The emperors, with their usual modesty, assumed it as the mark of their divinity; and under this respectable patronage it passed, like many other Pagan superstitions and customs, into the use of the Church." The emperors here get rather more than a fair share of the blame due to them. It was not the emperors that brought "Pagan superstition" into the Church, so much as the Bishop of Rome. See Chap. VII. Sect. II.

resembled the Virgin Mary, that would never have excused idolatry. But when it is evident that the goddess enshrined in the Papal Church for the supreme worship of its votaries, is that very Babylonian queen who set up Nimrod, or Ninus "the Son," as the rival of Christ, and who in her own person was the incarnation of every kind of licentiousness, how dark a character does that stamp on the Roman idolatry. What will it avail to migitate the heinous character of that idolatry, to say that the child she holds forth to adoration is called by the name of Jesus? When she was worshipped with her child in Babylon of old, that child was called by a name as peculiar to Christ, as distinctive of His glorious character, as the name of Jesus. He was called "Zoro-ashta," "the seed of the woman." But that did not hinder the hot anger of God from being directed against those in the days of old who worshipped that "image of jealousy, provoking to jealousy."* Neither can the giving of the

Fig. 26.

name of Christ to the infant in the arms of the Romish Madonna, make it less the "image of jealousy," less offensive to the Most High, less fitted to provoke His high displeasure, when it is evident that that infant is worshipped as the child of her who was adored as Queen of Heaven, with all the attributes of divinity, and was at the same time the "Mother of harlots and abominations of the earth." Image-worship in every case the Lord abhors; but image-worship of such a kind as this must be peculiarly abhorrent to His holy soul. Now, if the facts I have adduced be true, is it wonderful that such dreadful threatenings should be directed in the Word of God against the Romish apostacy, and that the vials of this tremendous wrath are

* Ezek. viii. 3. There have been many speculations about what this "image of jealousy" could be. But when it is known that the grand feature of ancient idolatry was just the worship of the Mother and the child, and that child as the Son of God incarnate, all is plain. Compare verses 3 and 5 with verse 14, and it will be seen that the "women weeping for Tammuz" were weeping close beside the image of jealousy.

destined to be outpoured upon its guilty head? If these things be true (and gainsay them who can), who will venture now to plead for Papal Rome, or to call her a Christian Church? Is there one, who fears God, and who reads these lines, who would not admit that Paganism alone could ever have inspired such a doctrine as that avowed by the Melchites at the Nicene Council, that the Holy Trinity consisted of "the Father, the Virgin Mary, and the Messiah their Son"?* Is there one who would not shrink with horror from such a thought? What, then, would the reader say of a Church that teaches its children to adore such a Trinity as that contained in the following lines?—

> "Heart of Jesus I adore thee;
> Heart of Mary, I implore thee;
> Heart of Joseph, pure and just;
> IN THESE THREE HEARTS I PUT MY TRUST."†

If this is not Paganism, what is there that can be called by such a name? Yet this is the Trinity which *now* the Roman Catholics of Ireland from tender infancy are taught to adore. This is the Trinity which, in the latest books of catechetical instruction is presented as the grand object of devotion to the adherents of the Papacy. The manual that contains this blasphemy comes forth with the express "*Imprimatur*" of "Paulus Cullen," Popish Archbishop

* *Quarterly Journal of Prophecy*, July, 1852, p. 244.

† *What every Christian must Know and Do.* By the Rev. J. FURNISS. Published by James Duffy, Dublin. The edition of this Manual of Popery quoted above, besides the blasphemy it contains, contains most immoral principles, teaching distinctly the harmlessness of fraud, if only kept within due bounds. On this account, a great outcry having been raised against it, I believe this edition has been withdrawn from *general* circulation. The genuineness of the passage above given is, however, beyond all dispute. I received myself from a friend in Liverpool a copy of the edition containing these words, which is now in my possession, having previously seen them in a copy in the possession of the Rev. Richard Smyth of Armagh. It is not in Ireland, however, only, that such a trinity is exhibited for the worship of Romanists. In a Card, or Fly-leaf, issued by the Popish priests of Sunderland, now lying before me, with the heading "Paschal Duty, St. Mary's Church, Bishopwearmouth, 1859," the following is the 4th admonition given to the "Dear Christians" to whom it is addressed:—

"4. And never forget the acts of a good Christian, recommended to you so often during the renewal of the Mission.

> Blessed be Jesus, Mary, and Joseph.
> Jesus, Mary, and Joseph, I give you my heart, my life, and my soul.
> Jesus, Mary, and Joseph, assist me always; and in my last agony,
> Jesus, Mary, and Joseph, receive my last breath. Amen."

To induce the adherents of Rome to perform this "act of a good Christian," a considerable bribe is held out. In p. 30 of Furniss's Manual above referred to, under the head "Rule of Life," the following passage occurs:—"In the morning, before you get up, make the sign of the cross, and say, Jesus, Mary, and Joseph, I give you my heart and my soul. (Each time you say this prayer, you get an indulgence of 100 days, which you can give to the souls in Purgatory)!" I must add that the title of Furniss's book, as given above, is the title of Mr. Smyth's copy. The title of the copy in my possession is "*What every Christian must Know.*" London: Richardson & Son, 147 Strand. Both copies alike have the blasphemous words given in the text, and both have the "Imprimatur" of "Paulus Cullen."

of Dublin. Will any one after this say that the Roman Catholic Church must still be called Christian, because it holds the doctrine of the Trinity? So did the Pagan Babylonians, so did the Egyptians, so do the Hindoos at this hour, in the very same sense in which Rome does. They all admitted A trinity, but did they worship THE Triune Jehovah, the King Eternal, Immortal, and Invisible? And will any one say with such evidence before him, that Rome does so? Away then, with the deadly delusion that Rome is Christian! There might once have been some palliation for entertaining such a supposition; but every day the "Grand Mystery" is revealing itself more and more in its true character. There is not, and there cannot be, any safety for the souls of men in "Babylon." "Come out of her, my people," is the loud and express command of God. Those who disobey that command, do it at their peril.

CHAPTER III.

FESTIVALS.

SECTION I.—CHRISTMAS AND LADY-DAY.

IF Rome be indeed the Babylon of the Apocalypse, and the Madonna enshrined in her sanctuaries be the very queen of heaven, for the worshipping of whom the fierce anger of God was provoked against the Jews in the days of Jeremiah, it is of the last consequence that the fact should be established beyond all possibility of doubt; for that being once established, every one who trembles at the Word of God must shudder at the very thought of giving such a system, either individually or nationally, the least countenance or support. Something has been said already that goes far to prove the identity of the Roman and Babylonian systems; but at every step the evidence becomes still more overwhelming. That which arises from comparing the different festivals is peculiarly so.

The festivals of Rome are innumerable; but five of the most important may be singled out for elucidation—viz., Christmas-day, Lady-day, Easter, the Nativity of St. John, and the Feast of the Assumption. Each and all of these can be proved to be Babylonian. And first, as to the festival in honour of the birth of Christ, or Christmas. How comes it that that festival was connected with the 25th of December? There is not a word in the Scriptures about the precise day of His birth, or the time of the year when He was born. What is recorded there, implies that at what time soever His birth took place, it *could* not have been on the 25th of December. At the time that the angel announced His birth to the shepherds of Bethlehem, they were feeding their flocks by night in the open fields. Now, no doubt, the climate of Palestine is not so severe as the climate of this country; but even there, though the heat of the day be considerable, the cold of the night, from December to February, is very piercing,* and it was *not* the custom for the shepherds of Judea to watch their flocks in the open fields *later* than about the end of October.† It is in the last degree incredible, then,

* *London Tract Society's Commentary*, vol. i. p. 472. ALFORD'S *Greek Testament*, vol. i. p. 412. GRESWELL, vol. i., *Dissert.* xii. pp. 381-437.

† GILL, in his *Commentary* on Luke ii. 8, has the following:—"There are two sorts of cattle with the Jews . . . . there are the cattle of the house that lie in the city; the cattle of the wilderness are they that lie in the pastures. On which one of the commentators (MAIMONIDES, *in Misn. Betza*, cap. 5, sect. 7), observes, 'These lie in the pastures, which are in the villages, all the days of the cold and heat, and do not go into the cities until the rains descend.' The first rain falls in the month Marchesvan, which answers to the latter part of our

that the birth of Christ could have taken place at the end of December. There is great unanimity among commentators on this point. Besides Barnes, Doddridge, Lightfoot, Joseph Scaliger, and Jennings, in his "Jewish Antiquities," who are all of opinion that December 25th could not be the right time of our Lord's nativity, the celebrated Joseph Mede pronounces a very decisive opinion to the same effect. After a long and careful disquisition on the subject, among other arguments he adduces the following:—"At the birth of Christ every woman and child was to go to be taxed at the city whereto they belonged, whither some had long journeys; but the middle of winter was not fitting for such a business, especially for women with child, and children to travel in. Therefore, Christ could not be born in the depth of winter. Again, at the time of Christ's birth, the shepherds lay abroad watching with their flocks in the night time; but this was not likely to be in the middle of winter. And if any shall think the winter wind was not so extreme in these parts, let him remember the words of Christ in the gospel, 'Pray that your flight be not in the winter.' If the winter was so bad a time to flee in, it seems no fit time for shepherds to lie in the fields in, and women and children to travel in."* Indeed, it is admitted by the most learned and candid writers of all parties† that the day of our Lord's birth cannot be determined,‡ and that

October and the former part of November. . . . . From whence it appears that Christ must be born before the middle of October, since the first rain was not yet come." KITTO, on Deut. xi. 14 (*Illustrated Commentary*, vol. i. p. 398), says that the "first rain," is in "autumn," "that is, in September or October." This would make the time of the removal of the flocks from the fields somewhat earlier than I have stated in the text; but there is no doubt that it could not be later than there stated, according to the testimony of Maimonides, whose acquaintance with all that concerns Jewish customs is well known.

* MEDE's *Works*, 1672. *Discourse* xlviii. The above argument of Mede goes on the supposition of the well-known reasonableness and consideration by which the Roman laws were distinguished.

† Archdeacon WOOD, in *Christian Annotator*, vol. iii. p. 2. LORIMER's *Manual of Presbytery*, p. 130. Lorimer quotes Sir Peter King, who, in his *Enquiry into the Worship of the Primitive Church*, &c., infers that no such festival was observed in that Church, and adds—"It seems improbable that they should celebrate Christ's nativity when they disagreed about the month and the day when Christ was born." See also Rev. J. RYLE, in his *Commentary* on Luke, chap. ii., Note to verse 8, who admits that the time of Christ's birth is uncertain, although he opposes the idea that the flocks could not have been in the open fields in December, by an appeal to Jacob's complaint to Laban, "By day the drought consumed me, and the frost by night." Now the whole force of Jacob's complaint against his churlish kinsman lay in this, that Laban made him do what no other man would have done, and, therefore, if he refers to the cold nights of winter (which, however, is not the common understanding of the expression), it proves just the opposite of what it is brought by Mr. Ryle to prove—viz., that it was *not* the custom for shepherds to tend their flocks in the fields by night in winter.

‡ GIESELER, vol. i. p. 54, and Note. CHRYSOSTOM (*Monitum in Hom. de Natal. Christi*), writing in Antioch about A.D. 380, says: "It is not yet *ten* years since this day was made known to us" (Vol. ii., p. 352). "What follows," adds Gieseler, "furnishes a remarkable illustration of the ease with which customs of recent date could assume the character of apostolic institutions." Thus proceeds Chrysostom: "Among those inhabiting the west, it was known before from ancient and primitive times, and to the dwellers from Thrace to Gadeira [Cadiz]

within the Christian Church no such festival as Christmas was ever heard of *till the third* century, and that not till the *fourth* century was far advanced did it gain much observance. How, then, did the Romish Church fix on December the 25th as Christmas-day? Why, thus: Long before the fourth century, and long before the Christian era itself, a festival was celebrated among the *heathen*, at that precise time of the year, in honour of the birth of the son of the Babylonian queen of heaven; and it may fairly be presumed that, in order to conciliate the heathen, and to swell the number of the nominal adherents of Christianity, the same festival was adopted by the Roman Church, giving it only the name of Christ. This tendency on the part of Christians to meet Paganism half-way was very early developed; and we find Tertullian, even in his day, about the year 230, bitterly lamenting the inconsistency of the disciples of Christ in this respect, and contrasting it with the strict fidelity of the Pagans to their own superstition. "By us," says he, "who are strangers to Sabbaths,* and new moons, and festivals, once acceptable to God, the Saturnalia, the feasts of January, the *Brumalia*, and Matronalia, are now frequented; gifts are carried to and fro, new year's day presents are made with din, and sports and banquets are celebrated with uproar; oh, how much more faithful are the heathen to *their* religion, who take special care to adopt no solemnity from the Christians."† Upright men strove to stem the tide, but in spite of all their efforts, the apostacy went on, till the Church, with the exception of a small remnant, was submerged under Pagan superstition. That Christmas was originally a Pagan festival, is beyond all doubt. The time of the year, and the ceremonies with which it is still celebrated, prove its origin. In Egypt, the son of Isis, the Egyptian title for the queen of heaven, was born at this very time, "about the time of the winter solstice."‡ The very name by which Christmas is popularly known among ourselves—Yule-day §—proves at once its Pagan and Babylonian origin. "Yule" is the Chaldee name for an "infant" or "little child;" ‖ and as the 25th of Decem-

it was previously familiar and well-known," that is, the birth-day of our Lord, which was unknown at Antioch in the east, on the very borders of the Holy Land, where He was born, was perfectly well known in all the European region of the west, from Thrace even to Spain!

* He is speaking of Jewish Sabbaths.

† TERTULLIAN, *De Idololatria*, c. 14, vol. i. p. 682. For the excesses connected with the *Pagan* practice of the *first foot* on New Year's day, see GIESELER, vol. i. sect. 79, Note.

‡ WILKINSON'S *Egyptians*, vol. iv. p. 405. PLUTARCH (*De Iside*, vol. ii. p. 377, B), states that the Egyptian priests pretended that the birth of the divine son of Isis, at the end of December, was premature. But this is evidently just the counterpart of the classic story of Bacchus, who, when his mother Semele was consumed by the fire of Jove, was said to have been rescued in his *embryo* state from the flames that consumed her. The foundation of the story being entirely taken away in a previous note (see p. 59), the superstructure of course falls to the ground

§ MALLET, vol. i. p. 130.

‖ From Eöl, an "infant." The pronunciation here is the same as in eön of Gideon. In Scotland, at least in the Lowlands, the Yule-cakes are also called Nūr-cakes (the *u* being pronounced as the French *u*). Now in Chaldee Noūr

ber was called by our Pagan Anglo-Saxon ancestors, "Yule-day," or the "Child's day," and the night that preceded it, "Mother-night," * long before they came in contact with Christianity, that sufficiently proves its real character. Far and wide, in the realms of Paganism, was this birth-day observed. This festival has been commonly believed to have had only an astronomical character, referring simply to the completion of the sun's yearly course, and the commencement of a new cycle.† But there is indubitable evidence that the festival in question had a much higher reference than this—that it commemorated not merely the figurative birth-day of the sun in the renewal of its course, but the birth-day of the grand Deliverer. Among the Sabeans of Arabia, who regarded the moon, and not the sun, as the visible symbol of the favourite object of their idolatry, the same period was observed as the birth festival. Thus we read in Stanley's *Sabean Philosophy:* "On the 24th of the tenth month," that is December, according to our reckoning, "the Arabians celebrated the BIRTH-DAY OF THE LORD—that is the Moon."‡ The Lord Moon was the great object of Arabian worship, and that Lord Moon, according to them was *born* on the 24th of December, which clearly shows that the *birth* which they celebrated had no necessary connection with the course of the sun. It is worthy of special note, too, that if Christmas-day among the ancient Saxons of this island, was observed to celebrate the birth of any Lord of the host of heaven, the case must have been precisely the same here as it was in Arabia. The Saxons, as is well known, regarded the *Sun* as a *female* divinity, and the Moon as a male.§ It must have been the birth-day of the Lord Moon, therefore, and not of the Sun, that was celebrated by them on the 25th of December, even as the birth-day of the same Lord Moon was observed by the Arabians on the 24th of December. The name of the Lord Moon in the East seems to have been Meni, for this appears the most natural interpretation of the Divine statement in Isaiah lxv. 11, "But ye are they that forsake my holy mountain, that prepare a temple for Gad, and that furnish the drink-offering unto Meni."‖ There is reason to believe that Gad refers to the sun-god, and that Meni in like manner designates the moon-divinity.¶ Meni, or Manai, signifies "The Numberer," and it is by

signifies "birth." Therefore, Nūr-cakes are "birth-cakes." The Scandinavian goddesses, called "Norns," who appointed children their destinies at their *birth*, evidently derived their name from the cognate Chaldee word "Nor," a child.

* SHARON TURNER'S *Anglo-Saxons*, vol. i. p. 219.

† SALVERTÉ, *Des Sciences Occultes*, p. 491.

‡ STANLEY, p. 1066, col. 1.

§ SHARON TURNER, vol. i. p. 213. Turner cites an Arabic poem which proves that a female sun and a masculine moon were recognised in Arabia as well as by the Anglo-Saxons.—(*Ibid.*)

‖ In the authorised version *Gad* is rendered "that troop," and *Meni*, "that number;" but the most learned admit that this is incorrect, and that the words are proper names.

¶ See KITTO, vol. iv. p. 66, end of Note. The name Gad evidently refers, in the first instance, to the war-god, for it signifies to *assault;* but it also signifies "the assembler;" and under both ideas it is applicable to Nimrod, whose general character was that of the sun-god, for he was the first grand warrior; and, under

the changes of the moon that the months are numbered: Psalm civ. 19, "He appointed the *moon* for seasons: the sun knoweth the time of its going down." The name of the "Man of the Moon," or the god who presided over that luminary among the Saxons, was Mané, as given in the "Edda,"* and Mani, in the "Voluspa."† That it was the birth of the "Lord Moon" that was celebrated among our ancestors at Christmas, we have remarkable evidence in the name that is still given in the lowlands of Scotland to the feast on the last day of the year, which seems to be a remnant of the old birth festival for the cakes then made are called Nūr-Cakes, or *Birth*-cakes. That name is Hogmanay.‡ Now, "Hog-Manai" in Chaldee signifies "The feast of the Numberer;" in other words, The festival of Deus Lunus, or of the Man of the Moon. To show the connection between country and country, and the inveterate endurance of old customs, it is

the name of Phoroneus, he was celebrated for having first gathered mankind into social communities. (See *ante*, p. 51.) The name Meni, "the numberer," on the other hand, seems just a synonym for the name of Cush or Chūs, which, while it signifies "to cover" or "hide," signifies also "to count or number." The true proper meaning of the name Cush is, I have no doubt, "The numberer" or "Arithmetician;" for while Nimrod his son, as the "*mighty*" one, was the grand propagator of the Babylonian system of idolatry, by force and power, he, as Hermes (see *ante*, pp. 25, 26), was the real concocter of that system, for he is said to have "taught men the proper mode of approaching the Deity with prayers and sacrifice" (WILKINSON, vol. v. p. 10); and seeing idolatry and astronomy were intimately combined, to enable him to do so with effect, it was indispensable that he should be pre-eminently skilled in the science of *numbers*. Now, Hermes (that is Cush) is said to have "first discovered numbers, and the art of reckoning, geometry, and astronomy, the games of chess and hazard" (*Ibid*. p. 3); and it is in all probability from reference to the meaning of the name of Cush, that some called "NUMBER the father of gods and men" (*Ibid*. vol. iv. p. 196). The name Meni is just the Chaldee form of the Hebrew "Mené," the "numberer" for in Chaldee *i* often takes the place of the final *e*. As we have seen reason to conclude with Gesenius, that Nebo, the great prophetic god of Babylon, was just the same god as Hermes (see *ante*, p. 25), this shows the peculiar emphasis of the first words in the Divine sentence that sealed the doom of Belshazzar, as representing the primeval god—"MENE, MENE, Tekel, Upharsin," which is as much as covertly to say, "The numberer is numbered." As the *cup* was peculiarly the symbol of Cush (see *ante*, p. 49), hence the pouring out of the *drink-offering* to him as the god of the *cup;* and as he was the great Diviner, hence the divinations as to the future year, which Jerome connects with the divinity referred to by Isaiah. Now Hermes, in Egypt as the "numberer," was identified with the moon that numbers the months. He was called "Lord of the moon" (BUNSEN, vol. i. p. 394); and as the "dispenser of time" (WILKINSON, vol. v. p. 11), he held a "palm branch, emblematic of a year" (*Ibid*. p. 2). Thus, then, if Gad was the "sun-divinity," Meni was very naturally regarded as "The Lord Moon."

* MALLET, vol. ii. p. 24. Edin. 1809.

† Supplement to IDA PFEIFFER's *Iceland*, pp. 322, 323.

‡ See JAMIESON's *Scottish Dictionary, sub voce*. Jamieson gives a good many speculations from different authors in regard to the meaning of the term "Hogmanay"; but the following extract is all that it seems necessary to quote:—"Hogmanay, the name appropriated by the vulgar to the last day in the year. Sibb thinks that the term may be .... allied to the Scandinavian Hoeg-tid, a term applied to Christmas, *and various other festivals of the Church*." As the Scandinavian "tid" means "time," and "hoeg-tid" is applied to festivals of the Church in general, the meaning of this expression is evidently "festival-time;" but that shows that "hoeg" has just the meaning which I have attached to Hog—the Chaldee meaning.

worthy of remark, that Jerome, commenting on the very words of Isaiah already quoted, about spreading "a table for Gad," and "pouring out a drink-offering to Meni," observes that it "was the custom so late as his time [in the fourth century], in all cities especially in Egypt and at Alexandria, to set tables, and furnish them with various luxurious articles of food, and with goblets containing a mixture of new wine, *on the last day of the month and the year*, and that the people drew omens from them in respect of the fruitfulness of the year."* The Egyptian year began at a different time from ours; but this is as near as possible (only substituting whisky for wine), the way in which Hogmanay is still observed on the *last* day of the *last* month of our year in Scotland. I do not know that any omens are drawn from anything that takes place at that time, but everybody in the south of Scotland is personally cognisant of the fact, that, on Hogmanay, or the evening before New Year's day, among those who observe old customs, a table is spread, and that while buns and other dainties are provided by those who can afford them, oat cakes and cheese are brought forth among those who never see oat cakes but on this occasion, and that strong drink forms an essential article of the provision.

Even where the sun was the favourite object of worship, as in Babylon itself and elsewhere, at this festival he was worshipped not merely as the orb of day, but as God incarnate.† It was an essential principle of the Babylonian system, that the Sun or Baal was the one only God.‡ When, therefore, Tammuz was worshipped as God incarnate, that implied also that he was an incarnation of the Sun. In the Hindoo mythology, which is admitted to be essentially Babylonian, this comes out very distinctly. There, Surya, or the Sun, is represented as being incarnate, and *born* for the purpose of subduing the enemies of the gods, who, without such a birth, could not have been subdued.§

It was no mere astronomic festival, then, that the Pagans celebrated at the winter solstice. That festival at Rome was called the feast of Saturn, and the mode in which it was celebrated there, showed whence it had been derived. The feast, as regulated by Caligula, lasted five days;|| loose reins were given to *drunkenness*

* HIERONYM, vol. ii. p. 217.

† PLUTARCH, *De Iside*, vol. ii. sect. 52, p. 372; D. MACROB. *Saturn.*, lib. i. cap. 21, p. 71.

‡ MACROBIUS, *Sat.*, lib. i. cap. 23, p. 72, E.

§ See the *Sanscrit Researches* of Col. VANS KENNEDY, p. 438. Col. K., a most distinguished Sanscrit scholar, brings the Brahmins from Babylon (*Ibid.* p. 157). Be it observed, the very name Surya, given to the sun over all India, is connected with this birth. Though the word had originally a different meaning, it was evidently identified by the priests with the Chaldee "Zero," and made to countenance the idea of the *birth* of the "Sun-god." The Pracrit name is still nearer the Scriptural name of the promised "seed." It is "Suro." It has been seen, in a previous Chapter (p. 77), that in Egypt also the *Sun* was represented as *born* of a goddess.

|| Subsequently the number of the days of the Saturnalia was increased to seven. See JUSTUS LIPSIUS, *Opera*, tom. ii., *Saturnal*, lib. i. cap. 4.

and revelry, slaves had a temporary emancipation,* and used all manner of freedoms with their masters.† This was precisely the way in which, according to Berosus, the drunken festival of the month Thebeth, answering to our December, in other words, the festival of Bacchus, was celebrated in Babylon. "It was the custom," says he, "during the five days it lasted, for masters to be in subjection to their servants, and one of them ruled the house, clothed in a purple garment like a king." ‡ This "purple-robed" servant was called "Zoganes," § the "Man of sport and wantonness," and answered exactly to the "Lord of Misrule," that in the dark ages, was chosen in all Popish countries to head the revels of Christmas. The wassailling bowl of Christmas had its precise counterpart in the "Drunken festival" of Babylon; and many of the other observances still kept up among ourselves at Christmas came from the very same quarter. The candles, in some parts of England, lighted on Christmas-eve, and used so long as the festive season lasts, were equally lighted by the Pagans on the eve of the festival of the Babylonian god, to do honour to him: for it was one of the distinguishing peculiarities of his worship to have lighted wax-candles on his altars.‖ The Christmas tree, now so common among us, was equally common in Pagan Rome and Pagan Egypt. In Egypt that tree was the palm-tree; in Rome it was the fir; ¶ the palm-tree denoting the Pagan Messiah, as Baal-Tamar, the fir referring to him as Baal-Berith. The mother of Adonis, the Sun-God and great mediatorial divinity, was mystically said to have been changed into a tree, and when in that state to have brought forth her divine son.** If the mother was a tree, the son must have been recognised as the "Man the branch." And this entirely accounts for the putting of the Yule Log into the fire on Christmas-eve, and the appearance of the Christmas-tree the next morning. As Zero-ashta, "The seed of the woman," which name also signified *Ignigena*, or "born of the fire," he has to enter the fire on "Mother-night," that he may be born the next day out of it, as the "Branch of God," or the Tree that brings all divine gifts to men. But why, it may be asked, does he enter the fire under the symbol of a Log? To understand this, it

* If Saturn, or Kronos, was, as we have seen reason to believe, *Phoroneus*, "The emancipator" (see *ante*, pp. 51, 52), the "temporary emancipation" of the slaves at his festival was exactly in keeping with his supposed character.

† ADAM'S *Roman Antiquities*, "Religion, Saturn." See STATIUS, *Sylv.*, lib. i. c. vi. v. 4, pp. 65, 66. The words of Statius are :—

"Saturnus mihi compede exolutâ
Et multo gravidus mero December
Et ridens jocus, et sales protervi
Adsint."

‡ In ATHENÆUS, xiv. p. 639, C.

§ From "Tzohkh," "to sport and wanton," and "anesh," "man," or perhaps "anes" may only be a termination signifying "the doer," from *an* "to act upon." To the initiated, it had another meaning.

‖ CRABB'S *Mythology*, "Saturn," p. 12.

¶ Berlin Correspondent of *London Times*, December 23, 1853.

** OVID, *Metam.*, lib. x. v. 500-513.

must be remembered that the divine child born at the winter solstice was born as a new incarnation of the great god (after that god had been cut in pieces), on purpose to revenge his death upon his murderers.* Now the great god, cut off in the midst of his power and glory, was symbolised as a huge tree, stripped of all its branches, and cut down almost to the ground.† But the great serpent, the symbol of the life restoring ‡ Æsculapius, twists itself around the dead stock (see Fig. 27),§ and lo, at its side up sprouts a young tree —a tree of an entirely different kind, that is destined never to be cut down by hostile power—even the palm-tree, the well-known symbol of victory. The Christmas-tree, as has been stated, was generally at Rome a different tree, even the fir; but the very same idea as was implied in the palm-tree was implied in the Christmas-fir; for that covertly symbolised the new-born God as Baal-berith, ‖ "Lord of the Covenant," and thus shadowed forth the perpetuity and everlasting nature of his power, now that after having fallen before his enemies, he had risen triumphant over them all. Therefore, the 25th of December, the day that was observed at Rome as the day when the victorious god reappeared on earth, was held at the *Natalis invicti solis*, "The birth-day of the unconquered Sun." ¶ Now the Yule Log is the dead stock of Nimrod, deified as the sun-god, but cut down by his enemies; the Christmas-tree is Nimrod *redivivus*—the slain god come to life again. In the light reflected by the above statement on customs that still linger among us, the origin of which has been lost in the midst of hoar antiquity, let the reader look at the singular practice still kept up in the South on Christmas-eve, of

Fig. 27.

* See *ante*, p. 69.

† "Ail," or "Il," a synonym for Gheber, the "mighty" one (Exodus xv. 15), signifies also a wide-spreading tree, or a stag with branching horns (see PARKHURST, *sub voce*). Therefore, at different times, the great god is symbolised by a stately tree, or by a stag. In the accompanying woodcut, the cutting off of the mighty one is symbolised by the cutting down of the tree. On an Ephesian coin (SMITH, p. 289), he is symbolised by a stag cut asunder; and there a palm-tree is represented as springing-up at the side of the stag, just as here it springs up at the side of the dead trunk. In SANCHUNIATHON, Kronis is expressly called "Ilos"—*i.e.*, "The mighty one." The great god being cut off, the cornucopia at the left of the tree is empty; but the palm-tree repairs all.

‡ The reader will remember that Æsculapius is generally represented with a stick or a stock of a tree at his side, and a serpent twining around it. The figure in the text evidently explains the origin of this representation. For his character as the life-restorer, see PAUSANIAS, lib. ii., *Corinthiaca*, cap. 26; and VIRGIL, *Æneid*, lib. vii. ll. 769-773, pp. 364, 365.

§ From MAURICE'S *Indian Antiquities*, vol. vi. p. 368. 1796.

‖ *Baal-bereth*, which differs only in one letter from *Baal-berith*, "Lord of the Covenant," signifies "Lord of the fir-tree."

¶ GIESELER, p. 42, Note.

kissing under the misletoe bough. That misletoe bough in the Druidic superstition, which, as we have seen, was derived from Babylon, was a representation of the Messiah, "The man the branch." The misletoe was regarded as a divine branch *—a branch that came from heaven, and grew upon a tree that sprung out of the earth. Thus by the engrafting of the celestial branch into the earthly tree, heaven and earth, that sin had severed, were joined together, and thus the misletoe bough became the token of Divine reconciliation to man, the *kiss* being the well-known token of pardon and reconciliation. Whence could such an idea have come? May it not have come from the eighty-fifth Psalm, ver. 10, 11, "Mercy and truth are met together; righteousness and peace have KISSED each other. Truth shall spring out of the earth [in consequence of the coming of the promised Saviour], and righteousness shall look down from heaven"? Certain it is that that Psalm was written soon after the Babylonish captivity; and as multitudes of the Jews, after that event, still remained in Babylon under the guidance of inspired men, such as Daniel, as a part of the Divine word it must have been communicated to them, as well as to their kinsmen in Palestine. Babylon was, at that time, the centre of the civilised world; and thus Paganism, corrupting the Divine symbol as it ever has done, had opportunities of sending forth its debased counterfeit of the truth to all the ends of the earth, through the Mysteries that were affiliated with the great central system in Babylon. Thus the very customs of Christmas still existent cast surprising light at once on the revelations of grace made to all the earth, and the efforts made by Satan and his emissaries to materialise, carnalise, and degrade them.

In many countries the boar was sacrificed to the god, for the injury a boar was fabled to have done him. According to one version of the story of the death of Adonis, or Tammuz, it was, as we have seen, in consequence of a wound from the tusk of a boar that he died.† The Phrygian Attes, the beloved of Cybele, whose story was identified with that of Adonis, was fabled to have perished

* In the Scandinavian story of Balder (see *ante*, p. 57), the misletoe branch is *distinguished* from the lamented god. The Druidic and Scandinavian myths somewhat differed; but yet, even in the Scandinavian story, it is evident that some marvellous power was attributed to the misletoe branch; for it was able to do what nothing else in the compass of creation could accomplish; it slew the divinity on whom the Anglo-Saxons regarded "the empire" of their "heaven" as "depending." Now, all that is necessary to unravel this apparent inconsistency, is just to understand "the branch" that had such power, as a symbolical expression for the *true* Messiah. The Bacchus of the Greeks came evidently to be recognised as the "*seed of the serpent;*" for he is said to have been brought forth by his mother in consequence of intercourse with Jupiter, when that god had appeared in the form of a serpent.—(See DYMOCK'S *Classical Dictionary, sub voce* "Deoïs.") If the character of Balder was the same, the story of his death just amounted to this, that the "seed of the serpent" had been slain by the "seed of the woman." This story, of course, must have originated with his enemies. But the idolaters took up what they could not altogether deny, evidently with the view of explaining it away.

† For the mystic meaning of the story of the boar, see *ante*, p. 65.

in like manner, by the tusk of a boar.* Therefore, Diana, who though commonly represented in popular myths only as the huntress Diana, was in reality the great mother of the gods,† has frequently the boar's head as her accompaniment, in token not of any mere success in the chase, but of her triumph over the grand enemy of the idolatrous system, in which she occupied so conspicuous a place. According to Theocritus, Venus was reconciled to the boar that killed Adonis, because when brought in chains before her, it pleaded so pathetically that it had not killed her husband of malice prepense, but only through accident.‡ But yet, in memory of the deed that the mystic boar had done, many a boar lost its head or was offered in sacrifice to the offended goddess. In Smith, Diana is represented with a boar's head lying beside her, on the top of a heap of stones,§ and in the accompanying woodcut (Fig. 28),‖ in which the Roman Emperor Trajan is represented burning incense to the same goddess,

Fig. 28.

the boar's head forms a very prominent figure. On Christmas-day the Continental Saxons offered a boar in sacrifice to the Sun,¶ to propitiate her** for the loss of her beloved Adonis. In Rome a similar observance had evidently existed; for a boar formed the

* Pausanias, lib. vii., *Achaica*, cap. 7.
† See *ante*, pp. 29, 30.
‡ Theocritus, *Idyll* xxx. v. 21, 45.
§ Smith's *Class. Dict.*, p. 112.
‖ From Kitto's *Illustrated Commentary*, vol. iv. p. 137.
¶ *Times*' Berlin Correspondent, December 23, 1853.
** The reader will remember the Sun was a *goddess*. Mallet says, "They offered the largest hog they could get to Frigga"—*i.e.*, the mother of Balder the lamented one.—(Vol. i. p. 132.) In Egypt swine were offered *once a-year*, at the feast of the Moon, to the Moon, and Bacchus or Osiris; and to them only it was lawful to make such an offering.—Ælian, x. 16, p. 562.

great article at the feast of Saturn, as appears from the following words of Martial :—

"That boar will make you a good Saturnalia."*

Hence the boar's head is still a standing dish in England at the Christmas dinner, when the reason of it is long since forgotten. Yea, the "Christmas goose" and "Yule cakes" were essential articles in the worship of the Babylonian Messiah, as that worship was practised both in Egypt and at Rome (Fig. 29). Wilkinson, in reference to Egypt, shows that "the favourite offering" of Osiris was "a goose,"† and moreover, that the "goose could not be eaten except in the depth of winter."‡ As to Rome, Juvenal says, "that Osiris, if offended, could be pacified only by a large goose and a thin

Fig. 29.

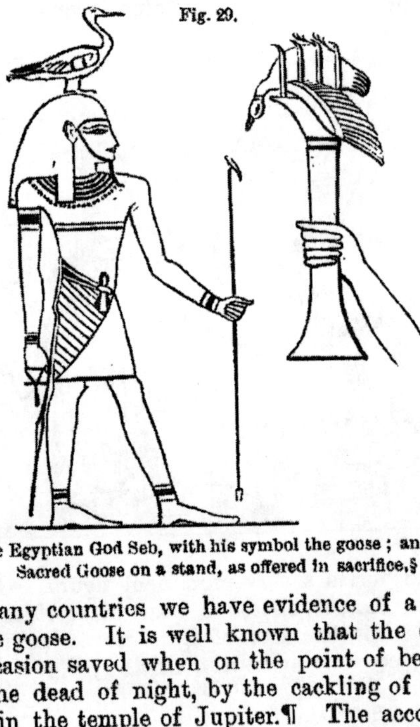

The Egyptian God Seb, with his symbol the goose; and the Sacred Goose on a stand, as offered in sacrifice.§

cake."|| In many countries we have evidence of a sacred character attached to the goose. It is well known that the capitol of Rome was on one occasion saved when on the point of being surprised by the Gauls in the dead of night, by the cackling of the geese sacred to Juno, kept in the temple of Jupiter.¶ The accompanying woodcut (Fig. 30)** proves that the goose in Asia Minor was the symbol of Cupid, just as it was the symbol of Seb in Egypt. In India, the goose occupied a similar position; for in that land we read of the

* Iste tibi faciet bona Saturnalia porcus."—MARTIAL, p. 754.

† WILKINSON, vol. v. p. 353. ‡ *Ibid.* vol. ii. p. 380.

§ From WILKINSON, vol. vi. plate 31; and goose on stand, from the same, vol. v. p. 353.

|| JUVENAL, *Satires*, vi. 539, 540, p. 129.

¶ LIVIUS, *Historia*, lib. v. cap. 47, vol. i. p. 388.

** From BARKER and AINSWORTH'S *Lares and Penates of Cilicia*, chap. iv. p. 220.

sacred "Brahmany goose," or goose sacred to Brahma.* Finally, the monuments of Babylon show † that the goose possessed a like mystic character in Chaldea, and that it was offered in sacrifice there, as well as in Rome or Egypt, for there the priest is seen with the goose in the one hand, and his sacrificing knife in the other.‡ There can be no doubt, then, that the Pagan festival at the winter solstice—in other words, Christmas—was held in honour of the birth of the Babylonian Messiah.

The consideration of the next great festival in the Popish calendar gives the very strongest confirmation to what has now been said. That festival, called Lady-day, is celebrated at Rome on the 25th of March, in alleged commemoration of the miraculous conception of our Lord in the womb of the Virgin, on the day when the angel was sent to announce to her the distinguished honour that was to be bestowed upon her as the mother of the Messiah. But who could tell when this annunciation was made? The Scripture gives no clue

Fig. 30.

at all in regard to the time. But it mattered not. Before our Lord was either conceived or born, that very day now set down in the Popish calendar for the "Annunciation of the Virgin" was observed in *Pagan* Rome in honour of Cybele, the *Mother* of the Babylonian Messiah.§ Now, it is manifest that Lady-day and Christmas-day

* MOOR's *Pantheon*, p. 10.

† KITTO's *Illustrated Commentary*, vol. iv. p. 31.

‡ The symbolic meaning of the offering of the goose is worthy of notice. "The goose," says Wilkinson, "signified in hieroglyphics a *child* or *son*;" and Horapollo says (i. 53, p. 276), "It was chosen to denote a *son*, from its love to its young, being always *ready to give itself up to the chasseur, in order that they might be preserved*; for which reason the Egyptians thought it right to revere this animal."—WILKINSON's *Egyptians*, vol. v. p. 227. Here, then, the true meaning of the symbol is a *son*, who voluntarily gives himself up as a sacrifice for those whom he loves—viz., the Pagan Messiah.

§ AMMIANUS MARCELLINUS, lib. xxiii. cap. 3, p. 355, and MACROB., *Sat.*, lib. i. cap. 3, p. 47, G, H. The fact stated in the paragraph above casts light on a festival held in Egypt, of which no satisfactory account has yet been given. That festival was held in commemoration of "the entrance of Osiris into the moon." Now, Osiris, like Surya in India, was just the Sun.—(PLUTARCH, *De Iside et*

stand in intimate relation to one another. Between the 25th of March and the 25th of December there are exactly nine months. If, then, the false Messiah was conceived in March and born in December, can any one for a moment believe that the conception and birth of the true Messiah can have so exactly synchronised, not only to the month, but to the day? The thing is incredible. Lady-day and Christmas-day, then, are purely Babylonian.

SECTION II.—EASTER.

Then look at Easter. What means the term Easter itself? It is not a Christian name. It bears its Chaldean origin on its very forehead. Easter is nothing else than Astarte, one of the titles of Beltis, the queen of heaven, whose name, as pronounced by the people of Nineveh, was evidently identical with that now in common use in this country. That name, as found by Layard on the Assyrian monuments, is Ishtar.* The worship of Bel and Astarte was very early introduced into Britain, along with the Druids, "the priests of the groves." Some have imagined that the Druidical worship was first introduced by the Phenicians, who, centuries before the Christian era, traded to the tin-mines of Cornwall. But the unequivocal traces of that worship are found in regions of the British islands where the Phenicians never penetrated, and it has everywhere left indelible marks of the strong hold which it must have had on the early British mind. From Bel, the 1st of May is still called Beltane in the Almanac;† and we have customs still lingering at this day among us, which prove how exactly the worship of Bel or Moloch (for both titles belonged to the same god) had been observed even in the northern parts of this island. "The late Lady Baird, of Fern Tower, in Perthshire," says a writer in "Notes and Queries," thoroughly

Osiride, sect. 52, vol. ii. p. 372, D.) The moon, on the other hand, though most frequently the symbol of the god Hermes or Thoth, was also the symbol of the goddess Isis, the queen of heaven. The learned Bunsen seems to dispute this; but his own admissions show that he does so without reason.—(Vol. i. pp. 414, 416.) And Jeremiah xliv. 17 seems decisive on the subject. The entrance of Osiris into the moon, then, was just the *sun's* being *conceived* by Isis, the queen of heaven, that, like the Indian Surya, he might in due time be born as the grand deliverer. (See note, p. 96.) Hence the very name Osiris; for, as Isis is the Greek form of H'isha, "the woman," so Osiris, as read at this day on the Egyptian monuments, is He-siri, "the seed." It is no objection to this to say that Osiris is commonly represented as the husband of Isis; for, as we have seen already (p. 22), Osiris is at once the *son* and *husband* of his mother. Now, this festival took place in Egypt generally in March, just as Lady-day, or the first great festival of Cybele, was held in the same month in Pagan Rome. We have seen that the common title of Cybele at Rome was Domina, or "the Lady" (OVID, *Fasti*, lib. iv. 340), as in Babylon it was Beltis (EUSEB. *Præp. Evang.*, lib. ix. cap. 41, vol. ii. p. 58), and from this, no doubt, comes the name "Lady-day" as it has descended to us.

* LAYARD'S *Nineveh and Babylon*, p. 629.

† See OLIVER & BOYD'S *Edinburgh Almanac*, 1860.

versed in British antiquities,* "told me, that every year, at Beltane (or the 1st of May), a number of men and women assemble at an ancient Druidical circle of stones on her property near Crieff. They light a fire in the centre, each person puts a bit of oat-cake in a shepherd's bonnet; they all sit down, and draw blindfold a piece from the bonnet. One piece has been previously blackened, and whoever gets that piece has to jump through the fire in the centre of the circle, and pay a forfeit. This is, in fact, a part of the ancient worship of Baal, and the person on whom the lot fell was previously burnt as a sacrifice. Now, the passing through the fire represents that, and the payment of the forfeit redeems the victim." If Baal was thus worshipped in Britain, it will not be difficult to believe that his consort Astarté was also adored by our ancestors, and that from Astarté, whose name in Nineveh was Ishtar, the religious solemnities of April, as now practised, are called by the name of Easter—that month, among our Pagan ancestors, having been called Easter-monath. The festival, of which we read in Church history, under the name of Easter, in the third or fourth centuries, was quite a different festival from that now observed in the Romish Church, and *at that time* was not known by any such name as Easter.† It was called Pasch, or the Passover, and though not of Apostolic institution,‡ was very early observed by many professing Christians, in commemoration of the death and resurrection of Christ. That festival agreed originally with the time of the Jewish Passover, when Christ was crucified, a period which, in the days of Tertullian, at the end of the second century, was believed to have been the 23rd of March.§ That festival was not idolatrous, and it was preceded by no Lent. "It ought to be known," said Cassianus, the monk of Marseilles, writing in the fifth century, and contrasting the primitive Church with the Church in his day, "that the observance of the forty days had no existence, so long as the perfection of that primitive Church remained inviolate."‖ Whence, then, came this observance? The forty days' abstinence of Lent was directly borrowed from the worshippers of the Babylonian goddess. Such a Lent of forty days, "in the spring of the year," is still observed by the Yezidis or Pagan Devil-worshippers of Koordistan,¶ who have

* The Right Hon. Lord John Scott.

† The name Easter is peculiar to the British Islands.

‡ Socrates, the ancient ecclesiastical historian, after a lengthened account of the different ways in which Easter was observed in different countries in his time —*i.e.*, the fifth century—sums up in these words:—"Thus much already laid down may seem a sufficient treatise to prove that the celebration of the feast of Easter began everywhere more of custom than by any commandment either of Christ or any Apostle."—(*Hist. Ecclesiast.*, lib. v. cap. 22.) Every one knows that the name "Easter," used in our translation of Acts xii. 4, refers not to any Christian festival, but to the Jewish Passover. This is one of the few places in our version where the translators show an undue bias.

§ Gieseler, vol. i. p. 55, Note. In Gieseler the time is printed "25th of March," but the Latin quotation accompanying it shows that this is a typographical mistake for "23rd."

‖ *Ibid.* vol. ii. p. 42, Note.

¶ Layard's *Nineveh and Babylon*, p. 93.

inherited it from their early masters, the Babylonians. Such a Lent of forty days was held in spring by the Pagan Mexicans, for thus we read in Humboldt,* where he gives account of Mexican observances: "Three days after the vernal equinox . . . . began a solemn fast of *forty days* in honour of the sun." Such a Lent of forty days was observed in Egypt, as may be seen on consulting Wilkinson's *Egyptians.*† This Egyptian Lent of forty days, we are informed by Landseer, in his *Sabean Researches*, was held expressly in commemoration of Adonis or Osiris, the great mediatorial god.‡ At the same time, the rape of Proserpine seems to have been commemorated, and in a similar manner; for Julius Firmicus informs us that, for "forty nights" the "wailing for Proserpine" continued;§ and from Arnobius we learn that the fast which the Pagans observed, called "Castus" or the "sacred" fast, was, by the Christians in his time, believed to have been primarily in imitation of the long fast of Ceres, when for many days she determinedly refused to eat on account of her "excess of sorrow" (*violentia mœroris*),‖ that is, on account of the loss of her daughter Proserpine, when carried away by Pluto, the god of hell. As the stories of Bacchus, or Adonis and Proserpine, though originally distinct, were made to join on and fit in to one another, so that Bacchus was called Liber, and his wife Ariadne, Libera¶ (which was one of the names of Proserpine),** it is highly probable that the forty days' fast of Lent was made in later times to have reference to both. Among the Pagans this Lent seems to have been an indispensable preliminary to the great annual festival in commemoration of the death and resurrection of Tammuz, which was celebrated by alternate weeping and rejoicing, and which, in many countries, was considerably later than the Christian festival, being observed in Palestine and Assyria in June, therefore called the "month of Tammuz;" in Egypt, about the middle of May, and in Britain, some time in April. To conciliate the Pagans to nominal Christianity, Rome, pursuing its usual policy, took measures to get the Christian and Pagan festivals amalgamated, and, by a complicated but skilful adjustment of the calendar, it was found no difficult matter, in general, to get Paganism and Christianity—now far sunk in idolatry—in this as in so many other things, to shake hands. The instrument in accomplishing this amalgamation was the abbot Dionysius the Little,†† to whom also we owe it, as modern chronologers have demonstrated, that the date of the Christian era, or of the birth of Christ Himself, was moved FOUR YEARS from the true time. Whether this was done through ignorance or design may be

* HUMBOLDT's *Mexican Researches*, v. i. p. 404.

† WILKINSON's *Egyptian Antiquities*, vol. i. p. 278.

‡ LANDSEER's *Sabean Researches*, p. 112.

§ *De Errore*, p. 70.

‖ ARNOBIUS, *Adversus Gentes*, lib. v. p. 403. See also what precedes in the same book in regard to Proserpine.

¶ OVID, *Fasti*, lib. iii. l. 512, vol. iii. p. 184.

** SMITH's *Classical Dictionary*, "Liber and Libera," p. 381.

†† About A.D. 525.

matter of question; but there seems to be no doubt of the fact, that the birth of the Lord Jesus was made full four years later than the truth.* This change of the calendar in regard to Easter was attended with momentous consequences. It brought into the Church the grossest corruption and the rankest superstition in connection with the abstinence of Lent. Let any one only read the atrocities that were commemorated during the "sacred fast" or Pagan Lent, as described by Arnobius and Clemens Alexandrinus,† and surely he must blush for the Christianity of those who, with the full knowledge of all these abominations, "went down to Egypt for help" to stir up the languid devotion of the degenerate Church, and who could find no more excellent way to "revive" it, than by borrowing from so polluted a source; the absurdities and abominations connected with which the early Christian writers had held up to scorn. That Christians should ever think of introducing the Pagan abstinence of Lent was a sign of evil; it showed how low they had sunk, and it was also a cause of evil; it inevitably led to deeper degradation. Originally, even in Rome, Lent, with the preceding revelries of the Carnival, was entirely unknown; and even when fasting before the Christian Pasch was held to be necessary, it was by slow steps that, in this respect, it came to conform with the ritual of Paganism. What may have been the period of fasting in the Roman Church before the sitting of the Nicene Council does not very clearly appear, but for a considerable period after that Council, we have distinct evidence that it did not exceed three weeks.‡ The words of Socrates, writing on this very subject, about A.D. 450, are these: "Those who inhabit the princely city of Rome fast together before Easter three weeks, excepting the Saturday and Lord's-day."§ But at last, when the worship of Astarte was rising into the ascendant, steps were taken to get the whole Chaldean Lent of six weeks, or

* GIESELER, vol. i. p. 54. Gieseler adduces as authorities for the statement in the text, G. A. HAMBERGER, *De Epochæ Christianæ ortu et auctore* (in MARTINI *Thesaur. Dissertat.*, T. iii., P. i. p. 241); JO. G. JANI, *Historia Æræ Dionysianæ*, *Viteb.*, 1715, 4, and IDELER'S *Chronologie*, ii. 366 ff. This is the statement also commonly made in all the standard English chronologies.

† CLEMENS ALEXANDRINUS, *Protrepticos*, p. 13.

‡ GIESELER, speaking of the Eastern Church in the second century, in regard to Paschal observances, says: "In it [the Paschal festival in commemoration of the death of Christ] they [the Eastern Christians] eat unleavened bread, probably like the Jews, eight days throughout. . . . . There is no trace of a yearly festival of a *resurrection* among them, for this was kept every Sunday" (*Catholic Church*, sect. 53, p. 178, Note 35). In regard to the Western Church, at a somewhat later period—the age of Constantine—fifteen days seem to have been observed in religious exercises in connection with the Christian Paschal feast, as appears from the following extracts from Bingham, kindly furnished to me by a friend, although the period of *fasting* is not stated. Bingham (*Origin. Eccles.*, vol. ix. p. 94) says: "The solemnities of Pasch [are] the week before and the week after Easter Sunday—one week of the Cross, the other of the resurrection. The ancients speak of the Passion and Resurrection Pasch as a fifteen days' solemnity. Fifteen days was enforced by *law* by the Empire, and commanded to the universal Church. . . . . Scaliger mentions a law of Constantine, ordering two weeks for Easter, and a vacation of all legal processes" (BINGHAM, ix. p. 95).

§ SOCRATES, *Hist. Eccles.*, lib. v. cap. 22, p. 234.

forty days, made imperative on all within the Roman empire of the West. The way was prepared for this by a Council held at Aurelia in the time of Hormisdas, Bishop of Rome, about the year 519, which decreed that Lent should be solemnly kept before Easter.* It was with the view, no doubt, of carrying out this decree that the calendar was, a few years after, readjusted by Dionysius. This decree could not be carried out all at once. About the end of the sixth century, the first decisive attempt was made to enforce the observance of the new calendar. It was in Britain that the first attempt was made in this way;† and here the attempt met with vigorous resistance. The difference, in point of time, betwixt the Christian Pasch, as observed in Britain by the native Christians, and the Pagan Easter enforced by Rome, at the time of its enforcement, was a whole month;‡ and it was only by violence and bloodshed, at last, that the Festival of the Anglo-Saxon or Chaldean goddess came to supersede that which had been held in honour of Christ.

Such is the history of Easter. The popular observances that still attend the period of its celebration amply confirm the testimony of history as to its Babylonian character. The hot cross buns of Good Friday, and the dyed eggs of Pasch or Easter Sunday, figured in the

* DR. MEREDITH HANMER'S *Chronographia*, subjoined to his translation of EUSEBIUS, p. 592. London, 1636.

† GIESELER, vol. i. p. 54.

‡ CUMMIANUS, quoted by Archbishop USSHER, *Sylloge*, p. 34. Those who have been brought up in the observance of Christmas and Easter, and who yet abhor from their hearts all Papal and Pagan idolatry alike, may perhaps feel as if there were something "untoward" in the revelations given above in regard to the origin of these festivals. But a moment's reflection will suffice entirely to banish such a feeling. They will see, that if the account I have given be true, it is of no use to ignore it. A few of the facts stated in these pages are already known to Infidel and Socinian writers of no mean mark, both in this country and on the Continent, and these are using them in such a way as to undermine the faith of the young and uninformed in regard to the very vitals of the Christian faith. Surely, then, it must be of the last consequence, that the truth should be set forth in its own native light, even though it may somewhat run counter to preconceived opinions, especially when that truth, justly considered, tends so much at once to strengthen the rising youth against the seductions of Popery, and to confirm them in the faith once delivered to the Saints. If a heathen could say, "Socrates I love, and Plato I love, but I love truth more," surely a truly Christian mind will not display less magnanimity. Is there not much, even in the aspect of the times, that ought to prompt the earnest inquiry, if the occasion has not arisen, when efforts, and strenuous efforts, should be made to purge out of the National Establishment in the south those observances, and everything else that has flowed in upon it from Babylon's golden cup? There are men of noble minds in the Church of Cranmer, Latimer, and Ridley, who love our Lord Jesus Christ in sincerity, who have felt the power of His blood, and known the comfort of His Spirit. Let them, in their closets, and on their knees, ask the question, at their God and at their own consciences, if they ought not to bestir themselves in right earnest, and labour with all their might till such a consummation be effected. Then, indeed, would England's Church be the grand bulwark of the Reformation—then would her sons speak with her enemies in the gate—then would she appear in the face of all Christendom, "clear as the sun, fair as the moon, and terrible as an army with banners." If, however, nothing effectual shall be done to stay the plague that is spreading in her, the result must be disastrous, not only to herself, but to the whole empire.

Chaldean rites just as they do now. The "buns," known too by that identical name, were used in the worship of the queen of heaven, the goddess Easter, as early as the days of Cecrops, the founder of Athens—that is, 1500 years before the Christian era. "One species of sacred bread," says Bryant,* "which used to be offered to the gods, was of great antiquity, and called Boun." Diogenes Laertius, speaking of this offering being made by Empedocles, describes the chief ingredients of which it was composed, saying, "He offered one of the sacred cakes called Boun, which was made of fine flour and honey."† The prophet Jeremiah takes notice of this kind of offering when he says, "The children gather wood, the fathers kindle the fire, and the women knead their dough, to make cakes to the queen of heaven."‡ The hot cross buns are not now *offered*, but *eaten*, on the festival of Astarte; but this leaves no doubt as to whence they have been derived. The origin of the Pasch eggs is just as clear. The ancient Druids bore an egg, as the sacred emblem of their order.§ In the

Fig. 31.

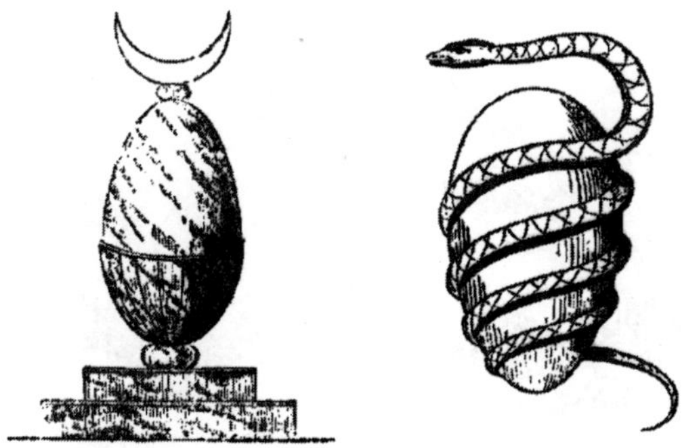

Sacred Egg of Heliopolis; and Typhon's Egg. From BRYANT'S *Mythology*, vol. iii. p. 62.

Dionysiaca, or mysteries of Bacchus, as celebrated in Athens, one part of the nocturnal ceremony consisted in the consecration of an egg.‖ The Hindoo fables celebrate their mundane egg as of a golden colour.¶ The people of Japan make their sacred egg to have been brazen.** In China, at this hour, dyed or painted eggs are used on

* *Mythology*, vol. i. p. 373.

† LAERTIUS, p. 227, B.

‡ Jeremiah vii. 18. It is from the very word here used by the prophet that the word "*bun*" seems to be derived. The Hebrew word, with the points, was pronounced Khavan, which in Greek became sometimes Kapan-os (PHOTIUS, *Lexeon Syllogè*, Part i. p. 130); and, at other times, Khabōn (NEANDER, in KITTO'S *Biblical Cyclopædia*, vol. i. p. 237). The first shows how Khvan, pronounced as one syllable, would pass into the Latin *panis*, "bread," and the second how, in like manner, Khvōn would become Bōn or Bun. It is not to be overlooked that our common English word Loa has passed through a similar process of formation. In Anglo-Saxon it was Hlaf.

§ DAVIES'S *Druids*, p. 208.

‖ *Ibid.* p. 207.

¶ Col. KENNEDY, p. 223.

** COLEMAN, p. 340.

sacred festivals, even as in this country.* In ancient times eggs were used in the religious rites of the Egyptians and the Greeks, and were hung up for mystic purposes in their temples.† (Fig. 31.) From Egypt these sacred eggs can be distinctly traced to the banks of the Euphrates. The classic poets are full of the fable of the mystic egg of the Babylonians; and thus its tale is told by Hyginus, the Egyptian, the learned keeper of the Palatine library at Rome, in the time of Augustus, who was skilled in all the wisdom of his native country: "An egg of wondrous size is said to have fallen from heaven into the river Euphrates. The fishes rolled it to the bank, where the doves having settled upon it, and hatched it, out came Venus, who afterwards was called the Syrian Goddess"‡—that is, Astarte. Hence the egg became one of the symbols of Astarte or Easter; and accordingly, in Cyprus, one of the chosen seats of the worship of Venus, or Astarte, the egg of wondrous size was represented on a grand scale. (See Fig. 32.)§

The occult meaning of this mystic egg of Astarte, in one of its

Fig. 32.

aspects (for it had a twofold significance), had reference to the ark‖ during the time of the flood, in which the whole human race were shut up, as the chick is enclosed in the egg before it is hatched. If any be inclined to ask, how could it ever enter the minds of men to employ such an extraordinary symbol for such a purpose, the answer is, first, The sacred egg of Paganism, as already indicated (p. 108), is well known as the "mundane egg," that is, the egg in which the *world* was shut up. Now the *world* has two distinct meanings—it means either the material earth, or the *inhabitants* of the earth. The latter meaning of the term is seen in Gen. xi. 1, "The whole earth was of one language and of one speech," where the meaning is that the whole people of the world were so. If then the *world* is

* My authority for the above statement is the Rev. James Johnston, of Glasgow, formerly missionary at Amoy, in China.

† WILKINSON, vol. iii. p. 20, and PAUSANIAS, lib. iii., *Laconica*, cap. 16.

‡ HYGINUS, *Fabulæ*, pp. 148, 149.

§ From LANDSEER's *Sabean Researches*, p. 80. London, 1823.

‖ BRYANT, vol. iii. p. 161.

seen shut up in an egg, and floating on the waters, it may not be difficult to believe, however the idea of the *egg* may have come, that the egg thus floating on the wide universal sea might be Noah's family that contained the whole world in its bosom. Then the application of the word *egg* to the ark comes thus:—The Hebrew name for an egg is Baitz, or in the feminine (for there are both genders), Baitza. This, in Chaldee and Phenician, becomes Baith or Baitha,* which in these languages is also the usual way in which the name of a *house* is pronounced.† The *egg* floating on the waters that contained the *world*, was the *house* floating on the waters of the deluge, with the elements of the new world in its bosom. The coming of the egg from heaven evidently refers to the preparation of the ark by express appointment of God; and the same thing seems clearly implied in the Egyptian story of the mundane egg which was said to have come out of the *mouth* of the great god.‡ The doves resting on the egg need no explanation. This, then, was the meaning of the mystic egg in one aspect. As, however, everything that was good or beneficial to mankind was represented in the Chaldean mysteries, as in some way connected with the Babylonian goddess, so the greatest blessing to the human race, which the ark contained in its bosom, was held to be Astarte, who was the great civiliser and benefactor of the world. Though the deified queen, whom Astarte represented, had no actual existence till some centuries after the flood, yet through the doctrine of metempsychosis, which was firmly established in Babylon, it was easy for her worshippers to be made to believe that, in a previous incarnation, she had lived in the Antediluvian world, and passed in safety through the waters of the flood. Now the Romish Church adopted this mystic egg of Astarte, and consecrated it as a symbol of Christ's resurrection. A form of prayer was even appointed to be used in connection with it, Pope Paul V. teaching his superstitious votaries thus to pray at Easter:— "Bless, O Lord, we beseech thee, this thy creature of *eggs*, that it may become a wholesome sustenance unto thy servants, eating it in remembrance of our Lord Jesus Christ, &c."§ Besides the mystic egg, there was also another emblem of Easter, the goddess queen of Babylon, and that was the Rimmon or "pomegranate." With the Rimmon or "pomegranate" in her hand, she is frequently represented in ancient medals, and the house of Rimmon, in which the King of Damascus, the Master of Naaman, the Syrian, worshipped, was in all likelihood a temple of Astarte, where that goddess with the Rimmon was publicly adored. The pomegranate is a fruit that

* In the later Chaldee, the name of an egg is commonly Baiaa, or Baietha in the emphatic form; but Baith is also formed exactly according to rule from Baitz, just as Kaitz, "summer," in Chaldee, becomes Kaith, and many other words.

† The common word "Beth," "house," in the Bible without the points, is "Baith," as may be seen in the name of Bethel, as given in Genesis xxxv. 1, of the Greek Septuagint, where it is "Baith-el."

‡ Bunsen, vol. i. p. 377.

§ *Scottish Guardian*, April, 1844.

is full of seeds; and on that account it has been supposed that it was employed as an emblem of that vessel in which the germs of the new creation were preserved, wherewith the world was to be sown anew with man and with beast, when the desolation of the deluge had passed away. But upon more searching inquiry, it turns out that the Rimmon or "pomegranate" had reference to an entirely different thing. Astarte, or Cybele, was called also Idaia Mater,* and the sacred mount in Phrygia, most famed for the celebration of her mysteries, was named Mount Ida—that is, in Chaldee, the sacred language of these mysteries, the Mount of *Knowledge*. "Idaia Mater," then, signifies "the Mother of *Knowledge*"—in other words, our Mother Eve, who first coveted the "*knowledge* of good and evil," and actually *purchased* it at so dire a price to herself and to all her children. Astarte, as can be abundantly shown, was worshipped not only as an incarnation of the Spirit of God, but also of the mother of mankind.† When, therefore, the mother of the gods, and the mother of *knowledge*, was represented with the fruit of the pomegranate in her extended hand (see Fig. 33), inviting those who ascended the sacred mount to initiation in her mysteries, can there be a doubt what that fruit was intended to signify? Evidently, it must accord with her assumed character; it must be the fruit of the "Tree of Knowledge"—the fruit of that very

Fig. 33.‡

> "Tree, whose mortal taste
> Brought death into the world, and all our woe."

The knowledge to which the votaries of the Idaean goddess were admitted, was precisely of the same kind as that which Eve derived from the eating of the forbidden fruit, the practical knowledge of all that was morally evil and base. Yet to Astarte, in this character, men were taught to look at their grand benefactress, as gaining for them knowledge, and blessings connected with that knowledge, which otherwise they might in vain have sought from Him, who is the Father of lights, from whom cometh down every good and perfect

* DYMOCK's *Classical Dictionary, sub voce.*

† For proof on this subject, see Appendix, Note J.

‡ From BRYANT, vol. iii. p. 276. Bryant gives the title of the above figure as "Juno, *Columba*, and Rhoia;" but from Pausanias we learn that the bird on the sceptre of Hera, or Juno, when she was represented with the pomegranate, was not the Columba or Dove, but the Cuckoo (PAUSAN., lib. ii., *Corinthiaca*, cap. 17); from which it appears, that when Hera or Juno was thus represented, it was not as the incarnation of the Spirit of God, but as the mother of *mankind*, that she was represented. But into the story of the cuckoo I cannot enter here.

gift. Popery inspires the same feeling in regard to the Romish queen of heaven, and leads its devotees to view the sin of Eve in much the same light as that in which Paganism regarded it. In the Canon of the Mass, the most solemn service in the Romish Missal, the following expression occurs, where the sin of our first parent is apostrophised: "*O beata culpa, quæ talem meruisti redemptorem.*"* "Oh blessed fault, which didst procure such a Redeemer!" The idea contained in these words is purely Pagan. They just amount to this: "Thanks be to Eve, to whose sin we are indebted for the glorious Saviour." It is true the idea contained in them is found in the same words in the writings of Augustine; but it is an idea utterly opposed to the spirit of the Gospel, which only makes sin the more exceeding sinful, from the consideration that it needed such a ransom to deliver from its awful curse. Augustine had imbibed many Pagan sentiments, and never got entirely delivered from them. It is wonderful that one so good and so enlightened as Merle D'Aubigné should see no harm in such words!

As Rome cherishes the same feelings as Paganism did, so it has adopted also the very same symbols, so far as it has the opportunity. In this country, and most of the countries of Europe, no pomegranates grow; and yet, even here, the superstition of the Rimmon must, as far as possible, be kept up. Instead of the pomegranate, therefore, the orange is employed; and so the Papists of Scotland join oranges with their eggs at Easter; and so also, when Bishop Gillis of Edinburgh went through the vain-glorious ceremony of washing the feet of twelve ragged Irishmen a few years ago at Easter, he concluded by presenting each of them with two eggs and an orange.

Now, this use of the orange as the representative of the fruit of Eden's "dread probationary tree," be it observed, is no modern invention; it goes back to the distant times of classic antiquity. The gardens of the Hesperides in the West, are admitted by all who have studied the subject, just to have been the counterpart of the paradise of Eden in the East. The description of the sacred gardens, as situated in the Isles of the Atlantic, over against the coast of Africa, shows that their legendary site exactly agrees with the Cape Verd or Canary Isles, or some of that group; and, of course, that the "golden fruit" on the sacred tree, so jealously guarded, was none other than the orange. Now, let the reader mark well: According to the classic Pagan story, there was no serpent in that garden of delight in the "islands of the blest," to TEMPT mankind to violate their duty to their great benefactor, by eating of the sacred tree which he had reserved as the test of their allegiance. No; on the contrary, it was the Serpent, the symbol of the Devil, the Principle of evil, the Enemy of man, that *prohibited* them from eating the precious fruit—that strictly watched it—that would not allow it to be touched. Hercules, one form of the Pagan Messiah—not the primitive, but the Grecian Hercules—pitying man's unhappy

* MERLE D'AUBIGNÉ's *Reformation*, vol. i. p. 179.

state, slew or subdued the serpent, the envious being that grudged mankind the use of that which was so necessary to make them at once perfectly happy and wise, and bestowed upon them what otherwise would have been hopelessly beyond their reach. Here, then, God and the devil are exactly made to change places. Jehovah, who *prohibited* man from eating of the tree of knowledge, is symbolised by the serpent, and held up as an ungenerous and malignant being, while he who emancipated man from Jehovah's yoke, and gave him of the fruit of the forbidden tree—in other words, Satan under the name of Hercules—is celebrated as the good and gracious Deliverer of the human race. What a mystery of iniquity is here! Now all this is wrapped up in the sacred *orange* of Easter.

SECTION III.—THE NATIVITY OF ST. JOHN.

The Feast of the Nativity of St. John is set down in the Papal calendar for the 24th of June, or Midsummer-day. The very same period was equally memorable in the Babylonian calendar as that of one of its most celebrated festivals. It was at Midsummer, or the summer solstice, that the *month* called in Chaldea, Syria, and Phenicia by the name of "Tammuz" began; and on the *first* day—that is, on or about the 24th of June—one of the grand original festivals of Tammuz was celebrated.* For different reasons, in different countries, other periods had been devoted to commemorate the death and reviving of the Babylonian god; but *this*, as may be inferred from the *name* of the month, appears to have been the real time when his festival was primitively observed in the land where idolatry had its birth. And so strong was the hold that this festival, with its peculiar rites, had taken of the minds of men, that, even when other days were devoted to the great events connected with the Babylonian Messiah, as was the case in some parts of our own land, this sacred season could not be allowed to pass without the due observance of some, at least, of its peculiar rites. When the Papacy sent its emissaries over Europe, towards the end of the sixth century, to gather in the Pagans into its fold, this festival was found in high favour in many countries. What was to be done with it? Were they to wage war with it? No. This would have been contrary to the famous advice of Pope Gregory I., that, by all means they should meet the Pagans half-way, and so bring them into the Roman Church.† The Gregorian policy was carefully observed; and so Midsummer-day, that had been hallowed by Paganism to the worship of Tammuz, was incorporated as a sacred Christian festival in the Roman calendar.

But still a question was to be determined, What was to be the *name* of this Pagan festival, when it was baptised, and admitted into the ritual of Roman Christianity? To call it by its old name of Bel

* STANLEY'S *Sabæan Philosophy*, p. 1065. In Egypt the month corresponding to Tammuz—viz., Epep—began June 25.—WILKINSON, vol. iv. p. 14.

† BOWER'S *Lives of the Popes*, vol. ii. p. 523.

or Tammuz, at the early period when it seems to have been adopted, would have been too bold. To call it by the name of Christ was difficult, inasmuch as there was nothing special in His history at that period to commemorate. But the subtlety of the agents of the Mystery of Iniquity was not to be baffled. If the name of Christ could not be conveniently tacked to it, what should hinder its being called by the name of His forerunner, John the Baptist? John the Baptist was born six months before our Lord. When, therefore, the Pagan festival of the winter solstice had once been consecrated as the birthday of the Saviour, it followed, as a matter of course, that if His forerunner was to have a festival at all, his festival must be at this very season; for between the 24th of June and the 25th of December—that is, between the summer and the winter solstice—there are just six months. Now, for the purposes of the Papacy, nothing could be more opportune than this. One of the many sacred names by which Tammuz or Nimrod was called, when he reappeared in the Mysteries, after being slain, was Oannes.* The name of John the Baptist, on the other hand, in the sacred language adopted by the Roman Church, was Joannes. To make the festival of the 24th of June, then, suit Christians and Pagans alike, all that was needful was just to call it the festival of Joannes; and thus the Christians would suppose that they were honouring John the Baptist, while the Pagans were still worshipping their old god Oannes, or Tammuz. Thus, the very period at which the great summer festival of Tammuz was celebrated in ancient Babylon, is at this very hour observed in the Papal Church as the Feast of the Nativity of St. John. And the *fête* of St. John begins exactly as the festal day began in Chaldea. It is well known that, in the East, the day began in the *evening*. So, though the 24th be set down as the nativity, yet it is on St. John's Eve—that is, on the evening of the 23rd—that the festivities and solemnities of that period begin.

Now, if we examine the festivities themselves, we shall see how purely Pagan they are, and how decisively they prove their real descent. The grand distinguishing solemnities of St. John's Eve are the Midsummer fires. These are lighted in France, in Switzerland, in Roman Catholic Ireland, and in some of the Scottish isles of the West, where Popery still lingers. They are kindled throughout all the grounds of the adherents of Rome, and flaming brands are carried about their corn-fields. Thus does Bell, in his *Wayside Pictures*, describe the St. John's fires of Brittany, in France:—"Every *fête* is

* Berosus, *apud* Bunsen's *Egypt*, vol. i. p. 707. To identify Nimrod with Oannes, mentioned by Berosus as appearing out of the sea, it will be remembered that Nimrod has been proved to be Bacchus. Then, for proof that Nimrod or Bacchus, on being overcome by his enemies, was fabled to have taken refuge in the sea (see Chap. IV. Sect. I.), When, therefore, he was represented as reappearing, it was natural that he should reappear in the very character of Oannes as a Fish-god. Now, Jerome calls Dagon, the well-known Fish-god, *Piscem mœroris* (Bryant, vol. iii. p. 179), "the fish of *sorrow*," which goes far to identify that Fish-god with Bacchus, the "Lamented one;" and the identification is complete when Hesychius tells us that some called Bacchus Ichthys, or "The fish" (*sub voce* "Bacchos," p. 179).

marked by distinct features peculiar to itself. That of St. John is perhaps, on the whole, the most striking. Throughout the day the poor children go about begging contributions for lighting the fires of Monsieur St. Jean, and towards evening one fire is gradually followed by two, three, four; then a thousand gleam out from the hill-tops, till the whole country glows under the conflagration. Sometimes the priests light the first fire in the market place; and sometimes it is lighted by an angel, who is made to descend by a mechanical device from the top of the church, with a flambeau in her hand, setting the pile in a blaze, and flying back again. The young people dance with a bewildering activity about the fires; for there is a superstition among them that, if they dance round nine fires before midnight, they will be married in the ensuing year. Seats are placed close to the flaming piles for the dead, whose spirits are supposed to come there for the melancholy pleasure of listening once more to their native songs, and contemplating the lively measures of their youth. Fragments of the torches on those occasions are preserved as spells against thunder and nervous diseases; and the crown of flowers which surmounted the principal fire is in such request as to produce tumultuous jealousy for its possession."* Thus is it in France. Turn now to Ireland. "On that great festival of the Irish peasantry, St. John's Eve," says Charlotte Elizabeth, describing a particular festival which she had witnessed, "it is the custom, at sunset on that evening, to kindle immense fires throughout the country, built, like our bonfires, to a great height, the pile being composed of turf, bogwood, and such other combustible substances as they can gather. The turf yields a steady, substantial body of fire, the bogwood a most brilliant flame, and the effect of these great beacons blazing on every hill, sending up volumes of smoke from every point of the horizon, is very remarkable. Early in the evening the peasants began to assemble, all habited in their best array, glowing with health, every countenance full of that sparkling animation and excess of enjoyment that characterise the enthusiastic people of the land. I had never seen anything resembling it; and was exceedingly delighted with their handsome, intelligent, merry faces; the bold bearing of the men, and the playful but really modest deportment of the maidens; the vivacity of the aged people, and the wild glee of the children. The fire being kindled, a splendid blaze shot up; and for a while they stood contemplating it with faces strangely disfigured by the peculiar light first emitted when the bogwood was thrown on it. After a short pause, the ground was cleared in front of an old blind piper, the very *beau ideal* of energy, drollery, and shrewdness, who, seated on a low chair, with a well-plenished jug within his reach, screwed his pipes to the liveliest tunes, and the endless jig began. But something was to follow that puzzled me not a little. When the fire burned for some hours and got low, an indispensable part of the ceremony commenced. Every one present of the peasantry passed through it, and several children were thrown across the sparkling

* *Wayside Pictures*, p. 225.

embers; while a wooden frame of some eight feet long, with a horse's head fixed to one end, and a large white sheet thrown over it, concealing the wood and the man on whose head it was carried, made its appearance. This was greeted with loud shouts as the 'white horse;' and having been safely carried, by the skill of its bearer, several times through the fire with a bold leap, it pursued the people, who ran screaming in every direction. I asked what the horse was meant for, and was told it represented 'all cattle.' Here," adds the authoress, "was the old Pagan worship of Baal, if not of Moloch too, carried on openly and universally in the heart of a nominally Christian country, and by millions professing the Christian name! I was confounded, for I did not then know that Popery is only a crafty adaptation of Pagan idolatries to its own scheme."*

Such is the festival of St. John's Eve, as celebrated at this day in France and in Popish Ireland. Such is the way in which the votaries of Rome pretend to commemorate the birth of him who came to prepare the way of the Lord, by turning away His ancient people from all their refuges of lies, and shutting them up to the necessity of embracing that kingdom of God that consists not in any mere external thing, but in "righteousness, and peace, and joy in the Holy Ghost." We have seen that the very sight of the rites with which that festival is celebrated, led the authoress just quoted at once to the conclusion that what she saw before her was truly a relic of the Pagan worship of Baal. The history of the festival, and the way in which it is observed, reflect mutual light upon each other. Before Christianity entered the British Isles, the Pagan festival of the 24th of June was celebrated among the Druids by blazing fires in honour of their great divinity, who, as we have already seen, was Baal. "These Midsummer fires and sacrifices," says Toland, in his *Account of the Druids*, "were [intended] to obtain a blessing on the fruits of the earth, now becoming ready for gathering; as those of the first of May, that they might prosperously grow; and those of the last of October were a thanksgiving for finishing the harvest."† Again, speaking of the Druidical fires at Midsummer, he thus proceeds: "To return to our carn-fires, it was customary for the lord of the place, or his son, or some other person of distinction, to take the entrails of the sacrificed animals in his hands, and, walking barefoot over the coals thrice after the flames had ceased, to carry them straight to the Druid, who waited in a whole skin at the altar. If the nobleman escaped harmless, it was reckoned a good omen, welcomed with loud acclamations; but if he received any hurt, it was deemed unlucky both to the community and himself." "Thus, I have seen," adds Toland, "the people running and leaping through the St. John's fires in Ireland; and not only proud of passing unsinged, but, as if it were some kind of *lustration*, thinking themselves in an especial manner blest by the ceremony, of whose original, nevertheless, they were wholly ignorant, in their imperfect imitation of it."‡ We have seen reason already (p. 51) to conclude that Phoroneus, "the

* *Personal Recollections*, pp. 112-115. † TOLAND'S *Druids*, p. 107. ‡ *Ibid.* p. 112.

first of mortals that reigned"—*i.e.*, Nimrod and the Roman goddess Feronia—bore a relation to one another. In connection with the fires of "St. John," that relation is still further established by what has been handed down from antiquity in regard to these two divinities; and, at the same time, the origin of these fires is elucidated. Phoroneus is described in such a way as shows that he was known as having been connected with the origin of fire-worship. Thus does Pausanias refer to him:—"Near this image [the image of Biton] they [the Argives] enkindle a fire, for they do not admit that fire was given by Prometheus, to men, but ascribe the invention of it to Phoroneus."* There must have been something tragic about the death of this fire-inventing Phoroneus, who "first gathered mankind into communities;"† for, after describing the position of his sepulchre, Pausanias adds: "Indeed, even at present they perform funeral obsequies to Phoroneus;"‡ language which shows that his death must have been celebrated in some such way as that of Bacchus. Then the character of the worship of Feronia, as coincident with fire-worship, is evident from the rites practised by the priests at the city lying at the foot of Mount Soracte, called by her name. "The priests," says Bryant, referring both to Pliny and Strabo as his authorities, "with their feet naked, walked over a large quantity of live coals and cinders."§ To this same practice we find Aruns in Virgil referring, when addressing Apollo, the sun-god, who had his shrine at Soracte, where Feronia was worshipped, and who therefore must have been the same as Jupiter Anxur, her contemplar divinity, who was regarded as a "youthful Jupiter," even as Apollo was often called the "young Apollo":—

"O patron of Soracte's high abodes,
Phœbus, the ruling power among the gods,
Whom first we serve; whole woods of unctuous pine
Are felled for thee, and to thy glory shine.
By thee protected, with our naked soles,
Through flames unsinged we march and tread the kindled coals."||

Thus the St. John's fires, over whose cinders old and young are made to pass, are traced up to "the first of mortals that reigned."

It is remarkable, that a festival attended with all the essential rites of the fire-worship of Baal, is found among Pagan nations, in regions most remote from one another, about the very period of the month of Tammuz, when the Babylonian god was anciently celebrated. Among the Turks, the fast of Ramazan, which, says Hurd, begins on the 12th of June, is attended by an illumination of burning lamps.¶ In China,

* PAUSAN., lib. ii., *Corinthiaca*, cap. 19.

† *Ibid.* cap. 15.

‡ *Ibid.* cap. 20.

§ BRYANT, vol. i. p. 237.

|| DRYDEN'S *Virgil, Æneid*, Book xi. ll. 1153-1158. "The young Apollo," when "born to introduce law and order among the Greeks," was said to have made his appearance at Delphi "*exactly in the middle of summer*."—(MÜLLER'S *Dorians*, vol. i. pp. 295, 296.)

¶ HURD'S *Rites and Ceremonies*, p. 346, col. i. The time here given by Hurd would not in itself be decisive as a proof of agreement with the period of the

where the Dragon-boat festival is celebrated in such a way as vividly to recall to those who have witnessed it, the weeping for Adonis, the solemnity begins at Midsummer.* In Peru, during the reign of the Incas, the feast of Raymi, the most magnificent feast of the Peruvians, when the sacred fire every year used to be kindled anew from the sun, by means of a concave mirror of polished metal, took place at the very same period. Regularly as Midsummer came round, there was first, in token of mourning, "for three days, a general fast, and no fire was allowed to be lighted in their dwellings," and then, on the fourth day, the mourning was turned into joy, when the Inca, and his court, followed by the whole population of Cuzco, assembled at early dawn in the great square to greet the rising of the sun. "Eagerly," says Prescott, "they watched the coming of the deity, and no sooner did his first yellow rays strike the turrets and loftiest buildings of the capital, than a shout of gratulation broke forth from the assembled multitude, accompanied by songs of triumph, and the wild melody of barbaric instruments, that swelled louder and louder as his bright orb, rising above the mountain range towards the east, shone in full splendour on his votaries."† Could this alternate mourning and rejoicing, at the very time when the Babylonians mourned and rejoiced over Tammuz, be accidental? As Tammuz was the Sun-divinity incarnate, it is easy to see how such mourning and rejoicing should be connected with the worship of the sun. In Egypt, the festival of the burning lamps, in which many have already been constrained to see the counterpart of the festival of St. John, was avowedly connected with the mourning and rejoicing for Osiris. "At Saïs," says Herodotus,‡ "they show the sepulchre of him whom I do not think it right to mention on this occasion." This is the invariable way in which the historian refers to Osiris, into whose mysteries he had been initiated, when giving accounts of any of the rites of his worship. "It is in the sacred enclosure behind the temple of Minerva, and close to the wall of this temple, whose whole length it occupies.§ They also meet at Saïs, to offer sacrifice during a certain night, when every one lights, in *the open air*, a number of lamps around his house. The lamps consist of small cups filled with salt and oil, having a wick floating in it which burns all night. This festival is called the festival of burning lamps. The Egyptians who are unable to attend also observe the sacrifice, and burn lamps at home, so that not only at Saïs, but *throughout Egypt, the same illumination takes place.* They assign a sacred reason for the festival celebrated on this night, and for the respect they have for it."‖ Wilkinson,¶ in quoting this passage of Herodotus, expressly identifies

original festival of Tammuz; for a friend who has lived for three years in Constantinople informs me that, in consequence of the disagreement between the Turkish and the solar year, the fast of Ramazan ranges in succession through all the different months in the year. The fact of a yearly illumination in connection with religious observances, however, is undoubted.

* See *ante*, p. 57.

† PRESCOTT'S *Conquest of Peru*, vol. i. p. 69.

‡ *Historia*, lib. ii. p. 176.

§ *Ibid.*

‖ HERODOTUS, lib. ii. c. 62, p. 127.

¶ WILKINSON, vol. v. p. 308.

this festival with the lamentation for Osiris, and assures us that "it was considered of the greatest consequence to do honour to the deity by the proper performance of this rite."

Among the Yezidis, or Devil-worshippers of Modern Chaldea, the same festival is celebrated at this day, with rites probably almost the same, so far as circumstances will allow, as thousands of years ago, when in the same regions the worship of Tammuz was in all its glory. Thus graphically does Mr. Layard describe a festival of this kind at which he himself had been present: "As the twilight faded, the Fakirs, or lower orders of priests, dressed in brown garments of coarse cloth, closely fitting to their bodies, and wearing black turbans on their heads, issued from the tomb, each bearing a light in one hand, and a pot of oil, with a bundle of cotton wick in the other. They filled and trimmed lamps placed in niches in the walls of the court-yard and scattered over the buildings on the sides of the valley, and even on isolated rocks, and in the hollow trunks of trees. Innumerable stars appeared to glitter on the black sides of the mountain and in the dark recesses of the forest. As the priests made their way through the crowd to perform their task, men and women passed their right hands through the flame; and after rubbing the right eyebrow with the part which had been *purified by the sacred element*, they devoutly carried it to their lips. Some who bore children in their arms anointed them in like manner, whilst others held out their hands to be touched by those who, less fortunate than themselves, could not reach the flame. . . . . As night advanced, those who had assembled—they must now have amounted to nearly five thousand persons—lighted torches, which they carried with them as they wandered through the forest. The effect was magical: the varied groups could be faintly distinguished through the darkness—men hurrying to and fro—women with their children seated on the house-tops—and crowds gathering round the pedlars, who exposed their wares for sale in the court-yard. Thousands of lights were reflected in the fountains and streams, glimmered amongst the foliage of the trees, and danced in the distance. As I was gazing on this extraordinary scene, the hum of human voices was suddenly hushed, and a strain, solemn and *melancholy*, arose from the valley. It resembled some majestic chant which years before I had listened to in the cathedral of a distant land. Music so *pathetic and so sweet* I never before heard in the East. The voices of men and women were blended in harmony with the soft notes of many flutes. At measured intervals the song was broken by the loud clash of cymbals and tambourines; and those who were within the precincts of the tomb then joined in the melody. . . . . The tambourines, which were struck simultaneously, only interrupted at intervals the song of the priests. As the time quickened they broke in more frequently. The chant gradually gave way to a lively melody, which, increasing in measure, was finally lost in a confusion of sounds. The tambourines were beaten with extraordinary energy—the flutes poured forth a rapid flood of notes—the voices were raised to the highest pitch—the men outside joined in the cry—whilst the women made the rocks resound with the shrill *tahlehl*.

"The musicians, giving way to the excitement, threw their instruments into the air, and strained their limbs into every contortion, until they fell exhausted to the ground. I never heard a more frightful yell than that which rose in the valley. It was midnight. I gazed with wonder upon the extraordinary scene around me. Thus were probably celebrated ages ago the mysterious rites of the Corybantes, when they met in some consecrated grove."* Layard does not state at what period of the year this festival occurred; but his language leaves little doubt that he regarded it as a festival of Bacchus; in other words, of the Babylonian Messiah, whose tragic death, and subsequent restoration to life and glory, formed the corner-stone of ancient Paganism. The festival was avowedly held in honour at once of Sheikh Shems, or the Sun, and of the Sheik Adi, or "Prince of Eternity," around whose *tomb* nevertheless the solemnity took place, just as the lamp festival in Egypt, in honour of the sun-god Osiris, was celebrated in the precincts of the *tomb* of that god at Saïs.

Now, the reader cannot fail to have observed that in this Yezidi festival, men, women, and children were "PURIFIED" by coming in contact with "*the sacred element*" of fire. In the rites of Zoroaster, the great Chaldean god, fire occupied precisely the same place. It was laid down as an essential principle in his system, that "he who approached to fire would receive a light from divinity,"† and that "through divine fire all the stains produced by generation would be purged away."‡ Therefore it was that "children were made to pass through the fire to Moloch" (Jer. xxxii. 35), to purge them from original sin, and through this purgation many a helpless babe became a victim to the bloody divinity. Among the Pagan Romans, this purifying by passing through the fire was equally observed; "for," says Ovid, enforcing the practice, "Fire purifies both the shepherd and the sheep."§ Among the Hindoos, from time immemorial, fire has been worshipped for its purifying efficacy. Thus a worshipper is represented by Colebrooke, according to the sacred books, as addressing the fire: "Salutation to thee [O fire!], who dost seize oblations, to thee who dost shine, to thee who dost scintillate, may thy auspicious flame burn our foes; mayest thou, the PURIFIER, be auspicious unto us."‖ There are some who maintain a "perpetual fire," and perform daily devotions to it, and in "concluding the sacraments of the gods," thus every day present their supplications to it: "Fire, thou dost expiate a sin against the gods; may this oblation be efficacious. Thou dost expiate a sin against man; thou dost expiate a sin against the *manes* [departed spirits];

* LAYARD'S *Nineveh and its Remains*, vol. i. pp. 290-294.

† TAYLOR'S *Jamblichus*, p. 247.

‡ PROCLUS, in *Timaeo*, p. 805.

§ OVID, *Fasti*, lib. iv. 785-794 inclusive.

‖ COLEBROOKE'S "Religious Ceremonies of Hindus," in *Asiatic Researches*, vol. vii. p. 260.

thou dost expiate a sin against my own soul; thou dost expiate repeated sins; thou dost expiate every sin which I have committed, whether wilfully or unintentionally; may this oblation be efficacious."* Among the Druids, also, fire was celebrated as the purifier. Thus, in a Druidic song, we read, "They celebrated the praise of the holy ones in the presence of the *purifying fire*, which was made to ascend on high."† If, indeed, a blessing was expected in Druidical times from lighting the carn-fires, and making either young or old, either human beings or cattle, pass through the fire, it was simply in consequence of the purgation from sin that attached to human beings and all things connected with them, that was believed to be derived from this passing through the fire. It is evident that this very same belief about the "*purifying*" efficacy of fire is held by the Roman Catholics of Ireland, when they are so zealous to pass both themselves and their children through the fires of St. John.‡ Toland testifies that it is as a "*lustration*" that these fires are kindled; and all who have carefully examined the subject must come to the same conclusion.

Now, if Tammuz was, as we have seen, the same as Zoroaster, the god of the ancient "fire-worshippers," and if his festival in Babylon so exactly synchronised with the feast of the Nativity of St. John, what wonder that that feast is still celebrated by the blazing "Baal-fires," and that it presents so faithful a copy of what was condemned by Jehovah of old in His ancient people when they "made their children pass through the fire to Moloch"? But who that knows anything of the Gospel would call such a festival as this a Christian festival? The Popish priests, if they do not openly teach, at least allow their deluded votaries to believe, as firmly as ever ancient fire worshipper did, that material fire can purge away the guilt and stain of sin. How that tends to rivet upon the minds of their benighted vassals one of the most monstrous but profitable fables of their system, will come to be afterwards considered.

The name Oannes could be known only to the initiated as the name of the Pagan Messiah; and at first, some measure of circumspection was necessary in introducing Paganism into the Church. But, as time went on, as the Gospel became obscured, and the darkness became more intense, the same caution was by no means so necessary. Accordingly, we find that, in the dark ages, the Pagan Messiah has not been brought into the Church in a mere clandestine manner. Openly and avowedly under his well-known classic names of Bacchus and Dionysus, has he been canonised, and set up for the worship of the "faithful." Yes, Rome, that professes to be pre-eminently the Bride of Christ, the only Church in which salvation is to be found, has had the unblushing effrontery to give the grand

* COLEBROOKE's "Religious Ceremonies of Hindus" in *Asiatic Researches*, vol. vii. p. 273.

† DAVIES's *Druids*, "Song to the Sun," pp. 369, 370.

‡ "I have seen parents," said the late Lord John Scott in a letter to me, "*force* their children to go through the Baal-fires."

Pagan adversary of the Son of God, UNDER HIS OWN PROPER NAME, a place in her calendar. The reader has only to turn to the Roman calendar, and he will find that this is a literal fact; he will find that October the 7th is set apart to be observed in honour of "St. Bacchus the Martyr." Now, no doubt, Bacchus *was* a "martyr"; he died a violent death; he lost his life for religion; but the religion for which he died was the religion of the fire-worshippers; for he was put to death, as we have seen from Maimonides, for maintaining the worship of the host of heaven. This patron of the heavenly host, and of fire worship (for the two went always hand in hand together), has Rome canonised; for that this "St. Bacchus the Martyr" was the identical Bacchus of the Pagans, the god of drunkenness and debauchery, is evident from the *time* of his festival; for October the 7th follows soon after the end of the vintage. At the end of the vintage in autumn, the old Pagan Romans used to celebrate what was called the "Rustic Festival" of Bacchus;* and about that very time does the Papal festival of "St. Bacchus the Martyr" occur.

As the Chaldean god has been admitted into the Roman calendar under the name of Bacchus, so also is he canonised under his other name of Dionysus.† The Pagans were in the habit of worshipping the same god under different names; and, accordingly, not content with the festival to Bacchus, under the name by which he was most commonly known at Rome, the Romans, no doubt to please the Greeks, celebrated a rustic festival to him, two days afterwards, under the name of Dionysus Eleuthereus, the name by which he was worshipped in Greece.‡ That "rustic" festival was briefly called by the name of Dionysia; or, expressing its object more fully, the name became "Festum Dionysi Eleutherei rusticum"—*i.e.*, the "*rustic* festival of Dionysus Eleuthereus."§ Now, the Papacy in its excess of zeal for saints and saint-worship, has actually split Dionysus Eleuthereus into two, has made two several saints out of the *double name* of one Pagan divinity; and more than that, has made the innocent epithet "Rusticum," which, even among the heathen, had no pretensions to divinity at all, a third; and so it comes to pass that, under date of October the 9th, we read this entry in the calendar: "The festival of St. Dionysius,‖ and of his companions, St. Eleuther and St. Rustic."¶ Now this Dionysius, whom Popery has so marvellously furnished with two companions, is the famed St. Denys, the patron saint of Paris; and a comparison of

* See extracts from *Legend of St. Peter's Chair*, by ANTHONY RICH, Esq., in Dr. BEGG'S admirable *Handbook of Popery*, pp. 114, 115. See also SALVERTÉ, *Essai sur Noms*, tom. ii. p. 54.

† Dionysus, as is well known, is the Latin form of the Greek Dionüsos.

‡ PAUSANIAS, *Attica*, p. 46, and TOOKE'S *Pantheon*, p. 58.

§ BEGG'S *Handbook of Popery*, p. 115.

‖ Though Dionysus was the proper classic name of the *god*, yet in Post-classical, or Low Latin, his name is found Dionysius, just as in the case of the Romish saint.

¶ See Calendar in *Missale Romanum*, Oct. 9th: "Dionysii, Rustici et Eleutherii Mart." and Oct. 7th, "Sergii, Bacchi, Marcelli et Apuleii Mart."

the history of the Popish saint and the Pagan god will cast no little light on the subject. St. Denys, on being beheaded and cast into the Seine, so runs the legend, after floating a space on its waters, to the amazement of the spectators, took up his head in his hand, and so marched away with it to the place of burial. In commemoration of so stupendous a miracle, a hymn was duly chanted for many a century in the Cathedral of St. Denys, at Paris, containing the following verse :—

"Se cadaver mox erexit,
Truncus truncum caput vexit,
Quem ferentem hoc direxit
Angelorum legio."*

At last, even Papists began to be ashamed of such an absurdity being celebrated in the name of religion; and in 1789, "the office of St. Denys" was abolished. Behold, however, the march of events. The world has for some time past been progressing back again to the dark ages. The Romish Breviary, which had been given up in France, has, within the last six years, been reimposed by Papal authority on the Gallican Church, with all its lying legends, and this among the rest of them; the Cathedral of St. Denys is again being rebuilt, and the old worship bids fair to be restored in all its grossness.† Now, how could it ever enter the minds of men to invent so monstrous a fable? The origin of it is not far to seek. The Church of Rome represented her canonised saints, who were said to have suffered martyrdom by the sword, as headless images or statues with the severed head borne in the hand. "I have seen," says Eusèbe Salverté, "in a church of Normandy, St. Clair; St. Mithra, at Arles, in Switzerland, all the soldiers of the Theban legion represented with their heads in their hands. St. Valerius is thus figured at Limoges, on the gates of the cathedral, and other monuments. The grand seal of the canton of Zurich represents, in the same attitude, St. Felix, St. Regula, and St. Exsuperantius. *There* certainly is the origin of the pious fable which is told of these martyrs, such as St. Denys and many others besides."‡ This was the *immediate* origin of the story of the dead saint rising up and marching away with his head in his hand. But it turns out that this very mode of representation was borrowed from Paganism, and borrowed in such a way as identifies the Papal St. Denys of Paris with the Pagan Dionysus, not only of Rome but of Babylon. Dionysus or Bacchus, in one of his transformations, was represented as Capricorn, the "goat-horned fish;" and there is reason to believe

* "The corpse immediately arose; the trunk bore away the dissevered head, guided on its way by a legion of angels" (SALVERTÉ, *Des Sciences Occultes*, Note, p. 48). In Salverté, the first word of the third line of the above Latin verse is "Quo," but as this does not make sense, and is evidently an error, I have corrected it into "Quem."

† The statement in the last clause of the above sentence referred to the position of matters five years ago. Probably by this time the rebuilding of the Cathedral of St. Denys is finished.

‡ SALVERTÉ, *Des Sciences Occultes*, pp. 47, 48.

that it was in this very form that he had the name of Oannes. In this form in India, under the name "Souro," that is evidently "the seed," he is said to have done many marvellous things.* Now, in the Persian Sphere he was not only represented mystically as Capricorn, but also in the human shape; and then exactly as St. Denys is represented by the Papacy. The words of the ancient writer who describes this figure in the Persian Sphere are these: "Capricorn, the third Decan. *The half of the figure without a head, because its head is in its hand.*"† Nimrod had his head cut off; and in commemoration of that fact, which his worshippers so piteously bewailed, his image in the Sphere was so represented. That dissevered head, in some of the versions of his story, was fabled to have done as marvellous things as any that were done by the lifeless trunk of St. Denys. Bryant has proved, in his story of Orpheus, that it is just a slightly-coloured variety of the story of Osiris.‡ As Osiris was cut in pieces in Egypt, so Orpheus was torn in pieces in Thrace. Now, when the mangled limbs of the latter had been strewn about the field, his head, floating on the Hebrus, gave proof of the miraculous character of him that owned it. "Then," says Virgil:—

> "Then, when his head from his fair shoulders torn,
> Washed by the waters, was on Hebrus borne,
> Even then his trembling voice invoked his bride,
> With his last voice, 'Eurydice,' he cried;
> 'Eurydice,' the rocks and river banks replied."§

There is diversity here, but amidst that diversity there is an obvious unity. In both cases, the head dissevered from the lifeless body occupies the foreground of the picture; in both cases, the miracle is in connection with a river. Now, when the festivals

* HUMBOLDT'S *Mexico*, vol. i. pp. 339, 340. For Oannes and Souro, see further in Appendix, Note K.

† Note to SALVERTÉ, *Des Sciences Occultes*, p. 47.

‡ BRYANT, vol. ii. pp. 419-423. The very name Orpheus is just a synonym for Bel, the name of the great Babylonian god, which, while originally given to Cush, became hereditary in the line of his deified descendants. Bel signifies "to mix," as well as "to confound," and "Orv" in Hebrew, which in Chaldee becomes Orph (see PARKHURST'S *Chaldee Grammar in Lexicon*, p. 40), signifies also "to mix." But "Orv," or "Orph," signifies besides "a willow-tree;" and therefore, in exact accordance with the mystic system, we find the symbol of Orpheus among the Greeks to have been a willow-tree. Thus, Pausanias, after referring to a representation of Actæon, says, "If again you look to the lower parts of the picture, you will see after Patroclus, Orpheus sitting on a hill, with a harp in his left hand, and in his right hand the *leaves of a willow-tree*" (PAUSANIAS, lib. x., *Phocica*, cap. 30); and again, a little further on, he says: "He is represented leaning on the trunk of this tree." The willow-leaves in the right hand of Orpheus, and the willow-tree on which he leans, sufficiently show the meaning of his name.

§ *Georgics*, Book iv. vol. i. ll. 759-766, and in original, ll. 523-527. The edition of Dryden, which I commonly quote, has in the first line, "Then with;" but as this does not agree with the construction of the sentence, I have given the passage as it stands in Baxter's London edition of 1807, which is evidently the correct reading.

of "St. Bacchus the Martyr," and of "St. Dionysius and Eleuther," so remarkably agree with the *time* when the festivals of the Pagan god of wine were celebrated, whether by the name of Bacchus, or Dionysus, or Eleuthereus, and when the mode of representing the modern Dionysius and the ancient Dionysus are evidently the very same, while the legends of both so strikingly harmonise, who can doubt the real character of these Romish festivals? They are not Christian. They are Pagan; they are unequivocally Babylonian.

SECTION IV.—THE FEAST OF THE ASSUMPTION.

If what has been already said shows the carnal policy of Rome at the expense of truth, the circumstances attending the festival of the Assumption show the daring wickedness and blasphemy of that Church still more; considering that the doctrine in regard to this festival, so far as the Papacy is concerned, was not established in the dark ages, but three centuries after the Reformation, amid all the boasted light of the nineteenth century. The doctrine on which the festival of the Assumption is founded, is this: that the Virgin Mary saw no corruption, that in body and in soul she was carried up to heaven, and now is invested with all power in heaven and in earth. This doctrine has been unblushingly avowed in the face of the British public, in a recent pastoral of the Popish Archbishop of Dublin. This doctrine has now received the stamp of Papal Infallibility, having been embodied in the late blasphemous decree that proclaims the "Immaculate Conception." Now, it is impossible for the priests of Rome to find one shred of countenance for such a doctrine in Scripture. But, in the Babylonian system, the fable was ready made to their hand. There it was taught that Bacchus went down to hell, rescued his mother from the infernal powers, and carried her with him in triumph to heaven.* This fable spread wherever the Babylonian system spread; and, accordingly, at this day, the Chinese celebrate, as they have done from time immemorial, a festival in honour of a Mother, who

* APOLLODORUS, lib. iii. cap. 5, p. 266. We have seen that the great goddess, who was worshipped in Babylon as "The Mother," was in reality the *wife* of Ninus, the great god, the prototype of Bacchus. In conformity with this, we find a somewhat similar story told of Ariadne, the wife of Bacchus, as is fabled of Semelé his mother. "The garment of Thetis," says Bryant (vol. ii. p. 99), "contained a description of some notable achievements in the first ages; and a particular account of the apotheōsis, of Ariadne, who is described, whatever may be the meaning of it, as *carried by Bacchus to heaven*." A similar story is told of Alcmēné, the mother of the Grecian Hercules, who was quite distinct, as we have seen, from the primitive Hercules, and was just one of the forms of Bacchus, for he was a "great tippler;" and the "Herculean goblets" are proverbial.—(MÜLLER's *Dorians*, vol. i. p. 462.) Now the mother of this Hercules is said to have had a resurrection. "Jupiter" [the father of Hercules], says Müller, "raised Alcmēné from the dead, and conducted her to the islands of the blest, as the wife of Rhadamanthus." (*Ibid*. p. 443.)

by her son was rescued from the power of death and the grave. The festival of the Assumption in the Romish Church is held on the 15th of August. The Chinese festival, founded on a similar legend, and celebrated with lanterns and chandeliers, as shown by Sir J. F. Davis in his able and graphic account of China, is equally celebrated in the month of August.* Now, when the mother of the Pagan Messiah came to be celebrated as having been thus "*Assumed*," then it was that, under the name of the "Dove,"† she was worshipped as the Incarnation of the Spirit of God, with whom she was identified. As such she was regarded as the source of all holiness, and the grand "PURIFIER," and, of course, was known herself as the "Virgin" mother, "PURE AND UNDEFILED."‡ Under the name of Proserpine (with whom, though the Babylonian goddess was originally distinct, she was identified), while celebrated, as the *mother* of the first Bacchus, and known as "Pluto's honoured wife," she is also addressed, in the "Orphic Hymns," as

> "Associate of the seasons, essence bright,
> All-ruling VIRGIN, bearing heavenly light."§

Whoever wrote these hymns, the more they are examined the more does it become evident, when they are compared with the most ancient doctrine of Classic Greece, that their authors understood and thoroughly adhered to the genuine theology of Paganism. To the fact that Proserpine was currently worshipped in Pagan Greece, though well-known to be the wife of Pluto, the god of hell, under the name of "The Holy Virgin," we find Pausanias, while describing the grove Carnasius, thus bearing testimony: "This grove contains a statue of Apollo Carneus, of Mercury carrying a ram, and of Proserpine, the daughter of Ceres, who is called 'The HOLY VIRGIN.'"‖ The purity of this "Holy Virgin" did not consist merely in freedom from actual sin, but she was especially distinguished for her "immaculate conception;" for Proclus says, "She is called Corè, through the purity of her essence, and her UNDEFILED transcendency in her GENERATIONS."¶ Do men stand amazed at the recent decree? There is no real reason to wonder. It was only in following out the Pagan doctrine previously adopted and interwoven with the whole system of Rome to its logical consequences, that that decree has been issued, and that the Madonna of Rome has been formally pronounced at last, in every sense of the term, absolutely "IMMACULATE."

* *China*, vol. i. pp. 354, 355.

† See *ante*, p. 79.

‡ PROCLUS, in TAYLOR'S *Note upon Jamblichus*, p. 136.

§ *Orphic Hymns*, 28th, p. 109. These hymns are thought by some to have been composed by Neo-Platonists after the Christian era, who are said to have corrupted the true doctrine of their predecessors. I doubt this. At anyrate, I allege nothing from them that is not amply borne out by authority of the highest kind.

‖ PAUSAN., lib. iv., *Messenica*, cap. 33, p. 362.

¶ PROCLUS, in additional note to TAYLOR'S *Orphic Hymns*, p. 198.

Now, after all this, is it possible to doubt that the Madonna of Rome, with the child in her arms, and the Madonna of Babylon, are one and the same goddess? It is notorious that the Roman Madonna is worshipped as a goddess, yea, is the supreme object of worship. Will not, then, the Christians of Britain revolt at the idea of longer supporting this monstrous Babylonian Paganism? What Christian constituency could tolerate that its representative should vote away the money of this Protestant nation for the support of such blasphemous idolatry?* Were not the minds of men judicially blinded, they would tremble at the very thought of incurring the guilt that this land, by upholding the corruption and wickedness of Rome, has for years past been contracting. Has not the Word of God, in the most energetic and awful terms, doomed the New Testament Babylon? And has it not equally declared, that those who *share* in Babylon's *sins*, shall *share* in Babylon's *plagues?* (Rev. xviii. 4.)

The guilt of idolatry is by many regarded as comparatively slight and insignificant guilt. But not so does the God of heaven regard it. Which is the commandment of all the ten that is fenced about with the most solemn and awful sanctions? It is the second: "Thou shalt not make unto thee any graven image, or any likeness of anything that is in the heaven above, or that is in the earth beneath, or that is in the water under the earth: thou shalt not bow down thyself to them, nor serve them: *for I the Lord thy God am a jealous God, visiting the iniquity of the fathers upon the children unto the third and fourth generation of them that hate me.*" These words were spoken by God's own lips, they were written by God's own finger on the tables of stone: not for the instruction of the seed of Abraham only, but of all the tribes and generations of mankind. *No other commandment has such a threatening attached to it as this.* Now, if God has threatened to visit the SIN OF IDOLATRY ABOVE ALL OTHER SINS, and if we find the heavy judgments of God pressing upon us as a nation, while this very sin is crying to heaven against us, ought it not to be a matter of earnest inquiry, if among all our other national sins, which are both many and great, this may not form "the very head and front of our offending"? What though we do not ourselves bow down to stocks and stones? Yet if we, making a profession the very opposite, encourage, and foster, and maintain that very idolatry which God has so fearfully threatened with His wrath, our guilt, instead of being the less, is only so much the greater, for it is a sin against the light. Now, the facts are manifest

* It is to be lamented that Christians in general seem to have so little sense either of the gravity of the present crisis of the Church and the world, or of the duty lying upon them as Christ's witnesses, to testify, and that *practically*, against the public sins of the nation. If they would wish to be stimulated to a more vigorous discharge of duty in this respect, let them read an excellent and well-timed little work recently issued from the press, entitled *An Original Interpretation of the Apocalypse*, where the Apocalyptic statements in regard to the character, life, death, and resurrection of the Two Witnesses, are briefly but forcibly handled.

to all men. It is notorious, that in 1845 anti-Christian idolatry was incorporated in the British Constitution, in a way in which for a century and a-half it had not been incorporated before. It is equally notorious, that *ever since*, the nation has been visited with one succession of judgments after another. Ought we then to regard this coincidence as merely accidental? Ought we not rather to see in it the fulfilment of the threatening pronounced by God in the Apocalypse? This is at this moment an intensely practical subject. If our sin in this matter is not nationally recognised, if it is not penitently confessed, if it is not put away from us; if, on the contrary, we go on increasing it, if now for the first time since the Revolution, while so manifestly dependent on the God of battles for the success of our arms, we affront Him to His face by sending idol priests into our camp, then, though we have national fasts, and days of humiliation without number, they cannot be accepted; they may procure us a temporary respite, but we may be certain that "the Lord's anger will not be turned away, His hand will be stretched out still."*

* The above paragraph first appeared in the spring of 1855, when the empire had for months been looking on in amazement at the "horrible and heart-rending" disasters in the Crimea, caused simply by the fact, that official men in that distant region "could not find their hands," and when at last a day of humiliation had been appointed. The reader can judge whether or not the events that have *since* occurred have made the above reasoning out of date. The few years of impunity that have elapsed since the Indian mutiny, with all its horrors, was suppressed, show the long-suffering of God. But if that long-suffering is despised (which it manifestly is, while the guilt is daily increasing), the ultimate issue must just be so much the more terrible.

CHAPTER IV.

DOCTRINE AND DISCIPLINE.

WHEN Linacer, a distinguished physician, but bigoted Romanist, in the reign of Henry VIII., first fell in with the New Testament, after reading it for a while, he tossed it from him with impatience and a great oath, exclaiming, "Either this book is not true, or we are not Christians." He saw at once that the system of Rome and the system of the New Testament were directly opposed to one another; and no one who impartially compares the two systems can come to any other conclusion. In passing from the Bible to the Breviary, it is like passing from light to darkness. While the one breathes glory to God in the highest, peace on earth, and good will to men, the other inculcates all that is dishonouring to the Most High, and ruinous to the moral and spiritual welfare of mankind. How came it that such pernicious doctrines and practices were embraced by the Papacy? Was the Bible so obscure or ambiguous that men naturally fell into the mistake of supposing that it required them to believe and practise the very opposite of what it did? No; the doctrine and discipline of the Papacy were never derived from the Bible. The fact that wherever it has the power, it lays the reading of the Bible under its ban, and either consigns that choicest gift of heavenly love to the flames, or shuts it up under lock and key, proves this of itself. But it can be still more conclusively established. A glance at the main pillars of the Papal system will sufficiently prove that its doctrine and discipline, in all essential respects, have been derived from Babylon. Let the reader now scan the evidence.

SECTION I.—BAPTISMAL REGENERATION.

It is well known that regeneration by baptism is a fundamental article of Rome, yea, that it stands at the very threshold of the Roman system. So important, according to Rome, is baptism for this purpose, that, on the one hand, it is pronounced of "absolute necessity for salvation,"* insomuch that infants dying without it cannot be admitted to glory; and on the other, its virtues are so great, that it is declared in all cases infallibly to "regenerate us by

* Bishop HAY'S *Sincere Christian*, vol. i. p. 363. There are two exceptions to this statement; the case of an infidel converted in a heathen land, where it is impossible to get baptism, and the case of a martyr "baptised," as it is called, "in his own blood;" but in all other cases, whether of young or old, the necessity is "*absolute.*"

a new spiritual birth, making us children of God:"*—it is pronounced to be "the *first* door by which we enter into the fold of Jesus Christ, the *first* means by which we receive the grace of reconciliation with God; therefore the merits of His death are by baptism applied to our souls in so superabundant a manner, as fully to satisfy Divine justice for all demands against us, whether for original or actual sin."† Now, in both respects this doctrine is absolutely anti-Scriptural; in both it is purely Pagan. It is anti-Scriptural, for the Lord Jesus Christ has expressly declared that infants, without the slightest respect to baptism or any external ordinance whatever, *are* capable of admission into all the glory of the heavenly world: "Suffer the little children to come unto Me, and forbid them not; for of *such is the kingdom of heaven.*" John the Baptist, while yet in his mother's womb was so filled with joy at the advent of the Saviour, that, as soon as Mary's salutation sounded in the ears of his own mother, the unborn babe "leaped in the womb for joy." Had that child died at the birth, what could have excluded it from "the inheritance of the saints in light" for which it was so certainly "made meet"? Yet the Roman Catholic Bishop Hay, in defiance of every principle of God's Word, does not hesitate to pen the following: "Question: What becomes of young children who die without baptism? Answer: If a young child were put to death for the sake of Christ, this would be to it the *baptism of blood,* and carry it to heaven; but except in this case, as such infants are incapable of having the desire of baptism, with the other necessary dispositions, if they are not actually baptised with water, THEY CANNOT GO TO HEAVEN."‡ As this doctrine never came from the Bible, whence came it? It came from heathenism. The classic reader cannot fail to remember where, and in what melancholy plight, Æneas, when he visited the infernal regions, found the souls of unhappy infants who had died before receiving, so to speak, "the rites of the Church":—

> "*Before the gates* the cries of babes new-born,
> Whom fate had from their tender mothers torn,
> Assault his ears."§

These wretched babes, to glorify the virtue and efficacy of the mystic rites of Paganism, are excluded from the Elysian Fields, the paradise of the heathen, and have among their nearest associates no better company than that of guilty suicides:—

> "The next in place and punishment are they
> Who prodigally threw their souls away,
> Fools, who, repining at their wretched state,
> And loathing anxious life, suborned their fate."‖

* Bishop HAY'S *Sincere Christian,* vol. i. p. 356.

† *Ibid.* p. 358.

‡ *Ibid.* vol. i. p. 362.

§ *Æneid,* Book vi. ll. 576-578, DRYDEN.—In Original, ll. 427-429.

‖ *Virgil,* Book vi. 586-589, DRYDEN'S Translation. — Original, ll. 434-436. Between the infants and the suicides one other class is interposed,—that is, those

So much for the *lack* of baptism. Then as to its *positive* efficacy when obtained, the Papal doctrine is equally anti-Scriptural. There are professed Protestants who hold the doctrine of Baptismal Regeneration; but the Word of God knows nothing of it. The Scriptural account of baptism is, *not* that it *communicates* the new birth, but that it is the appointed means of signifying and *sealing* that new birth where it already exists. In this respect baptism stands on the very same ground as circumcision. Now, what says God's Word of the efficacy of circumcision? This it says, speaking of Abraham: "He received the sign of circumcision, a seal of the righteousness of the faith which he had, yet being uncircumcised" (Romans iv. 11). Circumcision was not intended to *make* Abraham righteous; he was righteous already before he was circumcised. But it was intended to *declare* him righteous, to give him the more abundant evidence in his own consciousness of his being so. Had Abraham not been righteous *before* his circumcision, his circumcision could not have been a *seal*, could not have given confirmation to that which did not exist. So with baptism, it is "a seal of the righteousness of the faith" which the man "has before he is baptised:" for it is said, "He that believeth, and is baptised, shall be saved" (Mark xvi. 16). Where faith exists, if it be genuine, it is the evidence of a new heart, of a *regenerated nature;* and it is only on the profession of that faith and regeneration in the case of an adult, that he is admitted to baptism. Even in the case of infants, who can make no profession of faith or holiness, the administration of baptism is not for the purpose of regenerating them, or *making* them holy, but of *declaring* them "holy," in the sense of being fit for being consecrated, even in infancy, to the service of Christ, just as the whole nation of Israel, in consequence of their relation to Abraham, according to the flesh, were "holy unto the Lord." If they were not, in that figurative sense, "holy," they would not be fit subjects for baptism, which is the "*seal*" of a holy state. But the Bible pronounces them, in consequence of their descent from believing parents, to be "holy," and that even where only one of the parents is a believer: "The unbelieving husband is sanctified by the wife, and the unbelieving wife is sanctified by the husband; else were your children unclean, but now they are HOLY" (1 Cor. vii. 14). It is in consequence of, and solemnly to declare, that "holiness," with all the responsibilities attaching to it, that they are baptised. That "holiness," however, is very different from the "holiness" of the new nature; and although the very fact of baptism, if Scripturally viewed and duly improved, is, in the hand of the good Spirit of God, an important *means* of making that "holiness" a glorious reality, in the highest sense of the term, yet it does not in all cases necessarily secure their spiritual regeneration. God may, or may not, as He sees fit, give the new heart, before, or at, or after baptism; but manifest it is, that thousands who have been duly baptised are still unregenerate, are

who on earth have been unjustly condemned to die. Hope is held out for these, but no hope is held out for the babes.

still in precisely the same position as Simon Magus, who, after being canonically baptised by Philip, was declared to be "in the gall of bitterness and the bond of iniquity" (Acts viii. 23). The doctrine of Rome, however, is, that all who are canonically baptised, however ignorant, however immoral, if they only give implicit faith to the Church, and surrender their consciences to the priests, are as much regenerated as ever they can be, and that children coming from the waters of baptism are entirely purged from the stain of original sin. Hence we find the Jesuit missionaries in India boasting of making converts by thousands, by the mere fact of baptising them, without the least previous instruction, in the most complete ignorance of the truths of Christianity, on their mere profession of submission to Rome. This doctrine of Baptismal Regeneration also is essentially Babylonian. Some may perhaps stumble at the idea of regeneration at all having been known in the Pagan world; but if they only go to India, they will find at this day, the bigoted Hindoos, who have never opened their ears to Christian instruction, as familiar with the term and the idea as ourselves. The Brahmins make it their distinguishing boast that they are "twice-born"* men, and that, as such, they are sure of eternal happiness. Now, the same was the case in Babylon, and there the new birth was conferred by baptism. In the Chaldean mysteries, *before* any instruction could be received, it was required first of all, that the person to be initiated submit to baptism in token of blind and implicit obedience. We find different ancient authors bearing direct testimony both to the fact of this baptism and the intention of it. "In certain sacred rites of the heathen," says Tertullian, especially referring to the worship of Isis and Mithra, "the mode of initiation is by baptism."† The term "initiation" clearly shows that it was to the Mysteries of these divinities he referred. This baptism was by immersion, and seems to have been rather a rough and formidable process; for we find that he who passed through the purifying waters, and other necessary penances, "*if he survived*, was then admitted to the knowledge of the Mysteries."‡ To face this ordeal required no little courage on the part of those who were initiated. There was this grand inducement, however, to submit, that they who were thus baptised were, as Tertullian assures us, promised, as the consequence, "REGENERATION, and the pardon of all their perjuries."§ Our own Pagan ancestors, the worshippers of Odin, are known to have practised baptismal rites, which, taken in connection with their avowed object in practising them, show that, originally, at least, they must have believed that the natural guilt and corruption of their new-born children could be washed away by sprinkling them with water, or by plunging them, as soon as born, into lakes or rivers.‖ Yea,

* See *Asiatic Researches*, vol. vii. p. 271.

† TERTULL., *De Baptismo*, vol. i. p. 1204.

‡ *Eliae Comment.* in S. GREG. NAZ., Orat. iv.; GREGORII NAZIANZENI *Opera*, p. 245.

§ TERTULL., *De Baptismo*, vol. i. p. 1205.

‖ See MALLET on Anglo-Saxon Baptism, *Antiquities*, vol. i. p. 335.

on the other side of the Atlantic, in Mexico, the same doctrine of baptismal regeneration was found in full vigour among the natives, when Cortez and his warriors landed on their shores.* The ceremony of Mexican baptism, which was beheld with astonishment by the Spanish Roman Catholic missionaries, is thus strikingly described in Prescott's *Conquest of Mexico*:—"When everything necessary for the baptism had been made ready, all the relations of the child were assembled, and the midwife, who was the person that performed the rite of baptism,† was summoned. At early dawn, they met together in the court-yard of the house. When the sun had risen, the midwife, taking the child in her arms, called for a little earthen vessel of water, while those about her placed the ornaments, which had been prepared for baptism, in the midst of the court. To perform the rite of baptism, she placed herself with her face toward the west, and immediately began to go through certain ceremonies. . . . . After this she sprinkled water on the head of the infant, saying, 'O my child, take and receive the water of the Lord of the world, which is our life, which is given for the increasing and renewing of our body. *It is to wash and to purify.* I pray that these heavenly drops may enter into your body, and dwell there; that they may destroy and remove from you all the evil and sin which was given you before the beginning of the world, since all of us are under its power.' . . . . She then washed the body of the child with water, and spoke in this manner: 'Whencesoever thou comest, thou that art hurtful to this child, leave him and depart from him, for he now liveth anew, and is BORN ANEW; now he is purified and cleansed afresh, and our mother Chalchivitlycue [the goddess of water] bringeth him into the world.' Having thus prayed, the midwife took the child in both hands, and, lifting him towards heaven, said, 'O Lord, thou seest here thy creature, whom thou hast sent into the world, this place of sorrow, suffering, and penitence. Grant him, O Lord, thy gifts and inspiration, for thou art the Great God, and with thee is the great goddess.'"‡ Here is the *opus operatum* without mistake. Here is baptismal regeneration and exorcism too,§ as thorough and complete as any Romish priest or lover of Tractarianism could desire. Does the reader ask what evidence is there that Mexico had derived this doctrine from Chaldea? The evidence is decisive. From the researches of Humboldt we find that the Mexicans celebrated Wodan as the founder of their race, just as our own ancestors did. The Wodan

* HUMBOLDT'S *Mexican Researches*, vol. i. p. 185.

† As baptism is absolutely necessary to salvation, Rome also authorises midwives to administer baptism. In Mexico the midwife seems to have been a "priestess."

‡ PRESCOTT'S *Mexico*, vol. iii. pp. 339, 340.

§ In the Romish ceremony of baptism, the first thing the priest does is to exorcise the devil out of the child to be baptised in these words, "*Depart from him thou unclean spirit, and give place to the Holy Ghost the Comforter.*"—(*Sincere Christian*, vol. i. p. 365.) In the New Testament there is not the slightest hint of any such exorcism accompanying Christian baptism. It is purely Pagan.

or Odin of Scandinavia can be proved to be the Adon of Babylon.* The Wodan of Mexico, from the following quotation, will be seen to be the very same: "According to the ancient traditions collected by the Bishop Francis Nunez de la Vega," says Humboldt, "the Wodan of the Chiapanese [of Mexico] was grandson of that illustrious old man, who at the time of the great deluge, in which the greater part of the human race perished, was saved on a raft, together with his family. Wodan co-operated in the construction of the great edifice which had been undertaken by men to reach the skies; the execution of this rash project was interrupted; each family received from that time a different language; and the great spirit Teotl ordered Wodan to go and people the country of Anahuac."† This surely proves to demonstration whence originally came the Mexican mythology and whence also that doctrine of baptismal regeneration which the Mexicans held in common with the Egyptian and Persian worshippers of the Chaldean Queen of Heaven. Prescott, indeed, has cast doubts on the genuineness of this tradition, as being too exactly coincident with the Scriptural history to be easily believed.

Fig. 34.

But the distinguished Humboldt, who had carefully examined the matter, and who had no prejudice to warp him, expresses his full belief in its correctness; and even from Prescott's own interesting pages, it may be proved in every essential particular, with the single exception of the name of Wodan, to which he makes no reference. But, happily, the fact that that name had been borne by some illustrious hero among the supposed ancestors of the Mexican race, is put beyond all doubt by the singular circumstance that the Mexicans had one of their days called Wodansday, exactly as we ourselves have.‡ This, taken in connection with all the circumstances, is a very striking proof, at once of the unity of the human race, and of the wide-spread diffusion of the system that began at Babel.

If the question arise, How came it that the Babylonians themselves adopted such a doctrine as regeneration by baptism, we have light also on that. In the Babylonian Mysteries, the commemoration of the flood, of the ark, and the grand events in the life of Noah, was mingled with the worship of the Queen of Heaven and her son. Noah, as having lived in two worlds, both before the flood and after it, was called "Diphues," or "twice-born,"§ and was represented as a god with two heads looking in opposite directions, the one old, and *the other young* (Fig. 34).|| Though we have seen that the two-

* For proof, see Appendix, Note L.
† HUMBOLDT's *Researches*, vol. i. p. 320.
‡ *Ibid.* vol. i. p. 319.
§ BRYANT, vol. iii. p. 21.
|| *Ibid.* p. 84.

headed Janus in one aspect had reference to Cush and his son, Nimrod, viewed as one god, in a two-fold capacity, as the Supreme, and Father of all the deified "mighty ones," yet, in order to gain for him the very authority and respect essential to constitute him properly the head of the great system of idolatry that the apostates inaugurated, it was necessary to represent him as in some way or other identified with the great patriarch, who was the Father of all, and who had so miraculous a history. Therefore in the legends of Janus, we find mixed up with other things derived from an entirely different source, statements not only in regard to his being the "Father of the world," but also his being "the inventor of ships,"* which plainly have been borrowed from the history of Noah; and therefore, the remarkable way in which he is represented in the figure here presented to the reader may confidently be concluded to have been primarily suggested by the history of the great Diluvian patriarch, whose integrity in his *two-fold* life is so particularly referred to in the Scripture, where it is said (Gen. vi. 9), "Noah was a just man, and perfect in his *generations*," that is, in his life before the flood, and in his life after it. The whole mythology of Greece and Rome, as well as Asia, is full of the history and deeds of Noah, which it is impossible to misunderstand. In India, the god Vishnu, "the Preserver," who is celebrated as having miraculously preserved one righteous family at the time when the world was drowned, not only has the story of Noah wrought up with his legend, but is called by his very name. Vishnu is just the Sanscrit form of the Chaldee "Ish-nuh," "the man Noah," or the "Man of *rest*."† In the case of Indra, the "king of the gods," and *god of rain*, which is evidently only another form of the same god, the name is found in the precise form of Ishnu. Now, the very legend of Vishnu, that pretends to make him no mere creature, but the supreme and "eternal god," shows that this interpretation of the name is no mere unfounded imagination. Thus is he celebrated in the "Matsya Puran:" "The sun, the wind, the ether, all things incorporeal, were absorbed into his Divine essence; and the universe being consumed, the eternal and omnipotent god, having assumed an ancient form, REPOSED mysteriously upon the surface of that (universal) *ocean*. But no one is capable of knowing whether that being was then visible or invisible, or what the holy name of that person was, or what the cause of his mysterious SLUMBER. Nor can any one tell how long he thus REPOSED until he conceived the thought of acting; for no one saw him, no one approached him, and none can penetrate the mystery of his real essence."‡ In conformity with this ancient legend, Vishnu is still represented as *sleeping* four months every year. Now, connect this story with the name of

* BRYANT, vol. iii. p. 78.

† We find the very word *Ish*, "man," used in Sanscrit with the digamma prefixed: Thus *Visham*pati, "Lord of *men*."—See WILSON's *India 3000 Years Ago*, p. 59.

‡ Col. KENNEDY's *Hindoo Mythology*, p. 228.

Noah, the man of "Rest," and with his personal history during the period of the flood, when the world was destroyed, when for forty days and forty nights all was chaos, when neither sun nor moon nor twinkling star appeared, when sea and sky were mingled, and all was one wide universal "ocean," on the bosom of which the patriarch floated, when there was no human being to "approach" him but those who were with him in the ark, and "the mystery of his real essence is penetrated" at once, "the holy name of that person" is ascertained, and "his mysterious slumber" fully accounted for. Now, wherever Noah is celebrated, whether by the name of Saturn,* "the hidden one,"—for that name was applied to him as well as to Nimrod, on account of his having been "hidden" in the ark, in the "day of the Lord's fierce anger,"—or "Oannes," or "Janus," the "Man of the Sea," he is generally described in such a way as shows that he was looked upon as Diphues, "twice-born," or "regenerate." The "twice-born" Brahmins, who are all so many gods upon earth, by the very title they take to themselves, show that the god whom they *represent*, and to whose prerogatives they lay claim, had been known as the "twice-born" god. The connection of "regeneration" with the history of Noah, comes out with special evidence in the accounts handed down to us of the Mysteries as celebrated in Egypt. The most learned explorers of Egyptian antiquities, including Sir Gardiner Wilkinson, admit that the story of Noah was mixed up with the story of Osiris.† The ship of Isis, and the *coffin* of Osiris, floating on the waters, point distinctly to that remarkable event. There were different periods, in different places in Egypt, when the fate of Osiris was lamented; and at one time there was more special reference to the personal history of "the mighty hunter before the Lord," and at another to the awful catastrophe through which Noah passed. In the great and solemn festival called "The Disappearance of Osiris," it is evident that it is Noah himself who was then supposed to have been lost. The time when Osiris was "shut up in his coffin," and when that coffin was set afloat on the waters, as stated by Plutarch, agrees exactly with the period when Noah entered the ark. That time was "the 17th day of the month Athyr, when the overflowing of the Nile had ceased, when the nights were growing long and the days decreasing."‡ The month Athyr was the second month after the autumnal equinox, at which time the civil year of the Jews and the patriarchs began. According to this statement, then, Osiris was "shut up in his coffin" on the 17th day of the second month of the patriarchal year. Compare this with the Scriptural account of Noah's entering into the ark, and it will be seen how remarkably they agree (Gen. vii. 11), "In the six hundredth year of Noah's life, in the SECOND MONTH, in the SEVENTEENTH DAY of the month, were all the fountains of the great deep broken up; in the self-same day entered Noah into

* BRYANT, vol. iii. p. 75.
† WILKINSON, vol. iv. p. 340.
‡ PLUTARCH, *De Iside et Osiride*, vol. ii. p. 336, D.

the ark." The period, too, that Osiris (otherwise Adonis) was believed to have been shut up in his coffin, was precisely the same as Noah was confined in the ark, a whole year.* Now, the statements of Plutarch demonstrate that, as Osiris at this festival was looked upon as *dead* and *buried* when put into his ark or coffin, and committed to the deep, so, when at length he came out of it again, that new state was regarded as a state of "new life," or "REGENERATION."† There seems every reason to believe that by the ark and the flood God actually gave to the patriarchal saints, and especially to righteous Noah, a vivid typical representation of the power of the blood and Spirit of Christ, at once in saving from wrath, and cleansing from all sin—a representation which was a most cheering "*seal*" and confirmation to the faith of those who really believed. To this Peter seems distinctly to allude, when he says, speaking of this very event, "The like figure whereunto baptism doth also now save us." Whatever primitive truth the Chaldean priests held, they utterly perverted and corrupted it. They willingly overlooked the fact, that it was "the righteousness of the faith" which Noah "had *before*" the flood, that carried him safely through the avenging waters of that dread catastrophe, and ushered him, as it were, from the womb of the ark, by a new birth, into a new world, when on the ark resting on Mount Ararat, he was released from his long confinement. They led their votaries to believe that, if they only passed through the baptismal waters, and the penances therewith connected, that of itself would make them like the second father of mankind, "Diphueis," "twice-born," or "regenerate," would entitle them to all the privileges of "righteous" Noah, and give them that "new birth" (*palingenesia*)‡ which their consciences told them they so much needed. The Papacy acts on precisely the same principle; and from this very source has its doctrine of baptismal regeneration been derived, about which so much has been written and so many controversies been waged. Let men contend as they may, this, and this only, will be found to be the real origin of the anti-Scriptural dogma.§

The reader has seen already how faithfully Rome has copied the Pagan exorcism in connection with baptism. All the other peculi-

* APOLLODORUS, lib. iii. c. xiv., vol. i. pp. 356, 357. THEOCRITUS, *Idyll* xv., ll. 103, 104, pp. 190, 191, *Poetae Graeci Minores*. Theocritus is speaking of Adonis as delivered by Venus from Acheron, or the infernal regions, after being there for a year; but as the scene is laid in Egypt, it is evident that it is Osiris he refers to, as he was the Adonis of the Egyptians.

† PLUTARCH, *De Iside et Osiride*, vol. ii. pp. 356-367, *et quæ sequuntur*. It was in the character of Pthah-Sokari-Osiris that he was represented as having been thus "*buried*" in the waters. (See WILKINSON, vol. iv. p. 256.) In his own character, simply as Osiris, he had another burial altogether.

‡ PLUTARCH, *De Iside*, vol. ii. p. 364, F.

§ There have been considerable speculations about the meaning of the name Shinar, as applied to the region of which Babylon was the capital. Do not the facts above stated cast light on it? What so likely a derivation of this name as to derive it from "shené," "to repeat," and "naar," "childhood." The land of "Shinar," then, according to this view, is just the land of the "Regenerator."

arities attending the Romish baptism, such as the use of salt, spittle, chrism, or anointing with oil, and marking the forehead with the sign of the cross, are equally Pagan. Some of the continental advocates of Rome have *admitted* that some of these at least have not been derived from *Scripture*. Thus Jodocus Tiletanus of Louvaine, defending the doctrine of "Unwritten Tradition," does not hesitate to say, "We are not satisfied with that which the apostles or the Gospel do declare, but we say that, as well before as after, there are divers matters of importance and weight accepted and received out of a doctrine which is nowhere set forth in writing. For we do blesse the water wherewith we baptize, and the oyle wherewith we annoynt; yea, and besides that, him that is christened. And (I pray you) out of what Scripture have we learned the same? Have we it not of a secret and unwritten ordinance? And further, what Scripture hath taught us to grease with oyle? Yea, I pray you, whence cometh it, that we do dype the childe three times in the water? Doth it not come out of this hidden and undisclosed doctrine, which our forefathers have received closely without any curiosity, and do observe it still."* This learned divine of Louvaine, of course, maintains that "the hidden and undisclosed doctrine" of which he speaks, was the "unwritten word" handed down through the channel of infallibility, from the Apostles of Christ to his own time. But, after what we have already seen, the reader will probably entertain a different opinion of the source from which the hidden and undisclosed doctrine must have come. And, indeed, Father Newman himself admits, in regard to "holy water" (that is, water impregnated with "salt," and consecrated), and many other things that were, as he says, "the very instruments and appendages of demon-worship"—that they were all of "Pagan" origin, and "sanctified by adoption into the Church."† What plea, then, what palliation can he offer, for so extraordinary an adoption? Why, this: that the Church had "confidence in the power of Christianity to resist the infection of evil," and to transmute them to "an evangelical use." What right had the Church to entertain any such "confidence"? What fellowship could light have with darkness? what concord between Christ and Belial? Let the history of the Church bear testimony to the vanity, yea, impiety of such a hope. Let the progress of our inquiries shed light upon the same. At the present stage, there is only one of the concomitant rites of baptism to which I will refer—viz., the use of "*spittle*" in that ordinance; and an examination of the very words of the Roman ritual, in applying it, will prove that its use in baptism *must* have come from the Mysteries. The following is the account of its application, as given by Bishop Hay ‡:—"The priest recites another exorcism, and at the end of it touches the ear and nostrils of the person to be baptised with a little *spittle*, saying, 'Ephpheta, that is,

* *Review of Epistle of* Dr. Gentianus Harvet, p. 19 B, and 20 A.

† Newman's *Development*, pp. 359, 360.

‡ *Sincere Christian*, vol. i. p. 368.

Be thou opened into an *odour of sweetness;* but be thou put to flight, O Devil, for the judgment of God will be at hand.'" Now, surely the reader will at once ask, what possible, what conceivable connection can there be between *spittle* and an "*odour of sweetness*"? If the secret doctrine of the Chaldean mysteries be set side by side with this statement, it will be seen that, absurd and nonsensical as this collocation of terms may appear, it was not at random that "*spittle*" and an "*odour of sweetness*" were brought together. We have seen already how thoroughly Paganism was acquainted with the attributes and work of the promised Messiah, though all that acquaintance with these grand themes was used for the purpose of corrupting the minds of mankind, and keeping them in spiritual bondage. We have now to see that, as they were well aware of the *existence* of the Holy Spirit, so, intellectually, they were just as well acquainted with His *work*, though their knowledge on that subject was equally debased and degraded. Servius, in his comments upon Virgil's *First Georgic*, after quoting the well-known expression, "Mystica vannus Iacchi," "the mystic fan of Bacchus," says that that "mystic fan" symbolised the "purifying of souls."* Now, how could the fan be a symbol of the purification of souls? The answer is, The fan is an instrument for producing "wind"; † and in Chaldee, as has been already observed, it is one and the same word which signifies "wind" and the "Holy Spirit." There can be no doubt, that, from the very beginning, the "wind" was one of the Divine patriarchal emblems by which the power of the Holy Ghost was shadowed forth, even as our Lord Jesus Christ said to Nicodemus, "The *wind* bloweth where it listeth, and thou hearest the sound thereof, but canst not tell whence it cometh or whither it goeth: so is every one that is born of the *Spirit.*" Hence, when Bacchus was represented with "the mystic fan," that was to declare him to be the mighty One with whom was "the residue of the Spirit." Hence came the idea of purifying the soul by means of the wind, according to the description of Virgil, who represents the stain and pollution of sin as being removed in this very way:—

> "For this are various penances enjoined,
> And some are hung to bleach upon the WIND." ‡

Hence the priests of Jupiter (who was originally just another form of Bacchus), (see Fig. 35), were called Flamens,§—that is Breathers, or bestowers of the Holy Ghost, by breathing upon their votaries.

Now, in the Mysteries, the "*spittle*" was just another symbol for the same thing. In Egypt, through which the Babylonian system

* SERVIUS, vol. ii. p. 197.

† There is an evident allusion to the "mystic fan" of the Babylonian god, in the doom of Babylon, as pronounced by Jeremiah li. 1, 2:—"Thus saith the Lord, Behold, I will raise up against Babylon, and against them that dwell in the midst of them that rise up against me, a destroying *wind;* and will send unto Babylon *fanners*, that shall *fan* her, and shall empty her land."

‡ DRYDEN'S *Virgil, Æneid*, Book vi. vs. 1002, 1003; in Original, ll. 739-741.

§ From "Flo," "I breathe."

passed to Western Europe, the name of the "Pure or Purifying Spirit" was "Rekh."* But "Rekh" also signified "spittle";† so that to anoint the nose and ears of the initiated with "spittle," according to the mystic system, was held to be anointing them with the "Purifying Spirit." That Rome in adopting the "spittle" actually copied from some Chaldean ritual in which "spittle" was the appointed emblem of the "Spirit," is plain from the account which she gives in her own recognised formularies of the reason for anointing the *ears* with it. The reason for anointing the *ears* with "*spittle*," says Bishop Hay, is because "by the grace of baptism, the ears of our soul are opened to hear the Word of God, and the *inspirations of His Holy Spirit*."‡ But what, it may be asked, has the "spittle" to do with the "odour of sweetness"? I answer, The very word "Rekh," which signified the "Holy Spirit," and was

Fig. 35.§

visibly represented by the "spittle," was intimately connected with "Rikh," which signifies a "fragrant smell," or "odour of sweetness." Thus, a knowledge of the Mysteries gives sense and a consistent meaning to the cabalistic saying addressed by the Papal baptiser to the person about to be baptised, when the "spittle" is daubed on his nose and ears, which otherwise would have no mean-

* Bunsen, vol. i. pp. 475, 476, and 516.

† Parkhurst's *Lexicon*, p. 703.

‡ *Sincere Christian*, vol. i. p. 368.

§ From *Pompeii*, vol. ii. p. 150. The reader will remember that Jupiter, as "Jupiter puer," or "Jupiter the boy," was worshipped in the arms of the goddess Fortuna, just as Ninus was worshipped in the arms of the Babylonian goddess, or Horus in the arms of Isis (see *ante*, p. 20). Moreover, Cupid, who, as being the son of Jupiter, is Vejovis—that is, as we learn from Ovid (vol. iii. p. 179, in a Note to *Fasti*, lib. iii. v. 408), "Young Jupiter"—is represented, as in the above cut, not only with the wine-cup of Bacchus, but with the Ivy garland, the distinctive mark of the same divinity, around him.

ing at all—"*Ephpheta, Be thou opened into an odour of sweetness.*" While this was the primitive truth concealed under the "spittle," yet the whole spirit of Paganism was so opposed to the spirituality of the patriarchal religion, and indeed intended to make it void, and to draw men utterly away from it, while pretending to do homage to it, that among the multitude in general the magic use of "spittle" became the symbol of the grossest superstition. Theocritus shows with what debasing rites it was mixed up in Sicily and Greece;* and Persius thus holds up to scorn the people of Rome in his day for their reliance on it to avert the influence of the "evil eye":—

"Our superstitions with our life begin;
The obscene old grandam, or the next of kin,
The new-born infant from the cradle takes,
And first of spittle a lustration makes;
Then in the spawl her middle finger dips,
Anoints the temples, forehead, and the lips,
Pretending force of magic to prevent (*urentes oculos*)
By virtue of her nasty excrement."—DRYDEN.†

While thus far we have seen how the Papal baptism is just a reproduction of the Chaldean, there is still one other point to be noticed, which makes the demonstration complete. That point is contained in the following tremendous curse fulminated against a man who committed the unpardonable offence of leaving the Church of Rome, and published grave and weighty reasons for so doing: "May the Father, who creates man, curse him! May the Son, who suffered for us, curse him! May the *Holy Ghost who suffered for us in baptism*, curse him!"‡ I do not stop to show how absolutely and utterly opposed such a curse as this is to the whole spirit of the Gospel. But what I call the reader's attention to is the astounding statement that "the Holy Ghost suffered for us in baptism." Where in the whole compass of Scripture could warrant be found for such an assertion as this, or anything that could even suggest it? But let the reader revert to the Babylonian account of the personality of the Holy Ghost, and the amount of blasphemy contained in this language will be apparent. According to the Chaldean doctrine, Semiramis, the wife of Ninus or Nimrod, when exalted to divinity under the name of the Queen of Heaven, came, as we have seen, to be worshipped as Juno, the "Dove"—in other words, the Holy Spirit incarnate. Now, when her husband, for his blasphemous rebellion against the majesty of heaven, was cut off, for a season it was a time of tribulation also for her. The fragments of ancient history that have come down to us give an account of her trepidation and flight, to save herself from her adversaries. In the fables of the mythology, this flight was mystically represented in accordance with what was attributed

* THEOCRITUS, *Idyll* ii. 61, pp. 126, 127.

† PERSIUS, *Satires*, ii. v. 30-34, in Original.

‡ The above is from the curse fulminated against Mr. Hogan of Philadelphia for leaving the Church of Rome, and assigning his reasons for doing so.—See BEGG'S *Handbook*, p. 152. See also BLAKENEY'S *Popery in its Social Aspect*, p. 126, and Note to p. 127.

to her husband. The bards of Greece represented Bacchus, when overcome by his enemies, as taking refuge in the depths of the ocean (see Fig. 36).* Thus, Homer :—

"In a mad mood, while Bacchus blindly raged,
Lycurgus drove his trembling bands, confused,
O'er the vast plains of Nusa. They in haste
Threw down their sacred implements, and fled
In fearful dissipation. Bacchus saw
Rout upon rout, and, lost in wild dismay,
Plunged in the deep. Here Thetis in her arms
Received him shuddering at the dire event."†

In Egypt, as we have seen, Osiris, as identified with Noah, was represented, when overcome by his grand enemy Typhon, or the "Evil One," as passing through the waters. The poets represented Semiramis as sharing in his distress, and likewise seeking safety in the same way. We have seen already, that, under the name of Astarte, she was said to have come forth from the wondrous egg that was found floating on the waters of the Euphrates. Now Manilius

Fig. 36.

tells, in his *Astronomical Poetics*, what induced her to take refuge in these waters. "Venus plunged into the Babylonian waters," says

* From BRYANT: the first figure, the divided bull, is from vol. iii. p. 303; the second, the god on the fish, from the same vol., p. 338. The former is just another symbol of that which is represented by the mighty tree cut asunder (see *ante*, p. 97). That tree represented Nimrod as "the mighty one" cut in pieces in the midst of his power and glory. The divided man-bull symbolises him as "The *prince*" who was cut asunder in like manner; for the name for a prince and a bull is the same. The fish over the bull shows the transformation he was supposed to undergo when put to death by his enemies; for the story of Melikerta, who with his mother Ino was cast into the sea, and became a sea-god (SMITH'S *Class. Dict.*, "Athamas," p. 100), is just another version of the story of Bacchus, for Ino was the foster-mother of Bacchus (SMITH, *sub voce* "Dionysus," p. 226). Now, on the second medal, Melikerta, under the name of Palæmon, is represented as triumphantly riding on the fish, his sorrows being over, with the fir-tree, or pine, the emblem of Baal-berith, "Lord of the Covenant," as his ensign. This, compared with what is stated in p. 98 about the Christmas-tree, shows how the fir-tree came to be recognised in the character of the Christmas-tree. The name Ghelas above the divided bull and the fish is equivocal. As applied to the fish, it comes from Ghela, "to exult or leap for joy," as dolphins and such like fishes do in the sea; as applied to the divinity, whom both the fish and the bull represented, it comes from Ghela, "to reveal," for that divinity was the "revealer of goodness and truth" (WILKINSON, vol. iv. p. 189).

† HOMER, *Iliad*, vi. v. 133. See BRYANT'S *Mythology*, vol. iv. p. 57.

he, "to shun the fury of the snake-footed Typhon."* When Venus Urania, or Dioné,† the "Heavenly Dove," plunged in deep distress into these waters of Babylon, be it observed what, according to the Chaldean doctrine, this amounted to. It was neither more nor less than saying that the Holy Ghost incarnate in deep tribulation entered these waters, and that on purpose that these waters might be fit, not only by the temporary abode of the Messiah in the midst of them, but by the Spirit's efficacy thus imparted to them, for giving new life and regeneration, *by baptism*, to the worshippers of the Chaldean Madonna. We have evidence that the purifying virtue of the waters, which in Pagan esteem had such efficacy in cleansing from guilt and regenerating the soul, was derived in part from the passing of the Mediatorial god, the sun-god and god of fire, through these waters during his humiliation and sojourn in the midst of them; and that the Papacy at this day retains the very custom which had sprung up from that persuasion. So far as heathenism is concerned, the following extracts from Potter and Athenæus speak distinctly enough: "Every person," says the former, "who came to the solemn sacrifices [of the Greeks] was purified by water. To which end, at the entrance of the temples there was commonly placed a vessel full of holy water."‡ How did this water get its holiness? This water "was consecrated," says Athenæus, "by putting into it a BURNING TORCH taken from the altar."§ The *burning torch* was the express symbol of the god of fire; and by the light of this torch, so indispensable for consecrating "the holy water," we may easily see whence came one great part of the purifying virtue of "the water of the loud resounding sea," which was held to be so efficacious in purging away the guilt and stain of sin,||—even from the sun-god having taken refuge in its waters. Now this very same method is used in the Romish Church for consecrating the water for baptism. The unsuspicious testimony of Bishop Hay leaves no doubt on this point: "It" [the water kept in the baptismal font], says he, "is blessed on the eve of Pentecost, because it is the Holy Ghost who gives to the waters of baptism the power and efficacy of sanctifying our souls, and because the baptism of Christ is 'with the Holy Ghost, and with fire' (Matt. iii. 11). In blessing the waters, a LIGHTED TORCH is put into the font."¶ Here, then, it is manifest that the baptismal *regenerating* water of Rome is consecrated just as the *regenerating* and *purifying* water of the Pagans was. Of what avail is it for Bishop Hay to say, with the view of sanctifying superstition and "making apostacy plausible," that this is done "to represent the fire of Divine love, which is communicated to the soul by baptism, and the light of good example, which all who are baptised ought to give."** This is the fair face put on the matter; but the fact still remains

* MANILIUS, *Astronom.*, lib. iv. v. 579-582, p. 146.

† OVID, *Fasti*, lib. ii. 461.

‡ POTTER'S *Antiquities*, vol. i. p. 195. § ATHENÆUS, lib. ix. p. 409.

|| "All human ills," says Euripides, in a well-known passage, "are washed away by the sea."

¶ HAY'S *Sincere Christian*, vol. i. p. 365. ** *Ibid.*

that while the Romish doctrine in regard to baptism is purely Pagan, in the ceremonies connected with the Papal baptism one of the essential rites of the ancient fire-worship is still practised at this day, just as it was practised by the worshippers of Bacchus, the Babylonian Messiah. As Rome keeps up the remembrance of the fire-god passing through the waters and giving virtue to them, so when it speaks of the "Holy Ghost *suffering* for us in baptism," it in like manner commemorates the part which Paganism assigned to the Babylonian goddess when she plunged into the waters. The sorrows of Nimrod, or Bacchus, when in the waters were meritorious sorrows. The sorrows of his wife, in whom the Holy Ghost miraculously dwelt, were the same. The sorrows of the Madonna, then, when in these waters, fleeing from Typhon's rage, were the birth-throes by which children were born to God. And thus, even in the Far West, Chalchivitlycue, the Mexican "goddess of the waters," and "mother" of all the regenerate, was represented as purging the new-born infant from original sin, and "bringing it anew into the world."* Now, the Holy Ghost was idolatrously worshipped in Babylon under the form of a "Dove." Under the same form, and with equal idolatry, the Holy Ghost is worshipped in Rome. When, therefore, we read, in opposition to every Scripture principle, that "*the Holy Ghost suffered for us in baptism,*" surely it must now be manifest who is that Holy Ghost that is really intended. It is no other than Semiramis, the very incarnation of lust and all uncleanness.

SECTION II.—JUSTIFICATION BY WORKS.

The worshippers of Nimrod and his queen were looked upon as regenerated and purged from sin by baptism, which baptism received its virtue from the sufferings of these two great Babylonian divinities. But yet in regard to justification, the Chaldean doctrine was that it was by works and merits of men themselves that they must be justified and accepted of God. The following remarks of Christie in his observations appended to Ouvaroff's *Eleusinian Mysteries*, show that such was the case: "Mr. Ouvaroff has suggested that one of the great objects of the Mysteries was the presenting to fallen man the means of his return to God. These means were the cathartic virtues—(*i.e.*, the virtues by which sin is removed), by the exercise of which a corporeal life was to be vanquished. Accordingly the Mysteries were termed Teletæ, 'perfections,' because they were supposed to induce a perfectness of life. Those who were purified by them were styled Teloumenoi and Tetelesmenoi, that is, 'brought . . . . to perfection,' which depended on the exertions of the individual."† In the *Metamorphosis* of Apuleius, who was himself initiated in the mysteries of Isis, we find this same doctrine of human merits distinctly set forth. Thus the goddess is herself represented

* See *ante*, p. 133.

† Ouvaroff, pp. 183, 184.

as addressing the hero of his tale: "If you shall be found to DESERVE the protection of my divinity by *sedulous obedience, religious devotion,* and *inviolable chastity,* you shall be sensible that it is possible for me, and me alone, to extend your life beyond the limits that have been appointed to it by your destiny."* When the same individual has received a proof of the supposed favour of the divinity, thus do the onlookers express their congratulations: "Happy, by Hercules! and thrice blessed he to have MERITED, by the innocence and probity of his past life, such special patronage of heaven."† Thus was it in life. At death, also, the grand passport into the unseen world was still through the merits of men themselves, although the name of Osiris was, as we shall by-and-by see, given to those who departed in the faith. "When the bodies of persons of distinction" [in Egypt], says Wilkinson, quoting Porphyry, "were embalmed, they took out the intestines and put them into a vessel, over which (after some other rites had been performed for the dead) one of the embalmers pronounced an invocation to the sun in behalf of the deceased." The formula, according to Euphantus, who translated it from the original into Greek, was as follows: "O thou Sun, our sovereign lord! and all ye Deities who have given life to man, receive me, and grant me an abode with the eternal gods. During the whole course of my life I have scrupulously worshipped the gods my father taught me to adore; I have ever honoured my parents, who begat this body; I have killed no one; I have not defrauded any, nor have I done any injury to any man."‡ Thus the merits, the obedience, or the innocence of man was the grand plea. The doctrine of Rome in regard to the vital article of a sinner's justification is the very same. Of course this of itself would prove little in regard to the affiliation of the two systems, the Babylonian and the Roman; for, from the days of Cain downward, the doctrine of human merit and of self-justification has everywhere been indigenous in the heart of depraved humanity. But, what is worthy of notice in regard to this subject is, that in the two systems, it was *symbolised* in precisely the same way. In the Papal legends it is taught that St. Michael the Archangel has committed to him the balance of God's justice,§ and that in the two opposite scales of that balance the merits and the demerits of the departed are put that they may be fairly weighed, the one over against the other, and that as the scale turns to the favourable or unfavourable side they may be justified or condemned as the case may be. Now, the Chaldean doctrine of justification, as we get light on it from the monuments of Egypt, is symbolised in precisely the same way, except that in the land of Ham the scales of justice were committed to the charge of the god Anubis instead of St. Michael the Archangel, and that the good deeds and the bad seem to have been weighed separately, and a distinct record made of each, so that when both were summed up and

* *Metam.*, cap. 11. † *Ibid.*

‡ WILKINSON, vol. v. pp. 463, 464.

§ *Review of Epistle of* DR. GENTIANUS HARVET, Book II. chap. xiv.

the balance struck, judgment was pronounced accordingly. Wilkinson states that Anubis and his scales are often represented; and that in some cases there is some difference in the *details*. But it is evident from his statements, that the *principle* in all is the same. The following is the account which he gives of one of these judgment scenes, previous to the admission of the dead to Paradise: "Cerberus is present as the guardian of the gates, near which the scales of justice are erected; and Anubis, the director of the weight, having placed a vase representing the good actions of the deceased in one scale, and the figure or emblem of truth in the other, proceeds to ascertain his claims for admission. If, on being weighed, he is found wanting, he is rejected, and Osiris, the judge of the dead, inclining his sceptre in token of condemnation, pronounces judgment upon him, and condemns his soul to return to earth under the form of a pig or some unclean animal. . . . . But if, when the SUM of his deeds are recorded by Thoth [who stands by to mark the results of the different weighings of Anubis], his virtues so far PREDOMINATE as to entitle him to admission to the mansions of the blessed, Horus, taking in his hand the tablet of Thoth, introduces him to the presence of Osiris, who, in his palace, attended by Isis and Nepthys, sits on his throne in the midst of the waters, from which rises the lotus, bearing upon its expanded flowers the four Genii of Amenti."* The same mode of symbolising the justification by works had evidently been in use in Babylon itself; and, therefore, there was great force in the Divine handwriting on the wall, when the doom of Belshazzar went forth: "*Tekel*," "Thou art weighed in the balances, and art found wanting." In the Parsee system, which has largely borrowed from Chaldea, the principle of weighing the good deeds over against the bad deeds is fully developed. "For three days after dissolution," says Vaux, in his *Nineveh and Persepolis*, giving an account of Parsee doctrines in regard to the dead, "the soul is supposed to flit round its tenement of clay, in hopes of reunion; on the fourth, the Angel Seroch appears, and conducts it to the bridge of Chinevad. On this structure, which they assert connects heaven and earth, sits the Angel of Justice, to weigh the actions of mortals; when the good deeds prevail, the soul is met on the bridge by a dazzling figure, which says, 'I am thy good angel; I was pure originally, but thy good deeds have rendered me purer;' and passing his hand over the neck of the blessed soul, leads it to Paradise. If iniquities preponderate, the soul is met by a hideous spectre, which howls out, 'I am thy evil genius; I was impure from the first, but thy misdeeds have made me fouler; through thee we shall remain miserable until the resurrection;' the sinning soul is then dragged away to hell, where Ahriman sits to taunt it with its crimes."† Such is the doctrine of Parseeism. The same is the case in China, where Bishop Hurd, giving an account of the Chinese descriptions of the infernal regions, and of the figures that refer to them, says, "One of them always

* WILKINSON'S *Egyptians*, vol. v. p. 447.

† VAUX, p. 113.

represents a sinner in a pair of scales, with his iniquities in the one, and his good works in another." "We meet with several such representations," he adds, "in the Grecian mythology."* Thus does Sir J. F. Davis describe the operation of the principle in China: "In a work of some note on morals, called *Merits and Demerits Examined*, a man is directed to keep a debtor and creditor account with himself of the acts of each day, and at the end of the year to wind it up. If the balance is in his favour, it serves as the foundation of a stock of merits for the ensuing year: and if against him, it must be liquidated by future good deeds. Various lists and comparative tables are given of both good and bad actions in the several relations of life; and benevolence is strongly inculcated in regard first to man, and, secondly, to the brute creation. To cause another's death is reckoned at one hundred on the side of demerit; while a single act of charitable relief counts as one on the other side. . . . . To save a person's life ranks in the above work as an exact set-off to the opposite act of taking it away; and it is said that this deed of merit will prolong a person's life twelve years."†

While such a mode of justification is, on the one hand, in the very nature of the case, utterly demoralising, there never could by means of it, on the other, be in the bosom of any man whose conscience is aroused, any solid feeling of comfort, or assurance as to his prospects in the eternal world. Who could ever tell, however good he might suppose himself to be, whether the "*sum* of his good actions" would or would not counterbalance the amount of sins and transgressions that his conscience might charge against him. How very different the Scriptural, the god-like plan of "justification by faith," and "faith alone, without the deeds of the law," absolutely irrespective of human merits, simply and solely through the "righteousness of Christ, that is unto all and upon all them that believe," that delivers at once and for ever "from all condemnation," those who accept of the offered Saviour, and by faith are vitally united to Him. It is not the will of our Father in heaven, that His children in this world should be ever in doubt and darkness as to the vital point of their eternal salvation. Even a genuine saint, no doubt, may for a season, if need be, be in heaviness through manifold temptations, but such is not the natural, the normal state of a healthful Christian, of one who knows the fulness and the freeness of the blessings of the Gospel of peace. God has laid the most solid foundation for all His people to say, with John, "We have KNOWN and believed the love which God hath to us" (1 John iv. 16); or with Paul, "I am PERSUADED that neither death, nor life, nor angels, nor principalities, nor powers, nor things present, nor things to come, nor height, nor depth, nor any other creature, shall be able to separate us from the love of God, which is in Christ Jesus" (Rom. viii. 38, 39). But this no man can ever say, who "goes about to establish his own righteousness" (Rom. x. 3), who seeks, in any shape, to be justified

* HURD's *Rites and Ceremonies*, p. 64, col. i.

† DAVIS's *China*, vol. ii. chap. "Religion—Buddhism."

by works. Such assurance, such comfort, can come only from a simple and believing reliance on the free, unmerited grace of God, given *in and along* with Christ, the unspeakable gift of the Father's love. It was this that made Luther's spirit to be, as he himself declared, "as free as a flower of the field,"* when, single and alone, he went up to the Diet of Worms, to confront all the prelates and potentates there convened to condemn the doctrine which he held. It was this that in every age made the martyrs go with such sublime heroism not only to prison but to death. It is this that emancipates the soul, restores the true dignity of humanity, and cuts up by the roots all the imposing pretensions of priestcraft. It is this only that can produce a life of loving, filial, hearty obedience to the law and commandments of God; and that, when nature fails, and when the king of terrors is at hand, can enable poor, guilty sons of men, with the deepest sense of unworthiness, yet to say, "O death, where is thy sting? O grave, where is thy victory? Thanks be unto God, who giveth us the victory through Jesus Christ our Lord" (1 Cor. xv. 55, 57).

Now, to all such confidence in God, such assurance of salvation, spiritual despotism in every age, both Pagan and Papal, has ever shown itself unfriendly. Its grand object has always been to keep the souls of its votaries away from direct and immediate intercourse with a living and merciful Saviour, and consequently from assurance of His favour, to inspire a sense of the necessity of human mediation, and so to establish itself on the ruins of the hopes and the happiness of the world. Considering the pretensions which the Papacy makes to absolute infallibility, and the supernatural powers which it attributes to the functions of its priests, in regard to regeneration and the forgiveness of sins, it might have been supposed, as a matter of course, that all its adherents would have been encouraged to rejoice in the continual assurance of their personal salvation. But the very contrary is the fact. After all its boastings and high pretensions, perpetual doubt on the subject of a man's salvation, to his life's end, is inculcated as a duty; it being peremptorily decreed as an article of faith by the Council of Trent, "That *no man* can know with infallible assurance of faith that he HAS OBTAINED the grace of God."† This very decree of Rome, while directly opposed to the Word of God, stamps its own lofty claims with the brand of imposture; for if no man who has been regenerated by its baptism, and who has received its absolution from sin, can yet have any *certain assurance* after all that "the grace of God" has been *conferred* upon him, what can be the worth of its *opus operatum?* Yet, in seeking to keep its devotees in continual doubt and uncertainty as to their final state, it is "wise after its generation.' In the Pagan system, it was the priest alone who could at all pretend

* Quoted in *Edinburgh Review*, January, 1839.

† *Concilium Tridentinum. Decretum de Justificatione.* Articulus ix. See SARPI'S *History of Council of Trent*, translated into French by COURAYER, vol. i. p. 353.

to anticipate the operation of the scales of Anubis; and, in the confessional, there was from time to time, after a sort, a mimic rehearsal of the dread weighing that was to take place at last in the judgment scene before the tribunal of Osiris. There the priest sat in judgment on the good deeds and bad deeds of his penitents; and, as his power and influence were founded to a large extent on the mere principle of slavish dread, he took care that the scale should generally turn in the wrong direction, that they might be more subservient to his will in casting in a due amount of good works into the opposite scale. As he was the grand judge of what these works should be, it was his interest to appoint what should be most for the selfish aggrandisement of himself, or the glory of his order; and yet so to weigh and counterweigh merits and demerits, that there should always be left a large balance to be settled, not only by the man himself, but by his heirs. If any man had been allowed to believe himself beforehand absolutely sure of glory, the priests might have been in danger of being robbed of their dues after death—an issue by all means to be guarded against. Now, the priests of Rome have in every respect copied after the priests of Anubis, the god of the scales. In the confessional, when they have an object to gain, they make the sins and transgressions good weight; and then, when they have a man of influence, or power, or wealth to deal with, they will not give him the slightest hope till round sums of money, or the founding of an abbey, or some other object on which they have set their heart, be cast into the other scale. In the famous letter of Père La Chaise, the confessor of Louis XIV. of France, giving an account of the method which he adopted to gain the consent of that licentious monarch to the revocation of the Edict of Nantes, by which such cruelties were inflicted on his innocent Huguenot subjects, we see how the fear of the scales of St. Michael operated in bringing about the desired result :—"Many a time since," says the accomplished Jesuit, referring to an atrocious sin of which the king had been guilty, "many a time since, when I have had him at confession, *I have shook hell about his ears, and made him sigh, fear and tremble,* before I would give him absolution. By this I saw that he had still an inclination to me, and was willing to be under my government; so I set the baseness of the action before him by telling the whole story, and how wicked it was, and that it could not be forgiven till he had done some good action to BALANCE that, and expiate the crime. Whereupon he at last asked me what he must do. I told him that he must root out all heretics from his kingdom."* This was the "good action" to be cast into the *scale* of St. Michael the Archangel, to "BALANCE" his crime. The king, wicked as he was—sore against his will—consented; the "good action" was cast in, the "heretics" were extirpated; and the king was absolved. But yet the absolution was not such but that, when he went the way of all the earth, there was still much to be cast in before the scales could be fairly adjusted. Thus Paganism

* MACGAVIN's *Protestant*, p. 841, col. 2.

and Popery alike "make merchandise of the souls of men" (Rev. xviii. 13). Thus the one with the scales of Anubis, the other with the scales of St. Michael, exactly answer to the Divine description of Ephraim in his apostacy: "Ephraim is a merchant, the balances of deceit are in his hand" (Hosea xii. 7). The Anubis of the Egyptians was precisely the same as the Mercury of the Greeks *—the "god of thieves." St. Michael, in the hands of Rome, answers exactly to the same character. By means of him and his scales, and their doctrine of human merits, they have made what they call the house of God to be nothing else than a "den of thieves." To rob men of their money is bad, but infinitely worse to cheat them also of their souls.

Into the scales of Anubis, the ancient Pagans, by way of securing their justification, were required to put not merely good deeds, properly so called, but deeds of austerity and self-mortification inflicted on their own persons, for averting the wrath of the gods.† The scales of St. Michael inflexibly required to be balanced in the very same way. The priests of Rome teach that when sin is forgiven, the *punishment* is not thereby fully taken away. However perfect may be the pardon that God, through the priests, may bestow, yet punishment, greater or less, still remains behind, which men must endure, and that to "*satisfy the justice of God.*" Again and again has it been shown that man cannot do anything to satisfy the justice of God, that to that justice he is hopelessly indebted, that he "has" absolutely "nothing to pay;" and more than that, that there is no need that he should attempt to pay one farthing; for that, in behalf of all who believe, Christ has finished transgression, made an end of sin, and made *all* the satisfaction to the broken law that that law could possibly demand. Still Rome insists that every man must be punished for his own sins, and that God *cannot be satisfied* ‡ without groans and sighs, lacerations of the flesh, tortures of the body, and penances without number, on the part of the offender, however broken in heart, however contrite that offender may be. Now, looking simply at the Scripture, this perverse demand for self-torture on the part of those for whom Christ has made a *complete* and *perfect* atonement, might seem exceedingly strange; but, looking at the real character of the god whom the Papacy has set up for the worship of its deluded devotees, there is nothing in the least strange about it. That god is Moloch, the god of barbarity and blood. Moloch signifies "king"; and Nimrod was the first after the flood that violated the patriarchal system, and set up as "king" over his fellows. At first he was worshipped as the "revealer of goodness and truth," but by-and-by his worship was made to correspond with

* WILKINSON'S *Egyptians*, vol. v. pp. 9, 10.

† See what is said about Penance in connection with the Confessional, in Chapter I. pp. 9, 10.

‡ Bishop HAY'S *Sincere Christian*, vol. i. p. 270. The words of Bishop Hay are: "But He absolutely demands that, by penitential works, we PUNISH ourselves for our shocking ingratitude, and satisfy the Divine justice for the abuse of His mercy." The established modes of "punishment," as is well known, are just such as are described in the text.

his dark and forbidding countenance and complexion. The name Moloch originally suggested nothing of cruelty or terror; but now the well-known rites associated with that name have made it for ages a synonym for all that is most revolting to the heart of humanity, and amply justify the description of Milton:—

"First Moloch, horrid king, besmeared with blood
Of human sacrifice, and parents' tears,
Though, for the noise of drums and timbrels loud,
Their children's cries unheard, that passed through fire
To his grim idol."*

In almost every land the bloody worship prevailed; "horrid cruelty," hand in hand with abject superstition, filled not only "the dark places of the earth," but also regions that boasted of their enlightenment. Greece, Rome, Egypt, Phenicia, Assyria, and our own land under the savage Druids, at one period or other in their history, worshipped the same god and in the same way. Human victims were his most acceptable offerings; human groans and wailings were the sweetest music in his ears; human tortures were believed to delight his heart. His image bore, as the symbol of "majesty," a *whip*,† and with whips his worshippers, at some of his festivals, were required unmercifully to scourge themselves. "After the ceremonies of sacrifice," says Herodotus, speaking of the feast of Isis at Busiris, "the whole assembly, to the amount of many thousands, scourge themselves; but in whose honour they do this I am not at liberty to disclose."‡ This reserve Herodotus generally uses, out of respect to his oath as an initiated man; but subsequent researches leave no doubt as to the god "in whose honour" the scourgings took place. In Pagan Rome the worshippers of Isis observed the same practice in honour of Osiris. In Greece, Apollo, the Delian god, who was identical with Osiris,§ was propitiated

* *Paradise Lost*, Book I. ll. 392-396, p. 13.

† See woodcut of Osiris, p. 44.

‡ HERODOTUS, lib. ii. cap. 61, p. 127, A.

§ We have seen already (p. 69) that the Egyptian Horus was just a new incarnation of Osiris or Nimrod. Now, Herodotus calls Horus by the name of Apollo (lib. ii. p. 171, C). Diodorus Siculus, also (lib. i. p. 15), says that "Horus, the son of Isis, is interpreted to be Apollo." Wilkinson seems, on one occasion, to call this identity of Horus and Apollo in question; but he elsewhere admits that the story of Apollo's "combat with the serpent Pytho is evidently derived from the Egyptian mythology" (vol. iv. p. 395), where the allusion is to the representation of Horus piercing the snake with a spear. From divers considerations, it may be shown that this conclusion is correct:—1. Horus, or Osiris, was the sun-god, so was Apollo. 2. Osiris, whom Horus represented, was the great Revealer; the Pythian Apollo was the god of oracles. 3. Osiris, in the character of Horus, was born when his mother was said to be persecuted by the malice of her enemies. Latona, the mother of Apollo, was a fugitive for a similar reason when Apollo was born. 4. Horus, according to one version of the myth, was said, like Osiris, to have been cut in pieces (PLUTARCH, vol. ii., *De Iside*, p. 358, E). In the classic story of Greece, this part of the myth of Apollo was generally kept in the background; and he was represented as victor in the conflict with the serpent; but even there it was sometimes admitted that he had suffered a violent death, for by Porphyry he is said to have been slain by the serpent, and

with similar penances by the sailors who visited his shrine, as we learn from the following lines of Callimachus in his hymn to Delos:—

"Soon as they reach thy soundings, down at once
They drop slack sails and all the naval gear.
The ship is moored; nor do the crew presume
To quit thy sacred limits, till they've passed
A fearful penance; with the galling whip
Lashed thrice around thine altar."*

Over and above the scourgings, there were also slashings and cuttings of the flesh required as propitiatory rites on the part of his worshippers. "In the solemn celebration of the Mysteries," says Julius Firmicus, "all things in order had to be done, which the youth either did or *suffered* at his death."† Osiris was cut in pieces; therefore, to imitate his fate, so far as living men might do so, they were required to cut and wound their own bodies. Therefore, when the priests of Baal contended with Elijah, to gain the favour of their god, and induce him to work the desired miracle in their behalf, "they cried aloud and cut themselves, after their manner, with knives and with lancets, till the blood gushed out upon them."‡ In Egypt, the natives in general, though liberal in the use of the whip, seem to have been sparing of the knife; but even there, there were men also who mimicked on their own persons the dismemberment of Osiris. "The Carians of Egypt," says Herodotus, in the place already quoted, "treat themselves at this solemnity with still more severity, for they cut themselves in the face with swords."§ To this practice, there can be no doubt, there is a direct allusion in the command in the Mosaic law, "Ye shall make no cuttings in your flesh for the dead."|| These cuttings in the flesh are largely practised in the worship of the Hindoo divinities, as propitiatory rites or meritorious penances. They are well known to have been practised in the rites of Bellona,¶ the

Pythagoras affirmed that he had seen his tomb at Tripos in Delphi (BRYANT, vol. ii. p. 187). 5. Horus was the war-god. Apollo was represented in the same way as the great god represented in Layard, with the bow and arrow, who was evidently the Babylonian war-god, Apollo's well-known title of "Arcitenens,"—"The bearer of the bow," having evidently been borrowed from that source. Fuss tells us (pp. 354, 355) that Apollo was regarded as the inventor of the art of shooting with the bow, which identifies him with Sagittarius, whose origin we have already seen. 6. Lastly, from Ovid (*Metam.*, lib. i. fab. 8, l. 442, vol. ii. p. 39) we learn that, before engaging with Python, Apollo had used his arrows only on fallow-deers, stags, &c. All which sufficiently proves his substantial identification with the mighty *Hunter of Babel.*

* CALLIMACHUS, in Original, v. 318-321, vol. i. p. 134.

† JULIUS FIRMICUS, p. 18.

‡ 1 Kings xviii. 28.

§ HERODOTUS, lib. ii. cap. 61, p. 127, A and B.

|| Leviticus xix. 28. Every person who died in the faith was believed to be identified with Osiris, and called by his name.—WILKINSON, vol. iv. p. 167, Note.

¶ "The priests of Bellona," says Lactantius, "sacrificed not with any other men's blood but their own, their shoulders being lanced, and with both hands brandishing naked swords, they ran and leaped up and down like mad men."—Lib. i. cap. 2, p. 52.

"sister" or "wife of the Roman war-god Mars," whose name, "The lamenter of Bel," clearly proves the original of her husband to whom the Romans were so fond of tracing back their pedigree. They were practised also in the most savage form in the gladiatorial shows, in which the Roman people, with all their boasted civilisation, so much delighted. The miserable men who were doomed to engage in these bloody exhibitions, did not do so generally of their own free will. But yet, the principle on which these shows were conducted was the very same as that which influenced the priests of Baal. They were celebrated as propitiatory sacrifices. From Fuss we learn that "gladiatorial shows were sacred" to Saturn;* and in Ausonius we read that "the amphitheatre claims its gladiators for itself, when at the end of December they PROPITIATE with their blood the sickle-bearing Son of Heaven."† On this passage, Justus Lipsius, who quotes it, thus comments: "Where you will observe two things, both, that the gladiators fought on the Saturnalia, and that they did so for the purpose of appeasing and PROPITIATING Saturn."‡ "The reason of this," he adds, "I should suppose to be, that Saturn is not among the celestial but the infernal gods. Plutarch, in his book of 'Summaries,' says, that 'the Romans looked upon Kronos as a subterranean and infernal God.'"§ There can be no doubt that this is so far true, for the name of Pluto is only a synonym for Saturn, "The Hidden One."‖ But yet, in the light of the real history of the historical Saturn, we find a more satisfactory reason for the barbarous custom that so much disgraced the escutcheon of Rome in all its glory, when mistress of the world, when such multitudes of men were

"Butchered to make a Roman holiday."

When it is remembered that Saturn himself was cut in pieces, it is easy to see how the idea would arise of offering a welcome sacrifice to him by setting men to cut one another in pieces on his birthday, by way of propitiating his favour.

The practice of such penances, then, on the part of those of the Pagans who cut and slashed themselves, was intended to propitiate and please their god, and so to lay up a stock of merit that might tell in their behalf in the scales of Anubis. In the Papacy, the penances are not only intended to answer the same end, but, to a large extent, they are identical. I do not know, indeed, that they use the *knife* as the priests of Baal did; but it is certain that they look upon the shedding of their own *blood* as a most meritorious penance, that gains them high favour with God, and wipes away

* *Roman Antiquities*, p. 359.

† AUSONIUS, *Eclog.* i. p. 156.

‡ LIPSIUS, tom. ii. *Saturnal.*, lib. i. cap. 5.

§ PLUTARCH, vol. ii. p. 266.

‖ The name Pluto is evidently from "Lut," to hide, which, with the Egyptian definite article prefixed, becomes "P'Lut." The Greek πλουτος, "wealth," "the *hidden* thing," is obviously formed in the same way. Hadés is just another synonym of the same name.

many sins. Let the reader look at the pilgrims at Lough Dergh, in Ireland, crawling on their bare knees over the sharp rocks, and leaving the bloody tracks behind them, and say what substantial difference there is between that and cutting themselves with knives. In the matter of scourging themselves, however, the adherents of the Papacy have literally borrowed the lash of Osiris. Everyone has heard of the Flagellants, who publicly scourge themselves on the festivals of the Roman Church, and who are regarded as saints of the first water. In the early ages of Christianity such flagellations were regarded as purely and entirely Pagan. Athenagoras, one of the early Christian Apologists, holds up the Pagans to ridicule for thinking that sin could be atoned for, or God propitiated, by any such means.* But now, in the high places of the Papal Church, such practices are regarded as the grand means of gaining the favour of God. On Good Friday, at Rome and Madrid, and other chief seats of Roman idolatry, multitudes flock together to witness the performances of the saintly whippers, who lash themselves till the blood gushes in streams from every part of their body.† They pretend to do this in honour of Christ, on the festival set apart professedly to commemorate His death, just as the worshippers of Osiris did the same on the festival when they lamented for his loss.‡ But can any man of the least Christian enlightenment believe that the exalted Saviour can look on such rites as doing honour to Him, which pour contempt on His all-perfect atonement, and represent His most "precious blood" as needing to have its virtue *supplemented* by that of blood drawn from the backs of wretched and misguided sinners? Such offerings were altogether fit for the worship of Moloch; but they are the very opposite of being fit for the service of Christ.

It is not in one point only, but in manifold respects, that the ceremonies of "Holy Week" at Rome, as it is termed, recall to memory the rites of the great Babylonian god. The more we look at these rites, the more we shall be struck with the wonderful resemblance that subsists between them and those observed at the Egyptian festival of burning lamps and the other ceremonies of the fire-worshippers in different countries. In Egypt the *grand illumination* took place beside the sepulchre of Osiris at Saïs.§ In Rome in "Holy Week," a sepulchre of Christ also figures in connection with a brilliant illumination of burning tapers.|| In Crete, where the tomb of Jupiter was exhibited, that tomb was an object of worship to the Cretans.¶ In Rome, if the devotees do

* ATHENAGORAS, *Legatio pro Christ.*, s. 14, p. 134.

† HURD's *Rites and Ceremonies*, p. 175; and *Rome in the 19th Century*, vol. iii. p. 161.

‡ The priests of Cybele at Rome observed the same practice.—*Ibid.* p. 251, Note.

§ WILKINSON, vol. iv. p. 328.

|| *Rome in the 19th Century*, vol. iii. pp. 145, 150.

¶ "A vanis Cretensibus adhuc mortui Jovis tumulus adoratur."—FIRMICUS, lib. ii. p. 23.

not worship the so-called sepulchre of Christ, they worship what is entombed within it.* As there is reason to believe that the Pagan festival of burning lamps was observed in commemoration of the ancient fire-worship, so there is a ceremony at Rome in the Easter week, which is an unmistakable act of fire-worship, when a *cross of fire* is the grand object of worship. This ceremony is thus graphically described by the authoress of *Rome in the 19th Century:* "The effect of the blazing cross of fire suspended from the dome above the confession or tomb of St. Peter's, was strikingly brilliant at night. It is covered with innumerable lamps, which have the effect of one blaze of fire. . . . . The whole church was thronged with a vast multitude of all classes and countries, from royalty to the meanest beggar, all gazing upon this one object. In a few minutes the Pope and all his Cardinals descended into St. Peter's, and room being kept for them by the Swiss guards, the aged Pontiff . . . . prostrated himself in silent adoration before the CROSS OF FIRE. A long train of Cardinals knelt before him, whose splendid robes and attendant train-bearers, formed a striking contrast to the humility of their attitude." † What could be a more clear and unequivocal act of fire-worship than this? Now, view this in connection with the fact stated in the following extract from the same work, and how does the one cast light on the other:—"With Holy Thursday our miseries began [that is, from crowding]. On this disastrous day we went before nine to the Sistine chapel . . . . and beheld a procession led by the inferior orders of clergy, followed up by the Cardinals in superb dresses, bearing long wax tapers in their hands, and ending with the Pope himself, who walked beneath a crimson canopy, with his head uncovered, bearing the Host in a box; and this being, as you know, the real flesh and blood of Christ, was carried from the Sistine chapel through the intermediate hall to the Paulina chapel, where it was deposited in the sepulchre prepared to receive it beneath the altar. . . . . I never could learn why Christ was to be buried before He was dead, for, as the crucifixion did not take place till Good Friday, it seems odd to inter Him on Thursday. His body, however, is laid in the sepulchre, in all the churches of Rome, where this rite is practised, on Thursday forenoon, and it remains there till Saturday at mid-day, when, for some reason best known to themselves, He is supposed to rise from the grave amidst the firing of cannon, and blowing of trumpets, and jingling of bells, which have been carefully tied up ever since the dawn of Holy Thursday, lest the devil should get into them." ‡ The worship of the cross of fire on Good Friday explains at once the anomaly otherwise so perplexing, that Christ should be buried on Thursday, and rise from the dead on Saturday. If the festival of Holy Week be really, as its rites declare, one of the old festivals of Saturn, the Babylonian fire-

* *Rome in the 19th Century*, vol. iii. p. 145.

† *Ibid.* pp. 148, 149. We shall yet see that the *cross* is the express symbol of Tammuz, the sun-god and god of fire. See Sect. VI. of the next Chapter.

‡ *Ibid.* pp. 144, 145.

god, who, though an infernal god, was yet Phoroneus, the great "Deliverer," it is altogether natural that the god of the Papal idolatry, though called by Christ's *name*, should rise from the dead on his *own* day—the *Dies Saturni*, or "Saturn's day." * On the day before the *Miserērē* is sung with such overwhelming pathos, that few can listen to it unmoved, and many even swoon with the emotions that are excited. What if this be at bottom only the old song of Linus,† of whose very touching and melancholy character Herodotus speaks so strikingly? Certain it is, that much of the pathos of that *Miserērē* depends on the part borne in singing it by the *sopranos;* and equally certain it is that Semiramis, the wife of him who, historically, was the original of that god whose tragic death was so pathetically celebrated in many countries, enjoys the fame, such as it is, of having been the inventress of the practice from which *soprano singing* took its rise.‡

Now, the flagellations which form an important part of the penances that take place at Rome on the evening of Good Friday, formed an equally important part in the rites of that fire-god, from which, as we have seen, the Papacy has borrowed so much. These flagellations, then, of "Passion Week," taken in connection with the other ceremonies of that period, bear their additional testimony to the real character of that god whose death and resurrection Rome then celebrates. Wonderful it is to consider that, in the very high place of what is called Catholic Christendom, the essential rites at this day are seen to be the very rites of the old Chaldean fire-worshippers.

SECTION III.—THE SACRIFICE OF THE MASS.

If baptismal regeneration, the initiating ordinance of Rome, and justification by works, be both Chaldean, the principle embodied in the "unbloody sacrifice" of the mass is not less so. We have evidence that goes to show the Babylonian origin of the idea of that "unbloody sacrifice" very distinctly. From Tacitus § we learn that no blood

* The above account referred to the ceremonies as witnessed by the authoress in 1817 and 1818. It would seem that some change has taken place since then, caused probably by the very attention called by her to the gross anomaly mentioned above; for Count Vlodaisky, formerly a Roman Catholic priest, who visited Rome in 1845, has informed me that in that year the resurrection took place, not at mid-day, but at nine o'clock on the evening of Saturday. This may have been intended to make the inconsistency between Roman practice and Scriptural fact appear somewhat less glaring. Still the fact remains, that the resurrection of Christ, as celebrated at Rome, takes place, not on His own day—"The Lord's day"—but—on the day of Saturn, the god of fire!

† A surname of one of the three Linuses was Narcissus (in Greek, Narkissos).—(CLINTON'S *Fasti Hellenici*, Appendix, vol. i. p. 343.) Now "Naar" signifies "child," and "Kissos," as we have seen (p. 49), is Cush, so that Nar-kissos is "The child of Cush."

‡ AMMIANUS MARCELLINUS, lib. xiv. cap. 6, p. xxv.

§ *Historia*, lib. ii. cap. 3, vol. iii. p. 106.

was allowed to be offered on the altars of Paphian Venus. Victims were used for the purposes of the Haruspex, that presages of the issues of events might be drawn from the inspection of the entrails of these victims; but the altars of the Paphian goddess were required to be kept pure from blood. Tacitus shows that the Haruspex of the temple of the Paphian Venus was brought from *Cilicia*, for his knowledge of her rites, that they might be duly performed according to the supposed will of the goddess, the Cilicians having peculiar knowledge of her rites. Now, Tarsus, the capital of Cilicia, was built by Sennacherib, the Assyrian king, in express imitation of Babylon.* Its religion would naturally correspond; and when we find "unbloody sacrifice" in Cyprus, whose priest came from Cilicia, that, in the circumstances, is itself a strong presumption that the "unbloody sacrifice" came to it through Cilicia from Babylon. This presumption is greatly strengthened when we find from Herodotus that the peculiar and abominable institution of Babylon in prostituting virgins in honour of Mylitta, was observed also in Cyprus in honour of Venus.† But the positive testimony of Pausanias brings this presumption to a certainty. "Near this," says that historian, speaking of the temple of Vulcan at Athens, "is the temple of Celestial Venus, who was first worshipped by the Assyrians, and after these by the Paphians in Cyprus, and the Phenicians who inhabited the city of Ascalon in Palestine. But the Cythereans venerated this goddess in consequence of learning her sacred rites from the Phenicians."‡ The Assyrian Venus, then—that is, the great goddess of Babylon—and the Cyprian Venus were one and the same, and consequently the "bloodless" altars of the Paphian goddess show the character of the worship peculiar to the Babylonian goddess, from whom she was derived. In this respect the goddess-queen of Chaldea differed from her son, who was worshipped in her arms. *He* was, as we have seen, represented as delighting in blood. But *she*, as the mother of grace and mercy, as the celestial "Dove," as "the hope of the whole world,"§ was averse to blood, and was represented in a benign and gentle character. Accordingly, in Babylon she bore the name of Mylitta ||—that is, "The Mediatrix."¶ Every one who reads the Bible, and sees how expressly it declares that, as there is only "one God," so there is only "one Mediator between God and man" (1 Tim. ii. 5), must marvel how it could ever have entered the mind of any one to bestow on Mary, as is done by the Church of Rome, the character of the "Mediatrix." But the character ascribed to

* BUNSEN, vol. i. p. 718.

† HEROD., *Historia*, lib. i. cap. 199, p. 92.

‡ PAUSANIAS, lib. i. *Attica*, cap. 14.

§ *Nonni Dionysiaca*, in BRYANT, vol. iii. p. 226.

|| HERODOT., lib. i. cap. 199.

¶ Mylitta is the same as Melitta, the feminine of Melitz, "a mediator," which in Chaldee becomes Melitt. Melitz is the word used in Job xxxiii. 23, 24: "If there be a messenger with him, an *interpreter* (Heb. Melitz, "*a mediator*"), one among a thousand, to show unto man his uprightness, then he is gracious unto him, and saith, Deliver him from going down to the pit; I have found a ransom." For further evidence on this point, see Appendix, Note J.

the Babylonian goddess as Mylitta sufficiently accounts for this. In accordance with this character of Mediatrix, she was called Aphrodîté—that is, "the wrath-subduer"*—who by her charms could soothe the breast of angry Jove, and soften the most rugged spirits of gods or mortal-men. In Athens she was called Amarusia †—that is, "The Mother of gracious acceptance."‡ In Rome she was called "Bona Dea," "the good goddess," the mysteries of this goddess being celebrated by women with peculiar secrecy. In India the goddess Lakshmi, "the Mother of the Universe," the consort of Vishnu, is represented also as possessing the most gracious and genial disposition; and that disposition is indicated in the same way as in the case of the Babylonian goddess. "In the festivals of Lakshmi," says Coleman, "no *sanguinary sacrifices are offered.*"§ In China, the great gods, on whom the final destinies of mankind depend, are held up to the popular mind as objects of dread; but the goddess Kuanyin, "the goddess of mercy,"‖ whom the Chinese of Canton recognise as bearing an analogy to the Virgin of Rome, is described as looking with an eye of compassion on the guilty, and interposing to save miserable souls even from torments to which in the world of spirits they have been doomed.¶ Therefore she is regarded with peculiar favour by the Chinese. This character of the goddess-mother has evidently radiated in all directions from Chaldea. Now, thus we see how it comes that Rome represents Christ, the "Lamb of God," meek and lowly in heart, who never brake the bruised reed, nor quenched the smoking flax—who spake words of sweetest encouragement to every mourning penitent—who wept over Jerusalem—who prayed for His murderers—as a stern and inexorable judge, before whom the sinner "might grovel in the dust, and still never be sure that his prayers would be heard,"** while Mary is set off in the most winning and engaging light, as the hope of the guilty, as the grand refuge of sinners; how it is that the former is said to have "reserved justice and judgment to Himself," but to have committed the exercise of all mercy to His Mother! †† The most standard devotional works of Rome are pervaded by this very principle, exalting the compassion and gentleness of the mother at the expense of the loving character of the Son. Thus, St. Alphonsus Liguori tells his readers that the sinner that ventures to come directly to Christ may come with dread and apprehension of His wrath; but let him only employ the mediation of the Virgin with her Son, and she has only to "*show*" that Son

* From Chaldee "aph," "wrath," and "radah," "to subdue;" "radîté" is the feminine emphatic.

† PAUSANIAS, lib. i., *Attica*, cap. 31, p. 72.

‡ From "Ama," "mother," and "Retza," "to accept graciously," which in the participle active is "Rūtza." Pausanias expresses his perplexity as to the meaning of the name Amarusia as applied to Diana, saying, "Concerning which appellation I never could find any one able to give a satisfactory account." The sacred tongue plainly shows the meaning of it.

§ *Hindoo Mythology*, p. 61.

‖ Sir J. F. DAVIS, vol. ii. p. 67.

¶ *Ibid.* vol. ii. p. 61.

** Sermon of an Italian Priest, in *Evangelical Christendom*, May, 1853.

†† *British Reformers*, "Jewell," p. 209.

"*the breasts that gave Him suck*,"* and His wrath will immediately be appeased. But where in the Word of God could such an idea have been found? Not surely in the answer of the Lord Jesus to the woman who exclaimed, "Blessed is the womb that bare thee, and the paps that thou hast sucked!" Jesus answered and said unto her, "*Yea, rather*, blessed are they that hear the Word of God and keep it" (Luke xi. 27, 28). There cannot be a doubt that this answer was given by the prescient Saviour, to check in the very bud every idea akin to that expressed by Liguori. Yet this idea, which is not to be found in Scripture, which the Scripture expressly repudiates, was widely diffused in the realms of Paganism. Thus we find an exactly parallel representation in the Hindoo mythology in regard to the god Siva and his wife Kali, when that god appeared as a little child. "Siva," says the Lainga Puran, "appeared as an infant in a cemetery, surrounded by ghosts, and on beholding him, Kali (his wife) took him up, and, *caressing him, gave him her breast*. He sucked the nectareous fluid; but becoming ANGRY, in order to divert and PACIFY him, Kali *clasping him to her bosom*, danced with her attendant goblins and demons amongst the dead, until he was *pleased and delighted;* while Vishnu, Brahma, Indra, and all the gods, bowing themselves, praised with laudatory strains the god of gods, Kal and Parvati."† Kali, in India, is the goddess of destruction; but even into the myth that concerns this goddess of destruction, the power of the goddess *mother*, in appeasing an offended god, by means only suited to PACIFY a peevish child, has found an introduction. If the Hindoo story exhibits its "god of gods" in such a degrading light, how much more honouring is the Papal story to the Son of the Blessed, when it represents Him as needing to be *pacified* by His mother exposing to Him "the breasts that He has sucked." All this is done only to exalt the Mother, as *more* gracious and *more* compassionate than her glorious Son. Now, this was the very case in Babylon: and to this character of the goddess queen her favourite offerings exactly corresponded. Therefore, we find the women of Judah represented as simply "burning incense, pouring out drink-offerings, and offering *cakes* to the queen of heaven" (Jeremiah xliv. 19). The cakes were "the unbloody sacrifice" she required. That "unbloody sacrifice" her votaries not only offered, but when admitted to the higher mysteries, they partook of, swearing anew fidelity to her. In the fourth century, when the queen of heaven, under the name of Mary, was beginning to be worshipped in the Christian Church, this "unbloody sacrifice" also was brought in. Epiphanius states that the practice of offering and eating it began among the women of Arabia;‡ and at that time it was well known to have been adopted from the Pagans. The very shape of the unbloody sacrifice of Rome may indicate whence it came. It is a small thin, *round* wafer; and on its *roundness* the

* *Catholic Layman*, July, 1856.

† LAINGA PURAN, *apud* KENNEDY'S *Ancient and Hindoo Mythology*, p. 338, Note.

‡ EPIPHANIUS, *Adversus Hæreses*, vol. i. p. 1054.

Church of Rome lays so much stress, that, to use the pithy language of John Knox in regard to the wafer-god, "If, in making the *roundness* the ring be broken, then must another of his fellow-cakes receive that honour to be made a god, and the crazed or cracked miserable cake, that once was in hope to be made a god, must be given to a baby to play withal."* What could have induced the Papacy to insist so much on the "*roundness*" of its "unbloody sacrifice"? Clearly not any reference to the Divine institution of the Supper of our Lord; for in all the accounts that are given of it, no reference whatever is made to the *form* of the bread which our Lord took, when He blessed and break it, and gave it to His disciples, saying, "Take, eat; this is My body: this do in remembrance of Me." As little can it be taken from any regard to injunctions about the form of the Jewish Paschal bread; for no injunctions on that subject are given in the books of Moses. The importance, however, which Rome attaches to the *roundness* of the wafer, must have a reason; and that reason will be found, if we look at the altars of Egypt. "The thin, *round* cake," says Wilkinson, "occurs on all

Fig. 37.

altars."† Almost every jot or tittle in the Egyptian worship had a symbolical meaning. The *round disk*, so frequent in the sacred emblems of Egypt, symbolised the *sun*. Now, when Osiris, the sun-divinity, became incarnate, and was born, it was not merely that he should give his life as a *sacrifice* for men,‡ but that he might also be the life and *nourishment* of the souls of men. It is universally admitted that Isis was the original of the Greek and Roman Ceres. But Ceres, be it observed, was worshipped not simply as the *discoverer* of corn; she was worshipped as "the MOTHER of Corn."§ The child she brought forth was He-Siri, "the Seed," or, as he was most frequently called in Assyria, "Bar," which signifies at once "the *Son*" and "the *Corn*." (Fig. 37.)‖ The uninitiated might reverence Ceres for the gift of material corn to nourish their *bodies*, but the

* BEGG'S *Handbook of Popery*, p. 259.

† WILKINSON'S *Egyptians*, vol. v. p. 353.

‡ See *ante*, p. 102, Note, in regard to the symbolical meaning of the goose.

§ "Genitrix, or Mater frugum." See PYPER'S *Gradus ad Parnassum*, "Ceres"; also OVID, *Metam.*, lib. vi. v. 117, 118.

‖ The ear of corn in the above medal from BRYANT (vol. v. p. 384), is alongside of Ceres; but usually it is held in her hand. The god on the reverse is the same as that ear. See page 73, in regard to "Beltis and the *Shining* Bar."

initiated adored her for a higher gift—for food to nourish their souls—for giving them that bread of God that cometh down from heaven—for the life of the world, of which, "if a man eat, he shall never die." Does any one imagine that it is a mere *New Testament* doctrine, that Christ is the "bread of life"? There never *was*, there never *could* be, spiritual life in any soul, since the world began, at least since the expulsion from Eden, that was not nourished and supported by a continual feeding by faith on the Son of God, "in whom it hath pleased the Father that all fulness should dwell" (Col. i. 19), "that out of His fulness we might receive, and grace for grace" (John i. 16). Paul tells us that the manna of which the Israelites ate in the wilderness was to them a type and lively symbol of "the bread of life;" (1 Cor. x. 3), "They did all eat the same *spiritual* meat"—*i.e.*, meat which was intended not only to support their natural lives, but to point them to Him who was the life of their souls. Now, Clement of Alexandria, to whom we are largely indebted for all the discoveries that, in modern times, have been made in Egypt, expressly assures us that, "in their *hidden character*, the enigmas of the Egyptians were VERY SIMILAR TO THOSE OF THE JEWS." * That the initiated Pagans actually believed that the "Corn" which Ceres bestowed on the world was not the "Corn" of this earth, but the Divine "Son," through whom alone spiritual and eternal life could be enjoyed, we have clear and decisive proof. The Druids were devoted worshippers of Ceres, and as such they were celebrated in their mystic poems as "bearers of the ears of corn." † Now, the following is the account which the Druids give of their great divinity, under the form of "*Corn.*" That divinity was represented as having, in the first instance, incurred, for some reason or other, the displeasure of Ceres, and as fleeing in terror from her. In his terror, "he took the form of a bird, and mounted into the air. That element afforded him no refuge; for *The Lady*, in the form of a sparrow-hawk, was gaining upon him—she was just in the act of pouncing upon him. Shuddering with dread, he perceived a heap of clean wheat upon a floor, dropped into the midst of it, and assumed the form of a *single grain*. Ceridwen [*i.e.*, the British Ceres] took the form of a black high-crested hen, descended into the wheat, scratched him out, distinguished, and swallowed him. And, as the history relates, she was pregnant of him nine months, and when delivered of him, she found him *so lovely a babe*, that she had not resolution to put him to death." ‡ Here it is evident that the *grain of corn*, is expressly identified with "*the lovely babe*;" from which it is still further evident that Ceres, who, to the profane vulgar was known only as the Mother of "Bar," "the Corn," was known to the initiated as the Mother of "Bar," "the Son." And now, the reader will be prepared to understand the full significance of the representation in the Celestial sphere of "the

* CLEMENS ALEXANDRINUS, *Stromata*, v. 7, vol. iii. p. 56.

† DAVIES'S *British Druids*, p. 504.

‡ "Song of Taliesin," DAVIES'S *British Druids*, p. 230.

Virgin with the ear of wheat in her hand." That *ear of wheat* in the Virgin's *hand* is just another symbol for the *child* in the *arms* of the Virgin Mother.

Now, this Son, who was symbolised as "Corn," was the SUN-divinity incarnate, according to the sacred oracle of the great goddess of Egypt: "No mortal hath lifted my veil. The fruit which I have brought forth is the SUN."* What more natural, then, if this incarnate divinity is symbolised as the "*bread* of God," than that he should be represented as a "*round* wafer," to identify him with the Sun? Is this a mere fancy? Let the reader peruse the following extract from Hurd, in which he describes the embellishments of the Romish altar, on which the sacrament or consecrated wafer is deposited, and then he will be able to judge:—"A plate of silver, in the form of a SUN, is fixed opposite to the SACRAMENT on the altar; which, with the light of the tapers, makes a most brilliant appearance."† What has that "brilliant" "*Sun*" to do there, on the altar, over against the "*sacrament*," or *round* wafer? In Egypt, the *disk* of the Sun was represented in the temples, and the sovereign and his wife and children were represented as adoring it. Near the small town of Babain, in Upper Egypt, there still exists in a grotto, a representation of a sacrifice to the sun, where two priests are seen worshipping the sun's image, as in the accompanying woodcut (Fig. 38).‡ In the great temple of Babylon, the golden image of the Sun was exhibited for the worship of the Babylonians.§ In the temple of Cuzco, in Peru, the disk of the sun was fixed up in flaming gold upon the wall,|| that all who entered might bow down before it. The Pæonians of Thrace were sun-worshippers; and in their worship they adored an image of the sun in the form of a disk at the top of a long pole.¶ In the worship of Baal, as practised by the idolatrous Israelites in the days of their apostacy, the worship of the sun's image was equally observed; and it is striking to find that the image of the sun, which apostate Israel worshipped, was erected *above the altar*. When the good king Josiah set about the work of reformation, we read that his servants in carrying out the work, proceeded thus (2 Chron. xxxiv. 4): "And they brake down the *altars* of Baalim in his

Fig. 38.

* BUNSEN'S *Egypt*, vol. i. pp. 386, 387.

† HURD'S *Rites and Ceremonies*, p. 196, col. i.

‡ From MAURICE'S *Indian Antiquities*, vol. iii. p. 309. 1793.

§ See *ante*, p. 62.

|| PRESCOTT'S *Peru*, vol. i. p. 64. ¶ BRYANT, vol. i. p. 259.

presence, and the images (margin, SUN-IMAGES) that were on high above them, he cut down." Benjamin of Tudela, the great Jewish traveller, gives a striking account of sun-worship even in comparatively modern times, as subsisting among the Cushites of the East, from which we find that the image of the sun was, even in his day, worshipped on the altar. "There is a temple," says he, "of the posterity of Chus, addicted to the contemplation of the stars. They worship the sun as a god, and the whole country, for half-a-mile round their town, is filled with great altars dedicated to him. By the dawn of morn they get up and run out of town, to wait the rising sun, to whom, *on every altar*, there is a *consecrated image*, not in the likeness of a man, but *of the solar orb*, framed by magic art. These orbs, as soon as the sun rises, take fire, and resound with a great noise, while everybody there, men and women, hold censers in their hands, and all burn incense to the sun." * From all this, it is manifest that the image of the sun above, or on the altar, was one of the recognised symbols of those who worshipped Baal or the Sun. And here, in a so-called Christian Church, a brilliant plate of silver, "in the form of a SUN," is so placed on the altar, that every one who adores at that altar must bow down in lowly reverence before that image of the "*Sun*." Whence, I ask, could that have come, but from the ancient sun-worship, or the worship of Baal? And when the wafer is so placed that the silver "SUN" is fronting the "*round*" wafer, whose "*roundness*" is so important an element in the Romish Mystery, what can be the meaning of it, but just to show to those who have eyes to see, that the "Wafer" itself is only another symbol of Baal, or the Sun. If the sun-divinity was worshipped in Egypt as "the Seed," or in Babylon as the "Corn," precisely so is the wafer adored in Rome. "Bread-*corn* of the elect, have mercy upon us," is one of the appointed prayers of the Roman Litany, addressed to the wafer, in the celebration of the mass.† And one at least of the imperative requirements as to the way in which that wafer is to be partaken of, is the very same as was enforced in the old worship of the Babylonian divinity. Those who partake of it are required to partake absolutely fasting. This is very stringently laid down. Bishop Hay, laying down the law on the subject, says that it is indispensable, "that we be fasting from midnight, so as to have taken nothing into our stomach from twelve o'clock at night before we receive, neither food, nor drink, nor medicine."‡ Considering that our Lord Jesus Christ instituted the Holy Communion immediately after His disciples had partaken of the paschal feast, such a strict requirement of fasting might seem very unaccountable. But look at this provision in regard to the "unbloody sacrifice" of the mass in the light of the Eleusinian Mysteries, and it is accounted for at once; for there the first question put to those who sought initiation was, "Are you fasting?"§ and

* Quoted by Translator of SAVARY'S *Letters*, vol. ii. pp. 562, 563, Note.

† *Protestant*, p. 269, col. 2.

‡ *Sincere Christian*, vol. ii. sect. iii. p. 34.

§ POTTER, vol. i., *Eleusiania*, p. 356.

unless that question was answered in the affirmative, no initiation could take place. There is no question that fasting is in certain circumstances a Christian duty; but while neither the letter nor the spirit of the Divine institution requires any such stringent regulation as the above, the regulations in regard to the Babylonian Mysteries make it evident whence this requirement has really come.

Although the god whom Isis or Ceres brought forth, and who was offered to her under the symbol of the wafer or thin round cake, as "the bread of life," was in reality the fierce, scorching Sun, or terrible Moloch, yet in that offering all his terror was veiled, and everything repulsive was cast into the shade. In the appointed symbol he is offered up to the benignant Mother, who tempers judgment with mercy, and to whom all spiritual blessings are ultimately referred; and blessed by that mother, he is given back to be feasted upon, as the staff of life, as the nourishment of her worshippers' souls. Thus the Mother was held up as the favourite divinity. And thus, also, and for an entirely similar reason, does the Madonna of Rome entirely eclipse her son as the "Mother of grace and mercy."

In regard to the Pagan character of the "unbloody sacrifice" of the mass, we have seen not little already. But there is something yet to be considered, in which the working of the mystery of iniquity will still further appear. There are letters on the wafer that are worth reading. These letters are I. H. S. What mean these mystical letters? To a Christian these letters are represented as signifying, "*Iesus Hominum Salvator*," "Jesus the Saviour of men." But let a Roman worshipper of Isis (for in the age of the emperors there were innumerable worshippers of Isis in Rome) cast his eyes upon them, and how will he read them? He will read them, of course, according to his own well-known system of idolatry: "*Isis, Horus, Seb*," that is, "The Mother, the Child, and the Father of the gods,"—in other words, "The Egyptian Trinity." Can the reader imagine that this double sense is accidental? Surely not. The very same spirit that converted the festival of the Pagan Oannes into the feast of the Christian Joannes, retaining at the same time all its ancient Paganism, has skilfully planned the initials I. H. S. to pay the *semblance* of a tribute to Christianity, while Paganism in reality has all the *substance* of the homage bestowed upon it.

When the women of Arabia began to adopt this wafer and offer the "unbloody sacrifice," all genuine Christians saw at once the real character of their sacrifice. They were treated as heretics, and branded with the name of Collyridians, from the Greek name for the cake which they employed. But Rome saw that the heresy might be turned to account; and therefore, though condemned by the sound portion of the Church, the practice of offering and eating this "unbloody sacrifice" was patronised by the Papacy; and now, throughout the whole bounds of the Romish communion, it has superseded the simple but most precious sacrament of the Supper instituted by our Lord Himself.

Intimately connected with the sacrifice of the mass is the subject of transubstantiation; but the consideration of it will come more conveniently at a subsequent stage of this inquiry.

SECTION IV.—EXTREME UNCTION.

The last office which Popery performs for living men is to give them "extreme unction," to anoint them in the name of the Lord, after they have been shriven and absolved, and thus to prepare them for their last and unseen journey. The pretence for this "unction" of dying men is professedly taken from a command of James in regard to the visitation of the sick; but when the passage in question is fairly quoted it will be seen that such a practice could never have arisen from the apostolic direction—that it must have come from an entirely different source. "Is any sick among you?" says James (v. 14, 15), "let him call for the elders of the church; and let them pray over him, anointing him with oil in the name of the Lord: and the prayer of faith shall save the sick, and the Lord shall RAISE HIM UP." Now, it is evident that this prayer and anointing were intended for the *recovery* of the sick. Apostolic men, for the laying of the foundations of the Christian Church, were, by their great King and Head, invested with miraculous powers—powers which were intended only for a time, and were destined, as the apostles themselves declared, while exercising them, to "vanish away" (1 Cor. xiii. 8). These powers were every day exercised by the "elders of the Church," when James wrote his epistle, and that for *healing* the bodies of men, even as our Lord Himself did. The "extreme unction" of Rome, as the very expression itself declares, is *not* intended for any such purpose. It is not intended for healing the sick, or "*raising them up;*" for it is *not* on any account to be administered till *all hope of recovery* is gone, and death is visibly at the very doors. As the object of this anointing is the very opposite of the Scriptural anointing, it must have come from a quite different quarter. That quarter is the very same from which the Papacy has imported so much heathenism, as we have seen already, into its own foul bosom. From the Chaldean Mysteries, extreme unction has obviously come. Among the many names of the Babylonian god was the name "Beël-samen," "Lord of Heaven,"* which is the name of the sun, but also of course of the sun-god. But Beël-samen also properly signifies "Lord of Oil," and was evidently intended as a synonym of the Divine name, "The Messiah." In Herodotus we find a statement made which this name alone can fully explain. There an individual is represented as having dreamt that the sun had anointed her father.† That the sun should anoint any one is

* "Lord of Heaven" is properly "Beël-shemin," but in Sanchuniathon it is given exactly as the name of the "Lord of Oil" (pp. 12, 13).—EUSEB., *Praep. Evang.*, lib. i. cap. 10, p. 39.

† HERODOTUS, lib. iii. cap. 124.

certainly not an idea that could naturally have presented itself; but when the name "Beël-samen," "Lord of Heaven," is seen also to signify "Lord of Oil," it is easy to see how that idea would be suggested. This also accounts for the fact that the body of the Babylonian Belus was represented as having been preserved in his sepulchre in Babylon till the time of Xerxes, floating in oil.* And for the same reason, no doubt, it was that at Rome the "statue of Saturn" was "made hollow, and *filled with oil*."†

The olive branch, which we have already seen to have been one of the symbols of the Chaldean god, had evidently the same hieroglyphical meaning; for, as the olive was the oil-tree, so an olive branch emblematically signified a "son of oil," or an "anointed one" (Zech. iv. 12-14). Hence the reason that the Greeks, in coming before their gods in the attitude of suppliants deprecating their wrath and entreating their favour, came to the temple on many occasions bearing an olive branch in their hands. As the olive branch was one of the recognised symbols of their Messiah, whose great mission it was to make peace between God and man, so, in bearing this branch of the anointed one, they thereby testified that in the *name* of that anointed one they came seeking peace. Now, the worshippers of this Beël-samen, "Lord of Heaven," and "Lord of Oil," were anointed in the name of their god. It was not enough that they were anointed with "spittle"; they were also anointed with "magical ointments" of the most powerful kind; and these ointments were the means of introducing into their bodily systems such drugs as tended to excite their imaginations and add to the power of the magical drinks they received, that they might be prepared for the visions and revelations that were to be made to them in the Mysteries. These "*unctions*," says Salverté, "were exceedingly frequent in the ancient ceremonies. . . . . Before consulting the oracle of Trophonius, they were rubbed with oil over the whole body. This preparation certainly concurred to produce the desired vision. Before being admitted to the Mysteries of the Indian sages, Apollonius and his companion were rubbed with an oil so powerful that *they felt as if bathed with fire*."‡ This was professedly an unction in the name of the "Lord of Heaven," to fit and prepare them for being admitted *in vision* into his awful presence. The very same reason that suggested such an unction before initiation on this present scene of things, would naturally plead more powerfully still for a special "*unction*" when the individual was called, not in vision, but in reality, to face the "Mystery of mysteries," his personal introduction into the world unseen and eternal. Thus the Pagan system naturally developed itself into "extreme unction."§ Its votaries were *anointed* for their last journey, that by the double influence of superstition and powerful stimulants introduced into the frame by the only way in which it might then be possible, their minds might

* CLERICUS, *Philosoph. Orient.*, lib. i., *De Chaldæis*, sect. i. cap. 4.
† SMITH'S *Classical Dictionary*, p. 679.
‡ SALVERTÉ, *Des Sciences Occultes*, p. 282.
§ *Quarterly Journal of Prophecy*, p. 6, January, 1853.

be fortified at once against the sense of guilt and the assaults of the king of terrors. From this source, and this alone, there can be no doubt came the "extreme unction" of the Papacy, which was entirely unknown among Christians till corruption was far advanced in the Church.*

SECTION V.—PURGATORY AND PRAYERS FOR THE DEAD.

"Extreme unction," however, to a burdened soul, was but a miserable resource, after all, in the prospect of death. No wonder, therefore, that something else was found to be needed by those who had received all that priestly assumption could pretend to confer, to comfort them in the prospect of eternity. In every system, therefore, except that of the Bible, the doctrine of a purgatory after death, and prayers for the dead, has always been found to occupy a place. Go wherever we may, in ancient or modern times, we shall find that Paganism leaves hope after death for sinners, who, at the time of their departure, were consciously unfit for the abodes of the blest. For this purpose a middle state has been feigned, in which, by means of purgatorial pains, guilt unremoved in time may in a future world be purged away, and the soul be made meet for final beatitude. In Greece the doctrine of a purgatory was inculcated by the very chief of the philosophers. Thus Plato, speaking of the future judgment of the dead, holds out the hope of final deliverance for *all*, but maintains that, of "those who are judged," "some" must *first* "proceed to a subterranean place of judgment, where they shall *sustain the punishment they have deserved*;" while others, in consequence of a favourable judgment, being elevated at once into a certain celestial place, "shall pass their time in a manner becoming the life they have lived in a human shape."† In Pagan Rome, purgatory was equally held up before the minds of men; but there, there seems to have been no hope held out to any of exemption from its pains. Therefore, Virgil, describing its different tortures, thus speaks:—

> "Nor can the grovelling mind,
> In the dark dungeon of the limbs confined,
> Assert the native skies, or own its heavenly kind.
> Nor death itself can wholly wash their stains;
> But long-contracted filth, even in the soul, remains
> The relics of inveterate vice they wear,
> And spots of sin obscene in *every face* appear.
> For this are various penances enjoined;
> And some are hung to bleach upon the wind,
> Some plunged in water, *others purged in fires*,
> Till all the dregs are drained, and all the rust expires.
> *All* have their Manés, and those Manés bear.

* Bishop GIBSON says that it was not known in the Church for a thousand years.—*Preservative against Popery*, vol. viii. p. 255.

† PLATO, *Phaedrus*, p. 249, A, B.

The few so cleansed to these abodes repair,
And breathe in ample fields the soft Elysian air.
Then are they happy, when by length of time
The scurf is worn away of each committed crime;
No speck is left of their habitual stains,
But the pure ether of the soul remains."*

In Egypt, substantially the same doctrine of purgatory was inculcated. But when once this doctrine of purgatory was admitted into the popular mind, then the door was opened for all manner of priestly extortions. Prayers for the dead ever go hand in hand with purgatory; but no prayers can be completely efficacious without the interposition of the priests; and no priestly functions can be rendered unless there be *special pay* for them. Therefore, in every land we find the Pagan priesthood "devouring widows' houses," and making merchandise of the tender feelings of sorrowing relatives, sensitively alive to the immortal happiness of the beloved dead. From all quarters there is one universal testimony as to the burdensome character and the *expense* of these posthumous devotions. One of the oppressions under which the poor Romanists in Ireland groan, is the periodical special devotions, for which they are required to pay, when death has carried away one of the inmates of their dwelling. Not only are there funeral services and funeral dues for the repose of the departed, at the time of burial, but the priest pays repeated visits to the family for the same purpose, which entail heavy expense, beginning with what is called "the month's mind," that is, a service in behalf of the deceased when a month after death has elapsed. Something entirely similar to this had evidently been the case in ancient Greece; for, says Müller in his *History of the Dorians*, "the Argives sacrificed on the thirtieth day [after death] to Mercury as the conductor of the dead."† In India many and burdensome are the services of the Srádd'ha, or funeral obsequies for the repose of the dead; and for securing the due efficacy of these, it is inculcated that "donations of cattle, land, gold, silver, and other things," should be made by the man himself at the approach of death; or, "if he be too weak, by another in his name."‡ Wherever we look, the case is nearly the same. In Tartary, "The Gurjumi, or prayers for the dead," says the *Asiatic Journal*, "are very expensive."§ In Greece, says Suidas,|| "the greatest and most *expensive* sacrifice was the mysterious sacrifice called the Teleté," a sacrifice which, according to Plato, "was offered for the living and the *dead*, and was supposed to free them from all the evils to which the wicked are liable when they have left this world."¶ In Egypt the exactions of the priests for funeral dues and masses for the dead were far from being trifling.

* DRYDEN's *Virgil*, Book vi. ll. 995-1012, vol. ii. p. 536; in Original, ll. 730-747.

† *Dorians*, vol. ii. p. 405. MÜLLER states that the Argives sacrificed *also* immediately after death.

‡ *Asiatic Researches*, vol. vii. pp. 239, 240.

§ *Asiatic Journal*, vol. xvii. p. 143.

|| SUIDAS, vol. ii. p. 879, B.

¶ PLATO, vol. ii. pp. 364, 365.

"The priests," says Wilkinson, "induced the people to expend large sums on the celebration of funeral rites; and *many who had barely sufficient to obtain the necessaries of life* were anxious to save something for the expenses of their death. For, besides the embalming process, which sometimes cost a talent of silver, or about £250 English money, the tomb itself was purchased at an immense expense; and numerous demands were made upon the estate of the deceased, for the celebration of prayer and other services for the soul."* "The ceremonies," we find him elsewhere saying, "consisted of a sacrifice similar to those offered in the temples, vowed for the deceased to one or more gods (as Osiris, Anubis, and others connected with Amenti); incense and libation were also presented; and a prayer was sometimes read, the relations and friends being present as mourners. They even joined their prayers to those of the priest. The priest who officiated at the burial service was selected from the grade of Pontiffs, who wore the leopard skin; but various other rites were performed by one of the minor priests to the mummies, previous to their being lowered into the pit of the tomb after that ceremony. Indeed, they continued to be administered at intervals, *as long as the family paid for their performance*."† Such was the operation of the doctrine of purgatory and prayers for the dead among avowed and acknowledged Pagans; and in what essential respect does it differ from the operation of the same doctrine in Papal Rome? There are the same extortions in the one as there were in the other. The doctrine of purgatory is purely Pagan, and cannot for a moment stand in the light of Scripture. For those who die in Christ no purgatory *is*, or *can* be, needed; for "the blood of Jesus Christ, God's Son, cleanseth from ALL sin." If this be true, where can there be the need for any other cleansing? On the other hand, for those who die without personal union to Christ, and consequently unwashed, unjustified, unsaved, there can be no other cleansing; for, while "he that hath the Son hath life, he that hath not the Son hath *not* life," and never *can* have it. Search the Scripture through, and it will be found that, in regard to all who "*die in their sins*," the decree of God is irreversible: "Let him that is unjust be unjust still, and let him that is filthy be filthy still." Thus the whole doctrine of purgatory is a system of pure bare-faced Pagan imposture, dishonouring to God, deluding men who live in sin with the hope of atoning for it after death, and cheating them at once out of their property and their salvation. In the Pagan purgatory, fire, water, wind, were represented (as may be seen from the lines of Virgil) ‡ as combining to purge away the stain of sin. In the purgatory of the Papacy, ever since the days of Pope Gregory, FIRE itself has been the grand means of purgation.§ Thus, while the purgatorial fires of the future world are just the carrying out of the principle embodied in the blazing and

* WILKINSON, vol. ii. p. 94.
† *Ibid.* vol. v. pp. 383, 384.
‡ See *ante*, p. 167.
§ *Catechismus Romanus*, pars i., art. 5, sect. 5, p. 50.

purifying Baal-fires of the eve of St. John, they form another link in identifying the system of Rome with the system of Tammuz or Zoroaster, the great God of the ancient fire-worshippers.

Now, if baptismal regeneration, justification by works, penance as a satisfaction to God's justice, the unbloody sacrifice of the mass, extreme unction, purgatory, and prayers for the dead, were all derived from Babylon, how justly may the general system of Rome be styled Babylonian? And if the account already given be true, what thanks ought we to render to God, that, from a system such as this, we were set free at the blessed Reformation! How great a boon is it to be delivered from trusting in such refuges of lies as could no more take away sin than the blood of bulls or of goats! How blessed to feel that the blood of the Lamb, applied by the Spirit of God to the most defiled conscience, completely purges it from dead works and from sin! How fervent ought our gratitude to be, when we know that, in all our trials and distresses, we may come boldly unto the throne of grace, in the name of no creature, but of God's eternal and well-beloved Son; and that that Son is exhibited as a most tender and compassionate high priest, who is TOUCHED with a feeling of our infirmities, having been in all points tempted like as we are, yet without sin. Surely the thought of all this, while inspiring tender compassion for the deluded slaves of Papal tyranny, ought to make us ourselves stand fast in the liberty wherewith Christ has made us free, and quit ourselves like men, that neither we nor our children may ever again be entangled in the yoke of bondage.

CHAPTER V.

RITES AND CEREMONIES.

SECTION I.—IDOL PROCESSIONS.

THOSE who have read the account of the last idol procession in the capital of Scotland, in John Knox's *History of the Reformation*, cannot easily have forgot the tragi-comedy with which it ended. The light of the Gospel had widely spread, the Popish idols had lost their fascination, and popular antipathy was everywhere rising against them. "The images," says the historian, "were stolen away in all parts of the country; and in Edinburgh was that great idol called Sanct Geyle [the patron saint of the capital], first drowned in the North Loch, after burnt, which raised no small trouble in the town."* The bishops demanded of the Town Council either "to get them again the old Sanct Geyle, or else, upon their (own) expenses, to make a new image."† The Town Council *could* not do the one, and the other they absolutely *refused* to do; for they were now convinced of the sin of idolatry. The bishops and priests, however, were still mad upon their idols; and, as the anniversary of the feast of St. Giles was approaching, when the saint used to be carried in procession through the town, they determined to do their best, that the accustomed procession should take place with as much pomp as possible. For this purpose, "a marmouset idole" was borrowed from the Grey friars, which the people, in derision, called "Young Sanct Geyle," and which was made to do service instead of the old one. On the appointed day, says Knox, "there assembled priests, friars, canons . . . . with taborns and trumpets, banners, and bagpipes; and who was there to lead the ring but the Queen Regent herself, with all her shavelings, for honour of that feast. West about goes it, and comes down the High Street, and down to the Canno Cross."‡ As long as the Queen was present, all went to the heart's content of the priests and their partisans. But no sooner had majesty retired to dine, than some in the crowd, who had viewed the whole concern with an evil eye, "drew nigh to the idol, as willing to help to bear him, and getting the fertour (or barrow) on their shoulders, began to shudder, thinking that thereby the idol should have fallen. But that was provided and prevented by the iron nails [with which it was fastened to the fertour]; and so began one to cry, 'Down with the idol, down with it;' and so without

* KNOX, vol. i. p. 256. † *Ibid.* vol. i. p. 258.

‡ *Ibid.* vol. i. p. 259.

delay it was pulled down. Some brag made the priests' patrons at the first; but when they saw the feebleness of their god, for one took him by the heels, and dadding * his head to the calsay,† left Dagon without head or hands, and said, 'Fye upon thee, thou young Sanct Geyle, thy father would have tarried ‡ four such [blows];' this considered, we say, the priests and friars fled faster than they did at Pinkey Cleuch. There might have been seen so sudden a fray as seldom has been seen amongst that sort of men within this realm; for down goes the crosses, off goes the surplice, round caps corner with the crowns. The Grey friars gaped, the Black friars blew, the priests panted and fled, and happy was he that first gat the house; for such ane sudden fray came never amongst the generation of Antichrist within this realm before." §

Such an idol procession among a people who had begun to study and relish the Word of God, elicited nothing but indignation and scorn. But in Popish lands, among a people studiously kept in the dark, such processions are among the favourite means which the Romish Church employs to bind its votaries to itself. The long processions with images borne on men's shoulders, with the gorgeous dresses of the priests, and the various habits of different orders of monks and nuns, with the aids of flying banners and the thrilling strains of instrumental music, if not too closely scanned, are well fitted "plausibly to amuse" the worldly mind, to gratify the love for the picturesque, and when the emotions thereby called forth are dignified with the names of piety and religion, to minister to the purposes of spiritual despotism. Accordingly, Popery has ever largely availed itself of such pageants. On joyous occasions, it has sought to consecrate the hilarity and excitement created by such processions to the service of its idols; and in seasons of sorrow, it has made use of the same means to draw forth the deeper wail of distress from the multitudes that throng the procession, as if the mere loudness of the cry would avert the displeasure of a justly offended God. Gregory, commonly called the Great, seems to have been the first who, on a *large scale*, introduced those religious processions into the Roman Church. In 590, when Rome was suffering under the heavy hand of God from the pestilence, he exhorted the people to unite publicly in supplication to God, appointing that they should meet at daybreak in SEVEN DIFFERENT COMPANIES, according to their respective ages, SEXES, and stations, and walk in seven different processions, reciting litanies or supplications, till they all met at one place.‖ They did so, and proceeded singing and uttering the words, "Lord, have mercy upon us," carrying along with them, as Baronius relates, by Gregory's express command, an image of the Virgin.¶ The very idea of such processions was an affront to the majesty of heaven; it implied that

* Knocking. † Pavement. ‡ Abode or withstood. § KNOX, vol. i. p. 260.

‖ This is the origin of what is called *Litania Septemplex*, or "The Sevenfold Litany."

¶ BARONIUS, *Annales*, 590, tom. viii. pp. 6, 7.

God who is a Spirit "saw with eyes of flesh," and might be moved by the imposing picturesqueness of such a spectacle, just as sensuous mortals might. As an experiment it had but slender success. In the space of one hour, while thus engaged, eighty persons fell to the ground, and breathed their last.* Yet this is now held up to Britons as "the more excellent way" for deprecating the wrath of God in a season of national distress. "Had this calamity," says Dr. Wiseman, referring to the Indian disasters, "had this calamity fallen upon our forefathers in Catholic days, one would have seen the streets of this city [London] trodden in every direction by penitential processions, crying out, like David, when pestilence had struck the people." If this allusion to David has any pertinence or meaning, it must imply that David, in the time of pestilence, headed some such "penitential procession." But Dr. Wiseman knows, or ought to know, that David did nothing of the sort, that his penitence was expressed in no such way as by processions, and far less by idol processions, as "in the Catholic days of our forefathers," to which we are invited to turn back. This reference to David, then, is a mere blind, intended to mislead those who are not given to Bible reading, as if such "penitential processions" had something of Scripture warrant to rest upon. The *Times*, commenting on this recommendation of the Papal dignitary, has hit the nail on the head. "The historic idea," says that journal, "is simple enough, and as old as old can be. We have it in Homer—the procession of Hecuba and the ladies of Troy to the shrine of Minerva, in the Acropolis of that city." It was a time of terror and dismay in Troy, when Diomede, with resistless might, was driving everything before him, and the overthrow of the proud city seemed at hand. To avert the apparently inevitable doom, the Trojan Queen was divinely directed

"To lead the assembled train
Of Troy's chief matrons to Minerva's fane."

And she did so :—

"Herself . . . . the long procession leads ;
The train majestically slow proceeds.
Soon as to Ilion's topmost tower they come,
And awful reach the high Palladian dome,
Antenor's consort, fair Theano, waits
As Pallas' priestess, and unbars the gates.
With hands uplifted and imploring eyes,
They fill the dome with supplicating cries." †

Here is a precedent for "penitential processions" in connection with idolatry entirely to the point, such as will be sought for in vain in the history of David, or any of the Old Testament saints. Religious processions, and especially processions with images, whether of a jubilant or sorrowful description, are purely Pagan. In the

* Baronius, *Annales*, 590, tom. viii. p. 7.

† *Iliad*, Book vi. Pope's Translation, vol. ii. pp. 455-468.

Word of God we find two instances in which there were processions practised with Divine sanction; but when the object of these processions is compared with the avowed object and character of Romish processions, it will be seen that there is no analogy between them and the processions of Rome. The two cases to which I refer are the seven days' encompassing of Jericho, and the procession at the bringing up of the ark of God from Kirjath-jearim to the city of David. The processions, in the first case, though attended with the symbols of Divine worship, were not intended as acts of religious worship, but were a miraculous mode of conducting war, when a signal interposition of Divine power was to be vouchsafed. In the other, there was simply the removing of the ark, the symbol of Jehovah's presence, from the place where, for a long period, it had been allowed to lie in obscurity, to the place which the Lord Himself had chosen for its abode; and on such an occasion it was entirely fitting and proper that the transference should be made with all religious solemnity. But these were simply occasional things, and have nothing at all in common with Romish processions, which form a regular part of the Papal ceremonial. But, though Scripture speaks nothing of religious processions in the approved worship of God, it refers once and again to Pagan processions, and these, too, accompanied with images; and it vividly exposes the folly of those who can expect any good from gods that cannot move from one place to another, unless they are carried. Speaking of the gods of Babylon, thus saith the prophet Isaiah (chap. xlvi. 6), "They lavish gold out of the bag, and weigh silver in the balance, and hire a goldsmith; and he maketh it a god: they fall down, yea, they worship. *They bear him upon the shoulder, they carry him*, and set him in his place, and he standeth; from his place he shall not remove." In the sculptures of Nineveh these processions of idols, borne on men's shoulders, are forcibly represented,* and form at once a striking illustration of the prophetic language, and of the real *origin* of the Popish processions. In Egypt, the same practice was observed. In "the procession of shrines," says Wilkinson, "it was usual to carry the statue of the principal deity, in whose honour the procession took place, together with that of the king, and the figures of his ancestors, borne in the same manner, on men's shoulders."† But not only are the processions in general identified with the Babylonian system. We have evidence that these processions trace their origin to that very disastrous event in the history of Nimrod, which has already occupied so much of our attention. Wilkinson says "that Diodorus speaks of an Ethiopian festival of Jupiter, when his statue was carried in procession, probably to commemorate the supposed refuge of the gods in that country, which," says he, "may have been a memorial of the flight of the Egyptians with their gods."‡ The passage of Diodorus, to which

* LAYARD'S *Nineveh and its Remains*, vol. ii. p. 451.

† WILKINSON, vol. v. p. 273.

‡ *Ibid.* vol. v. p. 274.

Wilkinson refers, is not very decisive as to the object for which the statues of Jupiter and Juno (for Diodorus mentions the shrine of Juno as well as of Jupiter) were annually carried into the land of Ethiopia, and then, after a certain period of sojourn there, were brought back to Egypt again.* But, on comparing it with other passages of antiquity, its object very clearly appears. Eustathius says, that at the festival in question, "according to some, the ***Ethiopians*** used to fetch the images of Zeus, and other gods from the great temple of Zeus at Thebes. With these images they went about at a certain period in Libya, and celebrated a splendid festival for twelve gods."† As the festival was called an Ethiopian festival; and as it was Ethiopians that both carried away the idols and brought them back again, this indicates that the idols must have been Ethiopian idols; and as we have seen that Egypt was under the power of Nimrod, and consequently of the Cushites or Ethiopians, when idolatry was for a time put down in Egypt, ‡ what would this carrying of the idols into Ethiopia, the land of the Cushites, that was solemnly commemorated every year, be, but just the natural result of the temporary suppression of the idol-worship inaugurated by Nimrod. In Mexico, we have an account of an exact counterpart of this Ethiopian festival. There, at a certain period, the images of the gods were carried out of the country in a mourning procession, as if taking their leave of it, and then, after a time, they were brought back to it again with every demonstration of joy.§ In Greece, we find a festival of an entirely similar kind, which, while it connects itself with the Ethiopian festival of Egypt on the one hand, brings that festival, on the other, into the closest relation to the penitential procession of Pope Gregory. Thus we find Potter referring first to a "Delphian festival in memory of a JOURNEY of Apollo;"‖ and then under the head of the festival called Apollonia, we thus read: "To Apollo, at Ægialea on this account: Apollo having obtained a victory over Python, went to Ægialea, accompanied with his sister Diana; but, *being frightened from thence, fled into Crete.* After this, the Ægialeans were infected with an epidemical distemper; and, being advised by the prophets to appease the two offended deities, sent SEVEN boys and as many virgins to entreat them to return. [Here is the typical germ of 'The Sevenfold Litany' of Pope Gregory.] Apollo and Diana accepted their piety, ... and it became a *custom* to appoint chosen boys and virgins, to make a solemn procession, in show, as if they designed to bring back Apollo and Diana, which continued till Pausanias's time."¶ The contest between Python and Apollo, in Greece, is just the counterpart of that between Typho and Osiris

* DIODORUS, lib. i. sect. 97, p. 62.

† EUSTATHIUS on HOMER'S *Iliad*, lib. i. ll. 423-425, quoted in SMITH'S (larger) *Classical Dictionary, sub voce* "Ethiopia."

‡ See *ante*, pp. 63-65.

§ HUMBOLDT, vol. i. pp. 381, 382.

‖ POTTER, vol. i. p. 360.

¶ *Ibid.* p. 334.

in Egypt; in other words, between Shem and Nimrod. Thus we see the real meaning and origin of the Ethiopian festival, when the Ethiopians carried away the gods from the Egyptian temples. That festival evidently goes back to the time when Nimrod being cut off, idolatry durst not show itself except among the devoted adherents of the "Mighty hunter" (who were found in his own family—the family of Cush), when, with great weepings and lamentations, the idolaters fled with their gods on their shoulders, to hide themselves where they might.* In commemoration of the suppression of idolatry, and the unhappy consequences that were supposed to flow from that suppression, the first part of the festival, as we get light upon it both from Mexico and Greece, had consisted of a procession of mourners; and then the mourning was turned into joy, in memory of the happy return of these banished gods to their former exaltation. Truly a worthy origin for Pope Gregory's "Sevenfold Litany" and the Popish processions.

SECTION II.—RELIC WORSHIP.

Nothing is more characteristic of Rome than the worship of relics. Wherever a chapel is opened, or a temple consecrated, it cannot be thoroughly complete without some relic or other of he-saint or she-saint to give sanctity to it. The relics of the saints and rotten bones of the martyrs form a great part of the wealth of the Church. The grossest impostures have been practised in regard to such relics; and the most drivelling tales have been told of their wonder-working powers, and that too by Fathers of high name in the records of Christendom. Even Augustine, with all his philosophical acuteness and zeal against some forms of false doctrine, was deeply infected with the grovelling spirit that led to relic worship. Let any one read the stuff with which he concludes his famous "City of God," and he will in no wise wonder that Rome has made a saint of him, and set him up for the worship of her devotees. Take only a specimen or two of the stories with which he bolsters up the prevalent delusions of his day: "When the Bishop Projectius brought the relics of St. Stephen to the town called Aquæ Tibiltinæ, the people came in great crowds to honour them. Amongst these was a blind woman, who entreated the people to lead her to the bishop who had the HOLY RELICS. They did so, and the bishop gave her some flowers which he had in his hand. She took them, and put them to her eyes, and immediately her sight was restored, so that she passed speedily on before all the others, no longer requiring to be guided."† In Augustine's day, the formal "*worship*" of the relics was not yet established; but the martyrs to whom they were supposed to have belonged were already invoked with prayers and supplications, and that with the high approval of the Bishop of Hippo, as the following story will abundantly show: Here, in Hippo, says he, there was a

* In regard to "the flight of the gods," see also Chapter VII.

† *De Civitate*, lib. xxii. cap. 8, vol. ix. p. 875, B and C.

poor and holy old man, by name Florentius, who obtained a living by tailoring. This man once lost his coat, and not being able to purchase another to replace it, he came to the shrine of the Twenty Martyrs, in this city, and prayed aloud to them, beseeching that they would enable him to get another garment. A crowd of silly boys who overheard him, followed him at his departure, scoffing at him, and asking him whether he had begged fifty pence from the martyrs to buy a coat. The poor man went silently on towards home, and as he passed near the sea, he saw a large fish which had been cast up on the sand, and was still panting. The other persons who were present allowed him to take up this fish, which he brought to one Catosus, a cook, and a good Christian, who bought it from him for three hundred pence. With this he meant to purchase wool, which his wife might spin, and make into a garment for him. When the cook cut up the fish, he found within its belly a ring of gold, which his conscience persuaded him to give to the poor man from whom he bought the fish. He did so, saying, at the same time, "Behold how the Twenty Martyrs have clothed you!"* Thus did the great Augustine inculcate the worship of dead men, and the honouring of their wonder-working relics. The "silly children" who "scoffed" at the tailor's prayer seem to have had more sense than either the "holy old tailor" or the bishop. Now, if men professing Christianity were thus, in the fifth century, paving the way for the worship of all manner of rags and rotten bones; in the realms of Heathendom the same worship had flourished for ages before Christian saints or martyrs had appeared in the world. In Greece, the superstitious regard to relics, and especially to the bones of the deified heroes, was a conspicuous part of the popular idolatry. The work of Pausanias, the learned Grecian antiquary, is full of reference to this superstition. Thus, of the shoulder-blade of Pelops, we read that, after passing through divers adventures, being appointed by the oracle of Delphi, as a divine means of delivering the Eleans from a pestilence under which they suffered, it "was committed," as a sacred relic, "to the custody" of the man who had fished it out of the sea, and of his posterity after him.† The bones of the Trojan Hector were preserved as a precious deposit at Thebes. "They" [the Thebans], says Pausanias, "say that his [Hector's] bones were brought hither from Troy, in consequence of the following oracle: 'Thebans, who inhabit the city of Cadmus, if you wish to reside in your country, blest with the possession of blameless wealth, bring the bones of Hector, the son of Priam, into your dominions from Asia, and reverence the hero agreeably to the mandate of Jupiter.'"‡

* *De Civitate*, lib. xxii., cap. 8, vol. ix. pp. 874, 875. This story of the fish and the ring is an old Egyptian story.—(WILKINSON, vol. i. pp. 186, 187.) Catosus, "the good Christian," was evidently a tool of the priests, who could *afford* to give him a ring to put into the fish's belly. The miracle would draw worshippers to the shrine of the Twenty Martyrs, and thus bring grist to their mill, and amply repay them.

† PAUSANIAS, lib. v., *Prior Eliaca*, cap. 13, p. 408.

‡ *Ibid.* lib. ix., *Bœotica*, cap. 18, p. 746.

Many other similar instances from the same author might be adduced. The bones thus carefully kept and reverenced were all believed to be miracle-working bones. From the earliest periods, the system of Buddhism has been propped up by relics, that have wrought miracles at least as well vouched as those wrought by the relics of St. Stephen, or by the "Twenty Martyrs." In the "Mahawanso," one of the great standards of the Buddhist faith, reference is thus made to the enshrining of the relics of Buddha: "The vanquisher of foes having perfected the works to be executed within the relic receptacle, convening an assembly of the priesthood, thus addressed them: 'The works that were to be executed by me, in the relic receptacle, are completed. To-morrow, I shall enshrine the relics. Lords, bear in mind the relics.'"* Who has not heard of the Holy Coat of Trèves, and its *exhibition* to the people? From the following, the reader will see that there was an exactly similar exhibition of the Holy Coat of Buddha: "Thereupon (the nephew of the Naga Rajah) by his supernatural gift, springing up into the air to the height of seven palmyra trees, and stretching out his arm brought to the spot where he was poised, the Dupathupo (or shrine) in which the DRESS laid aside by Buddho, as Prince Siddhatto, on his entering the priesthood, was enshrined . . . . and EXHIBITED IT TO THE PEOPLE."† This "Holy Coat" of Buddha was no doubt as genuine, and as well entitled to worship, as the "Holy Coat" of Trèves. The resemblance does not stop here. It is only a year or two ago since the Pope presented to his beloved son, Francis Joseph of Austria, a "TOOTH" of "St. Peter," as a mark of his special favour and regard.‡ The *teeth* of Buddha are in equal request among his worshippers. "King of Devas," said a Buddhist missionary, who was sent to one of the principal courts of Ceylon to demand a relic or two from the Rajah, "King of Devas, thou possessest the right canine *tooth relic* (of Buddha), as well as the right collar bone of the divine teacher. Lord of Devas, demur not in matters involving the salvation of the land of Lanka."§ Then the miraculous efficacy of these relics is shown in the following: "The Saviour of the world (Buddha) even after he had attained to Parinibanan or final emancipation (*i.e.*, after his death), by means of a corporeal relic, performed *infinite acts to the utmost perfection*, for the spiritual comfort and mundane prosperity of mankind. While the Vanquisher (Jeyus) yet lived, what must he not have done?"‖ Now, in the *Asiatic Researches*, a statement is made in regard to these relics of Buddha, which marvellously reveals to us the real origin of this Buddhist relic worship. The statement is this: "The bones or limbs of Buddha were scattered all over the world, like those of Osiris and Jupiter Zagreus. To collect them was the first

* POCOCKE'S *India in Greece*, p. 307.

† *Ibid.* pp. 307, 308.

‡ *Original Interpretation of the Apocalypse*, p. 72.

§ POCOCKE, p. 321.

‖ *Ibid.* p. 321, and Note.

duty of his descendants and followers, and then to entomb them. Out of filial piety, the remembrance of this mournful search was yearly kept up by a fictitious one, with all possible marks of grief and sorrow till a priest announced that the sacred relics were at last found. This is practised to this day by several Tartarian tribes of the religion of Buddha; and the expression of the bones of the Son of the Spirit of heaven is peculiar to the Chinese and some tribes in Tartary."* Here, then, it is evident that the worship of relics is just a part of those ceremonies instituted to commemorate the tragic death of Osiris or Nimrod, who, as the reader may remember, was divided into fourteen pieces, which were sent into so many different regions infected by his apostacy and false worship, to operate *in terrorem* upon all who might seek to follow his example. When the apostates regained their power, the very first thing they did was to seek for these dismembered *relics* of the great ringleader in idolatry, and to entomb them with every mark of devotion. Thus does Plutarch describe the search: "Being acquainted with this event [viz., the dismemberment of Osiris], Isis set out once more in search of the scattered members of her husband's body, using a boat made of the papyrus rush in order more easily to pass through the lower and fenny parts of the country. . . . . And one reason assigned for the different sepulchres of Osiris shown in Egypt is, that wherever any one of his scattered limbs was discovered she buried it on the spot; though others suppose that it was owing to an artifice of the queen, who presented each of those cities with an image of her husband, in order that, if Typho should overcome Horus in the approaching contest, he might be unable to find the real sepulchre. Isis succeeded in recovering all the different members, with the exception of one, which had been devoured by the Lepidotus, the Phagrus, and the Oxyrynchus, for which reason these fish are held in abhorrence by the Egyptians. To make amends, she consecrated the Phallus, and instituted a solemn festival to its memory."† Not only does this show the real origin of relic worship; it shows also that the *multiplication* of relics can pretend to the most venerable antiquity. If, therefore, Rome can boast that she has sixteen or twenty holy coats, seven or eight arms of St. Matthew, two or three heads of St. Peter, this is nothing more than Egypt could do in regard to the relics of Osiris. Egypt was *covered* with sepulchres of its martyred god; and many a leg and arm and skull, all vouched to be genuine, were exhibited in the rival burying-places for the adoration of the Egyptian faithful. Nay, not only were these Egyptian relics sacred themselves, they CONSECRATED THE VERY GROUND in which they were entombed. This fact is brought out by Wilkinson, from a statement of Plutarch:‡ "The Temple of this deity at Abydos," says he, "was also particularly honoured, and so holy was the place considered by the Egyptians, that persons living

* *Asiatic Researches*, vol. x. pp. 128, 129.

† PLUTARCH, vol. ii. p. 358, A.

‡ *Ibid.* sect. 20, vol. ii. p. 359, A.

at some distance from it sought, and perhaps with difficulty obtained, permission to possess a sepulchre within its Necropolis, in order that, after death, *they might repose* in GROUND HALLOWED BY THE TOMB of this great and mysterious deity."* If the places where the relics of Osiris were buried were accounted peculiarly holy, it is easy to see how naturally this would give rise to the *pilgrimages* so frequent among the heathen. The reader does not need to be told what merit Rome attaches to such *pilgrimages* to the tombs of saints, and how, in the Middle Ages, one of the most favourite ways of washing away sin was to undertake a pilgrimage to the shrine of St. Jago di Compostella in Spain, or to the Holy Sepulchre in Jerusalem.† Now, in the Scripture there is not the slightest trace of any such thing as a *pilgrimage* to the tomb of saint, martyr, prophet, or apostle. The very way in which the Lord saw fit to dispose of the body of Moses in burying it Himself in the plains of Moab, so that no man should ever know where his sepulchre was, was evidently designed to rebuke every such feeling as that from which such *pilgrimages* arise. And considering *whence* Israel had come, the Egyptian ideas with which they were infected, as shown in the matter of the golden calf, and the high reverence they must have entertained for Moses, the wisdom of God in so disposing of his body must be apparent. In the land where Israel had so long sojourned, there were great and pompous *pilgrimages* at certain seasons of the year, and these often attended with gross excesses. Herodotus tells us, that in his time the multitude who went annually on pilgrimage to Bubastis amounted to 700,000 individuals, and that then more wine was drunk than at any other time in the year.‡ Wilkinson thus refers to a similar pilgrimage to Philae: "Besides the celebration of the great mysteries which took place at Philae, a grand ceremony was performed at a particular time, when the priests, in solemn procession, visited his tomb, and crowned it with flowers.§ Plutarch even pretends that all access to the island was forbidden at every other period, and that no bird would fly over it, or fish swim near this CONSECRATED GROUND."‖ This seems not to have been a procession merely of the priests in the immediate neighbourhood of the tomb, but a truly national *pilgrimage;* for, says Diodorus, "the sepulchre of Osiris at Philae is revered by all the priests throughout Egypt."¶ We have not the same minute information about the relic worship in Assyria or Babylon; but we have enough to show that, as it was the Babylonian god that was worshipped in Egypt under the name of Osiris, so in his own country there was the same superstitious reverence paid to his relics. We have seen already, that when the Babylonian Zoroaster died, he was said voluntarily to have given his life as a sacrifice, and to have "charged his countrymen to *preserve his remains,*" assuring them

* WILKINSON, vol. iv. p. 346.

† *Evangelical Christendom*, Ann. 1855, vol. ix. p. 201.

‡ HERODOTUS, *Historia*, lib. ii. cap. 60, pp. 126, 127.

§ PLUTARCH, vol. ii. p. 359, B.

‖ WILKINSON'S *Egyptians*, vol. iv. p. 346.

¶ DIODORUS, lib. i. p. 13.

that on the observance or neglect of this dying command, the fate of their empire would hinge.* And, accordingly, we learn from Ovid, that the "Busta Nini," or "Tomb of Ninus," long ages thereafter, was one of the monuments of Babylon.† Now, in comparing the death and fabled resurrection of the false Messiah with the death and resurrection of the true, when he actually appeared, it will be found that there is a very remarkable contrast. When the false Messiah died, limb was severed from limb, and his bones were scattered over the country. When the death of the true Messiah took place, Providence so arranged it that the body should be kept entire, and that the prophetic word should be exactly fulfilled—"a bone of Him shall not be broken." When, again, the false Messiah was pretended to have had a resurrection, that resurrection was in a *new* body, while the old body, with all its members, was left behind, thereby showing that the resurrection was nothing but a pretence and a sham. When, however, the true Messiah was "declared to be the Son of God with power, by the resurrection from the dead," the tomb, though jealously watched by the armed unbelieving soldiery of Rome, was found to be absolutely empty, and no dead body of the Lord was ever afterwards found, or even pretended to have been found. The resurrection of Christ, therefore, stands on a very different footing from the resurrection of Osiris. Of the body of Christ, of course, in the nature of the case, there could be no relics. Rome, however, to carry out the Babylonian system, has supplied the deficiency by means of the relics of the saints; and now the relics of St. Peter and St. Paul, of St. Thomas A'Beckett and St. Lawrence O'Toole, occupy the very same place in the worship of the Papacy as the relics of Osiris in Egypt, or of Zoroaster in Babylon.

SECTION III.—THE CLOTHING AND CROWNING OF IMAGES.

In the Church of Rome, the clothing and crowning of images form no insignificant part of the ceremonial. The sacred images are not represented, like ordinary statues, with the garments formed of the same material as themselves, but they have garments put on them from time to time, like ordinary mortals of living flesh and blood. Great expense is often lavished on their drapery; and those who present to them splendid robes are believed thereby to gain their signal favour, and to lay up a large stock of merit for themselves. Thus, in September, 1852, we find the Duke and Duchess of Montpensier celebrated in the *Tablet*, not only for their charity in "giving 3000 reals in alms to the poor," but especially, and *above all*, for their piety in "*presenting the Virgin with a magnificent dress of tissue of gold, with white lace and a silver crown.*" Somewhat about

* SUIDAS, in *Zoroastres*, vol. i. pp. 1133, 1134. See further on this subject in Chap. VII. Sect. I., in connection with what is said about Phaëthon.

† *Metamorphoses*, lib. iv. l. 88, vol. ii. p. 278.

the same time the piety of the dissolute Queen of Spain was testified by a similar benefaction, when she deposited at the feet of the Queen of Heaven the homage of the dress and jewels she wore on a previous occasion of solemn thanksgiving, as well as the dress in which she was attired when she was stabbed by the assassin Merino. "The mantle," says the Spanish journal *Espana*, "exhibited the marks of the wound, and its ermine lining was stained with the precious blood of Her Majesty. In the basket (that bore the dresses) were likewise the jewels which adorned Her Majesty's head and breast. Among them was a diamond stomacher, so exquisitely wrought, and so dazzling, that it appeared to be wrought of a single stone."* This is all sufficiently childish, and presents human nature in a most humiliating aspect; but it is just copied from the old Pagan worship. The same clothing and adorning of the gods went on in Egypt, and there were sacred persons who alone could be permitted to interfere with so high a function. Thus, in the Rosetta Stone we find these sacred functionaries distinctly referred to: "The chief priests and prophets, and those who have access to the adytum to *clothe the gods*, ... assembled in the temple at Memphis, established the following decree."† The "clothing of the gods" occupied an equally important place in the sacred ceremonial of ancient Greece. Thus, we find Pausanias referring to a present made to Minerva: "In after times, Laodicè, the daughter of Agapēnor, sent a veil to Tegea, to Minerva Alea." The epigram [inscription] on this offering indicates, at the same time, the origin of Laodicè:—

> "Laodicè, from Cyprus, the divine,
> To her paternal wide-extended land,
> This veil—an offering to Minerva—sent."‡

Thus, also, when Hecuba, the Trojan queen, in the instance already referred to, was directed to lead the penitential procession through the streets of Troy to Minerva's temple, she was commanded not to go empty-handed, but to carry along with her, as her most acceptable offering—

> "The largest mantle your full wardrobes hold,
> Most prized for art, and laboured o'er with gold."

The royal lady punctually obeyed:—

> "The Phrygian queen to her rich wardrobe went,
> Where treasured odours breathed a costly scent;
> There lay the vestures of no vulgar art;
> Sidonian maids embroidered every part,
> Whom from soft Sydon youthful Paris bore,
> With Helen touching on the Tyrian shore.
> Here, as the Queen revolved with careful eyes
> The various textures and the various dyes,
> She chose a veil that shone superior far,
> And glowed refulgent as the morning star."§

* BEGG's *Handbook*, pp. 272, 273.

† Line vi. *apud* WILKINSON, vol. i. p. 265, Note.

‡ PAUSANIAS, lib. viii., *Arcadica*, cap. 5, p. 607.

§ HOMER's *Iliad*, Book vi., POPE's Translation, pp. 466-468.

There is surely a wonderful resemblance here between the piety of the Queen of Troy and that of the Queen of Spain. Now, in ancient Paganism there was a mystery couched under the clothing of the gods. If gods and goddesses were so much pleased by being clothed, it was because there had once been a time in their history when they stood greatly in *need* of clothing. Yes, it can be distinctly established, as has been already hinted, that ultimately the great god and great goddess of Heathenism, while the facts of their own history were interwoven with their idolatrous system, were worshipped also as incarnations of our great progenitors, whose disastrous fall stripped them of their primeval glory, and made it needful that the hand Divine should cover their nakedness with clothing specially prepared for them. I cannot enter here into an elaborate proof of this point; but let the statement of Herodotus be pondered in regard to the annual ceremony, observed in Egypt, of slaying a ram, and clothing the FATHER OF THE GODS with its skin.* Compare this statement with the Divine record in Genesis about the clothing of the "Father of *Mankind*" in a coat of sheepskin; and after all that we have seen of the deification of dead men, can there be a doubt what it was that was thus annually commemorated? Nimrod himself, when he was cut in pieces, was necessarily stripped. That exposure was identified with the nakedness of Noah, and ultimately with that of Adam. His sufferings were represented as *voluntarily* undergone for the good of mankind. His nakedness, therefore, and the nakedness of the "Father of the gods," of whom he was an incarnation, was held to be a *voluntary* humiliation too. When, therefore, his suffering was over, and his humiliation past, the clothing in which he was invested was regarded as a meritorious clothing, available not only for himself, but for all who were initiated in his mysteries. In the sacred rites of the Babylonian god, both the exposure and the clothing that were represented as having taken place, in his own history, were repeated on all his worshippers, in accordance with the statement of Firmicus, that the initiated underwent what their god had undergone.† First, after being duly prepared by magic rites and ceremonies, they were ushered, in a state of absolute nudity, into the innermost recesses of the temple. This appears from the following statement of Proclus: "In the most holy of the mysteries, they say that the mystics at first meet with the many-shaped genera [*i.e.*, with evil demons], which are hurled forth before the gods: but on entering the interior parts of the temple, unmoved and guarded by the mystic rites, they genuinely receive in their bosom divine illumination, and, DIVESTED OF THEIR GARMENTS, participate, as they would say, of a divine nature."‡ When the initiated, thus "illuminated" and made partakers of a "divine nature," after being "divested of their garments," were clothed anew, the garments with which they were invested were

* HERODOTUS, *Historia*, lib. ii. cap. 42, p. 119, A and B.

† FIRMICUS, *De Errore*, p. 18.

‡ TAYLOR'S *Jamblichus*, Note, p. 148. See Appendix, Note M.

looked upon as "sacred garments," and possessing distinguished virtues. "The coat of skin" with which the Father of mankind was divinely invested after he was made so painfully sensible of his nakedness, was, as all intelligent theologians admit, a typical emblem of the glorious righteousness of Christ—"the garment of salvation," which is "unto all and upon all them that believe." The garments put upon the initiated after their disrobing of their former clothes, were evidently intended as a *counterfeit* of the same. "The garments of those initiated in the Eleusinian Mysteries," says Potter, "were accounted *sacred*, and of no less efficacy to avert evils than charms and incantations. They were never cast off till completely worn out."* And of course, if possible, in these "*sacred garments*" they were buried; for Herodotus, speaking of Egypt, whence these mysteries were derived, tells us that "religion" prescribed the garments of the dead.† The efficacy of "sacred garments" as a means of salvation and delivering from evil in the unseen and eternal world, occupies a foremost place in many religions. Thus the Parsees, the fundamental elements of whose system came from the Chaldean Zoroaster, believe that "the *sadra* or *sacred vest*" tends essentially to "preserve the departed soul from the calamities accruing from Ahriman," or the Devil; and they represent those who neglect the use of this "*sacred vest*" as suffering in their souls, and "uttering the most dreadful and appalling cries," on account of the torments inflicted on them "by all kinds of reptiles and noxious animals, who assail them with their teeth and stings, and give them not a moment's respite."‡ What could have ever led mankind to attribute such virtue to a "*sacred vest*"? If it be admitted that it is just a perversion of the "sacred garment" put on our first parents, all is clear. This, too, accounts for the superstitious feeling in the Papacy, otherwise so unaccountable, that led so many in the dark ages to fortify themselves against the fears of the judgment to come, by seeking to be buried in a monk's dress. "To be buried in a friar's cast-off habit, accompanied by letters enrolling the deceased in a monastic order, was accounted a sure deliverance from eternal condemnation! In 'Piers the Ploughman's Creed,' a friar is described as wheedling a poor man out of his money by assuring him that, if he will only contribute to his monastery,

'St. Francis himself shall fold thee in his cope,
And present thee to the Trinity, and pray for thy sins.'"§

In virtue of the same superstitious belief, King John of England was buried in a monk's cowl;‖ and many a royal and noble personage besides, "before life and immortality" were anew "brought to light" at the Reformation, could think of no better way to cover their naked and polluted souls in prospect of death, than by wrapping

* POTTER'S *Greek Antiquities*, vol. i. p. 356.
† HERODOTUS, lib. ii. cap. 81, p. 134, B.
‡ WILSON'S *Parsee Religion*, pp. 164, 441, and 442.
§ *British Reformers*, "Bilney," p. 258, Note. ‖ *Ibid.*

themselves in the garment of some monk or friar as unholy as themselves. Now, all these refuges of lies, in Popery as well as Paganism, taken in connection with the clothing of the saints of the one system, and of the gods of the other, when traced to their source, show that since sin entered the world, man has ever felt the need of a better righteousness than his own to cover him, and that the time was when all the tribes of the earth knew that the only righteousness that could avail for such a purpose was "the righteousness of God," and that of "God manifest in the flesh."

Intimately connected with the "clothing of the images of the saints" is also the "*crowning*" of them. For the last two centuries, in the Popish communion, the festivals for *crowning* the "sacred images" have been more and more celebrated. In Florence, a few years ago, the image of the Madonna with the child in her arms was "*crowned*" with unusual pomp and solemnity.* Now, this too arose out of the facts commemorated in the history of Bacchus or Osiris. As Nimrod was the first king after the Flood, so Bacchus was celebrated as the first who wore a crown.† When, however, he fell into the hands of his enemies, as he was stripped of all his glory and power, he was stripped also of his *crown*. The "falling of the *crown* from the head of Osiris" was specially commemorated in Egypt. That crown at different times was represented in different ways, but in the most famous myth of Osiris it was represented as a "Melilot garland."‡ Melilot is a species of trefoil; and trefoil in the Pagan system was one of the emblems of the Trinity. Among the Tractarians at this day, trefoil is used in the same symbolical sense as it has long been in the Papacy, from which Puseyism has borrowed it. Thus, in a blasphemous Popish representation of what is called God the Father (of the fourteenth century), we find him represented as wearing a crown with three points, each of which is surmounted with a leaf of white clover (Fig. 39).§ But long before Tractarianism or Romanism was known, trefoil was a sacred symbol. The clover leaf was evidently a symbol of high import among the ancient Persians; for thus we find Herodotus referring to it, in describing the rites of the Persian Magi—"If any (Persian) intends to offer to a god, he leads the animal to a consecrated spot. Then, dividing the victim into parts, he boils the flesh, and lays it upon the most tender herbs, especially TREFOIL. This done, a magus—

Fig. 39.

* *Bulwark*, 1852-53, pp. 154-157.

† PLINY, *Hist. Nat.*, lib. xvi. p. 377. Under the name of Saturn, also, the same thing was attributed to Nimrod. See *ante*, p. 35, Note.

‡ PLUTARCH, *De Iside*, vol. ii. p. 356, E.

§ From DIDRON's *Iconography*, vol. i. p. 296.

without a magus no sacrifice can be performed—sings a sacred hymn."* In Greece, the clover, or trefoil, in some form or other, had also occupied an important place; for the rod of Mercury, the conductor of souls, to which such potency was ascribed, was called "Rabdos Tripetēlos," or "the *three-leaved rod*."† Among the British Druids the white clover leaf was held in high esteem as an emblem of their Triune God,‡ and was borrowed from the same Babylonian source as the rest of their religion. The Melilot, or trefoil garland, then, with which the head of Osiris was bound, was the crown of the Trinity—the crown set on his head as the representative of the Eternal—"The crown of all the earth," in accordance with the voice divine at his birth, "The Lord of all the earth is born." Now, as that "Melilot garland," that crown of universal dominion, fell "from his head" before his death, so, when he rose to new life, the crown must be again set upon his head, and his universal dominion solemnly avouched. Hence, therefore, came the solemn crowning of the statues of the great god, and also the laying of the "chaplet" on his altar, as a trophy of his recovered "dominion." But if the great god was crowned, it was needful also that the great goddess should receive a similar honour. Therefore it was fabled that when Bacchus carried his wife Ariadne to heaven, in token of the high dignity bestowed upon her, he set a crown upon her head;§ and the remembrance of this crowning of the wife of the Babylonian god is perpetuated to this hour by the well-known figure in the sphere called *Ariadnæa corona*,‖ or "Ariadne's crown." This is, beyond question, the real source of the Popish rite of crowning the image of the Virgin.

From the fact that the Melilot garland occupied so conspicuous a place in the myth of Osiris, and that the "chaplet" was laid on his altar, and his tomb was "crowned"¶ with flowers, arose the custom, so prevalent in heathenism, of adorning the altars of the gods with "chaplets" of all sorts, and with a gay profusion of flowers.** Side by side with this reason for decorating the altars with flowers, there was also another. When in

"That fair field
Of Enna, Proserpine gathering flowers,
Herself, a fairer flower, by gloomy Dis,
Was gathered;"

and all the flowers she had stored up in her lap were lost, the loss thereby sustained by the world not only drew forth her own tears, but was lamented in the Mysteries as a loss of no ordinary kind, a loss which not only stripped her of her own spiritual glory, but

* *Historia*, lib. i. cap. 132, pp. 62, 63.
† HOMER, *Hymn to Mercury*, ll. 526, 527.
‡ DAVIES'S *Druids*, p. 448.
§ OVID, *Fasti*, lib. iii. l. 513, vol. iii. p. 184.
‖ MANILIUS, lib. v. v. 21, p. 164.
¶ WILKINSON, vol. iv. p. 345.
** *Ibid.* vol. v. p. 368.

blasted the fertility and beauty of the earth itself.* That loss, however, the wife of Nimrod, under the name of Astarte, or Venus, was believed to have more than repaired. Therefore, while the sacred "chaplet" of the discrowned god was placed in triumph anew on his head and on his altars, the recovered flowers which Proserpine had lost were also laid on these altars along with it, in token of gratitude to that mother of grace and goodness, for the beauty and the temporal blessings that the earth owed to her interposition and love.† In Pagan Rome especially this was the case. The altars were profusely adorned with flowers. From that source directly the Papacy has borrowed the custom of adorning the altar with flowers; and from the Papacy, Puseyism, in Protestant England, is labouring to introduce the custom among ourselves. But, viewing it in connection with its source, surely men with the slightest spark of Christian feeling may well blush to think of such a thing. It is not only opposed to the genius of the Gospel dispensation, which requires that they who worship God, who is a Spirit, "worship Him in spirit and in truth;"‡ but it is a direct symbolising with those who rejoiced in the *re-establishment* of Paganism in *opposition* to the worship of the one living and true God.

SECTION IV.—THE ROSARY AND THE WORSHIP OF THE SACRED HEART.

Every one knows how thoroughly Romanist is the use of the rosary; and how the devotees of Rome mechanically tell their prayers upon their beads. The rosary, however, is no invention of the Papacy. It is of the highest antiquity, and almost universally found among Pagan nations. The rosary was used as a sacred instrument among the ancient Mexicans.§ It is commonly employed among the Brahmins of Hindustan; and in the Hindoo sacred books reference is made to it again and again. Thus, in an account of the death of Sati, the wife of Shiva, we find the rosary introduced: "On hearing of this event, Shiva fainted from grief; then, having recovered, he hastened to the banks of the river of heaven, where he

* OVID, *Metamorphoses*, lib. v. fab. 6, ll. 391-395, and fab. 8, ll. 468-473. Ovid speaks of the tears which Proserpine shed when, on her robe being torn from top to bottom, all the flowers which she had been gathering up in it fell to the ground, as showing only the simplicity of a girlish mind. But this is evidently only for the uninitiated. The lamentations of Ceres, which were intimately connected with the fall of these flowers, and the *curse* upon the ground that immediately followed, indicated something entirely different. But on that I cannot enter here.

† Lucretius, addressing Venus, says, "Tibi suaveis dædala tellus summittit flores."—Lib. i. v. 6, 7, p. 2.

‡ It is evident that this expression does not mean merely that they should worship Him in sincerity, but in simplicity, as opposed to the Jewish symbolical worship.

§ HUMBOLDT, vol. ii. p. 20.

beheld lying the body of his beloved Sati, arrayed in white garments, *holding a rosary in her hand*, and glowing with splendour, bright as burnished gold."* In Thibet it has been used from time immemorial, and among all the millions in the East that adhere to the Buddhist faith. The following, from Sir John F. Davis, will show how it is employed in China: "From the Tartar religion of the Lamas, the rosary of 108 beads has become a part of the ceremonial dress attached to the nine grades of official rank. It consists of a necklace of stones and coral, nearly as large as a pigeon's egg, descending to the waist, and distinguished by various beads, according to the quality of the wearer. There is a small rosary of eighteen beads, of inferior size, *with which the bonzes count their prayers and ejaculations exactly as in the Romish ritual.* The laity in China sometimes wear this at the wrist, perfumed with musk, and give it the name of Heang-choo, or fragrant beads."† In Asiatic Greece the rosary was commonly used, as may be seen from the image of the Ephesian Diana.‡ In Pagan Rome the same appears to have been the case. The necklaces which the Roman ladies wore were not merely ornamental bands about the neck, but hung down the breast,§ just as the modern rosaries do; and the name by which they were called indicates the use to which they were applied. "*Monilé*," the ordinary word for a necklace, can have no other meaning than that of a "Remembrancer." Now, whatever might be the pretence, in the first instance, for the introduction of such "Rosaries" or "Remembrancers," the very idea of such a thing is thoroughly Pagan.‖ It supposes that a certain number of prayers must be regularly gone over; it overlooks the grand demand which God makes for the heart, and leads those who use them to believe that form and routine are everything, and that "they must be heard for their much speaking."

In the Church of Rome a new kind of devotion has of late been largely introduced, in which the beads play an important part, and which shows what new and additional strides in the direction of the old Babylonian Paganism the Papacy every day is steadily making. I refer to the "Rosary of the Sacred Heart." It is not very long since the worship of the "Sacred Heart" was first introduced; and now, everywhere it is the favourite worship. It was so in ancient Babylon, as is evident from the Babylonian system as it appeared in Egypt. There also a "Sacred Heart" was venerated. The "Heart" was one of the sacred symbols of Osiris when he was born again, and appeared as Harpocrates, or the infant divinity,¶ borne in the arms of his mother Isis. Therefore, the fruit of the Egyptian Perséa was peculiarly sacred to him, from its resemblance to the

* *Vaivashi Puran*, KENNEDY, p. 332.

† *China*, vol. i. p. 391. ‡ See Woodcut, Fig. 8, p. 29.

§ "Dat *longa* monilia collo."—OVID, *Metam.*, lib. x. l. 264, vol. ii. p. 498.

‖ "Rosary" itself seems to be from the Chaldee "Ro," "thought," and "Shareh," "director."

¶ The name Harpocrates, as shown by Bunsen, signifies "Horus, the *child*."

HUMAN HEART."* Hence this infant divinity was frequently represented with a heart, or the heart-shaped fruit of the Perséa, in one of his hands.† (Fig. 40.) The accompanying woodcut is from *Pompeii;* but the following extract from John Bell's criticism on the antiques in the Picture Gallery of Florence, will show that the boyish divinity had been represented elsewhere also in ancient times in the same manner. Speaking of a statue of Cupid, he says it is "a fair, full, fleshy, round boy, in fine and sportive action, *tossing back a heart.*"‡ Thus the boy-god came to be regarded as the "god of the heart," in other words, as Cupid, or the god of love. To identify this infant divinity, with his father "the mighty hunter," he was equipped with "bow and arrows;" and in the hands of the poets, for the amusement of the profane vulgar, this sportive boy-god was celebrated as taking aim with his gold-tipped shafts at the hearts of mankind. His real character, however, as the above statement shows, and as we have seen reason already to conclude, was far higher and of a very different kind. He was the woman's seed. Venus and her son Cupid, then, were none other than the Madonna and the child.§ Looking at the subject in this light, the real force and meaning of the language will appear, which Virgil puts into the mouth of Venus, when addressing the youthful Cupid:—

Fig. 40.

"My son, *my strength*, whose mighty power alone
Controls the thunderer on his awful throne,
To thee thy much afflicted mother flies,
And on thy succour and thy faith relies."||

From what we have seen already as to the *power and glory* of the Goddess Mother being entirely built on the divine character attributed to her *Son*, the reader must see how exactly this is brought out, when the Son is called "THE STRENGTH" of his Mother. As the boy-god, whose symbol was the *heart*, was recognised as the god of childhood, this very satisfactorily accounts for one of the peculiar customs of the Romans. Kennett tells us, in his *Antiquities*, that the Roman youths, in their tender years, used to wear a golden ornament suspended from their necks, called *bulla*, which

* PLUTARCH, *De Iside*, vol. ii. p. 378, C. † *Pompeii*, vol. ii. p. 177.

‡ JOHN BELL'S *Italy*, p. 269. Edinburgh, 1825.

§ The following lines of Ovid will show that *he* distinctly identified Venus and Cupid with the Babylonian "Mother and Child:"

"Terribilem quondam fugiens Typhona Dione
Tunc cum pro cœlo Jupiter arma tulit,
Venit ad *Euphraten*, comitata Cupidine parvo,
Inque Palæstinæ margine sedit aquæ."
Fasti, lib. ii. 461-464, vol. iii. p. 113.

|| *Æneid*, Book i. 937-940. DRYDEN'S Translation, vol. ii. p. 335; in Original, ll. 668-670.

was hollow, and *heart*-shaped.* Barker, in his work on Cilicia, while admitting that the Roman bulla was *heart*-shaped,† further states, that "it was usual at the birth of a child to name it after some divine personage, who was supposed to receive it under his care;" but that the "name was not retained beyond infancy, when the bulla was given up."‡ Who so likely to be the god under whose guardianship the Roman children were put, as the god under one or other of his many names whose express symbol they wore, and who, while he was recognised as the great and mighty war-god, was *also* exhibited himself in his favourite form as a little child?

The veneration of the "sacred heart" seems also to have extended to India, for there Vishnu, the Mediatorial god, in one of his forms, with the mark of the wound in his *foot*,§ in consequence of which he died, and for which such lamentation is annually made, is represented as wearing a *heart* suspended on his breast (Fig. 41).‖ Is it asked, How came it that the "Heart" became the recognised symbol of the Child of the great Mother? The answer is, "The Heart" in Chaldee is "BEL"; and as, at first, after the check given to idolatry, almost all the most important elements of the Chaldean system were introduced under a veil, so under that veil they continued to be shrouded from the gaze of the uninitiated, after the first reason—the reason of fear—had long ceased to operate. Now, the worship of the "Sacred Heart" was just, under a symbol, the worship of the "Sacred *Bel*," that mighty one of Babylon, who had died a martyr for idolatry; for Harpocrates, or Horus, the infant god, was regarded as Bel, born again.¶ That this was in very deed the case, the following extract from Taylor, in one of his notes to his translation of the *Orphic Hymns*, will show. "While Bacchus," says he, was "beholding himself" with admiration "in a mirror, he was miserably torn to pieces by the Titans, who, not content with this cruelty, first boiled his members in water, and afterwards roasted them in the fire; but while they were tasting his

Fig. 41.

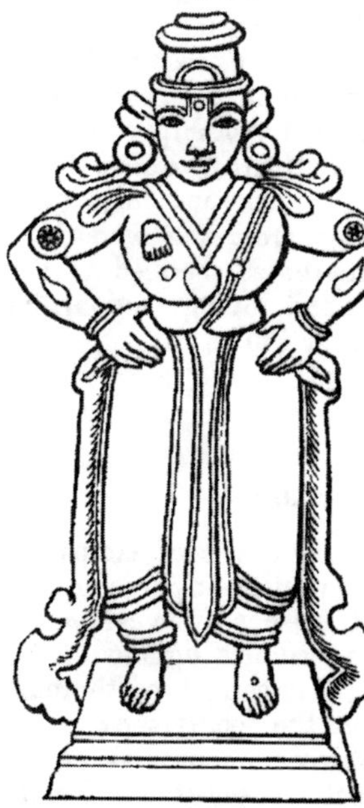

* Pp. 300, 301.

† *Lares and Penates of Cilicia*, p. 147.

‡ *Ibid.* p. 166.

§ See *ante*, in regard to the death of Crishna, one of the forms of Vishnu, p. 61.

‖ From MOOR'S *Pantheon*, Plate 11, Fig. 6.

¶ See *ante*, p. 69.

flesh thus dressed, Jupiter, excited by the steam, and perceiving the cruelty of the deed, hurled his thunder at the Titans, but committed his members to Apollo, the brother of Bacchus, that they might be properly interred. And this being performed, Dionysius [*i.e.*, Bacchus], (whose HEART, during his laceration, was snatched away by Minerva and preserved) by a new REGENERATION, again emerged, and he being restored to his pristine life and integrity, afterwards filled up the number of the gods." * This surely shows, in a striking light, the peculiar *sacredness* of the *heart* of Bacchus; and that the regeneration of his *heart* has the very meaning I have attached to it—viz., the new birth or new incarnation of Nimrod or Bel. When Bel, however, was born again as a child, he was, as we have seen, represented as an incarnation of the sun. Therefore, to indicate his connection with the fiery and burning sun, the "sacred heart" was frequently represented as a "heart of *flame*." † So the "Sacred Heart" of Rome is actually worshipped as a *flaming* heart, as may be seen on the rosaries devoted to that worship. Of what use, then, is it to say that the "Sacred Heart" which Rome worships is called by the name of "Jesus," when not only is the devotion given to a material image borrowed from the worship of the Babylonian Antichrist, but when the attributes ascribed to that "Jesus" are *not* the attributes of the living and loving Saviour, but the genuine attributes of the ancient Moloch or Bel?

SECTION V.—LAMPS AND WAX-CANDLES.

Another peculiarity of the Papal worship is the use of lamps and wax-candles. If the Madonna and child are set up in a niche, they must have a lamp to burn before them; if mass is to be celebrated, though in broad daylight, there must be wax-candles lighted on the altar; if a grand procession is to be formed, it cannot be thorough and complete without lighted tapers to grace the goodly show. The use of these lamps and tapers comes from the same source as all the rest of the Papal superstition. That which caused the "Heart," when it became an emblem of the incarnate Son, to be represented as a heart on *fire*, required also that burning lamps and lighted candles should form part of the worship of that Son; for so, according to the established rites of Zoroaster, was the sun-god worshipped.‡ When every Egyptian on the same night was required to light a lamp before his house in the open air, this was an act of homage to the sun, that had veiled its glory by enshrouding itself in a human form.§ When the Yezidis of Koordistan, at this day, once a-year celebrate their festival of "burning lamps," that, too, is to the

* TAYLOR'S *Mystic Hymns of Orpheus.* Note, p. 88.
† See Fig. 4, p. 17, with flaming heart in one of the hands.
‡ See third Note.
§ See *ante*, p. 118.

honour of Sheikh Shems, or the Sun.* Now, what on these high occasions was done on a grand scale was also done on a smaller scale, in the individual acts of worship to their god, by the lighting of lamps and tapers before the favourite divinity. In Babylon, this practice had been exceedingly prevalent, as we learn from the Apocryphal writer of the Book of Baruch. "They (the Babylonians)," says he, "light up lamps to their gods, and that in greater numbers, too, than they do for themselves, although the gods cannot see one of them, and are senseless as the beams of their houses."† In Pagan Rome, the same practice was observed. Thus we find Licinius, the Pagan Emperor, before joining battle with Constantine, his rival, calling a council of his friends in a thick wood, and there offering sacrifices to his gods, "lighting up wax-tapers" before them, and at the same time, in his speech, giving his gods a hint, that if they did not give him the victory against Constantine, his enemy and theirs, he would be under the necessity of abandoning their worship, and lighting up no more "wax-tapers to their honour."‡ In the Pagan processions, also, at Rome, the wax-candles largely figured. "At these solemnities," says Dr. Middleton, referring to Apuleius as his authority, "at these solemnities, the chief magistrate used frequently to assist, in robes of ceremony, attended by the priests in surplices, *with wax-candles in their hands*, carrying upon a pageant or thensa, the images of their gods, dressed out in their best clothes; these were usually followed by the principal youth of the place, in white linen vestments or surplices, singing hymns in honour of the gods whose festivals they were celebrating, accompanied by crowds of all sorts that were initiated in the same religion, all with flambeaux or *wax-candles* in their hands."§ Now, so thoroughly and exclusively Pagan was this custom of lighting up lamps and candles in daylight, that we find Christian writers, such as Lactantius, in the fourth century, exposing the absurdity of the practice, and deriding the Romans "for lighting up candles to God, as if He lived in the dark."‖ Had such a custom at that time gained the least footing among Christians, Lactantius could never have ridiculed it as he does, as a practice peculiar to Paganism. But what was unknown to the Christian Church in the beginning of the fourth century, soon thereafter began to creep in, and now forms one of the most marked peculiarities of that community that boasts that it is the "Mother and mistress of all Churches."

While Rome uses both lamps and wax-candles in her sacred rites, it is evident, however, that she attributes some pre-eminent virtue to

* Identified with Sheik Adi. See *Nineveh and Babylon*, p. 81, and *Nineveh and its Remains*, vol. i. pp. 289, 290.

† BARUCH, vi. 19, 20. The above is from Diodati's Translation. The common English version, so far as the point in hand is concerned, is substantially the same.

‡ EUSEBIUS, *Vita Constantini*, lib. ii. 5, p. 183.

§ MIDDLETON'S *Letter from Rome*, p. 189. APULEIUS, vol. i., *Metam.*, cap. ix. pp. 1014-1016, and cap. x. pp. 1019-1021.

‖ LACTANTIUS, *Institut.*, lib. vi. cap. 2, p. 289.

the latter above all other lights. Up to the time of the Council of Trent, she thus prayed on Easter Eve, at the blessing of the Easter candles: "Calling upon thee in thy works, this holy Eve of Easter, we offer most humbly unto thy Majesty this sacrifice; namely, a fire not defiled with the fat of flesh, nor polluted with unholy oil or ointment, nor attainted with any profane fire; but we offer unto thee with obedience, proceeding from perfect devotion, a fire of wrought WAX and wick, kindled and made to burn in honour of thy name. This so great a MYSTERY therefore, and the marvellous sacrament of this holy eve, must needs he extolled with due and deserved praises." * That there *was* some occult "Mystery," as is here declared, couched under the "wax-candles," in the original system of idolatry, from which Rome derived its ritual, may be well believed, when it is observed with what unanimity nations the most remote have agreed to use *wax-candles* in their sacred rites. Among the Tungusians, near the Lake Baikal in Siberia, "*wax-tapers* are placed before the Burchans," the gods or idols of that country.† In the Molucca Islands, wax-tapers are used in the worship of Nito, or Devil, whom these islanders adore. "Twenty or thirty persons having assembled," says Hurd, "they summon the Nito, by beating a small consecrated drum, whilst two or more of the company light up *wax-tapers*, and pronounce several mysterious words, which they consider as able to conjure him up."‡ In the worship of Ceylon, the use of wax-candles is an indispensable requisite. "In Ceylon," says the same author, "some devotees, who are not priests, erect chapels for themselves, but in each of them they are obliged to have an image of Buddha, and light up tapers or *wax-candles* before it, and adorn it with flowers."§ A practice thus so general must have come from some primeval source, and must have originally had some mystic reason at the bottom of it. The wax-candle was, in fact, a *hieroglyphic*, like so many other things which we have already seen, and was intended to exhibit the Babylonian god in one of the essential characters of the Great Mediator. The classic reader may remember that one of the gods of primeval antiquity was called Ouranos,|| that is, "The Enlightener." In this very character

* "Office for Easter Eve," in *Review of Epistle of* Dr. GENTIANUS HARVET *of Louvaine*, p. 229, B, and 230, A.

† *Asiatic Journal*, vol. xvii. pp. 593, 596.

‡ *Rites and Ceremonies*, p. 91, col. 1.

§ *Ibid.* p. 95, col. 2.

|| From *Aor* or *our*, "light," and *ân*, "to act upon" or produce, the same as our English particle *en*, "to make." *Ouranos*, then, is "The Enlightener." This Ouranos is, by Sanchuniathon, the Phœnician, called the *son* of Elioun—*i.e.*, as he himself, or Philo-Byblius, interprets the name, "The Most High."—(SANCH., pp. 16-19.) Ouranos, in the physical sense, is "The Shiner;" and by Hesychius (*sub voce* "Akmōn") it is made equivalent to *Kronos*, which also has the same meaning, for *Krn*, the verb from which it comes, signifies either "to put forth horns," or "to send forth rays of light;" and, therefore, while the epithet Kronos, or "The Horned One," had primarily reference to the physical power of Nimrod as a "mighty" king; when that king was deified, and made "Lord of Heaven," that name, Kronos, was still applied to him in his new character as "The Shiner or Lightgiver." The distinction made by Hesiod between Ouranos

was Nimrod worshipped when he was deified. As the Sun-god he was regarded not only as the illuminator of the material world, but as the enlightener of the *souls* of men, for he was recognised as the revealer of "goodness and truth."* It is evident, from the Old Testament, not less than the New, that the proper and personal name of our Lord Jesus Christ is, "The Word of God," as the Revealer of the heart and counsels of the Godhead. Now, to identify the Sun-god with the Great Revealer of the Godhead, while under the name of Mithra, he was exhibited in sculpture as a Lion; that Lion had a *Bee* represented between his lips.† (Fig. 42.) The bee between the *lips* of the Sun-god was intended to point him out as "the Word;" for Dabar, the expression which signifies in Chaldee a "Bee," signifies also a "Word"; and the position of that bee in the *mouth* leaves no doubt as to the idea intended to be conveyed. It was intended to impress the belief that Mithra (who, says Plutarch, was worshipped as *Mesītēs*, "The Mediator"),‡ in his character as Ouranos, "The Enlightener," was no other than that glorious one of whom the Evangelist John says, "In the beginning was the Word, and the Word was with God, and the Word was God. The same was in the beginning with God. . . . In Him was life; and the life was THE LIGHT OF MEN." The Lord Jesus Christ ever was the revealer of the Godhead, and must have been known to the patriarchs as such; for the same Evangelist says, "No man hath seen God at any time: the only-begotten Son, which is in the bosom of the Father, He hath *declared*," that is, He hath *revealed* "Him." Before the Saviour came, the ancient Jews commonly spoke of the Messiah, or the Son of God, under the name of Dabar, or the "Word." This will appear from a consideration of what is stated in the 3rd chapter of 1st Samuel. In the first verse of that chapter it is said, "The WORD of the Lord was precious in those days; there was no open vision," that is, in consequence of the sin of Eli, the Lord had not, for a long time, revealed Himself in vision to him, as He did to the prophets. When the Lord had called

Fig. 42.

and Kronos, is no argument against the real substantial identity of these divinities originally as *Pagan* divinities; for Herodotus (*Hist.*, lib. ii. cap. 53) states that Hesiod had a hand in "*inventing* a theogony" for the Greeks, which implies that some at least of the details of that theogony must have come from his own fancy; and, on examination, it will be found, when the veil of allegory is removed, that Hesiod's "Ouranos," though introduced as one of the Pagan gods, was really at bottom the "God of Heaven," the living and true God. See what is said in regard to Hesiod's "Titan" in Chap. VII. Sect. V.

* WILKINSON, vol. iv. p. 189.

† DUPUIS, *De l'origine des tous les cultes*, vol. iv. p. 194. The above figure is from HYDE, *De Vetere Religione Persarum*, p. 113.

‡ PLUTARCH, *De Iside*, vol. ii. p. 369.

Samuel, this "vision" of the God of Israel was restored (though not to Eli), for it is said in the last verse (v. 21), "And the Lord APPEARED again in Shiloh; for the Lord *revealed* Himself to Samuel by the WORD of the Lord." Although the Lord *spake* to Samuel, this language implies more than speech, for it is said, "The Lord *appeared*"—*i.e.*, was *seen*. When the Lord *revealed* Himself, or was *seen* by Samuel, it is said that it was "by (Dabar) the Word of the Lord." The "Word of the Lord" to be visible, must have been the personal "Word of God," that is, Christ.* This had evidently been a primitive name by which He was known; and therefore it is not wonderful that Plato should speak of the second person of his Trinity under the name of the Logos, which is just a translation of "Dabar," or "the Word."† Now, the light of the wax-candle, as the light from Dabar, "the Bee," was set up as the *substitute* of the light of Dabar "the Word." Thus the apostates turned away from the "True Light," and set up a shadow in His stead. That this was really the case is plain; for, says Crabb, speaking of Saturn, "on his altars were placed wax-tapers lighted, because by Saturn men were reduced from the darkness of error to the light of truth."‡ In Asiatic Greece, the Babylonian god was evidently recognised as the Light-giving "Word," for there we find the Bee occupying such a position as makes it very clear that it was a symbol of the great Revealer. Thus we find Müller referring to the symbols connected with the worship of the Ephesian Diana: "Her constant symbol is the bee, which is not otherwise attributed to Diana. . . . . The chief priest himself was called Essēn, or the *king-bee.*"§ The character of the chief priest shows the character of the god he represented. The contemplar divinity of Diana, the tower-bearing goddess, was of course the same divinity as invariably accompanied the Babylonian goddess: and this title of the priest shows that the Bee which appeared on her medals was just another symbol for her child, as the "Seed of the Woman," in his assumed character, as *Dabar*, "The Word" that enlightened the souls of men. That this is the precise "Mystery" couched under the wax-candles burning on the altars of the Papacy, we have very remarkable evidence from its own formularies; for, in the very same place in which the "Mystery" of the wax-candle is spoken of, thus does Rome refer to the Bee, by which the wax is produced: "Forasmuch as we do marvellously wonder, in considering the first beginning of this substance, to wit, wax-

* After the Babylonish captivity, as the Chaldee Targums or Paraphrases of the Old Testament show, Christ was commonly called by the title "The Word of the Lord." In these Targums of later Chaldee, the term for "The Word" is "Mimra"; but this word, though a synonym for that which is used in the Hebrew Scriptures, is never used there. Dabar is the word employed. This is so well recognised that, in the Hebrew translation of John's Gospel in Bagster's Polyglott, the first verse runs thus: "In the beginning was the Word (Dabar)."

† *Platonis Opera*, vol. i. p. 85, E.

‡ CRABB'S *Mythology*, p. 12.

§ MÜLLER'S *Dorians*, vol. i. pp. 403, 404. Oxford, 1830.

tapers, then must we of necessity greatly extol the original of Bees, for . . . . they gather the flowers with their feet, yet the flowers are not injured thereby; they bring forth no young ones, but deliver their young swarms through their *mouths*, like as Christ (for a wonderful example) is proceeded from His Father's MOUTH."* Here it is evident that Christ is referred to as the "Word of God;" and how could any imagination ever have conceived such a parallel as is contained in this passage, had it not been for the equivoque between "Dabar," "the Bee," and "Dabar," "the Word." In a Popish work already quoted, the *Pancarpium Marianum*, I find the Lord Jesus expressly called by the name of the Bee. Referring to Mary, under the title of "The Paradise of Delight," the author thus speaks: "In this Paradise that celestial Bee, that is, the *incarnate Wisdom*, did feed. Here it found that dropping honeycomb, with which the whole bitterness of the corrupted world has been turned into sweetness."† This blasphemously represents the Lord Jesus as having derived everything necessary to bless the world from His mother! Could this ever have come from the Bible? No. It must have come only from the source where the writer learned to call "the incarnate Wisdom" by the name of the Bee. Now, as the

* *Review of Epistle of* DR. GENTIANUS HARVET *of Louvaine*, pp. 349, B, and 350, A. This work, which is commonly called *The Beehive of the Roman Church*, contains the original Latin of the passage translated above. The passage in question is to be found in at least two Roman Missals, which, however, are now very rare—viz., one printed at Vienna in 1506, fol. 75, p. 2, with which the quotation in the text has been compared and verified; and one printed at Venice in 1522. These dates are antecedent to the establishment of the Reformation; and it appears that this passage was expunged from subsequent editions, as being unfit to stand the searching scrutiny to which everything in regard to religion was subjected in consequence of that great event. The ceremonial of blessing the candles, however, which has no place in the *Pontificale Romanum* in the Edinburgh Advocates' Library, is to be found in the *Pontificale Romanum*, Venice, 1543, p. 195, and in *Pontificale Romanum*, Venice, 1572, p. 183. In the ceremony of blessing the candles, given in the *Roman Missal*, printed at Paris, 1677, at p. 181 and following pages, there is great praise of the Bee, strongly resembling the passage quoted in the text. The introduction of such an extraordinary formula into a religious ceremony is of very ancient date, and is distinctly traced to an Italian source; for, in the works of the Popish Bishop Ennodius, who occupied an Italian diocese in the sixth century, we find the counterpart of that under consideration. Thus, in a prayer in regard to the "Easter Candle," the reason for offering up the wax-candle is expressly declared to be, because that through means of the bees that produce the wax of which it is made, "earth has an image of what is PECULIAR TO HEAVEN" (*meretur habere terra quod cœli est*) (ENNOD. *Opera*, p. 456), and that in regard to the very subject of GENERATION; the bees being able, "through the virtue of herbs, to pour forth their young through their MOUTHS with less waste of time than all other creatures do in the ordinary way" ("prolem . . . . quam herbarum lucro, diligentius possunt ore profligare quam *semine*"). (*Ibid.*) This prayer contains the precise idea of the prayer in the text; and there is only one way of accounting for the origin of such an idea. It must have come from a Chaldean Liturgy.

For discovering this first link in the chain of evidence on this important point, now happily brought to perfection by another hand, I am indebted to my brother, Mr. Hislop, of Blair Lodge, from whose zealous and recondite researches on many other points this work has derived no slight advantage.

† *Pancarpium*, cap. 29, p. 122.

equivoque from which such a name applied to the Lord Jesus springs, is founded only on the Babylonian tongue, it shows whence his theology has come, and it proves also to demonstration that this whole prayer about the blessing of wax-candles must have been drawn from a Babylonian prayer-book. Surely, at every step, the reader must see more and more the exactitude of the Divine name given to the woman on the seven mountains, "Mystery, Babylon the Great!"

SECTION VI.—THE SIGN OF THE CROSS.

There is yet one more symbol of the Romish worship to be noticed, and that is the sign of the cross. In the Papal system, as is well known, the sign of the cross and the image of the cross are all in all. No prayer can be said, no worship engaged in, no step almost can be taken, without the frequent use of the sign of the cross. The cross is looked upon as the grand charm, as the great refuge in every season of danger, in every hour of temptation as the infallible preservative from all the powers of darkness. The cross is adored with all the homage due only to the Most High; and for any one to call it, in the hearing of a genuine Romanist, by the Scriptural term, "the accursed tree," is a mortal offence. To say

Fig. 43.

1.* 2.† 3.‡ 4. 5.

that such a superstitious feeling for the sign of the cross, such worship as Rome pays to a wooden or a metal cross, ever grew out of the saying of Paul, "God forbid that I should glory, save in the cross of our Lord Jesus Christ"—that is, in the doctrine of Christ crucified—is a mere absurdity, a shallow subterfuge and pretence. The magic virtues attributed to the so-called sign of the cross, the worship bestowed on it, never came from such a source. The same sign of the cross that Rome now worships was used in the Babylonian Mysteries, was applied by Paganism to the same magic purposes, was honoured with the same honours. That which is now called the Christian cross was originally no Christian emblem at all, but was the mystic Tau of the Chaldeans and Egyptians—the true original form of the letter T—the initial of the name of Tammuz—which, in Hebrew, radically the same as ancient Chaldee, as found on coins, was formed as in No. 1 of the accompanying woodcut (Fig. 43); and in Etrurian and Coptic, as in Nos. 2 and 3. That

* From KITTO'S *Biblical Cyclopædia*, vol. i. p. 495.
† From Sir W. BETHAM'S *Etruria*, vol. i. p. 54.
‡ From BUNSEN, vol. i. p. 450.

mystic Tau was marked in baptism on the foreheads of those initiated in the Mysteries,* and was used in every variety of way as a most sacred symbol. To identify Tammuz with the sun it was joined sometimes to the circle of the sun, as in No. 4; sometimes it was *inserted* in the circle, as in No. 5.† Whether the Maltese cross, which the Romish bishops append to their names as a symbol of their episcopal dignity, is the letter T, may be doubtful; but there seems no reason to doubt that that Maltese cross is an express symbol of the sun; for Layard found it as a sacred symbol in Nineveh in such a connection as led him to identify it with the sun.‡ The mystic Tau, as the symbol of the great divinity, was called "the sign of life;" it was used as an amulet over the heart;§ it was marked on the official garments of the priests, as on the official garments of the priests of Rome; it was borne by kings in their hand, as a token of their dignity or divinely-conferred authority.‖

Fig. 44.

The Vestal virgins of Pagan Rome wore it suspended from their necklaces, as the nuns do now.¶ The Egyptians did the same, and many of the barbarous nations with whom they had intercourse, as the Egyptian monuments bear witness. In reference to the adorning of some of these tribes, Wilkinson thus writes: "The girdle was sometimes highly ornamented; men as well as women wore ear-

* TERTULLIAN, *De Præscript. Hæret.* cap. 40, vol. ii. p. 54, and Note. The language of Tertullian implies that those who were initiated by baptism in the Mysteries were marked on the forehead in the same way as his Christian countrymen in Africa, who had begun by this time to be marked in baptism with the sign of the cross.

† STEPHEN'S *Central America*, vol. ii. p. 344, Plate 2.

‡ LAYARD'S *Nineveh and Babylon*, p. 211; *Nineveh and its Remains*, vol. ii. p. 446.

§ WILKINSON, vol. i. p. 365, Plate.

‖ See woodcut of King in next Chapter, p. 214.

¶ PÈRE LAFITAN, *Mœurs des Sauvages Ameriquains*, vol. i. p. 442.

rings; and they frequently had a *small cross* suspended to a necklace, or to the collar of their dress. The adoption of this last was not peculiar to them; it was also appended to, or figured upon, the robes of the Rot-n-no; and traces of it may be seen in the fancy ornaments of the Rebo, showing that it was already in use as *early as the fifteenth century before the Christian era*."* (Fig. 44.) There is hardly a Pagan tribe where the cross has not been found. The cross was worshipped by the Pagan Celts long before the incarnation and death of Christ.† "It is a fact," says Maurice, "not less remarkable than well-attested, that the Druids in their groves were accustomed to select the most stately and beautiful tree as an emblem of the Deity they adored, and having cut the side branches, they affixed two of the largest of them to the highest part of the trunk, in such a manner that those branches extended on each side like the arms of a man, and, together with the body, presented the appearance of a HUGE CROSS, and on the bark, in several places, was also inscribed the letter Thau."‡ It was worshipped in Mexico for ages before the Roman Catholic missionaries set foot there, large stone crosses being erected, probably to the "god of rain."§ The cross thus widely worshipped, or regarded as a sacred emblem, was the unequivocal symbol of Bacchus, the Babylonian Messiah, for he was represented with a head-band covered with crosses (see Fig. 45).‖ This symbol of the Babylonian god is reverenced at this day in all the wide wastes of Tartary, where Buddhism prevails, and the way in which it is represented among them forms a striking commentary on the language applied by Rome to the Cross. "The cross," says Colonel Wilford, in the *Asiatic Researches*, "though not an object of *worship* among the Baud'has or Buddhists, is a favourite emblem and device among them. It is exactly the cross of the Manicheans, with leaves and flowers springing from it. This cross, putting forth leaves and flowers (and fruit also, as I am told), is called the divine tree, the tree of the gods, the tree of life and knowledge, and productive of whatever is good and desirable,

Fig. 45.

* WILKINSON, vol. i. p. 376.

† CRABB's *Mythology*, p. 163.

‡ MAURICE's *Indian Antiquities*, vol. vi. p. 49.

§ PRESCOTT's *Conquest of Mexico*, vol. i. p. 242.

‖ The above figure is the head of that which is given in p. 48, *ante*, only magnified, that the crosses may be more distinctly visible. Let the reader turn back from this point, and read over again what is said in p. 154 about the worship at Rome on Good Friday of the "cross of fire," and the full significance of that worship will now appear.

and is placed in the terrestrial paradise."* (Fig. 46.)† Compare this with the language of Rome applied to the cross, and it will be seen how exact is the coincidence. In the Office of the Cross, it is called the "Tree of life," and the worshippers are taught thus to address it: "Hail, O Cross, triumphal wood, true salvation of the world, among trees there is none like thee in leaf, flower, and bud.

Fig. 46.

. . . . O Cross, our only hope, increase righteousness to the godly and pardon the offences of the guilty."‡ Can any one, reading

* *Asiatic Researches*, vol. x. p. 124.

† The two at the top are Standards of Pagan barbarous nations of the East, from BRYANT'S *Mythology*, vol. iii. p. 327. The *black* one in the middle, "The sacred Egyptian Tau or Sign of Life," from WILKINSON, vol. v. p. 283. The two lowest are Buddhist Crosses, from *Asiatic Researches*, vol. x. p. 124.

‡ *Review of Epistle of* Dr. GENTIANUS HARVET *of Louvaine*, p. 251, A. The following is one of the stanzas of the above hymn in the original:—

"O crux, lignum triumphale
Mundi vera salus, vale,
Inter ligna nullum tale
Fronde, flore, germine."

The above was actually versified by the Romanisers in the Church of England, and published along with much besides from the same source, some years ago, in a volume entitled *Devotions on the Passion*. The *London Record*, of April, 1842, gave the following as a specimen of the "*Devotions*" provided by these "wolves in sheep's clothing" for members of the Church of England:—

"O faithful cross, thou peerless tree,
No forest yields the like of thee,
Leaf, flower, and bud;
Sweet is the wood, and sweet the weight
And sweet the nails that penetrate
Thee, thou sweet wood."

the gospel narrative of the crucifixion, possibly believe that that narrative of itself could ever germinate into such extravagance of "leaf, flower, and bud," as thus appears in this Roman Office? But when it is considered that the Buddhist, like the Babylonian cross, was the recognised emblem of Tammuz, who was known as the misletoe branch, or "All-heal," then it is easy to see how the sacred Initial should be represented as covered with leaves, and how Rome, in adopting it, should call it the "Medicine which preserves the healthful, heals the sick, and does what mere human power alone could never do."*

Now, this Pagan symbol seems first to have crept into the Christian Church in Egypt, and generally into Africa. A statement of Tertullian, about the middle of the third century, shows how much, by that time, the Church of Carthage was infected with the old leaven.† Egypt especially, which was never thoroughly evangelised appears to have taken the lead in bringing in this Pagan symbol. The first form of that which is called the *Christian Cross*, found on *Christian* monuments there, is the unequivocal Pagan Tau, or Egyptian "Sign of life." Let the reader peruse the following statement of Sir G. Wilkinson: "A still more curious fact may be mentioned respecting this hieroglyphical character [the Tau], that the early Christians of Egypt adopted it in lieu of the cross, which was *afterwards* substituted for it, prefixing it to inscriptions in the same manner as the cross in *later times*. For, though Dr. Young had some scruples in believing the statement of Sir A. Edmonstone, that it holds that position in the sepulchres of the great Oasis, I can attest that such is the case, and that numerous inscriptions, headed by the *Tau*, are preserved to the present day on early Christian monuments."‡ The drift of this statement is evidently this, that in Egypt the earliest form of that which has since been *called* the cross, was no other than the "Crux Ansata," or "Sign of life," borne by Osiris and all the Egyptian gods; that the *ansa* or "handle" was afterwards dispensed with, and that it became the simple Tau, or ordinary cross, as it appears at this day, and that the design of its first employment on the sepulchres, therefore, could have no reference to the crucifixion of the Nazarene, but was simply the result of the attachment to old and long-cherished Pagan symbols, which is always strong in those who, with the adoption of the Christian name and profession, are still, to a large extent, Pagan in heart and feeling. This, and this only, is the origin of the worship of the "cross."

This, no doubt, will appear all very strange and very incredible to those who have read Church history, as most have done to a large extent, even amongst Protestants, through Romish spectacles; and especially to those who call to mind the famous story told of the miraculous appearance of the cross to Constantine on the day before

* From hymn already quoted.

† TERTULLIAN, *De Corona Militis*, cap. iii., vol. ii. p. 80.

‡ WILKINSON, vol. v. pp. 283, 284.

the decisive victory at the Milvian bridge, that decided the fortunes of avowed Paganism and nominal Christianity. That story, as commonly told, if true, would certainly give a Divine sanction to the reverence for the cross. But that story, when sifted to the bottom, according to the common version of it, will be found to be based on a delusion—a delusion, however, into which so good a man as Milner has allowed himself to fall. Milner's account is as follows:—"Constantine, marching from France into Italy against Maxentius, in an expedition which was likely either to exalt or to ruin him, was oppressed with anxiety. Some god he thought needful to protect him; the God of the Christians he was most inclined to respect, but he wanted some satisfactory proof of His real existence and power, and he neither understood the means of acquiring this, nor could he be content with the atheistic indifference in which so many generals and heroes since his time have acquiesced. He prayed, he implored with such vehemence and importunity, and God left him not unanswered. While he was marching with his forces in the afternoon, the trophy of the cross appeared very luminous in the heavens, brighter than the sun, with this inscription, 'Conquer by this.' He and his soldiers were astonished at the sight; but he continued pondering on the event till night. And Christ appeared to him when asleep with the same sign of the cross, and directed him to make use of the symbol as his military ensign."* Such is the statement of Milner. Now, in regard to the "trophy of the cross," a few words will suffice to show that it is utterly unfounded. I do not think it necessary to dispute the fact of some miraculous sign having been given. There may, or there may not, have been on this occasion a "*dignus vindice nodus*," a crisis worthy of a Divine interposition. Whether, however, there was anything out of the ordinary course, I do not inquire. But this I say, on the *supposition* that Constantine in this matter acted in good faith, and that there actually *was* a miraculous appearance in the heavens, that it was not the sign of the cross that was seen, but quite a different thing, the *name* of Christ. That this was the case, we have at once the testimony of Lactantius, who was the tutor of Constantine's son Crispus—the earliest author who gives any account of the matter, and the indisputable evidence of the standards of Constantine themselves, as handed down to us on medals struck at the time. The testimony of Lactantius is most decisive: "Constantine was warned in a dream to make the celestial sign of God upon his soldiers' shields, and so to join battle. He did as he was bid, and with the transverse letter X circumflecting the head of it, he marks *Christ* or their shields. Equipped with this sign, his army takes the sword."† Now, the

* *Church History*, vol. ii. p. 41. Milner refers to EUSEB. *Constant.* xvii. But this is an error; it is *De Vita Constant.* lib. i. cap. 28, 29, p. 173.

† LACTANTIUS, *De mortibus Persecutorum*, 44, pp. 565, 566. The exact words of Lactantius are as follows:—"Commonitus est in quiete Constantinus, ut cœleste signum Dei notaret in scutis, atque ita prœlium committeret. Fecit ut jussus est et transversâ X literâ summo capite circumflexo, Christum scutis notat. Quo signo armatus exercitus capit ferrum."

letter X was just the initial of the *name* of Christ, being equivalent in Greek to CH. If, therefore, Constantine did as he was bid, when he made "the celestial sign of God" in the form of "the letter X," it was that "letter X," as the symbol of "*Christ*," and *not* the sign of the cross, which he saw in the heavens. When the Labarum, or far-famed standard of Constantine itself, properly so called, was made, we have the evidence of Ambrose, the well-known Bishop of Milan, that that standard was formed on the very principle contained in the statement of Lactantius—viz., simply to display the Redeemer's name. He calls it "Labarum, hoc est Christi sacratum nomine signum."*—"The Labarum, that is, the ensign consecrated by the NAME of Christ."† There is not the slightest allusion to any cross—to anything but the simple name of Christ. While we have these testimonies of Lactantius and Ambrose, when we come to examine the standard of Constantine, we find the accounts of both authors fully borne out; we find that that standard, bearing on it these very words, "*Hoc signo victor eris*," "In this sign thou shalt be a conqueror," said to have been addressed from heaven to the emperor, has nothing at all in the shape of a cross, but "the letter X." In the Roman Catacombs, on a Christian monument to "Sinphonia and her sons," there is a distinct allusion to the story of the vision; but that allusion also shows that the X, and not the cross, was regarded as the "heavenly sign." The words at the head of the inscription are these:—

"IN HOC VINCES ‡
X."

Nothing whatever but the X is here given as the "Victorious Sign." There are some examples, no doubt, of Constantine's standard, in which there is a cross-*bar*, from which the flag is suspended, that contains that "letter X;"§ and Eusebius, who wrote when superstition and apostacy were working, tries hard to make it appear that that cross-bar was the essential element in the ensign of Constantine. But this is obviously a mistake; that cross-bar was nothing new, nothing peculiar to Constantine's standard. Tertullian shows‖ that that cross-bar was found long before on the *vexillum*, the Roman Pagan

* *Ambrosii Opera*, vol. iv. p. 327.

† *Epistle of Ambrose to the Emperor Theodosius about the proposal to restore the Pagan altar of Victory in the Roman Senate.* The subject of the Labarum has been much confused through ignorance of the meaning of the word. Bryant *assumes* (and I was myself formerly led away by the assumption) that it was applied to the standard bearing the crescent and the cross, but he produces no evidence for the assumption; and I am now satisfied that none can be produced. The name Labarum, which is generally believed to have come from the East, treated as an Oriental word, gives forth its meaning at once. It evidently comes from *Lab*, "to vibrate," or "move to and fro," and *âr* "to be active." Interpreted thus, Labarum signifies simply a banner or flag, "waving to and fro" in the wind, and this entirely agrees with the language of Ambrose "an *ensign* consecrated by the *name* of Christ," which implies a banner.

‡ "In this thou shalt overcome."

§ Dr. MAITLAND'S *Church in the Catacombs*, p. 169.

‖ *Apologeticus Adv. Gentes*, cap. 16. vol. i. pp. 368, 369.

standard, that carried a flag; and it was used simply for the purpose of displaying that flag. If, therefore, that cross-bar was the "celestial sign," it needed no voice from heaven to direct Constantine to make it; nor would the making or displaying of it have excited any particular attention on the part of those who saw it. We find no evidence at all that the famous legend, "In this overcome," has any reference to this cross-bar; but we find evidence the most decisive that that legend does refer to the X. Now, that that X was not intended as the sign of the cross, but as the initial of Christ's name, is manifest from this, that the Greek P, equivalent to our R, is inserted in the middle of it, making by their union CHR. Any one who pleases may satisfy himself of this by examining the plates given in Mr. Elliot's *Horæ Apocalypticæ*.* The standard of Constantine, then, was just the *name* of Christ. Whether the device came from earth or from heaven—whether it was suggested by human wisdom or Divine, supposing that Constantine was sincere in his Christian profession, nothing more was implied in it than a literal embodiment of the sentiment of the Psalmist, "In the *name* of the Lord will we display our banners." To display that name on the standards of Imperial Rome was a thing absolutely new; and the sight of that *name*, there can be little doubt, nerved the Christian soldiers in Constantine's army with more than usual fire to fight and conquer at the Milvian bridge.

In the above remarks I have gone on the supposition that Constantine acted in good faith as a Christian. His good faith, however, has been questioned; † and I am not without my suspicions that the X *may* have been intended to have one meaning to the Christians and another to the Pagans. It is certain that the X was the symbol of the god Ham in Egypt, and as such was exhibited on the breast of his image.‡ Whichever view be taken, however, of Constantine's sincerity, the supposed Divine warrant for reverencing the sign of the cross entirely falls to the ground. In regard to the X, there is no doubt that, by the Christians who knew nothing of secret plots or devices, it was generally taken, as Lactantius declares, as equivalent to the name of "*Christ*." In this view, therefore, it had no very great attractions for the Pagans, who, even in worshipping Horus, had always been accustomed to make use of the mystic Tau or cross, as the "sign of life," or the magical charm that secured all that was good, and warded off everything that was evil. When, therefore, multitudes of the Pagans, on the conversion of Constantine, flocked into the Church, like the semi-Pagans of Egypt, they brought along with them their predilection for the old symbol. The consequence was, that in no great length of time, as apostacy proceeded, the X which in itself was not an unnatural symbol of Christ, the true Messiah, and which had once been regarded as such, was allowed to go entirely into disuse, and the Tau, the sign of the cross, the indis-

* *Horæ*, vol. i. pp. 226, 240.

† By GAVAZZI, in his publication entitled *The Free Word*.

‡ See WILKINSON, vol. vi., "Khem."

putable sign of Tammuz, the false Messiah, was everywhere *substituted* in its stead. Thus, by the "sign of the cross," Christ has been crucified anew by those who profess to be His disciples. Now, if these things be matter of historic fact, who can wonder that, in the Romish Church, "the sign of the cross" has always and everywhere been seen to be such an instrument of rank superstition and delusion?

There is more, much more, in the rites and ceremonies of Rome that might be brought to elucidate our subject. But the above may suffice.*

* If the above remarks be well founded, surely it cannot be right that this sign of the Cross, or emblem of Tammuz, should be used in Christian baptism. At the period of the Revolution, a Royal Commission, appointed to inquire into the Rites and Ceremonies of the Church of England, numbering among its members *eight* or *ten* bishops, strongly recommended that the use of the cross, as tending to superstition, should be laid aside. If such a recommendation was given then, and that by such authority as members of the Church of England must respect, how much ought that recommendation to be enforced by the new light which Providence has cast on the subject!

CHAPTER VI.

RELIGIOUS ORDERS.

SECTION I.—THE SOVEREIGN PONTIFF.

THE gift of the ministry is one of the greatest gifts which Christ has bestowed upon the world. It is in reference to this that the Psalmist, predicting the ascension of Christ, thus loftily speaks of its blessed results: "Thou hast ascended up on high; Thou hast led captivity captive; Thou hast received *gifts for men*, even for the rebellious, that the Lord God might dwell among them" (Eph. iv. 8-11). The Church of Rome, at its first planting, had the divinely-bestowed gift of a Scriptural ministry and government; and then "its faith was spoken of throughout the whole world;" its works of righteousness were both rich and abundant. But, in an evil hour, the Babylonian element was admitted into its ministry, and thenceforth, that which had been intended as a blessing, was converted into a curse. Since then, instead of sanctifying men, it has only been the means of demoralising them, and making them "twofold more the children of hell" than they would have been if they had been left simply to themselves.

If there be any who imagine that there is some occult and mysterious virtue in an apostolic succession that comes through the Papacy, let them seriously consider the real character of the Pope's own orders, and of those of his bishops and clergy. From the Pope downwards, all can be shown to be *now* radically Babylonian. The College of Cardinals, with the Pope at its head, is just the counterpart of the Pagan College of Pontiffs, with its "Pontifex Maximus," or "Sovereign Pontiff," which had existed in Rome from the earliest times, and which is known to have been framed on the model of the grand original Council of Pontiffs at Babylon. The Pope *now* pretends to supremacy in the Church as the successor of Peter, to whom it is alleged that our Lord exclusively committed the keys of the kingdom of heaven. But here is the important fact that, *till* the Pope was invested with the title, which for a *thousand* years had had attached to it the power of the keys of Janus and Cybele,* no such claim to pre-eminence, or anything approaching to it, was ever publicly made on his part, on *the ground of his being the possessor of*

* It was only in the second century before the Christian era that the worship of Cybele, *under that name*, was introduced into Rome; but the same goddess, under the name of Cardea, with the "*power of the key*," was worshipped in Rome, along with Janus, ages before.—OVID'S *Fasti*, vol. iii. l. 101, p. 346.

the keys bestowed on Peter. Very early, indeed, did the bishops of Rome show a proud and ambitious spirit; but, for the first three centuries, their claim for superior honour was founded simply on the dignity of their see, as being that of the imperial city, the capital of the Roman world. When, however, the seat of empire was removed to the East, and Constantinople threatened to eclipse Rome, some new ground for maintaining the dignity of the Bishop of Rome must be sought. That new ground was found when, about 378, the Pope fell heir to the keys that were the symbols of two well-known Pagan divinities at Rome. Janus bore a key,* and Cybele bore a key;† and these are the two keys that the Pope emblazons on his arms as the ensigns of his spiritual authority. How the Pope came to be regarded as wielding the power of these keys will appear in the sequel; but that he did, in the popular apprehension, become entitled to that power at the period referred to is certain. Now, when he had come in the estimation of the *Pagans*, to occupy the place of the representatives of Janus and Cybele, and therefore to be entitled to bear their keys, the Pope saw that if he could only get it believed among the *Christians* that *Peter alone* had the power of the keys, and that he was Peter's successor, then the sight of these keys would keep up the delusion, and thus, though the temporal dignity of Rome as a *city* should decay, his own dignity as the *bishop* of Rome would be more firmly established than ever. On this policy it is evident he acted. Some time was allowed to pass away, and then, when the secret working of the Mystery of iniquity had prepared the way for it, for the first time did the Pope publicly assert his pre-eminence, as founded on the keys given to Peter. About 378 was he raised to the position which gave him, in Pagan estimation, the power of the keys referred to. In 431, and not before, did he publicly lay claim to the possession of Peter's keys.‡ This, surely, is a striking coincidence. Does the reader ask how it was possible that men could give credit to such a baseless assumption? The words of Scripture, in regard to this very subject, give a very solemn but satisfactory answer (2 Thess. ii. 10, 11): "Because they received not the love of the truth, that they might be saved. . . . . For this cause God shall send them strong delusion, that they should believe a lie." Few lies could be more gross; but, in course of time, it came to be widely believed; and now, as the statue of Jupiter is worshipped at Rome as the veritable image of Peter, so the keys of Janus and Cybele have for ages been devoutly believed to represent the keys of the same apostle.

While nothing but judicial infatuation can account for the credulity of the Christians in regarding these keys as emblems of an exclusive power given by Christ to the Pope through Peter, it is not

* OVID's *Fasti*, lib. i. ll. 95, 99, vol. iii. p. 18.

† TOOKE's *Pantheon*, "Cybele," p. 153.

‡ In proof of the fact that this claim was first made in 431, see ELLIOT's *Horæ*, vol. iii. p. 139. In 429 he gave a hint at it, but it was only in 431 that this claim was broadly and distinctly made.

difficult to see how the *Pagans* would rally round the Pope all the more readily when they heard him found his power on the possession of *Peter's* keys. The keys that the Pope bore *were* the keys of a "Peter" well known to the Pagans initiated in the Chaldean Mysteries. That Peter the apostle was ever Bishop of Rome has been proved again and again to be an arrant fable. That he ever even set foot in Rome is at the best highly doubtful. His visit to that city rests on no better authority than that of a writer at the end of the second century or beginning of the third—viz., the author of the work called *The Clementines*,* who gravely tells us that on the occasion of his visit, finding Simon Magus there, the apostle challenged him to give proof of his miraculous or magical powers, whereupon the sorcerer flew up into the air, and Peter brought him down in such haste that his leg was broken.† All historians of repute have at once rejected this story of the apostolic encounter with the magician as being destitute of all contemporary evidence; but as the visit of Peter to Rome rests on the same authority, it must stand or fall along with it, or, at least, it must be admitted to be extremely doubtful. But, while this is the case with Peter the *Christian*, it can be shown to be by no means doubtful that before the Christian era, and downwards, there *was* a "Peter" at Rome, who occupied the highest place in the *Pagan* priesthood. The priest who explained the Mysteries to the initiated was sometimes called by a Greek term, the Hierophant; but in primitive Chaldee, the real language of the Mysteries, his title, as pronounced without the points, was "Peter"—*i.e.*, "the interpreter."‡ As the revealer of that which was hidden, nothing was more natural than that, while opening up the esoteric doctrine of the Mysteries, he should be decorated with the keys of the two divinities whose mysteries he unfolded.§ Thus we may see how the keys of Janus and Cybele would come to be known as the keys of Peter, the "interpreter" of the Mysteries. Yea, we have the strongest evidence that, in countries far removed from one another, and far distant from Rome, these keys were known by initiated Pagans not merely as the "keys of Peter," but as the keys of a Peter identified with Rome. In the Eleusinian Mysteries at Athens, when the candidates for initiation were instructed in the secret doctrine of Paganism, the explanation of that doctrine was read to them out of a book called by ordinary writers the "Book Petroma;" that is, as we are told, a book formed of stone.‖ But this is evidently just a play upon words, according to the usual spirit of Paganism, intended to amuse the vulgar. The nature of the case, and the history of the Mysteries, alike show that this book could be none other than the "Book Pet-Roma;" that is, the "Book of the Grand Interpreter," in other words, of Hermes

* GIESELER, vol. i. pp. 206-208. † See BOWER, vol. i. pp. 1, 2.

‡ PARKHURST'S *Hebrew Lexicon*, p. 602.

§ The Turkish Muftis, or "interpreters" of the *Koran*, derive that name from the very same verb as that from which comes *Miftah*, a key.

‖ POTTER'S *Antiquities*, vol. i., *Mysteries*, p. 356.

Trismegistus, the great "Interpreter of the Gods." In Egypt, from which Athens derived its religion, the books of Hermes were regarded as the divine fountain of all true knowledge of the Mysteries.* In Egypt therefore, Hermes was looked up to in this very character of Grand Interpreter, or "Peter-Roma."† In Athens, Hermes, as is well known, occupied precisely the same place,‡ and, of course, in the sacred language, must have been known by the same title. The priest, therefore, that in the name of Hermes explained the Mysteries, must have been decked not only with the keys of Peter, but with the keys of "Peter-Roma." Here, then, the famous "Book of Stone" begins to appear in a new light, and not only so, but to shed new light on one of the darkest and most puzzling passages of Papal history. It has always been a matter of amazement to candid historical inquirers how it could ever have come to pass that the name of Peter should be associated with *Rome* in the way in which it is found from the fourth century downwards—how so many in different countries had been led to believe that Peter, who was an "apostle of the *circumcision*," had apostatised from his Divine commission, and become bishop of a *Gentile* Church, and that he should be the spiritual ruler in Rome, when no satisfactory evidence could be found for his ever having been in Rome at all. But the book of "Peter-Roma" accounts for what otherwise is entirely inexplicable. The existence of such a title was too valuable to be overlooked by the Papacy; and, according to its usual policy, it was sure, if it had the opportunity, to turn it to the account of its own aggrandisement. And that opportunity it had. When the Pope came, as he did, into intimate connection with the Pagan priesthood; when they came at last, as we shall see they did, under his control,

* The following are the authorities for the statement in the text :—"Jamblichus says that Hermes [*i.e.*, the Egyptian] was the god of all celestial knowledge, which, being communicated by him to his priests, authorised them to inscribe their commentaries with the name of Hermes" (WILKINSON, vol. v., chap. xiii. pp. 9, 10). Again, according to the fabulous accounts of the Egyptian Mercury, he was reported . . . . to have taught men the proper mode of approaching the Deity with prayers and sacrifice (WILKINSON, vol. v., chap. xiii. p. 10). Hermes Trismegistus seems to have been regarded as a new incarnation of Thoth, and possessed of higher honours. The principal books of this Hermes, according to Clemens of Alexandria, were treated by the Egyptians with the most profound respect, and carried in their religious processions (CLEM., ALEX., *Strom.*, lib. vi., vol. iii. pp. 214-219).

† In Egypt, "Petr" was used in this very sense. See BUNSEN, vol. i., *Hieroglyph*, p. 545, where *Ptr* is said to signify "to show." The interpreter was called Hierophantes, which has the very idea of "showing" in it.

‡ The Athenian or Grecian Hermes is celebrated as "The source of invention. . . . . He bestows, too, mathesis on souls, by unfolding the will of the father of Jupiter, and this he accomplishes as the angel or messenger of Jupiter. . . . . He is the guardian of disciplines, because the invention of geometry, reasoning, and language is referred to this god. He presides, therefore over every species of erudition, leading us to an intelligible essence from this mortal abode, governing the different herds of souls" (PROCLUS in *Commentary on First Alcibiades*, in the Notes on TAYLOR'S *Orphic Hymns*, pp. 64, 65). The Grecian Hermes was so essentially the revealer or interpreter of divine things, that Hermeneutes, an interpreter, was currently said to come from his name (HYGINUS, Note to page 114).

what more natural than to seek not only to reconcile Paganism and Christianity, but to make it appear that the Pagan "Peter-Roma," with his keys, meant "Peter of Rome," and that that "Peter of Rome" was the very apostle to whom the Lord Jesus Christ gave the "keys of the kingdom of heaven"? Hence, from the mere jingle of words, persons and things essentially different were confounded; and Paganism and Christianity jumbled together, that the towering ambition of a wicked priest might be gratified; and so, to the blinded Christians of the apostacy, the Pope was the representative of Peter the apostle, while to the initiated Pagans, he was only the representative of Peter, the interpreter of their well-known Mysteries.* Thus was the Pope the express counterpart of "Janus, the double-faced." Oh! what an emphasis of meaning in the Scriptural expression, as applied to the Papacy, "The Mystery of Iniquity"!

The reader will now be prepared to understand how it is that the Pope's Grand Council of State, which assists him in the government of the Church, comes to be called the College of Cardinals. The term Cardinal is derived from *Cardo*, a hinge. Janus, whose key the Pope bears, was the god of doors and hinges, and was called Patulcius and Clusius, "the opener and the shutter."† This had a blasphemous meaning, for he was worshipped at Rome as the grand mediator. Whatever important business was in hand, whatever deity was to be invoked, an invocation first of all must be addressed to Janus,‡ who was recognised as the "God of gods,"§ in whose mysterious divinity the characters of father and son were combined,‖ and without that no prayer could be heard—the "door of heaven" could not be opened.¶ It was this same god whose worship prevailed so exceedingly in Asia Minor at the time when our Lord sent, by his servant John, the seven Apocalyptic messages to the churches established in that region. And, therefore, in one of these messages we find Him tacitly rebuking the profane ascription of His own peculiar dignity to that divinity, and asserting His exclusive claim to the prerogative usually attributed to His rival. Thus, Rev. iii. 7: "And to the angel of the church in Philadelphia write: These things saith he that is holy, he that is true, he that hath the key of David, *he that openeth, and no man shutteth; and shutteth, and no man openeth.*" Now, to this Janus, as Mediator, worshipped in Asia Minor, and equally, from very early times, in Rome, belonged the government of the world; and, "all power in heaven, in earth, and the sea," according to Pagan ideas, was vested in him.** In this character he was said to have "*jus vertendi cardinis*"—the "power of turning the hinge"—of opening the doors of heaven, or of opening

* For evidence in regard to the *title* of the interpreter of the Mysteries, see BRYANT'S *Mythology*, vol. i. pp. 308-311, 356, 359-362.

† LEMPRIERE, *sub voce*.

‡ OVID, *Fasti*, lib. i. ll. 171, 172, vol. iii. p. 24.

§ So called in the *Hymns of the Salii*, MACROB., *Sat.*, lib. i. c. 9, p. 54, col. 2, H.

‖ See *ante*, pp. 28 (Note) and 134.

¶ OVID, *Fasti*, lib. i. ll. 117-121.

** *Ibid.* lib. i. ll. 117, 120, 125.

or shutting the gates of peace or war upon earth. The Pope, therefore, when he set up as the High-priest of Janus, assumed also the "*jus vertendi cardinis*," "the power of turning the hinge,"—of opening and shutting in the blasphemous Pagan sense. Slowly and cautiously at first was this power asserted; but the foundation being laid, steadily, century after century, was the grand superstructure of priestly power erected upon it. The Pagans who saw what strides, under Papal directions, Christianity, as professed in Rome, was making towards Paganism, were more than content to recognise the Pope as possessing this power; they gladly encouraged him to rise, step by step, to the full height of the blasphemous pretensions befitting the representative of Janus—pretensions which, as all men know, are *now*, by the unanimous consent of Western Apostate Christendom, recognised as inherent in the office of the Bishop of Rome. To enable the Pope, however, to rise to the full plenitude of power which he now asserts, the co-operation of others was needed. When his power increased, when his dominion extended, and especially after he became a temporal sovereign, the key of Janus became too heavy for his single hand—he needed some to share with him the power of the "hinge." Hence his privy councillors, his high functionaries of state, who were associated with him in the government of the Church and the world, got the now well-known title of "Cardinals"—the priests of the "*hinge*." This title had been previously borne by the high officials of the Roman Emperor, who, as "Pontifex Maximus," had been himself the representative of Janus, and who delegated his powers to servants of his own. Even in the reign of Theodosius, the Christian Emperor of Rome, the title of Cardinal was borne by his Prime Minister.* But now both the name and the power implied in the name have long since disappeared from all civil functionaries of temporal sovereigns; and those only who aid the Pope in wielding the key of Janus—in opening and shutting—are known by the title of Cardinals, or priests of the "*hinge*."

I have said that the Pope became the representative of Janus, who, it is evident, was none other than the Babylonian Messiah. If the reader only considers the blasphemous assumptions of the Papacy, he will see how exactly it has copied from its original. In the countries where the Babylonian system was most thoroughly developed, we find the Sovereign Pontiff of the Babylonian god invested with the very attributes now ascribed to the Pope. Is the Pope called "*God upon earth*," the "Vice-God," and "Vicar of Jesus Christ"? The King in Egypt, who was Sovereign-Pontiff,† was, says Wilkinson, regarded with the highest reverence as "THE REPRESENTATIVE OF THE DIVINITY ON EARTH." ‡ Is the Pope "Infallible," and does the Church of Rome, in consequence, boast that it has always been

* PARKHURST, *Lexicon*, p. 627.

† Wilkinson shows that the king had the right of enacting laws, and of managing all the affairs of *religion* and the State (vol. ii. p. 22), which proves him to have been Sovereign Pontiff.

‡ WILKINSON'S *Egyptians*, vol. ii. p. 68.

"unchanged and unchangeable"? The same was the case with the Chaldean Pontiff, and the system over which he presided. The Sovereign Pontiff, says the writer just quoted, was believed to be "INCAPABLE OF ERROR,"* and, in consequence, there was "the greatest respect for the sanctity of old edicts;" and hence, no doubt, also the origin of the custom that "the laws of the Medes and Persians could not be altered." Does the Pope receive the adorations of the Cardinals? The king of Babylon, as Sovereign Pontiff, was adored in like manner.† Are kings and ambassadors required to kiss the Pope's *slipper?* This, too, is copied from the same pattern; for, says Professor Gaussen, quoting Strabo and Herodotus, "the kings of Chaldea wore on their feet *slippers* which the kings they conquered used to *kiss.*"‡ In fine, is the Pope addressed by the title of "Your Holiness"? So also was the Pagan Pontiff of Rome. The title seems to have been common to *all* the Pontiffs. Symmachus, the last Pagan representative of the Roman Emperor, as Sovereign Pontiff, addressing one of his colleagues or fellow-pontiffs, on a step of promotion he was about to obtain, says, "I hear that YOUR HOLINESS (*sanctitatem tuam*) is to be called out by the sacred letters."§

Peter's keys have now been restored to their rightful owner. Peter's chair must also go along with them. That far-famed chair came from the very same quarter as the cross-keys. The very same reason that led the Pope to assume the Chaldean keys naturally led him also to take possession of the vacant chair of the Pagan Pontifex Maximus. As the Pontifex, by virtue of his office, had been the Hierophant, or Interpreter of the Mysteries, his chair of office was as well entitled to be called "Peter's" chair as the Pagan keys to be called "the keys of Peter;" and so it was called accordingly. The real pedigree of the far-famed chair of Peter will appear from the following fact: "The Romans had," says Bower, "as they thought, till the year 1662, a pregnant proof, not only of Peter's erecting their

* WILKINSON'S *Egyptians*. The "Infallibility" was a natural result of the popular belief in regard to the relation in which the Sovereign stood to the gods: for, says Diodorus Siculus, speaking of Egypt, the king was believed to be "a partaker of the divine nature" (lib. i. cap. 7, p. 57).

† From the statements of Layard (*Nineveh and its Remains*, vol. ii. pp. 472-474, and *Nineveh and Babylon*, p. 361), it appears that as the king of Egypt was the "Head of the religion and the state," so was the king of Assyria, which included Babylon. Then we have evidence that he was worshipped. The sacred images are represented as adoring him (LAYARD, *Nineveh and its Remains*, vol. ii. p. 464), which could not have been the case if his own subjects did not pay their homage in that way. Then the adoration claimed by Alexander the Great evidently came from this source. It was directly in imitation of the adoration paid to the Persian kings that he required such homage. Quint. Curtius says (lib. viii. cap. 5, pp. 592, 593), "Volebat . . . . itaque *more Persarum* Macedonas venerabundos ipsum salutare prosternentes humi corpora." From Xenophon we have evidence that this Persian custom came from Babylon. It was when Cyrus had entered Babylon that the Persians, for the *first* time, testified their homage to him by adoration; for, "before this," says Xenophon (*Cyropæd.*, lib. viii. p. 215, C), "none of the Persians had given adoration to Cyrus."

‡ GAUSSEN on *Daniel*, vol. i. p. 114.

§ SYMMACHUS, *Epistolæ*, lib. vi. 31, p. 240.

chair, but of his sitting in it himself; for, till that year, the very chair on which they believed, or would make others believe, he had sat, was shown and exposed to public adoration on the 18th of January, the festival of the said chair. But while it was cleaning, in order to set it up in some conspicuous place of the Vatican, the twelve labours of Hercules unluckily appeared on it!"* and so it had to be laid aside. The partisans of the Papacy were not a little disconcerted by this discovery; but they tried to put the best face on the matter they could. "Our worship," said Giacomo Bartolini, in his *Sacred Antiquities of Rome*, while relating the circumstances of the discovery, "Our worship, however, was not misplaced, since it was not to the wood we paid it, but to the prince of the apostles, St. Peter," that had been supposed to sit in it.† Whatever the reader may think of this apology for chair-worship, he will surely at least perceive, taking this in connection with what we have already seen, that the hoary fable of Peter's chair is fairly exploded. In modern times, Rome seems to have been rather unfortunate in regard to Peter's chair; for, even after that which bore the twelve labours of Hercules had been condemned and cast aside, as unfit to bear the light that the Reformation had poured upon the darkness of the Holy See, that which was chosen to replace it was destined to reveal still more ludicrously the barefaced impostures of the Papacy. The former chair was borrowed from the Pagans; the next appears to have been purloined from the Mussulmans; for when the French soldiers under General Bonaparte took possession of Rome in 1795, they found on the back of it, in Arabic, this well-known sentence of the Koran, "There is no God but God, and Mahomet is His Prophet."‡

The Pope has not merely a chair to *sit* in; but he has a chair to be *carried* in, in pomp and state, on men's shoulders, when he pays a visit to St. Peter's, or any of the churches of Rome. Thus does an eye-witness describe such a pageant on the Lord's Day, in the head-quarters of Papal idolatry: "The drums were heard beating without. The guns of the soldiers rung on the stone pavement of the house of God, as, at the bidding of their officer, they grounded, shouldered, and presented arms. How unlike the Sabbath—how unlike religion—how unlike the suitable preparation to receive a minister of the meek and lowly Jesus! Now, moving slowly up, between the two armed lines of soldiers, appeared a long procession of ecclesiastics, bishops, canons, and cardinals, preceding the Roman pontiff, who was borne on a gilded chair, clad in vestments resplendent as the sun. His bearers were twelve men clad in crimson, being immediately preceded by several persons carrying a cross, his mitre, his triple crown, and other insignia of his office. As he was borne

* BOWER's *History of the Popes*, vol. i. p. 7.

† BARTOLINI, *Antichità Sacré di Roma*, p. 32, *Ibid.*

‡ Lady MORGAN's *Italy*, vol. iii. p. 81. Dr. Wiseman tried to dispute this; but, as the *Times*, I think, remarked, "the lady had evidently the best of the argument."

along on the shoulders of men, amid the gaping crowds, his head was shaded or canopied by two immense fans, made of peacock's feathers, which were borne by two attendants."* Thus is it with the Sovereign Pontiff of Rome at this day; only that, frequently, over and above being shaded by the fan, which is just the "Mystic fan of Bacchus," his chair of state is also covered with a regular canopy. Now, look back through the vista of three thousand years, and see how the Sovereign Pontiff of Egypt used to pay a visit to the temple of his god. "Having reached the precincts of the temple," says Wilkinson, "the guards and royal attendants selected to be the representatives of the whole army entered the courts. . . . . Military bands played the favourite airs of the country; and the numerous standards of the different regiments, the banners floating on the wind, the bright lustre of arms, the immense concourse of people, and the imposing majesty of the lofty towers of the propylæa, decked with their bright-coloured flags, streaming above the cornice, pre-

Fig. 47.

sented a scene seldom, we may say, equalled on any occasion, in any country. The most striking feature of this pompous ceremony was the brilliant cortege of the monarch, who was either borne in his chair of state by the principal officers of state, under a rich canopy, or walked on foot, overshadowed with rich flabella and fans of waving plumes."† We give, as a woodcut, from Wilkinson (Fig. 47),‡ the central portion of one of his plates devoted to such an Egyptian procession, that the reader may see with his own eyes how exactly the Pagan agrees with the well-known account of the Papal ceremonial.

So much for Peter's chair and Peter's keys. Now Janus, whose key the Pope usurped with that of his wife or mother Cybele, was also Dagon. Janus, the two-headed god, "who had lived in two

* Begg's *Handbook of Popery*, p. 24.
† Wilkinson, vol. v. pp. 285, 286.
‡ From *Ibid.* vol. vi. Plate 76.

worlds," was the Babylonian divinity as an incarnation of Noah. Dagon, the fish-god, represented that deity as a manifestation of the same patriarch who had lived so long in the waters of the deluge. As the Pope bears the key of Janus, so he wears the mitre of Dagon. The excavations of Nineveh have put this beyond all possibility of doubt. The Papal mitre is entirely different from the mitre of Aaron and the Jewish high priests. That mitre was a turban. The two-horned mitre, which the Pope wears, when he sits on the high altar at Rome and receives the adoration of the Cardinals, is the very mitre worn by Dagon, the fish-god of the Philistines and Babylonians. There were two ways in which Dagon was anciently represented. The one was when he was depicted as half-man half-fish; the upper part being entirely human, the under part ending in the tail of a fish. The other was, when, to use the words of Layard, "the head of the fish formed a *mitre* above that of the man, while its scaly, fan-like tail fell as a cloak behind, leaving the human limbs and feet exposed."* Of Dagon in this form Layard gives a repre-

Fig. 48.

sentation in his last work, which is here represented to the reader (Fig. 48); and no one who examines his mitre, and compares it with the Pope's as given in Elliot's *Horæ*,† can doubt for a moment that from that, and no other source, has the pontifical mitre been derived. The gaping jaws of the fish surmounting the head of the man at Nineveh are the unmistakable counterpart of the horns of the Pope's mitre at Rome. Thus was it in the East, at least five hundred years before the Christian era. The same seems to have been the case also in Egypt; for Wilkinson, speaking of a fish of the species of Silurus, says "that one of the Genii of the Egyptian Pantheon appears under a *human form*, with the head of this fish." ‡ In the West, at a later period, we have evidence that the Pagans had detached the fish-head mitre from the body of the fish, and used that mitre alone to adorn the head of the great Mediatorial god; for on several Maltese Pagan coins that god, with the well-known attributes of Osiris, is represented with nothing of the fish save the

* LAYARD's *Babylon and Nineveh*, p. 343.

† 4th Edit., vol. iii. pt. 4, Plate 27.

‡ WILKINSON, vol. v. p. 253.

mitre on his head (Fig. 49); * very nearly in the same form as the mitre of the Pope, or of a Papal bishop at this day. Even in China, the same practice of wearing the fish-head mitre had evidently once prevailed; for the very counterpart of the Papal mitre, as worn by

Fig. 49.

the Chinese Emperor, has subsisted to modern times. "Is it known," asks a well-read author of the present day, in a private communication to me, "that the Emperor of China, in all ages, even to the present year, as high priest of the nation, once a-year prays for and blesses the whole nation, having his priestly robes on and his mitre on his head, the same, the very same, as that worn by the Roman Pontiff for near 1200 years? Such is the fact." † In proof of this statement the accompanying figure of the Imperial mitre (Fig. 50) ‡ is produced—which is the very facsimile of the Popish Episcopal Mitre, in a front view. The reader must bear in mind, that even in Japan, still farther distant from Babel than China itself, one of the divinities is represented with the same symbol of might as prevailed in Assyria —even the bull's horns, and is called "The ox-headed Prince of Heaven." § If the symbol of Nimrod, as Kronos, "The Horned one," is thus found in Japan, it cannot be surprising that the symbol of Dagon should be found in China.

Fig. 50.

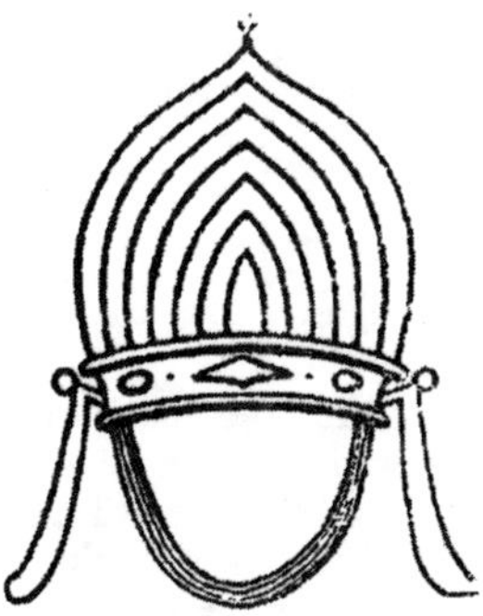

But there is another symbol of the Pope's power which must not be overlooked, and that is the pontifical crosier. Whence came the crosier? The answer to this, in the first place, is, that the

* From BRYANT, vol. v. p. 384. See also woodcut of Ceres and the ear of corn, Fig. 37, p. 160, of this vol.

† A. TRIMEN, Esq., the distinguished architect, London, author of *Church and Chapel Architecture.*

‡ From HAGER, on *Chinese Hieroglyphics*, B xxxv. in British Museum, copied for me by Mr. Trimen's son, Mr. L. B. Trimen. The words of Hager, are :—"In like manner the sacrificial mitre of the Chinese Emperor (the Pontifex Maximus of his nation), which was of old represented under this form [and then the above figure is given] (—*Philos. Transact.* at tab. 41—), bearing a strong resemblance to the Roman Episcopal Mitre," &c., &c.

§ KEMPFER'S *Japan*, in PINKERTON'S *Collection*, vol. vii. p. 776.

Pope stole it from the Roman augur. The classical reader may remember, that when the Roman augurs consulted the heavens, or took prognostics from the aspect of the sky, there was a certain instrument with which it was indispensable that they should be equipped. That instrument with which they described the portion of the heavens on which their observations were to be made, was curved at the one end, and was called "*lituus.*" Now, so manifestly was the "*lituus,*" or crooked rod of the Roman augurs, identical with the pontifical crosier, that Roman Catholic writers themselves, writing in the Dark Ages, at a time when disguise was thought unnecessary, did not hesitate to use the term "*lituus*" as a synonym for the "crosier."* Thus a Papal writer describes a certain Pope or Papal bishop as "*mitrâ lituoque decorus,*" adorned with the mitre and the augur's rod, meaning thereby that he was "adorned with the mitre and the *crosier.*" But this lituus, or divining-rod, of the Roman augurs, was, as is well known, borrowed from the Etruscans, who, again, had derived it, along with their religion, from the Assyrians. As the Roman augur was distinguished by his crooked

Fig. 51.

rod, so the Chaldean soothsayers and priests, in the performance of their magic rites, were generally equipped with a crook or crosier. This magic crook can be traced up directly to the first king of Babylon, that is, Nimrod, who, as stated by Berosus, was the first that bore the title of a Shepherd-king.† In Hebrew, or the Chaldee of the days of Abraham, "Nimrod the Shepherd," is just Nimrod "He-Roè"; and from this title of the "mighty hunter before the Lord," have no doubt been derived, both the name of Hero itself, and all that Hero-worship which has since overspread the world. Certain it is that Nimrod's deified successors have generally been represented with the crook or crosier. This was the case in Babylon and Nineveh, as the extant monuments show. The accompanying figure (Fig. 51) ‡ from Babylon shows the crosier in its ruder guise.

* See *Gradus ad Parnassum*, compiled by G. PYPER, a member of the Society of Jesus, *sub vocibus Lituus Episcopus et Pedum*, pp. 372, 464.

† BEROSUS *apud* ABYDENUS, in CORY'S *Fragments*, p. 32. See also EUSEB., *Chron.*, Pars. i. pp. 46, 47.

‡ From KITTO'S *Biblical Cyclopædia*, vol. i. p. 272.—See also KITTO'S *Illustrated Commentary*, vol. iv. p. 31, where another figure from Babylon is given with a similar crosier.

In Layard, it may be seen in a more ornate form, and nearly resembling the papal crosier as borne at this day.* This was the case in Egypt, after the Babylonian power was established there, as the statues of Osiris with his crosier bear witness,† Osiris *himself* being frequently represented *as* a crosier with an eye above it.‡ This is the case among the negroes of Africa, whose god, called the Fetiche, is represented in the form of a crosier, as is evident from the following words of Hurd: "They place Fetiches before their doors, and these titular deities are made in the form of *grapples* or *hooks*, which we generally make use of to shake our fruit trees."§ This is the case at this hour in Thibet, where the Lamas or Theros bear, as stated by the Jesuit Huc, a crosier, as the ensign of their office. This is the case even in the far-distant Japan, where, in a description of the idols of the great temple of Miaco, the spiritual capital, we find this statement: "Their heads are adorned with rays of glory, and some of them have *shepherd's crooks* in their hands, pointing out that they are the guardians of mankind against all the machinations of evil spirits."‖ The crosier of the Pope, then, which he bears as an emblem of his office, as the great shepherd of the sheep, is neither more nor less than the augur's crooked staff, or magic rod of the priests of Nimrod.

Now, what say the worshippers of the apostolic succession to all this? What think they now of their vaunted orders as derived from *Peter of Rome?* Surely they have much reason to be proud of them. But what, I further ask, would even the old Pagan priests say, who left the stage of time while the martyrs were still battling against their gods, and, rather than symbolise with them, "loved not their lives unto the death," if they were to see the present aspect of the so-called Church of European Christendom? What would Belshazzar himself say, if it were possible for him to "revisit the glimpses of the moon," and enter St. Peter's at Rome, and see the Pope in his pontificals, in all his pomp and glory? Surely he would conclude that he had only entered one of his own well-known temples, and that all things continued as they were at Babylon, on that memorable night, when he saw with astonished eyes the handwriting on the wall: "Mene, mene, tekel, Upharsin."

* *Nineveh and Babylon*, p. 361. Layard seems to think the instrument referred to, which is borne by the king, "attired as high priest in his sacrificial robes," a sickle; but any one who attentively examines it will see that it is a crosier, adorned with studs, as is commonly the case even now with the Roman crosiers, only, that instead of being held erect, it is held downwards.

† The well-known name Pharaoh, the title of the Pontiff-kings of Egypt, is just the Egyptian form of the Hebrew He-Roè. Pharaoh in Genesis, without the points, is "Phe-Roé." Phe is the Egyptian definite article. It was not shepherd-*kings* that the Egyptians abhorred, but Roi-Tzan, "shepherds of *cattle*" (Gen. xlvi. 34). Without the article Roé, a "shepherd," is manifestly the original of the French Roi, a king, whence the adjective royal; and from Ro, which signifies to "act the shepherd," which is frequently pronounced Reg—(with *Sh*, which signifies "He who is," or "who does," affixed)—comes Regsh, "He who acts the shepherd," whence the Latin Rex, and Regal.

‡ Plutarch, vol. ii. p. 354, F.

§ Hurd, p. 374, col. 2.

‖ *Ibid.* p. 104, col. 2.

SECTION II.—PRIESTS, MONKS, AND NUNS.

If the head be corrupt, so also must be the members. If the Pope be essentially Pagan, what else can be the character of his clergy? If they derive their orders from a radically corrupted source, these orders must partake of the corruption of the source from which they flow. This might be inferred independently of any special evidence; but the evidence in regard to the Pagan character of the Pope's clergy is as complete as that in regard to the Pope himself. In whatever light the subject is viewed, this will be very apparent.

There is a direct contrast between the character of the ministers of Christ, and that of the Papal priesthood. When Christ commissioned His servants, it was "to feed His sheep, to feed His lambs," and that with the Word of God, which testifies of Himself, and contains the words of eternal life. When the Pope ordains his clergy, he takes them bound to *prohibit*, except in special circumstances, the reading of the Word of God "in the vulgar tongue," that is, in a language which the people can understand. He gives them, indeed, a commission; and what is it? It is couched in these astounding words: "Receive the power of sacrificing for the living and the dead."* What blasphemy could be worse than this? What more derogatory to the *one* sacrifice of Christ, whereby "He hath perfected for ever them that are sanctified"? (Heb. x. 14). This is the real distinguishing function of the popish priesthood. At the remembrance that this power, in these very words, had been conferred on him, when ordained to the priesthood, Luther used, in after years, with a shudder, to express his astonishment that "the earth had not opened its mouth and swallowed up both him who uttered these words, and him to whom they were addressed."† The sacrifice which the papal priesthood are empowered to offer, as a "true propitiatory sacrifice" for the sins of the living and the dead, is just the "unbloody sacrifice" of the mass, which was offered up in Babylon long before it was ever heard of in Rome.

Now, while Semiramis, the real original of the Chaldean Queen of Heaven, to whom the "unbloody sacrifice" of the mass was first offered, was in her own person, as we have already seen, the very paragon of impurity, she at the same time affected the greatest favour for that kind of sanctity which looks down with contempt on God's holy ordinance of marriage. The Mysteries over which she presided were scenes of the rankest pollution; and yet the higher orders of the priesthood were bound to a life of celibacy, as a life of peculiar and pre-eminent holiness. Strange though it may seem, yet the voice of antiquity assigns to that abandoned queen the invention of clerical celibacy, and that in the most stringent form.‡ In some countries,

* D'AUBIGNÉ's *Reformation*, vol. i. B. ii. cap. 4, p. 171.

† *Ibid.* vol. i. p. 171.

‡ AMMIANUS MARCELLINUS. "Semiramis teneros mares castravit omnium prima," lib. xiv. cap. 6, p. xxvi.

as in Egypt, human nature asserted its rights, and though the general system of Babylon was retained, the yoke of celibacy was abolished, and the priesthood were permitted to marry. But every scholar knows that when the worship of Cybele, the Babylonian goddess, was introduced into Pagan Rome, it was introduced in its primitive form, with its celibate clergy.* When the Pope appropiated to himself so much that was peculiar to the worship of that goddess, from the very same source, also, he introduced into the priesthood under his authority the binding obligation of celibacy. The introduction of such a principle into the Christian Church had been distinctly predicted as one grand mark of the apostacy, when men should "depart from the faith, and speaking lies in hypocrisy, having their consciences seared with a hot iron, should *forbid to marry.*" The effects of its introduction were most disastrous.† The records of all nations where priestly celibacy has been introduced have proved that, instead of ministering to the *purity* of those condemned to it, it has only plunged them in the deepest pollution. The history of Thibet, and China, and Japan, where the Babylonian institute of priestly celibacy has prevailed from time immemorial, bears testimony to the abominations that have flowed from it.‡ The excesses committed by the celibate priests of Bacchus in Pagan Rome in their secret Mysteries, were such that the Senate felt called upon to expel them from the bounds of the Roman republic.§ In Papal Rome the same abominations have flowed from priestly celibacy, in connection with the corrupt and corrupting system of the confessional, insomuch that all men who have examined the subject have been compelled to admire the amazing significance of the name divinely bestowed on it, both in a literal and figurative sense, "Babylon the Great, THE MOTHER OF HARLOTS AND ABOMINATIONS OF THE EARTH."‖ Out of a thousand facts of a similar kind, let one only be adduced, vouched for by the distinguished Roman Catholic historian De Thou. When Pope Paul V. meditated the suppression of the licensed brothels in the "Holy City," the Roman Senate petitioned against his carrying his design into effect, on the ground that the existence of such places was the only means of *hindering the priests from seducing their wives and daughters ! !* ¶

These celibate priests have all a certain mark set upon them at their ordination; and that is the clerical tonsure. The tonsure is the

* PAUSANIAS, lib. vii. cap. 17, p. 566 ; and KENNETT, Book ii. chap. vii., "Of the *Duumviri*," &c.

† See *Light of Prophecy*, chapters i. p. 28, and iv. p. 114 ; and *British Reformers*, "Jewell," p. 228.

‡ HAMEL'S *Travels in Corea*, in PINKERTON'S *Collection*, vol. vii. pp. 536, 537. See also *Description of Tibet* in same *Collection*, p. 554 ; CARON'S *Japan*, *Ibid.* p. 630 ; and KEMPFER'S *Japan*, *Ibid.* p. 747.

§ LIVY, lib. xxxix. 8 and 18, vol. v. pp. 196-207.

‖ Rev. xvii. 5. The Rev. M. H. Seymour shows that in 1836 the whole number of births in Rome was 4373, while of these no fewer than 3160 were foundlings ! What enormous profligacy does this reveal !—"Moral Results of the Romish System," p. xlix. in *Evenings with Romanists.*

¶ THUANUS, *Historia*, lib. xxxix. cap. 3, vol. ii. p. 483.

first part of the ceremony of ordination; and it is held to be a most important element in connection with the orders of the Romish clergy. When, after long contendings, the Picts were at last brought to submit to the Bishop of Rome, the acceptance of this tonsure as the tonsure of St. Peter on the part of the clergy was the visible symbol of that submission. Naitan, the Pictish king, having assembled the nobles of his court and the pastors of his church, thus addressed them: "I recommend all the clergy of my kingdom to receive the tonsure." Then, without delay, as Bede informs us, this important revolution was accomplished by royal authority.* He sent agents into every province, and caused all the ministers and monks to receive the *circular tonsure*, according to the Roman fashion, and thus to submit to Peter, "the most blessed Prince of the apostles." † "It was the mark," says Merle D'Aubigné, "that Popes stamped not on the forehead, but on the crown. A royal proclamation, and a few clips of the scissors, placed the Scotch, like a flock of sheep, beneath the crook of the shepherd of the Tiber."‡ Now, as Rome set so much importance on this tonsure, let it be asked what was the meaning of it? It was the visible inauguration of those who submitted to it as the priests of Bacchus. This tonsure cannot have the slightest pretence to Christian authority. It was indeed the "tonsure of Peter," but not of the Peter of Galilee, but of the Chaldean "Peter" of the Mysteries. *He* was a tonsured priest, for so was the god whose Mysteries he revealed. Centuries before the Christian era, thus spoke Herodotus of the Babylonian tonsure: "The Arabians acknowledge no other gods than Bacchus and Urania [*i.e.*, the Queen of Heaven], and they say that their hair was cut in the same manner as Bacchus's is cut; now, they cut it in a *circular form*, shaving it around the temples."§ What, then, could have led to this tonsure of Bacchus? Everything in his history was mystically or hieroglyphically represented, and that in such a way as none but the initiated could understand. One of the things that occupied the most important place in the Mysteries was the mutilation to which he was subjected when he was put to death. In memory of that, he was lamented with bitter weeping every year, as "Rosh-Gheza," "the mutilated Prince." But "Rosh-Gheza"‖ also signified the "clipped or shaved head." Therefore he was himself represented either with the one or the other form of tonsure; and his priests, for the same reason, at their ordination had their heads either clipped or shaven. Over all the world, where the traces of the Chaldean system are found, this tonsure or shaving of the head is always found along with it. The priests of Osiris, the Egyptian Bacchus, were always distinguished by the shaving of their heads.¶ In Pagan Rome,** in India, and even in China, the distinguishing mark of the Babylonian

* BEDE, lib. v. c. 21, p. 216. † *Ibid.* ‡ D'AUBIGNÉ, vol. v. p. 55.
§ HERODOTUS, lib. iii. cap. 8, p. 185, C.
‖ Gheza signifies either "shearing" or "shaving."
¶ MACROBIUS, lib. i. c. 23, p. 189.
** TERTULLIAN, vol. ii., *Carmina*, pp. 1105, 1106.

priesthood was the shaven head. Thus Gautama Buddha, who lived at least 540 years before Christ, when setting up the sect of Buddhism in India which spread to the remotest regions of the East, first shaved his own head, in obedience, as he pretended, to a Divine command, and then set to work to get others to imitate his example. One of the very titles by which he was called was that of the "Shaved-head."* "The *shaved-head*," says one of the Purans, "that he might perform the orders of Vishnu, formed a number of disciples, and of *shaved-heads* like himself." The high antiquity of this tonsure may be seen from the enactment in the Mosaic law against it. The Jewish priests were expressly forbidden to make any baldness upon their heads (Lev. xxi. 5), which sufficiently shows that, even so early as the time of Moses, the "shaved-head" had been already introduced. In the Church of Rome the heads of the ordinary priests are only *clipped*, the heads of the monks or regular clergy are *shaven*, but both alike, at their consecration, receive the *circular tonsure*, thereby identifying them, beyond all possibility of doubt, with Bacchus, "the mutilated Prince."† Now, if the priests of Rome take away the key of knowledge, and lock up the Bible from the people; if they are ordained to offer the Chaldean sacrifice in honour of the Pagan Queen of Heaven; if they are bound by the Chaldean

* Col. KENNEDY, "Buddha," in *Hindoo Mythology*, pp. 263, 264.

† It has been already shown (p. 18, Note) that among the Chaldeans the one term "Zero" signified at once "a circle" and "the seed." "Suro," "the seed," in India, as we have seen, was the sun-divinity incarnate. When that seed was represented in human form, to identify him with the sun, he was represented with the circle, the well-known emblem of the sun's annual course, on some part of his person. Thus our own god Thor was represented with a blazing circle on his breast.—(WILSON'S *Parsi Religion*, p. 31.) In Persia and Assyria the circle was represented sometimes on the breast, sometimes round the waist, and sometimes in the hand of the sun-divinity.—(BRYANT, vol. ii., Plates, pp. 216, 406, 409; and LAYARD'S *Nineveh and Babylon*, p. 160.) In India it is represented at the tip of the finger.—(MOOR'S *Pantheon*, Plate 13, "Vishnu.") Hence the circle became the emblem of Tammuz born again, or "the seed." The *circular* tonsure of Bacchus was doubtless intended to point him out as "Zero," or "the seed," the grand deliverer. And the *circle* of light around the head of the so-called pictures of Christ was evidently just a different form of the very same thing, and borrowed from the very same source. The ceremony of tonsure, says Maurice, referring to the practice of that ceremony in India, "was an old practice of the priests of Mithra, who *in their tonsures imitated the solar disk*."—(*Antiquities*, vol. vii. p. 851. London, 1800.) As the sun-god was the great *lamented* god, and had his hair cut in a circular form, and the priests who lamented him had their hair cut in a similar manner, so in different countries those who lamented the dead and cut off their hair in honour of them, cut it in a circular form. There were traces of that in Greece, as appears from the *Electra* of Sophocles (line 52, pp. 108, 109); and Herodotus particularly refers to it as practised among the Scythians when giving an account of a royal funeral among that people. "The body," says he, "is enclosed in wax. They then place it on a carriage, and remove it to another district, where the persons who receive it, like the Royal Scythians, cut off a part of their ear, *shave their heads in a circular form*," &c.—(*Hist.*, lib. iv. cap. 71, p. 279.) Now, while the Pope, as the grand representative of the false Messiah, received the circular tonsure himself, so all his priests to identify them with the same system are required to submit to the same *circular* tonsure, to mark them in their measure and their own sphere as representatives of that same false Messiah.

law of celibacy, that plunges them in profligacy; if, in short, they are all marked at their consecration with the distinguishing mark of the priests of the Chaldean Bacchus, what right, what possible right, can they have to be called ministers of Christ?

But Rome has not only her ordinary secular clergy, as they are called; she has also, as every one knows, other religious orders of a different kind. She has innumerable armies of monks and nuns all engaged in her service. Where can there be shown the least warrant for such an institution in Scripture? In the religion of the Babylonian Messiah their institution was from the earliest times. In that system there were monks and nuns in abundance. In Thibet and Japan, where the Chaldean system was early introduced, monasteries are still to be found, and with the same disastrous results to morals as in Papal Europe.* In Scandinavia, the priestesses of Freya, who were generally kings' daughters, whose duty it was to watch the sacred fire, and who were bound to perpetual virginity, were just an order of nuns.† In Athens there were virgins maintained at the public expense, who were strictly bound to single life.‡ In Pagan Rome, the Vestal virgins, who had the same duty to perform as the priestesses of Freya, occupied a similar position. Even in Peru, during the reign of the Incas, the same system prevailed, and showed so remarkable an analogy, as to indicate that the Vestals of Rome, the nuns of the Papacy, and the Holy Virgins of Peru, must have sprung from a common origin. Thus does Prescott refer to the Peruvian nunneries: "Another singular analogy with Roman Catholic institutions is presented by the virgins of the sun, the elect, as they were called. These were young maidens dedicated to the service of the deity, who at a tender age were taken from their homes, and introduced into convents, where they were placed under the care of certain elderly matrons, *mamaconas*,§ who had grown grey within their walls. It was their duty to watch over the sacred fire obtained at the festival of Raymi. From the moment they entered the establishment they were cut off

* See *ante*, Notes to p. 220, and also *History of Tonquin*, in PINKERTON, vol. ix. p. 766. There are some, and Protestants, too, who begin to speak of what they call the benefits of monasteries in rude times, as if they were hurtful only when they fall into "decrepitude and corruption"! Enforced celibacy, which lies at the foundation of the monastic system, is of the very *essence* of the Apostacy, which is divinely characterised as the "Mystery of Iniquity." Let such Protestants read 1 Tim. iv. 1-3, and surely they will never speak more of the abominations of the monasteries as coming only from their "decrepitude"!

† MALLET, vol. i. p. 141.

‡ POTTER'S *Antiquities*, vol. i. p. 369.

§ Mamacona, "Mother Priestess," is almost pure Hebrew, being derived from *Am* a "mother," and *Cohn*, "a priest," only with the feminine termination. Our own Mamma, as well as that of Peru, is just the Hebrew *Am* reduplicated. It is singular that the usual style and title of the Lady Abbess in Ireland is the "Reverend Mother." The term Nun itself is a Chaldean word. Ninus, the son in Chaldee is either Nin or Non. Now, the feminine of Non, a "son," is Nonna, a "daughter," which is just the Popish canonical name for a "Nun," and Nonnus, in like manner, was in early times the designation for a monk in the East.—(GIESELER, vol. ii. p. 14, Note.)

from all communication with the world, even with their own family and friends. . . . . Woe to the unhappy maiden who was detected in an intrigue! By the stern law of the Incas she was to be *buried alive.*" This was precisely the fate of the Roman Vestal who was proved to have violated her vow. Neither in Peru, however, nor in Pagan Rome was the obligation to virginity so stringent as in the Papacy. It was not perpetual, and therefore not so exceedingly demoralising. After a time, the nuns might be delivered from their confinement, and marry; from all hopes of which they are absolutely cut off in the Church of Rome. In all these cases, however, it is plain that the principle on which these institutions were founded was originally the same. "One is astonished," adds Prescott, "to find so close a resemblance between the institutions of the American Indian, the ancient Roman, and the modern Catholic."*

Prescott finds it difficult to account for this resemblance; but the one little sentence from the prophet Jeremiah, which was quoted at the commencement of this inquiry, accounts for it completely: "Babylon hath been a golden cup in the Lord's hand, that hath made ALL THE EARTH drunken" (Jer. li. 7). This is the Rosetta stone that has helped already to bring to light so much of the secret iniquity of the Papacy, and that is destined still further to decipher the dark mysteries of every system of heathen mythology that either has been or that is. The statement of this text can be proved to be a literal fact. It can be proved that the idolatry of the whole earth is one, that the sacred language of all nations is radically Chaldean—that the GREAT GODS of every country and clime are called by Babylonian names—and that all the Paganisms of the human race are only a wicked and deliberate, but yet most instructive corruption of the primeval gospel first preached in Eden, and through Noah, afterwards conveyed to all mankind. The system, first concocted in Babylon, and thence conveyed to the ends of the earth, has been modified and diluted in different ages and countries. *In Papal Rome only is it now found nearly pure and entire.* But yet, amid all the seeming variety of heathenism, there is an astonishing oneness and identity, bearing testimony to the truth of God's Word. The overthrow of all idolatry cannot now be distant. But before the idols of the heathen shall be finally cast to the moles and to the bats, I am persuaded that they will be made to fall down and worship "the Lord the king," to bear testimony to His glorious truth, and with one loud and united acclaim, ascribe salvation, and glory, and honour, and power unto Him that sitteth upon the throne, and to the Lamb, for ever and ever.

* PRESCOTT'S *Peru*, vol. i. p. 103.

CHAPTER VII.

THE TWO DEVELOPMENTS HISTORICALLY AND PROPHETICALLY CONSIDERED.

HITHERTO we have considered the history of the Two Babylons chiefly in detail. Now we are to view them as organised systems. The idolatrous system of the ancient Babylon assumed different phases in different periods of its history. In the prophetic description of the modern Babylon, there is evidently also a development of different powers at different times. Do these two developments bear any typical relation to each other? Yes, they do. When we bring the religious history of the ancient Babylonian Paganism to bear on the prophetic symbols that shadow forth the organised working of idolatry in Rome, it will be found that it casts as much light on this view of the subject as on that which has hitherto engaged our attention. The powers of iniquity at work in the modern Babylon are specifically described in chapters xii. and xiii. of the Revelation; and they are as follows:—I. The Great Red Dragon; II. The Beast that comes up out of the sea; III. The Beast that ascendeth out of the earth; and IV. The Image of the Beast.* In all these respects it will be found, on inquiry, that, in regard to succession and order of development, the Paganism of the Old Testament Babylon was the exact type of the Paganism of the New.

SECTION I.—THE GREAT RED DRAGON.

This formidable enemy of the truth is particularly described in Rev. xii. 3: "And there appeared another wonder in heaven, a great red dragon." It is admitted on all hands that this is the first grand enemy that in Gospel times assaulted the Christian Church. If the terms in which it is described, and the deeds attributed to it, are considered, it will be found that there is a great analogy between it and the first enemy of all, that appeared against the ancient Church of God soon after the Flood. The term dragon, according to the associations currently connected with it, is somewhat apt to mislead the reader, by recalling to his mind the fabulous dragons of the Dark Ages, equipped with wings. At the time this Divine description was

* I purposely omit the consideration of the "Beast from the bottomless pit" (Rev. xvii. 8). The reader will find an argument on that subject in the *Red Republic*.

given, the term dragon had no such meaning among either profane or sacred writers. "The dragon of the Greeks," says Pausanias, "was only a large snake;"* and the context shows that this is the very case here; for what in the third verse is called a "dragon," in the fourteenth is simply described as a "serpent." Then the word rendered "Red" properly means "Fiery"; so that the "Red Dragon" signifies the "Fiery Serpent" or "Serpent of Fire." Exactly so does it appear to have been in the first form of idolatry, that, under the patronage of Nimrod, appeared in the ancient world. The "Serpent of Fire" in the plains of Shinar seems to have been the grand object of worship. There is the strongest evidence that apostacy among the sons of Noah began in fire-worship, and that in connection with the symbol of the serpent.

We have seen already, on different occasions, that fire was worshipped as the enlightener and the purifier. Now, it was thus at the very beginning; for Nimrod is singled out by the voice of antiquity as *commencing* this fire-worship.† The identity of Nimrod and Ninus has already been proved; and under the name of Ninus, also, he is represented as originating the same practice. In a fragment of Apollodorus it is said that "Ninus taught the Assyrians to worship fire."‡ The sun, as the great source of light and heat, was worshipped under the name of Baal. Now, the fact that the sun under that name, was worshipped in the earliest ages of the world, shows the audacious character of these first beginnings of apostacy. Men have spoken as if the worship of the sun and of the heavenly bodies was a very excusable thing, into which the human race might very readily and very innocently fall. But how stands the fact? According to the primitive language of mankind, the sun was called "Shemesh"—that is, "the Servant"—that name, no doubt, being divinely given, to keep the world in mind of the great truth that, however glorious was the orb of day, it was, after all, the appointed *Minister* of the bounty of the great unseen Creator to His creatures upon earth. Men knew this, and yet with the full knowledge of it, they put the servant in the place of the Master; and called the sun Baal—that is, the Lord—and worshipped him accordingly. What a meaning, then, in the saying of Paul, that, "*when they knew God*, they glorified Him not as God;" but "changed the truth of God into a lie, and worshipped and served the creature more than the Creator, who is God over all, blessed for ever." The beginning, then, of sun-worship, and of the worship of the host of heaven, was a sin against the light—a presumptuous, heaven-daring sin. As the sun in the heavens was the great object of worship, so *fire* was worshipped as its earthly representative. To this primeval fire-worship Vitruvius alludes when he says that "men were first formed into states and communities by meeting around fires."§

* PAUSANIAS, lib. ii., *Corinthiaca*, cap. 28, p. 175.
† JOHANN. CLERICUS, tom. ii. p. 199, and VAUX, p. 8.
‡ MÜLLER, *Frag.*, 68, vol. i. p. 440.
§ VITRUVIUS, lib. ii. cap. 1, vol. ii. p. 36, &c.

And this is exactly in conformity with what we have already seen (p. 117) in regard to Phoroneus, whom we have identified with Nimrod, that while he was said to be the "inventor of fire," he was also regarded as the first that "gathered mankind into communities."

Along with the sun, as the great fire-god, and, in due time, identified with him, was the serpent worshipped. (See Fig. 52.)* "In the mythology of the primitive world," says Owen, "the serpent is universally the symbol of the sun."† In Egypt, one of the commonest symbols of the sun, or sun-god, is a disc with a serpent around it.‡ The original reason of that identification seems just to have been that, as the sun was the great enlightener of the *physical* world, so the serpent was held to have been the great enlightener of the *spiritual*, by giving mankind the "knowledge of good and evil." This, of course, implies tremendous depravity on the part of the ringleaders in such a system, considering the period when it began; but such appears to have been the real meaning of the identification. At all events, we have evidence, both Scriptural and profane, for the fact, that the worship of the serpent began side by side with the worship of fire and the sun. The inspired statement of Paul seems decisive on the subject. It was, he says, "*when men knew God, but glorified Him not as God*," that they changed the glory of God, not only into an image made like to corruptible man, but into the likeness of "*creeping things*"—that is, of *serpents* (Rom. i. 23). With this profane history exactly coincides. Of profane writers, Sanchuniathon, the Phœnician, who is believed to have lived about the time of Joshua, says—"Thoth first attributed something of the divine nature to the serpent and the serpent tribe, in which he was followed by the Phœnicians and Egyptians. For this animal was esteemed by him to be the most *spiritual* of all the reptiles, and of a FIERY nature, inasmuch as it exhibits an incredible celerity, moving by its spirit, without either hands or feet. . . . . Moreover, it is long-lived, and has the quality of RENEWING ITS YOUTH . . . . as Thoth has laid down in the sacred books; upon which accounts this animal is introduced in the sacred rites and Mysteries."§

Fig. 52.

Now, Thoth, it will be remembered, was the counsellor of Thamus, that is, Nimrod.|| From this statement, then, we are led to the

* From Phœnician Coin, in MAURICE'S *Indian Antiquities*, vol. vi. p. 368. London, 1796.

† OWEN, *apud* DAVIES'S *Druids*, in Note, p. 437.

‡ BUNSEN, *Hieroglyphics*, vol. i. p. 497.

§ SANCHUNIATHON, lib. i. pp. 46-49.

|| See page 56.

conclusion that serpent-worship was a part of the primeval apostacy of Nimrod. The "FIERY NATURE" of the serpent, alluded to in the above extract, is continually celebrated by the heathen poets. Thus Virgil, "availing himself," as the author of *Pompeii* remarks, "of the divine nature attributed to serpents,"* describes the sacred serpent that came from the tomb of Anchises, when his son Æneas had been sacrificing before it, in such terms as illustrate at once the language of the Phœnician, and the "Fiery Serpent" of the passage before us:—

> "Scarce had he finished, when, with speckled pride,
> A serpent from the tomb began to glide;
> His hugy bulk on seven high volumes rolled,
> Blue was his breadth of back, but streaked with scaly gold.
> Thus, riding on his curls, he seemed to pass
> *A rolling fire along, and singe the grass.*"†

It is not wonderful, then, that fire-worship and serpent-worship should be conjoined. The serpent, also, as "renewing its youth" every year, was plausibly represented to those who wished an excuse for idolatry as a meet emblem of the sun, the great regenerator, who every year regenerates and renews the face of nature, and who, when deified, was worshipped as the grand Regenerator of the *souls* of men.

In the chapter under consideration, the "great fiery serpent" is represented with all the emblems of royalty. All its heads are encircled with "crowns or diadems;" and so in Egypt, the serpent of fire, or serpent of the sun, in Greek was called the Basilisk, that is, the "*royal* serpent," to identify it with Moloch, which name, while it recalls the ideas both of *fire* and *blood*, properly signifies "*the King.*" The Basilisk was always, among the Egyptians, and among many nations besides, regarded as "the very type of majesty and dominion."‡ As such, its image was worn affixed to the head-dress of the Egyptian monarchs; and it was not lawful for any one else to wear it.§ The sun identified with this serpent was called "P'ouro,"‖ which signifies at once "the Fire" and "the King," and from this very name the epithet "Purros," the "Fiery," is given to the "Great seven-crowned serpent" of our text.¶

Thus was the Sun, the Great Fire-god, identified with the Serpent. But he had also a human representative, and that was Tammuz, for whom the daughters of Israel lamented, in other words Nimrod. We have already seen the identity of Nimrod and Zoroaster. Now,

* Vol. ii. p. 114.

† DRYDEN'S *Virgil*, Book v. ll. 111-116, vol. ii. pp. 460, 461; in Original, ll. 84-88.

‡ WILKINSON, vol. iv. p. 239.

§ Implied in *Ibid.* vol. iv. p. 239.

‖ BUNSEN, vol. i. pp. 407, 457.

¶ The word Purros in the text does not *exclude* the idea of "*Red*," for the sun-god was painted *red* to identify him with Moloch, at once the god of *fire* and god of *blood*.—(WILKINSON, vol. iv. pp. 288-296.) The primary leading idea, however, is that of *Fire*.

Zoroaster was not only the head of the Chaldean Mysteries, but, as all admit, the head of the fire-worshippers.* The title given to Nimrod, as the first of the Babylonian kings, by Berosus, indicates the same thing. That title is Alorus,† that is, "the god of fire."‡ As Nimrod, "the god of fire," was Molk-Gheber, or, "the Mighty king," inasmuch as he was the *first* who was called Moloch, or King, and the *first* who began to be "mighty" (*Gheber*) on the earth, we see at once how it was that the "passing through the fire to Moloch" originated, and how the god of fire among the Romans came to be called "Mulkiber."§ It was only after his death, however, that he appears to have been deified. Then, retrospectively, he was worshipped as the child of the Sun, or the Sun incarnate. In his own life-time, however, he set up no higher pretensions than that of being Bol-Kahn, or Priest of Baal, from which the other name of the Roman fire-god Vulcan is evidently derived.‖ Everything in the history of Vulcan exactly agrees with that of Nimrod. Vulcan was "the most ugly and deformed" of all the gods.¶ Nimrod, over all the world, is represented with the features and complexion of a negro. Though Vulcan was so ugly, that when he sought a wife, "all the beautiful goddesses rejected him with horror;" yet "Destiny, the irrevocable, interposed, and pronounced the decree, by which [Venus] the most beautiful of the goddesses, was united to the most unsightly of the gods."** So, in spite of the black and Cushite features of Nimrod, he had for his queen Semiramis, the most beautiful of women. The wife of Vulcan was noted for her infidelities and licentiousness; the wife of Nimrod was the very same.†† Vulcan was the head and chief of the Cyclops, that is, "the kings of flame."‡‡ Nimrod was the head of the fire-worshippers. Vulcan was the forger of the thunderbolts by which such havoc was made among the enemies of the gods. Ninus, or Nimrod, in his wars with the king of Bactria, seems to have carried on the conflict in a similar way. From Arnobius we learn, that when the Assyrians under Ninus made war against the Bactrians, the warfare was waged not only by the sword and bodily strength, but by magic and by means derived from the secret instructions of the

* In regard to Zoroaster as head of the fire worshippers, see Appendix, Note N.

† BUNSEN, vol. i. p. 710.

‡ BRYANT, vol. i. p. 10, and vol. iv. p. 152. Bryant derives the name Alorus from Al-Aur, "god of fire." I incline to think that, from the analogy of the name that succeeds it, it comes from Al-Hor, "The burning god;" but the meaning is the same either way.

§ Commonly spelled Mulciber (OVID, *Art. Am.*, lib. ii. l. 562, vol. i. p. 535); but the Roman c was hard. From the epithet "Gheber," the Parsees, or fire-worshippers of India, are still called "Guebres."

‖ OVID, *De Art. Am.*, *Ibid.*, *Nota.*

¶ *Heathen Mythology Illustrated*, p. 66.

** *Ibid.* p. 75.

†† Nimrod, as universal king, was Khuk-hold, "King of the world." As such, the emblem of his power was the bull's horns. Hence the origin of the Cuckhold's horns.

‡‡ Kuclops, from Khuk, "king," and Lohb, "flame." The image of the great god was represented with *three* eyes—one in the forehead; hence the story of the Cyclops with the one eye in the forehead.

Chaldeans.* When it is known that the historical Cyclops are, by the historian Castor, traced up to the very time of Saturn or Belus, the first king of Babylon,† and when we learn that Jupiter (who was worshipped in the very same character as Ninus, "the child"),‡ when fighting against the Titans, "received from the Cyclops aid" by means of "dazzling lightnings and thunders," we may have some pretty clear idea of the magic arts derived from the Chaldean Mysteries, which Ninus employed against the Bactrian king. There is evidence that, down to a late period, the priests of the Chaldean Mysteries knew the composition of the formidable Greek fire, which burned under water, and the secret of which has been lost;§ and there can be little doubt that Nimrod, in erecting his power, availed himself of such or similar scientific secrets, which he and his associates alone possessed.

In these, and other respects yet to be noticed, there is an exact coincidence between Vulcan, the god of fire of the Romans, and Nimrod the fire-god of Babylon. In the case of the classic Vulcan, it is only in his character of the fire-god as a physical agent that he is popularly represented. But it was in his spiritual aspects, in cleansing and regenerating the souls of men, that the fire-worship told most effectually on the world. The power, the popularity, and skill of Nimrod, as well as the seductive nature of the system itself, enabled him to spread the delusive doctrine far and wide, and he was represented under the well-known name of Phaëthon,‖ as on the point of "setting the whole world on fire," or (without the poetical metaphor) of involving all mankind in the guilt of fire-worship. The extraordinary prevalence of the worship of the fire-god in the early ages of the world, is proved by legends found over all the earth, and by facts in almost every clime. Thus, in Mexico, the natives relate, that in primeval times, just after the first age, the world was burnt up with fire.¶ As their history, like the Egyptian, was written in Hieroglyphics, it is plain that this must be symbolically understood. In India, they have a legend to the very same effect, though somewhat varied in its form. The Brahmins say that, in a very remote period of the past, one of the gods shone with such insufferable splendour, "inflicting distress on the universe by his effulgent beams, brighter than a thousand worlds,"** that, unless another more potent god had interposed and cut off his head, the

* Arnobius, lib. i. p. 327, col. 1.

† Eusebius, *Chronicon*. Armenian Translation, Pars. i. p. 81.

‡ See *ante*, p. 139.

§ Salverté, *Des Sciences Occultes*, p. 415.

‖ Phaëthon is called an Ethiopian—*i.e.*, a Cushite. For explanation of his story, see Appendix, Note O.

¶ Humboldt's *Mexico*, vol. ii. pp. 21, 22.

** Skanda Puran, and Padma Puran, *apud* Kennedy's *Hindoo Mythology*, p. 275. In the myth, this divinity is represented as the fifth head of Brahmà; but as this head is represented as having gained the knowledge that made him so insufferably proud by perusing the Vedas produced by the other four heads of Brahmà, that shows that he must have been regarded as having a distinct individuality.

result would have been most disastrous. In the Druidic Triads of the old British Bards, there is distinct reference to the same event. They say that in primeval times a "tempest of fire arose, which split the earth asunder to the great deep," from which none escaped but "the select company, shut up together in the enclosure with the strong door," with the great "patriarch distinguished for his integrity,"* that is evidently with Shem, the leader of the faithful—who preserved their "integrity" when so many made shipwreck of faith and a good conscience. These stories all point to one and the same period, and they show how powerful had been this form of apostacy. The Papal purgatory and the fires of St. John's Eve, which we have already considered, and many other fables or practices still extant, are just so many relics of the same ancient superstition.

It will be observed, however, that the Great Red Dragon, or Great Fiery Serpent, is represented as standing before the Woman with the crown of twelve stars, that is, the true Church of God, "*To devour her child as soon as it should be born.*" Now, this is in exact accordance with the character of the Great Head of the system of fire-worship. Nimrod, as the representative of the devouring fire to which human victims, and especially children, were offered in sacrifice, was regarded as the great child-devourer. Though, at his first deification, he was set up himself as Ninus, or the child, yet, as the first of mankind that was deified, he was, of course, the actual father of all the Babylonian gods; and, therefore, in that character he was afterwards universally regarded.† As the Father of the gods, he was, as we have seen, called Kronos; and every one knows that the classical story of Kronos was just this, that, "*he devoured his sons as soon as they were born.*"‡ Such is the analogy between type and antitype. This legend has a further and deeper meaning; but, as applied to Nimrod, or "The Horned One,"§ it just refers to the fact, that, as the representative of Moloch or Baal, infants were the most acceptable offerings at his altar. We have ample and melancholy evidence on this subject from the records of antiquity. "The Phenicians," says Eusebius, "every year sacrificed their beloved and only-begotten children to Kronos or Saturn,‖ and the Rhodians also often did the same." Diodorus Siculus states that the Carthaginians, on one occasion, when besieged by the Sicilians, and sore pressed, in order to rectify, as they supposed, their error in having somewhat departed from the ancient custom of Carthage, in this respect, hastily "chose out two hundred of the noblest of their children, and publicly sacrificed them" to this god.¶ There is

* DAVIES's *Druids*, p. 226.

† Phaëthon, though the child of the sun, is also called the Father of the gods.—(LACTANTIUS, *De Falsa Religione*, lib. i. cap. 5, p. 10.) In Egypt, too, Vulcan was the Father of the gods.—(AMMIANUS MARCELLINUS, lib. xvii. cap. 4, p. 163.)

‡ LEMPRIERE, "Saturn."

§ See woodcut, Fig. 10, p. 33.

‖ EUSEB. *De Laud. Constantini*, cap. xiii. p. 267, A, C.

¶ DIODORUS, lib. xx. pp. 739, 740.

reason to believe that the same practice obtained in our own land in the times of the Druids. We know that they offered human sacrifices to their bloody gods. We have evidence that they made "their children pass through the fire to Moloch," and that makes it highly probable that they also offered them in sacrifice; for, from Jeremiah xxxii. 35, compared with Jeremiah xix. 5, we find that these two things were parts of one and the same system. The god whom the Druids worshipped was Baal, as the blazing Baal-fires show, and the last-cited passage proves that *children* were offered in sacrifice to Baal. When "the fruit of the body" was thus offered, it was "for the sin of the soul." And it was a principle of the Mosaic law, a principle no doubt derived from the patriarchal faith, that the priest must partake of whatever was offered as a sin-offering (Numbers xviii. 9, 10). Hence, the priests of Nimrod or Baal were necessarily required to eat of the human sacrifices; and thus it has come to pass that "Cahna-Bal,"* the "Priest of Baal," is the established word in our own tongue for a devourer of human flesh.†

Now, the ancient traditions relate that the apostates who joined in the rebellion of Nimrod made war upon the faithful among the sons of Noah. Power and numbers were on the side of the fire-worshippers. But on the side of Shem and the faithful was the mighty power of God's Spirit. Therefore many were convinced of their sin, arrested in their evil career; and victory, as we have already seen, declared for the saints. The power of Nimrod came to an end,‡ and with that, for a time, the worship of the sun, and the

* The word Cahna is the emphatic form of Cahn. Cahn is "*a* priest," Cahna is "*the* priest."

† From the historian Castor (in Armenian translation of EUSEBIUS, pars. i. p. 81) we learn that it was under Bel, or Belus, that is Baal, that the Cyclops lived; and the Scholiast on Æschylus (p. 32, *ante*, Note) states that these Cyclops were the brethren of Kronos, who was also Bel or Bal, as we have elsewhere seen (p. 32). The eye in their forehead shows that originally this name was a name of the great god; for that eye in India and Greece is found the characteristic of the supreme divinity. The Cyclops, then, had been representatives of that God—in other words, priests, and priests of Bel or Baal. Now, we find that the Cyclops were well-known as cannibals, *Referre ritus Cyclopum*, "to bring back the rites of the Cyclops," meaning to revive the practice of eating human flesh.—(OVID, *Metam.*, xv. 93, vol. ii. p. 132.)

‡ The wars of the *giants* against *heaven*, referred to in ancient heathen writers, had primary reference to this war against the *saints;* for men cannot make war upon God except by attacking the people of God. The ancient writer Eupolemus, as quoted by Eusebius (*Præparatio Evang.*, lib. i. cap. 17, vol. ii. p. 19), states, that the builders of the tower of Babel were these *giants;* which statement amounts nearly to the same thing as the conclusion to which we have already come, for we have seen that the "mighty ones" of Nimrod were "the giants" of antiquity (see *ante*, p. 54, Notes). Epiphanius records (lib. i., vol. i. p. 7) that Nimrod was a ringleader among these giants, and that "conspiracy, sedition, and tyranny were carried on under him." From the very necessity of the case, the faithful must have suffered most, as being most opposed to his ambitious and sacrilegious schemes. That Nimrod's reign terminated in some very signal catastrophe, we have seen abundant reason already to conclude. The following statement of Syncellus confirms the conclusions to which we have already come as to the nature of that catastrophe; referring to the arresting of the tower-building scheme, Syncellus (*Chronographia*, vol. i. p. 77) proceeds thus: "But

fiery serpent associated with it. The case was exactly as stated here in regard to the antitype (Rev. xii. 9): "The great dragon," or fiery serpent, was "cast out of heaven to the earth, and his angels were cast out with him;" that is, the Head of the fire-worship, and all his associates and underlings, were cast down from the power and glory to which they had been raised. Then was the time when the whole gods of the classic Pantheon of Greece were fain to flee and hide themselves from the wrath of their adversaries.* Then it was, that, in India, Indra, the king of the gods, Surya, the god of the sun, Agni, the god of fire, and all the rabble rout of the Hindu Olympus, were driven from heaven, wandered over the earth,† or hid themselves in forests,‡ disconsolate, and ready to "perish of hunger."§ Then it was that Phaëthon, while driving the chariot of the sun, when on the point of setting the world on fire, was smitten by the Supreme God, and cast headlong to the earth, while his sisters, the daughters of the sun, inconsolably lamented him, as, "the women wept for Tammuz." Then it was, as the reader must be prepared to see, that Vulcan, or Molk-gheber, the classic "god of fire," was so ignominiously hurled down from heaven, as he himself relates in Homer, speaking of the wrath of the King of Heaven, which in this instance must mean God Most High:—

> "I felt his matchless might,
> Hurled headlong downwards from the ethereal height;
> Tossed all the day in rapid circles round,
> Nor, till the sun descended, touched the ground.
> Breathless I fell, in giddy motion lost.
> The Sinthians raised me on the Lemnian coast."‖

The lines, in which Milton refers to this same downfall, though he gives it another application, still more beautifully describe the greatness of the overthrow:—

> "In Ausonian land
> Men called him Mulciber; and how he fell
> From heaven, they fabled. Thrown by angry Jove
> Sheer o'er the crystal battlements; from morn

Nimrod would still obstinately stay (when most of the other tower-builders were dispersed), and reside upon the spot; nor could he be withdrawn from the tower, still having the command over no contemptible body of men. Upon this, we are informed, that the tower, being beat upon by violent winds, gave way, and by the just judgment of God, crushed him to pieces." Though this could not be literally true, for the tower stood for many ages, yet there is a considerable amount of tradition to the effect that the tower in which Nimrod gloried was overthrown by *wind*, which gives reason to suspect that this story, when *properly understood*, had a real meaning in it. Take it figuratively, and remembering that the same word which signifies the *wind* signifies also the *Spirit of God*, it becomes highly probable that the meaning is, that his lofty and ambitious scheme, by which, in Scriptural language, he was seeking to "mount up to heaven," and "set his nest among the stars," was overthrown for a time by the Spirit of God, as we have already concluded, and that, in that overthrow he himself perished.

* OVID, *Metamorphoses*, lib. v., fab. 5, ll. 321-323.

† KENNEDY'S *Hindoo Mythology*, p. 336. ‡ COLEMAN, p. 89.

§ KENNEDY'S *Hindoo Mythology*, p. 350.

‖ POPE'S *Homer*, *Iliad*, Book i. ll. 750-765, vol. i. p. 39.

To noon he fell, from noon to dewy eve,
A summer's day; and, with the setting sun,
Dropped from the zenith, like a falling star,
On Lemnos, the Ægean isle."*

These words very strikingly show the tremendous fall of Molkgheber, or Nimrod, "the Mighty King," when "suddenly he was cast down from the height of his power, and was deprived at once of his kingdom and his life."† Now, to this overthrow there is very manifest allusion in the prophetic apostrophe of Isaiah to the king of Babylon, exulting over his approaching downfall: "How art thou fallen from heaven, O Lucifer, son of the morning!" The Babylonian king pretended to be a representative of Nimrod or Phaëthon; and the prophet, in these words, informs him, that, as certainly as the god in whom he gloried had been cast down from his high estate, so certainly should he. In the classic story, Phaëthon is said to have been consumed with lightning (and, as we shall see by-and-by, Æsculapius also died the same death); but the lightning is a mere metaphor for the *wrath of God*, under which his life and his kingdom had come to an end. When the history is examined, and the figure stripped off, it turns out, as we have already seen, that he was judicially *slain with the sword.*‡

Such is the language of the prophecy, and so exactly does it correspond with the character, and deeds, and fate of the ancient type. How does it suit the antitype? Could the power of Pagan Imperial Rome—that power that first persecuted the Church of Christ, that stood by its soldiers around the tomb of the Son of God Himself, to devour Him, if it had been possible, when He should be brought forth, as the *first-begotten* from the dead,§ to rule all nations—be

* *Paradise Lost*, lib. i. ll. 738-745.

† The Greek poets speak of two downfalls of Vulcan. In the one case he was cast down by Jupiter, in the other by Juno. When Jupiter cast him down, it was for rebellion; when Juno did so, one of the reasons specially singled out for doing so was his "malformation," that is, his ugliness.—(HOMER's *Hymn to Apollo*, ll. 316-318, p. 37 of Hymn.) How exactly does this agree with the story of Nimrod: First he was personally cast down, when, by Divine authority, he was slain. Then he was cast down, in effigy, by Juno, when his image was degraded from the arms of the Queen of Heaven, to make way for the fairer child.—See *ante*, p. 69.

‡ See pages 62-65. Though Orpheus was commonly represented as having been *torn in pieces*, he too was fabled to have been killed by lightning.—(PAUSANIAS, *Bœotica*, cap. xxx. p. 768.) When Zoroaster died, he also is said in the myth to have perished by lightning (SUIDAS, vol. i. pp. 1133, 1134); and therefore, in accordance with that myth, he is represented as charging his countrymen to preserve not his body, but his "*ashes*." The death by lightning, however, is evidently a mere figure.

§ The birth of the Man-child, as given above, is different from that usually given: but let the reader consider if the view which I have taken does not meet all the requirements of the case. I think there will be but few who will assent to the opinion of Mr. Elliot, which in substance amounts to this, that the Man-child was Constantine the Great, and that when Christianity, in his person sat down on the throne of Imperial Rome, that was the fulfilment of the saying, that the child brought forth by the woman, amid such pangs of travail, was "caught up to God and His throne." When Constantine came to the empire, the Church indeed, as foretold in Daniel xi. 34, "was holpen with a little help;" but that was all. The

represented by a "Fiery Serpent"? Nothing could more lucidly show it forth. Among the lords many, and the gods many, worshipped in the imperial city, the two grand objects of worship were the "Eternal Fire," kept perpetually burning in the temple of

Christianity of Constantine was but of a very doubtful kind, the Pagans seeing nothing in it to hinder but that when he died, he should be enrolled among their gods.—(EUTROPIUS, x. pp.131-133.) But even though it had been better, the description of the woman's child is far too high for Constantine, or any Christian emperor that succeeded him on the imperial throne. "The Man-child, born to rule all nations with a rod of iron," is unequivocally Christ (see Psalms ii. 9; Rev. xix. 15). True believers, as one with Him in a subordinate sense, share in that honour (Rev. ii. 27); but to Christ alone, *properly*, does that prerogative belong; and I think it must be evident that it is *His* birth that is here referred to. But those who have contended for this view have done injustice to their cause by representing this passage as referring to His *literal* birth in Bethlehem. When Christ was born in Bethlehem, no doubt Herod endeavoured to cut Him off, and Herod was a subject of the Roman Empire. But it was not from any respect to Cæsar that he did so, but simply from fear of danger to his own dignity as King of Judea. So little did Cæsar sympathise with the slaughter of the children of Bethlehem, that it is recorded that Augustus, on hearing of it, remarked that it was "better to be Herod's hog than to be his child."—(MACROBIUS, *Saturnalia*, lib. ii. cap. 4, p. 77, B.) Then, even if it were admitted that Herod's bloody attempt to cut off the infant Saviour was symbolised by the Roman dragon, "standing ready to devour the child as soon as it should be born," where was there anything that could correspond to the statement that the child, to save it from that dragon, "was caught up to God and His throne"? The flight of Joseph and Mary with the Child into Egypt could never answer to such language. Moreover, it is worthy of special note, that when the Lord Jesus was born in Bethlehem, He was born, in a very important sense *only* as "King of the *Jews*." "Where is He that is born King of the Jews?" was the inquiry of the wise men that came from the East to seek Him. All His life long, He appeared in no other character; and when He died, the inscription on His cross ran in these terms: "This is the King of the Jews." Now, this was no accidental thing. Paul tells us (Rom. xv. 8) that "Jesus Christ was a minister of the *circumcision* for the truth of God, to confirm the promises made unto the fathers." Our Lord Himself plainly declared the same thing. "I am not sent," said He to the Syrophœnician woman, "save to the lost sheep of the house of Israel;" and, in sending out His disciples during His personal ministry, this was the charge which He gave them: "Go not in the way of the Gentiles, and into any city of the Samaritans enter ye not." It was *only* when He was "begotten from the dead," and "declared to be the Son of God with power," by His victory over the grave, that He was revealed as "the Man-child, born to rule all nations." Then said He to His disciples, when He had risen, and was about to ascend on high: "All power is given unto Me in heaven and in earth: go ye therefore, and teach *all* nations." To this glorious "birth" from the tomb, and to the birth-pangs of His Church that preceded it, our Lord Himself made distinct allusion on the night before He was betrayed (John xvi. 20-22), "Verily, verily, I say unto you, That ye shall weep and lament, but the world shall rejoice; and ye shall be sorrowful, but your sorrow shall be turned into joy. *A woman when she is in travail hath sorrow, because her hour is come;* but as soon as she is delivered of the child, she remembereth no more the anguish, for joy that a MAN is born into the world. *And ye now therefore have sorrow;* but I will see you again, and your heart shall rejoice." Here the grief of the apostles, and, of course, all the true Church that sympathised with them during the hour and power of darkness, is compared to the pangs of a travailing woman; and their joy, when the Saviour should see them again after His resurrection, to the joy of a mother when safely delivered of a *Man-child.* Can there be a doubt, then, what the symbol before us means, when the woman is represented as travailing in pain to be delivered of a "Man-child, that was to rule all nations," and when it is said that that "*Man-child* was caught up to God and His throne"?

Vesta, and the sacred Epidaurian Serpent. In Pagan Rome, this fire-worship and serpent-worship were sometimes separate, sometimes conjoined; but both occupied a pre-eminent place in Roman esteem. The fire of Vesta was regarded as one of the grand safeguards of the empire. It was pretended to have been brought from Troy by Æneas, who had it confided to his care by the shade of Hector,* and was kept with the most jealous care by the Vestal virgins, who, for their charge of it, were honoured with the highest honours. The temple where it was kept, says Augustine, "was the most sacred and most reverenced of all the temples of Rome."† The fire that was so jealously guarded in that temple, and on which so much was believed to depend, was regarded in the very same light as by the old Babylonian fire-worshippers. It was looked upon as the purifier, and in April every year, at the Palilia, or feast of Pales, both men and cattle, for this purpose, were made to pass through the fire.‡ The Epidaurian snake, that the Romans worshipped along with the fire, was looked on as the divine representation of Æsculapius, the child of the Sun.§ Æsculapius, whom that sacred snake represented, was evidently, just another name for the great Babylonian god. His fate was exactly the same as that of Phaëthon. He was said to have been smitten with lightning for raising the dead.‖ It is evident that this could never have been the case in a physical sense, nor could it easily have been believed to be so. But view it in a spiritual sense, and then the statement is just this, that he was believed to raise men who were dead in trespasses and sins to newness of life. Now, this was exactly what Phaëthon was pretending to do, when he was smitten for setting the world on fire. In the Babylonian system there was a symbolical death,¶ that all the initiated had to pass through, before they got the new life which was implied in regeneration, and that just to declare that they had passed from death unto life. As the passing through the fire was both a purgation from sin and the means of regeneration, so it was also for raising the dead that Phaëthon was smitten. Then, as Æsculapius was the child of the Sun, so was Phaëthon.** To symbolise this relationship, the head of the image of Æsculapius was generally encircled with rays.†† The Pope thus encircles the heads of the pretended images of Christ; but the real source of these irradiations is patent to all acquainted either with the literature or the art of Rome. Thus speaks Virgil of Latinus:—

* VIRGIL'S *Æneid*, Book ii. ll. 296, 297, p. 78.

† *De Civitate*, lib. iii. cap. 28, vol. ix. p. 110.

‡ OVID, *Fasti*, lib. iv. ll. 722-743.

§ *Ibid. Metam.*, lib. xv. ll. 736-745.

‖ *Ibid.* and *Æneid*, lib. vii. ll. 769-773, pp. 364, 365.

¶ WILKINSON, vol. i. p. 267, and APULEIUS, *Metam.*, cap. xi.

** The birth of Æsculapius in the myth was just the same as that of Bacchus. His mother was consumed by lightning, and the infant was rescued from the lightning that consumed her, as Bacchus was snatched from the flames that burnt up his mother.—LEMPRIERE.

†† DYMOCK, *sub voce*.

"And now, in pomp, the peaceful kings appear,
Four steeds the chariot of Latinus bear,
Twelve golden beams around his temples play,
To mark his lineage from the god of day."*

The "golden beams" around the head of Æsculapius were intended to mark the same, to point him out as the child of the Sun, or the Sun incarnate. The "golden beams" around the heads of pictures and images called by the name of Christ, were intended to show the Pagans that they might safely worship them, as the images of their well-known divinities, though called by a different name. Now Æsculapius, in a time of deadly pestilence, had been invited from Epidaurus to Rome. The god, under the form of a large serpent, entered the ship that was sent to convey him to Rome, and having safely arrived in the Tiber, was solemnly inaugurated as the guardian god of the Romans.† From that time forth, in private as well as in public, the worship of the Epidaurian snake, the serpent that represented the Sun-divinity incarnate, in other words, the "Serpent of Fire," became nearly universal. In almost every house the sacred serpent, which was a harmless sort, was to be found. "These serpents nestled about the domestic altars," says the author of *Pompeii*, "and came out, like dogs or cats, to be patted by the visitors, and beg for something to eat. Nay, at table, if we may build upon insulated passages, they crept about the cups of the guests, and, in hot weather, ladies would use them as live boas, and twist them round their necks for the sake of coolness. . . . These sacred animals made war on the rats and mice, and thus kept down one species of vermin; but as they bore a charmed life, and no one laid violent hands on them, they multiplied so fast, that, like the monkeys of Benares, they became an intolerable nuisance. The frequent fires at Rome were the only things that kept them under."‡ The reader will find, in the accompanying woodcut (Fig. 53), a representation of Roman fire-worship and serpent-worship at once separate and conjoined.§ The reason of the double representation of the god I cannot here enter into; but it must be evident, from the words of Virgil already quoted, that the figures in the upper compartment, having their heads encircled with rays, represent the fire-god, or Sun-divinity; and what

Fig. 53.

* DRYDEN'S *Virgil*, Book xii. ll. 245-248, vol. iii. p. 775; in Original, ll. 161-164.
† LACTANTIUS, *De Origine Erroris*, p. 82.
‡ *Pompeii*, vol. ii. pp. 114, 115.
§ *Ibid.* vol. ii. p. 105.

is worthy of special note is, that these fire-gods are *black*,* the colour thereby identifying them with the Æthiopian or *black* Phaëthon; while, as the author of *Pompeii* himself admits, these same black fire-gods are in the under compartment represented by two huge serpents. Now, if this worship of the sacred serpent of the Sun, the great fire-god, was so universal in Rome, what symbol could more graphically portray the idolatrous power of Pagan Imperial Rome than the "Great Fiery Serpent"? No doubt it was to set forth this very thing that the Imperial standard itself—the standard of the Pagan Emperor of Rome, as Pontifex Maximus, Head of the great system of fire-worship and serpent-worship—was a serpent elevated on a lofty pole, and so coloured, as to exhibit it as a recognised symbol of fire-worship.†

As Christianity spread in the Roman Empire, the powers of light and darkness came into collision (Rev. xii. 7, 8):—"Michael and his angels fought against the dragon; and the dragon fought and his angels, and prevailed not; neither was their place found any more in heaven. And the great dragon was cast out; . . . . he was cast out into the earth, and his angels were cast out with him." The "great serpent of fire" was cast out, when, by the decree of Gratian, Paganism throughout the Roman empire was abolished—when the fires of Vesta were extinguished, and the revenues of the Vestal virgins were confiscated—when the Roman Emperor (who though for more than a century and a-half a professor of Christianity, had been "Pontifex Maximus," the very head of the idolatry of Rome, and as such, on high occasions, appearing invested with all the idolatrous insignia of Paganism), through force of conscience abolished his own office.‡ While Nimrod was personally and *literally* slain by the sword, it was through the sword of the Spirit that Shem overcame the *system* of fire-worship, and so bowed the hearts of men, as to cause it for a time to be utterly extinguished. In like manner did the Dragon of fire, in the Roman Empire, receive a deadly wound from a sword, and that the *sword* of the

Fig. 54.

* "All the faces in his (MAZOIS's) engraving are quite black."—(*Pompeii*, vol. ii. p. 106.) In India, the infant Crishna (emphatically the *black* god), in the arms of the goddess Devaki, is represented with the woolly hair and marked features of the Negro or African race (see Fig. 54; from MOOR, Plate 59).

† AMMIANUS MARCELLINUS, lib. xvi. cap. 12, p. 145. (See Appendix, Note P.)

‡ ZOSIMI *Hist.*, lib. iv. p. 761.

Spirit, which is the Word of God. There is thus far an exact analogy between the type and the antitype.

But not only is there this analogy. It turns out, when the records of history are searched to the bottom, that when the head of the Pagan idolatry of Rome was slain with the sword by the extinction of the office of Pontifex Maximus, the last Roman Pontifex Maximus was the ACTUAL, LEGITIMATE, SOLE REPRESENTATIVE OF NIMROD and his idolatrous system then existing. To make this clear, a brief glance at the Roman history is necessary. In common with all the earth, Rome at a very early prehistoric period, had drunk deep of Babylon's "golden cup." But above and beyond all other nations, it had had a connection with the idolatry of Babylon that put it in a position peculiar and alone. Long before the days of Romulus, a representative of the Babylonian Messiah, called by his name, had fixed his temple as a god, and his palace as a king, on one of those very heights which came to be included within the walls of that city which Remus and his brother were destined to found. On the Capitoline hill, so famed in after-days as the great high place of Roman worship, Saturnia, or the city of Saturn, the great Chaldean god, had in the days of dim and distant antiquity been erected.* Some revolution had then taken place—the graven images of Babylon had been abolished—the erecting of any idol had been sternly prohibited,† and when the twin founders of the now world-renowned city reared its humble walls, the city and the palace of their Babylonian predecessor had long lain in ruins. The ruined state of this sacred city, even in the remote age of Evander, is alluded to by Virgil. Referring to the time when Æneas is said to have visited that ancient Italian king, thus he speaks :—

> "Then saw two *heaps of ruins;* once they stood
> Two stately towns on either side the flood;
> *Saturnia* and Janicula's remains;
> And either place the founder's name retains."‡

The deadly wound, however, thus given to the Chaldean system, was destined to be healed. A colony of Etruscans, earnestly attached to the Chaldean idolatry, had migrated, some say from Asia Minor, others from Greece, and settled in the immediate neighbourhood of Rome.§ They were ultimately incorporated in the Roman state, but long before this political union took place they exercised the most powerful influence on the religion of the Romans. From the very first their skill in augury, soothsaying, and all science, real or

* AURELIUS VICTOR, *Origo Gent. Roman.*, cap. 3.

† PLUTARCH (in *Hist. Numæ*, vol. i. p. 65) states, that Numa forbade the making of images, and that for 170 years after the founding of Rome, no images were allowed in the Roman temples.

‡ *Æneid*, lib. viii. ll. 467-470, vol. iii. p. 608.

§ DIONYSIUS HALICARN., vol. i. p. 22, Sir W. Betham (*Etruria Celtica*, vol. i. p. 47) opposes the Lydian origin of the Etrurians; but Layard (*Nineveh and Babylon*, chap. xxiv. p. 563) seems to have set the question at rest in favour of their Oriental extraction, or at least their close connection with the East.

pretended, that the augurs or soothsayers monopolised, made the Romans look up to them with respect. It is admitted on all hands that the Romans derived their knowledge of augury, which occupied so prominent a place in every public transaction in which they engaged, chiefly from the Tuscans,* that is, the people of Etruria, and at first none but natives of that country were permitted to exercise the office of a Haruspex, which had respect to all the rites essentially involved in sacrifice.† Wars and disputes arose between Rome and the Etruscans; but still the highest of the noble youths of Rome were sent to Etruria to be instructed in the sacred science which flourished there.‡ The consequence was, that under the influence of men whose minds were moulded by those who clung to the ancient idol-worship, the Romans were brought back again to much of that idolatry which they had formerly repudiated and cast off. Though Numa, therefore, in setting up his religious system, so far deferred to the prevailing feeling of his day and forbade image-worship, yet in consequence of the alliance subsisting between Rome and Etruria in sacred things, matters were put in train for the ultimate subversion of that prohibition. The college of Pontiffs, of which he laid the foundation,§ in process of time came to be substantially an Etruscan college, and the Sovereign Pontiff that presided over that college, and that controlled all the public and private religious rites of the Roman people in all essential respects, became in spirit and in practice an Etruscan Pontiff.

Still the Sovereign Pontiff of Rome, even after the Etruscan idolatry was absorbed into the Roman system, was only an offshoot from the grand original Babylonian system. He was a devoted worshipper of the Babylonian god; but he was not the legitimate representative of that God. The true legitimate Babylonian Pontiff had his seat beyond the bounds of the Roman empire. That seat, after the death of Belshazzar, and the expulsion of the Chaldean priesthood from Babylon by the Medo-Persian kings, was at Pergamos, where afterwards was one of the seven churches of Asia.‖ There, in consequence, for many centuries was "Satan's seat" (Rev. ii. 13). There, under favour of the deified¶ kings of Pergamos, was

* KENNETT'S *Antiquities*, Part ii., Book ii. chap. 3, p. 67, and ADAM'S *Antiquities*, "Ministers of Religion," p. 255.

† KENNETT'S *Antiquities*, Book ii. chap. 4, p. 69.

‡ CICERO, *De Divinatione*, lib. i. cap. 41, vol. iii. pp. 34, 35.

§ LIVY, lib. iv. cap. 4, vol. i. p. 260.

‖ BARKER and AINSWORTH'S *Lares and Penates of Cilicia*, chap. viii. p. 232. Barker says, "The defeated Chaldeans fled to Asia Minor, and fixed their central college at Pergamos." Phrygia, that was so remarkable for the worship of Cybele and Atys, formed part of the kingdom of Pergamos. Mysia also was another, and the Mysians, in the *Paschal Chronicle*, are said to be descended from Nimrod. The words are, "Nebrod, the huntsman and giant—from whence came the Mysians."—(*Pasch. Chron.* vol. i. p. 50.) Lydia, also, from which Livy and Herodotus say the Etrurians came, formed part of the same kingdom. For the fact that Mysia, Lydia, and Phrygia were constituent parts of the kingdom of Pergamos, see SMITH'S *Classical Dictionary*, p. 542.

¶ The kings of Pergamos, in whose dominions the Chaldean Magi found an asylum, were evidently by them, and by the general voice of Paganism that

his favourite abode, there was the worship of Æsculapius, under the form of the serpent, celebrated with frantic orgies and excesses, that elsewhere were kept under some measure of restraint. At first, the Roman Pontiff had no immediate connection with Pergamos and the hierarchy there; yet, in course of time, the Pontificate of Rome and the Pontificate of Pergamos came to be identified. Pergamos itself became part and parcel of the Roman empire, when Attalus III., the last of its kings, at his death, left by will all his dominions to the Roman people, B.C. 133.* For some time after the kingdom of Pergamos was merged in the Roman dominions, there was no one who could set himself openly and advisedly to lay claim to all the dignity inherent in the old title of the kings of Pergamos. The original powers even of the Roman Pontiffs seem to have been by that time abridged,† but when Julius Cæsar, who had previously been elected Pontifex Maximus,‡ became also, as Emperor, the supreme civil ruler of the Romans, then, as head of the Roman state, and head of the Roman religion, all the powers and functions of the *true legitimate Babylonian Pontiff* were supremely vested in him, and he found himself in a position to assert these powers. Then he seems to have laid claim to the divine dignity of Attalus, as well as the kingdom that Attalus had bequeathed to the Romans, as centring in himself; for his well-known watchword, "*Venus Genetrix*," which meant that Venus was the mother of the Julian race, appears to have been intended to make him "The Son" of the great goddess, even as the "Bull-horned" Attalus had been regarded.§ Then, on certain occasions, in the exercise of his high pontifical office, he appeared of course in all the pomp of the Babylonian costume, as Belshazzar himself might have done, in robes of scarlet,|| with the crosier of Nimrod in his hand, wearing the mitre of Dagon and bearing the keys of Janus and Cybele.¶ Thus did

sympathised with them, put into the vacant place which Belshazzar and his predecessors had occupied. They were hailed as the representatives of the old Babylonian god. This is evident from the statements of Pausanias. First, he quotes the following words from the oracle of a prophetess called Phaënnis, in reference to the Gauls: "But divinity will still more seriously afflict those that dwell near the sea. However, in a short time after, Jupiter will send them a defender, the beloved son of a Jove-nourished bull, who will bring destruction on all the Gauls." —(Lib. x., *Phocica*, cap. xv. p. 833.) Then on this he comments as follows: "Phaënnis, in this oracle, means by the son of a bull, Attalus, king of Pergamos, whom the oracle of Apollo called Taurokerōn," or bull-horned.—(*Ibid.*) This title given by the Delphian god, proves that Attalus, in whose dominions the Magi had their chief seat, had been set up and recognised in the very character of Bacchus, the Head of the Magi. Thus the vacant seat of Belshazzar was filled, and the broken chain of the Chaldean succession renewed.

* SMITH'S *Classical Dictionary*, p. 542.

† NIEBUHR, vol. iii. p. 27.

‡ DYMOCK, *sub voce* "Julius Cæsar," p. 460, col. 1.

§ The deification of the emperors that continued in succession from the days of Divus Julius, or the "Deified Julius," can be traced to no cause so likely as their representing the "Bull-horned" Attalus both as Pontiff and Sovereign.

|| That "scarlet" was the robe of honour in Belshazzar's time, see Dan. v. 7, 29.

¶ That the *key* was one of the symbols used in the Mysteries, the reader will

matters continue, as already stated, even under so-called Christian emperors; who, as a salve to their consciences, appointed a heathen as their substitute in the performance of the more *directly* idolatrous functions of the pontificate (that substitute, however, acting in their name and by their authority), until the reign of Gratian, who, as shown by Gibbon, was the first that refused to be arrayed in the idolatrous pontifical attire, or to act as Pontifex.* Now, from all this it is evident that, when Paganism in the Roman empire was abolished, when the office of Pontifex Maximus was suppressed, and all the dignitaries of paganism were cast down from their seats of influence and of power, which they had still been allowed in some measure to retain, this was not merely the casting down of the Fiery Dragon of Rome, but the casting down of the Fiery Dragon of Babylon. It was just the enacting over again, in a symbolical sense, upon the true and sole legitimate successor of Nimrod, what had taken place upon himself, when the greatness of his downfall gave rise to the exclamation, "How art thou fallen from heaven, O Lucifer, son of the morning!"

SECTION II.—THE BEAST FROM THE SEA.

The next great enemy introduced to our notice is the Beast from the Sea (Rev. xiii. 1):—"I stood," says John, "upon the sand of the sea-shore, and saw a beast rise up out of the sea." The seven heads and ten horns on this beast, as on the great dragon, show that this power is essentially the same beast, but that it has undergone a circumstantial change. In the old Babylonian system, after the worship of the god of fire, there speedily followed the worship of the god of water or the sea. As the world formerly was in danger of being burnt up, so now it was in equal danger of being drowned. In the Mexican story it is said to have actually been so. First, say they, it was destroyed by fire, and then it was destroyed by water.† The Druidic mythology gives the same account; for the Bards affirm that the dreadful tempest of fire that split the earth asunder, was rapidly succeeded by the bursting of the Lake Llion, when the waters of the

find on consulting TAYLOR'S *Note on Orphic Hymn to Pluto*, where that divinity is spoken of as "keeper of the keys." Now the Pontifex, as "Hierophant," was "arrayed in the habit and adorned with the symbols of the great Creator of the world, of whom in these Mysteries he was supposed to be the substitute."—(MAURICE'S *Antiquities*, vol. iii. p. 356.) The Primeval or Creative god was mystically represented as Androgyne, as combining in his own person both sexes (*Ibid.* vol. v. p. 933), being therefore both Janus and Cybele at the same time. In opening up the Mysteries, therefore, of this mysterious divinity, it was natural that the Pontifex should bear the key of both these divinities. Janus himself, however, as well as Pluto, was often represented with more than one key. The edition of Maurice above referred to is London, 1793-94.

* The original authority of Zosimus has already been given for this statement. The reader may find the same fact stated in GIBBON, vol. iii. p. 397, Note.

† HUMBOLDT'S *Researches*, vol. ii. pp. 21, 23.

abyss poured forth and "overwhelmed the whole world."* In Greece we meet with the very same story. Diodorus Siculus tells us that, in former times, "a monster called Ægides, who vomited flames, appeared in Phrygia; hence spreading along Mount Taurus, the conflagration burnt down all the woods as far as India; then, with a retrograde course, swept the forests of Mount Lebanon, and extended as far as Egypt and Africa; at last a stop was put to it by Minerva. The Phrygians remembered well this CONFLAGRATION and the FLOOD which FOLLOWED it."† Ovid, too, has a clear allusion to the same fact of the fire-worship being speedily followed by the worship of water, in his fable of the transformation of Cycnus. He represents *King* Cycnus, an attached friend of Phaëthon, and consequently of fire-worship, as, after his friend's death, ***hating the fire***, and taking to the contrary element that of ***water***, through ***fear***, and so being transformed into a swan.‡ In India, the great deluge, which occupies so conspicuous a place in its mythology, evidently has the same symbolical meaning, although the story of Noah is mixed up with it; for it was during that deluge that "the lost Vedas," or sacred books, were recovered, by means of the great *god*, under the form of a FISH. The "loss of the Vedas" had evidently taken place at that very time of terrible disaster to the gods, when, according to the Purans, a great enemy of these gods, called Durgu, "abolished all religious ceremonies, the Brahmins, through fear, forsook the *reading of the Veda*, ... fire lost its energy, and the terrified stars retired from sight;"§ in other words, when idolatry, fire-worship, and the worship of the host of heaven had been suppressed. When we turn to Babylon itself, we find there also substantially the same account. In Berosus, the deluge is represented as coming ***after*** the time of Alorus, or the "god of fire," that is, Nimrod, which shows that there, too, this deluge was symbolical. Now, out of this deluge emerged Dagon, the fish-god, or god of the sea. The origin of the worship of Dagon, as shown by Berosus, was founded upon a legend, that, at a remote period of the past, when men were sunk in barbarism, there came up a BEAST CALLED OANNES FROM THE RED SEA, or Persian Gulf—half-man, half-fish—that civilised the Babylonians, taught them arts and sciences, and instructed them in politics and religion.‖ The worship of Dagon was introduced by the very parties—Nimrod, of course,

* DAVIES's *Druids*, Note at p. 555, compared with p. 142.

† DIODORUS, lib. iii., cap. 4, p. 142.

‡ Ille relicto
. . . .
Imperio, ripas virides, amnemque querelis
Eridanum implêrat, silvamque sororibus auctam,
. . . . . nec se cœloque Jovique
Credit, ut injuste missi memor ignis ab illo,
Stagna petit, patulosque lacus; ignemque perosus,
Quæ *colat*, elegit contraria flumina flammis.

Metam., lib. ii. v. 369-380, vol. ii. pp. 88, 89. The reader will notice the ambiguity of *colat*, as signifying either "to worship" or "to inhabit."

§ COLEMAN's *Hindu Mythology*, p. 89.

‖ BEROSUS, lib. i. p. 48.

excepted—who had previously seduced the world into the worship of fire. In the secret Mysteries that were then set up, while in the first instance, no doubt, professing the greatest antipathy to the prescribed worship of fire, they sought to regain their influence and power by scenic representations of the awful scenes of the Flood, in which Noah was introduced under the name of Dagon, or the Fish-god—scenes in which the whole family of man, both from the nature of the event and their common connection with the second father of the human race, could not fail to feel a deep interest. The concocters of these Mysteries saw that if they could only bring men back again to idolatry in any shape, they could soon work that idolatry so as substantially to re-establish the very system that had been put down. Thus it was, that, as soon as the way was prepared for it, Tammuz was introduced as one who had allowed himself to be slain for the good of mankind. A distinction was made between good serpents and bad serpents, one kind being represented as the serpent of Agathodæmon, or the good divinity, another as the serpent of Cacodæmon, or the evil one.* It was easy, then, to lead men on by degrees to believe that, in spite of all appearances to the contrary, Tammuz, instead of being the patron of serpent-worship in any evil sense, was in reality the grand enemy of the Apophis, or great malignant serpent that envied the happiness of mankind, and that in fact he was the very seed of the woman who was destined to bruise the serpent's head. By means of the metempsychosis, it was just as easy to identify Nimrod and Noah, and to make it appear that the great patriarch, in the person of this his favoured descendant, had graciously condescended to become incarnate anew, as Dagon, that he might bring mankind back again to the blessings they had lost when Nimrod was slain. Certain it is, that Dagon was worshipped in the Chaldean Mysteries, wherever they were established, in a character that represented both the one and the other.†

In the previous system, the grand mode of purification had been by fire. *Now*, it was by water that men were to be purified. Then began the doctrine of baptismal regeneration, connected, as we have seen, with the passing of Noah through the waters of the Flood. Then began the reverence for holy wells, holy lakes, holy rivers, which is to be found wherever these exist on the earth; which is not only to be traced among the Parsees, who, along with the worship of fire, worship also the Zereparankard, or Caspian Sea,‡ and among the Hindoos, who worship the purifying waters of the Ganges, and who count it the grand passport to heaven, to leave their dying relatives to be smothered in its stream; but which is seen in full force at this day in Popish Ireland, in the universal reverence for holy wells, and the annual pilgrimages to Loch Dergh, to wash away sin in its blessed waters; and which manifestly lingers also among our-

* WILKINSON, vol. iv. pp. 239 and 412. In Egypt, the Uræus, or the Cerastes, was the good serpent, the Apophis the evil one.—(WILKINSON, vol. v. p. 243.)

† DAVIES'S *Druids*, p. 180. Davies identifies Noah with Bacchus.

‡ WILSON'S *Parsi Religion*, pp. 192, 251, 252, 262, 305.

selves, in the popular superstition about witches which shines out in the well-known line of Burns—

"A running stream they daurna cross."

So much for the worship of water. Along with the water-worship, however, the old worship of fire was soon incorporated again. In the Mysteries, both modes of purification were conjoined. Though water-baptism was hold to regenerate, yet purification by fire was still held to be indispensable;* and, long ages after baptismal regeneration had been established, the children were still made "to pass through the fire to Moloch." This double purification both by fire and water was practised in Mexico, among the followers of Wodan.† This double purification was also commonly practised among the old Pagan Romans;‡ and, in course of time, almost everywhere throughout

* The name Tammuz, as applied to Nimrod or Osiris, was equivalent to Alorus, or the "god of fire," and seems to have been given to him as the great purifier by fire. Tammuz is derived from *tam*, "to make perfect," and *muz*, "fire," and signifies "Fire the perfecter," or "the perfecting fire." To this meaning of the name, as well as to the character of Nimrod as the *Father* of the gods, the Zoroastrian verse alludes when it says: "All things are the progeny of ONE FIRE. The FATHER perfected all things, and delivered them to the second mind, whom all nations of men call the first."—(CORY's *Fragments*, p. 242.) Here Fire is declared to be the *Father* of all; for all things are said to be its *progeny*, and it is also called the "*perfecter* of all things." The second mind is evidently the child who displaced Nimrod's image as an object of worship; but yet the agency of Nimrod, as the first of the gods, and the fire-god, was held indispensable for "perfecting" men. And hence, too, no doubt, the necessity of the fire of Purgatory to "*perfect*" men's souls at last, and to purge away all the sins that they have carried with them into the unseen world.

† HUMBOLDT's *Researches*, vol. i. p. 185.

‡ OVID, *Fasti*, lib. iv. ll. 794, 795, vol. iii. p. 274. It was not a little interesting to me, after being led by strict induction from circumstantial evidence to the conclusion that the purgation by fire was derived from the fire-worship of Adon or Tammuz, and that by water had reference to Noah's Flood, to find an express statement in Ovid, that such was the actual belief at Rome in his day. After mentioning, in the passage to which the above citation refers, various fanciful reasons for the twofold purgation by fire and water, he concludes thus: "For my part, I do not believe them; there are some (however) who say that the one is intended to commemorate Phaëthon, and the other the flood of Deucalion."

If, however, any one should still think it unlikely that the worship of Noah should be mingled in the ancient world with the worship of the Queen of Heaven and her son, let him open his eyes to what is taking place in Italy at this hour [in 1856] in regard to the worship of that patriarch and the Roman Queen of Heaven. The following, kindly sent me by Lord John Scott, as confirmatory of the views propounded in these pages, appeared in the *Morning Herald*, Oct. 26, 1855: "AN ARCHBISHOP'S PRAYER TO THE PATRIARCH NOAH.—POPERY IN TURIN.—For several consecutive years the vintage has been almost entirely destroyed in Tuscany, in consequence of the prevalent disease. The Archbishop of Florence has conceived the idea of arresting this plague by directing prayers to be offered, not to God, but to the patriarch Noah; and he has just published a collection, containing eight forms of supplication, addressed to this distinguished personage of the ancient covenant. 'Most holy patriarch Noah!' is the language of one of these prayers, 'who didst employ thyself in thy long career in cultivating the vine, and gratifying the human race with that precious beverage, which allays the thirst, restores the strength, and enlivens the spirits of us all, deign to regard our vines, which, following thine example, we have cultivated hitherto; and, while

the Pagan world, both the fire-worship and serpent-worship of Nimrod, which had been put down, was re-established in a new form, with all its old and many additional abominations besides.

Now, this god of the sea, when his worship had been firmly re-established, and all formidable opposition had been put down, was worshipped also as the great god of war, who, though he had died for the good of mankind, now that he had risen again, was absolutely invincible. In memory of this new incarnation, the 25th of December, otherwise Christmas Day, was, as we have already seen, celebrated in Pagan Rome as "*Natalis Solis invicti*," "the birth-day of the Unconquered Sun."* We have equally seen that the very name of the Roman god of war is just the name of Nimrod; for Mars and Mavors, the two well-known names of the Roman war-god, are evidently just the Roman forms of the Chaldee "Mar" or "Mavor," the Rebel.† Thus terrible and invincible was Nimrod when he reappeared as Dagon, the beast from the sea. If the reader looks at what is said in Rev. xiii. 3, he will see precisely the same thing: "And I saw one of his heads as it were wounded unto death; and his deadly wound was healed: and all the world wondered after the beast. And they worshipped the dragon, which gave power unto the beast, and they worshipped the beast, saying, Who is like unto the beast? who is able to make war with him?" Such, in all respects, is the analogy between the language of the prophecy and the ancient Babylonian type.

Do we find, then, anything corresponding to this in the religious history of the Roman empire after the fall of the old Paganism of that empire? Exactly in every respect. No sooner was Paganism legally abolished, the eternal fire of Vesta extinguished, and the old serpent cast down from the seat of power, where so long he had sat secure, than he tried the most vigorous means to regain his influence and authority. Finding that persecution of Christianity, as such,

thou beholdest them languishing and blighted by that disastrous visitation, which, before the vintage, destroys the fruit (in severe punishment for many blasphemies and other enormous sins we have committed), have compassion on us, and, prostrate before the lofty throne of God, who has promised to His children the fruits of the earth, and an abundance of corn and wine, entreat Him on our behalf; promise Him in our name, that, with the aid of Divine grace, we will forsake the ways of vice and sin, that we will no longer abuse His sacred gifts, and will scrupulously observe His holy law, and that of our holy Mother, the Catholic Church,' &c. The collection concludes with a new prayer, addressed to the Virgin Mary, who is invoked in these words: 'O immaculate Mary, behold our fields and vineyards! and, should it seem to thee that we merit so great a favour, stay, we beseech thee, this terrible plague, which, inflicted for our sins, renders our fields unfruitful, and deprives our vines of the honours of the vintage,' &c. The work contains a vignette, representing the patriarch Noah presiding over the operations of the vintage, as well as a notification from the Archbishop, granting an indulgence of forty days to all who shall devoutly recite the prayers in question.—*Christian Times.*" In view of such rank Paganism as this, well may the noble Lord already referred to remark, that surely here is the world turned backwards, and the worship of the old god Bacchus unmistakably restored!

* GIESELER, vol. ii. p. 42, Note.

† The Greeks chose as their war-god Arioch or Arius, the *grandson* of Nimrod.—(CEDRENUS, vol. i pp. 28, 29.)

in the meantime would not do to destroy the church symbolised by the sun-clothed Woman, he made another tack (Rev. xii. 15): "And the serpent cast out of his mouth a flood of water after the woman, that he might cause her to be carried away of the flood." The symbol here is certainly very remarkable. If this was the dragon of *fire*, it might have been expected that it would have been represented, according to popular myths, as vomiting fire after the woman. But it is not so. It was a *flood of water* that he cast out of his mouth. What could this mean? As the water came out of the *mouth* of the dragon—that must mean doctrine, and of course, *false* doctrine. But is there nothing more specific than this? A single glance at the old Babylonian type will show that the water cast out of the mouth of the serpent must be the *water of baptismal regeneration*. Now, it was precisely at this time, when the old Paganism was suppressed, that the doctrine of regenerating men by baptism, which had been working in the Christian Church before, threatened to spread like a deluge over the face of the Roman empire.* It was then precisely that our Lord Jesus Christ began to be popularly called Ichthys, that is, "the Fish,"† manifestly to identify him with Dagon. At the end of the fourth century, and from that time forward, it was taught, that he who had been washed in the baptismal font was thereby born again, and made pure as the virgin snow.

This flood issued not merely from the mouth of Satan, the old serpent, but from the mouth of him who came to be recognised by the Pagans of Rome as the visible head of the old Roman Paganism. When the Roman fire-worship was suppressed, we have seen that the office of Pontifex Maximus, the head of that Paganism, was abolished. That was "the wounding unto death" of the head of the Fiery Dragon. But scarcely had that head received its deadly wound, when it began to be healed again. Within a few years after the Pagan title of Pontifex had been abolished, it was revived, and that by the very Emperor that had abolished it, and was bestowed, with all the Pagan associations clustering around it, upon the Bishop of Rome,‡ who, from that time forward, became the grand agent in pouring over professing Christendom, first the ruinous doctrine of baptismal regeneration, and then all the other doctrines of Paganism derived from ancient Babylon. When this Pagan title was bestowed on the Roman bishop, it was not as a mere empty title of honour it was bestowed, but as a title to which formidable power was annexed. To the authority of the Bishop of Rome in this new character, as Pontifex, when associated "with five

* From about A.D. 360, to the time of the Emperor Justinian, about 550, we have evidence both of the promulgation of this doctrine, and also of the deep hold it came at last to take of professing Christians. See GIESELER, vol. ii., Second Period, "Public Worship," p. 145.

† AUGUSTINE, *De Civitate*, lib. xviii. cap. 23, vol. ix. p. 665.

‡ *Codex Theodosianus*, lib. xvi. tit. 1, leg. 2. See also leg. 3. The reader will notice, that while the Bishop of Rome alone is called Pontifex, the heads of the other churches referred to are simply "Episcopi."

or seven other bishops" as his counsellors, bishops, and even metropolitans of foreign churches over extensive regions of the West, in Gaul not less than in Italy, were subjected; and civil pains were attached to those who refused to submit to his pontifical decisions.* Great was the danger to the cause of truth and righteousness when such power was, by imperial authority, vested in the Roman bishop, and that a bishop so willing to give himself to the propagation of false doctrine. Formidable, however, as the danger was, the true Church, the Bride, the Lamb's wife (so far as that Church was found within the bounds of the Western Empire), was wonderfully protected from it. That Church was for a time saved from the peril, not merely by the mountain fastnesses in which many of its devoted members found an asylum, as Jovinian, Vigilantius, and the Waldenses, and such-like faithful ones, in the wilderness among the Cottian Alps, and other secluded regions of Europe, but also not a little, by a signal interposition of Divine Providence in its behalf. That interposition is referred to in these words (Rev. xii. 16): "The earth opened her mouth and swallowed up the flood, which the dragon cast out of his mouth." What means the symbol of the "earth's opening its mouth"? In the natural world, when the earth opens its mouth, there is an earthquake; and an "earthquake," according to the figurative language of the Apocalypse, as all admit, just means a great political convulsion. Now, when we examine the history of the period in question, we find that the fact exactly agrees with the prefiguration; that soon after the Bishop of Rome became Pontiff, and, as Pontiff, set himself so zealously to bring in Paganism into the Church, those political convulsions began in the civil empire of Rome, which never ceased till the framework of that empire was broken up, and it was shattered to pieces. But for this the spiritual power of the Papacy might have been firmly established over all the nations of the West, long before the time it actually was so. It is clear, that immediately after Damasus, the Roman bishop, received his pontifical power, the predicted "apostacy" (1 Tim. iv. 3), so far as Rome was concerned, was broadly developed. Then were men "forbidden to marry,"† and "commanded to abstain from meats."‡ Then, with a factitious doctrine of sin, a factitious holiness also was inculcated, and people were led to believe that all baptised persons were necessarily regenerated. Had the Roman Empire of the West remained under one civil head, backed by that civil head, the Bishop

* *Rescript of Gratian, in answer to application of Roman Council,* in GIESELER, vol. i., Second Period, div. i. chap. 3, "Hierarchy in the West," p. 434, Note 12. See also BOWER, "Damasus," A.D. 378. For the demands of the Roman Council, see *Ibid.* vol. i. p. 209. This rescript was prior to the decree in the Codex above referred to, which decree runs in the name of Valentinian and Theodosius, as well as of Gratian, who had associated them with himself.

† The celibacy of the clergy was enacted by Syricius, Bishop of Rome, A.D. 385.—(GIESELER, vol. i., Second Period, div. i. chap. 4, "Monachism," vol. ii. p. 20; and BOWER's *Lives of the Popes*, vol. i. p. 235.)

‡ Against the use of flesh and wine, see what is said at the same period by Jerome, the great advocate of the Papacy.—(HIERONYMUS, *Adv. Jovin.*, lib. ii., throughout the book, vol. i. pp. 360-380.)

of Rome might very soon have infected all parts of that empire with the Pagan corruption he had evidently given himself up to propagate. Considering the cruelty* with which Jovinian, and all who opposed the Pagan doctrines in regard to marriage and abstinence, were treated by the Pontifex of Rome, under favour of the imperial power, it may easily be seen how serious would have been the consequences to the cause of truth in the Western Empire had this state of matters been allowed to pursue its natural course. But now the great Lord of the Church interfered. The "revolt of the Goths," and the sack of Rome by Alaric the Goth in 410, gave that shock to the Roman Empire which issued, by 476, in its complete upbreaking and the extinction of the imperial power. Although, therefore, in pursuance of the policy previously inaugurated, the Bishop of Rome was formally recognised, by an imperial edict in 445, as "Head of all the Churches of the West," all bishops being commanded "to hold and observe as a law whatever it should please the Bishop of Rome to ordain or decree;"† the convulsions of the empire, and the extinction, soon thereafter, of the imperial power itself, to a large extent nullified the disastrous effects of this edict. The "earth's opening its mouth," then—in other words, the breaking up of the Roman Empire into so many independent sovereignties—was a benefit to true religion, and prevented the flood of error and corruption, that had its source in Rome, from flowing as fast and as far as it would otherwise have done. When many different wills in the different countries were substituted for the *one* will of the Emperor, on which the Sovereign Pontiff leaned, the influence of that Pontiff was greatly neutralised. "Under these circumstances," says Gieseler, referring to the influence of Rome in the different kingdoms into which the empire was divided, "under these circumstances, the Popes could not directly interfere in ecclesiastical matters; and their communications with the established Church of the country depended entirely on the royal pleasure."‡ The Papacy at last overcame the effects of the earthquake, and the kingdoms of the West were engulfed in that flood of error that came out of the mouth of the dragon. But the overthrow of the imperial power, when so zealously propping up the spiritual despotism of Rome, gave the true Church in the West a lengthened period of comparative freedom, which otherwise it could not have had. The Dark Ages would have come sooner, and the darkness would have been more intense, *but for* the Goths and Vandals, and the political convulsions that attended their irruptions. They were raised up to scourge an apostatising community, *not* to persecute the saints of the Most High, though these, too, may have occasionally suffered in the common distress. The hand of Providence may be distinctly seen, in that, at so critical a moment, the earth opened its mouth and helped the Woman.

To return, however, to the memorable period when the pontifical

* See BowER, "Syricius," vol. i. p. 256. † Bower, vol. ii. p. 14.

‡ Gieseler, vol. ii., Second Period, div. ii. c. 6, "German Nations," p. 157.

title was bestowed on the Bishop of Rome. The circumstances in which that Pagan title was bestowed upon Pope Damasus, were such as might have been not a little trying to the faith and integrity of a much better man than he. Though Paganism was legally abolished in the Western Empire of Rome, yet in the city of the Seven Hills it was still rampant, insomuch that Jerome, who knew it well, writing of Rome at this very period, calls it "the sink of all superstitions."* The consequence was, that, while everywhere else throughout the empire the Imperial edict for the abolition of Paganism was respected, in Rome itself it was, to a large extent, a dead letter. Symmachus, the prefect of the city, and the highest patrician families, as well as the masses of the people, were fanatically devoted to the old religion; and, therefore, the Emperor found it necessary, in spite of the law, to connive at the idolatry of the Romans. How strong was the hold that Paganism had in the Imperial city, even after the fire of Vesta was extinguished, and State support was withdrawn from the Vestals, the reader may perceive from the following words of Gibbon: "The image and altar of Victory were indeed removed from the Senate-house; but the Emperor yet spared the statues of the gods which were exposed to public view; four hundred and twenty-four temples or chapels still remained to satisfy the devotion of the people, and in every quarter of Rome the delicacy of the Christians was offended by the fumes of idolatrous sacrifice."† Thus strong was Paganism in Rome, even after State support was withdrawn about 376. But look forward only about fifty years, and see what has become of it. The name of Paganism has almost entirely disappeared; insomuch that the younger Theodosius, in an edict issued A.D. 423, uses these words: "The Pagans that remain, although now we may believe there are none."‡ The words of Gibbon in reference to this are very striking. While fully admitting that, notwithstanding the Imperial laws made against Paganism, "no peculiar hardships" were imposed on "the sectaries who credulously received the fables of Ovid, and obstinately rejected the miracles of the Gospel," he expresses his surprise at the rapidity of the revolution that took place among the Romans from Paganism to Christianity. "The ruin of Paganism," he says—and his dates are from A.D. 378, the year when the Bishop of Rome was made Pontifex, to 395—"The ruin of Paganism, in the age of Theodosius, is perhaps the only example of the total *extirpation* of any ancient and popular superstition; and may therefore deserve to be considered as a singular event in the history of the human mind." . . . . After referring to the hasty conversion of the senate, he thus proceeds: "The edifying example of the Anician family [in embracing Christianity] was soon imitated by the rest of the nobility. . . . . The citizens who subsisted by their own industry, and the populace who were supported by the public liberality, filled the churches of

* *Comment. in Epist. ad Galat.*, iv. 3, tom. iii. p. 138, col. 1.

† *Decline and Fall*, chap. xxviii., vol. v. p. 87.

‡ *Codex Theodosianus*, xvi. 10, 22, p. 1625.

the Lateran and Vatican with an incessant throng of devout proselytes. The decrees of the senate, which proscribed the worship of idols, were ratified by the *general consent* of the Romans; the splendour of the capitol was defaced, and the solitary temples were abandoned to ruin and contempt. Rome submitted to the yoke of the Gospel. . . . . The generation that arose in the world, after the promulgation of Imperial laws, was ATTRACTED within the pale of the Catholic Church, and so RAPID, yet so GENTLE was the fall of Paganism, that only twenty-eight years after the death of Theodosius [the elder], the faint and minute vestiges were no longer visible to the eye of the legislator."* Now, how can this great and rapid revolution be accounted for? Is it because the Word of the Lord has had free course and been glorified? Then, what means the new aspect that the Roman Church has now begun to assume? In exact proportion as Paganism has disappeared from *without* the Church, in the very same proportion it appears *within* it. Pagan dresses for the priests, Pagan festivals for the people, Pagan doctrines and ideas of all sorts, are everywhere in vogue.† The testimony of the same historian, who has spoken so decisively about the rapid conversion of the Romans to the profession of the Gospel, is not less decisive on this point. In his account of the Roman Church, under the head of "Introduction of Pagan Ceremonies," he thus speaks: "As the objects of religion were gradually reduced to the standard of the imagination, the rites and ceremonies were introduced that seemed most powerfully to affect the senses of the vulgar. If, in the beginning of the fifth century, Tertullian or Lactantius had been suddenly raised from the dead, to assist at the festival of some popular saint or martyr, they would have gazed with astonishment and indignation on the profane spectacle which had succeeded to the pure and spiritual worship of a Christian congregation. As soon as the doors of the church were thrown open, they must have been offended by the smoke of incense, the perfume of flowers, and the glare of lamps and tapers, which diffused at noon-day a gaudy, superfluous, and, in their opinion, sacrilegious light."‡ Gibbon has a great deal more to the same effect. Now, can any one believe that this was accidental? No. It was evidently the result of that unprincipled policy, of which, in the course of this inquiry, we have already seen such innumerable instances on the part of the Papacy.§ Pope Damasus saw that, in a city pre-eminently given to idolatry, if he was to maintain the Gospel pure and entire, he must be willing to bear the cross, to encounter hatred and ill-will, to endure hardness as a good soldier of Jesus Christ. On the other hand, he could not but equally see, that if bearing the *title*, around which, for so many ages, all the hopes and affections of Paganism had

* *Decline and Fall*, chap. xxviii., vol. v. pp. 90–93, and p. 112.

† GIESELER, vol. ii. pp. 40, 45.

‡ *Decline and Fall*, chap. xxviii., vol. v. pp. 121, &c.

§ Gibbon distinctly admits this. "It must ingenuously be confessed," says he, "that the ministers of the Catholic Church imitated the profane model they were so impatient to destroy."

clustered, he should give its votaries reason to believe that he was willing to act up to the original spirit of that title, he might count on popularity, aggrandisement and glory. Which alternative, then, was Damasus likely to choose? The man that came into the bishopric of Rome, as a thief and a robber, over the dead bodies of above a hundred of his opponents,* could not hesitate as to the election he should make. The result shows that he had acted in character, that, in assuming the Pagan title of Pontifex, he had set himself at whatever sacrifice of truth to justify his claims to that title in the eyes of the Pagans, as the legitimate representative of their long line of pontiffs. There is no possibility of accounting for the facts on any other supposition. It is evident also that he and his successors were ACCEPTED in that character by the Pagans, who, in flocking into the Roman Church, and rallying around the new Pontiff, did not change *their* creed or worship, but brought *both* into the Church along with them. The reader has seen how complete and perfect is the copy of the old Babylonian Paganism, which, under the patronage of the Popes, has been introduced into the Roman Church. He has seen that the god whom the Papacy worships as the Son of the Highest, is not only, in spite of a Divine command, worshipped under the form of an image, made, as in the days of avowed Paganism, by art and man's device, but that attributes are ascribed to Him which are the very *opposite* of those which belong to the merciful Saviour, but which attributes are precisely those which were ascribed to Moloch, the fire-god, or Ala Mahozim, "the god of fortifications."† He has seen that, about the very time when the Bishop of Rome was invested with the Pagan title of Pontifex, the Saviour began to be called Ichthys, or "the Fish," thereby identifying Him with Dagon, or the Fish-god ; ‡ and that, ever since, advancing step by step, as circumstances would permit, what has gone under the name of the worship of Christ, has just been the worship of that same Babylonian divinity, with all its rites and pomps and ceremonies, precisely as in ancient Babylon. Lastly, he has seen that the Sovereign Pontiff of the so-called Christian Church of Rome has so wrought out the *title* bestowed upon him in the end of the fourth century, as to be now dignified, as for centuries he has been, with the very "names of blasphemy" originally bestowed on the old Babylonian pontiffs.§

* BOWER'S *Lives of the Popes*, vol. i., "Damasus," pp. 180-183 inclusive.

† See Chapter IV. p. 154.

‡ Bacchus himself was called by the very name "Ichthys."—(HESYCHIUS, p. 179.)

§ The reader who has seen the first edition of this work, will perceive that, in the above reasoning, I found nothing upon the formal appointment by Gratian of the Pope as Pontifex, with direct authority over the *Pagans*, as was done in that edition. That is not because I do not believe that such an appointment was made, but because, at the present moment, some obscurity rests on the subject. The Rev. Barcroft Boake, a very learned minister of the Church of England in Ceylon, when in this country, communicated to me his researches on the subject, which have made me hesitate to assert that there was any formal authority given to the Bishop of Rome over the *Pagans* by Gratian. At the same time, I am

Now, if the circumstances in which the Pope has risen to all this height of power and blasphemous assumption, be compared with a prediction in Daniel, which, for want of the true key has never been understood, I think the reader will see how literally in the history of the Popes of Rome that prediction has been fulfilled. The prediction to which I allude is that which refers to what is commonly called the "Wilful King" as described in Dan. xi. 36, and succeeding verses. That "Wilful King" is admitted on all hands to be a king that arises in Gospel times, and in Christendom, but has generally been supposed to be an Infidel Antichrist, not only opposing the truth but opposing Popery as well, and every thing that assumes the very name of Christianity. But now, let the prediction be read in the light of the facts that have passed in review before us, and it will be seen how very different is the case (ver. 36): "And the king shall do according to his will; and he shall exalt himself and magnify himself above every god, and shall speak marvellous things against the God of gods, and shall prosper till the indignation be accomplished: for that that is determined shall be done. Neither shall he regard the god of his fathers, nor the desire of women, nor regard any god: for he shall magnify himself above all." So far these words give an exact description of the Papacy, with its pride, its blasphemy, and forced celibacy and virginity. But the words that follow, according to any sense that the commentators have put upon them, have never hitherto been found capable of being made to agree either with the theory that the Pope was intended, or any other theory whatever. Let them, however, only be literally rendered, and compared with the Papal history, and all is clear, consistent, and harmonious. The inspired seer has declared that, in the Church of Christ, some one shall arise

still convinced that the original statement was substantially true. The late Mr. Jones, in the *Journal of Prophecy*, not only referred to the *Appendix to the Codex Theodosianus*, in proof of such an appointment, but, in elucidation of the words of the *Codex*, asserted in express terms that there was a contest for the office of Pontifex, and that there were two candidates, the one a Pagan, Symmachus, who had previously been Valentinian's deputy, and the other the Bishop of Rome.—(*Quarterly Journal of Prophecy*, Oct. 1852, p. 328.) I have not been able to find Mr. Jones's authority for this statement; but the statement is so circumstantial, that it cannot easily be called in question without impugning the veracity of him that made it. I have found Mr. Jones in error on divers points, but in no error of such a nature as this; and the character of the man forbids such a supposition. Moreover, the language of the *Appendix* cannot easily admit of any other interpretation. But, even though there were no formal appointment of Bishop Damasus to a pontificate extending over the Pagans, yet it is clear that, by the rescript of Gratian (the authenticity of which is fully admitted by the accurate Gieseler), he was made the supreme spiritual authority in the *Western* Empire, *in all religious questions*. When, therefore, in the year 400, Pagan *priests* were, by the Christian Emperor of the West, from political motives, "acknowledged as *public officers*" (*Cod. Theod.*, xii. 1, *ad* POMPEJANUM, *Procons. Africæ*, p. 1262), these Pagan priests necessarily came under the jurisdiction of the Bishop of Rome, as there was then no other tribunal but his for determining all matters affecting religion. In the text, however, I have made no allusion to this. The argument, as I think the reader will admit, is sufficiently decisive without it.

who shall not only aspire to a great height, but shall actually reach it, so that "he shall do according to his will;" his will shall be supreme in opposition to all law, human and Divine. Now, if this king is to be a pretended successor of the fisherman of Galilee, the question would naturally arise, How could it be possible that he should ever have the means of rising to such a height of power? The words that follow give a distinct answer to that question: "He shall not REGARD* any god, for he shall magnify himself above all. BUT, in *establishing* himself, shall he honour the god of fortifications (*Ala Mahozim*), and a god, whom his fathers knew not, shall he honour with gold and silver, and with precious stones and pleasant things. Thus shall he make into strengthening bulwarks† [for himself] the people of a strange god, whom he shall acknowledge and increase with glory; and he shall cause them to rule over many, and he shall divide the land for gain." Such is the prophecy. Now, this is exactly what the Pope did. Self-aggrandisement has ever been the grand principle of the Papacy; and, in "*establishing*" himself, it was just the "God of Fortifications" that he honoured. The worship of that god he introduced into the Roman Church; and, by so doing, he converted that which otherwise would have been a source of weakness to him, into the very tower of his strength—he made the very Paganism of Rome by which he was surrounded the bulwark of his power. When once it was proved that the Pope was willing to adopt Paganism under Christian names, the Pagans and Pagan priests would be his most hearty and staunch defenders. And when the Pope began to wield lordly power over the Christians, who were the men that he would recommend—that he would promote—that he would advance to honour and power? Just the very people most devoted to "the worship of the strange god" which he had introduced into the Christian Church. Gratitude and self-interest alike would conspire to this. Jovinian, and all who resisted the Pagan ideas and Pagan practices, were excommunicated and persecuted.‡ Those only who were heartily attached to the apostacy (and none could now be more so than genuine Pagans) were favoured and advanced. Such men were sent from Rome in all directions, even as far as Britain, to restore the reign of Paganism—they were magnified with high titles, the lands were divided among them, and all to promote "the gain" of the Romish see, to bring in "Peter's pence" from the ends of the earth to the Roman Pontiff. But it is still further said, that the self-magnifying king was to "honour a god, whom his fathers knew not, with gold and silver and precious stones." The principle on which transubstantiation

* The reader will observe, it is not said he shall not *worship* any god; the reverse is evident; but that he shall not *regard* any, that his own glory is his highest end.

† The word here is the same as above rendered "fortifications."

‡ GIBBON, vol. v. p. 176, states that he was persecuted and exiled, and that as the enemy of celibacy and fasts, that is, such fasts as Rome enforced. See also in regard to his excommunication, BOWER, vol. i. p. 256; and MILNER, *Church History*, cent. 5th, cap. 10, vol. ii., Note, p. 476.

was founded is unquestionably a Babylonian principle, but there is no evidence that that principle was applied in the way in which it has been by the Papacy. Certain it is, that we have evidence that no such wafer-god as the Papacy worships was ever worshipped in Pagan Rome. "Was any man ever so mad," says Cicero, who himself was a Roman augur and a priest—"was any man ever so mad as to take that which he feeds on for a god?"* Cicero could not have said this if anything like wafer-worship had been established in Rome. But what was too absurd for Pagan Romans is no absurdity at all for the Pope. The host, or consecrated wafer, is the great god of the Romish Church. That host is enshrined in a box adorned with gold and silver and precious stones. And thus it is manifest that "a god" whom even the Pope's *Pagan* "fathers knew not," he at this day honours in the very way that the terms of the prediction imply that he would. Thus, in every respect, when the Pope was invested with the Pagan title of Pontifex, and set himself to make that title a reality, he exactly fulfilled the prediction of Daniel recorded more than 900 years before.

But to return to the Apocalyptic symbols. It was out of the mouth of the "Fiery Dragon" that "the flood of water" was discharged. The Pope, as he is now, was at the close of the fourth century the only representative of Belshazzar, or Nimrod, on the earth; for the Pagans manifestly ACCEPTED him as such. He was equally, of course, the legitimate successor of the *Roman* "Dragon of fire." When, therefore, on being dignified with the title of Pontifex, he set himself to propagate the old Babylonian doctrine of baptismal regeneration, that was just a direct and formal fulfilment of the Divine words, that the great Fiery Dragon should "cast out of his mouth a flood of water to carry away the Woman with the flood." He, and those who co-operated with him in this cause, paved the way for the erecting of that tremendous civil and spiritual despotism which began to stand forth full in the face of Europe in A.D. 606, when, amid the convulsions and confusions of the nations, tossed like a tempestuous sea, the Pope of Rome was made Universal Bishop; and when the ten chief kingdoms of Europe recognised him as Christ's Vicar upon earth, the only centre of unity, the only source of stability to their thrones. Then by his own act and deed, and by the *consent* of the UNIVERSAL PAGANISM of Rome, he was actually the representative of Dagon; and as he bears upon his head at this day the mitre of Dagon, so there is reason to believe he did then.† Could there, then, be a more exact fulfilment of chap. xiii. 1: "And I stood upon the sand of the sea, and saw a beast rise up out

* CICERO, *De Natura Deorum*, lib. iii. cap. 16, vol. ii. p. 500.

† It is from this period only that the well-known 1260 days can begin to be counted; for not before did the Pope appear as Head of the ten-horned beast, and head of the Universal Church. The reader will observe that though the beast above referred to has passed through the sea, it still retains its primitive characteristic. The head of the apostacy at first was Kronos, "The *Horned* One." The head of the apostacy is Kronos still, for he is the beast "with seven heads and *ten horns*."

of the sea, having seven heads and ten horns, and upon his horns ten crowns, and upon his heads the names of blasphemy. . . . . And I saw one of his heads as it had been wounded to death; and his deadly wound was healed, and all the world wondered after the beast"?

SECTION III.—THE BEAST FROM THE EARTH.

This beast is presented to our notice (Rev. xiii. 11): "And I beheld another beast coming up out of the earth; and he had two horns like a lamb, and he spake as a serpent." Though this beast is *mentioned* after the beast from the sea, it does not follow that he came into *existence* after the sea-beast. The work he did seems to show the very contrary; for it is by his instrumentality that mankind are led (ver. 12) "to worship the first beast" after that beast had received the deadly wound, which shows that he must have been in existence before. The reason that he is mentioned second, is just because, as he exercises all the powers of the first beast, and leads all men to worship him, so he could not properly be described till that beast had first appeared on the stage. Now, in ancient Chaldea there was the type, also, of this. That god was called in Babylon Nebo, in Egypt Nub or Num,* and among the Romans Numa, for Numa Pompilius, the great priest-king of the Romans, occupied precisely the position of the Babylonian Nebo. Among the Etrurians, from whom the Romans derived the most of their rites, he was called Tages, and of this Tages it is particularly recorded, that just as John saw the beast under consideration "come up out of the earth," so Tages was a child suddenly and miraculously born out of a furrow or hole in the ground.† In Egypt, this God was represented with the head and horns of a ram (Fig. 55).‡ In Etruria he seems to have been represented in a somewhat similar way; for there we find a Divine and miraculous child exhibited wearing the ram's horns (Fig. 56).§ The name Nebo, the grand distinctive name of this god, signifies "The Prophet," and as such, he gave oracles, practised augury, pretended to miraculous powers, and was an adept in magic. He was the great wonder-worker, and answered exactly to the terms of the prophecy, when it is said (ver. 13), "he doeth great wonders, and causeth fire to come down from heaven in the sight of men." It was in this very character that the Etrurian Tages was known; for it was he who was said

* In Egypt, especially among the Greek-speaking population, the Egyptian *b* frequently passed into an *m*.—See BUNSEN, vol. i. pp. 273, 472.

† AMMIANUS MARCELLINUS, lib. xxi. cap. 1, p. 264.

‡ From WILKINSON, Plate 22, "Amun." By comparing this figure with what is said in WILKINSON, vol. iv. pp. 235, 238, it will be seen, that though the above figure is called by the name of "Amun," the *ram's head* makes it out as having the attributes of Noub.

§ From *Antiquités Etrusques.* Par. F. A. DAVID. Vol. v. Plate 57. I am indebted for the above, and many other things that have helped to elucidate this work, to my friend and neighbour, the Rev. A. Peebles, of Colliston.

to have taught the Romans augury, and all the superstition and wonder-working jugglery connected therewith.* As in recent times, we hear of weeping images and winking Madonnas, and innumerable prodigies besides, continually occurring in the Romish Church, in proof of this papal dogma or that, so was it also in the system of Babylon. There is hardly a form of "pious fraud" or saintly imposture practised at this day on the banks of the Tiber, that cannot be proved to have had its counterpart on the banks of the Euphrates, or in the systems that came from it. Has the image of the Virgin been seen to shed tears? Many a tear was shed by the Pagan images. To these tender-hearted idols Lucan alludes, when,

Fig. 55.

Fig. 56.

speaking of the prodigies that occurred during the civil wars, he says:—

> "Tears shed by gods, our country's patrons,
> And sweat from Larés, told the city's woes."†

Virgil also refers to the same, when he says:—

> "The weeping statues did the wars foretell,
> And holy sweat from brazen idols fell."‡

When in the consulship of Appius Claudius, and Marcus Perpenna, Publius Crassus was slain in a battle with Aristonicus, Apollo's statue at Cumæ shed tears for four days without intermission.§ The

* Ovid, *Metam.*, lib. xv. ll. 558, 559, p. 760.
† Lucan, *Civ. Bell.*, lib. i. v. 356, 357, p. 41.
‡ *Georgics*, Book i. l. 480, p. 129.
§ Augustine, *De Civitate*, lib. iii. cap. 11, vol. ix. p. 86.

gods had also their merry moods, as well as their weeping fits. If Rome counts it a divine accomplishment for the sacred image of her Madonna to "wink," it was surely not less becoming in the sacred images of Paganism to relax their features into an occasional grin. That they did so, we have abundant testimony. Psellus tells us that, when the priests put forth their magic powers, "then statues *laughed*, and lamps were spontaneously enkindled."* When the images made merry, however, they seemed to have inspired other feelings than those of merriment into the breasts of those who beheld them. "The Theurgists," says Salverté, "caused the appearance of the gods in the air, in the midst of gaseous vapour, disengaged from fire. The Theurgis Maximus undoubtedly made use of a secret analogous to this, when, in the fumes of the incense which he burned before the statue of Hecate, the image was seen to laugh so naturally *as to fill the spectators with terror*."† There were times, however, when different feelings were inspired. Has the image of the Madonna been made to look benignantly upon a favoured worshipper, and send him home assured that his prayer was heard? So did the statues of the Egyptian Isis. They were so framed, that the goddess could shake the silver serpent on her forehead, and nod assent to those who had preferred their petitions in such a way as pleased her.‡ We read of Romish saints that showed their miraculous powers by crossing rivers or the sea in most unlikely conveyances. Thus, of St. Raymond it is written that he was transported over the sea on his cloak.§ Paganism is not a whit behind in this matter; for it is recorded of a Buddhist saint, Sura Acharya, that, when "he used to visit his flocks west of the Indus, he floated himself across the stream upon his mantle."‖ Nay, the gods and high priests of Paganism showed far more buoyancy than even this. There is a holy man, at this day, in the Church of Rome, somewhere on the Continent, who rejoices in the name of St. Cubertin, who so overflows with spirituality, that when he engages in his devotions there is no keeping his body down to the ground, but, spite of all the laws of gravity, it rises several feet into the air. So was it also with the renowned St. Francis of Assisi,¶ Petrus à Martina,** and Francis of Macerata,†† some centuries ago. But both St. Cubertin and St. Francis and his fellows are far from being original in this superhuman devotion. The priests and magicians in the Chaldean Mysteries anticipated them not merely by centuries, but by thousands of years. Coelius Rhodiginus says, "that, according to the Chaldeans, luminous rays, emanating from the soul, do sometimes divinely penetrate the body, which is then of itself raised

* Psellus *on Demons*, pp. 40, 41.

† Eunapius, p. 73.

‡ Juvenal's *Satires*, vi. l. 537.

§ Newman's *Lectures*, 285-287, *apud* Begg's *Handbook of Popery*, p. 93.

‖ Todd's *Western India*, p. 277.

¶ Eusebe Salverté, p. 37.

** *Flores Seraphici*, p. 158.

†† *Ibid.* p. 391.

above the earth, and that this was the case with Zoroaster."* The disciples of Jamblichus asserted that they had often witnessed the same miracle in the case of their master, who, when he prayed was raised to the height of ten cubits from the earth.† The greatest miracle which Rome pretends to work, is when, by the repetition of five magic words, she professes to bring down the body, blood, soul, and divinity of our Lord Jesus Christ from heaven, to make Him really and corporeally present in the sacrament of the altar. The Chaldean priests pretended, by their magic spells, in like manner, to bring down their divinities into their statues, so that their "real presence" should be visibly manifested in them. This they called "the making of gods;"‡ and from this no doubt comes the blasphemous saying of the Popish priests, that they have power "to create their Creator." There is no evidence, so far as I have been able to find, that, in the Babylonian system, the thin round cake of wafer, the "unbloody sacrifice of the mass," was ever regarded in any other light than as a *symbol*, that ever it was held to be *changed into the god* whom it represented. But yet the doctrine of transubstantiation is clearly of the very essence of Magic, which pretended, on the pronunciation of a few potent words, to change one substance into another, or by a dexterous juggle, wholly to remove one substance, and to substitute another in its place. Further, the Pope, in the plenitude of his power, assumes the right of wielding the lightnings of Jehovah, and of blasting by his "fulminations" whoever offends him. Kings, and whole nations, believing in this power, have trembled and bowed before him, through fear of being scathed by his spiritual thunders. The priests of Paganism assumed the very same power; and, to enforce the belief of their spiritual power, they even attempted to bring down the literal lightnings from heaven; yea, there seems some reason to believe that they actually succeeded, and anticipated the splendid discovery of Dr. Franklin.§ Numa Pompilius is said to have done so with complete success. Tullus Hostilius, his successor, imitating his example, perished in the attempt, himself and his whole family being struck, like Professor Reichman in recent times, with the lightning he was endeavouring to draw down.|| Such were the wonder-working powers attributed in the Divine Word to the beast that was to come up from the earth; and by the old Babylonian type these very powers were all pretended to be exercised.

* SALVERTÉ, p. 37. The story of the above-mentioned Francis of Macerata, is the exact counterpart of the story of Zoroaster; for not only was he raised aloft in prayer, but his body became luminous at the same time, "*flammamque capiti insidentem*," a "flame resting on his head" (*Flores Ser*. p. 391).

† *Ibid.*

‡ AUGUSTINE, *De Civitate*, lib. viii. cap. 26, vol. ix. p. 284, col. 2.

§ See SALVERTÉ, p. 382.

|| *Ibid.* p. 383; LIVY, *Historia*, lib. i. cap. 31, vol. i. p. 46; PLINY, lib. xxviii. p. 684. The means appointed for drawing down the lightning were described in the books of the Etrurian Tages. Numa had copied from these books, and had left commentaries behind him on the subject, which Tullus had misunderstood, and hence the catastrophe.

Now, in remembrance of the birth of the god out of a "hole in the earth," the Mysteries were frequently celebrated in caves under ground. This was the case in Persia, where, just as Tages was said to be born out of the ground, Mithra was in like manner fabled to have been produced from a cave in the earth.* Numa of Rome himself pretended to get all his revelations from the nymph Egeria, in a cave.† In these caves men were first initiated in the secret Mysteries, and by the signs and lying wonders there presented to them, they were led back, after the death of Nimrod, to the worship of that god in its new form. This Apocalyptic beast, then, that "comes up out of the earth," agrees in all respects with that ancient god born from a "hole in the ground;" for no words could more exactly describe his doing than the words of the prediction (ver. 13): "He doeth great wonders, and causeth fire to come down from heaven in the sight of men, ... and he causeth the earth and them that dwell therein to worship the first beast, whose deadly wound was healed." This wonder-working beast, called Nebo, or "the Prophet," as the prophet of idolatry, was, of course, the "*false* prophet." By comparing the passage before us with Rev. xix. 20, it will be manifest that this beast that "came up out of the earth" is expressly called by that very name: "And the beast was taken, and with him the *false prophet* that wrought miracles before him, with which he deceived them that received the mark of the beast, and them that worshipped his image." As it was the "beast from the earth" that "wrought miracles" before the first beast, this shows that "the beast from the earth" is the "false prophet;" in other words, is "Nebo."

If we examine the history of the Roman empire, we shall find that here also there is a precise accordance between type and antitype. When the deadly wound of Paganism was healed, and the old Pagan title of Pontiff was restored, it was, through means of the corrupt clergy, symbolised, as is generally believed, and justly under the image of a beast with horns, like a lamb; according to the saying of our Lord, "Beware of false prophets, that shall come to you in sheep's clothing, but inwardly they are ravening wolves." The clergy, as a corporate body, consisted of two grand divisions—the regular and secular clergy answering to the two horns or powers of the beast, and combining also, at a very early period, both temporal and spiritual powers. The bishops, as heads of these clergy, had large temporal powers, long before the Pope gained his temporal crown. We have the distinct evidence of both Guizot and Gibbon to this effect. After showing that before the fifth century, the clergy had not only become distinct from, but independent of the people, Guizot adds: "The Christian clergy had moreover another and very different

* JUSTIN MARTYR, vol. ii. p. 193. It is remarkable that, as Mithra was *born* out of a *cave*, so the idolatrous nominal Christians of the East represent our Saviour as having in like manner been born in a cave.—(See KITTO'S *Cyclopædia*, "Bethlehem," vol. i. p. 327.) There is not the least hint of such a thing in the Scripture.

† LEMPRIERE.

source of influence. The bishops and priests became the *principal municipal magistrates*. . . . If you open the code, either of Theodosius or Justinian, you will find numerous regulations which remit municipal affairs to the clergy and the bishops." Guizot makes severel quotations. The following extract from the Justinian code is sufficient to show how ample was the civil power bestowed upon the bishops: "With respect to the yearly affairs of cities, whether they concern the ordinary revenues of the city, either from funds arising from the property of the city, or from private gifts or legacies, or from any other source; whether public works, or depôts of provisions or aqueducts, or the maintenance of baths or ports, or the construction of walls or towers, or the repairing of bridges or roads, or trials, in which the city may be engaged in reference to public or private interests, we ordain as follows:—The very pious bishop, and three notables, chosen from among the first men of the city, shall meet together; they shall each year examine the works done; they shall take care that those who conduct them, or who have conducted them, shall regulate them with precision, render their accounts, and show that they have duly performed their engagements in the administration, whether of the public monuments, or of the sums appointed for provisions or baths, or of expenses in the maintenance of roads, aqueducts, or any other work."* Here is a large list of functions laid on the spiritual shoulders of "the very pious bishop," not one of which is even hinted at in the Divine enumeration of the duties of a bishop, as contained in the Word of God. (See 1 Tim. iii. 1-7; and Tit. i. 5-9.) How did the bishops, who were originally appointed for purely spiritual objects, contrive to grasp at such a large amount of temporal authority? From Gibbon we get light as to the real origin of what Guizot calls this "prodigious power." The author of the *Decline and Fall* shows, that soon after Constantine's time, "the Church" [and consequently the bishops, especially when they assumed to be a separate order from the other clergy] gained great temporal power through the right of asylum, which had belonged to the Pagan temples, being transferred by the Emperors to the Christian churches. His words are: "The fugitive, and even the guilty, were permitted to implore either the justice or mercy of the Deity and His ministers."† Thus was the foundation laid of the invasion of the rights of the civil magistrate by ecclesiastics, and thus were they encouraged to grasp at all the powers of the State. Thus, also, as is justly observed by the authoress of *Rome in the 19th Century*, speaking of the right of asylum, were "the altars perverted into protection towards the very crimes they were raised to banish from the world."‡ This is a very striking thing, as showing how the temporal power of the Papacy, in its very first beginnings, was founded on "lawlessness," and is an additional proof to the many that might be alleged, that

* GUIZOT, *History of Civilisation*, vol. i. sect. ii. pp. 36, 37.

† GIBBON, vol. iii. chap. xx. p. 287.

‡ *Rome in the 19th Century*, vol. i. pp. 246, 247.

the Head of the Roman system, to whom all bishops are subject, is indeed ὁ ἄνομος, "The Lawless One" (2 Thess. ii. 8), predicted in Scripture as the recognised Head of the "Mystery of Iniquity." All this temporal power came into the hands of men, who, while professing to be ministers of Christ, and followers of the Lamb, were seeking simply their own aggrandisement, and, to secure that aggrandisement, did not hesitate to betray the cause which they professed to serve. The spiritual power which they wielded over the souls of men, and the secular power which they gained in the affairs of the world, were both alike used in opposition to the cause of pure religion and undefiled. At first these false prophets, in leading men astray, and seeking to unite Paganism and Christianity, *wrought under-ground*, mining like the mole in the dark, and secretly perverting the simple, according to the saying of Paul, "The *Mystery* of Iniquity doth already work." But by-and-by, towards the end of the fourth century, when the minds of men had been pretty well prepared, and the aspect of things seemed to be favourable for it, the wolves in sheep's clothing appeared above ground, brought their secret doctrines and practices, by little and little, into the light of day, and century after century, as their power increased, by means of all "deceivableness of unrighteousness," and "signs and lying wonders," deluded the minds of the worldly Christians, made them believe that their anathema was equivalent to the curse of God; in other words, that they could "bring down fire from heaven," and thus "caused the earth, and them that dwelt therein, to worship the beast whose deadly wound was healed."* When "the deadly wound" of the Pagan beast was healed, and the beast from the sea appeared, it is said that this beast from the earth became the recognised, accredited executor of the will of the great sea beast (v. 12), "And he exerciseth all the power of the first beast before him," literally "in his presence"—under his inspection. Considering who the first beast is, there is great force in this expression "in his presence." The beast that comes up from the sea, is "the little horn," that "has eyes like the eyes of man" (Dan. vii. 8); it is Janus Tuens, "All-seeing Janus," in other words, the Universal Bishop or "Universal Overseer," who, from his throne on the seven hills, by means of the organised system of the confessional, *sees* and *knows* all that is done, to the utmost bounds of his wide dominion. Now, it was just exactly about the time that the Pope became universal bishop, that the custom began of systematically investing the chief bishops of the Western empire with the Papal livery, the pallium, "for the purpose," says Gieseler, "of symbolising and

* Though the Pope be the great Jupiter Tonans of the Papacy, and "fulminates" from the Vatican, as his predecessor was formerly believed to do from the Capitol, yet it is not *he* in reality that brings down the fire from heaven, but his clergy. But for the influence of the clergy in everywhere blinding the minds of the people, the Papal thunders would be but "bruta fulmina" after all. The symbol, therefore, is most exact, when it attributes the "bringing down of the fire from heaven," to the beast from the earth, rather than to the beast from the sea.

strengthening their connection with the Church of Rome."* That pallium, worn on the shoulders of the bishops, while on the one hand it was the livery of the Pope, and bound those who received it to act as the functionaries of Rome, deriving all their authority from him, and exercising it under his superintendence, as the "Bishop of bishops," on the other hand, was in reality the visible investiture of these wolves with the sheep's clothing. For what was the pallium of the Papal bishop? It was a dress made of wool, blessed by the Pope, taken from the holy lambs kept by the nuns of St. Agnes, and woven by their sacred hands,† that it might be bestowed on those whom the Popes delighted to honour, for the purpose, as one of themselves expressed it, of "joining them to our society in the one *pastoral sheepfold*."‡ Thus commissioned, thus ordained by the universal Bishop, they did their work effectually, and brought the earth and them that dwelt in it, "to worship the beast that received the wound by a sword and did live." This was a *part* of this beast's predicted work. But there was another, and not less important, which remains for consideration.

SECTION IV.—THE IMAGE OF THE BEAST.

Not merely does the beast from the earth lead the world to worship the first beast, but (ver. 14) he prevails on them that dwell on the earth to make "an IMAGE to the beast, which had the wound by a sword, and did live." In meditating for many years on what might be implied in "the image of the beast," I could never find the least satisfaction in all the theories that had ever been propounded, till I fell in with an unpretending but valuable work, which I have noticed already, entitled *An Original Interpretation of the Apocalypse*. That work, evidently the production of a penetrating mind deeply read in the history of the Papacy, furnished at once the solution of the difficulty. There the image of the beast is pro-

* GIESELER, vol. ii., 2nd Period, Division 2nd, Sect. 117. From Gieseler we learn that so early as 501, the Bishop of Rome had laid the *foundation* of the *corporation* of bishops by the bestowal of the pallium; but, at the same time, he expressly states that it was only about 602, at the ascent of Phocas to the imperial throne—that Phocas that made the Pope Universal Bishop—that the Popes began to bestow the pallium, that is, of course, systematically, and on a large scale.

† *Rome in the 19th Century*, vol. iii. p. 214. In the present day, the pallium is given only to the Archbishops; Gieseler, in passage already quoted, shows that it was given to simple bishops as well.

‡ GIESELER, vol. ii., "Papacy," p. 255. The reader who peruses the early letters of the Popes in bestowing the pallium, will not fail to observe the wide difference of meaning between "the one pastoral sheepfold" ("uno pastorali ovili"), above referred to, and "The one sheepfold" of our Lord. The former really means a sheepfold consisting of pastors or shepherds. The papal letters unequivocally imply the organisation of the bishops, as a distinct corporation, altogether independent of the Church, and dependent only on the Papacy, which seems remarkably to agree with the terms of the prediction in regard to the beast from the earth.

nounced to be the Virgin Mother, or the Madonna.* This at first sight may appear a very unlikely solution; but when it is brought into comparison with the religious history of Chaldea, the unlikelihood entirely disappears. In the old Babylonian Paganism, there was an *image* of the Beast from the sea; and when it is known what that image was, the question will, I think, be fairly decided. When Dagon was first set up to be worshipped, while he was represented in many different ways, and exhibited in many different characters, the favourite form in which he was worshipped, as the reader well knows, was that of a child in his mother's arms. In the natural course of events, the mother came to be worshipped along with the child, yea, to be the favourite object of worship. To justify this worship, as we have already seen, that mother, of course, must be raised to divinity, and divine powers and prerogatives ascribed to her. Whatever dignity, therefore, the son was believed to possess a like dignity was ascribed to her. Whatever name of honour he bore, a similar name was bestowed upon her. He was called Belus, "the Lord;" she, Beltis, "My Lady."† He was called Dagon,‡ the "Merman"; she, Derketo,§ the "Mermaid." He, as the World-king, wore the bull's horns;‖ she, as we have already seen, on the authority of Sanchuniathon, put on her own head a *bull's* head, as the ensign of royalty.¶ He, as the Sun-god, was called Beël-samen, "Lord of heaven;"** she, as the Moon-goddess, Melkat-ashemin, "Queen of heaven."†† He was worshipped in Egypt as the "Revealer of goodness and truth;"‡‡ she, in Babylon, under the symbol of the Dove, as the goddess of gentleness and mercy,§§ the "Mother of gracious acceptance,"‖‖ "merciful and benignant to men."¶¶ He, under the name of Mithra, was worshipped as Mesītes,*** or "The Mediator;" she, as Aphrodite, or the "Wrath-subduer," was called Mylitta, "the Mediatrix."††† He was represented as crushing the great serpent under his heel;‡‡‡ she, as bruising the serpent's head in her hand.§§§ He, under the name Janus, bore a key, as the opener and shutter of the gates of the invisible world.‖‖‖ She, under the name of Cybele, was invested

* *Original Interpretation of the Apocalypse*, p. 123.

† See *ante*, p. 20, Note.

‡ See *ante*, p. 114, Note.

§ KITTO'S *Cyclopædia*, vol. i. pp. 251, 252.

‖ See *ante*, pp. 32-36.

¶ EUSEBIUS, *Præparatio Evangelii*, lib. i. cap. 10, vol. i. p. 45. This statement is remarkable, as showing that the horns which the great goddess wore were really intended to exhibit her as the express image of Ninus, or "the Son." Had she worn merely the cow's horns, it might have been supposed that these horns were intended only to identify her with the moon. But the *bull's* horns show that the intention was to represent her as equal in her sovereignty with Nimrod, or Kronos, the "Horned one."

** See *ante*, p. 165.

†† Jeremiah vii. 18, and PARKHURST'S *Hebrew Lexicon*, pp. 402, 403.

‡‡ See *ante*, p. 72.

§§ See *ante*, p. 78.

‖‖ See *ante*, p. 158. The Chaldean meaning of the name Amarusia, signifying "Mother of gracious acceptance," shows it to have come from Babylon.

¶¶ LUCIUS AMPELIUS, in BRYANT, vol. iii. p. 161.

*** See *ante*, p. 194.

††† See *ante*, p. 158.

‡‡‡ See *ante*, p. 60.

§§§ See *ante*, p. 75.

‖‖‖ See *ante*, p. 210.

with a *like* key, as an emblem of the same power.* He, as the cleanser from sin, was called the "Unpolluted god;"† she, too, had the power to wash away sin, and, though the mother of the seed, was called the "Virgin, pure and undefiled."‡ He was represented as "Judge of the dead;" she was represented as standing by his side, at the judgment-seat, in the unseen world.§ He, after being killed by the sword, was fabled to have risen again,|| and ascended up to heaven.¶ She, too, though history makes her to have been killed with the sword by one of her own sons,** was nevertheless, in the myth, said to have been carried by her son bodily to heaven,†† and to have been made Pambasileia, "Queen of the universe."‡‡ Finally, to clench the whole, the name by which she was now known was Semelé, which, in the Babylonian language, signifies "THE IMAGE."§§ Thus, in every respect, to the very least jot and tittle, she became the express image of the Babylonian "beast that had the wound by a sword, and did live."

After what the reader has already seen in a previous part of this work, it is hardly necessary to say that it is this very goddess that is now worshipped in the Church of Rome under the name of Mary. Though that goddess is called by the name of the mother of our Lord, all the attributes given to her are derived simply from the Babylonian Madonna, and *not* from the Virgin Mother of Christ.||||

* TOOKE's *Pantheon*, p. 153. That the key of Cybele, in the esoteric story, had a corresponding meaning to that of Janus, will appear from the character above assigned to her as the Mediatrix.

† Proclus, speaking of Saturn, says, "Purity therefore indicates this .... transcendency of Saturn, his undefiled union with the intelligible. This *purity* and the *undefiled*, which he possesses," &c., in Notes to TAYLOR's *Orphic Hymns*, p. 176.

‡ See *ante*, p. 125.

§ WILKINSON, vol. iv. pp. 314, 315.

|| *Ibid.* vol. iv. p. 190.

¶ *Ibid.* p. 256. See also *ante*, p. 57.

** MOSES OF CHORENE, lib. i. cap. 16, p. 48. "Ninyas enim occasionem nactus matrem (Semiramida) necavit." In like manner, Horus, in Egypt, is said to have cut off his mother's head, as Bel in Babylon also cut asunder the great primeval goddess of the Babylonians.—(BUNSEN, vol. i. pp. 436, 708.)

†† See *ante*, p. 125.

‡‡ *Orphic Hymns*, "Hymn to Semelé," No 43.

§§ Apollodorus states that Bacchus, on carrying his mother to heaven, called her Thuōné (APOLLODORUS, lib. iii. cap. 5, p. 266), which was just the feminine of his own name, Thuōneus—in Latin Thyoneus.—(OVID, *Metam.*, lib. iv. l. 13.) Thuōneus is evidently from the passive participle of *Thn*, "to lament," a synonym for "Bacchus," "The lamented *god.*" Thuōné, in like manner, is "The lamented *goddess.*" The Roman Juno was evidently known in this very character of the "Image"; for there was a temple erected to her in Rome, on the Capitoline hill, under the name of "Juno Moneta." Moneta is the emphatic form of one of the Chaldee words for an "image"; and that this was the real meaning of the name, will appear from the fact that the Mint was contained in the precincts of that temple.—(See SMITH's "Juno," p. 358.) What is the use of a mint but just to stamp "*images*"? Hence the connection between Juno and the Mint.

|||| The very way in which the Popish Madonna is represented is plainly copied from the idolatrous representations of the Pagan goddess. The great god used to be represented as sitting or standing in the cup of a Lotus-flower. (See BRYANT, vol. iii. p. 180, where Harpocrates is thus represented; and VAUX's *Handbook of British Museum*, p. 429, where Cupid is sitting on a flower.) In India, the very same mode of representation is common; Brahma being often seen

There is not one line or one letter in all the Bible to countenance the idea that Mary should be worshipped, that she is the "refuge of sinners," that she was "immaculate," that she made atonement for sin when standing by the cross, and when, according to Simeon, "a sword pierced through her own soul also;" or that, after her death, she was raised from the dead and carried in glory to heaven. But in the Babylonian system all this was found; and all this is now incorporated in the system of Rome. The "sacred heart of Mary" is exhibited as pierced through with a sword, *in token*, as the apostate Church teaches, that her anguish at the crucifixion was as true an atonement as the death of Christ;—for we read in the Devotional office or Service-book, adopted by the "Sodality of the

Fig. 57.

Fig. 58.

sacred heart," such blasphemous words as these, "Go, then, devout client! go to the heart of Jesus, but let your way be through the heart of Mary; *the sword of grief which pierced her soul opens you a passage;* enter by the wound which love has made;"*—again we

seated on a Lotus-flower, said to have sprung from the navel of Vishnu. The great goddess, in like manner, must have a similar couch; and, therefore, in India, we find Lakshmi, the "Mother of the Universe," sitting on a Lotus, borne by a tortoise (see Fig. 57; from COLEMAN'S *Mythology*, plate 23). Now, in this very thing, also, Popery has copied from its Pagan model; for, in the *Pancarpium Marianum*, p. 88, the Virgin and child are represented sitting in the cup of a tulip (see Fig. 58).

* *Memoir of Rev. Godfrey Massy*, pp. 91, 92. In the *Paradisus sponsi et sponsæ*, by the author of *Pancarpium Marianum*, the following words, addressed to the Virgin, occur in illustration of a plate representing the crucifixion, and Mary, at the foot of the Cross, with the *sword in her breast*, "*Dilectus tuus filius carnem tu vero animam immolasti: immo corpus et animam*" (p. 181); "Thy beloved son did

hear one expounder of the new faith, like M. Genoude in France, say that "Mary was the repairer of the guilt of Eve, as our Lord was the repairer of the guilt of Adam;" * and another—Professor Oswald of Paderbon—affirm that Mary was not a human creature like us, that she is "the Woman, as Christ is the Man," that "Mary is co-present in the Eucharist, and that it is indisputable that, according to the Eucharistic doctrine of the Church, this presence of Mary in the Eucharist is *true and real*, not merely ideal or figurative;" † and, further, we read in the Pope's decree of the Immaculate Conception, that that same Madonna, for this purpose "wounded with the sword," rose from the dead, and being assumed up on high, became Queen of Heaven. If all this be so, who can fail to see that in that apostate community is to be found what precisely answers to the making and setting up in the heart of Christendom, of an "Image to the beast that had the wound by a sword and did live"?

If the inspired terms be consulted, it will be seen that this was to be done by some public general act of apostate Christendom; (ver. 14), "Saying to them that dwell on the earth, that they should make an image to the beast;" and they made it. Now, here is the important fact to be observed, that this never *was* done, and this never could have been done, till eight years ago: for this plain reason, that till then the Madonna of Rome was never recognised as combining all the characters that belonged to the Babylonian "IMAGE of the beast." Till then it was not admitted even in Rome, though this evil leaven had been long working, and that strongly, that Mary was truly immaculate, and consequently she could not be the perfect counterpart of the Babylonian Image. What, however, had never been done before, was done in December, 1854. Then bishops from all parts of Christendom, and representatives from the ends of the earth, met in Rome; and with only four dissentient voices, it was decreed that Mary, the mother of God, who died, rose from the dead, and ascended into heaven, should henceforth be worshipped as the Immaculate Virgin, "conceived and born without sin." This was the formal setting up of the Image of the beast, and that by the general consent of "the men that dwell upon the earth." Now, this beast being set up, it is said, that the beast from the earth gives life and *speech* to the Image, implying, first, that it has neither life nor voice in itself; but that, nevertheless, through means of the beast from the earth, it is to have both life and voice, and to be an effective agent of the Papal clergy, who will make it speak exactly as they please. Since the Image has been set up, its voice has been everywhere heard throughout the Papacy. Formerly decrees ran less or more in the name of Christ. Now all things are pre-eminently done in the name of the Immaculate Virgin. Her voice is every-

sacrifice his flesh; thou thy soul—yea, both body and soul." This does much more than put the sacrifice of the Virgin on a level with that of the Lord Jesus, it makes it greater far. This, in 1617, was the creed only of Jesuitism; *now* there is reason to believe it to be the general creed of the Papacy.

* *Missionary Record of the Free Church*, 1855.

† *Ibid.*

where heard—her voice is supreme. But, be it observed, when that voice is heard, it is not the voice of mercy and love, it is the voice of cruelty and terror. The decrees that come forth under the name of the Image, are to this effect (ver. 17), that "no man might buy or sell, save he that had the mark, or the name of the beast, or the number of his name." No sooner is the image set up than we see this very thing begun to be carried out. What was the Concordat in Austria, that so speedily followed, but this very thing? That concordat, through the force of unexpected events that have arisen, has not yet been carried into effect; but if it were, the results would just be what is predicted—that no man in the Austrian dominions should "buy or sell" without the mark in some shape or other. And the very fact of such an intolerant concordat coming so speedily on the back of the Decree of the Immaculate Conception, shows what is the natural fruit of that decree. The events that soon thereafter took place in Spain showed the powerful working of the same persecuting spirit there also. During the last few years, the tide of spiritual despotism might have seemed to be effectually arrested; and many, no doubt, have indulged the persuasion that, crippled as the temporal sovereignty of the Papacy is, and tottering as it seems to be, that power, or its subordinates, could never persecute more. But there is an amazing vitality in the Mystery of Iniquity; and no one can ever tell beforehand what apparent impossibilities it may accomplish in the way of arresting the progress of truth and liberty, however promising the aspect of things may be. Whatever may become of the temporal sovereignty of the Roman states, it is by no means so evident this day, as to many it seemed only a short while ago, that the overthrow of the spiritual power of the Papacy is imminent, and that its power to persecute is finally gone. I doubt not but that many, constrained by the love and mercy of God, will yet obey the heavenly voice, and flee out of the doomed communion, before the vials of Divine wrath descend upon it. But if I have been right in the interpretation of this passage, then it follows that it must yet become more persecuting than ever it has been, and that that intolerance, which, immediately after the setting up of the Image, began to display itself in Austria and Spain, shall yet spread over all Europe; for it is not said that the Image of the beast should merely *decree*, but should "*cause* that as many as would not worship the Image of the beast should be killed" (ver. 15). When this takes place, that evidently is the time when the language of verse 8 is fulfilled, "And all that dwell on the earth shall worship the beast, whose names are not written in the book of life of the Lamb slain from the foundation of the world." It is impossible to get quit of this by saying, "This refers to the Dark Ages; this was fulfilled before Luther." I ask, had the men who dwelt on the earth set up the Image of the beast before Luther's days? Plainly not. The decree of the Immaculate Conception was the deed of yesterday. The prophecy, then, refers to our own times—to the period on which the Church is now entering. In other words, the slaying of the witnesses, the grand trial of the saints, IS STILL TO COME.*

SECTION V.—THE NAME OF THE BEAST, THE NUMBER OF HIS NAME,—THE INVISIBLE HEAD OF THE PAPACY.

Dagon and the Pope being now identified, this brings us naturally and easily to the long-sought name and number of the beast, and confirms, by entirely new evidence, the old Protestant view of the subject. The name "Lateinos" has been generally accepted by Protestant writers, as having many elements of probability to recommend it. But yet there has been always found a certain deficiency, and it has been felt that something was wanting to put it beyond all possibility of doubt. Now, looking at the subject from the Babylonian point of view, we shall find both the name and number of the beast brought home to us in such a way as leaves nothing to be desired on the point of evidence. Osiris, or Nimrod, whom the Pope represents, was called by many different titles, and therefore, as Wilkinson remarks,† he was much in the same position as his wife, who was called "Myrionymus," the goddess with "ten thousand names." Among these innumerable names, how shall we ascertain *the* name at which the Spirit of God points in the enigmatical language that speaks of the name of the beast, and the number of his name? If we know the Apocalyptic name of the *system*, that will lead us to the name of the *head* of the system. The name of the system is "Mystery" (Rev. xvii. 5). Here, then, we have the key that at once unlocks the enigma. We have now only to inquire what was the name by which Nimrod was known *as* the god of the Chaldean Mysteries. That name, as we have seen, was Saturn. Saturn and Mystery are both Chaldean words, and they are correlative terms. As Mystery signifies the Hidden system, so Saturn signifies the Hidden god.‡ To those who were initiated the god was revealed; to all else he was hidden. Now, the name Saturn in Chaldee is pronounced Satūr; but, as every Chaldee scholar knows, consists only of four letters, thus —Stūr. This name contains exactly the Apocalyptic number 666:—

S = 60
T = 400
U = 6
R = 200
——— 666

* See Appendix, Note Q.

† Vol. iv. p. 179.

‡ In the Litany of the Mass, the worshippers are taught thus to pray: "GOD HIDDEN, and my Saviour, have mercy upon us."—(M'GAVIN's *Protestant*, vol. ii. p. 79, 1837.) Whence can this invocation of the "God Hidden" have come, but from the ancient worship of Saturn, the "Hidden God"? As the Papacy has canonised the Babylonian god by the name of St. Dionysius, and St. Bacchus, the "martyr," so by this very name of "Satur" is he also enrolled in the calendar; for March 29th is the festival of "St. Satur," the martyr.—(CHAMBERS's *Book of Days*, p. 435.)

If the Pope is, as we have seen, the legitimate representative of Saturn, the number of the Pope, as head of the Mystery of Iniquity, is just 666. But still further it turns out, as shown above, that the original name of Rome itself was Saturnia, "the city of Saturn." This is vouched alike by Ovid,* by Pliny,† and by Aurelius Victor.‡ Thus, then, the Pope has a double claim to the name and number of the beast. He is the *only* legitimate representative of the original Saturn at this day in existence, and he reigns in the very city of the seven hills where the Roman Saturn formerly reigned; and, from his residence in which, the whole of Italy was "long after called by his name," being commonly named "the Saturnian land." But what bearing, it may be said, has this upon the name Lateinos, which is commonly believed to be the "name of the beast"? Much. It proves that the common opinion is thoroughly well-founded. Saturn and Lateinos are just synonymous, having precisely the same meaning, and belonging equally to the same god. The reader cannot have forgotten the lines of Virgil, which showed that Lateinos, to whom the Romans or Latin race traced back their lineage, was represented with a *glory* around his head, to show that he was a "child of the Sun."§ Thus, then, it is evident that, in popular opinion, the *original* Lateinos had occupied the very same position as Saturn did in the Mysteries, who was equally worshipped as the "offspring of the Sun." Moreover, it is evident that the Romans knew that the name "Lateinos" signified the "Hidden One," for their antiquarians invariably affirm that Latium received its name from Saturn "lying *hid*" there.‖ On etymological grounds, then, even on the testimony of the Romans, Lateinos is equivalent to the "Hidden One;" that is, to Saturn, the "god of Mystery."¶

* *Fasti*, lib. vi. ll. 31-34, vol. iii. p. 342. † *Hist. Nat.*, lib. iii. 5, p. 55.

‡ AUREL. VICT., *Origo Gent. Roman*, cap. iii. § See *ante*, p. 236.

‖ OVID, *Fasti*, lib. i. l. 238, vol. iii. p. 29; also VIRGIL, *Æneid* lib. viii. l. 319, &c., p. 384.

¶ Latium Latinus (the Roman form of the Greek Lateinos), and Lateo, "to lie hid," all alike come from the Chaldee "Lat," which has the same meaning. The name "Lat," or the hidden one, had evidently been given, as well as Saturn, to the Great Babylonian god. This is evident from the name of the fish Latus, which was worshipped along with the Egyptian Minerva, in the city of Latopolis in Egypt, now Esneh (WILKINSON, vol. iv. p. 284, and vol. v. p. 253), that fish Latus evidently just being another name for the fish-god Dagon. We have seen that Ichthys, or the Fish, was one of the names of Bacchus; and the Assyrian goddess Atergatis, with her son Ichthys is said to have been cast into the lake of Ascalon.—(*Vossius de Idololatria*, lib. i. cap. xxiii. p. 89, also ATHENÆUS, lib. viii. cap. viii. p. 346, E.) That the sun-god Apollo had been known under the name of Lat, may be inferred from the Greek name of his mother-wife Lētō, or in Doric, Lātō, which is just the feminine of Lat. The Roman name Latona confirms this, for it signifies "The lamenter of Lat," as Bellona signifies "The lamenter of Bel." The Indian god Siva, who, as we have seen, is sometimes represented as a child at the breast of its mother, and has the same bloody character as Moloch, or the Roman Saturn, is called by this very name, as may be seen from the following verse made in reference to the image found in his celebrated temple at Somnaut:

> "This image grim, whose name was LAUT,
> Bold Mahmoud found when he took Sumnaut."
> —BORROW's *Gypsies in Spain, or Zincali*, vol. ii. p. 113.

While Saturn, therefore, is the name of the beast, and contains the mystic number, Lateinos, which contains the same number, is just as peculiar and distinctive an appellation of the same beast. The Pope, then, as the head of the beast, is equally Lateinos or Saturn, that is, the head of the Babylonian "Mystery." When, therefore, the Pope requires all his services to be performed in the "*Latin* tongue," that is as much as to say that they must be performed in the language of "Mystery"; when he calls his Church the *Latin* Church, that is equivalent to a declaration that it is the Church of "Mystery." Thus, by this very name of the Pope's own choosing, he has with his own hands written upon the very forehead of his apostate communion its divine Apocalyptic designation, "MYSTERY—Babylon the great." Thus, also, by a process of the purest induction, we have been led on from step to step, till we find the mystic number 666 unmistakably and "indelibly marked" on his own forehead, and that he who has his seat on the seven hills of Rome has exclusive and indefeasible claims to be regarded as the *Visible* head of the beast.

The reader, however, who has carefully considered the language that speaks of the name and number of the Apocalyptic beast, must have observed that, in the terms that describe that name and number, there is still an enigma that ought not to be overlooked. The words are these: "Let him that hath understanding count the number of the beast—for it is the number of a *man*" (Rev. xiii. 18). What means the saying, that the "number of the beast is the number of a *man*"? Does it merely mean that he has been called by a name that has been borne by some individual man before? This is the sense in which the words have been generally understood. But surely this would be nothing very distinctive—nothing that might not equally apply to innumerable names. But view this language in connection with the ascertained facts of the case, and what a Divine light at once beams from the expression. Saturn, the hidden god,—the god of the Mysteries, whom the Pope represents, whose secrets were revealed only to the initiated,—was identical with Janus, who was publicly known to all Rome, to the uninitiated and initiated alike, as the grand Mediator, the opener and the shutter, who had the key of the invisible world. Now, what means the name Janus? That name, as Cornificius in Macrobius shows, was properly Eanus;* and in ancient Chaldee, E-anush signifies

As Lat was used as a synonym for Saturn, there can be little doubt that Latinus was used in the same sense. Virgil makes the Latinus, who was the contemporary of Æneas, third in descent from Saturn:

> "Rex arva Latinus et urbes
> Jam senior longa placidus in pace regebat.
> Hunc Fauno et Mympha genitum Laurente Maricâ
> Accipimus. Fauno Picus pater, isque parentem
> Te, Saturne, refert."
>
> —*Æneid*, lib. vii. ll. 45-49, p. 323.

The deified kings were called after the gods from whom they professed to spring, and *not* after their territories. The same, we may be sure, was the case with Latinus.

* *Saturnalia*, lib. i. cap. 9, p. 54, G.

"the Man." By that very name was the Babylonian beast from the sea called, when it first made its appearance.* The name E-anush, or "the Man," was applied to the Babylonian Messiah, as identifying him with the promised seed of the Woman. The name of "the Man," as applied to a *god*, was intended to designate him as the "*god-man*." We have seen that in India, the Hindoo Shasters bear, that in order to enable the gods to overcome their enemies, it was needful that the Sun, the supreme divinity, should be incarnate, and born of a Woman.† The classical nations had a legend of precisely the same nature. "There was a current tradition in heaven," says Apollodorus, "that the giants could never be conquered except by the help of a *man*."‡ That man, who was believed to have conquered the adversaries of the gods, was Janus, the god-man. In consequence of his assumed character and exploits, Janus was invested with high powers, made the keeper of the gates of heaven, and arbiter of men's eternal destinies. Of this Janus, this Babylonian "man," the Pope, as we have seen, is the legitimate representative; his key, therefore, he bears, with that of Cybele, his mother-wife; and to all his blasphemous pretensions he at this hour lays claim. The very fact, then, that the Pope founds his claim to universal homage on the possession of the keys of heaven, and that in a sense which empowers him, in defiance of every principle of Christianity, to open and shut the gates of glory, according to his mere sovereign will and pleasure, is a striking and additional proof that he is that head of the beast from the sea, whose number, as identified with Janus, is the number of a *man*, and amounts exactly to 666.

But there is something further still in the name of Janus or Eanus, not to be passed over. Janus, while manifestly worshipped as the Messiah or god-man, was also celebrated as "Principium Deorum,"§ the source and fountain of all the Pagan gods. We have already in this character traced him backward through Cush to Noah; but to make out his claim to this high character, in its proper completeness, he must be traced even further still. The Pagans knew, and could not but know, at the time the Mysteries were concocted, in the days of Shem and his brethren, who, through the Flood, had passed from the old world to the new, the whole story of Adam, and therefore it was necessary, if a deification of mankind there was to be, that his pre-eminent dignity, as the *human* "Father of gods and *men*," should not be ignored. Nor was it. The

* The name, as given in Greek by Berosus, is O-annés (p. 48); but this is just the very way we might expect "He-anesh," "the man," to appear in Greek. He-siri, in Greek, becomes Osiris; and He-sarsiphon, Osarsiphon; and, in like manner, He-anesh naturally becomes Oannés. In the sense of a "Man-god," the name Oannés is taken by Barker (*Lares and Penates*, p. 224). We find the conversion of the H' into O' among our own immediate neighbours, the Irish; what is now O'Brien and O'Connell was originally H'Brien and H'Connell.—(*Sketches of Irish History*, p. 72.)

† See *ante*, Chapter III. p. 96.

‡ *Bibliotheca*, lib. i. in PARKHURST, *sub voce* "aaz," No. v.; see also MACROBIUS, *Saturnalia*, lib. i. cap. 20, in regard to "Hercules the *man*."

§ TERENTIANUS MAURUS in BRYANT, vol. iii. p. 82.

Mysteries were full of what he did, and what befel him; and the name E-anush, or, as it appeared in the Egyptian form, Ph'anesh,* "The man," was only another name for that of our great progenitor. The name of Adam in the Hebrew of Genesis almost always occurs with the article before it, implying "The Adam," or "The man." There is this difference, however—"The Adam" refers to man unfallen, E-anush, "The man," to "fallen man." E-anush, then, as "Principium deorum," "The fountain and father of the gods," is "FALLEN Adam."† The principle of Pagan idolatry went directly to exalt *fallen* humanity, to consecrate its lusts, to give men license to live after the flesh, and yet, after such a life, to make them sure of eternal felicity. E-anus, the "fallen man," was set up as the human Head of this system of corruption—this "Mystery of Iniquity." Now, from this we come to see the real meaning of the name, applied to the divinity commonly worshipped in Phrygia along with Cybele in the very same character as this same Janus, who was at once the Father of the gods, and the Mediatorial divinity. That name was Atys, or Attis, or Attes,‡ and the meaning will evidently appear from the meaning of the well-known Greek word Atè, which signifies "error of sin," and is obviously derived from the Chaldean Hata, "to sin." Atys or Attes, formed from the same verb, and in a similar way, signifies "The Sinner." The reader will remember that Rhea or Cybele was worshipped in Phrygia under the name of Idaia Mater, "The mother of knowledge," and that she bore in her hand, as her symbol, the pomegranate, which we have seen reason to conclude to have been in Pagan estimation the fruit of the "forbidden tree."§ Who, then, so likely to have been the contemplar divinity of that "Mother of knowledge" as Attes, "The sinner," even her own husband, whom she induced to share with her in her sin, and partake of her fatal knowledge, and who thereby became in true and proper sense, "The man of sin,"—"the man by

* WILKINSON, vol. iv. p. 191.

† Anesh *properly* signifies only the *weakness* or *frailty* of fallen humanity; but any one who consults OVID, *Fasti*, "Kal. Jun.," ll. 100, &c., vol. iii. p. 346, as to the character of Janus, will see that when E-anush was deified, it was not simply as Fallen man with his *weakness*, but Fallen man with his *corruption*.

‡ SMITH'S *Classical Dictionary*, "Atys," p. 107. The identification of Attes with Bacchus or Adonis, who was at once the Father of the gods, and the Mediator, is proved from divers considerations.—1. While it is certain that the favourite god of the Phrygian Cybele was Attes, whence he was called "Cybelius Attes," from Strabo, lib. x. p. 452, we learn that the divinity worshipped along with Cybele in Phrygia, was called by the very name of Dionusos or Bacchus. 2. Attes was *represented* in the very same way as Bacchus. In Bryant there is an inscription to him along with the Idaean goddess, that is Cybele, under the name of "Attis the Minotaur" (*Mythol.*, vol. ii. p. 109, Note). Bacchus was bull-horned; it is well known that the Minotaur, in like manner, was half-man, half-bull. 3. He was represented in the *exoteric* story, as perishing in the same way as Adonis by a wild boar (PAUSAN., lib. vii., *Achaica*, cap. 17). 4. In the rites of Magna Mater or Cybele, the priests invoked him as the "Deus propitius, Deus sanctus," "the merciful God, the holy God" (ARNOBIUS, lib. i. in *Maxima Biblioth. Patrum*, in Ed. Adv. Lib., tom. iii. p. 435, Lugd., 1677), the very character which Bacchus or Adonis sustained as the mediatorial god.

§ See *ante*, p. 111.

whom sin entered the world, and death by sin, and so death passed upon all, because all have sinned."* Now to Attes, this "Man of sin," after passing through those sorrows and sufferings, which his worshippers yearly commemorated, the distinguishing characteristics and glories of the Messiah were given. He was identified with the sun,† the one only god; he was identified with Adonis; and to him as thus identified, the language of the Sixteenth Psalm, predicting the triumph of our Saviour Christ over death and the grave, was in all its greatness applied: "Thou wilt not leave my soul in hell, nor suffer thine Holy One to see corruption." It is sufficiently known that the first part of this statement was applied to Adonis; for the annual weeping of the women for Tammuz was speedily turned into rejoicings, on account of his fabled return from Hades, or the infernal regions. But it is not so well known that Paganism applied to its mediatorial god the predicted incorruption of the *body* of the Messiah. But that this was the fact, we learn from the distinct testimony of Pausanias. "Agdistis," that is Cybele, says he, "obtained from Jupiter, that no part of the body of Attes should either *become putrid or waste away.*"‡ Thus did Paganism apply to Attes "the sinner," the incommunicable honour of Christ, who came to "save His people from their sins"—as contained in the Divine language uttered by the "sweet psalmist of Israel," a thousand years before the Christian era. If, therefore, the Pope occupies, as we have seen, the very place of Janus "the man," how clear is it, that he equally occupies the place of Attes, "the sinner," and then how striking in this point of view the name "Man of sin," as divinely given by prophecy (2 Thess. ii. 3) to him who was to be the head of the Christian apostacy, and who was to concentrate in that apostacy all the corruption of Babylonian Paganism?

The Pope is thus on every ground demonstrated to be the *visible* head of the beast. But the beast has not only a visible, but an invisible head that governs it. That invisible head is none other than Satan, the head of the first grand apostacy that began in heaven itself. This is put beyond doubt by the language of Rev. xiii. 4: "And they worshipped the Dragon which gave power unto the beast, saying, Who is like unto the beast? Who is able to make war with him?" This language shows that the worship of the dragon is commensurate with the worship of the beast. That the

* The whole story of Attes can be proved in detail to be the story of the Fall. Suffice it here only to state that, even on the surface, his sin was said to be connected with undue love for "a nymph, whose fate depended on a *tree*" (OVID, *Fasti*, lib. iv., Ludi Megalenses). The love of Attes for this nymph was in one aspect an *offence* to Cybele, but, in another, it was the love of Cybele herself; for Cybele has two distinct fundamental characters—that of the Holy Spirit, and also that of our mother Eve (see Appendix, Note G). "The nymph whose fate depended on a *tree*" was evidently Rhea, the mother of mankind.

† BRYANT, vol. i. p. 387, Note. The ground of the identification of Attis with the sun evidently was, that as Hata signifies *to sin*, so Hatah, which signifies *to burn*, is in pronunciation nearly the same. In illustration of the name Attes, or Attis, as "The Sinner," see Appendix, Note R.

‡ PAUSAN., lib. vii., *Achaica*, cap. 17.

dragon is primarily Satan, the arch-fiend himself, is plain from the statement of the previous chapter (Rev. xii. 9): "And the Dragon was cast out, that old serpent, called the Devil, and Satan, which deceiveth the whole world." If, then, the Pope be, as we have seen, the visible head of the beast, the adherents of Rome, in worshipping the Pope, of necessity worship also the Devil. With the Divine statement before us, there is no possibility of escaping from this. And this is exactly what we might expect on other grounds. Let it be remembered that the Pope, as the head of the Mystery of Iniquity, is "the son of perdition," Iscariot, the false apostle, the traitor. Now, it is expressly stated, that before Judas committed his treason, "Satan," the prince of the Devils, "entered into him," took complete and entire possession of him. From analogy, we may expect the same to have been the case here. Before the Pope could even conceive such a scheme of complicated treachery to the cause of his Lord, as has been proved against him, before he could be qualified for successfully carrying that treacherous scheme into effect, Satan himself must enter into him. The Mystery of Iniquity was to practise and prosper according "to the working"—*i.e.*, literally, "according to the *energy* or mighty power of Satan" (2 Thess. ii. 9).* Therefore Satan himself, and not any subordinate spirit of hell, must preside over the whole vast system of consecrated wickedness; he must personally take possession of him who is its visible head, that the system may be guided by his diabolical subtlety, and "energised" by his super-human power. Keeping this in view, we see at once how it is that, when the followers of the Pope worship the beast, they worship also the "dragon that gave power to the beast."

Thus, altogether independent of historical evidence on this point, we are brought to the irresistible conclusion that the worship of Rome is one vast system of Devil-worship. If it be once admitted that the Pope is the head of the beast from the sea, we are bound, on the mere testimony of God, without any other evidence whatever, to receive this as a fact, that, consciously or unconsciously, those who worship the Pope are *actually* worshipping the Devil. But, in truth, we have historical evidence, and that of a very remarkable kind, that the Pope, as head of the Chaldean Mysteries, is as directly the representative of Satan, as he is of the false Messiah of Babylon. It was long ago noticed by Irenæus, about the end of the second century, that the name Teitan contained the mystic number 666; and he gave it as his opinion, that Teitan was "by far the most probable name" of the beast from the sea.† The grounds of his

* The very term "energy" here employed, is the term continually used in the Chaldean books, describing the inspiration coming from the gods and demons to their worshippers.—(TAYLOR'S *Jamblichus*, p. 163, *et passim.*)

† IRENÆUS, lib. v. cap. 30, p. 802. Though the name Teitan was originally derived from Chaldee, yet it became thoroughly naturalised in the Greek language. Therefore, to give the more abundant evidence on this important subject, the Spirit of God seems to have ordered it, that the number of Teitan should be found according to the Greek computation, while that of Satūr is found by the Chaldee.

opinion, as stated by him, do not carry much weight; but the opinion itself he may have derived from others who had better and more valid reasons for their belief on this subject. Now, on inquiry, it will actually be found, that while Saturn was the name of the *visible* head, Teitan was the name of the *invisible* head of the beast. Teitan is just the Chaldean form of Sheitan,* the very name by which Satan has been called from time immemorial by the Devil-worshippers of Kurdistan;† and from Armenia or Kurdistan, this Devil-worship embodied in the Chaldean Mysteries came westward to Asia Minor, and thence to Etruria and Rome. That Teitan was actually known by the classic nations of antiquity to be Satan, or the spirit of wickedness, and originator of moral evil, we have the following proofs: The history of Teitan and his *brethren*, as given in Homer and Hesiod, the two earliest of all the Greek writers, although later legends are obviously mixed up with it, is evidently the exact counterpart of the Scriptural account of Satan and his angels. Homer says, that "all the gods of Tartarus," or Hell, "were called Teitans."‡ Hesiod tells us how these Teitans, or "gods of hell," came to have their dwelling there. The chief of them having committed a certain act of wickedness against his father, the supreme god of heaven, with the sympathy of many others of the "sons of heaven," that father "called them all by an opprobrious name, Teitans,"§ pronounced a curse upon them, and then, in consequence of that curse, they were "cast down to hell," and "bound in chains of darkness" in the abyss.|| While this is the earliest account of Teitan and his followers among the Greeks, we find that, in the Chaldean system, Teitan was just a synonym for Typhon, the malignant Serpent or Dragon, who was universally regarded as the Devil, or author of all wickedness. It was Typhon, according to the Pagan version of the story, that killed Tammuz, and cut him in pieces; but Lactantius, who was thoroughly acquainted with the subject, upbraids his Pagan countrymen for "worshipping a child torn in pieces by the Teitans."¶ It is undeniable, then, that Teitan, in Pagan belief, was identical with the Dragon, or Satan.**

* The learned reader has no need of examples in proof of this frequent Chaldean transformation of the Sh or S into T; but for the common reader, the following may be adduced: Hebrew, Shekel, to weigh, becomes Tekel in Chaldee; Hebrew, Shabar, to break—Chaldee, Tabar; Hebrew, Seraphim—Chaldee, Teraphim, the Babylonian counterfeit of the Divine Cherubim or Seraphim; Hebrew, Asar, to be rich—Chaldee, Atar; Hebrew, Shani, second—Chaldee, Tanin, &c.

† WALPOLE'S *Ansayri*, vol. i. p. 397. LAYARD'S *Nineveh*, vol. i. pp. 287, 288. See also REDHOUSE'S *Turkish Dictionary, sub voce* "Satan," p. 303. The Turks came from the Euphrates.

‡ HOMER, *Iliad*, lib. xiv. l. 279, p. 549.

§ HESIOD, *Theogonia*, l. 207, pp. 18, 19.

|| *Ibid.* ll. 717, 729, pp. 56-59. I think the reader will see that Ouranos, or Heaven, against whom the Titans rebelled, was just God.

¶ LACTANTIUS, *De Falsa Religione*, p. 221; CLEMENS ALEXANDRINUS also, vol. i. p. 30.

** We have seen that Shem was the *actual* slayer of Tammuz. As the grand adversary of the Pagan Messiah, those who hated him for his deed called him for

In the Mysteries, as formerly hinted, an important change took place as soon as the way was paved for it. First, Tammuz was worshipped as the bruiser of the serpent's head, meaning thereby that he was the appointed destroyer of Satan's kingdom. Then the dragon himself, or Satan, came to receive a certain measure of worship, to "console him," as the Pagans said, "for the loss of his power," and to prevent him from hurting them;* and last of all the dragon, or Teitan or Satan, became the supreme object of worship, the Titania, or rites of Teitan, occupying a prominent place in the Egyptian Mysteries,† and also in those of Greece.‡ How vitally important was the place that these rites of Teitan or Satan occupied, may be judged of from the fact that Pluto, the god of Hell (who, in his *ultimate* character, was just the grand Adversary), was looked up to with awe and dread as the great god on whom the destinies of mankind in the eternal world did mainly depend; for it was said that to Pluto it belonged "to purify souls after death."§ Purgatory having been in Paganism, as it is in Popery, the grand hinge of priestcraft and superstition, what a power did this opinion attribute to the "god of Hell"! No wonder that the serpent, the Devil's grand instrument in seducing mankind, was in all the earth worshipped with such extraordinary reverence, it being laid down in the Octateuch of Ostanes, that "serpents were the supreme of all gods and the princes of the Universe."‖ No wonder that it came at last to be firmly believed that the Messiah, on whom the hopes of the world depended, was *Himself* the "seed of the serpent"! This was manifestly the case in Greece; for the current story there came to be, that the first Bacchus was brought forth in consequence of a connexion on the part of his mother with the father of the gods, in the form of a "speckled snake."¶ That "father of the gods" was manifestly "the god of hell;" for Proserpine, the mother of Bacchus, that miraculously conceived and brought forth the wondrous child—whose rape by Pluto occupied such a place in the Mysteries—was worshipped *as* the wife of the god of Hell, as we have already seen, under the name of the "Holy Virgin."** The

that very deed by the name of the Grand Adversary of all, Typhon, or the Devil. "If they called the Master of the house Beelzebub," no wonder that his servant was called by a similar name.

* PLUTARCH, *De Iside*, vol. ii. p. 362. † *Ibid.* vol. ii. p. 364.

‡ POTTER'S *Antiquities*, vol. i., *sub voce* "Titania," p. 400.

§ TAYLOR'S *Pausanias*, vol. iii. p. 321, Note.

‖ EUSEBIUS, *Præparatio Evang.*, lib. i. vol. i. p. 50.

¶ OVID, *Metam.*, lib. vi. l. 114. So deeply was the idea of "the seed of the serpent" being the great World-king imprinted on the Pagan mind, that when a man set up to be a god upon earth, it was held essential to establish his title to that character, that he prove himself to be the "serpent's seed." Thus, when Alexander the Great claimed divine honours, it is well known that his mother Olympias, declared that he was not sprung from King Philip, her husband, but from Jupiter, in the form of a serpent. In like manner, says the authoress of *Rome in the 19th Century*, vol. i. p. 388, the Roman emperor, "Augustus, pretended that he was the son of Apollo, and that the god had assumed the form of a serpent for the purpose of giving him birth."—*Vid.* SUET. AUGUSTUS.

** See *ante*, p. 126.

story of the seduction of Eve* by the serpent is plainly imported into this legend, as Julius Firmicus and the early Christian apologists did with great force cast in the teeth of the Pagans of their day; but very different is the colouring given to it in the Pagan legend from that which it has in the Divine Word. Thus the grand Thimblerigger, by dexterously shifting the peas, through means of men who began with great professions of abhorrence of his character, got himself almost everywhere recognised as in very deed "the god of this world." So deep and so strong was the hold that Satan had contrived to get of the ancient world in this character, that even when Christianity had been proclaimed to man, and the true light had shone from Heaven, the very doctrine we have been considering raised its head among the professed disciples of Christ. Those who held this doctrine were called Ophiani or Ophites, that is, serpent-worshippers. "These heretics," says Tertullian, "magnify the serpent to such a degree as to prefer him even to Christ Himself; for he, say they, gave us the first knowledge of good and evil. It was from a perception of his power and majesty that Moses was induced to erect the brazen serpent, to which whosoever looked was healed. Christ Himself, they affirm, in the Gospel imitates the sacred power of the serpent, when He says that, 'As Moses lifted up the serpent in the wilderness even so must the Son of Man be lifted up.'† They introduce it when they bless the Eucharist." These wicked heretics avowedly worshipped the old serpent, or Satan, as the grand benefactor of mankind, for revealing to them the knowledge of good and evil. But this doctrine they had just brought along with them from the Pagan world, from which they had come, or from the Mysteries, as they came to be received and celebrated in Rome. Though Teitan, in the days of Hesiod and in early Greece, was an "opprobrious name," yet in Rome, in the days of the Empire and before, it had become the very reverse. "The splendid or glorious Teitan" was the way in which Teitan was spoken of at Rome. This was the title commonly given to the Sun, both as the orb of day and viewed as a divinity. Now, the reader has seen already that another form of the sun-divinity, or Teitan, at Rome, was the Epidaurian snake, worshipped under the name of "Æsculapius," that is, "the man-instructing serpent."‡ Here, then, in

* We find that Semele, the mother of the Grecian Bacchus, had been identified with Eve; for the name of Eve had been given to her, as Photius tells us that "Pherecydes called Semele, Hué."—(PHOT. *Lex.*, pars ii. p. 616.) Hué is just the Hebrew name for Eve, without the points.

† TERTULLIAN, *De Præscript. adv. Hæreticos*, cap. 47, vol. ii. pp. 63, 64.

‡ Aish-shkul-apé, from *Aish*, "man"; *shkul*, "to instruct;" and *Aphé*, or *Apé*, "a serpent." The Greek form of this name, Asklepios, signifies simply "the instructing snake," and comes from *A*, "the," *skl*, "to teach," and *hefi*, "a snake," the Chaldean words being thus modified in Egypt. The name Asclepios, however, is capable of another sense, as derived from *Aaz*, "strength," and *Khlep*, "to renew;" and, therefore, in the exoteric doctrine, Asclepios was known simply as "the strength-restorer," or the Healing God. But, as identified with the serpent, the true meaning of the name seems to be that which is first stated. Macrobius, giving an account of the mystic doctrine of the ancients, says that

Rome was Teitan, or Satan, identified with the "serpent that taught mankind," that opened their eyes (when, of course, they were blind), and gave them "the knowledge of good and evil." In Pergamos, and in all Asia Minor, from which directly Rome derived its knowledge of the Mysteries, the case was the same. In Pergamos, especially, where pre-eminently "*Satan's* seat was," the sun-divinity, as is well known, was worshipped under the form of a serpent and under the name of Æsculapius, "the man-instructing serpent." According to the fundamental doctrine of the Mysteries, as brought from Pergamos to Rome, the sun was the one only god.* Teitan, or Satan, then, was thus recognised as the one only god; and of that only god, Tammuz or Janus, in his character as the Son, or the woman's seed, was just an incarnation. Here, then, the grand secret of the Roman Empire is at last brought to light—viz., the real name of the tutelar divinity of Rome. That secret was most jealously guarded; insomuch that when Valerius Soranus, a man of the highest rank, and, as Cicero declares, "the most learned of the Romans," had incautiously divulged it, he was remorselessly put to death for his revelation. Now, however, it stands plainly revealed.

Fig. 59.

A symbolical representation of the worship of the Roman people, from *Pompeii*, strikingly confirms this deduction by evidence that appeals to the very senses. Let the reader cast his eyes on the woodcut herewith given (Fig. 59).† We have seen already that it is admitted by the author of *Pompeii*, in regard to a former representation, that the serpents in the under compartment are only another way of exhibiting the dark divinities represented in the upper compartment. Let the same principle be admitted here, and it follows that the swallows, or birds pursuing the flies, represent the same thing as the serpents do below. But the serpent, of which there is a double representation, is unquestionably the serpent of Æsculapius. The fly-destroying swallow, therefore, must represent the same divinity. Now, every one knows what was the name by which "the Lord of the fly," or fly-destroying god of the Oriental world was called. It was Beel-zebub.‡ This name, as signifying

Æsculapius was that beneficent influence of the sun which pervaded the souls of men.—(*Sat.*, lib. i. cap. 23.) Now the *Serpent* was the symbol of the enlightening sun.

* MACROBIUS, *Saturnalia*, lib. i. cap. 17, 23, pp. 65, C, and 72, 1, 2.

† From *Pompeii*, vol. ii. p. 141.

‡ KITTO'S *Illustrated Commentary*, vol. ii. p. 317.

"Lord of the Fly," to the profane meant only the power that destroyed the swarms of flies when these became, as they often did in hot countries, a source of torment to the people whom they invaded. But this name, as identified with the serpent, clearly reveals itself as one of the distinctive names of Satan. And how appropriate is this name, when its mystic or esoteric meaning is penetrated. What is the real meaning of this familiar name? Baal-zebub just means "The restless Lord,"* even that unhappy one who "goeth to and fro in the earth, and walketh up and down in it," who "goeth through dry places seeking rest, and finding none." From all this, the inference is unavoidable that Satan, in his own proper name, *must* have been the great god of their secret and mysterious worship, and this accounts for the extraordinary mystery observed on the subject.† When, therefore, Gratian abolished the legal provision for the support of the fire-worship and serpent-worship of Rome, we see how exactly the Divine prediction was fulfilled (Rev. xii. 9): "And the great dragon was cast out, that old serpent called the DEVIL, and SATAN, which deceiveth the whole world: he was cast out into the earth, and his angels were cast out with him."‡ Now, as the Pagan Pontifex, to whose powers and

* See CLAVIS STOCKII, *sub voce* "Zebub," where it is stated that the word zebub, as applied to the fly, comes from an Arabic root, which signifies to move from place to place, as flies do, without settling anywhere. Baal-zebub, therefore, in its secret meaning, signifies, "Lord of restless and unsettled motion."

† I find Lactantius was led to the conclusion that the Æsculapian serpent was the express symbol of Satan, for, giving an account of the bringing of the Epidaurian snake to Rome, he says: "Thither [*i.e.*, to Rome] the Demoniarches [or Prince of the Devils] in his own proper shape, without disguise, was brought; for those who were sent on that business brought back with them a dragon of amazing size."—(*De Origine Erroris*, lib. ii. cap. 16, p. 108.)

‡ The facts stated above cast a very singular light on a well-known superstition among ourselves. Everybody has heard of St. Swithin's day, on which, if it rain, the current belief is, that it will rain in uninterrupted succession for six weeks. And who or what was St. Swithin that *his* day should be connected with forty days' uninterrupted rain? for six weeks is just the round number of weeks equivalent to forty days. It is evident, in the first place, that he was no Christian saint, though an Archbishop of Canterbury in the tenth century is said to have been called by his name. The patron saint of the forty days' rain was just Tammuz or Odin, who was worshipped among our ancestors as the incarnation of Noah, in whose time it rained forty days and forty nights without intermission. Tammuz and St. Swithin, then, must have been one and the same. But, as in Egypt, and Rome, and Greece, and almost everywhere else, long before the Christian era, Tammuz had come to be recognised as an incarnation of the Devil, we need not be surprised to find that St. Swithin is no other than St. Satan. One of the current forms of the grand adversary's name among the Pagans was just Sytan or Sythan. This name, as applied to the Evil Being, is found as far to the east as the kingdom of Siam. It had evidently been known to the Druids, and that in connection with the flood; for they say that it was the son of Seithin that, under the influence of drink, let in the sea over the country so as to overwhelm a large and populous district.—(DAVIES'S *Druids*, p. 198.) The Anglo-Saxons, when they received that name, in the very same way as they made Odin into Wodin, would naturally change Sythan into Swythan: and thus, in St. Swithin's day and the superstition therewith connected, we have at once a striking proof of the wide extent of Devil-worship in the heathen world, and of the thorough acquaintance of our Pagan ancestors with the great Scriptural fact of the forty days' incessant rain at the Deluge.

prerogatives the Pope had served himself heir, was thus the High-priest of Satan, so, when the Pope entered into a league and alliance with that system of Devil-worship, and consented to occupy the very position of that Pontifex, and to bring all its abominations into the Church, as he has done, he necessarily became the Prime Minister of the Devil, and, of course, came as thoroughly under his power as ever the previous Pontiff had been.* How exact the fulfilment of the Divine statement that the coming of the Man of Sin was to be "after the working or energy of Satan." Here, then, is the grand conclusion to which we are compelled, both on historical and Scriptural grounds, to come: As the mystery of godliness is God manifest in the flesh, so the mystery of iniquity is—so far as such a thing is possible—the Devil incarnate.

If any one thinks it incredible that Satan should thus be canonised by the Papacy in the Dark Ages, let me call attention to the pregnant fact that, even in comparatively recent times, the Dragon—the Devil's universally recognised symbol—was worshipped by the Romanists of Poictiers under the name of "the good St. Vermine"!!—(*Notes of the Society of the Antiquaries of France*, vol. i. p. 464, *apud* SALVERTÉ, p. 475.)

* This gives a new and darker significance to the mystic Tau, or sign of the cross. At first it was the emblem of Tammuz, at last it became the emblem of Teitan, or Satan himself.

CONCLUSION.

I HAVE now finished the task I proposed to myself. Even yet the evidence is not nearly exhausted; but, upon the evidence which has been adduced, I appeal to the reader if I have not proved every point which I engaged to demonstrate. Is there one, who has candidly considered the proof that has been led, that now doubts that Rome is the Apocalyptic Babylon? Is there one who will venture to deny that, from the foundation to the topmost stone, it is essentially a system of Paganism. What, then, is to be the practical conclusion from all this?

1. Let every Christian henceforth and for ever treat it as an outcast from the pale of Christianity. Instead of speaking of it as a Christian Church, let it be recognised and regarded as the Mystery of Iniquity, yea, as the very Synagogue of Satan. With such overwhelming evidence of its real character, it would be folly—it would be worse—it would be treachery to the cause of Christ—to stand merely on the defensive, to parley with its priests about the lawfulness of Protestant orders, the validity of Protestant sacraments, or the possibility of salvation apart from its communion. If Rome is now to be admitted to form a portion of the Church of Christ, where is the system of Paganism that has ever existed, or that now exists, that could not put in an equal claim? On what grounds could the worshippers of the original Madonna and child in the days of old be excluded "from the commonwealth of Israel," or shown to be "strangers to the covenants of promise"? On what grounds could the worshippers of Vishnu at this day be put beyond the bounds of such wide catholicity? The ancient Babylonians held, the modern Hindoos still hold, clear and distinct traditions of the Trinity, the Incarnation, the Atonement. Yet, who will venture to say that such nominal recognition of the cardinal articles of Divine revelation could relieve the character of either the one system or the other from the brand of the most deadly and God-dishonouring heathenism? And so also in regard to Rome. True, it nominally admits Christian terms and Christian names; but all that is apparently Christian in its system is *more* than neutralised by the malignant Paganism that it embodies. Grant that the bread the Papacy presents to its votaries can be proved to have been originally made of the finest of the wheat; but what then, if every particle of that bread is combined with prussic acid or strychnine? Can the excellence of the bread overcome the virus of the poison? Can there be anything but death, spiritual and eternal death, to those who continue to feed upon the poisoned food that it offers? Yes, here is the question, and let it be

fairly faced. Can there be salvation in a communion in which it is declared to be a fundamental principle, that the Madonna is "our greatest hope; yea, the SOLE GROUND OF OUR HOPE"?* The time is come when charity to the perishing souls of men, hoodwinked by a Pagan priesthood, abusing the name of Christ, requires that the truth in this matter should be clearly, loudly, unflinchingly proclaimed. The beast and the image of the beast alike stand revealed in the face of all Christendom; and now the tremendous threatening of the Divine Word in regard to their worship fully applies (Rev. xiv. 9, 10): "And the third angel followed them, saying, 'If any man worship the beast and his image, and receive his mark in his forehead, or in his hand, the same shall drink of the wine of the wrath of God, poured without mixture into the cup of His indignation; and he shall be tormented with fire and brimstone in the presence of the holy angels, and in the presence of the Lamb.'" These words are words of awful import; and woe to the man who is found finally under the guilt which they imply. These words, as has already been admitted by Elliott, contain a "chronological prophecy," a prophecy not referring to the Dark Ages, but to a period not far distant from the consummation, when the Gospel should be widely diffused, and when bright light should be cast on the character and doom of the apostate Church of Rome (ver. 6-8). They come, in the Divine chronology of events, immediately after an angel has proclaimed, "BABYLON IS FALLEN, IS FALLEN." We have, as it were, with our own ears heard this predicted "Fall of Babylon" announced from the high places of Rome itself, when the seven hills of the "Eternal City" reverberated with the guns that proclaimed, not merely to the citizens of the Roman republic, but to the wide world, that "PAPACY HAD FALLEN, *de facto* and *de jure*, from the temporal throne of the Roman State."† Now, it is in the order of the prophecy, *after* this fall of Babylon, that this fearful threatening comes. Can there, then, be a doubt that this threatening specially and peculiarly applies to this very time? Never till now was the real nature of the Papacy fully revealed; never till now was the Image of the beast set up. Till the Image of the beast was erected, till the blasphemous decree of the Immaculate Conception was promulged, no such apostacy had taken place, even in Rome, no such guilt had been contracted, as now lies at the door of the great Babylon. This, then, is a subject of infinite importance to every one within the pale of the Church of Rome—to every one also who is looking, as so many at present are doing, towards the City of the Seven Hills. If any one can prove that the Pope does not assume all the prerogatives and bear substantially all the blasphemous titles of that Babylonian beast that "had the wound by a sword, and did live," and if it can be shown that the Madonna,

* The language of the late Pope Gregory, substantially indorsed by the present Pontiff.

† The Apocalypse announces two *falls* of Babylon. The fall referred to above is evidently only the *first*. The prophecy clearly implies, that *after* the first fall it rises to a greater height than before; and therefore the necessity of the warning.

that has so recently with one consent been set up, is not in every essential respect the same as the Chaldean "Image" of the beast, they may indeed afford to despise the threatening contained in these words. But if neither the one nor the other can be proved (and I challenge the strictest scrutiny in regard to both), then every one within the pale of the Papacy may well tremble at such a threatening. Now, then, as never before, may the voice Divine, and that a voice of the tenderest love, be heard sounding from the Eternal throne to every adherent of the Mystic Babylon, "Come out of her, My people, that ye be not partakers of her sins, and that ye receive not of her plagues."

2. But if the guilt and danger of those who adhere to the Roman Church, believing it to be the only Church where salvation can be found, be so great, what must be the guilt of those who, with a Protestant profession, nevertheless uphold the doomed Babylon? The Constitution of this land requires our Queen to *swear*, before the crown can be put upon her head, before she can take her seat on the throne, that "she *believes*" that the essential doctrines of Rome are "*idolatrous.*" All the Churches of Britain, endowed and unendowed, alike with one voice declare the very same. They all proclaim that the system of Rome is a system of blasphemous idolatry. . . . . And yet the members of these Churches can endow and uphold, with Protestant money, the schools, the colleges, the chaplains of that idolatrous system. If the guilt of Romanists, then, be great, the guilt of Protestants who uphold such a system must be tenfold greater. That guilt has been greatly accumulating during the last three or four years. While the King of Italy, in the very States of the Church—what but lately were the Pope's own dominions—has been suppressing the monasteries (and in the space of two years no less than fifty-four were suppressed, and their property confiscated), the British Government has been acting on a policy the very reverse, has not only been conniving at the erection of monasteries, which are prohibited by the law of the land, but has actually been bestowing endowment on these illegal institutions under the name of Reformatories. It was only a short while ago, that it was stated, on authority of the *Catholic Directory*, that in the space of three years, fifty-two new convents were *added* to the monastic system of Great Britain,* almost the very number that the Italians had confiscated, yet Christian men and Christian Churches look on with indifference. Now, if ever there was an excuse for thinking lightly of the guilt contracted by our national support of idolatry, that excuse will no longer avail. The God of Providence, in India, has been demonstrating that He is the God of Revelation. He has been proving, to an awe-struck world, by events that made every ear to tingle, that every word of wrath, written three thousand years ago against idolatry, is in as full force at this day as when He desolated the covenanted people of Israel for their idols, and sold them into the hands of their enemies. If men begin to see that it

* Quoted in *Irish Covenanter*, February, 1862, p. 52.

is a dangerous thing for professing Christians to uphold the Pagan idolatry of India, they must be blind indeed if they do not equally see that it must be as dangerous to uphold the Pagan idolatry of Rome. Wherein does the Paganism of Rome differ from that of Hindooism? Only in this, that the Roman Paganism is the more complete, more finished, more dangerous, more insidious Paganism of the two.

I am afraid, that after all that has been said, not a few will revolt from the above comparative estimate of Popery and undisguised Paganism. Let me, therefore, fortify my opinion by the testimonies of two distinguished writers, well qualified to pronounce on this subject. They will, at least, show that I am not singular in the estimate which I have formed. The writers to whom I refer, are Sir George Sinclair of Ulbster, and Dr. Bonar of Kelso. Few men have studied the system of Rome more thoroughly than Sir George, and in his *Letters to the Protestants of Scotland* he has brought all the fertility of his genius, the *curiosa felicitas* of his style, and the stores of his highly cultivated mind, to bear upon the elucidation of his theme. Now, the testimony of Sir George is this: "Romanism is a refined system of Christianised heathenism, and chiefly differs from its prototype in being *more* treacherous, *more* cruel, *more* dangerous, *more* intolerant." * The mature opinion of Dr. Bonar is the very same, and that, too, expressed with the Cawnpore massacre particularly in view: "We are doing for Popery at home," says he, "what we have done for idolaters abroad, and in the end the results will be the same; *nay, worse;* for Popish cruelty, and thirst for the blood of the innocent, have been the most savage and merciless that the earth has seen. Cawnpore, Delhi, and Bareilly, are but dust in comparison with the *demoniacal brutalities* perpetrated by the Inquisition, and by the armies of Popish fanaticism." † These are the words of truth and soberness, that no man acquainted with the history of modern Europe can dispute. There is great danger of their being overlooked at this moment. It will be a fatal error if they be. Let not the pregnant fact be overlooked, that, while the Apocalyptic history runs down to the consummation of all things, in that Divine foreshadowing all the other Paganisms of the world are in a manner cast into the shade by the Paganism of Papal Rome. It is against Babylon that sits on the seven hills that the saints are forewarned; it is for worshipping the beast and his image pre-eminently, that "the vials of the wrath of God, that liveth and abideth for ever," are destined to be outpoured upon the nations. Now, if the voice of God has been heard in the late Indian calamities, the Protestantism of Britain will rouse itself to sweep away at once and for ever all national support, alike from the idolatry of Hindostan and the still more malignant idolatry of Rome. Then, indeed, there would be a lengthening of our tranquillity, then there would be hope that Britain would be exalted, and that its power would

* *First Series*, p. 121.

† *British Messenger*, Dec., 1857.

rest on a firm and stable foundation. But if we will not "hear the voice, if we receive not correction, if we refuse to return," if we persist in maintaining, at the national charge, "that image of jealousy provoking to jealousy," then, after the repeated and ever-INCREASING strokes that the justice of God has laid on us, we have every reason to fear that the calamities that have fallen so heavily upon our countrymen in India, may fall still more heavily upon ourselves, within our own borders at home; for it was when "the image of jealousy" was set up in Jerusalem by the elders of Judah, that the Lord said, "Therefore will I also deal in fury; mine eye shall not spare, neither will I have pity; and though they cry in mine ears with a loud voice, yet will I not hear them." He who let loose the Sepoys, to whose idolatrous feelings and antisocial propensities we have pandered so much, to punish us for the guilty homage we had paid to their idolatry, can just as easily let loose the Papal Powers of Europe, to take vengeance upon us for our criminal fawning upon the Papacy.

3. But, further, if the views established in this work be correct, it is time that the Church of God were aroused. Are the witnesses still to be slain, and has the Image of the Beast only within the last year or two been set up, at whose instigation the bloody work is to be done? Is this, then, the time for indifference, for sloth, for lukewarmness in religion? Yet, alas! how few are they who are lifting up their voice like a trumpet, who are sounding the alarm in God's holy mountain—who are bestirring themselves according to the greatness of the emergency—to gather the embattled hosts of the Lord to the coming conflict? The emissaries of Rome for years have been labouring unceasingly night and day, in season and out of season, in every conceivable way, to advance their Master's cause, and largely have they succeeded. But "the children of light" have allowed themselves to be lulled into a fatal security; they have folded their hands; they have gone to sleep as soundly as if Rome had actually disappeared from the face of the earth—as if Satan himself had been bound and cast into the bottomless pit, and the pit had shut its mouth upon him, to keep him fast for a thousand years. How long shall this state of things continue? Oh, Church of God, awake, awake! Open your eyes, and see if there be not dark and lowering clouds on the horizon that indicate an approaching tempest. Search the Scriptures for yourselves; compare them with the facts of history, and say, if there be not reason after all to suspect that there are sterner prospects before the saints than most seem to wot of. If it may turn out that the views opened up in these pages are Scriptural and well-founded, they are at least worthy of being made the subjects of earnest and prayerful inquiry. It never can tend to good to indulge an uninquiring and delusive feeling of safety, when, if they *be* true, the only safety is to be found in a timely knowledge of the danger and due preparation, by all activity, all zeal, all spirituality of mind, to meet it. On the supposition that peculiar dangers are at hand, and that God in His prophetic

Word has revealed them, His goodness is manifest. He has made known the danger, that, being forewarned, we may be forearmed; that, knowing our own weakness, we may cast ourselves on His Almighty grace; that we may feel the necessity of a fresh baptism of the Holy Ghost; that the joy of the Lord being our strength, we may be thorough and decided for the Lord, and for the Lord alone, that we may work, every one in his own sphere, with increased energy and diligence, in the Lord's vineyard, and save all the souls we can, while yet opportunity lasts, and the dark predicted night has not come, wherein no man can work. Though there be dark prospects before us, there is no room for despondency; no ground for any one to say that, with such prospects, effort is vain. The Lord can bless and prosper to His own glory, the efforts of those who truly gird themselves to fight His battles in the most hopeless circumstances; and, at the very time when the enemy cometh in like a flood, He can, by His Spirit, lift up a standard against him. Nay, not only is this a possible thing, there is reason, from the prophetic word, to believe that so it shall actually be; that the last triumph of the Man of Sin shall not be achieved without a glorious struggle first, on the part of those who are leal-hearted to Zion's King. But if we would really wish to do anything effectual in this warfare, it is indispensable that we know, and continually keep before our eyes, the stupendous character of that Mystery of Iniquity embodied in the Papacy that we have to grapple with. Popery boasts of being the "old religion;" and truly, from what we have seen, it appears that it is ancient indeed. It can trace its lineage far beyond the era of Christianity, back over 4000 years, to near the period of the Flood and the building of the Tower of Babel. During all that period its essential elements have been nearly the same, and these elements have a peculiar adaptation to the corruption of human nature. Most seem to think that Popery is a system merely to be scouted and laughed at; but the Spirit of God everywhere characterises it in quite a different way. Every statement in the Scripture shows that it was truly described when it was characterised as "Satan's Masterpiece"—the perfection of his policy for deluding and ensnaring the world. It is not the state-craft of politicians, the wisdom of philosophers, or the resources of human science, that can cope with the wiles and subtleties of the Papacy. Satan, who inspires it, has triumphed over all these again and again. Why, the very nations where the worship of the Queen of Heaven, with all its attendant abominations, has flourished most in all ages, have been precisely the most civilised, the most polished, the most distinguished for arts and sciences. Babylon, where it took its rise, was the cradle of astronomy. Egypt, that nursed it in its bosom, was the mother of all the arts; the Greek cities of Asia Minor, where it found a refuge when expelled from Chaldea, were famed for their poets and philosophers, among the former Homer himself being numbered; and the nations of the European Continent, where literature has long been cultivated, are now prostrate before it. Physical force, no doubt, is at present employed in its behalf; but the question arises, How comes it that this system, of all others, can so prevail as to get that physical force to obey its behests? No answer can be given but this, that Satan, the god of this world, exerts his highest power in its behalf. Physical force has not always been on the side of the Chaldean worship of the Queen of Heaven. Again and again has power been arrayed against it; but hitherto every obstacle it has surmounted, every difficulty it has overcome. Cyrus, Xerxes, and many of the Medo-Persian kings, banished its priests from Babylon, and laboured to root it out of their empire; but then it found a secure retreat in Pergamos, and "Satan's seat" was erected there. The glory of Pergamos and the cities of Asia Minor departed; but the worship of the Queen of Heaven did not wane. It took a higher flight, and seated itself on the throne of Imperial Rome. That throne was subverted. The Arian Goths came burning with fury against the worshippers of the Virgin Queen; but still that worship rose buoyant above all attempts to put it down, and the Arian Goths themselves were soon prostrate at the feet of the Babylonian goddess, seated in glory on the seven hills of Rome. In more modern times, the temporal powers of all the kingdoms of Europe have expelled the Jesuits, the chief promoters of this idolatrous worship, from their dominions. France, Spain, Portugal, Naples, Rome itself, have all adopted the same measures, and yet what do we see at this hour? The same Jesuitism and the worship of the Virgin exalted above almost every throne on the Continent. When we look over the history of the last 4000 years, what a meaning in the words of inspiration, that "the coming of the Man of Sin" is with the energy, "the mighty power of Satan." Now, is this the system that, year by year, has been rising into power in our own empire? And is it for a moment to be imagined that lukewarm, temporising, half-hearted Protestants can make any head against such a system? No; the time is come when Gideon's proclamation must be made throughout the camp of the Lord: "Whosoever is fearful and afraid, let him return and depart early from Mount Gilead." Of the old martyrs it is said, "They overcame by the blood of the Lamb and the word of their testimony, and they loved not their lives unto the death." The same self-denying, the same determined spirit, is needed now as much as ever it was. Are there none who are prepared to stand up, and in that very spirit to gird themselves for the great conflict that *must* come, before Satan shall be bound and cast into his prison-house? Can any one believe that such an event can take place without a tremendous struggle—that "the god of this world" shall quietly consent to resign the power that for thousands of years he has wielded, without stirring up all his wrath, and putting forth all his energy and skill to prevent such a catastrophe. Who, then, is on the Lord's side? If there be those who, within the last few years, have been revived and quickened—stirred up, not by mere human excitement, but by the Almighty grace of God's Spirit, what is the gracious design of this? Is it merely that they themselves may be delivered from the wrath to come? No; it is that, zealous for the glory of their Lord, they may act the parts of true witnesses, contend earnestly for the faith once delivered to the saints, and maintain the honour of Christ in opposition to him who blasphemously usurps his prerogatives. If the servants of Antichrist are faithful to their master, and unwearied in promoting his cause, shall it be said that the servants of Christ are less faithful to theirs? If none else will bestir themselves, surely to the generous hearts of the young and rising ministry of Christ, in the kindness of their youth, and the love of their espousals, the appeal shall not be made in vain, when the appeal is made in the name of Him whom their souls love, that in this grand crisis of the Church and of the world, they should "come to the help of the Lord—the help of the Lord against the mighty," that they should do what in them lies to strengthen the hands and encourage the hearts of those who are seeking to stem the tide of apostacy, and to resist the efforts of the men who are labouring with such zeal, and with so much of infatuated patronage on the part of "the powers that be," to bring this land back again under the power of the Man of Sin. To take such a part, and steadily and perseveringly to pursue it, amid so much growing lukewarmness, it is indispensable that the servants of Christ set their faces as a flint. But if they have grace so to do, they shall not do so without a rich reward at last; and in time they have the firm and faithful promise that "as their day is, so shall their strength be." For all who wish truly to perform their part as good soldiers of Jesus Christ, there is the strongest and richest encouragement. With the blood of Christ on the conscience, with the Spirit of Christ warm and working in the heart, with our Father's name on our forehead, and our life, as well as our lips, consistently bearing "testimony" for God, we shall be prepared for every event. But it is not common grace that will do for uncommon times. If there be indeed such prospects before us, as I have endeavoured to prove there are, then we must live, and feel, and act as if we heard every day resounding in our ears the words of the great Captain of our Salvation, "To him that overcometh will I grant to sit with Me on My throne, even as I also overcame, and am set down with My Father on His throne. Be thou faithful unto death, and I will give thee a crown of life."

Lastly, I appeal to every reader of this work, if it does not contain an argument for the divinity of the Scriptures, as well as an exposure of the impostures of Rome. Surely, if one thing more than another be proved in the previous pages, it is this, that the Bible is no cunningly devised fable, but that holy men of God of old spake and wrote as they were moved by the Holy Ghost. What can account for the marvellous unity in all the idolatrous systems of the world, but that the facts recorded in the early chapters of Genesis were real transactions, in which, as all mankind were involved, so all mankind have preserved in their various systems, distinct and undeniable memorials of them, though those who have preserved them have long lost the true key to their meaning? What, too, but Omniscience could have foreseen that a system, such as that of the Papacy, could ever effect an entrance into the Christian Church, and practise and prosper as it has done? How could it ever have entered into the heart of John, the solitary exile of Patmos, to imagine, that any of the professed disciples of that Saviour whom he loved, and who said, "My kingdom is not of this world," should gather up and systematise all the idolatry and superstition and immorality of the Babylon of Belshazzar, introduce it into the bosom of the Church, and, by help of it, seat themselves on the throne of the Cæsars, and there, as the high-priests of the Queen of Heaven, and gods upon earth, for 1200 years, rule the nations with a rod of iron? Human foresight could never have done this; but all this the exile of Patmos has done. His pen, then, must have been guided by Him who sees the end from the beginning, and who calleth the things that be not as though they were. And if the wisdom of God now shines forth so brightly from the Divine expression "Babylon the Great," into which such an immensity of meaning has been condensed, ought not that to lead us the more to reverence and adore the same wisdom that is in reality stamped on every page of the inspired Word? Ought it not to lead us to say with the Psalmist, "Therefore, I esteem *all* Thy commandments concerning all things to be right"? The commandments of God, to our corrupt and perverse minds, may sometimes seem to be hard. They may require us to do what is painful, they may require us to forego what is pleasing to flesh and blood. But, whether we know the reason of these commandments or no, if we only know that they come from "the only wise God, our Saviour," we may be sure that in the keeping of them there is great reward; we may go blindfold wherever the Word of God may lead us, and rest in the firm conviction that, in so doing, we are pursuing the very path of safety and peace. Human wisdom at the best is but a blind guide; human policy is a meteor that dazzles and leads astray; and they who follow it walk in darkness, and know not whither they are going; but he "that walketh uprightly," that walks by the rule of God's infallible Word, will ever find that "he walketh surely," and that whatever duty he has to perform, whatever danger he has to face, "great peace have all they that love God's law, and nothing shall offend them."

APPENDIX.

Note A, p. 6.

Woman with Golden Cup.

In Pausanias we find an account of a goddess represented in the very attitude of the Apocalyptic "Woman." "But of this stone [Parian marble] Phidias," says he, "made a statue of Nemesis; and on the head of the goddess there is a crown adorned with stags, and images of victory of no great magnitude. In her left hand, too, she holds a branch of an ash tree, and in her right a cup, in which Æthiopians are carved."—(Pausanias, lib. i., *Attica*, cap. 33, p. 81.) Pausanias declares himself unable to assign any reason why "the *Æthiopians*" were carved on the cup; but the meaning of the Æthiopians and the stags too will be apparent to all who read pp. 48, 49, and 50, &c., *ante*. We find, however, from statements made in the same chapter, that though Nemesis is commonly represented as the goddess of revenge, she must have been also known in quite a different character. Thus Pausanias proceeds, commenting on the statue: "But neither has this statue of the goddess wings. Among the Smyrneans, however, who possess the most holy images of Nemesis, I perceived afterwards that these statues had wings. For, as *this goddess principally pertains to lovers*, on this account they may be supposed to have given wings to Nemesis, as well as to love," *i.e.*, Cupid.—(*Ibid.*) The giving of wings to Nemesis, the goddess who "principally pertained to lovers," because Cupid, the *god* of love, bore them, implies that, in the opinion of Pausanias, she was the *counterpart* of Cupid, or the *goddess* of love—that is, Venus. While this is the inference naturally to be deduced from the words of Pausanias, we find it confirmed by an express statement of Photius, speaking of the statue of Rhamnusian Nemesis: "She was at first erected in the form of Venus, and therefore bore also the branch of an apple tree."—(Photii, *Lexicon*, pars. ii. p. 482.) Though a goddess of love and a goddess of revenge might seem very remote in their characters from one another, yet it is not difficult to see how this must have come about. The goddess who was revealed to the initiated in the Mysteries, in the most alluring manner, was also known to be most unmerciful and unrelenting in taking vengeance upon those who revealed these Mysteries; for every such one who was discovered was unsparingly put to death.—(Potter's *Antiquities*, vol. i., "Eleusinia," p. 354.) Thus, then, the cup-bearing goddess was at once Venus, the goddess of licentiousness, and Nemesis, the stern and unmerciful one to all who rebelled against her authority. How remarkable a type of the woman, whom John saw, described in one aspect as the "Mother of harlots," and in another as "Drunken with the blood of the saints"!

Note B, p. 6.

Hebrew Chronology.

Dr. Hales has attempted to substitute the longer chronology of the Septuagint for the Hebrew chronology. But this implies that the Hebrew Church, as a body, was not faithful to the trust committed to it in respect to the keeping of the Scriptures, which seems distinctly opposed to the testimony of our Lord in reference to these Scriptures (John v. 39 ; x. 35), and also to that of Paul (Rom. iii. 2), where there is not the least hint of unfaithfulness. Then we can find a reason that might induce the translators of the Septuagint in Alexandria to *lengthen* out the period of the ancient history of the world ; we can find no reason to induce the Jews in Palestine to *shorten* it. The Egyptians had long, fabulous eras in their history, and Jews dwelling in Egypt might wish to make their sacred history go as far back as they could, and the addition of just one hundred years in each case, as in the Septuagint, to the ages of the patriarchs, looks wonderfully like an intentional forgery ; whereas we cannot imagine why the Palestine Jews should make any change in regard to this matter at all. It is well known that the Septuagint contains innumerable gross errors and interpolations.

Bunsen casts overboard *all* Scriptural chronology whatever, whether Hebrew, Samaritan, or Greek, and sets up the unsupported dynasties of Manetho, as if they were sufficient to over-ride the Divine word as to a question of historical fact. But, if the Scriptures are not historically true, we can have no assurance of their truth at all. Now it is worthy of notice that, though Herodotus vouches for the fact that at one time there were no fewer than twelve contemporaneous kings in Egypt, Manetho, as observed by Wilkinson (vol. i. p. 148), has made no allusion to this, but has made his Thinite, Memphite, and Diospolitan dynasties of kings, and a long etcetera of other dynasties, all successive !

The period over which the dynasties of Manetho extend, beginning with Menes, the first king of these dynasties, is in itself a very lengthened period, and surpassing all rational belief. But Bunsen, not content with this, expresses his very confident persuasion that there had been long lines of powerful monarchs in Upper and Lower Egypt, "during a period of from two to four thousand years" (vol. i. p. 72), even before the reign of Menes. In coming to such a conclusion, he plainly goes upon the supposition that the name Mizraim, which is the Scriptural name of the land of Egypt, and is evidently derived from the name of the son of Ham, and grandson of Noah, is not, after all, the name of a *person*, but the name of the united *kingdom* formed under Menes out of "the two Misr," "Upper and Lower Egypt" (*Ibid.* p. 73), which had previously existed as separate kingdoms, the name *Misrim*, according to him, being a plural word. This derivation of the name Mizraim, or Misrim, as a plural word, infallibly leaves the impression that Mizraim, the son of Ham, must be only a mythical personage. But there is no real reason for thinking that Mizraim is a plural word, or that it became the name of "the land of Ham," from any other reason than because that land was also the land of Ham's son. Mizraim, as it stands in the Hebrew of Genesis, without the points, is Metzrim ; and Metzr-im signifies "The encloser or embanker of the *sea*" (the word being derived from *Im*, the same as *Yam*, "the sea," and *Tzr*, "to enclose," with the formative *M* prefixed).

If the accounts which ancient history has handed down to us of the original state of Egypt be correct, the first man who formed a settlement there *must* have done the very thing implied in this name. Diodorus Siculus tells us that, in primitive times, that which, when he wrote, "was

Egypt, was said to have been not a country, but *one universal sea*."—(DIOD., lib. iii. p. 106.) Plutarch also says (*De Iside*, vol. ii. p. 367) that Egypt was sea. From Herodotus, too, we have very striking evidence to the same effect. He excepts the province of Thebes from his statement; but when it is seen that "the province of Thebes" did not belong to Mizraim, or Egypt proper, which, says the author of the article "Mizraim" in *Biblical Cyclopædia*, p. 598, "properly denotes Lower Egypt;"* the testimony of Herodotus will be seen entirely to agree with that of Diodorus and Plutarch. His statemant is, that in the reign of the first king, "the whole of Egypt (except the province of Thebes) was an extended marsh. No part of that which is now situate beyond the lake Moeris was to be seen, the distance between which lake and the sea is a journey of seven days."—(HERODOT., lib. ii. cap. 4.) Thus all Mizraim or Lower Egypt was under water.

This state of the country arose from the unrestrained overflowing of the Nile, which, to adopt the language of Wilkinson (vol. i. p. 89), "formerly washed the foot of the sandy mountains of the Lybian chain." Now, before Egypt could be fit for being a suitable place for human abode—before it could become what it afterwards did become, one of the most fertile of all lands, it was indispensable that bounds should be set to the overflowings of the *sea* (for by the very name of the Ocean, or Sea, the Nile was anciently called,—DIODORUS, lib. i. p. 8), and that for this purpose great embankments should *enclose* or *confine* its waters. If Ham's son, then, led a colony into Lower Egypt and settled it there, this very work he must have done. And what more natural than that a name should be given him in memory of his great achievement? and what name so exactly descriptive as Metzr-im, "The embanker of the sea," or as the name is found at this day applied to *all* Egypt (WILKINSON, vol. i. p. 2), Musr or Misr? Names always tend to abbreviation in the mouths of a people, and, therefore, "The land of Misr" is evidently just "The land of the embanker." From this statement it follows that the "embanking of the sea"—the "enclosing" of it within certain bounds, was the *making* of it as a *river*, so far as lower Egypt was concerned. Viewing the matter in this light, what a meaning is there in the Divine language in Ezekiel xxix. 3, where judgments are denounced against the king of Egypt, the representative of Metzr-im, "The embanker of the sea," for his pride: "Behold, I am against thee, Pharaoh, king of Egypt, the great dragon that lieth in the midst of his rivers, which saith, My river is mine own, I have *made* it for myself."

When we turn to what is recorded of the doings of Menes, who, by Herodotus, Manetho, and Diodorus alike, is made the first historical king of Egypt, and compare what is said of *him*, with this simple explanation of the meaning of the name of Mizraim, how does the one cast light on the other? Thus does Wilkinson describle the great work which entailed fame on Menes, "who," says he, "is allowed by universal consent to have been the first sovereign of the country." "Having diverted the course of the Nile, which formerly washed the foot of the sandy mountains of the Lybian chain, he obliged it to run in the centre of the valley, nearly at an equal distance between the two parallel ridges of mountains which border it on the east and west; and built the city of Memphis in the bed of the ancient channel. This change was effected by constructing a dyke about a hundred stadia above the site of the projected city, whose lofty mounds and strong EMBANKMENTS turned the water to the eastward, and effectually CONFINED the river to its new bed. The dyke was carefully kept in

* The same view of the extent of Mizraim is taken by the Rev. R. JAMIESON in PAXTON'S *Illustrations of Scripture*, vol. i. p. 198; and in KITTO'S *Illustrated Comment.*, vol. iv. p. 110.

repair by succeeding kings; and, even as late as the Persian invasion, a guard was always maintained there, to overlook the necessary repairs, and to watch over the state of the embankments."—(*Egyptians*, vol. i. p. 89.)

When we see that Menes, the first of the acknowledged historical kings of Egypt, accomplished that very achievement which is implied in the name of Mizraim, who can resist the conclusion that Menes and Mizraim are only two different names for the same person? And if so, what becomes of Bunsen's vision of powerful dynasties of sovereigns "during a period of from two to four thousand years" before the reign of Menes, by which all Scriptural chronology respecting Noah and his sons was to be upset, when it turns out that Menes must have been Mizraim, the grandson of Noah himself? Thus does Scripture contain, within its own bosom, the means of vindicating itself; and thus do its minutest statements, even in regard to matters of fact, when thoroughly understood, shed surprising light on the dark parts of the history of the world.

NOTE C, p. 21.

Shing Moo and Ma Tsoopo of China.

The name of Shing Moo, applied by the Chinese to their "Holy Mother," compared with another name of the same goddess in another province of China, strongly favours the conclusion that Shing Moo is just a synonym for one of the well-known names of the goddess-mother of Babylon. Gillespie (in his *Land of Sinim*, p. 64) states that the Chinese goddess-mother, or "Queen of Heaven," in the province of Fuh-kien, is worshipped by seafaring people under the name of Ma Tsoopo. Now, "Ama Tzupah" signifies the "Gazing Mother;" and there is much reason to believe that Shing Moo signifies the same; for Mū was one of the forms in which Mut or Maut, the name of the great mother, appeared in Egypt (BUNSEN'S *Vocabulary*, vol. i. p. 471); and Shngh, in Chaldee, signifies "to look" or "gaze." The Egyptian Mū or Maut was symbolised either by a vulture, or an *eye* surrounded by a vulture's wings (WILKINSON, vol. v. p. 203). The symbolic meaning of the vulture may be learned from the Scriptural expression: "There is a path which no fowl knoweth, and which the vulture's eye hath not seen" (Job xxviii. 7). The vulture was noted for its sharp sight, and hence, the *eye* surrounded by the vulture's wings showed that, for some reason or other, the great mother of the gods in Egypt had been known as "The gazer." But the idea contained in the Egyptian symbol had evidently been borrowed from Chaldea; for Rheia, one of the most noted names of the Babylonian mother of the gods, is just the Chaldee form of the Hebrew Rhaah, which signifies at once "a gazing woman" and a "vulture." The Hebrew Rhaah itself is also, according to a dialectical variation, legitimately pronounced Rheah; and hence the name of the great goddess-mother of Assyria was sometimes Rhea, and sometimes Rheia. In Greece, the same idea was evidently attached to Athena or Minerva, whom we have seen to have been by some regarded as the Mother of the children of the sun (see *ante*, p. 20, Note). For one of her distinguishing titles was Ophthalmitis (SMITH'S *Classical Dictionary*, "Athena," p. 101), thereby pointing her out as the goddess of "the *eye*." It was no doubt to indicate the same thing that, as the Egyptian Maut wore a vulture on her head, so the Athenian Minerva was represented as wearing a helmet with two *eyes*, or eye-holes, in the front of the helmet.—(VAUX'S *Antiquities*, p. 186.)

Having thus traced the gazing mother over the earth, is it asked, What can have given origin to such a name as applied to the mother of the gods?

A fragment of Sanchuniathon (pp. 16-19), in regard to the Phenician mythology, furnishes us with a satisfactory reply. There it is said that Rheia conceived by Kronos, who was her own brother, and yet was known as the father of the gods, and in consequence brought forth a son who was called Mūth, that is, as Philo-Byblius correctly interprets the word, "Death." As Sanchuniathon expressly distinguishes this "father of the gods" from "Hypsistos," The Most High,* we naturally recall what Hesiod says in regard to his Kronos, the father of the gods, who, for a certain wicked deed, was called Titan, and cast down to hell.—(*Theogonia*, l. 207, p. 18.) The Kronos to whom Hesiod refers is evidently at bottom a different Kronos from the human father of the gods, or Nimrod, whose history occupies so large a place in this work. He is plainly none other than Satan himself; the name Titan, or Teitan, as it is sometimes given, being, as we have elsewhere concluded (pp. 275, 276), only the Chaldee form of Sheitan, the common name of the grand Adversary among the Arabs, in the very region where the Chaldean Mysteries were originally concocted,—that Adversary who was ultimately the real father of all the Pagan gods,—and who (to make the title of Kronos, "the Horned One," appropriate to *him* also) was symbolised by the Kerastes, or *Horned* serpent. All "the brethren" of this father of the gods, who were implicated in his rebellion against his own father, the "God of Heaven," were equally called by the "reproachful" name "Titans"; but, inasmuch as he was the ringleader in the rebellion, *he* was, of course, Titan by way of eminence. In this rebellion of Titan, the goddess of the earth was concerned, and the result was that (removing the figure under which Hesiod has hid the fact) it became naturally impossible that the God of Heaven should have children upon earth—a plain allusion to the Fall.

Now, assuming that this is the "Father of the gods," by whom Rhea, whose common title is that of the Mother of the gods, and who is also identified with Gē, or the Earth-goddess, had the child called Mūth, or Death, who could this "Mother of the gods" be, but just our Mother Eve? And the name Rhea, or "The Gazer," bestowed on her, is wondrously significant. It was as "the gazer" that the mother of mankind conceived by Satan, and brought forth that deadly birth, under which the world has hitherto groaned. It was through her *eyes* that the fatal connection was first formed between her and the grand Adversary, under the form of a serpent, whose name, Nahash, or Nachash, as it stands in the Hebrew of the Old Testament, also signifies "to view attentively," or "to gaze:" (Gen. iii. 6) "And when the woman *saw* that the tree was good for food, and *pleasant to the eyes*," &c., "she took of the fruit thereof, and did eat; and gave also unto her husband with her, and he did eat." Here, then, we have the pedigree of sin and death; "Lust, when it had conceived, brought forth sin; and sin, when it was finished, brought forth death" (James i. 15). Though Mūth, or Death, was the son of Rhea, this progeny of hers came to be regarded, not as Death in the abstract, but as the *god* of death; therefore, says Philo-Byblius, Mūth was interpreted not only as death, but as Pluto.—(SANCHUN., p. 24.) In the Roman mythology, Pluto was regarded as on a level, for honour, with Jupiter (OVID, *Fasti*, lib. vii. 578); and in Egypt, we have evidence that Osiris, "the seed of the woman," was the "Lord of heaven," and king of hell, or "Pluto" (WILKINSON, vol. iv. p. 63; BUNSEN, vol. i. pp. 431, 432); and it can be shown by a large induction of particulars (and the reader has somewhat of the evidence presented in this volume), that he was none other than the Devil himself,

* In reading Sanchuniathon, it is necessary to bear in mind what Philo-Byblius, his translator, states at the end of the *Phenician History*—viz., that history and mythology were mingled together in that work.

supposed to have become incarnate; who, though through the first transgression, and his connection with the woman, he had brought sin and death into the world, had, nevertheless, by means of them, brought innumerable benefits to mankind. As the name Pluto has the very same meaning as Saturn, "The hidden one," so, whatever other aspect this name had, as applied to the father of the gods, it is to Satan, the Hidden Lord of hell, ultimately that all came at last to be traced back; for the different myths about Saturn, when carefully examined, show that he was at once the Devil, the father of all sin and idolatry, who *hid* himself under the disguise of the serpent,—and Adam, who *hid* himself among the trees of the garden,—and Noah, who lay *hid* for a whole year in the ark,—and Nimrod, who was *hid* in the secrecy of the Babylonian Mysteries. It was to glorify Nimrod that the whole Chaldean system of iniquity was formed. He was known as Nin, "the son," and his wife as Rhea, who was called Ammas, "The Mother." The name Rhea, as applied to Semiramis, had another meaning from what it had when applied to her, who was really the primeval goddess, the "mother of gods and *men*." But yet, to make out the full majesty of her character, it was necessary that she should be identified with that primeval goddess; and, therefore, although the son she bore in her arms was represented as he who was born to destroy death, yet she was often represented with the very symbols of her who brought death into the world. And so was it also in the different countries where the Babylonian system spread.

Note D, p. 32.

Ala-Mahozim.

The name "Ala-Mahozim" is never, so far as I know, found in any ancient uninspired author, and in the Scripture itself it is found only in a prophecy. Considering that the design of prophecy is always to leave a certain obscurity before the event, though giving enough of light for the practical guidance of the upright, it is not to be wondered at that an unusual word should be employed to describe the divinity in question. But, though this precise name be not found, we have a synonym that can be traced home to Nimrod. In Sanchuniathon, pp. 24, 25, "Astarte, travelling about the habitable world," is said to have found "a star falling through the air, which she took up and consecrated in the holy island Tyre." Now what is this story of the falling star but just another version of the fall of Mulciber from heaven (see *ante*, p. 233), or of Nimrod from his high estate? for as we have already seen, Macrobius shows (*Saturn.*, lib. i., cap. 21, p. 70) that the story of Adonis—the lamented one—so favourite a theme in Phenicia, originally came from Assyria. The name of the great god in the holy island of Tyre, as is well known, was Melkart (Kitto's *Illus. Comment.*, vol. ii. p. 300), but this name, as brought from Tyre to Carthage, and from thence to Malta (which was colonised from Carthage), where it is found on a monument at this day, casts no little light on the subject. The name Melkart is thought by some to have been derived from Melek-eretz, or "king of the earth" (Wilkinson, vol. v. p. 18); but the way in which it is sculptured in Malta shows that it was really Melek-kart, "king of the walled city."—(See Wilkinson's Errata prefixed to vol. v.) Kir, the same as the Welsh Caer, found in Caer-narvon, &c., signifies "an encompassing wall," or a "city completely walled round;" and Kart was the feminine form of the same word, as may be seen in the different forms of the name of Carthage, which is sometimes Car-chēdon, and sometimes Cart-hada or Cart-hago. In the Book of

Proverbs we find a slight variety of the feminine form of Kart, which seems evidently used in the sense of a bulwark or a fortification. Thus (Prov. x. 15) we read: "A rich man's wealth is his strong *city*" (Karit), that is, his strong *bulwark* or *defence*. Melk-kart, then, "king of the walled city," conveys the very same idea as Ala-Mahozim. In GRUTER'S *Inscriptions*, as quoted by Bryant, we find a title also given to Mars, the Roman war-god, exactly coincident in meaning with that of Melkart. We have elsewhere seen abundant reason to conclude that the original of Mars was Nimrod (p. 44, Note). The title to which I refer confirms this conclusion, and is contained in the following Roman inscription on an ancient temple in Spain:—

"Malacæ Hispaniæ
MARTI CIRADINO
Templum communi voto
Erectum."

(See BRYANT, vol. ii. p. 454.) This title shows that the temple was dedicated to "Mars Kir-aden," the lord of "The Kir," or "walled city." The Roman C, as is well known, is hard, like K; and Adon, "Lord," is also Aden. Now, with this clue to guide us, we can unravel at once what has hitherto greatly puzzled mythologists in regard to the name of *Mars Quirinus* as distinguished from *Mars Gradivus*. The K in Kir is what in Hebrew or Chaldee is called Koph, a different letter from Kape, and is frequently pronounced as a Q. Quir-inus, therefore, signifies "belonging to the walled city," and refers to the security which was given to cities by encompassing walls. Gradivus, on the other hand, comes from "Grah," "conflict," and "divus," "god,"—a different form of *Deus*, which has been already shown to be a Chaldee term; and therefore signifies "God of battle." Both these titles exactly answer to the two characters of Nimrod, as the great city builder and the great warrior, and that both these distinctive characters were set forth by the two names referred to, we have distinct evidence in FUSS'S *Antiquities*, chap. iv. p. 348. "The Romans," says he, "worshipped two idols of the kind [that is, gods under the name of Mars], the one called Quirinus, the *guardian of the city and its peace;* the other called Gradivus, *greedy of war and slaughter*, whose temple stood beyond the city's boundaries."

NOTE E, p. 42.

Meaning of the name Centaurus.

The ordinary classical derivation of this name gives little satisfaction; for, even though it could be derived from words that signify "Bull-killers" (and the derivation itself is but lame), such a meaning casts no light at all on the history of the Centaurs. Take it as a Chaldee word, and it will be seen at once that the whole history of the primitive Kentaurus entirely agrees with the history of Nimrod, with whom we have already identified him. Kentaurus is evidently derived from Kehn, "a priest," and Tor, "to go round." "Kehn-Tor," therefore, is "Priest of the revolver," that is, of the sun, which, to appearance, makes a daily revolution round the earth. The name for a priest, as written, is just Khn, and the vowel is supplied according to the different dialects of those who pronounce it, so as to make it either Kohn, Kahn, or Kehn. Tor, "the revolver," as applied to the sun, is evidently just another name for the Greek Zen or Zan applied to Jupiter, as identified with the sun, which signifies the "Encircler" or "Encompasser,"—the very word from which comes our own word "Sun," which, in Anglo-Saxon, was Sunna (MALLET, *Glossary*, p. 565, London, 1847), and of which we find distinct traces in Egypt in the term *snnu* (BUNSEN'S *Vocab.*, vol. i. p. 546), as applied to the sun's orbit. The Hebrew Zon or Zawon, to "encircle," from which these words come, in Chaldee becomes Don or Dawon, and thus we penetrate the meaning of the name given by the Bœotians to the "Mighty hunter," Orion. That name was Kandaon, as appears from the following words of the Scholiast on Lycophron, quoted in BRYANT, vol. iv. p. 154: "Orion, whom the Bœotians call also Kandaon." Kahn-daon, then, and Kehn-tor, were just different names for the same office—the one meaning "Priest of the Encircler," the other, "Priest of the revolver"—titles evidently equivalent to that of Bol-kahn, or "Priest of Baal, or the Sun," which, there can be no doubt, was the distinguishing title of Nimrod. As the title of Centaurus thus exactly agrees with the known position of Nimrod, so the history of the father of the Centaurs does the same. We have seen already that, though Ixion was, by the Greeks, made the father of that mythical race, even they themselves admitted that the Centaurs had a much higher origin, and consequently that Ixion, which seems to be a Grecian name, had taken the place of an earlier name, according to that propensity particularly noticed by Salverté, which has often led mankind "to apply to personages known in one time and one country, myths which they have borrowed from another country and an earlier epoch" (*Des Sciences*, Appendix, p. 483). Let this only be admitted to be the case here —let only the name of Ixion be removed, and it will be seen that all that is said of the father of the Centaurs, or Horsemen-archers, applies exactly to Nimrod, as represented by the different myths that refer to the first progenitor of these Centaurs. First, then, Centaurus is represented as having been taken up to heaven (DYMOCK, *sub voce* "Ixion"), that is, as having been highly exalted through special favour of heaven; then, in that state of exaltation, he is said to have fallen in love with Nephelé, who passed under the name of Juno, the "Queen of Heaven." The story here is intentionally confused, to mystify the vulgar, and the order of events seems changed, which can easily be accounted for. As Nephelé in Greek signifies "a cloud," so the offspring of Centaurus are said to have been produced by a "cloud." But Nephelé, in the language of the country where the fable was orginally framed, signified "A fallen woman," and it is from that "fallen woman," therefore, that the Centaurs are really said to have sprung. Now, the story of Nimrod, as Ninus, is, that he fell in love with Semiramis when she was another man's wife, and took her for his own wife, whereby she became doubly fallen—fallen as a woman*—and fallen from the primitive faith in which she must have been brought up; and it is well known that this "fallen woman" was, under the name of Juno, or the Dove, after her death, worshipped among the Babylonians. Centaurus, for his presumption and pride, was smitten with lightning by the supreme God, and cast down to hell (DYMOCK, *sub voce* "Ixion"). This, then, is just another version of the story of Phaëthon, Æsculapius, and Orpheus, who were all smitten in like manner and for a similar cause. In the infernal world, the father of the Centaurs is represented as tied by serpents to a wheel which perpetually revolves, and thus makes his punishment eternal (DYMOCK, *Ibid.*). In the serpents there is evidently reference to one of the two emblems of the fire-worship of Nimrod. If *he* introduced the worship of the serpent, as I have endeavoured to show (p. 228), there was poetical justice in making the serpent an instrument of his punishment. Then the revolving wheel very clearly points to the name Centaurus itself,

* Nephelé was used, even in Greece, as the name of a woman, the *degraded* wife of Athamas being so called.—(SMITH'S *Class. Dict.*, *sub voce* "Athamas," p. 110).

as denoting the "Priest of the revolving sun." To the worship of the sun in the character of the "Revolver," there was a very distinct allusion not only in the circle which, among the Pagans, was the emblem of the sun-god, and the blazing wheel with which he was so frequently represented (WILSON'S *Parsi Religion*, p. 31), "but in the *circular* dances of the Bacchanalians. Hence the phrase, "Bassaridum *rotator* Evan"—"The *wheeling* Evan of the Bacchantes" (STATIUS, *Sylv.*, lib. ii., s. 7, v. 7, p. 118). Hence, also, the circular dances of the Druids as referred to in the following quotation from a Druidic song:—"Ruddy was the sea beach whilst the *circular revolution* was performed by the attendants and the white bands in graceful extravagance" (DAVIES'S *Druids*, p. 172). That this circular dance among the Pagan idolators really had reference to the circuit of the sun, we find from the distinct statement of Lucian in his treatise *On Dancing*, where, speaking of the circular dance of the ancient Eastern nations, he says, with express reference to the sun-god, "it consisted in a dance imitating this god" (LUCIAN, vol. ii. p. 278). We see then, here, a very specific reason for the circular dance of the Bacchæ, and for the ever-revolving wheel of the great Centaurus in the infernal regions.

NOTE F, p. 72.

Olenos, the Sin-Bearer.

In different portions of this work evidence has been brought to show that Saturn, "the father of gods and *men*," was in one aspect just our first parent Adam. Now, of Saturn it is said that he devoured all his children.* In the exoteric story, among those who knew not the actual fact referred to, this naturally appeared in the myth, in the shape in which we commonly find it—viz., that he devoured them all as soon as they were born. But that which was really couched under the statement, in regard to his devouring his children, was just the Scriptural fact of the Fall—viz., that *he destroyed them by eating*—not by eating *them*, but by eating the *forbidden fruit*. When this was the sad and dismal state of matters, the Pagan story goes on to say that the destruction of the children of the father of gods and men was arrested by means of his wife, Rhea. Rhea, as we have already seen, had really as much to do with the devouring of Saturn's children, as Saturn himself; but, in the progress of idolatry and apostacy, Rhea, or Eve, came to get glory at Saturn's expense. Saturn, or Adam, was represented as a morose divinity; Rhea, or Eve, exceedingly benignant; and, in her benignity, she presented to her husband a stone bound in swaddling bands, which he greedily devoured, and henceforth the children of the cannibal father were safe.† The stone bound in swaddling bands is, in the sacred language, "Ebn Hatūl;" but Ebn-Hat-tul ‡ also signifies "A sin-bearing son." This does not necessarily mean that Eve, or the mother of mankind, herself actually brought forth the promised seed (although there are many myths also to that effect), but that, having received the glad tidings herself, and embraced it, she presented it to her husband, who received it by faith from *her*, and that this laid the foundation of his own salvation and that of his posterity. The devouring on the part of Saturn

* Sometimes he is said to have devoured only his male children; but see SMITH'S (Larger) *Classical Dictionary*, *sub voce* "Hera," where it will be found that the female as well as the male were devoured.

† HESIOD, *Theogonia*, ll. 485, &c., pp. 38-41.

‡ Hata, "sin," is found also in Chaldee, Hat.—(See CLAVIS STOCKII, p. 1329.) Tul is from Ntl, "to support." If the reader will look at Horus with his swathes (BRYANT, vol. iii. plate 22); Diana with the bandages round her legs (see *ante*, p. 29); the symbolic bull of the Persians swathed in like manner (BRYANT, vol. i. plate 5, p. 367), and even the shapeless log of the Tahitians, used as a god and bound about with ropes (WILLIAMS, p. 31); he will see, I think, that there must be some important mystery in this swathing.

of the swaddled stone is just the symbolical expression of the eagerness with which Adam by faith received the good news of the woman's seed; for the act of faith, both in the Old Testament and in the New, is symbolised by *eating.* Thus Jeremiah says, "Thy words were found of me, and I did eat them, and Thy word was unto me the joy and rejoicing of my heart" (Jer. xv. 16). This also is strongly shown by our Lord Jesus Christ Himself, who, while setting before the Jews the indispensable necessity of eating His flesh, and feeding on Him, did at the same time say: "It is the Spirit that quickeneth; the flesh profiteth nothing: the words that I speak unto you, they are spirit, and they are life" (John vi. 63). That Adam eagerly received the good news about the promised seed, and treasured it up in his heart as the life of his soul, is evident from the name which he gave to his wife immediately after hearing it: "And Adam called his wife's name Eve, because she was the mother of all *living ones*" (Gen. iii. 20. See Dr. CANDLISH'S *Genesis*, p. 108).

The story of the swaddled stone does not end with the swallowing of it, and the arresting of the ruin of the children of Saturn. This swaddled stone was said to be "preserved near the temple of Delphi, where care was taken to anoint it daily with oil, and to cover it with wool" (MAURICE'S *Indian Antiquities*, vol. ii. p. 348). If this stone symbolised the "sin-bearing son," it of course symbolised also the Lamb of God, slain from the foundation of the world, in whose symbolic covering our first parents were invested when God clothed them in the coats of skins. Therefore, though represented to the eye as a stone, he must have the appropriate covering of wool. When represented as a branch, the branch of God, the branch also was wrapped in *wool* (POTTER, vol. i., *Religion of Greece*, chap. v. p. 208). The *daily* anointing with oil is very significant. If the stone represented the "sin-bearing son," what could the anointing of that "sin-bearing son" daily with oil mean, but just to point him out as the "Lord's Anointed," or the "Messiah," whom the idolaters worshipped in opposition to the *true* Messiah yet to be revealed?

One of the names by which this swaddled and anointed stone was called is very strikingly confirmatory of the above conclusion. That name is Baitulos. This we find from Priscian (lib. v., vol. i. p. 180, Note, and lib. vi., vol. i. p. 249), who, speaking of "that stone which Saturn is said to have devoured for Jupiter," adds, "*quem Græci* Βαιτυλον *vocant,*" whom the Greeks called "Baitulos." Now, "B'hai-tuloh"* signifies the "Life-restoring child."* The father of gods and men had destroyed his children by eating; but the reception of "the swaddled stone" is said to have "restored them to life" (HESIOD, *Theogon.*, l. 495, p. 41). Hence the name Baitulos; and this meaning of the name is entirely in accordance with what is said in Sanchuniathon (lib. i., cap. 6, p. 22) about the Baithulia made by the Phenician god Ouranos: "It was the god Ouranos who devised Baithulia, contriving stones that moved *as having life.*" If the stone Baitulos represented the "life-restoring child," it was natural that that stone should be made, if possible, to appear as having "life" in *itself.*

Now, there is a great analogy between this swaddled stone that represented the "sin-bearing son," and that Olenos mentioned by Ovid, who took on him guilt not his own, and in consequence was changed into

* From Tli, Tleh, or Tloh, "Infans puer" (CLAVIS STOCKII, *Chald.*, p. 1342), and Hia, or Haya, "to live, to restore life."—(GESENIUS, p. 310.) From Hia, "to live," with digamma prefixed, comes the Greek Βιος, life. That Hia, when adopted into Greek, was also pronounced Haya, we have evidence in the noun Hiim, "life," pronounced Hayyim, which in Greek is represented by αἱμα, "blood." The Mosaic principle, that "the blood was the life," is thus proved to have been known by others besides the Jews. Now Haya, "to live or restore life," with the digamma prefixed, becomes B'haya; and so in Egypt, we find that Bai signified "soul," or "spirit" (BUNSEN, vol. i. p. 375), which is the *living* principle. B'haitulos, then, is the "Life-restoring child." P'haya-n is the same god.

a stone. We have seen already that Olenos, when changed into a stone, was set up in Phrygia on the holy mountain of Ida. We have reason to believe that the stone which was fabled to have done so much for the children of Saturn, and was set up near the temple of Delphi, was just a representation of this same Olenos. We find that Olen was the first prophet at Delphi, who founded the first temple there (PAUSANIAS, lib. x., *Phocica*, cap. 5, p. 321). As the prophets and priests generally bore the names of the gods whom they represented (Hesychius expressly tells us that the priest who represented the great god under the name of the branch in the Mysteries was himself called by the name of Bacchus, p. 179), this indicates one of the ancient names of the god of Delphi. If, then, there was a sacred stone on Mount Ida called the stone of Olenos, and a sacred stone in the precincts of the temple of Delphi, which Olen founded, can there be a doubt that the sacred stone of Delphi represented the same as was represented by the sacred stone of Ida? The swaddled stone set up at Delphi is expressly called by Priscian, in the place already cited, "a god." This god, then, that in symbol was divinely anointed, and was celebrated as having restored to life the children of Saturn, father of gods and men, as identified with the Idæan Olenos, is proved to have been regarded as occupying the very place of the Messiah, the great Sin-bearer, who came to bear the sins of men, and took their place and suffered in their room and stead; for Olenos, as we have seen, voluntarily took on him guilt of which he was personally free.

Fig. 60.

While thus we have seen how much of the patriarchal faith was hid under the mystical symbols of Paganism, there is yet a circumstance to be noted in regard to the swaddled stone, that shows how the Mystery of Iniquity in Rome has contrived to import this swaddled stone of Paganism into what is called Christian symbolism. The Baitulos, or swaddled stone, was στρογγυλος λιθος (BRYANT, vol. ii. p. 20, Note), a round or globular stone. This globular stone is frequently represented swathed and bound, sometimes with more, sometimes with fewer bandages. In BRYANT, vol. iii. p. 246, where the goddess Cybele, is represented as "Spes Divina," or Divine hope, we see the foundation of this divine hope held out to the world in the representation of the swaddled stone at her right hand, bound with four different swathes. In DAVID'S *Antiquités Etrusques*, vol. iv. plate 27, we find a goddess represented with Pandora's box, the source of all ill, in her extended hand, and the swaddled globe depending from it; and in this case that globe has only two bandages, the one crossing the other. And what is this bandaged globe of Paganism but just the counterpart of that globe, with a band around it, and the mystic *Tau* or cross, on the top of it, that is called "the type of dominion," and is frequently represented, as in the accompanying woodcut (Fig. 60),* in the hands of the profane representations of God the Father. The reader does not now need to be told that the cross is the chosen sign and *mark*

* From DIDRON'S *Iconography*, vol. i. p. 301.

of that very God whom the swaddled stone represented; and that when that God was born, it was said, "The Lord of all the earth is born" (WILKINSON, vol. iv. p. 310). As the god symbolised by the swaddled stone not only restored the children of Saturn to life, but restored the lordship of the earth to Saturn himself, which by transgression he had lost, it is not to be wondered at that it is said of "these consecrated stones," that while "some were dedicated to Jupiter, and others to the sun," "they were considered in a more particular manner sacred to Saturn," the Father of the gods (MAURICE, vol. ii. p. 348), and that Rome, in consequence, has put the round stone into the hand of the image, bearing the profaned name of God the Father attached to it, and that from this source the bandaged globe, surmounted with the mark of Tammuz, has become the symbol of dominion throughout all Papal Europe.

NOTE G, p. 75.

The Identification of Rhea or Cybele and Venus.

In the exoteric doctrine of Greece and Rome, the characters of Cybele, the mother of the gods, and of Venus, the goddess of love, are generally very distinct, insomuch that some minds may perhaps find no slight difficulty in regard to the identification of these two divinities. But that difficulty will disappear, if the fundamental principle of the Mysteries be borne in mind—viz., that at bottom they recognised only Adad, "The One God" (see *ante*, pp. 14, 15, 16, Note). Adad being Triune, this left room, when the Babylonian Mystery of Iniquity took shape, for three different FORMS of divinity—the father, the mother, and the son; but all the multiform divinities with which the Pagan world abounded, whatever diversities there were among them, were resolved substantially into so many manifestations of one or other of these divine persons, or rather of two, for the first person was generally in the background. We have distinct evidence that this was the case. Apuleius tells us (vol. i. pp. 995, 996), that when he was initiated, the goddess Isis revealed herself to him as "The first of the celestials, and the uniform manifestation of the gods and goddesses . . . . WHOSE ONE SOLE DIVINITY the whole orb of the earth venerated, and under a manifold form, with different rites, and under a variety of appellations;" and going over many of these appellations, she declares herself to be at once "Pessinuntica, the mother of the gods [*i.e.*, Cybele], and Paphian Venus" (*Ibid.* p. 997). Now, as this was the case in the later ages of the Mysteries, so it must have been the case from the very beginning; because they SET OUT, and necessarily set out, with the doctrine of the UNITY of the Godhead. This, of course, would give rise to no little absurdity and inconsistency in the very nature of the case. Both Wilkinson and Bunsen, to get rid of the inconsistencies they have met with in the Egyptian system, have found it necessary to have recourse to substantially the same explanation as I have done. Thus we find Wilkinson saying: "I have stated that Amun-re and other gods took the form of different deities, which, though it appears at first sight to present some difficulty, may readily be accounted for when we consider that each of those whose figures or emblems were adopted, was only an EMANATION, or deified attribute of the SAME GREAT BEING to whom they ascribed various characters, according to the several offices he was supposed to perform" (WILKINSON, vol. iv. p. 245). The statement of Bunsen is to the same effect, and it is this: "Upon these premises, we think ourselves justified in concluding that the two series of gods were originally identical, and that, in the GREAT PAIR of gods, all these attributes were concentrated, from the development of which, in various personifications, that mythological system sprung up which we have been already considering" (BUNSEN, vol. i. p. 418).

The bearing of all this upon the question of the identification of Cybele and Astarte, or Venus, is important. Fundamentally, there was but one goddess—the Holy Spirit, represented as female, when the distinction of sex was wickedly ascribed to the Godhead, through a perversion of the great Scripture idea, that all the children of God are at once begotten of the Father, and born of the Spirit; and under this idea, the Spirit of God, as Mother, was represented under the form of a dove, in memory of the fact that that Spirit, at the creation, "fluttered"—for so, as I have observed, is the exact meaning of the term in Gen. i. 2—"on the face of the waters." This goddess, then, was called *Ops*, "the flutterer," or *Juno*, "The Dove," or *Khubelé*, "The binder with cords," which last title had reference to "the bands of love, the cords of a man" (called in Hosea xi. 4, "*Khubeli Adam*"), with which not only does God continually, by His providential goodness, *draw* men unto Himself, but with which our first parent Adam, through the Spirit's indwelling, while the covenant of Eden was unbroken, was sweetly bound to God. This theme is minutely dwelt on in Pagan story, and the evidence is very abundant; but I cannot enter

Fig. 61.

upon it here. Let this only be noticed, however, that the Romans joined the two terms Juno and Khubele—or, as it is commonly pronounced, Cybele—together; and on certain occasions invoked their supreme goddess, under the name of Juno Covella—(see STANLEY'S *Philosophy*, p. 1055)—that is, "The dove that binds with cords." In STATIUS (lib. v. *Sylv.* 1, v. 222, *apud* BRYANT, vol. iii. p. 325), the name of the great goddess occurs as Cybēle—

"Italo gemitus Almone Cybēle
Ponit, et Idæos jam non reminiscitur amnes."

If the reader looks, in Layard, at the triune emblem of the supreme Assyrian divinity, he will see this very idea visibly embodied. There the wings and tail of the dove have *two bands* associated with them instead of feet (LAYARD'S *Nineveh and its Remains*, vol. ii. p. 418; see also accompanying woodcut (Fig. 61), from BRYANT, vol. ii. p. 216; and KITTO'S *Bib. Cyclop.*, vol. i. p. 425).

In reference to events *after* the Fall, Cybele got a new idea attached to her name. Khubel signifies not only to "bind with cords," but also "to travail in birth;" and therefore Cybele appeared as the "Mother of the gods," by whom all God's children must be born anew or regenerated. But, for this purpose, it was held indispensable that there should be a union in the first instance with Rheia, "The gazer," the *human* "mother of gods and men," that the ruin she had introduced might be remedied. Hence the identification of Cybele and Rheia, which in all the Pantheons are declared to be only two different names of the same goddess (see LEMPRIERE'S *Classical Dictionary, sub voce*), though, as we have seen, these goddesses were in reality entirely distinct. This same principle was applied to all the other deified mothers. They were deified *only* through the supposed miraculous identification with them of Juno or Cybele—in other words, of the Holy Spirit of God. Each of these mothers had her own legend, and had special worship suited thereto; but, as in all cases, she was held to be an incarnation of the one Spirit of God, as the great Mother of all, the attributes of that one Spirit were always pre-supposed as belonging to her. This, then, was the case with the goddess recognised as Astarte or Venus, as well as with Rhea. Though there were points of difference between Cybele or Rhea, and Astarte or Mylitta, the Assyrian Venus, Layard shows that there were also distinct points of contact between them. Cybele or Rhea was remarkable for her turreted crown. Mylitta, or Astarte, was represented with a similar crown (LAYARD'S *Nineveh*, vol. ii. p. 456). Cybele, or Rhea, was drawn by lions; Mylitta, or Astarte, was represented as standing on a lion (*Ibid.*). The worship of Mylitta, or Astarte, was a mass of moral pollution (HERODOT., lib. i. cap. 199, p. 92). The worship of Cybele, under the name of Terra, was the same (AUGUSTINE, *De Civitate*, lib. vi. cap. 8, tom. ix., p. 203).

The first deified woman was no doubt Semiramis, as the first deified man was her husband. But it is evident that it was some time after the Mysteries began that this deification took place; for it was not till after Semiramis was dead that she was exalted to divinity, and worshipped under the form of a dove. When, however, the Mysteries were originally concocted, the deeds of Eve, who, through her connection with the serpent, brought forth *death*, must necessarily have occupied a place; for the Mystery of sin and death lies at the very foundation of all religion, and in the age of Semiramis and Nimrod, and Shem and Ham, all men must have been well acquainted with the facts of the Fall. At first the sin of Eve may have been admitted in all its sinfulness (otherwise men generally would have been shocked, especially when the general conscience had been quickened through the zeal of Shem); but when a woman was to be deified, the shape that the mystic story came to assume shows that that sin was softened, yea, that it changed its very character, and that by a perversion of the name given to Eve, as "the mother of all living ones," that is, all the regenerate (see Note I), she was glorified as the authoress of spiritual life, and, under the very name Rhea, was recognised as the mother of the gods. Now, those who had the working of the Mystery of Iniquity did not find it very difficult to show that this name Rhea, originally appropriate to the mother of *mankind*, was hardly less appropriate for her who was the *actual* mother of the *gods*, that is, of all the deified mortals. Rhea, in the active sense, signifies "the Gazing woman," but in the passive it signifies "The woman gazed at," that is, "The beauty,"* and thus, under one and the same term, the mother of mankind and the mother of the Pagan gods, that is, Semiramis, were amalgamated; insomuch, that now, as is well known, Rhea, is currently recognised as the "Mother of gods and *men*" (HESIOD, *Theogon.*, v. 453, p. 36). It is not wonderful, therefore, that the name Rhea is found applied to her, who, by the Assyrians, was worshipped in the very character of Astarte or Venus.

* In Esther ii. 9, we find the plural of Rhea evidently used in the sense of "beautiful." As applied to the "maidens" given to Esther, the Vulgate renders it "*speciosissimas*," and Parkhurst, *sub voce*, does the same.

NOTE H, p. 77.

The Virgin Mother of Paganism.

"Almost all the Tartar princes," says Salverté (*Des Sciences Occultes*, Appendix, Note A, sect. xii. p. 490), "trace their genealogy to a celestial virgin, impregnated by a sunbeam, or some equally miraculous means." In India, the mother of Surya, the sun-god, who was *born* to destroy the enemies of the gods (see *ante*, p. 96), is said to have become pregnant in this way, a beam of the sun having entered her womb, in consequence of which she brought forth the sun-god. Now the knowledge of this widely diffused myth casts light on the *secret* meaning of the name Aurora, given to the wife of Orion, to whose marriage with that "mighty hunter" Homer refers (*Odyssey*, lib. v. ll. 120, 121). While the name Aur-ora, in the physical sense, signifies also "pregnant with light;" and from "ohra," "to conceive" or be "pregnant," we have in Greek, the word 'οαρ for a wife. As Orion, according to Persian accounts, was Nimrod; and Nimrod, under the name of Ninus, was worshipped as the *son* of his wife, when he came to be deified as the sun-god, that name Aurora, as applied to his wife, is evidently intended to convey the very same idea as prevails in Tartary and India. These myths of the Tartars and Hindoos clearly prove that the Pagan idea of the miraculous conception had not come from any intermixture of Christianity with their superstition, but directly from the promise of "the seed of the woman." But how, it may be asked, could the idea of being pregnant with a sunbeam arise? There is reason to believe that it came from one of the natural names of the sun. From the Chaldean *zhr*, "to shine," comes, in the participle active, *zuhro* or *zuhré*, "the Shiner;" and hence, no doubt, from *zuhro*, "the Shiner," under the prompting of a designing priesthood, men would slide into the idea of *zuro*, "the seed,"—"the Shiner" and "the seed," according to the genius of Paganism, being thus identified. This was manifestly the case in Persia, where the sun was the great divinity; for the "Persians," says Maurice, "called God Suré" (*Antiquities*, vol. v. p. 22).

NOTE I, p. 77.

The Goddess Mother as a Habitation.

What could ever have induced mankind to think of calling the great Goddess-mother, or mother of gods and *men*, a House or Habitation? The answer is evidently to be found in a statement made in Gen. ii. 21, in regard to the formation of the mother of *mankind*: "And the Lord caused a deep sleep to fall upon Adam, and he slept, and he took one of his ribs, and closed up the flesh instead thereof. And the *rib* which the Lord God had taken from man, made (margin, literally BUILDED) he into a woman." That this history of the rib was well known to the Babylonians, is manifest from one of the names given to their primeval goddess, as found in Berosus (lib. i. p. 50). That name is Thalatth. But Thalatth is just the Chaldean form of the Hebrew Tzalaa, in the feminine,—the very word used in Genesis for the rib, of which Eve was formed; and the other name which Berosus couples with Thalatth, does much to confirm this; for that name, which is Omorka,* just signifies "The Mother of the world." When we have thus deciphered the meaning of the name Thalatth, as applied to

* From "*Am*," "mother," and "*arka*," "earth." The first letter *aleph* in both of these words is often pronounced as *o*. Thus the pronunciation of *a* in Am, "mother," is seen in the the Greek ωμος, a "shoulder." Am, "mother," comes from *am*, "to support," and from *am*, pronounced *om*, comes ωμος, the shoulder that *bears* burdens. Hence also the name Oma, as one of the names of Bona Dea. Oma is evidently the "Mother." See Note K.

the "mother of the world," that leads us at once to the understanding, of the name Thalasius,* applied by the Romans to the god of marriage, the origin of which name has hitherto been sought in vain. Thalatthi signifies "belonging to the rib," and, with the Roman termination, becomes Thalatthius or "Thalasius, the man of the rib." And what name more appropriate than this for Adam, as the god of marriage, who, when the rib was brought to him, said, "This is now bone of my bones, and flesh of my flesh: she shall be called Woman, because she was taken out of man." At first, when Thalatth, the rib, was *builded* into a woman, that "woman" was, in a very important sense, the "Habitation" or "Temple of God;" and had not the Fall intervened, all her children would, in consequence of mere natural generation, have been the children of God. The entrance of sin into the world subverted the original constitution of things. Still, when the promise of a Saviour was given and embraced, the renewed indwelling of the Holy Spirit was given too, *not* that *she* might thereby have any power in herself to bring forth children unto God, but *only* that she might duly act the part of a mother to a spiritually living offspring—to those whom God of His free grace should quicken, and bring from death unto life. Now, Paganism willingly overlooked all this; and taught, as soon as its votaries were prepared for receiving it, that this renewed indwelling of the Spirit of God in the woman, was identification, and so it deified her. Then Rhea, "the gazer," the mother of mankind, was identified with Cybele "the binder with cords," or Juno, "the Dove," that is, the Holy Spirit. Then, in the blasphemous Pagan sense, she became Athor, "the Habitation of God," or Sacca, or Sacta, "the tabernacle" or "temple," in whom dwelt "all the fulness of the Godhead bodily." Thus she became Heva, "The Living One;" not in the sense in which Adam gave that name to his wife after the Fall, when the hope of life out of the midst of death was so unexpectedly presented to her as well as to himself; but in the sense of the *communicator* of spiritual and eternal life to men; for Rhea was called the "*fountain* of the blessed ones."† The agency, then, of this deified woman was held to be indispensable for the begetting of spiritual children to God, in this, as it was admitted, fallen world. Looked at from this point of view, the meaning of the name given to the Babylonian goddess in 2 Kings xvii. 30, will be at once apparent. The name Succoth-benoth has very frequently been supposed to be a plural word, and to refer to booths or tabernacles used in Babylon for infamous purposes. But, as observed by Clericus (lib. i. *De Chaldæis*, sect. 2, cap. 37), who refers to the Rabbins as being of the same opinion, the context clearly shows that the name must be the name of an idol: (ver. 29, 30), "Howbeit every nation *made gods* of their own, and put them in the houses of the high places which the Samaritans had made, every nation in their cities wherein they dwelt. And the men of Babylon made Succoth-benoth." It is here evidently an idol that is spoken of; and as the name is feminine, that idol must have been the image of a goddess. Taken in this sense, then, and in the light of the Chaldean system as now unfolded, the meaning of "Succoth-benoth," as applied to the Babylonian goddess, is just "The tabernacle of child-bearing."‡ When the Babylonian system was developed, Eve was represented as the first that occupied this place, and the very name Benoth, that signifies "child-bearing," explains also how it came about that the Woman, who, as Hestia or Vesta, was herself called the "Habitation," got the credit of "having *invented the art of building houses*" (SMITH, *sub voce* "Hestia").

* CATULLUS, *Epithalamium*, p. 98.

† *Orphic Fragment*, in BRYANT, vol. iii. p. 238.

‡ That is, the Habitation in which the Spirit of God dwelt, for the purpose of begetting spiritual children.

Benah, the verb, from which Benoth comes, signifies at once to "bring forth children" and "to build houses;" the bringing forth of children being metaphorically regarded as the "building up of the house," that is, of the family.

While the Pagan system, so far as a Goddess-mother was concerned, was founded on this *identification* of the Celestial and Terrestrial mothers of the "blessed" immortals, each of these two divinities was still celebrated as having, in some sense, a distinct individuality; and, in consequence, all the different incarnations of the Saviour-seed were represented as born of two mothers. It is well-known that Bimater, or Two-mothered, is one of the distinguishing epithets applied to Bacchus. Ovid makes the reason of the application of this epithet to him to have arisen from the myth, that when in embryo, he was rescued from the flames in which his mother died, was sewed up into Jupiter's thigh, and then brought forth at the due time. Without inquiring into the secret meaning of this, it is sufficient to state that Bacchus had two goddess-mothers; for, not only was he conceived by Semele, but he was brought into the world by the goddess Ippa (PROCLUS in *Timæum*, lib. ii. sect. 124, pp. 292, 293). This is the very same thing, no doubt, that is referred to, when it is said that after his mother Semele's death, his aunt Ino acted the part of a mother and nurse unto him. The same thing appears in the mythology of Egypt, for there we read that Osiris, under the form of Anubis, having been brought forth by Nepthys, was adopted and brought up by the goddess Isis as her own son. In consequence of this, the favourite Triad came everywhere to be the two mothers and the son. In WILKINSON, vol. vi., plate 35, the reader will find a divine Triad, consisting of Isis and Nepthys, and the child of Horus between them. In Babylon, the statement of Diodorus (lib. ii. p. 69) shows that the Triad there at one period was two goddesses and the son—Hera, Rhea, and Zeus; and in the Capitol at Rome, in like manner, the Triad was Juno, Minerva, and Jupiter; while, when Jupiter was worshipped by the Roman matrons as "Jupiter puer," or "Jupiter the child," it was in company with Juno and the goddess Fortuna (CICERO, *De Divinatione*, lib. ii. cap. 41, vol. iii. p. 77). This kind of divine Triad seems to be traced up to very ancient times among the Romans; for it is stated both by Dionysius Halicarnassius and by Livy, that soon after the expulsion of the Tarquins, there was at Rome a temple in which were worshipped Ceres, Liber, and Libera (DION. HALICARN., vol. i. pp. 25, 26; and LIVY, vol. i. p. 233).

NOTE J, p. 110.

The Meaning of the name Astarte.

That Semiramis, under the name of Astarte, was worshipped not only as an incarnation of the Spirit of God, but as the mother of mankind, we have very clear and satisfactory evidence. There is no doubt that "the Syrian goddess" was Astarte (LAYARD'S *Nineveh and its Remains*, vol. ii. p. 456). Now, the Assyrian goddess, or Astarte, is identified with Semiramis by Athenagoras (*Legatio*, vol. ii. p. 179), and by Lucian (*De Dea Syria*, vol. iii. p. 382). These testimonies in regard to Astarte, or the Syrian goddess, being, in one aspect, Semiramis, are quite decisive. 1. The name Astarte, as applied to *her*, has reference to her as being Rhea, or Cybele, the tower-bearing goddess, the first, as Ovid says (*Opera*, vol. iii., *Fasti*, lib. iv. ll. 219, 220), that "made (towers) in cities;" for we find from Layard, at the page above referred to, that in the Syrian temple of Hierapolis, "she [Dea Syria or Astarte] was represented standing on a lion *crowned with towers*." Now, no name could more exactly picture forth the character of Semiramis, as queen of Babylon than the name of "Asht-tart," for that just means "The woman that made towers." It is admitted on all hands that the last syllable "tart" comes from the Hebrew verb "Tr." It has been always taken for granted, however, that "Tr" signifies only "to *go* round." But we have evidence that, in nouns derived from it, it also signifies "to *be* round," "to surround," or "encompass." In the masculine, we find "Tor" used for "a border or row of jewels round the head" (see PARKHURST, *sub voce* No. ii., and also GESENIUS). And in the feminine, as given in Hesychius (*Lexicon*, p. 925), we find the meaning much more decisively brought out: Τυρις ὁ περιβολος του τειχους. Turis is just the Greek form of Turit, the final *t*, according to the genius of the Greek language, being converted into *s*. Ash-turit, then, which is obviously the same as the Hebrew "Ashtoreth," is just "The woman that made the *encompassing wall.*" Considering how commonly the glory of that achievement, as regards Babylon, was given to Semiramis, not only by Ovid (*Opera Metam.*, lib. iv. fab. 4, l. 58, vol. ii. p. 177), but by Justin, Dionysius, Afer, and others, both the name and mural crown on the head of that goddess were surely very appropriate. In confirmation of this interpretation of the meaning of the name Astarte, I may adduce an epithet applied to the Greek Diana, who at Ephesus bore a turreted crown on her head, and was identified with Semiramis, which is not a little striking. It is contained in the following extract from Livy (lib. xliv. cap. 44, vol. vi. pp. 57, 58): "When the news of the battle [near Pydna] reached Amphipolis, the matrons ran together to the temple of Diana, whom they style Tauropolos, to implore her aid." Tauropolos, from Tor, "a tower," or "surrounding fortification," and Pol, "to make," plainly means the "tower-maker," or "maker of surrounding fortifications;" and to her as the goddess of fortifications, they would naturally apply when they dreaded an attack upon their city.

Semiramis, being deified as Astarte, came to be raised to the highest honours; and her change into a dove, as has been already shown (p. 79, *ante*), was evidently intended, when the distinction of sex had been blasphemously attributed to the Godhead, to identify her, under the name of the *Mother* of the gods, with that Divine Spirit, without whose agency no one can be born a child of God, and whose emblem, in the symbolical language of Scripture, was the Dove, as that of the Messiah was the Lamb. Since the Spirit of God is the source of all wisdom, natural as well as spiritual, arts and inventions and skill of every kind being attributed to Him (Exod. xxxi. 3, and xxxv. 31), so the Mother of the gods, in whom that Spirit was feigned to be incarnate, was celebrated as the originator of some of the useful arts and sciences (DIODORUS SICULUS, lib. iii. p. 134). Hence, also, the character attributed to the Grecian Minerva, whose name Athena, as we have seen reason to conclude, is only a synonym for Beltis, the well-known name of the Assyrian goddess (see *ante*, pp. 20, 21, Note). Athena, the Minerva of Athens, is universally known as the "goddess of wisdom," the inventress of arts and sciences. 2. The name Astarte signifies also the "Maker of *investigations*;" and in this respect was applicable to Cybele or Semiramis, as symbolised by the Dove. That this is one of the meanings of the name Astarte may be seen from comparing it with the cognate names Asterie and Astræa (in Greek Astraia), which are formed by taking the last member of the compound word in the masculine, instead of the feminine, Te i, or Tri (the latter being pronounced Trai or Træ), being the same in sense as Tart. Now, Asterie was the wife of Perseus, the Assyrian (HERODOTUS, lib. vi. p. 400), and who was the founder of Mysteries (BRYANT, vol. iii. pp. 267, 268). As Asterie was further represented as the daughter of Bel, this implies a position similar to that of Semiramis. Astræa, again, was the goddess of justice, who is identified with the heavenly virgin Themis, the name Themis signifying "the perfect one," who gave oracles (OVID, *Metam.*, lib. i. fab. 7, vol. ii. p. 30), and who, having lived on earth before the Flood, forsook it just before that catastrophe came on (*Ibid.* Note). Themis and Astræa are sometimes distinguished and sometimes identified; but both have the same character as goddesses of *justice* (see *Gradus ad Parnassum, sub voce* "Justitia"). The explanation of the discrepancy obviously is, that the Spirit has sometimes been viewed as incarnate, and sometimes not. When incarnate, Astræa is daughter of Themis. What name could more exactly agree with the character of a goddess of justice, than Ash-trai-a, "The maker of *investigations*," and what name could more appropriately shadow forth one of the characters of that Divine Spirit, who "*searcheth* all thing, yea, the deep things of God"? As Astræa, or Themis, was "Fatidica Themis," "Themis the prophetic," this also was another characteristic of the Spirit; for whence can any true oracle, or prophetic inspiration, come, but from the inspiring Spirit of God? Then, lastly, what can more exactly agree with the Divine statement in Genesis in regard to the Spirit of God, than the statement of Ovid, that Astræa was the last of the celestials who remained on earth, and that her forsaking it was the signal for the downpouring of the destroying deluge? The announcement of the coming Flood is in Scripture ushered in with these words: (Gen. vi. 3), "And the Lord said, My Spirit shall not always strive with man, for that he also is flesh: yet his days shall be an hundred and twenty years." All these 120 years, the Spirit was striving; when they came to an end, the Spirit strove no longer, forsook the earth, and left the world to its fate. But though the Spirit of God forsook the earth, it did not forsake the family of righteous Noah. It entered with the patriarch into the ark; and when that patriarch came forth from his long imprisonment, it came forth along with him. Thus the Pagans had a historical foundation for their myth of the dove resting on the symbol of the ark in the Babylonian waters, and the Syrian goddess, or Astarte—the same as Astræa—coming forth from it. Semiramis, then, as Astarte, worshipped as the dove, was regarded as the incarnation of the Spirit of God. 3. As Baal, Lord of Heaven, had his visible emblem, the *sun*, so she, as Beltis, Queen of Heaven, must have hers also—the *moon*, which in another sense was Asht-tart-e, "The maker of *revolutions*;" for there is no doubt that Tart very commonly signifies "going round." But, 4th, the whole system must be dovetailed together. As the mother of the *gods* was equally the mother of *mankind*, Semiramis, or Astarte, must also be identified with Eve; and the name Rhea, which, according to the *Paschal Chronicle*, vol. i. p. 65, was given to her, sufficiently proves her identification with Eve. As applied to the common mother of the human race, the name Astarte is singularly appropriate; for, as she was *Idaia mater*, "The mother of knowledge," the question is, "How did she come by that knowledge?" To this the answer can only be: "By the fatal *investigations* she made." It was a tremendous experiment she made, when, in opposition to the Divine command, and in spite of the threatened penalty, she ventured to "*search*" into that forbidden knowledge which her Maker in His goodness had kept from her. Thus she took the lead in that unhappy course of which the Scripture speaks—"God made man upright, but they have SOUGHT out many inventions" (Eccles. vii. 29). Now Semiramis, deified as the Dove, was Astarte in the most gracious and benignant form. Lucius Ampelius (in *Libro ad Macrinum apud* BRYANT, vol. iii. p. 161) calls her "*Deam benignam et misericordem hominibus ad vitam bonam*," "The goddess benignant and merciful to men" (bringing them) "to a good and happy life." In reference to this benignity of her character, both the titles, Aphroditè and Mylitta are evidently attributed to her. The first I have elsewhere explained as "The wrath-subduer" (*ante*, p. 158), and the second is in exact accordance with it. Mylitta, or, as it is in Greek, Mulitta, signifies "The Mediatrix." The Hebrew Melitz, which in Chaldee becomes Melitt, is evidently used in Job xxxiii. 23, in the sense of a Mediator; "the messenger, the *interpreter*" (Melitz), who is "gracious" to a man, and saith, "Deliver from going down to the pit: I have found a ransom," being really "The Messenger, the MEDIATOR." Parkhurst takes the word in this sense, and derives it from "Mltz," "to be sweet." Now, the feminine of Melitz is Melitza, from which comes Melissa, a "bee" (the *sweetener*, or producer of *sweetness*), and Melissa, a common name of the priestesses of Cybele, and as we may infer of Cybele, as Astarte, or Queen of Heaven, herself; for, after Porphyry has stated that "the ancients called the priestesses of Demeter, Melissæ," he adds, that they also "called the Moon Melissa" (*De antro Nympharum*, p. 18). We have evidence, further, that goes far to identify this title as a title of Semiramis. Melissa or Melitta (APOLLODORUS, vol. i. lib. ii. p. 110)—for the name is given in both ways —is said to have been the mother of Phoroneus, *the first that reigned*, in whose days the dispersion of mankind occurred, divisions having come in among them, whereas before, all had been in harmony and spoke one language (*Hyginus*, fab. 143, p. 114). There is no other to whom this can be applied but Nimrod; and as Nimrod came to be worshipped as Nin, the son of his own wife, the identification is exact. Melitta, then, the mother of Phoroneus, is the same as Mylitta, the well-known name of the Babylonian Venus; and the name, as being the feminine of Melitz, the Mediator, consequently signifies the *Mediatrix*. Another name also given to the mother of Phoroneus, "the first that reigned," is Archia (LEMPRIERE; see also SMITH, p. 572). Now Archia signifies "*Spiritual*" (from "Rkh," Heb. "Spirit," which in Egyptian also is "Rkh" (BUNSEN, vol. i. p. 516, No. 292); and in Chaldee, with the prosthetic *a* prefixed becomes Arkh).* From the same root also evidently comes the epithet Architis, as applied to the Venus that wept for Adonis.† Venus Architis is the spiritual Venus.‡ Thus, then, the mother-wife of the first king that reigned was known as Archia and Melitta, in other words, as the woman in whom the "Spirit of God" was incarnate; and thus appeared as the "Dea Benigna," "The *Mediatrix*" for sinful mortals. The first form of Astarte, as Eve, brought sin into the world; the second form before the Flood, was *avenging* as the goddess of justice. This form was "Benignant and Merciful." Thus, also, Semiramis, or Astarte, as Venus the goddess of love and beauty, became "The HOPE of the whole world," and men gladly had recourse to the "*mediation*" of one so tolerant of sin.

NOTE K, p. 124.

Oannes and Souro.

The reason for believing that Oannes, that was said to have been the first of the fabulous creatures that came up out of the sea and instructed the Babylonians, was represented as the goat-horned fish, is as follows: First, the name Oannes, as elsewhere shown, is just the Greek form of He-anesh, or "The man," which is a synonym for the name of our first

* The Hebrew Dem, *blood*, in Chaldee becomes Adem; and, in like manner, Rkh becomes Arkh.

† MACROBIUS, *Saturnal.*, lib. i., cap. 21, p. 70, F.

‡ From OUVAROFF (Sect. 6, p. 102, Note) we learn that the mother of the third Bacchus was Aura, and Phaëthon is said by Orpheus to have been the son περιμηκεος ἀερος of the "wide extended air" (LACTANTIUS, lib. i. cap. 5, p. 10). The connection in the sacred language between the wind, the air, and the spirit, sufficiently accounts for these statements, and shows their real meaning.

parent, Adam. Now, Adam can be proved to be the original of Pan, who was also called Inuus (see DYMOCK, *sub voce* "Inuus"), which is just another pronunciation of Anosh without the article, which, in our translation of Gen. v. 7, is made Enos. This name, as universally admitted, is the generic name for *man* after the Fall, as weak and diseased. The *o* in Enos is what is called the *vau*, which sometimes is pronounced *o*, sometimes *u*, and sometimes *v* or *w*. A legitimate pronunciation of Enos, therefore, is just Enūs or Enws, the same in sound as Inuus, the Ancient Roman name of Pan. The name Pan itself signifies "He who turned aside." As the Hebrew word for "uprightness" signifies "walking straight in the way," so every deviation from the *straight line* of duty was *Sin;* Hata, the word for sin, signifying generically "to go aside from the straight line." Pan, it is admitted, was the Head of the Satyrs—that is, "the first of the Hidden Ones," for Satyr and Satur, "the Hidden One," are evidently just the same word; and Adam was the first of mankind that *hid* himself. Pan is said to have loved a nymph called Pitho, or, as it is given in another form, Pitys (SMITH, *sub voce* "Pan"); and what is Pitho or Pitys but just the name of the beguiling woman, who, having been *beguiled* herself, acted the part of a *beguiler* to her husband, and induced him to take the step, in consequence of which he earned the name Pan, "The man that turned aside." Pitho or Pitys evidently come from Peth or Pet, "to beguile," from which verb also the famous serpent Python derived its name. This conclusion in regard to the personal identity of Pan and Pitho is greatly confirmed by the titles given to the wife of Faunus. Faunus, says Smith (*Ibid.*), is "merely another name for Pan."* Now, the wife of Faunus was called Oma, Fauna, and Fatna (*Ibid.*, *sub voce* "Bona Dea"), which names plainly mean "The mother that turned aside, being beguiled."† This beguiled mother is also called indifferently "the sister, wife, or daughter" of her husband; and how this agrees with the relations of Eve to Adam, the reader does not need to be told.

Now, a title of Pan was Capricornus, or "The goat-horned" (DYMOCK, *sub voce* "Pan"), and the origin of this title must be traced to what took place when our first parent became the Head of the Satyrs,—the "first of the Hidden ones." He *fled* to hide himself; and Berkha, "a fugitive," signifies also "a he-goat." Hence the origin of the epithet Capricornus, or "goat-horned," as applied to Pan. But as Capricornus in the sphere is generally represented as the "Goat-fish," if Capricornus represents Pan, or Adam, or Oannes, that shows that it must be Adam, after, through virtue of the metempsychosis, he had passed through the waters of the deluge; the goat, as the symbol of Pan, representing Adam, the *first* father of mankind, combined with the fish, the symbol of Noah, the *second* father of the human race; of both whom Nimrod, as at once Kronos, "the father of the gods," and Souro, "the seed," was a new incarnation. Among the idols of Babylon, as represented in KITTO'S *Illust. Commentary*, vol. iv. p. 31, we find a representation of this very Capricornus, or goat-horned fish; and Berosus tells us ("Berosiana," in BUNSEN, vol. i. p. 708), that the well-known representations of Pan, of which Capricornus is a modification, were found in Babylon in the most ancient times. A great deal more of evidence might be adduced on this subject; but I submit to the reader if the above statement does not sufficiently account for the origin of the remarkable figure in the Zodiac, "The goat-horned fish."

* In Chaldee the same letter that is pronounced P is also pronounced Ph, that is F, therefore Pan is just Faun.

† The name Fatua evidently comes from the same verb as Pitho or Pitys, that is Pet, or Phet. In the active sense we find Fatuus in common use in the well-known expression *Ignis fatuus*. In the passive sense it is seen in the phrase "A fatuous person."

NOTE L, p. 133.

The Identity of the Scandinavian Odin and Adon of Babylon.

1. Nimrod, or Adon, or Adonis, of Babylon, was the great war-god. Odin, as is well known, was the same. 2. Nimrod, in the character of Bacchus, was regarded as the god of wine; Odin is represented as taking no food but wine. For thus we read in the *Edda*: "As to himself he [Odin] stands in no need of food; wine is to him instead of every other aliment, according to what is said in these verses: The illustrious father of armies, with his own hand, fattens his two wolves; but the victorious Odin takes no other nourishment to himself than what arises from the unintermitted quaffing of wine" (MALLET, 20*th Fable*, vol. ii. p. 106). 3. The name of one of Odin's sons indicates the meaning of Odin's own name. Balder, for whose death such lamentations were made, seems evidently just the Chaldee form of Baal-zer, "The seed of Baal;" for the Hebrew *z*, as is well known, frequently, in the later Chaldee, becomes *d*. Now, Baal and Adon both alike signify "Lord"; and, therefore, if Balder be admitted to be the seed or son of Baal, that is as much as to say that he is the son of Adon; and, consequently, Adon and Odin must be the same. This, of course, puts Odin a step back; makes his son to be the object of lamentation and not himself; but the same was the case also in Egypt; for there Horus the *child* was sometimes represented as torn in pieces, as Osiris had been. Clemens Alexandrinus says (*Cohortatio*, vol. i. p. 30), "they lament an infant torn in pieces by the Titans." The lamentations for Balder are very plainly the counterpart of the lamentations for Adonis; and, of course, if Balder was, as the lamentations prove him to have been, the favourite form of the Scandinavian Messiah, he was Adon, or "Lord," as well as his father. 4. Then, lastly, the name of the other son of Odin, the mighty and warlike Thor, strengthens all the foregoing conclusions. Ninyas, the son of Ninus or Nimrod, on his father's death, when idolatry rose again, was, of course, from the nature of the mystic system, set up as Adon, "the Lord." Now, as Odin had a son called Thor, so the second Assyrian Adon had a son called Thouros (*Cedrenus*, vol. i. p. 29). The name Thouros seems just to be another form of Zoro, or Doro, "the seed;" for Photius tells us that among the Greeks Thoros signified "Seed" (*Lexicon*, pars i. p. 93). The D is often pronounced as Th,—Adon, in the pointed Hebrew, being pronounced Athon.

NOTE M, p. 183.

The Stripping of the Clothes of the Initiated in the Mysteries.

The passage given at the above page from Proclus is differently rendered by different translators. As I have quoted it, it is nearly the same as rendered by Taylor in his translation of Proclus. Taylor departs from the rendering of the Latin translator of the edition of Hamburgi, 1618, in regard to the word rendered "divested of their garments." That translator renders the word, which, in the original, is γυμνιτας, by "velites," or "light armed soldiers." But, on a careful examination of the passage, it will be found that Taylor's version, in regard to the meaning and application of this word, is perfectly correct, and that to interpret it as "light armed soldiers" entirely confounds the sense. In DONNEGAN'S *Greek Lexicon*, γυμνιτης is made synonymous with γυμνης, which in its primary signification is said to mean *naked*. In LIDDELL and SCOTT'S *Lexicon*, γυμνιτης is not given, but γυμνητης; and there γυμνητης is said, when a *noun*, to mean a *light armed soldier*, but when an *adjective*, to signify *naked*. Now, the context shows that γυμνιτας, or γυμνητας, must be used as an *adjective*. Further, the context, before and after, makes it evident that it must mean "stripped" or "divested of garments." The sentence itself states a comparison. I give the words of the comparison from the Latin version already referred to: Et *quemadmodum*. . . . [and then here come in the words I have quoted in the text] *eodem modo* puto et in ipsâ rerum universarum contemplatione rem se habere." Now, in the sentence before, the soul or person who properly gives himself to the contemplation of the universe and God, is said to do so thus: "Contrahens se totam in sui ipsius unionem, et in ipsum centrum universæ vitæ, et *multitudinem et varietatem* omnigenarum in ea comprehensarum facultatem AMOVENS, in ipsam summam ipsorum Entium speculam ascendit." Then, in the passage following the sentence in question, the same idea of the *removing* of everything that may hinder perfect union of soul is represented, "et omnibus OMISSIS atque NEGLECTIS," &c. Here the argument is, that *as* the initiated needed to be stripped naked, to get the full benefits of initiation, *so* the soul needs to *divest* itself of everything that may hinder it from rising to the contemplation of things as they really are.

There is only one other thing to be noticed, and that is the doubt that may arise in regard to the parenthetic words, "as they would say," whether, as they stand in the original, and as they are given by Taylor, they qualify the words preceding, or that follow after. As given in Taylor's translation, the words appear thus: "divested of their garments, as they would say, participate of divine nature." Here it is not clear which clause they must be held to affect. This can be ascertained only from the *usus loquendi*. Now, the *usus loquendi* in Proclus is very decisive in showing that they qualify *what follows*. Thus, in lib. i. cap. 3, p. 6, we find the following, την ἀκροτητα του νου, και (ὡς φασι) το ανθος—"The summit of the soul, and as (they say) the flower;" and again (*Ibid*. cap. 7, p. 16), και παντες (ὡς ειπειν) της ενθεου σοφιας μετειληφασι—"and all (so to speak) have partaken of the inspired wisdom." From these passages the usage of Proclus is clear, and, therefore, while keeping the *words* of Taylor's translation, I have arranged the last clause so as to bring out more clearly the real meaning of the original author.

NOTE N, p. 228.

Zoroaster, the Head of the Fire-Worshippers.

That Zoroaster was head of the fire-worshippers, the following, among other evidence, may prove. Not to mention that the name Zoroaster is almost a synonym for a fire-worshipper, the testimony of Plutarch is of weight: "Plutarchus agnoscit Zoroastrem apud Chaldæos Magos instituisse, *ad quorum imitationem* Persæ etiam sus habuerunt.* Arabica quoque Historia (ab Erpenio edita) tradit Zaradussit non *primum instituisse*, sed reformasse religionem Persarum et Magorum, qui divisi erant in plures sectas" (CLERICUS, lib. i., *De Chaldæis*, sect. i. cap. 2, vol. ii. p. 195); "Plutarch acknowledges that Zoroaster among the Chaldeans instituted the Magi, *in imitation of whom* the Persians also had their (Magi). The Arabian History also (edited by Erpenius) relates that Zaradussit, or Zerdusht, did not for the first time institute, but (only) reform the religion

* The great antiquity of the institution of the Magi is proved from the statement of Aristotle already referred to, as preserved in Theopompus, which makes them to have been "more ancient than the Egyptians," whose antiquity is well known.—(*Theopompi Fragmenta* in MÜLLER, vol. i. p. 280.)

of the Persians and Magi, who had been divided into many sects." The testimony of Agathias is to the same effect. He gives it as his opinion that the worship of fire came from the Chaldeans to the Persians, lib. ii. cap. 25, pp. 118, 119. That the Magi among the Persians were the guardians of "the sacred and eternal fire" may be assumed from Curtius (lib. iii. cap. 3, pp. 41, 42), who says that fire was carried before them "on silver altars;" from the statement of Strabo (*Geograph.*, lib. xv. p. 696), that "the Magi kept upon the altar a quantity of ashes and an immortal fire," and of Herodotus (lib. i. p. 63), that "without them, no sacrifice could be offered." The fire-worship was an essential part of the system of the Persian Magi (WILSON, *Parsee Religion*, pp. 228-235). This fire-worship the Persian Magi did not pretend to have invented; but their popular story carried the origin of it up to the days of Hoshang, the father of Tahmurs, who founded Babylon (WILSON, pp. 202, 203, and 579)—*i.e.*, the time of Nimrod. In confirmation of this, we have seen that a fragment of Apollodorus (Müller, 68) makes Ninus the head of the fire-worshippers. Layard, quoting this fragment, supposes Ninus to be different from Zoroaster (*Nineveh and its Remains*, vol. ii. p. 443, Note); but it can be proved, that though many others bore the name of Zoroaster, the lines of evidence all converge, so as to demonstrate that Ninus and Nimrod and Zoroaster were one. The legends of Zoroaster show that he was known not only as a Magus, but as a Warrior (ARNOBIUS, lib. i. p. 327). Plato says that Eros Armenius (whom CLERICUS, *De Chaldæis*, states, vol. ii. p. 195, to have been the same as the fourth Zoroaster) died and rose again after ten days, having been killed in battle; and that what he pretended to have learned in Hades, he communicated to men in his new life (PLATO, *De Republica*, lib. x. vol. ii. p. 614). We have seen the death of Nimrod, the original Zoroaster, was not that of a warrior slain in battle; but yet this legend of the warrior Zoroaster is entirely in favour of the supposition that the original Zoroaster, the original Head of the Magi, was not a priest merely, but a warrior-king. Everywhere are the Zoroastrians, or fire-worshippers, called Guebres or Gabrs. Now, Gen. x. 8 proves that Nimrod was the *first* of the "Gabrs."

As Zoroaster was head of the fire-worshippers, so Tammuz was evidently the same. We have seen evidence already that sufficiently proves the identity of Tammuz and Nimrod; but a few words may still more decisively prove it, and cast further light on the primitive fire-worship. 1. In the first place, Tammuz and Adonis are proved to be the same divinity. Jerome, who lived in Palestine when the rites of Tammuz were observed, up to the very time when he wrote, expressly identifies Tammuz and Adonis (vol. ii. p. 353), in his *Commentary on Ezekiel*, viii. 14, where the Jewish women are represented as weeping for Tammuz; and the testimony of Jerome on this subject is universally admitted. Then the mode in which the rites of Tammuz or Adonis were celebrated in Syria was essentially the same as the rites of Osiris. The statement of Lucian (*De Dea Syria*, vol. iii. p. 454) strikingly shows this, and Bunsen (vol. i. p. 443) distinctly admits it. The identity of Osiris and Nimrod, has been largely proved in the body of this work. When, therefore, Tammuz or Adonis is identified with Osiris, the identification of Tammuz with Nimrod follows of course. And then this entirely agrees with the language of Bion, in his *Lament for Adonis*, where he represents Venus as going in a frenzy of grief, like a Bacchant, after the death of Adonis, through the woods and valleys, and "calling upon her Assyrian husband" (BION, *Idyll*, Id. i. v. 24, in *Poetæ Minores Græci*, p. 304). It equally agrees with the statement of Maimonides, that when Tammuz was put to death, the grand scene of weeping for that death was in the temple of Babylon (see *ante*, p. 62). 2. Now, if Tammuz was Nimrod, the examination of the meaning of the name confirms the connection of Nimrod with the first fire-worship. After what has already been advanced, there needs no argument to show that, as the Chaldeans were the *first* who introduced the name and power of kings (SYNCELLUS, vol. i. p. 169), and as Nimrod was unquestionably the first of these kings, and the first, consequently, that bore the title of Moloch, or king, so it was in honour of him that the "children were made to pass through the fire to Moloch." But the intention of that passing through the fire was undoubtedly to purify. The name Tammuz has evidently reference to this, for it signifies "to perfect," that is, "to purify"* "by fire;" and if Nimrod was, as the *Paschal Chronicle* (vol. i. pp. 50, 51), and the general voice of antiquity, represent him to have been, the orginiator of fire-worship, this name very exactly expresses his character in that respect. It is evident, however, from the Zoroastrian verse, elsewhere quoted (*ante*, p. 245), that fire itself was worshipped as Tammuz, for *it* is called the "Father that perfected all things." In one aspect this represented fire as the Creative god; but in another, there can be no doubt that it had reference to the "perfecting" of men by "purifying" them. And especially it perfected those whom it consumed. This was the very idea that, from time immemorial till very recently, led so many widows in India to immolate themselves on the funeral piles of their husbands, the woman who thus burned herself being counted blessed, because she became *Suttee*†—*i.e.*, "Pure by burning." And this also, no doubt, reconciled the parents who actually sacrificed their children to Moloch, to the cruel sacrifice, the belief being cherished that the fire that consumed them also "*perfected*" them, and made them meet for eternal happiness. As both the passing *through* the fire, and the burning *in* the fire, were essential rites in the worship of Moloch or Nimrod, this is an argument that Nimrod was Tammuz. As the priest and representative of the perfecting or purifying fire, it was he that carried on the work of perfecting or purifying by fire, and so he was called by its name.

When we turn to the legends of India, we find evidence to the very same effect as that which we have seen with regard to Zoroaster and Tammuz as head of the fire-worshippers. The fifth head of Brahma, that was cut off for inflicting distress on the three worlds, by the "effulgence of its dazzling beams," referred to in the text of this work, identifies itself with Nimrod. The fact that that fifth head was represented as having read the Vedas, or sacred books produced by the other four heads, shows, I think, a succession.‡ Now, coming down from Noah, what would that succession

* From *tam*, "to perfect," and *muz*, "to burn." To be "pure in heart" in Scripture is just the same as to be "perfect in heart." The well-known name Deucalion, as connected with the flood, seems to be a correlative term of the water-worshippers. Dukh-kaleh signifies "to purify by washing," from Dukh, "to wash" (CLAVIS STOCKII, p. 223), and Khaleh, "to complete," or "perfect." The noun from the latter verb, found in 2 Chron. iv. 21, shows that the root means "to purify," "*perfect* gold" being in the Septuagint justly rendered "*pure* gold." There is a name sometimes applied to the king of the gods that has some bearing on this subject. That name is "Akmōn." What is the meaning of it? It is evidently just the Chaldee form of the Hebrew Khmn, "the burner," which becomes Akmōn in the same way as the Hebrew Dem, "blood," in Chaldee becomes "Adem." Hesychius says that Akmon is Kronos, *sub voce* "Akmōn." In Virgil (*Æneid*, lib. viii. l. 425) we find this name compounded so as to be an exact synonym for Tammuz, Pyracmon being the name of one of the three famous Cyclops whom the poet introduces. We have seen that the original Cyclops were Kronos and his brethren, and deriving the name from "Pur," the Chaldee form of Bur, "to purify," and "Akmōn," it just signifies "The purifying burner."

† MOOR'S *Pantheon*, "Siva," p. 43. The epithet for a woman that burns herself is *spelled* "Sati," but is *pronounced* "Suttee," as above.

‡ The Indian Vedas that now exist do not seem to be of very great antiquity as written documents; but the legend goes much further back than anything that took place in India. The antiquity of writing seems to be very great, but whether or not there was any written religious document in Nimrod's day, a Veda there must have been; for what is the meaning of the word "Veda"? It is evidently just the same as the Anglo-Saxon Edda with the digamma prefixed, and both alike evidently come from "Ed" a "Testimony," a "Religious

be? We have evidence from Berosus, that, in the days of Belus—that is, Nimrod—the custom of making representations like that of two-headed Janus, had begun.* Assume, then, that Noah, as having lived in two worlds, has his two heads. Ham is the third, Cush the fourth, and Nimrod is, of course, the fifth. And this fifth head was cut off for doing the very thing for which Nimrod actually was cut off. I suspect that this Indian myth is the key to open up the meaning of a statement of Plutarch, which, according to the terms of it, as it stands, is visibly absurd. It is as follows: Plutarch (in the fourth book of his *Symposiaca*, Quest. 5, vol. ii. p. 670, B) says that "the Egyptians were of the opinion that darkness was prior to light, and that the latter [viz., light] was produced from *mice*, in the fifth generation, at the time of the *new moon*." In India, we find that "a *new* moon" was produced in a different sense from the ordinary meaning of that term, and that the production of that new moon was not only important in Indian mythology, but evidently agreed in time with the period when the fifth head of Brahma scorched the world with its insufferable splendour. The account of its production runs thus: that the gods and mankind were entirely discontented with the moon which they had got, "*because it gave no light*," and besides the plants were poor and the fruits of no use, and that therefore they churned the White sea [or, as it is commonly expressed, "they churned the ocean"], when all things were mingled—*i.e.*, were thrown into confusion, and that then a new moon, with a new regent, was appointed, which brought in an entirely new system of things (*Asiatic Researches*, vol. ix. p. 98). From MAURICE'S *Indian Antiquities* (vol. ii. sect. 6, pp. 264-266), we learn that at this very time of the churning of the ocean, the earth was set on fire, and a great conflagration was the result. But the name of the moon in India is Soma, or Som (for the final *a* is only a breathing, and the word is found in the name of the famous temple of *Som*naut, which name signifies "Lord of the Moon"), and the moon in India is male. As this transaction is symbolical, the question naturally arises, who could be meant by the moon, or regent of the moon, who was cast off in the fifth generation of the world? The name Som shows at once who he must have been. Som is just the name of Shem; for Shem's name comes from Shom, "to appoint," and is legitimately represented either by the name Som, or Sem, as it is in Greek; and it was precisely to get rid of Shem (either after his father's death, or when the infirmities of old age were coming upon him) as the great instructor of the world, that is, as the great diffuser of spiritual light, that in the fifth generation the world was thrown into confusion and the earth set on fire. The propriety of Shem's being compared to the *moon* will appear if we consider the way in which his father Noah was evidently symbolised. The head of a family is divinely compared to the *sun*, as in the dream of Joseph (Genesis xxxvii. 9), and it may be easily conceived how Noah would, by his posterity in general, be looked up to as occupying the paramount place as the Sun of the world; and accordingly Bryant, Davies, Faber, and others, have agreed in recognising Noah as so symbolised by Paganism. When, however, his younger son—for Shem was younger than Japhet—(Genesis x. 21) was *substituted* for his father, to whom the world had looked up in comparison of the "greater light," Shem would naturally, especially by those who disliked him and rebelled against him, be compared to "the lesser light," or the moon.† Now, the

Record," or "Confession of Faith." Such a "Record" or "Confession," either "oral" or "written," must have existed from the beginning.

* *Berosiana* in BUNSEN, vol. i. p. 708.

† "As to a kingdom, the *Oriental Oneirocritics*, chap. 167, jointly say, that the sun is the symbol of the king, and the moon of the next to him in power." This sentence, extracted from DAUBUZ'S *Symbolical Dictionary* (p. 115), illustrated with judicious notes by my learned

production of light by *mice*, at this period, comes in exactly to confirm this deduction. A mouse in Chaldee is "Aakbar"; and Gheber, or Kheber, in Arabic, Turkish, and some of the other eastern dialects, becomes "Akbar," as in the well-known Moslem saying, "Allar Akbar," "God is Great." So that the whole statement of Plutarch, when stripped of its nonsensical garb, just amounts to this, that light was produced by the Guebres or fire-worshippers, when Nimrod was set up in opposition to Shem, as the representative of Noah, and the great enlightener of the world.

NOTE O, p. 230.

The Story of Phaëthon.

The identity of Phaëthon and Nimrod has much to support it besides the *prima facie* evidence arising from the statement that Phaëthon was an Ethiopian or Cushite, and the resemblance of his fate, in being cast down from heaven while driving the chariot of the sun, as "the child of the Sun," to the casting down of Molk Gheber, whose very name, as the god of fire, identifies him with Nimrod. 1. Phaëthon is said by Apollodorus (vol. i. p. 354) to have been the son of Tithonus; but if the meaning of the name Tithonus be examined, it will be evident that he was Tithonus himself. Tithonus was the husband of Aurora (DYMOCK, *sub voce*). In the physical sense, as we have already seen, Aur-ora signifies "The awakener of the light;" to correspond with this Tithonus signifies "The kindler of light," or "setter on fire."* Now "Phaëthon, the son of Tithonus," is in Chaldee "Phaëthon Bar Tithon." But this also signifies "Phaëthon, the son that set on fire." Assuming, then, the identity of Phaëthon and Tithonus, this goes far to identify Phaëthon with Nimrod; for Homer, as we have seen (*Odyssey*, lib. v. l. 121, p. 127), mentions the marriage of Aurora with Orion, the mighty Hunter, whose identity with Nimrod is established. Then the name of the celebrated son that sprang from the union between Aurora and Tithonus, shows that Tithonus, in his original character, must have been indeed the same as "the mighty hunter" of Scripture, for the name of that son was Memnon (MARTIAL, lib. viii., s. 21, p. 440, and OVID, *Metam.* lib. xiii. l. 517, vol. ii. p. 467), which signifies "The son of the spotted one,"† thereby identifying the father with Nimrod, whose emblem was the spotted leopard's skin. As Ninus or Nimrod was worshipped as the *son* of his own wife, and that wife Aurora, the goddess of the dawn, we see how exact is the reference to Phaëthon, when Isaiah, speaking of the King of Babylon, who was his representative, says, "How art thou fallen from heaven, O Lucifer, son of the morning" (Isa. xiv. 12). The marriage of Orion with Aurora; in other words, his setting up as "The kindler of light," or becoming the "author of fire-worship," is said by Homer to have been the *cause* of his death, he having in consequence perished under the wrath of the gods (*Odyss.* lib. v. l. 124, p. 127). 2. That Phaëthon was currently represented as the son of Aurora, the common story, as related by Ovid, sufficiently proves. While Phaëthon claimed to be the son of Phoebus, or the sun, he was reproached with being only the son of Merops—*i.e.*, of the mortal husband of his mother Clymene (OVID, *Metam.* lib. ii. ll. 179-184, and Note). The story implies that that mother gave herself out to be Aurora, not in the physical sense

friend, the Rev. A. Forbes, London, shows that the conclusion to which I had come before seeing it, in regard to the symbolical meaning of the *moon*, is entirely in harmony with Oriental modes of thinking. For some excellent remarks in regard to Babylon, see the same work, p. 38.

* From Tzet or Tzit, "to kindle," or "set on fire," which in Chaldee becomes Tit, and Thon, "to give."

† From Mem or Mom, "spotted," and Non, "a son."

of that term, but in its mystical sense; as "The woman pregnant with light;" and, consequently, her son was held up as the great "Light-bringer" who was to enlighten the world,—"Lucifer, the son of the morning," who was the pretended enlightener of the *souls* of men.* The name Lucifer, in Isaiah, is the very word from which Eleleus, one of the names of Bacchus, evidently comes. It comes from "Helel," which signifies "to irradiate" or "to bring light," and is equivalent to the name Tithōn. Now we have evidence that Lucifer, the son of Aurora, or the morning, was worshipped in the very same character as Nimrod, when he appeared in his new character as a little child; for there is an inscription extant in these words:—

"Bono Deo
Puero Phosphoro."

(See WILKINSON, vol. iv. p. 410.)

This Phaëthon, or Lucifer, who was cast down, is further proved to be Janus; for Janus is called "Pater Matutinus" (HORACE, *Sat.* ii. 6, 20, p. 674); and the meaning of this name will appear in one of its aspects when the meaning of the name of the *Dea Matuta* is ascertained. Dea Matuta signifies "The kindling or Light-bringing goddess," † and accordingly, by Priscian, she is identified with Aurora: "*Matuta, quæ significat Aurorame*" (PRISCIAN, ii. p. 591, *apud* Sir WILLIAM BETHAM'S *Etruria*, vol. ii. p. 53). Matutinus is evidently just the correlate of Matuta, goddess of the morning; Janus, therefore, as Matutinus, is "Lucifer, son of the morning." But further, Matuta is identified with Ino, after she had plunged into the sea, and had, along with her son Melikerta, been changed into a sea-divinity (*Gradus ad Parnassum, sub voce* "Ino"). Consequently her son Melikerta, "king of the walled city," is the same as Janus Matutinus, or Lucifer, Phaëthon, or Nimrod.

There is still another link by which Melikerta, the sea-divinity, or Janus Matutinus, is identified with the primitive god of the fire-worshippers. The most common name of Ino, or Matuta, after she had passed through the waters, was Leukothoë (OVID, *Metam.* lib. iv. ll. 541, 542). Now, Leukothoë or Leukothea has a double meaning, as it is derived either from "Lukhoth," which signifies "to light," or "set on fire," ‡ or from Lukoth "to glean." In the Maltese medal given (*ante*, p. 160), the reader will see both of these senses exemplified. The ear of corn, at the side of the goddess, which is more commonly held in her hand, while really referring in its hidden meaning to her being the Mother of Bar, "the son," to the uninitiated exhibits her as Spicilega, or "The Gleaner,"—"the popular name," says Hyde (*De Religione, Vet. Pers.*, p. 392), "for the female with the ear of wheat represented in the constellation *Virgo.*" In Bryant (vol. iii. p. 245), Cybele is represented with two or three ears of corn in her hand; for, as there were *three* peculiarly distinguished Bacchuses, there were con-

* The reader will see, from the following extracts from the *Pancarpium Marianum* that the Virgin of Rome is not only called by the name of Aurora, but that that name is evidently applied to her in two distinct sexes specified in the text: "O Aurora Maria, quæ a lumine incepisti, crevisti cum lumine, et nunquam lumine privaris. Sicut lux meridiana clara es. Dominum concepisti, qui dixit, Lux sum mundi" (cap. 41, p. 170). "Numquid *sol* justitiæ Christus, qui dixit. Lux sum mundi, operamini, dum dies est? Numquid hanc solis æterni lampadem aurora Maria consurgens invexit; surgite soporati?" (*Ibid.* p. 171.) These words contain both of the ideas in the name of the Pagan Aurora.

† Matuta comes from the same word as Tithonus—*i.e.*, Tzet, Tzit, or Tzut, which in Chaldee becomes Tet, Tit, or Tut, "to light" or "set on fire." From Tit, "to set on fire," comes the Latin Titio, "a firebrand;" and from Tut, with the formative M prefixed, comes Matuta—just as from Nasseh, "to forget," with the same formative prefixed, comes Manasseh, "forgetting," the name of the eldest son of Joseph (Gen. xli. 51). The root of this verb is commonly given as "Itzt"; but see BAKER'S *Lexicon* (p. 176), where it is also given as "Tzt." It is evidently from this root that the Sanscrit "Suttee" already referred to comes.

‡ In Hebrew, the verb is Lhth, but the Hebrew letter "He" frequently becomes in Chaldee Heth, with the power of *Kh*.

sequently as many "Bars," and she might therefore be represented with one, two, or three ears in her hand. But to revert to the Maltese medal just referred to, the *flames* coming out of the head of Lukothea, the "Gleaner," show that, though she has passed through the waters, she is still Lukhothea, "the Burner," or "Light-giver." And the rays around the mitre of the god on the reverse entirely agree with the character of that god as Eleleus, or Phaëthon—in other words, as "The Shining Bar." Now, this "Shining Bar," as Melikerta, "king of the walled city," occupies the very place of "Ala-Mahozim," whose representative the Pope is elsewhere (*ante*, p. 252) proved to be. But he is equally the Sea-divinity, who in that capacity wears the mitre of Dagon (compare woodcuts, pp. 160 and 216, where different forms of the same Maltese divinity are given). The fish-head mitre which the Pope wears shows that, in this character also, as the "Beast from the sea," he is the unquestionable representative of Melikerta.

NOTE P, p. 238.

The Roman Imperial Standard of the Dragon a Symbol of Fire-worship.

The passage of Ammianus Marcellinus, that speaks of that standard, calls it "purpureum signum draconis" (lib. xvi. cap. 12, p. 145). On this may be raised the question, Has the epithet *purpureum*, as describing the colour of the dragon, any reference to fire? The following extract from Salverté may cast some light upon it: "The dragon figured among the military ensigns of the Assyrians. Cyrus caused it to be adopted by the Persians and Medes. Under the Roman emperors, and under the emperors of Byzantium, each cohort or centuria bore for an ensign a dragon" (*Des Sciences Occultes*, Appendix, Note A, p. 486). There is no doubt that the dragon or serpent standard of the Assyrians and Persians had reference to fire-worship, the worship of fire and the serpent being mixed up together in both these countries (see LAYARD'S *Nineveh and its Remains*, vol. ii. pp. 468, 469). As the Romans, therefore, borrowed these standards evidently from these sources, it is to be presumed that they viewed them in the very same light as those from whom they borrowed them, especially as that light was so exactly in harmony with their own system of fire-worship. The epithet *purpureus* or "purple" does not indeed naturally convey the idea of *fire-colour* to *us*. But it does convey the idea of *red*; and *red* in one shade or another, among idolatrous nations, has almost with one consent been used to represent *fire*. The Egyptians (BUNSEN, vol. i. p. 290), the Hindoos (MOOR'S *Pantheon*, "Brahma," p. 6), the Assyrians (LAYARD'S *Nineveh, &c.*, vol. ii. chap. 3, p. 312, Note), all represented *fire* by *red*. The Persians evidently did the same, for when Quintus Curtius describes the Magi as following "the sacred and eternal fire," he describes the 365 youths, who formed the train of these Magi, as clad "puniceis amiculis," in "scarlet garments" (lib. iii. cap. 3, p. 42), the colour of these garments, no doubt, having reference to the *fire* whose ministers they were. *Puniceus* is equivalent to *purpureus*, for it was in Phenicia that the purpura, or purple-fish, was originally found. The colour derived from that purple-fish was *scarlet* (see KITTO'S *Illustrated Commentary on Exodus* xxxv. 35, vol. i. p. 215), and it is the very name of that Phenician purple-fish, "arguna," that is used in Daniel v. 16 and 19, where it is said that he that should interpret the handwriting on the wall should "be clothed in *scarlet*." The Tyrians had the art of making true purples, as well as scarlet; and there seems no doubt that *purpureus* is frequently used in the ordinary sense attached to our word purple. But the original meaning of the epithet is scarlet; and as bright scarlet colour is a natural colour to represent *fire*, so we have reason to believe that that colour, when used for robes of state among the Tyrians, had special reference to fire; for the Tyrian Hercules, who was regarded as the inventor of purple (BRYANT, vol. iii. p. 485), was regarded as "King of Fire," ανaξ πυρος (NONNUS *Dionysiaca*, lib. xl. l. 369, vol. ii. p. 223). Now, when we find that the *purpura* of Tyre produced the scarlet colour which naturally represented fire, and that *puniceus*, which is equivalent to *purpureus*, is evidently used for scarlet, there is nothing that forbids us to understand *purpureus* in the same sense here, but rather requires it. But even though it were admitted that the tinge was deeper, and *purpureus* meant the true purple, as *red*, of which it is a shade, is the established colour of fire, and as the serpent was the universally acknowledged symbol of fire-worship, the probability is strong that the use of a *red* dragon as the Imperial standard of Rome was designed as an emblem of that system of fire-worship on which the safety of the empire was believed so vitally to hinge.

NOTE Q, p. 268.

The Slaying of the Witnesses.

Is it past, or is it still to come? This is a vital question. The favourite doctrine at this moment is, that it is past centuries ago, and that no such dark night of suffering to the saints of God can ever come again, as happened just before the era of the Reformation. This is the cardinal principle of a work that has just appeared, under the title of *The Great Exodus*, which implies, that however much the truth may be assailed, however much the saints of God may be threatened, however their fears may be aroused, they have no real reason to fear, for that the Red Sea will divide, the tribes of the Lord will pass through dry shod, and all their enemies, like Pharaoh and his host, shall sink in overwhelming ruin. If the doctrine maintained by many of the soberest interpreters of Scripture for a century past, including such names as Brown of Haddington, Thomas Scott, and others, be well founded—viz., that the putting down of the testimony of the witnesses is still to come, this theory must not only be a delusion, but a delusion of most fatal tendency—a delusion that by throwing professors off their guard, and giving them an excuse for taking their ease, rather than standing in the high places of the field, and bearing bold and unflinching testimony for Christ, directly paves the way for that very extinction of the testimony which is predicted. I enter not into any historical disquisition as to the question, whether, as a matter of fact, it was true that the witnesses were slain before Luther appeared. Those who wish to see an historical argument on the subject may see it in the *Red Republic*, which I venture to think has not yet been answered. Neither do I think it worth while particularly to examine the assumption of Dr. Wylie, and I hold it to be a pure and gratuitous assumption, that the 1260 days during which the saints of God in Gospel times were to suffer for righteousness' sake, has any relation whatever, as a half period, to a *whole*, symbolised by the "Seven times" that passed over Nebuchadnezzar when he was suffering and chastened for his pride and blasphemy, as the representative of the "world power."* But to this only I call the reader's attention, that even on the

* The author does not himself make the humiliation of the Babylonian king a type of the humiliation of the Church. How then can he establish any typical relation between the "seven times" in the one case, and the "seven times" in the other? He seems to think it quite enough to establish that relation, if he can find one point of resemblance between Nebuchadnezzar, the humbled despot, and the "world-power" that *oppresses* the Church during the two periods of "seven times" respectively. That one point is the "madness" of the one and the other. It might be asked, Was, then, the "world power" in its right mind *before* "the seven times" began? But waiving that, here is the vital objection to this view:

theory of Dr. Wylie himself, the witnesses of Christ could not possibly have finished their testimony before the Decree of the Immaculate Conception came forth. The theory of Dr. Wylie, and those who take the same general view as he, is, that the "finishing of the testimony" means "completing the elements" of the testimony, bearing a full and complete testimony against the errors of Rome. Dr. Wylie himself admits that "the dogma of the 'Immaculate Conception' [which was given forth only during the last few years] declares Mary truly 'divine,' and places her upon the altars of Rome as practically the sole and supreme object of worship" (*The Great Exodus*, p. 109). This was NEVER done before, and therefore the errors and blasphemies of Rome were not complete until that decree had gone forth, if even then. Now, if the corruption and blasphemy of Rome were "incomplete" up to our own day, and if they have risen to a height which was never witnessed before, as all men instinctively felt and declared, when that decree was issued, how could the testimony of the witnesses be "*complete*" before Luther's day! It is nothing to say that the principle and the germ of this decree were in operation long before. The same thing may be

The madness in the case of Nebuchadnezzar was simply an *affliction;* in the other it was *sin.* The madness of Nebuchadnezzar did not, so far as we know, lead him to oppress a single individual; the madness of the "world-power," according to the theory, is essentially characterised by the oppression of the saints. Where, then, can there be the least analogy between the two cases? The "seven times" of the Babylonian king were seven times of *humiliation*, and *humiliation alone.* The suffering monarch cannot be a type of the suffering Church; and still less can his "seven times" of deepest humiliation, when all power and glory was taken from him, be a type of the "seven times" of the "world-power," when that "world-power" was to concentrate in itself all the glory and grandeur of the earth. This is one fatal objection to this theory. Then let the reader only look at the following sentence from the work under consideration, and compare it with historical fact, and he will see still more how unfounded the theory is: "It follows undeniably," says the author (pp. 184, 185), "that as the Church is to be tyrannised over by the idolatrous power throughout the whole of the seven times, she will be oppressed during the first half of the 'seven times,' by idolatry in the form of Paganism, and during the last half by idolatry in the form of Popery." Now, the first half, or 1260 years, during which the Church was to be oppressed by *Pagan* idolatry, ran out exactly, it is said, in A.D. 530 or 532; when suddenly Justinian changed the scene, and brought the new oppressor on the stage. But I ask where was the "world-power" to be found up to 530, maintaining "idolatry in the form of *Paganism*"? From the time of Gratian at least, who, about 376, formally abolished the worship of the gods, and confiscated their revenues, where was there any such *Pagan* power to persecute? There is certainly a very considerable interval between 376 and 532. The necessities of the theory require that Paganism, and that avowed Paganism, be it observed, shall be persecuting the Church straight away till 532; but for 156 years there was no such thing as a Pagan "world-power" in existence to persecute the Church. "The legs of the lame," says Solomon, "are not equal;" and if the 1260 years of Pagan persecution lack no less than 156 years of the predicted period, surely it must be manifest that the theory halts very much on one side at least. But I ask, do the facts agree with the theory, even in regard to the running out of the second 1260 years in 1792, at the period of the French Revolution? If the 1260 years of Papal oppression terminated then, and if then the Ancient of days came to *begin* the final judgment on the beast, He came also to do something else. This will appear from the language of Daniel: Dan. vii. 21, 22, "I beheld, and the same horn made war with the saints, and prevailed against them; until the Ancient of days came, and judgment was given to the saints of the Most High; *and the time came that the saints possessed the kingdom.*" This language implies that the judgment on the little horn, and the putting of the saints in possession "of the kingdom" are contemporaneous events. Long has the rule of the kingdoms of this world been in the hands of worldly men, that knew not God nor obeyed Him; but now, when He to whom the kingdom belongs comes to inflict judgment on His enemies, He comes also to transfer the rule of the kingdoms of this world from the hands of those who have abused it, into the hands of those that fear God and govern their public conduct by His revealed will. This is evidently the meaning of the Divine statement. Now, on the supposition that 1792 was the predicted period of the coming of the Ancient of days, it follows that, ever since, the principles of God's Word must have been leavening the governments of Europe more and more, and good and holy men, of the spirit of Daniel and Nehemiah, must have been advanced to the high places of power. But has it been so in point of fact? Is there one nation in all Europe that acts on Scriptural principles at this day? Does Britain itself do so? Why, it is notorious that it was just three years after the reign of righteousness, according to this theory, must have commenced that that unprincipled policy began that has left hardly a shred of appearance of respect for the honour of the "Prince of the Kings of the earth" in the public rule of this nation. It was in 1795 that Pitt, and the British Parliament, passed the Act for the erecting of the Roman Catholic College of Maynooth, which formed the beginning of a course that, year by year, has lifted the Man of Sin into a position of power in this land, that threatens, if Divine mercy do not miraculously interfere, to bring us speedily back again under complete thraldom to Antichrist. Yet, according to the theory of *The Great Exodus*, the very opposite of this ought to have been the case.

said of all the leading errors of Rome long before Luther's day. They were all in essence and substance very broadly developed, from near the time when Gregory the Great commanded the image of the Virgin to be carried forth in the processions that supplicated the Most High to remove the pestilence from Rome, when it was committing such havoc among its citizens. But that does in nowise prove that they were "complete," or that the witnesses of Christ could then "finish their testimony" by bearing a full and "complete testimony" against the errors and corruptions of the Papacy. I submit this view of the matter to every intelligent reader for his prayerful consideration. If we have not "understanding of the times," it is vain to expect that we "shall know what Israel ought to do." If we are saying "Peace and safety," when trouble is at hand, or underrating the nature of that trouble, we cannot be prepared for the grand struggle when that struggle shall come.

Note R, p. 274.

Attes, the Sinner.

We have seen that the name Pan signifies "to turn aside," and have concluded that as it is a synonym for Hata, "to sin," the proper generic meaning of which is "to turn aside from the straight line," that name was the name of our first parent, Adam. One of the names of Eve, as the primeval goddess, worshipped in ancient Babylon, while it gives confirmation to this conclusion, elucidates also another classical myth in a somewhat unexpected way. The name of that primeval goddess, as given by Berosus, is Thalatth, which, as we have seen, signifies "the rib." Adam's name, as her *husband*, would be "Baal-Thalatth," "Husband of the rib;" for Baal signifies Lord in the sense frequently of "*Husband.*" But "Baal-Thalatth," according to a peculiar Hebrew idiom already noticed (p. 38, Note), signifies also "He that halted or went sideways."* This is the remote origin of Vulcan's lameness; for Vulcan, as the "Father of the gods,"† needed to be identified with Adam, as well as the other "fathers of the gods," to whom we have already traced him. Now Adam, in consequence of his sin and departure from the straight line of duty, was, all his life after, in a double sense "Baal-Thalatth," not only the "Husband of the rib," but "The man that halted or walked sideways." In memory of this turning aside, no doubt it was that the priests of Baal (1 Kings xviii. 26) "*limped* at the altar," when supplicating their god to hear them (for that is the exact meaning in the original of the word rendered "*leaped*"—see Kitto's *Bib. Cyclop.*, vol. i. p. 261), and that the Druidic priests went *sideways* in performing some of their sacred rites, as appears from the following passage of Davies:—"The dance is performed with solemn festivity about the lakes, round which and the sanctuary the priests *move sideways*, whilst the sanctuary is earnestly invoking the gliding king, before whom the fair one retreats upon the veil that covers the huge stones" (*Druids*, p. 171). This Davies regards as connected with the story of Jupiter, the father of the gods, violating his own daughter in the form of a serpent (p. 561). Now, let the reader look at what is on the breast of the Ephesian Diana, as the *Mother* of the gods (*ante*, p. 29), and he will see a reference to *her* share in the same act of going aside; for there is the crab, and how does a crab go but *sideways?* This, then, shows the meaning of another of the signs of the Zodiac. Cancer commemorates the fatal turning aside of our first parent from the paths of righteousness, when the covenant of Eden was broken.

* The Chaldee Thalatth, "a rib" or a "side," comes from the verb Thalaa, the Chaldee form of Tzalaa, which signifies "to turn aside," "to halt," "to sidle," or "to walk sideways."

† For Vulcan as "the first of all the gods," see Minutius Felix, *Octavius*, p. 163.

The Pagans knew that this turning aside or going sideways, implied death—the death of the soul—("In the *day* thou eatest thereof, thou shalt surely die"); and, therefore, while at the spring festival of Cybele and Attes, there were great lamentations for the death of Attes, so on the Hilaria or rejoicing festival of the 25th of March—that is, Lady-day, the last day of the festival—the mourning was turned into joy, "on occasion of the dead god being restored to life again" (DUPUIS, *Origine de tous les Cultes*, tom. iv. pt. 1, p. 253, Paris, L'an iii. de la Republique [1794]). If Attes was he that by "his turning aside" brought sin and death into the world, what could the life be to which he was so speedily restored, but just that new and divine life which enters every soul when it is "*born again*," and so "passes from death unto life." When the promise was given that the seed of the woman should bruise the serpent's head, and Adam grasped it by faith, that, there can be no doubt, was evidence that the divine life was *restored*, and that he was *born again*. And thus do the very Mysteries of Attes, which were guarded with special jealousy, and the secret meaning of which Pausanias declares that he found it impossible, notwithstanding all his efforts, to discover (Lib. vii., *Achaica*, cap. 17), bear their distinct testimony, when once the meaning of the name of Attes is deciphered, to the knowledge which Paganism itself had of the real nature of the Fall, and of the essential character of that *death*, which was threatened in the primeval covenant.

This new *birth* of Attes laid the foundation for his being represented as a little child, and so being identified with Adonis, who, though he died a full-grown man, was represented in that very way. In the Eleusinian Mysteries, that commemorated the rape of Proserpine, that is, the seduction of Eve, the lamented god, or Bacchus, was represented as a babe at the breast of the great Mother, who by Sophocles is called Dēo (*Antigone*, v. 1121, Oxon. 1808). As Dēo or Dēmēte, applied to the Great Mother, is evidently just another form of Idaia Mater, "The Mother of Knowledge" (the verb "to know" being either *Daa* or *Idau*), this little child, in one of his aspects, was no doubt the same as Attes, and thus also Deōius, as his name is given (*ante*, p. 20). The Hilaria, or rejoicing festival of the 25th of March, or Lady-day, owed its gladness to the Annunciation of a birth yet to come, even the birth of the woman's seed; but, at the same time, the joy of that festival was enhanced by the immediate new birth that very day of Attes, "The sinner," or Adam, who, in consequence of his breach of the covenant, had become dead in "trespasses and sins."

INDEX.

OPINIONS OF THE PRESS.

"The volume before us on the subject of Romanism is able and interesting. The author is a 'full man.' His scholarship is ripe, and his historical research deep and accurate. Classical and Oriental literature and the records of antiquity, he employs with the skill and readiness of a master, to make good his positions. Rarely, indeed, within the same space, have we seen such a rich variety of learned and curious information arrayed in evidence against the assumptions, usages, doctrines, and pretended apostolical origin of Romanism. The tinsel garments of pretended sanctity he strips off, and the charm of sacred association he scatters to the winds."—*Evangelical Magazine.*

"This is a work of no common-place character. It clearly proves that the religion of the Church of Rome is the religion of ancient Babylon, tinted and varnished with the name of Christianity."—*Achill Herald.*

"Mr. Hislop's work entitles him to a place in the first ranks of those who have been honoured, by their discoveries, to throw intensely interesting light, in different ways, on some of the darkest pages of the world's history."—*Original Secession Magazine.*

"Mr. Hislop has displayed no small amount of historical and philological lore, which stamps him as a scholar of no mean rank. His felicity in tracing analogies is very remarkable."—*Scottish Press.*

"These papers (on the Moral Identity of Babylon and Rome) produced at the time a powerful impression: and their learned author has since prosecuted his inquiries more fully, and in a most interesting volume, just published, has set forth in ample detail the whole proofs and illustrations of his interesting and striking theory. . . . It gives one a strange and vivid idea of the inspiration of Scripture to read these remarkable pages."—*Dr. Begg, in Bulwark.*

"One of the most valuable contributions towards the settlement of the great controversy which we hold with Antichrist that has appeared for years. . . . The relation which mythology bears to mythology, and which all bear to Christian Theism, is beautifully, though apparently unconsciously, developed in Mr. Hislop's 'Two Babylons.'"—*Stanyan Bigg, in Devonshire Protestant.*

[SEE OVER.

"Mr. Hislop has collected a large mass of materials (many of them new and very striking) in proof of his position; and has arranged and stated his argument with a calmness, precision, and force, that greatly impress the reader."—*Christian Treasury.*

"This work is of no common erudition. . . . We have not for a considerable time met with any volume that presents the subjects in lights so striking and original. The author has performed a noble service to our common Protestantism, and is entitled to the thanks of every section of the true Church."—*Dr. Campbell, in British Standard.*

"We venture to say, no reader will rise from its perusal without a loftier reverence for God's truth, and a deeper conviction of the indelible brand that truth has stamped upon the Papal system. There is a touch of the sublime in finding the predictions of the seer of Patmos unloosed from their enigmatic mystery, when we bring together the early idolatrous worship of Chaldea, and the latest dogmas of Rome. The simple narrative of the two developments completes the circle—a luminous ring, which lights up the dark page of prophecy until it reads like a history written but yesterday." —*Northern Warder.*

"The vast amount of learning, and the philological research and comparison so fascinating to many minds, coupled with the striking analogies every now and then made apparent, render the book as attractive as a novel, and the reader is drawn on irresistibly to the end. Its pages form a mine of historical wealth, or rather a depository of ores and fossils dug from a vast number of sources, and labelled, classified, and arranged until, like specimens from the various strata of the earth's crust similarly laid out in a museum, and pieced together by the hands of a master in geology, the oneness of the source whence sprang the many systems of religion of ancient times is made manifest, as are the corruptions which in later ages have crept into the Church of the primitive Christians."—*Arbroath Guide.*

"This is a book of literary curiosities—of laborious researches and ingenious discourses. . . . A more able exposure of the abominations of Romanism has not appeared since the days of Luther. . . . Our author has evidently received a commission to apostate Rome similar to that of Ezekiel to apostate Jerusalem; and he has executed it with equal fidelity." —*Mr. Spurgeon, in Sword and Trowel.*